CURRENT ENGLISH FINANCIAL TERMS
A Mnemonic Aid to Expression

和英
金融用語辞典

花田　實編

The Japan Times, Ltd.

は　し　が　き

　すべて母国語以外の言葉による表現を安易に創作することに，大きな危険が伴うことは多言を要しません。また，各分野で使われる術語・慣用語句によらないで，表意の正確を期待することの無謀さについても同様でしょう。

　わが国ではこれまでにも，普通の語句や語法に関する限り，数多くの秀れた英語辞典類が出されています。ところが，通貨，財政を含め金融英語となりますと，これら一般の英語辞典では十分にカバーされていません。しかも，日を追っていよいよ増大している必要にもかかわらず，和英の金融用語辞典で世に出ているものはいまだにその数が極めて限られており，広い範囲で相当に専門的な要求に応えるには決して十分とはいえないのが現状であります。

　さて，この辞典は，そのような要求を出来る限り満足に近づけたいという意図をもって，さきに編みました『和英・経済英語辞典』（1976年，ジャパンタイムズ刊）を延長，拡大したものです。ただ，本来編者個人の備忘録を基礎として編まれた先の辞典は，後日の大方のご教示，ご批判を期待しつつ急ぎ上梓したものでしたから，勿論広いご利用を図って当初極力試みました補正の後にもその収録語彙の構成になお若干の個人的偏向を残していました。加えて，昨今いよいよ進展する本格的な金融・経済の国際化と自由化の下に，貿易摩擦論議と反保護貿易主義・運動，これに繋がるわが国に対する金融自由化と市場開放の要求，さらに一部は周期的とはいえ近年とみに顕現化した第三世界の累積債務問題，一方，国内ではサービス化経済の中で金融機関の新しい型の情報産業化，金融多岐化による証券市場への銀行の積極的参入，とその後の時流の変化に応じる語句の充足も，また待たれるところでした。

この基礎的な修正と，引き続きその後の実務上の要求に基づいた，特に金融面の説明用語句の拡充を行った結果が，この辞典です。もっとも，金融の説明にはこれと表裏一体を成す実体経済への言及がある程度不可欠でありますから，その範囲で必要な経済用語句を併せて収録してあります。これら金融・経済関係の術語・慣用語句のうち基礎的な語については，それぞれ連語（collocation）を示す用例を付しました。その中には，編者が日常業務の間に実際の必要から探索し，また常々探し求めていた語句・表現で，主に米・英両国政府・中央銀行その他の機関，国際機関の報告文から抜いて，後日の用にと書き留めておいたもののうちから，皆さんの参考になると思われるものも豊富に収めました。皆さんがいろいろな英語報告文を書かれる時に，必要な金融関係語句を，この辞典によって，思い起こし，その用法を再確認すると共に，用例に適宜の語句を代入，挿入することによって，最適の表現が得られるように，この辞典は編集してあります。これら各用例が，収録訳語と共に，彼岸の慣用語句を駆使して十分意を得た英文金融関係作文に，前身に増して，寄与するところがあればと願っています。

この補完改版を可能にされた多くの貴重なご示唆と有力なご支援を下さった皆様並びにジャパンタイムズ出版部の方々に，ここに再び，厚くお礼申します，と同時に，なお一層の改善のための引き続くご支援をお願い致します。

1985 年

編　者

凡　例

1.　見出し語は，ローマ字（ヘボン式）綴りによるアルファベット順に配列した。ただし，GNP ギャップ，IMF 協定など，ローマ字で始まる見出し語は，各セクションの先頭に置いた。

　　同一音のものは，漢字の画数の少ない順とした。

　[例]　**kanryū　還流**

　　　　kanryū　環流

　　また，同一綴りのものは，短音，長音の順とした。

　[例]　**yosō　予想**

　　　　yōso　要素

　　　　yōsō　様相

　　綴りの中で -ny- が連音するものは，連音しないものの後に置いた。

　[例]　**kin'yū　金融**

　　　　kinyū　記入

　　各項目内の内訳項目も，ローマ字表記は略したが，同じくアルファベット順に配列した。

2.　見出し項目・英訳語句とも同義の語句があるときはセミコロン（；）を介して列記した。

3.　訳語中（＝　）内の語句は，その直前の語句と代替できることを示す。

　[例]　policy actions（＝moves; measures）とあるのは policy actions のほかに policy moves とも policy measures とも用いられることを示す。

4.　見出し項目・訳語中とも（　）内の語句は省略できることを示す。

　[例]　(external) payments position とあるのは external payments position とも payments postion とも用いられることを示す。

5. 訳語句のうち使用される分野が限られているものには，その分野に応じて次の略語を付し区別した。

［会］	会計・経理	［証市］	特に証券市場	［英］	英国
［外］	外国為替・貿易	［統］	統計	［独］	ドイツ
［コン］	コンピューター	［日］	日本		
［市］	証券・商品市場	［米］	米国		

［例］［米・市］に続く語句は米国の市場用語として慣用されるもの，［日］に続く語句はわが国に特有の慣用語句であることを示す。

　　ただし，たとえば「損益計算書」，「直物為替」のように，使用分野を明らかに示す語句には略語を付していない。

6. 用例は各訳語の後に ¶ で示し，2つ以上の用例を掲げる場合は // を介して列記した。その配列は，表現が常用のもので，一般的なものから限定的なもの，品詞を変えて（名詞から動詞，形容詞などに）用いたもの，特殊ではあるが有用なもの，の順とした。

7. ［参考］に続く用例は当該見出し語を用いた用例ではないが，同趣意を示す文例である。

8. → に続く見出し語は，当該見出し語と同意であることを示し，［参考］→ に続く見出し語は，当該見出し語と類似の意であることを示す。

9. 用例はすべて外国新聞，雑誌，経済誌および BIS，ニューヨーク連銀その他国際金融機関の公式レポートに拠った。

目　　次

A

abeirabiriti アベイラビリティ (credit) availability; availability of credit
facilities ¶ The *availability of* the
rediscount *facilities* had been
suspended in March as part of restrictive credit policy. // The international *availability* of bank finance
is greater than before. // a new firm
constrained by *credit availability* //
the general *availability of credit* to
borrowers // severe tightness of
credit availability throughout U.S.
financial markets // desirable conditions of *credit availability* in the
credit market // the ready *availability* of monetary financing // The
ready *availability* of revenues leads
to easy expenditures. // The choice
of companies was constrained by
data *availability.*

abiseuri 浴びせ売り [市] bunched
sales

afutāsābisu アフターサービス after-
sales servicing ¶ The outlet offers
adequate *after-sales servicing.*

agari 揚り income; earning; return;
taking; receipt

agarisagari 上がり下がり ups and
downs; rises and falls; fluctuation

agaru 上がる →上昇; 物価

ageashi 上げ足 upward momentum; up-trend; upward tendency ¶
The dollar can sustain its recent
upward momentum.

agechō 揚超 net receipt; surplus;
excess of withdrawals over payments (on Treasury accounts; in the

government transactions with the
public) ¶ Tourists *receipts* are
expected to *net* over $1 billion.

agedomari 上げ止り [市] peaking
out; topping out ¶ Prices *peaked
out.* // The late-1980s date for a
topping-out of petroleum exports //
[参考] The market lost upside
momentum as prices edged lower.

ageru 上げる increase; raise; up-
raise; elevate; heighten; lift; uplift;
set up; move up; tilt up; take up;
boost; buoy; mount ¶ The discount
rates were *increased* from 2½ percent to 2¾ percent. // The Federal
Reserve discount rate was *raised*
marginally by ⅛ percent. // Higher
prices for fir *boosted* the average
lumber price to $75.88. // →上昇

agesōba 上げ相場 [市] bullish
(market) sentiment; rising quotations; long market

airo 隘路 bottleneck; constraint ¶
Supply *constraints* appeared in some
lines. // to cause *constraints* in production // Serious *bottlenecks* are
emerging in supply. // to break the
financial *bottleneck* // This sudden
demand has run slap into a supply
bottleneck. // The economy was con-
fronted with serious physical *bottlenecks.*

airosangyō 隘路産業 bottleneck
industry

aitai 相対 personal; vis-à-vis; mutual ¶ The Bank carried out selling
operations in securities *vis-à-vis* se-

curities companies.

aitaibaibai 相対売買 ［市］cross trade; negotiated transaction

aitaisaimu 相対債務 mutual debt; cross debt

aitaitorihiki 相対取引 →相対売買

aizu 合図 signal ¶ The Bank gave the discount market a firm *signal* that interest rates should not be allowed to fall. // This step is regarded as *signaling* a change in the current setting of monetary policy. // the *signal* for the beginning of an economic transformation for the country

aji 味 tone; atmosphere; sentiment ¶ The market was in a soft *tone*. // in a shade firmer *tone*

ajiadarāsai アジア・ダラー債 Asian-dollar bond

ajiadarāshijō アジア・ダラー市場 Asian-dollar market

ajiadoru アジア・ドル Asian dollar

ajiataiheiyōkeizaiken アジア太平洋経済圏 economic community in the Asian-Pacific area

ajitsukegai 味付買い ［市］support buying

akafunanishōken 赤船荷証券 red B/L

akaji 赤字 deficit; loss; red ink figure; gap; shortfall ¶ The current account balance, having shifted from a surplus of $83 billion in 1980 to a *deficit* of $10 billion in 1981, continues to move more deeply into *deficit*. // The balance ended in a *deficit* of $321 million. // Canada incurred a balance-of-payments *deficit* of $89 million. // The *deficit* on trade account reverted to a surplus. // The financial year put America $76 billion in the *red*. // The U.S.

budget *deficit* in 1977 was $47.5 billion. // The government is running a heavy *deficit*. // The U.S. will incur a non-trivial *deficit* next year. // Last year's trade *deficit* on agricultural products was of the order of $1 billion. // The government ran a cumulative budget *deficit* of ¥310 billion, and more *red ink* is expected next year. // The nation's current account *deficit* plunged from $29 million a year ago to $1,308 million. // The total accumulated Federal *deficit* is budgeted to reach Sw. Fr. 10.7 billion. // The current *deficit* goes on narrowing slowly, and may be reduced to less than a million dollars. // Western Europe's trade *deficit* with us shall remain modest. // Belgium's 1979 budget *deficit* may lie between B.fr. 80 and 90 billion. // a return to an unacceptably high current-account *deficit* // a marked swing into *deficit* on current account // The government expects the *shortfall* for 1979/80 to total S. Kr. 41.8 billion. // The balance of payments turned back into the *red* to the tune of nearly $500 m. // to record a large £15 billion *red-ink figure* // The trade *gap* fell each month. // to help close *gaps* in family budget

akajihoten 赤字補填 covering (= making good; filling up; making up) of a deficit

akajikin'yū 赤字金融 deficit-covering finance (=financing)

akajikoku 赤字国 deficit country; deficit-ridden nation

akajikōsai 赤字公債 bond issued for deficit financing; deficit-financing bond; deficit-covering bond; deficit bond ¶ The government is to issue *deficit-covering bonds*.

akajirosen 赤字路線 loss making railway line

akajiyosan 赤字予算 deficit budget; adverse budget; unbalanced budget

akajiyūshi 赤字融資 financing for deficit-covering; deficit financing; deficit-covering loan ¶ to use the money-creating powers of the banking system in full support of government *deficit financing* // Some $6 billion became available through institutional channels for *financing the deficit* of developing countries.

akajizaisei 赤字財政 deficit spending (by the government); deficit finance; deficit-ridden Treasury ¶ to rehabilitate the *deficit-ridden Treasury*

akajizandaka 赤字残高 deficit balance; adverse balance; unfavorable balance; red balance ¶ external payments in substantial *deficit balance* // The *deficit balance* accumulated sizably.

akinai 商内 business; trade; trading ¶ *Trading* remained subdued on lack of fresh incentive. // The volume of *business* was small. // The dollar remained firm in active *business*. // The recovery of the *trading* has been slow. // *Trading* slackened. // The stock market made a moderate advance in quiet *trading,* then advanced in heavy *trading*. // Maize and oats *trade* was lighter. // *Trading* was fairly active. // The international gold market was characterized by relatively calm *trading*.

akinaijakkan 商内若干 [市] some business done

akka 悪化 deterioration; worsen-ing; aggravation; exacerbation ¶ The sharp *deterioration* in economic activity was reflected in widespread lay-offs. // a *worsening* in the current account // The deficit balance *aggravated*. // Spiraling inflation was *exacerbated* by floating of the peso.

akka 悪貨 bad coin; bad money ¶ "*Bad money* drives out good." // *Bad coin* tends to drive the good out of circulation.

akuifujitsuhyōji 悪意不実表示 fraudulent misrepresentation

akuino 悪意の mala fide ¶ *mala fide*, not bona fide, possessors of the bonds

akujunkan 悪循環 spiral; vicious circle; vicious cycle ¶ to put an end to the *vicious* wage-price *circle* // the *vicious circle* of depreciating exchange rates and domestic inflation, and possible ways out of the perpetuating syndrome // to plunge the country into an inflation-cum-devaluation *spiral* // countries caught in a *vicious circle* set in motion // For the big cities, the *cycle* is depressingly *vicious*. // The economy is trapped in the *vicious circle* of external depreciation, price rises, external depreciation and so on. // to add a further twist to the wage-price *spiral* // the danger of a major new price/wage *spiral* being triggered // Increases in oil prices may generate a marked acceleration of the wage price *spiral*. // The normal *vicious circle* of high prices, more money and higher prices was in full swing. // to break the *vicious circle* of financial instability and structural deficiencies

akume 悪目 [市] setback ¶ The

market had its worst *setback* of the year.

akunuke あく抜け ［市］ getting rid of adverse (=bearish) factors

akuseiinfure 悪性インフレ virulent inflation; vicious inflation; malignant inflation; inflationary spiral ¶ →インフレーション

akuseputansu アクセプタンス acceptance ¶ bank *acceptances,* or banker's *acceptances*

akuzairyō 悪材料 adverse factor; unfavorable factor; bearish factor; bad news ¶ *Bad news* of poor business earnings was legitimate reason for the burst of selling.

amai 甘い ［市］ easy

ana 穴 deficit; loss ¶ to score a *loss* // to suffer a *loss* // to register a *deficit* of...

anaume 穴埋め stopgap; bridging; covering (= filling up; making up; supplying) a deficiency ¶ to borrow extra funds to *bridge* the shortfall in government revenues

anbunwariate 按分割当 pro rata (=proportional) allotment

ankanaseifu 安価な政府 cheap government

ankēto アンケート inquiry; questionnaire ¶ The results of the *inquiry* indicate that business opinion is distrustful. // Fourty-four *questionnaires* were returned, 83 percent of the number dispatched and the best ever response rate in the series.

ankētochōsa アンケート調査 questionnaire survey; survey by questionnaire; inquiry; inquiry survey; survey by inquiries ¶ a *questionnaire survey* conducted by the Association // Of the respondents, 38% *surveyed by questionnaire* rated fiscal policy as

"poor."

anmokunodōi 暗黙の同意 tacit consent

anrakusuijun 安楽水準 standard of comforts

ansokuchi 安息地 haven ¶ to make the United States a more attractive *haven* for funds // to move plants to tax *havens*

antei 安定 stability; steadiness ¶ to bring about greater *stability* in exchange relations // to enjoy an enormous degree of social *stability* // The improvement in the economic climate lacks *stability*. // to regain a much greater measure of *stability* than before // Greater currency *stability* will lead to enhanced political *stability*. // to maintain a sufficient degree of price *stability* // domestic monetary *stability* as well as *stability* on foreign exchange markets // Restoration of greater exchange rate *stability* must await the return of national economic *stability*. // Orders seem to have *steadied* at a level higher than expected. // ［参考］ The dollar returned to terra firma.

為替安定 foreign exchange stabilization; stabilization of foreign exchange rates

経済安定 economic stabilization

雇用安定 stabilization of employment

通貨安定 currency stabilization

通貨安定借款 currency stabilization loan

物価安定 price stabilization

物価水準の安定 stabilization of price levels

anteichinginsei 安定賃金制 stable wage system

anteijōken 安定条件 stability conditions

anteika 安定化 stabilization ¶ to formulate and inaugurate a wage-price *stabilization* program to expect *stabilization* of employment

anteikabu 安定株 investment holdings (of stock)

anteikabunushi 安定株主 strong stockholder

anteikachikeisan 安定価値計算 calculation on stabilized value

anteikakaku 安定価格 stabilized value; stable price

anteikaseisaku 安定化政策 stabilization policy

anteikeikaku 安定計画 stabilization program (=plan) ¶ to formulate and inaugurate a wage-price *stabilization program* // uncertainties about the future course of the *stabilization program*

anteikeizai 安定経済 stable economy

anteikeizaiseichō 安定経済成長 stable economic growth

anteikikin 安定基金 stabilization fund

anteikinkō 安定均衡 stable equilibrium

anteikōka 安定効果 stabilizing effect ¶ Price changes exerted a *stabilizing effect* on wholesale prices.

anteikyōkō 安定恐慌 stabilization crisis

anteirōdōryoku 安定労働力 stable labor force

anteisei 安定性 stability; steadiness ¶ Prices broadly have held about *stable.* // to avoid upsetting the *stability* of the financial system // The mixture of strength and weakness adds up to over-all *stability.* // three years of relative *stability* //

near-*stability* of prices // Prices are *steady* up and down the line. // the *steady* month-to-month gain // the price holding *steady* at $325 // The market then *steadied* down. // ［参考］ the sustained strength of final demand // well sustained exports

anteiseichō 安定成長 stable growth; sustainable growth; sound growth; steady growth; growth at a steady pace; growth with stability; sound and lasting growth ¶ the *steady, sustainable,* or *sound growth* of the economy // The economy can now look forward to a period of *sound growth* from a firm base. // a strategy aimed at *lasting growth with stability* // to facilitate a more *sustainable* pattern of economic *growth* // ［参考］ The economy is healthy and prosperous again on a lasting basis.

anteiseichōrosen 安定成長路線 stable-growth path; stabilized-growth track ¶ to place the economy on the right *track* of *sustainable growth*

anteiseiryoku 安定勢力 stabilizing force

anteishikyō 安定市況 stabilized market; stable market

anteishisan 安定資産 riskless asset

anteisōchi 安定装置 stabilizer; equilibrator

anteisōsa 安定操作 stabilizing operation (=transaction)

anteitaikakaku 安定帯価格 stable-zone price; price within the price range

anteitsūka 安定通貨 stable currency; stabilized currency; stable money

anteiyosanseisaku 安定予算政策

stabilizing budget policy

anzenben 安全弁 safety valve

anzenmō 安全網 safety net; security net ¶ This financial support facility will be in the nature of a *safety net* to be used as a last resort. // the $25 billion *"safety net"* fund designed to bolster European countries strained by high oil prices // A financial *"safety net"* was established to which deficit countries can turn for assistance as a last resort.

anzensei 安全性 safety; security ¶ U.S. government obligations offer the highest degree of *safety* of principal in terms of dollars. // to provide a large measure of *safety* for purchasing power // to profoundly affect *safety* of investment

anzenshihon 安全資本 security capital

anzen'yoyū 安全余裕 margin of safety

aoiroshinkoku 青色申告 [日] blue-form return

aoru あおる [市] bull the market

aoshingō 青信号 green light ¶ EEC Foreign Ministers formally gave the *green light* for the opening of negotiations with Canada for a new type of economic cooperation agreement.

aotenjō 青天井 [市] skyrocketing

aozorahō 青空法 [米] blue sky laws

aozorashijō 青空市場 open-air market

apāto アパート apartment house; condominium; multifamily structure (=dwelling)

apurōchi アプローチ approach ¶ The case for interdisciplinary *approach* to problems of the world's economic future seems to be incontestable. // the theoretical movement going beyond both the classical and the Marxist *approach*

徴候的アプローチ symptom approach

学際的アプローチ interdisciplinary approach

因果的アプローチ causality approach

社会・生態的アプローチ socio-ecological approach

システム的アプローチ systems approach

arabuafurikakeizaikaihatsuginkō アラブ・アフリカ経済開発銀行 Arab Bank for African Economic Development; ABAED

arabudoru アラブ・ドル Arab dollar ¶ to float *Arab dollar* bonds

arabuisuraeruboikottoiinkai アラブ・イスラエルボイコット委員会 Committee of Arab for Israel Boycott

arabukeizaishakaikaihatsukikin アラブ経済社会開発基金 Arab Fund for Economic and Social Development; AFESD

arabukokusaibōekikaihatsuginkō アラブ国際貿易開発銀行 Arab International Bank for Foreign Trade and Development

arabusekiyutōshikōsha アラブ石油投資公社 Arab Petroleum Investment Corporation

arabusekiyuyushutsukokukikō アラブ石油輸出国機構 Organization of Arab Petroleum Exporting Countries; OPEC

aremoyō 荒れ模様 [市] irregular fluctuation

aridaka 有高 (goods, cash, etc.) in

(=on) hand; goods in stock; balance in (=on) hand; holdings

arujekenshō アルジェ憲章 Charter of Algiers, 1967

aryūsangasukankyōkijun 亜硫酸ガス環境基準 environmental standards for sulfurous acid gas

ashibumi 足踏み marking time; stalemate; standstill; remaining; stationary ¶ The market this week was *marking time*. // to be almost *stationary* // The quotations for ferrous metals *stood still* for a while.

ashidori 足取り tendency; course; trend; progress of the price movement ¶ →歩み

ashidorihyō 足取表 price table

ashiohipparu 足を引っ張る to act as a drag ¶ Interest rates are *acting as a drag* on the dollar, not as a support.

asobikin 遊金 idle money

assennin 幹旋人 ［市］finder

asshinyashihei アッシニャ紙幣 assignats

asshuku 圧縮 squeeze; clampdown; diminution ¶ The *squeeze* on profits reduced company entertainment expenses. // a thaw in the 18-month long credit *squeeze* // The *squeeze* on company profits and liquidity meant that high rents could no longer be afforded. // Inflation *squeezed* company profit margins. // It would require a continued *clampdown* on Federal spending. // The budget plans a substantial *diminution* of the present large deficit. // a repetition of the severe credit *squeeze* of 1972 // to engage in a price-cost *squeeze* of the intermediate-product producers // ［参考］ negative influences to put a further

damper on share prices

asshukukichō 圧縮記帳 reduced-value entry (of acquired property)

atamakin 頭 金 down-payment; ［市］margin ¶ to *pay* \$500 *down*, that is, to make a *down-payment* of \$500

atamauchi 頭打ち tapering-off (=-out); hitting ceiling; topping-out; flattening (out) ¶ a distinct *tapering-off* of demand // anticipation of *tapering-off* of public sector activity // Exports began to *taper off*. // The loan volume is *peaking out*. // Surfboard sales have *peaked out*. // Industrial output has virtually *flattened out*. // Yield curves have been either *flattening* or actually sloping down. // →先細り

atobarmi 後払い deferred payment

atohizuke 後 日 付 dating backward; back-date ¶ to be *back-dated* to September 1

atoiresakidashihō 後入れ先出し法 last-in first-out method; Lifo

atsuenkōzai 圧延鋼材 rolled steel products

atsuminoarukeizai 厚みのある経済 solid economy

atsuryoku 圧 力 pressure; force; stress; strain; push ¶ Upward *pressures* on prices became more intense. // *Pressures* subsided somewhat. // *Pressure* is building up for a relaxation of restriction. // The *pressure* of home demand slackened. // Inflationary *forces* were brought under control. // Upward *pressures* on prices receded. // The yen resisted selling *pressure* which hit continental currencies. // It could raise international *pressure* for lower U.S. interest rates. // to cope with financial *strains* and *stresses* at year-end // The market *strains* continue. // to attenuate external inflationary *pressures* // The yen became the immediate focus of speculative *pressure.* // To counter selling *pressures* the Bank sold dollars. // The Canadian dollar is exposed to downward *pressure.* // Rising import prices aggravated price *pressures* in the domestic economy. // The depreciation of the dollar reduced the competitve *pressures* on price of domestically produced goods. // Inflationary monetary *pressures* mounted alarmingly. // Significant cost and price *pressures* are likely to persist. // to insulate certain prices from upward *pressures* through subsidies // *Pressure* on stocks has subsided. // The upward *push* of costs and prices was damped down rapidly.

atsuryokudantai 圧力団体 pressure group

autarukī アウタルキー autarchy (= autarky); economic self-sufficiency ¶ to retreat into overtly nationalistic and *autarchic* policies

autoraitosakimonotorihiki アウトライト先物取引 outright forward operation (=transaction; trading; dealing); outright forward exchange

autoraitotorihiki アウトライト取引 outright operation (=transaction; trading; dealing)

aya あや [市] technical change; lurch ¶ to smooth out monthly *lurches*

ayamodoshi あや戻し [市] faint recovery; technical rally (=rebound)

ayaoshi あや押し [市] technical reaction

ayumi 歩み trend; movement ¶ The *movement* of stock prices has tended upward. // The *trend* in prices reversed and recorded a marginal decline. // The *trend* of price *movements* is one of slight uprise.

ayumiyori 歩み寄り compromise ¶ The Minister called for a *compromise* between unions and employers over union demands for a shorter working week.

azukarinin 預かり人 depositee; depositary

azukarishōken 預かり証券 deposit certificate; warrant; warehouse receipt

azukaru 預かる receive in deposit; be deposited with; be entrusted with; receive in trust; receive in custody

azukeire 預け入れ inpayment ¶ Net *inpayments* to savings accounts (i.e., excluding interest credited) amounted to over DM10 billion between January and June.

azukekin 預け金 deposit ¶ *deposits* with a bank // →預金

azukeru 預ける deposit with (a bank, etc.); place in custody of (a bank, etc.)

B

B/C yūzansu B/C ユーザンス negotiation of bills of collection by an overseas branch of a Japanese bank

ba 場 [市] market; session; exchange
　後場 afternoon session; afternoon market; afternoon sale
　前場 morning session; morning market; morning sale

baaji 場味 [市] undertone ¶ The market has been firm in its *undertone*. // The *undertone* of the market is steady. // The market *undertone* is a shade softer.

baiasu バイアス bias ¶ →偏向
　上向バイアス upward bias

baibai 売買 buying and selling; purchase and sale; trade; dealing; transaction; bargain; marketing
　反対売買 counter-sale
　保税品売買 sale in bond
　委託売買 brokerage; agency transaction
　条件付売買 conditional sale
　仮装売買 washed sale
　見越売買 speculative transaction; trading on speculation
　なれあい売買 matched orders; wash
　成行相場売買 sale at daily market price
　指値売買 sale at limited price
　大量売買 bulk sale
　店頭売買 over-the-counter transaction; sale over the counter

baibaichūmonnodakiawase 売買注文の抱合せ marrying of buying and selling orders

baibaidaka 売買高 sales amount; turnover; trading; (trade) volume

baibaihōkokusho 売買報告書 bought and sold note

baibaiichininchūmon 売買一任注文 discretionary order

baibaijōken 売買条件 terms of transaction; terms and conditions of sale

baibaikakuteikabu 売買確定株 firm stock

baibaikanjō 売買勘定 trading account

baibaikeiyaku 売買契約 sales contract

baibaisaeki 売買差益 profit on own account tradings

baibaisakin 売買差金 margin

baibaishihō 売買仕法 transaction system

baibaishijō 売買市場 circulation market; trading market; secondary market

baibaishōken 売買証券 sales warrant

baibaishōsho 売買証書 bill of sale; contract note

baibaisōbanohiraki 売買相場の開き exchange margin; exchange difference; exchange spread

baibaison'ekikanjō 売買損益勘定 trading profit and loss account

baibaitan'i 売買単位 [市] even lot; regular lot

baibaitesūryō 売買手数料 brokerage; commission

baibaitetsuzuki 売買手続 transaction procedure

baibaitōjisha 売買当事者 parties to a sale

baibaiyakujō 売買約定 bargain

baibaiyakujōbi 売買約定日 contractual value date

baibaiyakujōkigen 売買約定期限 contractual resale (=reselling) date

baika 売価 selling price; sale price; labeled price ¶ at 80 percent of the *sale price; selling price* with 20 percent reduction

baika 買価 buying price; purchase price

baikai バイカイ [市] cross transaction; crossing at the going price

baikai 媒介 medium; vehicle; intermediary; intermediation ¶ *media* for investment, investment *vehicles*, like gold, which previously were looked upon as esoteric and too risky // the role of banks as financial *intermediaries* // Land is a very basic savings *medium*. // the dollar as a *vehicle* currency for transactions // Bank credits became viable *vehicles* for financing many types of investment projects. // Cofinancing provides a *vehicle* for helping a borrower establish its credit. // to serve as the *vehicle* for the transition to a free regime *intermediation* of financing, or financial *intermediation*

baikaihaijo 媒介排除 disintermediation

baikaitsūka 媒介通貨 vehicle currency (for international trade)

baikyaku 売却 sale; disposal

baikyakudaikin 売却代金 sales proceeds; proceeds from sales; proceeds of sales ¶ *proceeds from sales* of stocks // *sales proceeds* of stocks

baikyakueki 売却益 profit on sale

baikyakuiyoku 売却意欲 eagerness to sell; willingness to sell

baikyakujōken 売却条件 terms of sale

baikyakukachi 売却価値 salable value; realizable value

baikyakukanjō 売却勘定 sales account

baikyakunin 売却人 seller; vendor

baikyakuson 売却損 loss on sale

baikyakutsūchi 売却通知 notice of sale

baishō 賠償 compensation; indemnity; reparation

中間賠償 interim reparations

役務賠償 reparations in service

現物賠償 reparations in kind

現金賠償 reparations in cash

生産賠償 reparations by current production

戦争賠償 war reparations

baishōhoshōsho 賠償保証書 letter of indemnity

baishōiinkai 賠償委員会 reparations commission

baishōkōjō 賠償工場 plant for reparations

baishōkyōtei 賠償協定 reparations treaty

baishōmondai 賠償問題 reparations problem

baishōshisetsu 賠償施設 facilities designated as reparations

baishōtekkyo 賠償撤去 reparations removal

baishōtoritate 賠償取立て exaction of reparations; collection of reparations

baishū 買収 purchase; acquisition; buying up; take-over; buying out; buy-out; buying over; bribing; payout ¶ Japanese banks have *bought* 10 banks in California, yet, no foreign banks have *taken over* Japanese ones. // the potential price of the proposed *buyout* of the commodity business of the parent corporation

baishūkakaku 買収価格 purchase price

baiyaku 売約 sales contract

baiyakuzumi 売約済み sold

bakabu 場株 listed stock on the local market

bakkin 罰金 fine; penalty; forfeit; monetary penalty

bākuhātokehōan バーク・ハートケ法案 [米] Burke-Hartke bill

bakuhatsu 爆発 explosion ¶ to avert the trauma of *price explosions* that took place in the 1970s
物価爆発 price explosion
人口爆発 population explosion

bakuhatsutekinajuyō 爆発的な需要 burst of demand; explosion of demand; demand explosion

banare 〜離れ flight slipping away from (banks, etc.); getting rid of ¶ Men hurried to *get rid of* money for goods. // →離脱

bankufurōto バンク・フロート bank float; checks in process of collection ¶ to permit banks to count *bank float* as reserve cash

bannōtaishakutaishōhyō 万能貸借対照表 all-purpose balance sheet

bannōyaku 万能薬 panacea; cure-all; nostrum ¶ a *cure-all* for economic ills // It will not be a magic *cure-all* for world inflation. // Floating has turned out not to be a *panacea* for payments imbalances. // a *panacea* for all our economic woes

bappontekisochi 抜本的措置 radical measure

barani バラ荷 bulk cargo

baransutōshin バランス投信 balance fund

baratsuki ばらつき ill-balance; unevenness; disparity; inequality; differential ¶ an *ill-balanced* pace of improvement in different regions of the country // the *uneven* development between branches of industry

baromētā バロメーター barometer ¶ The *barometer* stood at 93.17, as compared with 88.18 in June. // The "cyclical *barometer*" measuring general economic activity in Belgium calculated by the National Bank of Belgium has now gone up. // At the end of January the "*barometer*" stood at 93.19. // Equipment investment is a fair *barometer* of business activity. // to be regarded as a rough *barometer* of business capital spending

barukuyusō バルク輸送 traffic in the bulk commodities; to carry the bulk commodities

bashotekikachi 場所的価値 place value ¶ the difference in *place values*

bashotekisaitei 場所的裁定 [外] arbitrage in space

bassokutekikinri 罰則的金利 penal(ty) rate

bātābōeki バーター貿易 barter trade

batachi 場立ち [市] floor clerk; floor trader; board man

bāzeruenjo バーゼル援助 Basle facilities

bāzerukyōtei バーゼル協定 Basle Agreement, 1961

beddotaun ベッド・タウン dormitory town; bedroom town; commuters' town

beidorukinkōkanseiteishi 米ドル

金交換性停止 suspension of the convertibility of the (U.S.) dollar into gold

beika 米価 rice price

実勢米価 actual rice price

公定米価 official rice price; ceiling rice price

適正米価 reasonable rice price

beika 米貨 American currency; the U.S. dollar; dollars

beikabarainihonkōsai 米貨払日本公債 Japanese dollar bond

beikachōsetsu 米価調節 regulation of the rice market; rice price regulation

beikakawase 米貨為替 dollar exchange

beikakōsai 米貨公債 dollar bond

beikasaiken 米貨債券 debenture in U.S. dollars

beikaseisaku 米価政策 rice price policy

beikashiharai 米貨支払 payable in dollars

beikategata 米貨手形 dollar bill

beikokukinkyūkeizaitaisaku 米国緊急経済対策 new U.S. economic policy; U.S. emergency economic (policy) measures; NEP

beikokunendo 米穀年度 rice year

beikokuyotakushōken 米国預託証券 American Depositary Receipt; ADR

beisaku 米作 rice crop

beisakutenkanshōrei 米作転換奨励 encouragement of a switch from rice to other crops

beisakuyosō 米作予想 estimated rice crop; rice crop estimate; forecast of the rice crop

beiton 米トン short ton

bengi 便宜 facility ¶ The credit market provides a capacious, fluid, and efficient *facility* for handling both domestic and international business. // the central bank discount or lending *facility* // the resort to the discount *facility* by member banks // full use of the *facilities* of the F.R. system for custody of marketable assets, transfer of funds and collection of cash items // the reconversion of productive *facilities* to peacetime needs // to forgo ordinary access to the lending *facilities* of the Federal Reserve system // No *facilities* are available for providing additional funds. // various types of long-term development financing *facilities* // Credit *facilities* are available from the Fund and elsewhere. // Overdraft *facilities* granted by the banks totaled S.Kr. 41,633 million. // to *facilitate* the clearance and collection of checks // the establishment of a now intermediate lending *facility* in the World Bank known as the Third Window // a drawing on the IMF under the compensatory financing *facility* for certain countries // The SDR could have become a useful monetary *facility*.

bengiatsukai 便宜扱い expedient treatment

bengichisekisen 便宜置籍船 ship flying a flag of convenience; flag-of-convenience vessel ¶ [参考] Liberia is one of the main ports of convenience registration.

bengisenseki 便宜船籍 flag of convenience

bengishugi 便宜主義 expediency

bengoshihiyō 弁護士費用 attorney's fees

bengoshiirairyō 弁護士依頼料 retaining fee; retainer

benrishōhin 便利商品 convenience goods

benriten 便利店 convenience store

bensai 弁済 payment; repayment; settlement; liquidation

bensaikanōmikomigaku 弁済可能見込額 probable amount of repayment

bensaikigen 弁済期限 maturity; date of repayment; due date

benshō 弁償 compensation; indemnification

benshōkin 弁償金 indemnity; compensation; damages

bēsu ベース basis; footing ¶ Imports on a license *basis* totaled $58 bn, and on a customs *basis* $42 bn. // the April increase in the consumer price index on a month-to-month *basis* // real output measured by GNP on a 1975＝100 *basis* // comparisons on a monthly average *basis* // The government treats foreign-controlled firms on an equal *footing* with domestic companies.

bēsuappu ベースアップ wage raise; raising average wage; increase in the regular wage; base-wage increase ¶ The agreement provided for a *base-wage increase* of 8½ percent plus an additional rise under a cost-of-living escalator clause.

betsudan'yokin 別段預金 special deposit

betsudōgaisha 別働会社 shell company; dummy company

betsukanjō 別勘定 separate account; separate bill

bichiku 備蓄 stockpile; buffer stock ¶ Moves were stepped up to expand raw material *stockpiles*. // to step up (＝expand) raw material *stockpiles* // to promote increased imports of crude oil for *stockpiles* // →緩衝在庫 戦略備蓄 strategic stockpile

bichikuyunyū 備蓄輸入 import for stockpiling

bichōsei 微調整 fine-tuning ¶ the day-to-day *fine-tuning* of monetary regulations // to seek to *fine-tune* the economy // the policy of *fine-tuning* demand through regulation // to try to *fine-tune* the economy

bidōkyūyosei ビドー給与制 Bedaux system

bihin 備品 furnishings; fittings and appliances

binbōsen 貧乏線 poverty line ¶ →貧困線

binjō 便乗 making the use; taking full advantage ¶ to raise prices *taking full advantage* of the increase in crude oil prices // price increases *making the use* of the rise in crude oil prices

binjōneage 便乗値上げ "me-too" price hikes; "free ride" price markups; jumping on the price-raising bandwagon; raising prices under the pretext of (higher oil prices); price hikes by utilizing (rises in oil prices)

biraku 微落 fractional decline; slight decline; marginal decline; slight fall; marginal dip

biruzuonrīseisaku ビルズ・オンリー政策 [米] bills-only policy

biryūshiosen 微粒子汚染 particulate pollution

bishiteki 微視的 micro(-scopic; -cosmic)

bitō 微騰 fractional advance; slight rise; marginal advance

bizō 微増 slight increase; edging up; marginal rise; fractional increase

bōage 棒上げ straight rise; uninterrupted upward move

bōbiki 棒引き →帳消し

bōchō 膨張 expansion; inflation; increase; swelling

歳出膨張 increase in expenditure ¶ to limit the *inflation* of bank deposits

通貨膨張 inflation; inflation of currency; currency expansion; monetary expansion

bōchōkeisū 膨張係数 coefficient of expansion

bōchōritsu 膨張率 rate of expansion

bōei 防衛 defense; self-protection ¶ market intervention under the U.S. package in *defense* of the dollar // the measures taken by the United States in *defense* of the dollar // President Nixon's *defend*-the-dollar program // consumers' scare-buying for *self-protection*

bōeigai 防衛買い ［市］ defensive buying

bōeikainyū 防衛介入 defensive intervention

bōeisaku 防衛策 defense measure; defense package ¶ the *package* of dollar *defense measures* announced on 1/11 // President Carter's dollar *defense package* // ［参考］ restrictions which were adopted in defense of the lira

bōeishishutsu 防衛支出 defense spending (=expenditure)

bōeitekibuki 防衛的武器 defensive weapons

bōeki 貿易 trade; foreign trade; international trade; export and import trade; overseas trade ¶ The trend of *overseas trade* was distorted by the dock strike. // *International*

trade showed remarkable resilience, with the value of world exports increasing substantially. // a more moderate rate of growth of *trade* between Japan and the U.S. // Despite measures to damp down exports and encourage imports, the *trade* surplus grew. // *Trade* performance in metal manufacturing improved last year. // ［参考］ the decline in the international performance of British industry

仲介貿易 intermediary (=intermediate) trade; merchanting trade

中継貿易 entrepot trade; transit trade; intermediary (=intermediate) trade

沿岸貿易 coastal trade; coastwise trade

外国貿易 foreign trade; overseas trade

保護貿易 protective trade

域内貿易 intra-trade

委託加工貿易 processing trade; processing deal

自由貿易 free trade

海外貿易 overseas trade

海上貿易 floating trade

加工貿易 processing trade; improvement trade

国内貿易 home trade; inland trade

国際貿易 international trade

協定貿易 trade by agreement

求償貿易 reciprocal trade; compensation trade; barter trade

無差別貿易 non-discriminative trade

二国間貿易 bilateral trade

覚え書貿易 memorandum trade

三角貿易 triangular trade

政府間貿易 government (to government) trade

世界貿易 world trade

商品貿易 merchandise trade; visible trade

双務貿易 bilateral trade

垂直貿易 vertical trade

多角的貿易 multilateral trade

通過貿易 transit trade

迂回貿易 roundabout trade

bōekiaitekoku 貿易相手国 trading partner (country); client state ¶ Germany was Switzerland's largest single *trading partner.* // a forward-looking and trustworthy *trading partner* // to open markets to imports from less affluent *trading partners*

bōekibukkashisū 貿易物価指数 unit value indexes of exports and imports

bōekifutaikeihi 貿易付帯経費 incidental expenses of trade; trade-related expenses

bōekigaikeijōtorihiki 貿易外経常取引 invisible current transactions

bōekigaishūshi 貿易外収支 invisible trade balance; services balance; invisible balance; balance of invisible trade

bōekigaitorihiki 貿易外取引 invisible trade; non-trade transaction

bōekigyōtaitōkeihyō 貿易業態統計表 statistic tables on foreign trade activity

bōekihikiuketegata 貿易引受手形 trade acceptance

bōekiizondo 貿易依存度 degree of dependence upon foreign trade

bōekijiri 貿易尻 balance of trade; trade balance

bōekijiyūka 貿易自由化 trade liberalization

bōekikakakushisū 貿易価格指数 external trade unit value indexes; unit value indexes of exports and imports

bōekikan 貿易館 trade museum

bōekikawaseseido 貿易為替制度 foreign trade and exchange legislations and systems

bōekikeitaibetsuyushutsunyū 貿易形態別輸出入 trade by type of contract

bōekikesson 貿易欠損 trade gaps; trade deficit ¶ There was a visible *trade gap* of Fl. 338 million in June against the *trade deficit* of Fl. 853 million in May.

bōekikin'yū 貿易金融 foreign trade financing

bōekikō 貿易港 trade port

bōekikyōtei 貿易協定 trade agreement

bōekimasatsu 貿易摩擦 trade friction

bōekirengō 貿易連合 trade federation

bōekisaikai 貿易再開 reopening of private foreign trade

bōekiseigen 貿易制限 trade restriction

bōekisensō 貿易戦争 trade war ¶ the opening gun of a full-scale *trade war*

bōekishin'yō 貿易信用 trade credit

bōekishō 貿易商 trader; trading merchant

bōekishūshi 貿易収支 trade balance; visible trade balance; balance of (visible) trade

bōekishūshijiri 貿易収支尻 foreign trade position; trade balance; merchandise trade position ¶ France's foreign *trade position* swung sharply into surplus. // The *trade balance* with these countries moved into a surplus in Germany's favor, in contrast to a deficit in the same period last year. // There was a *balance-of-trade* deficit of Fl. 2.1 billion. // countries in *balance-of-trade* difficulties // to restore equilibrium in the country's foreign *trade balance* // to strengthen Canada's already improving *merchandise-trade position*

bōekisūryōshisū 貿易数量指数 quantum indexes of exports and imports

bōekitegata 貿易手形 trade bill

bōekitōkei 貿易統計 foreign trade statistics

bōekitsūka 貿易通貨 trading currency; vehicle currency

bōgaikōsaku 妨害工作 obstructionism

bōgairieki 望外利益 windfall gain; windfall profit

bōgairijun 望外利潤 windfall profit

bōgairitoku 望外利得 windfall gain ¶ Any excess profits thus earned are treated as *windfall gains*.

bogaishisan 簿外資産 unlisted asset; hidden asset; secret assets

boka 簿価 book value

bōkeigaisha 傍系会社 collateral company; subsidiary company; subsidiary; affiliated company; affiliate ¶ foreign *affiliates* incorporated in Japan // Japanese *subsidiary companies* incorporated in the U.S.

bōkeino 傍系の collateral; affiliated; subsidiary

bokeru ぼける ［市］ slacken; weaken

boki 簿記 bookkeeping
複式簿記 double-entry bookkeeping
工業簿記 industrial bookkeeping
単式簿記 single-entry bookkeeping

bōkō 棒鋼 steel bar

bokuchiku 牧畜 stock raising; stock farming

bokuchikujō 牧畜場 stock farm

bonchō 凡調 ［市］ featureless; trendless

bondooiru ボンド・オイル bonded oil

bonyū 募入 ［証市］ allotment

bonyūsha 募入者 ［証市］ allottee

bōraku 暴落 nose-dive; heavy decline; heavy fall; collapse; plunge ¶ The value of the dollar *plunged* disastrously.

borantarîchēn ボランタリー・チェーン voluntary chain; VC

bōri 暴利 excessive profit; exorbitant interest; usury

bōritorishimarirei 暴利取締令 anti-profiteering ordinance

bōriya 暴利屋 profiteer

bōsage 棒下げ straight fall; slump; sudden fall; sharp break; tumbling

bosai 募債 flotation (=raising) of a loan; loan flotation ¶ →募集

bosaigaku 募債額 amount of loan

bosaihikiuke 募債引受け underwriting

bosaihikiukedan 募債引受団 underwriters; underwriting syndicate

bosaihikiukemōshikomisho 募債引受申込書 underwriting letter

bosaijōken 募債条件 terms of loan flotation

bosaikakaku 募債価格 issue price

bosaiseisaku 募債政策 loan policy

bōsengai 防戦買い defensive purchase; holding the market; supporting the market; support buying

boshoseiri 簿書整理 book regularization

boshū 募集 collection; recruitment; recruiting; ［証市］ offer(ing) to sell (=for sale; for subscription); placement; distribution ¶ an *offer to sell*, or a solicitation of an *offer* to buy securities

boshūannai 募集案内 ［証市］ offering circular ¶ the mis-statement or concealment of material facts in the *offering circulars* and other selling literature

boshūchōka 募集超過 oversubscription

boshūdairinin 募集代理人 ［証市］ placement agent

boshūdan 母集団 population; universe

  無限母集団 infinite population

  有限母集団 finite population

boshūgaku 募集額 amount to be raised

boshūhakkō 募集発行 issue by public offering ¶ to *offer* stocks *for public* subscription // *publicly offered* stocks

boshūhikiukekeiyaku 募集引受契約 underwriting agreement

boshūhikiukemōshikomisho 募集引受申込書 underwriting letter

boshūkōkoku 募集広告 advertisement for subscription

boshūuridashi 募集売出し sale (of securities) on a commission basis

boshūuridashitoriatsukaigyōmu 募集売出取扱業務 ［市］ business of distributor; distributing business

botayama ボタ山 (mound of) coalpit waste; pile of coal waste

buai 歩合 rate; percentage; commission

buaisan 歩合算 percentage calculation

buaiseitesūryō 歩合制手数料 performance fee

buaiukeoi 歩合請負 percentage contract

buhin 部品 components; spare parts

¶ demand for electronic *components* overseas // car *spare parts*

bukka 物価 commodity prices; prices

［上昇］ ¶ Wholesale *prices*, seasonally adjusted, increased 0.4 percent between May and June. // Consumer *prices* continued their rapid climb, increasing at a 7.6 percent annual rate. // Wholesale *prices* increased at a sharply accelerated pace. // The downward drift in the rate of *price* advances was broken by steel *price* rises. // *Prices* of producer goods rose faster (4.5 percent) from early 1969 to the autumn of 1975. // The *prices* of nonfood items soared at an annual rate of 7 percent. // The *price* gains were widespread, to show a mild upward tendency. // *Prices* edged up 0.2 percent and measured 5 percent above April last year. // The upward trend in *prices* has become stronger rather than weaker. // to recover a little from a sharp fall in April // a slight steepening of the mildly rising trend of domestic *prices*

［保合い］ ¶ *Prices* fluctuated narrowly around horizontal trends. // *Prices* remained in a narrow range. // *Prices* have been steady up and down the line. // *Prices* are maintained at the advanced levels reached in April. // *Prices* are unchanged at a level 2 percent higher than a year earlier. // The low point in *prices* has been passed. // The rise in *prices* was halted.

［下落］ ¶ *Prices* eased slightly. // The *price* fall was quite general, but most marked in metals. // *Prices* receded somewhat from the peaks reached in July.

狂乱物価　frenzied price spiral

bukkaantei　物価安定　price stabilization; price stability ¶ to maintain the already slow progress towards greater *price stability*

bukkaanteitai　物価安定帯　price stabilization zone

bukkaatsuryoku　物価圧力　price pressure; (up-)pressure on prices ¶ The pent-up *price pressures* will be released. // Major expansion in govt. demand puts *up-pressure on prices*.

bukkachinginsupairaru　物価賃金スパイラル　price-wage spiral ¶ Tax cuts may help in slowing down the *price-wage spiral.* // *A price-wage spiral* would then develop which would certainly aggravate the balance-of-payments situation.

bukkachōsetsu　物価調節　regulation of prices

bukkadōkō　物価動向　price developments; price trends; price movements; behavior of prices; price performance ¶ Overall *price developments* have recently been stable. // *Price developments* were more encouraging. // *Price performance* has been uneven. // recent and medium-term or longer run *price trends* // Prices have fluctuated narrowly around horizontal *trends*. // *Price movements* of a country of Norway's size must follow international *price movements* rather closely. // Some upward *movement in prices* has taken place. // The moderate behavior of consumers was reflected in the continued sidewise *movement of prices*. // The downward adjustments in prices of industrial materials left their mark on the *price*

performance and prompted a relaxation of demand management policies.

bukkahendō　物価変動　price fluctuation (=variation; change)

bukkahikisage　物価引下げ　reduction of prices

bukkahyō　物価表　price list

bukkajōshō　物価上昇　price rise; price advance; price boost; price hike; price increase; price upswing; price run-up; price upturn; price uptrend ¶ large-scale, huge, aggressive, frantic, rampant, rapid, sharp, or steep *rises in prices*

bukkajōshōatsuryoku　物価上昇圧力　inflationary pressure; pressure for price increases ¶ There are some potential factors that will increase *inflationary pressure* from the medium-term point of view. // to generate heavy *pressure for price increases* // factors that seemed to increase *pressure for price increase* // [参考] cooperation in keeping price hikes down // to check the relentless upward march of prices // Prices surged upwards.

bukkajōshōritsu　物価上昇率　rate of price increase; rate of increase in prices

bukkakugizuke　物価釘付け　price-pegging

bukkamitōshi　物価見通し　price forecast; prediction for prices

bukkanoantei　物価の安定　stability of prices; price stability; stabilization of prices; price stabilization

bukkanohanekaeri　物価のはね返り　reactionary rise in prices

bukkanokahōkōchokusei　物価の下方硬直性　downward rigidity of

prices

bukkaryūtsūkosuto 物価流通コスト physical distribution cost

bukkaseisaku 物価政策 price policy

巻き返し物価政策 roll-back policy

bukkashisū 物価指数 price index ¶ The *index* averaged 2.2 percent higher than in 1974. // The food *price index* (1970＝100) moved up 0.3 percent from the March figure. // The consumer *price index* climbed steeply again, rising at an annual rate of 5 percent despite a slight decline in food costs. // The wholesale *price index* jumped 0.4 percentage points, rebounding to the July level of 109.1 percent of the 1967-69 average. // A steep increase in petroleum prices lifted the January *price index* to a new high. // The *index* of wholesale *prices* of industrial commodities rose from mid-November to mid-December by 0.2 percent. // The *indexes* (＝indices) of export and import *prices* have wavered around horizontal trends. // As measured by the retail *price index*, prices rose by some 50 percent between January and April. // to give a slight downward tilt to the consumer *price index*

小売物価指数 retail price index

農村物価指数 price index of commodities in agricultural community

卸売物価指数 wholesale price index; W.P.I.

生産者物価指数 producer's price index

輸出入物価指数 export and import price indexes

bukkashisūsuraidosei 物価（指数）スライド制 indexation; indexing; indexing scheme ¶ wage *indexation* to living expenses or to prices // *schemes indexing* wages to inflation

bukkasuijun 物価水準 price level ¶ The moderate upward drift of the *price level* has run its course. // Retail prices have been maintained at the advanced *levels* reached in July. // The consumer *price level* will again rise slowly.

bukkataikei 物価体系 price structure

bukkataisaku 物価対策 measures against price rises; price stabilization measures

bukkatochinginnoakujunkan 物価と賃金の悪循環 price-wage spiral; vicious circle of wages and prices

bukkatōketsu 物価凍結 price freeze; freeze on prices

bukkatōki 物価騰貴 advance in prices; price rise; soaring prices; soaring high of prices ¶ →物価上昇

bukkatōseikaijo 物価統制解除 price decontrol

bukkatōseirei 物価統制令 price control ordinance

bukkenhaitō 物件配当 property dividend

bumon 部門 sector; segment; branch; line ¶ the private non-banking *sector* of the economy // across every *segment* of American life // various industrial *branches* // in some *lines* of industry // The 30 companies in this group span eight major *sectors* of industry. // within the broad *sectors* of the economy, and within important *segments* of each *sector* // the poorest *segments* of the population // various non-financial domestic *sectors* of the economy // The economy can be subdivided into four main *sectors* : the public sector, (central government, local authorities, public corporations), the personal *sector* (individuals and unincorporated businesses), the corporate business *sector*, (individual, commercial, and financial companies) and the overseas *sector* (foreigners).

bumonbetsukaikei 部門別会計 departmental accounting

bumonbetsurieki 部門別利益 departmental profit

bumonbetsuson'ekikeisansho 部門別損益計算書 multiple-step income statement; sectional income statement

bumonbunkatsu 部門分割 sectoring

bumonka 部門化 departmentalization

bumonkanjuyōshifutoinfure 部門間需要シフトインフレ sectorial demand-shift inflation

būmu ブーム boom ¶ Business reports reflect an extension of the *boom*. // The Government's disinflationary measures overcome the existing momentum of the *boom*. // The *boom* continues in Norway. // a less hectic development after three years of *boom* // The *boom* reached full force. // 1961 was the third *boom* year after a recession. // a brief period in the foothills of the next *boom* // Britain is now near the top of a roaring consumer *boom*. // By next spring, the consumer *boom* will be petering out. // The investment *boom* can peter out. // a consumer spending *boom* that was particularly bullish during the summer months
消費ブーム spending boom
投資ブーム investment boom

būmufurēshon ブームフレーション "boomflation"

bunbai 分売 distribution; offering
一次分売 primary distribution
二次分売 secondary distribution

bunbaidan 分売団 selling group; selling syndicate

bunbōgu 文房具 stationery and office utensils

bun'eki 分益 gain-sharing; crop sharing

bungyō 分業 division of labor; specialization
国際分業 international division of labor
産業内分業 intra-industry specialization
垂直的分業 vertical division of labor
水平的分業 horizontal division of labor

bunjō 分譲 allotment sale

bunjōchi 分譲地 lot (developed) for sale; land for allotment sales

bunjōjūtaku 分譲住宅 dwelling (built) for sale

bunka 分化 diversification; division ¶ to *diversify* and lighten human toil // the *division* of labor and the *division* of the product

bunkai 分解 analysis; decomposition; disintegration; dismantling; disaggregation ¶ to *disaggregate* capital according to type of capital or expected life

bunkakeikō 分化傾向 tiering; diversification ¶ to *diversify* monetary instruments // *diversification* and sophistication of people's taste // *tiering* money rates

bunkatsu 分割 partition; division; dismemberment; disaggregation; decomposition ¶ to *disaggregate*

exports by commodity group
株式分割　stock split; split-up
企業分割　split-up of business

bunkatsubarai 分割払い　easy payment; payment in installments ¶ the maximum number of months over which the borrower is to *pay* the balance in *installments* // →割賦

bunkatsubaraihanbaiten 分割払い販売店　tally shop

bunkatsubaraihōshiki 分割払い方式　[米] installment plan; [英] hire-purchase system ¶ Second hand cars are now subject to tighter *hire-purchase* conditions and must be paid for in twelve months. // There will be more severe regulations regarding *hire-purchase* on television sets, with deposits rising from 10 to 60 percent. // The selective relaxation of *purchase* and credit terms contributes to some recovery in sales of consumer durables.

bunkatsuchūmon 分割注文　split order

bunkatsufunazumi 分割船積み partial shipment

bunkatsuhanbai 分割販売　tally trade

bunkatsushoyūken 分割所有権　several ownerships

bunkatsusōzokusei 分割相続制　division of succession

bunkenka 分権化　decentralization ¶ *decentralization* of decision-making

bunkentekikanri 分権的管理　decentralized management

bunki 分岐　ramification ¶ manifold *ramifications* worrisome of the world debt situation

bunkyoku 分極　polarization ¶ a *polarization* of economies tending to make the strong stronger and to weaken the weak // a *polarization* of the world into surplus and deficit countries

bunpai 分配　distribution; share; split ¶ to ensure a more equitable *distribution* of income // to *distribute* the product more equally // the revenue *sharing* system // how to *split* those scarce dollars
富の分配　distribution of wealth
利益分配　division of profits; profit-sharing

bunpaichūmon 分配注文　give-out order

bunpaigaku 分配額　share

bunpairitsu 分配率　relative share

bunpu 分布　distribution ¶ The size-of-borrower *distribution* of bank lendings shifted from the largest to the intermediate category.
長方形分布　rectangular distribution
度数分布　frequency distribution
ふた山分布　bimodal distribution
非対称分布　asymmetrical distribution; skew distribution
一様分布　uniform distribution
株式分布　distribution of stocks
連続分布　continuous distribution
正規分布　normal distribution
所得分布　income distribution
対称分布　symmetrical distribution

bunretsukōka 分裂効果　polarization effect

bunri 分離　separation ¶ *separation* between capital and management // *separation* of investment and management, and of management and ownership // *separation* of securities business from banking businss
経営と所有の分離　separation of management and ownership

資本と経営の分離　separation between capital and administration
出資と経営の分離　separation of investment and management
財産分離　separation of property

bubrikazei 分離課税　separated taxation

bunrui 分類　classification; grouping; assortment; sorting ¶ a by-size *classification, classification* by size // The income *groupings, groupings* of countries by size of income, were fairly narrowly defined. // The selected countries were *grouped* into ten pairs with similar per capita incomes but contrasting tax levels. // to *group* under four broad headings // a breakdown by major commodity *groups* // household budget data which *group* households by income class

bunsan 分散　dissolution; dissipation; spread; breakup; distribution; diversification; dispersion; segmentation; fragmentation ¶ the *spreading* of the underwriting risks // a change in the *dispersion* of spreads among high and low-risk borrowers in the Euro-market // There is excessive *segmentation* of land-holdings in some areas. // a *fragmentation* of the international capital markets
機会分散　opportunity diversification
危険分散　risk diversification

bunsando 分散度 dispersion of prism; measure of dispersion

bunsanjunbisei 分散準備制　decentralized reserve system

bunsanritsu 分散率　index of dispersion; variance ratio

bunsantōshi 分散投資　diversified investment; diversification invest-

ment

bunseki 分析　analysis; assay ¶ to attempt an *analysis* // to make a previous *analysis* of it
微視的分析　microcosmic analysis; micro-analysis
分光分析　spectrometric analysis
貯蓄投資分析　saving-investment analysis
動態分析　dynamic analysis
限界分析　marginal analysis
ギャップ分析　gap analysis
平均分析　average analysis
比較分析　comparative analysis
比率分析　rate analysis
費用・効果分析　cost-benefit analysis
因果循環分析　recursive analysis
事後分析　ex-post analysis
時系列分析　time series analysis
実物分析　real analysis
事前分析　ex-ante analysis
回帰分析　regression analysis
価格分析　price analysis
貸手分析　analysis of lender's preference
過程分析　process analysis
活動分析　activity analysis
経営分析　analysis of operation
経過分析　sequence analysis
経験的分析　empirical analysis
計量経済モデル分析　econometric model analysis
経済分析　economic analysis
企業経営分析　financial statements analysis
期間分析　period analysis
均衡分析　equilibrium analysis
機能分析　functional analysis
国民所得分析　national income analysis
構造分析　structural analysis
巨視的分析　macrocosmic analysis; macro-analysis

マネー・フロー分析　money flow analysis; flow-of-funds analysis

マネー・サプライ分析　money supply analysis

横断面分析　cross-section analysis

ラグ分析　lag analysis

連立方程式分析　simultaneous equations analysis

作業分析　job analysis

成因分析　component analysis

市場分析　market analysis

信用分析　credit analysis

システム分析　systems analysis

職務分析　job analysis

所得分析　income analysis

損益分岐分析　break-even analysis

総体的経済分析　aggregate economic analysis

趨勢分析　trend analysis

定量分析　quantitative analysis

定性分析　qualitative analysis

定質分析　qualitative analysis

統計(的)分析　statistical analysis

投入・産出分析　input-output analysis

要因分析　factor analysis

財務諸表分析　financial statements analysis

bunsekiseisekihyō　分析成績表　assay report

bunsekisho　分析所　assay office

bunsekishōmeisho　分析証明書　assay certificate

bunsekitekiyosoku　分析的予測　analytical prediction

bunshogizō　文書偽造　forgery

bunson　分損　partial loss

buntan　分担　apportionment; partial charge; average

　損害の分担　apportionment of a loss

buntanbun　分担分　share to be borne

buntangaku　分担額　allotted amount; allotment; contribution

buntanjōkō　分担条項　contribution clause

buntankaison　分担海損　general average

buntankin　分担金　contribution

　国際機関への分担金　contributions to international institutions

bun'ya　分野　area; field; sector; branch; sphere ¶ to restrict credit to some *areas* of the economy // in a wide range of *fields* of industry // divergent developments of major dimentions in various *sectors* of the economy // a profitable *branch* of industry // to explore underdeveloped *fields* of industry // to afford a splendid *field* for activity // the *branch* that has specialized in... // to compete with other groups of banks in the latters' traditional *spheres*, such as small mortgages // in high priority *areas* // [参考] The February rise is broadly based across industry and market groupings.

buppinchōtatsu　物品調達　procurement of supplies and equipment

burasserukanzeihinmokubunruihyō　ブラッセル関税品目分類表　Brussel's Tariff Nomenclature; BTN

burasserukanzeijōkyohyō　ブラッセル関税譲許表　Brussel's Tariff Nomenclature; BTN

bureton'uzzukyōtei　ブレトン・ウッズ協定　Bretton Woods Agreement

bureton'uzzutaisei　ブレトン・ウッズ体制　Bretton Woods system; Bretton Woods regime ¶ the situation which existed in the days before the *Bretton Woods system* // The *Bretton Woods regime*, which served the world well for twenty-five years after the war, came to an end in the early 1970s.

burokku ブロック bloc ¶ the formation of closed trade *blocs* // economic *blocs* // *bloc*-building among nations

貿易ブロック   trade bloc

経済ブロック   economic bloc

burokkuka ブロック化 bloc-building

busshokugai 物色買い selective buying

busshi 物資 goods; materials; commodities

危険物資   hazardous substance

危急物資   critical materials

民需物資   civilian goods

busshibetsutekigōyusōhōshiki 物資別適合輸送方式 unit train service

busshidōin 物資動員 materials mobilization

busshiidōkeikaku 物資移動計画 plan for the transportation of goods

busshijukyūkeikaku 物資需給計画 plan for demand and supply of goods

busshikatsuyō 物資活用 utilization of materials

busshishūsanchi 物資集散地 distribution center

busshokugaininki 物色買人気 ［市］ selective strength ¶ *Selective strength* Monday sent the stock market to another new high for the year.

busshokusōba 物色相場 ［市］ selective market

butsunō 物納 payment in kind

buttekiryūtsūkosuto 物的流通コスト physical distribution cost; PD cost

buttekiryūtsūmō 物的流通網 physical distribution network

buttekisongai 物的損害 property damage

buzumiryōdateyokin 歩積両建預金 compulsory deposit as a condition for loans; bill discount deposit; insurance deposit against discount; compensating balance; compensatory balance ¶ the common practice to demand non-interest bearing *compensating balance* from corporate borrowers

byōdōshugi 平等主義 egalitarianism ¶ Developed countries tend to have a more *egalitarian* wage structure. // the *equalitarian*-minded head of assembly at Chrysler's plant

C

chakka 着荷 arrivals; receipts; goods arrived; goods received

chakkabarai 着荷払い payment on arrival

chakkawatashi 着荷渡し delivery on arrival

chakune 着値 c.i.f. price ¶ *¥100* per ton *c.i.f.* Kobe

chātābēsu チャーター・ベース charter base

chekkuraitā チェック・ライター check perforator

chienbaishōkin 遅延賠償金 indemnity for arrears

chienhaitōkin 遅延配当金 dividend in arrear(s); dividend arrears

chienhikiwatashi 遅延引渡し delayed delivery

chienrisoku 遅延利息 interest for arrears

chihō 地方 locality; district; region

chihōbunken 地方分権 decentralization of power

chihōbunkenshugi 地方分権主義 regionalism

chihōbun'yozei 地方分与税 partial tax transfer to local government

chihōchōkan 地方長官 prefectural governor

chihōchōkankaigi 地方長官会議 gubernatorial conference; governors' conference

chihōdairiten 地方代理店 local agent

chihōgikai 地方議会 prefectural assembly; municipal assembly; local assembly

chihōginkō 地方銀行 regional bank; provincial bank; country bank; local bank

chihōginkōdētatsūshinmō 地方銀行データ通信網 local banks' data communication system

chihōheikinji 地方平均時 local mean time

chihōhi 地方費 local expenditure

chihōjichi 地方自治 local self-government; local autonomy

chihōjichitai 地方自治体 local (public) authorities; local public entity; local government

chihōkakutoshi 地方核都市 local nucleus city

chihōkōeikigyō 地方公営企業 enterprises operated by local public organizations

chihōkōfukin 地方交付金 [米] revenue share

chihōkōfuzeikōfukin 地方交付税交付金 [日] distribution of local allocation tax; local allocation tax grant

chihōkōkyodantai 地方公共団体 local public authorities; local public body; local public entity

chihōkōkyōdantaikōshakōdanbumon 地方公共団体・公社・公団部門 local anthorities and public corporation sector

chihōsai 地方債 municipal bond; prefectural bond; local government bond

chihōsaibansho 地方裁判所 district court

chihōseikatsuken 地方生活圏 local activity zones

chihōtekidokusen 地方的独占 local monopoly

chihōzaisei 地方財政 local finance

chihōzaiseiheikōkōfukin 地方財政平衡交付金 [日] local finance equalization grants

chiikibunpu 地域分布 geographical distribution

chiikihyōjun 地域標準 regional standard

chiikikaihatsu 地域開発 regional development

chiikikankakusa 地域(間)格差 regional disparity (=differential) ¶ *Regional disparities* in living conditions narrowed. // to moderate or alleviate severe *disparities* in *regional* development // the extent and duration of the *regional disparities* // The *regional* wage *differentials*, wage *differentials* between *regions*, contracted.

chiikikeizai 地域経済 regional economy ¶ research related to the *regional economy*

chiikikōzō 地域構造 regional structure

chiikishakaisābisu 地域社会サービス community service

chiikitekishūchū 地域的集中 localization ¶ *localization* of industry and of labor

chiikitōgō 地域統合 regional integration

chiikitokkei 地域特恵 regional preferential duties

chiikiyōryō 地域容量 regional capacity

chijōken 地上権 superficies; surface rights

chika 地価 land price; land value

chikakōjiseido 地価公示制度 guide system of land value

chikashūsei 地価修正 revaluation of land

chikōshihyō 遅行指標 lagging indicator; laggard indicator ¶ The *laggard indicator* in the early economic recovery, housing, is expected to move toward an annual rate of some 1.5 million units.

chikugetsu 逐月 month after (= by) month ¶ Output increased *month after month.*

chikusan 畜産 animal husbandry

chikusanbutsushijikakakuseido 畜産物支持価格制度 price-support system for livestock products

chikusangyōsha 畜産業者 stockman

chikuseki 蓄積 accumulation; stock; stockpile; reservoir; heap; piling up; garner ¶ the cessation of inventory *accumulation* // the rich *accumulations* of material // *accumulating* reserves // *Stocks* were run down. // to be fully *stocked* with oil // a *stockpile* of war materials // a large *reservoir* of electric power // *cumulating*

force // to *heap* up products // to *pile* up goods in *heaps* // to *garner* trading profits from spot activity

本源的蓄積 primary accumulation

chikusekibaizō 蓄積倍増 doubling of accumulation

chikusekien 蓄積円 deposited yen

chin 賃 hire; wage; fare; charge; rate; freight; cartage; carriage; rent

chin'age 賃上げ wage increase; wage hike; pay raise; pay rise; wage claim ¶ The average *wage increases* negotiated for unionized workers amounted to 6.1 percent for the year. // to hold the *increase* in *pay* plus fringe benefits to a rate of 7% a year // claims for *pay raises* // an inflation-compensating *pay raise* // Employees are requested to keep their *wage claims,* and employers the *wage increases* granted, within the limits compatible with an increase in prices. // The ban on *pay raises* covers pay awards for merit, seniority and cost-of-living bonuses as well as negotiated *rises.* // Metal workers reached a significant agreement entailing an across-the-board *pay rise* of Lit. 25,000 a month.

物価上昇に見合った賃上げ pay increase kept pace with price rises

chin'ageritsu 賃上げ率 ratio of wage-hikes; rate of wage increases ¶ to hold the *increase* in *pay* plus fringe benefits to a *rate* of 7% a year // ［参考］ The average margin of raise was 18.4 percentage points less than last spring's settlement. // Settled pay raise amounts averaged 13.4%. // Wage and salary payment fell at an annual rate of $500 million. // There was considerable dispersion of pay settlements around the 5.8% figure. // Wage settlements have not kept with the rise in the consumer price index. // The level of wage settlements reached in this year's round of negotiations is lower than last year.

chin'ageyōkyū 賃上げ要求 claims for pay raise; wage claim; wage demand; pay demand ¶ The trade unions were quite restrained in their *wage demands*. // The workers have either settled their *wage claims* or have established a framework for such a settlement. // The trade unions presented rather moderate *wage claims*. // *Wage claims* in the pay round are considerably lower than they have been. // High unemployment held down *wage demands*. // large *pay demands* by the trade unions

chinetsuhatsuden 地熱発電 natural steam (electric power) generation; geothermal generation

chingin 賃金 wage; wage and salary; pay ¶ The once stagnant nominal *wages* are once again moving upward. // Only 15 percent of *wages* is earned by the top 10 percent of employees. // *Wages* rise as workers get older, provided they have stayed within the same firm. // Contractual *wages* for young graduates are at times higher in smaller firms.

安定賃金 stable wage

出来高賃金 piece (work) wage

一般業種別賃金 prevailing wage classified by occupation

法定賃金 legal minimum wage

時間当り賃金 hourly wages ¶ In April the index of minimum contractual *hourly wages* in industry (excluding family allowances)

worked out at 110.5. // Gross *hourly wages* in industry in April were 13.4% higher than 12 months earlier.

時間払賃金 time wage

時間外賃金 overtime wage

実質賃金 real wage

飢餓賃金 starvation wage

基本賃金 basic wage; regular wage; base wage

契約賃金 contractual (=contracted) wage

公正賃金 fair wage; just wage

名目賃金 nominal wage

年功序列型賃金 seniority order wage

利益均てん割賃金 profit sharing wage scale

最高賃金 maximum wage

最低賃金 minimum wage

生活維持賃金 subsistence wage

仕事別賃金 wages by job

品払賃金 wage (payment) in kind; truck system

奨励賃金 incentive wage

所定外賃金 wage drift

スライド賃金 wages in sliding scale

手取り賃金 take-home pay (in worker's envelope)

割増し賃金 extra wage; premium wage

chingintaikei 賃金体系 wage system; wage structure; wage constitution

chinginbakuhatsu 賃金爆発 wage explosion

chinginbēsu 賃金ベース wage standard

chinginbukkagaidorain 賃金物価ガイドライン wage-price guidelines ¶ Round two of the government's voluntary *wage-price guidelines* is being molded.

chinginbukkanoakujunkan 賃金・物価の悪循環 vicious circle of price and wages; wage-price spiral; wage-cost explosion

chinginbukkaseisaku 賃金・物価政策 pay and prices policy

chinginbukkasupairaru 賃金・物価スパイラル wage-price spiral ¶ the threat of a *wage-price spiral* that potentially undermine Italy's economic performance // A damaging *spiral* of *prices* and *wages* must be avoided at all costs. // the *spiral of wages* chasing prices and prices chasing wages

chinginbukkatōketsu 賃金・物価凍結 freeze on wages and prices; wage-price freeze

chinginbukkatōsei 賃金・物価統制 wage-price control

chinginhiyō 賃金費用 wage cost

chinginhōkyūseikatsusha 賃金俸給生活者 wage and salary earner ¶ Average unemployment reached 6% of the total number of *wage and salary earners.*

chinginhyō 賃金表 payroll ¶ to keep many people on the *payroll* // Smaller *payrolls* mean hardship for workers. // to be on or off the *payroll* // overpadding of public *payrolls* // to add a fair amount to its *payroll* // a large *payroll*

chinginkakusa 賃金格差 wage differential; wage disparity ¶ *Wage differentials* between firms and industries increased. // *Wage differentials* by industry and firms' size narrowed. // *wage differentials* by wage group and by sex // *wage disparity* by scale of enterprises // There is obviously some interindustry variation in *wage differentials.* // the unex-

plained male-female *wage differential*

地域別賃金格差 regional wage differentials

規模別賃金格差 wage disparity by scale of enterprises

chinginkirisage 賃金切下げ wage cut

chinginkōsei 賃金攻勢 wage offensive

chinginkōshō 賃金交渉 wage negotiation; wage bargaining; pay (raise) talks; wage offensive; labor offensive; wage round; pay round; bargaining round ¶ Managers and unions of major private railway companies began last-ditch *pay talks.* // *Wage negotiations* resulted in an increase of less than 10%. // The average growth of earnings during the current *bargaining round* will amount to roughly 7%. // Wage claims in the *pay round* beginning in August are expected to be considerably lower than they have been in the current *round.* // an early and moderate settlement in the current *wages* and incomes *negotiations*

chinginneageyōkyū 賃金値上げ要求 demand for higher wages; claims for pay raise ¶ →賃上げ要求

chinginnobukkasuraidosei 賃金の物価スライド制 wage indexation to prices; wage indexation to living expenses

chinginnoheijunka 賃金の平準化 wage standardization

chinginritsu 賃金率 wage scale; wage rate; pay scale ¶ disparities between the top and bottom of the public *pay scales* // relative increases in contractual hourly *wage rates* in the two countries // the gap between union and non-union labor *wage scales* // an average increase in contractual hourly *wage rates* of 5 to 5½% // The minimum wage is tied to average prevailing manufacturing *wage rates*. // The average *wage rate* for females is approximately two-thirds the average wage for males. // The *scale* of *wages* ranges from ten to twenty dollars a day. // Basic weekly *wage rates* rose by 4 percent.

出来高賃金率 price work wage rate

chinginrōdōsha 賃金労働者 wage-earner

chinginseikatsusha 賃金生活者 wage-earner; wage-worker

chinginseikeihirinkuhōshiki 賃金生計費リンク方式 cost-of-living indexation (system); indexation; indexing

chinginshiharaibo 賃金支払簿 payroll

chinginshiharaigaku 賃金支払額 wage bill ¶ Wage settlements gave rise to a year-on-year gain of 18% in the non-agricultural *wage bill*. // relatively low *wage-bills*

chinginshisū 賃金指数 wage rate index ¶ The *wage rate index* mainly covers lower paid workers.

chinginshotoku 賃金所得 wage income

chinginsuijun 賃金水準 wage level

chinginsutoppu 賃金ストップ wage pause; wage freeze

chingintessoku 賃金鉄則 iron law of wages; brazen law of wages, subsistence law of wages

chingintōketsu 賃金凍結 pay-freeze; wage-freeze

chingintōsō 賃金闘争 wage-hike

drive ¶ These employees stage yearly *wage-hike drives*.

chingin'uwanosebun 賃金上乗せ分 wage drift

chinginzenzōsei 賃金漸増制 escalator scale

chinpuka 陳腐化 obsolescence

非物質的陳腐化 moral obsolescence

経済的陳腐化 economic obsolescence

chinpukashita 陳腐化した obsolete; obsolescent; out-of-date; outmoded ¶ Higher oil prices made part of the capital stock *obsolete*. // functionally *obsolescent* railroad facilities // *obsolete* equipment requiring renovation // *out-of-date* technique of production management

chinpukashisan 陳腐化資産 obsolete assets

chinretsutenji 陳列展示 display and exhibits

chinrōdō 賃労働 wage labor

chinsei 鎮静 subsidence; diminution ¶ Inflation will *subside* a bit more than was commonly believed. // The drop in the price of gold was further evidence of a *diminution* of inflationary psychology. // *subsidence* of once rampant inflation // Inflation has now *subsided*. // Such a phenomenon is conducive to the *calming* of foreign exchange market conditions. // a market *cooling-off* in the economic climate // The economy was beginning to *cool*. // to *cool off* the accelerateing inflation now at work

chinseika 鎮静化 calming down; calm-down; cooling-off; dissipation ¶ to *cool down* the economic climate // the anticipated economic *calm-down* // The forces of inflation have been *dissipated*. // It looked as if *calm* had been restored to the monetary scene. // The business climate has *cooled off*.

chinshaku 賃借 lease; letting and hiring; charter; hire

chinshakuchi 賃借地 leased land

chinshakufudōsan 賃借不動産 leasehold estate

chinshakuhoken 賃借保険 leasehold insurance

chinshakuken 賃借権 right of lease

chinshakunin 賃借人 leasee; hirer; leaseholder; renter

chinshigoto 賃仕事 piece-work; job-work

chinshigotonin 賃仕事人 pieceworker

chintai 沈滞 reticence; doldrum ¶ Industrialists' *reticence* to invest helped to fuel the recession. // The economy is mired in the *doldrums* with supply outstripping demand. // Private investment is out of the *doldrums* if not actually experiencing a recovery.

chintai 賃貸 lease; hiring-out; charter

chintaikakaku 賃貸価格 rental value; value of lease

chintaikeiyaku 賃貸契約 lease contract

chintainin 賃貸人 lessor; renter

chintairyō 賃貸料 rent; charterage

chintairyōritsu 賃貸料率 rental rate

chintaishita 沈滞した dull; stagnant; slack; sluggish; inert; inactive; languid; torpid ¶ The economy continued (to be) *stagnant*. // The market declined in *sluggish* trading. // The economy *slackened*. // a distinct

dullness of activity in business // → 不況; 不冴え

chishikisangyō 知識産業 knowledge-intensive industry; knowledge industry

chishikishūyakuteki 知識集約的 knowledge-intensive ¶ an industrial structure that is more *knowledge-intensive* and higher value-added.

chissosankabutsu 窒素酸化物 nitrogen oxide

chisui 治水 flood control; riparian conservancy; river improvement; river conservancy

chisuikōgaku 治水工学 hydraulic engineering

chisuikōji 治水工事 riparian works; embankment works; levee (conservancy) works

chitaibaikasei 地帯売価制 zone pricing system

chitaiunchinsei 地帯運賃制 zone tariff system

chitekishokugyō 知的職業 profession; intellectual occupation

chitsujo 秩序 order ¶ These brought *order* out of chaos in the 1930's. // to maintain *order* on the DM/ dollar market // the concept of an all-encompassing new international economic *order* // New policies and mechanisms for insuring *orderly* evolution of the world economy are necessary. // to restore international monetary *order* // *orderly* marketing of exports // to establish a more *orderly* pattern of interest rates // to operate the market in *orderly* fashion // The international monetary *order* is sure to get more stable thereby. // This proved expedient for purposes of maintaining *orderly* market conditions.

chitsujoaru 秩序ある orderly ¶ to operate the market in an *orderly* fashion

chitsujoaruzenzō 秩序ある漸増 gradual and orderly increase

chōbatsutekikinri 懲罰的金利 penal rate; punitive high rate

chōbatsutekikōritsubuai 懲罰的高率歩合 punitive high rate

chōbo 帳簿 book; account-book

chōbogaishisan 帳簿外資産 non-ledger asset; concealed asset; hidden asset

chōbokakaku 帳簿価格 book value

chōboseiri 帳簿整理 adjustment of accounts

chochiku 貯蓄 saving; laying by; storing up; savings

不妊貯蓄 abortive savings

負の貯蓄 negative saving

法人貯蓄 corporate saving; business saving

事後的貯蓄 ex-post saving

自発的貯蓄 voluntary saving

事前的貯蓄 ex-ante saving

純貯蓄 net savings

企業貯蓄 corporate saving; business saving

強制的貯蓄 forced saving

任意貯蓄 voluntary saving

累積貯蓄 accumulated savings

政府貯蓄 government saving

総貯蓄 aggregate savings; gross savings

相互貯蓄 mutual savings

粗企業貯蓄 gross corporate (=business) saving

据置貯蓄 deferred savings; fixed savings

割増金付貯蓄 savings with premium

chochikuginkō 貯蓄銀行 savings bank

chochikujissenkatsudō 貯蓄実践活動 savings activity

chochikujissensoshiki 貯蓄実践組織 savings practice organization

chochikukikan 貯蓄機関 thrift institution; store-of-value institution ¶ specialized *thrift institutions,* including mutual savings banks, savings and loan associations, and credit unions

chochikuritsu 貯蓄率 savings rate; savings ratio; saving rate; ratio of saving to disposable income; private saving as a percentage of private disposable income ¶ Increased spending implies a drop in the *savings ratio,* i.e. private saving as a percentage of private disposable income. // The personal *saving rate* in the U.S. is in the range of 5% of disposable personal income.

chochikusaiken 貯蓄債券 savings debenture; saving bond

chochikuseikō 貯蓄性向 propensity to save

chochikuseiyokin 貯蓄性預金 time deposit

chochikushin 貯蓄心 thriftness; savings psychology ¶ to inculcate an enduring *savings psychology* among the people at large

chochikushinkeihatsu 貯蓄心啓発 inspiring and motivating the general public to practice savings

chochikushōrei 貯蓄奨励 saving encouragement; thrift encouragement; savings drive

chochikushōreisaku 貯蓄奨励策 savings promotion measures

chochikusuishinkikō 貯蓄推進機構 savings promotion organization

chochikusuishin'undō 貯蓄推進運動

savings promotion campaign; savings drive

chochikutōshinoshotokuketteiron 貯蓄投資の所得決定論 savings-investment theory of income determination

chochikutōshiron 貯蓄・投資論 saving-investment theory ¶ *saving-investment theory* of income determination

chochikutōshironsō 貯蓄・投資論争 savings-investment controversy

chochikuundō 貯蓄運動 savings campaign; savings drive

chochikuyokin 貯蓄預金 savings deposit

chochikuyūgūsochi 貯蓄優遇措置 preferential treatment for savings; favorable (tax) treatment for savings

chochikuzōkyō 貯蓄増強 savings promotion ¶ overall measures to *promote savings*

chōdefurēshon 超デフレーション hyper-deflation

chōfuku 重複 duplication; overlapping; to double; to overlap ¶ to avoid *duplication* of services and wasteful competition // Interbank deposits are merely a *duplication* of deposits of individuals and corporations.

chōfukubutsu 重複物 duplicate

chōfukuhoken 重複保険 double insurance

chōfukuhurikae 重複振替 double transfer

chōfukukanjō 重複勘定 overlapped account; double account; double-counting ¶ net of the *double-counting* that results from the redepositing of funds between banks

chōfukukazei 重複課税 double taxation

chōfukusaitei 重複裁定 compound arbitrage

chōfukutōshi 重複投資 overlapping investment

chōjiri 帳尻 balance of accounts; balance
貿易の帳尻 trade balance
銀行帳尻 bank balance

chōjirikessai 帳尻決済 settlement of balance

chōjunbōekihenkōtekiseichō 超順貿易偏向的成長 ultra-pro trade-biased growth

chōka 超過 excess; overage; overshooting ¶ the money supply *overshooting* the target range
引揚げ超過 net withdrawal of treasury funds; net receipts on Treasury accounts; withdrawal excess in the public-to-government balance
重量超過 overweight
支払超過 excess payment over receipt; net payment
資本超過 over-capitalization
積荷超過 overcharge; overloading
受取超過 excess receipt over payment; net receipt
輸入超過 excess of imports; adverse balance of trade
輸出超過 excess of exports; favorable balance of trade

chōkahakkō 超過発行 excess issue (over withdrawal)

chōkahoken 超過保険 excess insurance; over insurance

chōkahoshō 超過保証 over-certification

chōkajuyō 超過需要 excess demand

chōkakinmukyū 超過勤務給 overtime wage (=pay)

chōkakyōshutsu 超過供出 over-quota delivery

chōkanzenkoyō 超完全雇用 over-full employment; hyper-employment

chōkaritoku 超過利得 excess profit; excess windfall profit

chōkaritokuzei 超過利得税 excess profit tax

chōkasetsubinōryoku 超過設備能力 excess capacity

chōkashotoku 超過所得 excess income; excess revenue ¶ to reap *excess revenues* from the decontrol of oil prices

chōkasongaisaihoken 超過損害再保険 excess-of-loss reinsurance

chōkatenimotsu 超過手荷物 excess baggage; overweight baggage

chōkeshi 帳消し write-off; write-down; cancellation ¶ Most of the *write-offs* were on loans to private commercial enterprises. // *Write-offs* recovered in 1978 amounted to about $6.2 million, making net *write-offs* for the year about $342.8 million. // International loans and deposits *written off* last year totaled $405.7 million. // The World Bank has never had a *write-off* of a loan.

chōkifusai 長期負債 fixed liabilities; funded debt

chōkihadō 長期波動 long wave

chōkihendō 長期変動 secular change

chōkihoken 長期保険 long-term insurance

chōkikariirekin 長期借入金 long-term debt; long-term loans payable

chōkikashita 長期化した pro-tracted; prolonged ¶ the most *pro-tracted* and severe recession in the postwar period // pervasive and *prolonged* inflation

chōkikashitahikishime 長期化した引締め protracted credit restraint; protracted tight money policy

chōkikashitsukekin 長期貸付金 term loan; long-term loan; long-term receivable ¶ the extent to which banks can make *long-term loans* funded by short-term deposits

chōkikawase 長期為替 long exchange

chōkikeieikeikaku 長期経営計画 long-term management plan

chōkikeikaku 長期計画 long-range plan; long-term schedule; long-run program

chōkikinri 長期金利 long-term rate of interest; long-term interest rate; long-term rate

chōkikin'yūkikan 長期金融機関 financial institutions for long-term credit

chōkikin'yūshijō 長期金融市場 long-term credit market; capital market

chōkikōsai 長期公債 long-term government bond; funded debt

chokin 貯金 savings deposit
  天引き貯金 savings deducted at the source
  積立貯金 installment savings
  郵便貯金 postal savings

chokinbako 貯金箱 savings box; bank

chōkinkōyosan 超均衡予算 balanced budget with surplus

chōkinkōzaisei 超均衡財政 surplus finance

chokinkumiai 貯金組合 savings association

chōkinobebaraishin'yō 長期延払信用 long-term trade credit

chokintsūchō 貯金通帳 savings (deposit) passbook

chōkiseisanshijō 長期清算市場 futures market

chōkishasai 長期社債 long-term debenture; long-term bond

chōkishihonshūshi 長期資本収支 long-term capital balance; long-term capital transactions

chōkishikin 長期資金 long-term funds

chōkishintaku 長期信託 long-term trust

chōkishin'yōginkō 長期信用銀行 long-term credit bank

chōkitegata 長期手形 long-dated bill; long bill

chōkiteirishikinkashitsuke 長期低利資金貸付 long-term and low interest-rate loan

chōkiteitairiron 長期停滞理論 theory of secular stagnation

chōkiteki 長期的 long-term; long-range; long-run ¶ [参考] a strategic opportunity within an extended time frame

chōkitekifukinkō 長期的不均衡 secular disequilibrium

chōkitekikeikō 長期的傾向 secular trend

chōkitekikinkō 長期的均衡 secular equilibrium

chōkitekitenbō 長期的展望 long-term prospect; long-range outlook

chōkitorihiki 長期取引 long-term trading; dealing in futures

chōkiuntenshikinkashitsuke 長期運転資金貸付 lending of long-term operation funds

chōkiyoyaku 長期予約 long commitment

chokkeishokunōsoshiki 直系職能組織 line and functional organization

chokkeisoshiki 直系組織 line organization

chōkō 徴候 sign; indication ¶ *signs* of continued economic vigor abound // →兆し

chōkokkachūōginkō 超国家中央銀行 supranational central bank

chōkokkakikan 超国家機関 supranational institution (=organ); super-national institution (=organ)

chōkokusekikigyō 超国籍企業 supernational corporation →多国籍企業

chokusetsuaitaitorihiki 直接相対取引 central bank's securities selling operation vis-à-vis bank (or short-term credit broker); [外] bank-to-bank transaction

chokusetsuboshū 直接募集 [市] direct placement; allotment to shareholders ¶ *directly placed* new stocks

chokusetsusaitei 直接裁定 direct arbitrage

chokusetsutekikisei 直接的規制 direct control; direct (regulatory) action

chokusetsutōshi 直接投資 direct investment; equity investment ¶ *direct* U.S. *investments* abroad

chokusetsuzei 直接税 direct tax

chokuyunyū 直輸入 direct import

chokuyunyūhin 直輸入品 direct imports

chokuyunyūshō 直輸入商 direct importer

chokuyushutsu 直輸出 direct export

chokuyushutsuhin 直輸出品 direct exports

chokuyushutsushō 直輸出商 direct exporter

chōryokuhatsuden 潮力発電 tidal power generation

chōsa 調査 survey; research; exploration; investigation; factfinding ¶ an *exploration* of all possible means of financing

動機調査 motivation research

現地調査 on-the-spot survey

標本調査 sample survey

実地調査 field survey

縦深調査 (in-)depth survey

海外市場調査 foreign market research

環境調査 environmental research

家計調査 household budget survey

景気動向調査 survey of business trends

経済調査 economic research (=survey)

機械受注状況調査 survey of orders received for machinery

個人別賃金調査 individual wages survey

パネル調査 panel survey

労働力調査 labor force survey

世論調査 public opinion survey (= poll)

市場調査 market(ing) research (= survey)

士気調査 morale survey

自然環境保全調査 survey on the state of vegetation

消費者価格調査 consumer price survey

商況調査 business survey

出張調査 research visit

統計調査 statistical survey

売上高調査 sales research

chōsei 調整 alignment; regulation; governing; adjustment; coordination; modulation; tuning; reconcilement ¶ *alignment* periods of economic *adjustment* // required *adjustments* in production // to undergo difficult *adjustments* // read*justments* in the economy // The

economic *adjustment* has run true to form. // an *adjustment* of national energy policies // The Treasury *adjusted* its financing programs to the change in economic conditions. // the downward *adjustments* in prices // to secure the perfect *coordination* of fiscal and monetary policies // to *coordinate* all government programs // debt operations *coordinated* with monetary and fiscal policies // They help to facilitate *coordination* between fiscal, monetary, and other economic policies. // The Board of Governors fosters and *coordinates* the economic intelligence function of all the Reserve Banks. // the *coordination* of Federal Reserve policy with national stabilization policy // It has become difficult to *reconcile* the various targets. // *fine-tuning* of day-to-day monetary conditions // a more realistic *alignment* of wage demands with the prospective growth of real output // [参考] The U.S. GNP, after removing the impact of inflation, expanded at a seasonally adjusted annual rate of 8.3 percent.

微調整 fine-tuning

価格調整 price adjustment

年末調整 year-end adjustment

粗調整 rough-tuning

chōseiatsuryoku 調整圧力 adjustment discipline ¶ Business has been under rigorous *adjustment discipline*.

chōseibasukettohōshiki "調整バスケット"方式 "adjustable basket" technique

chōseihi 調整費 adjustment works expenses

chōseiinfure 調整インフレ adjustment inflation; controlled inflation;

induced inflation; artificial inflation ¶ the theory of *induced* or *artificial inflation* // ［参考］ an inflationary measure deliberately taken to stimulate business // open inflation against suppressed inflation

chōseikanōheika 調整可能平価 adjustable peg

chōseikatei 調整過程 adjustment process ¶ the economy in an *adjustment process*

chōseikikan 調整期間 adjustment period

chōseikikō 調整機構 adjustment mechanism

chōseikōmoku 調整項目 reconciliation item; adjustment item

chōseishikin 調整資金 adjustment fund

価格調整資金 price adjustment fund

chōseishokuhinten 調整食品店 delicatessen store

chōseishotoku 調整所得 adjusted income

chōseisōchi 調整装置 regulator; governor

chōseitekitorihiki 調整的取引 accommodating transaction

chōseizaigen 調整財源 adjustment funds

chōshūyaku 徴収役 collecting official

chōtatsu 調達 procurement; supply; raising; accommodation

域外調達 offshore procurement

特別調達 special procurement

chōteikinriseisaku 超低金利政策 ultra cheap money policy

chōten 頂点 highest; largest; apogee; zenith; top; ceiling; peak ¶ the economy at its *highest* postwar level, or at an *apogee*

chōwa 調和 coordination; alignment; harmony; concert ¶ *co-ordination* of exchange rate policies vis-à-vis third countries // to *co-ordinate* various Federal programs // well-*coordinated* fiscal and monetary policies // to bring long-term rates in better *alignment* with short-term rates // International levels of interest rates among countries are now more closely *aligned* than before. // Operations of the private sector must *harmonize* with the stabilization program. // to spoil *harmony* between labor and management // These steps were parts of a general and *concerted* credit policy.

chōwaheikin 調和平均 harmonic average; harmonic mean

chūchōkikashidashi 中長期貸出 term loans

chūchōkisai 中長期債 medium-to-long-term bonds

chūdō 中道 middle of the road ¶ He is a *middle-of-the-roader* but with leanings on the conservative side. // President Carter is pragmatic, *middle-of-the-road* and not doctrinaire.

chūgenshikin 中元資金 funds for customary midyear present

chūisū 中位数 median

chūka 鋳貨 coin ¶ issues of plated and debased *coins*

貿易鋳貨 trade coin

chūkai 仲介 intermediation ¶ *Intermediation* by the banks in Italy has grown. // the volume of *intermediation* carried out by the banks // The Euro-markets today are the ultimate in *intermediation* between lenders and borrowers, between savers and investors.

chūkaibōeki 仲介貿易 cross trade;

intermediary trade; merchanting trade

chūkaibōekikeiyaku 仲介貿易契約 merchanting trade contract; contract for merchant trade

chūkaisha 仲介者 intermediary; intermediate; inter-agent; go-between; middleman

chūkaitesūryō 仲介手数料 brokerage

chūkanbaishō 中間賠償 interim reparation

chūkanbōeki 中間貿易 intermediate trade

chūkanhaitō 中間配当 interim dividend

chūkanhōkoku 中間報告 interim report

chūkanhyōka 中間評価 interim appraisal

chūkanjuyō 中間需要 intermediate demand; wholesalers' demand

chūkankashitsukeginkō 中間貸付銀行 intermediate credit bank

chūkankeiki 中間景気 temporary boom; passing boom

chūkankin'yū 中間金融 interim finance

chūkanmokuhyō 中間目標 interim goal; intermediate target (of monetary policy) ¶ *interim goals* of economic policy actions

chūkannaikaku 中間内閣 interim cabinet; stop-gap cabinet

chūkansakushu 中間搾取 intermediary exploitation; indirect squeezing

chūkanseisanbutsu 中間生産物 intermediate product

chūkanshōnin 中間商人 middleman; broker ¶ to cut out the London Metal Exchange *middlemen* and sell its copper direct to customers.

chūkanshotokusō 中間所得層 middle income group

chūkansō 中間層 middle class

chūkeibōeki 中継貿易 entrepot trade

chūkeikichi 中継基地 staging terminal

chūkenchūshōkigyō 中堅中小企業 smaller, high-rated firms

chūkenkigyō 中堅企業 middle-market enterprise; middle-scale enterprise; medium-sized enterprise

chūkikashidashi 中期貸出 medium-term loan; intermediate term loan ¶ to make capital *loans* to business for *intermediate terms* of 2 to 10 years

chūkikeizaitenbō 中期経済展望 medium-range (=-term) economic outlook

chūkiteki 中期的 medium-term; intermediate ¶ near-term and *intermediate* prospects

chūkitenbō 中期展望 medium-term outlook ¶ The *medium-term outlook,* based on current assumptions, is unsatisfactory.

chūkitōshijunkan 中期投資循環 medium-term investment cycle ¶ As for private plant and equipment investment, a downward phase of the *medium-term investment cycle* has commenced. // The downswing of the *medium-term cycle* probably bottomed out.

chūkōnenrōdōsha 中高年労働者 middle and old-aged workers

chūmon 注文 order ¶ increased *orders* from European countries // The excessive backlog of *orders* has been reduced. // Markets became strongly competitive because of ample capacity and lagging *or-*

ders. // new *orders* received by durable goods manufacturers // New *orders* for durable goods continued to sag. // The pace of incoming *orders* is appreciably slower and *orders* in hand have reached a normal level. // Unfilled *orders* of producers of investment goods rose more slowly. // *Orders* on industries producing basic materials show signs of improvement. // Industrial *orders* had risen fast, and backlog of *orders* had been built up. // The spring and early summer seasonal slack in *orders* appears to be quite mild this year. // *Orders* placed with industry for machinery remained roughly on a plateau. // *Orders* placed with industry are running at a higher level than a year ago. // Foreign *orders* were filled first with the domestic market satisfied later. // to specialize in the execution of *orders* for blocks of stock less than 100 shares, the unit of trading on the floor

分割注文　split order
分配注文　give-out order
逆指値注文　stop-loss order
急ぎの注文　immediate order
確定注文　firm order
刻み注文　scale order
口頭注文　verbal order
見本注文　sample order
店任せ注文　customer's agreement
未消化注文　unfilled order; backlog of orders
成行注文　carte blanche order
指値注文　limit order
据置注文　open order
他店回し注文　give-out order
当日限りの注文　day order

chūmonchō 注文帳　order book

chūmonhassōchō 注文発送帳　order given

chūmonhin 注文品　goods ordered; article on order; made to order

chūmonseiritsutsūchijō 注文成立通知状　contract note

chūmonseisan 注文生産　order production

chūmonsho 注文書　order sheet

chūmonshoshiki 注文書式　order blank; order form

chūmontori 注文取り　canvasser; salesman

chūmon'ukeirechō 注文受入帳　orders acknowledged

chūnyū 注入　injection ¶ the central bank's direct *injection* of reserves into the banking system // The Bank of France made capital *injections* on the money market against first category paper.

chūōenzanshorisōchi 中央演算処理装置　[コン] central processing unit; CPU

chūōginkō 中央銀行　central bank

chūōginkōnochūritsusei 中央銀行の中立性　neutrality of the central bank

chūōginkōnomokuteki 中央銀行の目的　policy objectives of the central bank

chūōginkōshin'yō 中央銀行信用　central-bank credit ¶ a decline in recourse to *central-bank credit*

chūōginkōtsūka 中央銀行通貨　[独] central-bank money (including assets of the Confederation, but excluding credits and swaps) ¶ The volume of *central-bank money* in the usual sense (including borrowed funds) had gone up at a rate of only 1.3%. // The banks' demand for *central bank money* was large for seasonal reasons.

chūōginkōwaribikiritsu 中央銀行割引率 Bank rate; official discount rate

chūōseifukariirejuyō 中央政府借入需要 central government borrowing requirement; CGBR ¶ Britain's *CGBR* totalled 1.60 billion sterling in May.

chūōzaisei 中央財政 central goverment finance

chūrihhinokoonitachi チューリッヒの小鬼達 gnomes of Zurich

chūritsukasuru 中立化する neutralize ¶ Part of the concomitant liquidity expansion had to be *neutralized.* // Monetary instruments are used to *neutralize* the effects of autonomous changes in the monetary base.

chūritsuki 中立旗 neutral flag

chūritsukoku 中立国 neutral state; neutral

chūritsusei 中立性 in-between position; neutrality ¶ Policy-makers usually seem to have to take an *in-between position.*

chūritsuseinogensoku 中立性の原則 neutrality doctrine

chūritsusen 中立船 netural ship

chūritsusenshōmeisho 中立船証明書 certificate of neutrality; sea letters; pass

chūritsuteki 中立的 neutral; middle-of-the-road ¶ The influence of the public sector was virtually *neutral.* // a strategy that is *neutral* between the domestic and export markets // to declare a strict net *neutrality* against government intervention // a *neutral* fiscal policy // The 1976-77 budget is *neutral* because while raising the prices on

some items it cuts prices on others. // a *middle-of-the-road* anticyclical policy

chūritsutekirishiritsu 中立的利子率 neutral rate of interest

chūritsutekiseisaku 中立的政策 neutral policy ¶ The government assumed a *neutral policy* in compiling the national budget. // Monetary policy shifted from the restricitve posture to a position that has been described as a *neutral policy.*

chūritsutekitsukakyōkyū 中立的通貨供給 neutral money supply

chūsai 仲裁 arbitration; mediation; conciliation; intervention ¶ to settle the matter by *arbitration*
強制仲裁 compulsory arbitration
任意仲裁 voluntary arbitration

chūsaijōyaku 仲裁条約 arbitration treaty

chūsaikeiyaku 仲裁契約 arbitration agreement

chūsainin 仲裁人 arbitrator; mediator; peacemaker

chūsaisaitei 仲裁裁定 decision by arbitration; arbitration (award) ¶ The labor trouble will go to *arbitration.*

chūseikan 中勢観 intermediate-term market outlook

chūsenshōkan 抽籤償還 redemption by lot; redemption by drawing

chūsenshōkantōsenshōken 抽籤償還当籤証券 bond drawn for redemption

chūshinchi 中心地 center; hub; heartland ¶ a world financial *center* // its position as a gold market *hub* of the region // a *hub* of industry // Beirut has been eclipsed as a financial *center.* // The Great Lakes states constitute the U.S. industrial *heartland.*

chūshinchi 中心値 central value; mid-value

chūshinkabu 中心株 [市] market kingpin

chūshinkōgyōkoku 中進工業国 new industrializing countries; NICs

chūshinkoku 中進国 more developed countries; MDCs; medium nation; semi-advanced countries (=nations); more advanced developing countries (=nations); semi-industrialized countries

chūshinshugitaisei 〜中心主義体制 -centered system; -centric system ¶ Ethno*centric,* Poly*centric,* or Geo*centric* system

chūshinsōba 中心相場 prevailing rate; middle rate; median rate; medial rate; representative rate; central rate, pivot(al) rate ¶ to value at the market price *prevailing* on the day // latest indicative *middle rates* quoted between banks // median rate of spot dollars // to meet the bulk of the demand for dollars at the *median* trading *rate*

chūshōkigyō 中小企業 (medium and) small enterprises; small businesses; smaller businesses; medium and small business; businesses in medium and small markets; middle and small-market corporations

chūshōkigyōkankeikigentsukiyu-shutsutegata 中小企業関係期限付輸出手形 export usance bills drawn by small and medium-sized enterprises

chūshōkigyōkeieibunseki 中小企業経営分析 financial statements of small businesses

chūshōkigyōkikaishakkan 中小企業機械借款 equipment credit for small business

chūshōkigyōkin'yūbetsuwakuyū-shi 中小企業金融別枠融資 special loan for financing small business

chūshōkigyōkin'yūkikan 中小企業金融機関 financial institutions for small business

chūshōkigyōkōdokashikinkashitsū-keseido 中小企業高度化資金貸付制度 [日] loan system for the structural strengthening activities of smaller enterprises

chūshōkigyōmukesakimonoyoyaku-kankeigaikayotaku 中小企業向先物予約関係外貨預託 deposit of foreign currency with foreign exchange banks for facilitating forward exchange contract relating to exports by small enterprises

chūshōkigyōseiseihin 中小企業性製品 products supplied by medium and small enterprises; smaller enterprise products

chūshōkigyōsetsubikindaikashikin-kashitsuke 中小企業設備近代化資金貸付 [日] loans for the modernization of the equipment of smaller enterprises

chūshōkigyōtaisaku 中小企業対策 measures for small business

chūshōkigyōtankikeizaikansoku 中小企業短期経済観測 short-term economic survey of small businesses

chūshokuken 昼食券 lunch voucher

chūshōno 中小の medium and small(-scale); medium- and small-size; small-size; smaller

chūshōshōkōgyōsha 中小商工業者 medium and small traders and manufacturers

chūshotokukoku 中所得国 middle-income countries

chūshutsu 抽出(標本の) sampling; ［コン］extract
  枝分かれ型抽出 nested sampling
  比例抽出 proportionate sampling
  比例層抽出 proportional stratified sampling
  確立抽出 probability sampling
  系統的抽出 systematic sampling
  基本的抽出 fundamental sampling
  無作為抽出 random sampling
  無作為でない抽出 non-random sampling
  二段抽出 two-stage sampling; sub-sampling
  二重抽出 double sampling
  任意抽出 random sampling
  層化抽出 stratified sampling
  層化無作為抽出 stratified random sampling
  多段抽出 multi-stage sampling
  単純無作為抽出 simple random sampling
  多相抽出 multi-phase sampling
  点抽出 point sampling
  有意抽出 positive sampling; judgment sampling

chūshutsuritsu 抽出率 sampling ratio

chūtokaiyakuharaimodoshikinga-ku 中途解約払戻金額 surrender value

chūzō 鋳造 casting; founding; minting; coinage
  自由鋳造 free coinage
  貨幣鋳造 coinage
  制限鋳造 limited coinage

chūzōhō 鋳造法 casting process
  鋼の連続鋳造法 continuous casting

chūzōka 鋳造貨 metallic coin

chūzōsha 鋳造者 caster; founder

chūzōsho 鋳造所 foundry; mint
  活字鋳造所 type-foundry

D

dabutsuki だぶつき overabundance; overhang; glut; oversupply ¶ the dollar *overhang* in the exchange market

dai ～台 -mark; -level ¶ to pass the 500 yen-*mark* // the four percent-plus *level* // over the 10 percent-*mark* // Sales in dollars fell below the half million-*mark*. // Stock prices pierced the ¥5,000-*mark*. // Output recovered the $20,000 *level*. // The Dow Jones industrial index is hovering near the 1,000-*mark*. // The unemployment rate went down below the two percent *level* to 1.88 percent. // The number of foreign banks in London has topped the 300-*mark*.

daiarubijincsu ダイアル・ビジネス dial business

daiginkō 大銀行 major bank; big bank

daihakkai 大発会 opening session of the year

daihyōchi 代表値 central value

daihyōkengen'oyūsurutorishimari-yaku 代表権限を有する取締役 director who has authority to represent the company

daihyōtorishimariyaku 代表取締役 representing director

daii 代位 subrogation; substitution

daiibensai 代位弁済 subrogated

performance; subrogation; payment under guarantee; payment in subrogation

daiichijioroshiuridankai 第一次卸売段階 first stage wholesalers

daiichijisangyō 第一次産業 primary industry

daiichisekai 第一世界 "First World", or capitalist and industrialized world

daiichiteitō 第一抵当 first mortgage

daiinōfu 代位納付 payment in subrogation

daiisaiken 代位債権 subrogated right

daikibokigyō 大規模企業 large (-scale) corporations

daikibokourigyō 大規模小売業 large-scale retail trade

daikibokouritenpo 大規模小売店舗 big retailer

daikiboseisannorieki 大規模生産の利益 economies of large-scale production

daikigyōseiseihin 大企業性製品 larger enterprise products

daikin 代金 price; cost; bill

daikinhikikae 代金引替え cash on delivery; c.o.d.

daikinhikikaekozutsumi 代金引替小包 c.o.d. parcel

daikinhikikaenedan 代金引替値段 c.o.d. price

daikinhikikaeshō 代金引替証 c.o.d. certificate

daikinhikikaeshoruiwatashi 代金引替書類渡し document against payment; d/p.

daikinhikikaetesūryō 代金引替手数料 c.o.d. commission

daikinkaishūnogimu 代金回収の義務(輸出の) responsibility of collec-

tion of export proceeds; duty to collect export proceeds

daikintoritate 代金取立て collection of bills; collection of prices; bill collection

daikintoritatekawasetegata 代金取立為替手形 sales bill of exchange

daikintoritatetegata 代金取立手形 short bill; bill for collection

daikōgaisha 代行会社 clearing corporation

daikōkikan 代行機関 agency

daikōnin 代行人 representation; delegation; agency

daikōukewatashi 代行受渡 delivery by a clearing corporation

daikyōkō 大恐慌 the Great Depression (of the 1930s)

dainijisangyō 第二次産業 secondary industry

dainisekai 第二世界 "Second World", or Communist and industrialized world

dainōkai 大納会 closing session of the year

dairekutomāketingu ダイレクト・マーケティング direct marketing

dairi 代理 representation; agency; procuration; proxy ¶ The undersigned hereby constitutes and appoints them and lawful *proxies* of the undersigned.

dairigyōmu 代理業務 agency operations

dairihanbai 代理販売 sale by agent

dairiininjō 代理委任状 power of attorney; proxy

dairikashitsuke 代理貸付 agency loan

dairiken 代理権 proxy

dairikōkan 代理交換 clearing for non-member

dairinin 代理人 representative; agent; proxy; deputy
副代理人 subagent

dairisainyūchōshūkan 代理歳入徴収官 deputy revenue collector

dairishishutsukan 代理支出官 deputy disbursing official

dairishō 代理商 commission merchant; factor

dairiten 代理店 agency; agent
公金代理店 agency for governmental funds
公庫代理店 agency of public finance corporation
国債代理店 agency for government bonds
公社代理店 agency of public corporation
歳入代理店 national revenue agency

dairiten'azukekin 代理店預け金 deposits with agencies

dairitengari 代理店借り current credit accounts with agencies

dairitengashi 代理店貸し current debit accounts with agencies; due from (domestic) agencies

dairitenkanjō 代理店勘定 agency accounts

dairitenkitakukin 代理店寄託金 specified deposits with agencies

dairitentesūryō 代理店手数料 agent fee; agent commission

dairiuragaki 代理裏書き per procuration endorsement

daisangokushijō 第三国市場 third-country market

daisanjisangyō 第三次産業 tertiary industry

daisannomadoguchi 第三の窓口 an Intermediate Financing Facility (=the Third Window)

daisannotsūka 第三の通貨 third reserve component

daisansekai 第三世界 "Third World", or underdeveloped and poor world

daisanshaenoshiharaisābisu 第三者への支払サービス third-payment services

daishō 代償 price; compensation, reward; recompense; remuneration; indemnity; indemnification; reparation; sacrifice ¶ pecuniary *compensation*, or *compensation* money, for damage // *indemnity* for arrears // The bond had to accept considerable *sacrifice* in the shape of modification of terms. // The *price* paid by the public through bank failures at times was high.

daishōken 代証券 substitute bond

daishōyunyū 代償輸入 compensation import

daitai 代替 substitution; deplacement; replacement ¶ efficient domestic *substitution* for imports // The bank *substitutes* its own credit for that of the borrower or his customers. // to *substitute* a single federal system in place of the present dual system of state and national banks // New industries concentrate upon import *substitution*. // industrialization as a way of *substituting* for the oil exports // Petroleum gradually *displaced* coal as the leading fuel in the industrial world. // price-induced *substitution* of other materials for tin
技術代替 technical substitution
生産物代替 product substitution
輸入代替 import substitution

daitaibutsu 代替物 substitute ¶ some import *substitutes* and commodities containing imported inputs //

Adjustment and financing are alternative or *substitute* strategies. // Consumers went to local *substitutes* for imported products.

daitaienerugī 代替エネルギー alternative source of energy

daitaihin 代替品 substitute; alternate product ¶ products which can never be replaced by a domestically produced *substitute*

daitaijunbishisan 代替準備資産 alternative reserve assets

daitaikanjō 代替勘定 (IMF) Substitution Account

daitaikanōsei 代替可能性 substitutability

daitaikōka 代替効果 substitution effect

daitaisentaku 代替選択 substitution choice

daitaizai 代替財 competitive goods

daiware 台割れ falling below the mark; dropping below the level ¶ to *drop below* the 100 yen-*mark*

daiyaguramuhaisō ダイヤグラム配送 diagram delivery

daiyō 代用 substitution

daiyōdenpyō 代用伝票 substitute slip (=ticket)

daiyōhin 代用品 substitute article; substituting goods; substitute

daiyōnenryō 代用燃料 substitute fuel

daiyōnōfu 代用納付 (tax) payment by substitute

daiyōnōfushōken 代用納付証券 securities received for cash

daiyonsekai 第四世界 "Fourth World", or underdeveloped but immensely wealthy world

daiyōparupu 代用パルプ woodpulp substitute

daiyōshōken 代用証券 substitute

security; collateral security

daiyōshokuryō 代用食料 substitute for rice

daizu 大豆 soya beans: soybeans

dakan 兌換 conversion

dakanginkō 兌換銀行 bank of issue

dakanginkōken 兌換銀行券 convertible bank note

dakanjunbi 兌換準備 specie reserve

dakanken 兌換券 convertible note

dakankenhakkōzei 兌換券発行税 tax on bank note issue

dakankinken 兌換金券 convertible gold note

dakanseido 兌換制度 conversion system

dakanshihei 兌換紙幣 convertible note

daketsu 妥結 settlement ¶ reasonable *settlements* to be reached in the forthcoming wage negotiations // to encourage trade unions to make moderate wage *settlements* // Rates of increase in domestic prices and costs, including wage *settlements*, had clearly been picking up again.

dakiawase 抱合せ [外] marrying ¶ *marrying* of buying and selling orders

dakiawasehanbai 抱合せ販売 combination sale; package deal; tie-in sale ¶ merchandise sold on a *package deal* basis

danchi 団地 housing complex; collective housing area; housing project; apartment complex ¶ garden plaza of the high rise *apartment complex*

danchihoken 団地保険 apartment-house dwellers insurance

dankai 段階 stage; level; phase ¶

The newly announced measures are the first *stage* of policy aimed at holding the deficit down. // Price trends have entered the *stage* where vigilance is required. // The working year is negotiated at national *level*, and wage discussions are held at sectorial *level*. // to present at a ministerial-*level* OECD meeting the final form of a program // The present deal gave a first-*phase* wage rise of 8%, followed by a 2% second-*phase*. // Tariffs will be abolished in two *phases*, first from 1980 to 1983 and the second from 1983 to 1987. // Rostow's *stages* of (economic) growth (*phase*)

dankaiteki 段階的 phased; by degree; gradual; step by step ¶ a *phased* lifting of oil curbs // a *phasing*-out of the role of the dollar // a *gradual* strengthening of trade controls // a *step-by-step* relaxation of restraints

dankaitekihaishi 段階的廃止 phasing-out; gradual dismantling ¶ The anti-inflation controls will be *phased out*. // The wage and price control program was being *phased out*. // the Government's policy of *phasing out* all controls over industrial prices // Spain was moving towards a *phasing-out* of subsidies. // the *gradual dismantling*, in the first few months of the year, of the emergency measures

dankaitekiheikahendōsei 段階的平価変動制 crawling peg system

dankaitekihikisage 段階的引下げ step-by-step reduction; gradual reduction; reduction by degrees

dankaitekiikō 段階的移行 step-by-step transition; gradual transition;

phasing ¶ a soft landing *gradually phasing* into the long-term rate of growth

dankaitekikaishō 段階的解消 phasing-out ¶ Privileges are likely to be *phased out* with rising levels of income and industrialization. // the policy of *phasing out* the current budget deficit over three years // [参考] The employment figures are high in the first and milder phase of the recession.

dankaitekikyōseisochi 段階的強制措置 method of activation of graduated pressures

dankaitekisekkinhō 段階的接近法 successive approximation method

dankaitekishiharaijunbiritsu 段階的支払準備率 graduated reserve requirements

danpingu ダンピング dumping
隠蔽ダンピング concealed dumping
為替ダンピング exchange dumping
信用ダンピング credit dumping
ソシアルダンピング social dumping

danpingubōshikanzei ダンピング防止関税 anti-dumping duty; anti-dumping tariff

danryokuchi 弾力値 elasticity coefficient

danryokujōkō 弾力条項 elastic clause

danryokukanzei 弾力関税 elastic tariff

danryokusei 弾力性 flexibility; resilience; elasticity; maneuverability ¶ more *flexible* operation of monetary policies // the high demand *elasticity* for exports // *maneuverability* in government financing // a low world income *elasticity* of demand // The economy has demonstrated its basic strength and *resilience*. // Increases in the debt were limiting the *flexibility* of Danish economic policy. // Japan's "window guidance" ceilings on commercial-bank lending were administered with *flexibility*. // the interest *elasticity* of investment // The *elasticity* of employment to output rose significantly but is likely to decline. // Britain's income *elasticity* for imports is about 1.33 // There is little *elasticity* demand for oil. // the *elasticities* of export and import response to price, or cost, changes // Income *elasticities*, of demand for exports turned out to be quite high. // to have the *flexibility* to structure the transaction that suits a customer's needs // to encourage *flexibility* of interest rates to respond to market forces // a greater measure of *flexibility* in the World Bank operations

物価弾力性　elasticity of price

代替弾力性　elasticity of substitution

技術的代替の弾力性　elasticity of technical substitution

需要の弾力性　elasticity of demand

価格弾力性　price elasticity ¶ The long-term *price elasticity* of demand for exports in aggregate is 1.5-2.5. // an apparent lessening in companies' *price elasticity*

価格差別化における弾力性　elasticity in price discrimination

弧弾力性　arc elasticity

労働需要の弾力性　elasticity of demand for labor

産出量の弾力性　elasticity of output

商品代替の弾力性　elasticity of commodity substitution

租税の国民所得弾力性　elasticity of tax to national income

点弾力性　point elasticity

予想の弾力性　elasticity of expectation

輸出入弾力性　elasticity of export and import

danryokutekikyōkyū　弾力的供給　elastic supply

danryokutekiun'yō　弾力的運用　flexible operation

dansei　弾性　elasticity

danseikei　弾性計　elastometer

danseikyokugen　弾性極限　limit of elasticity

danseiritsu　弾性率　modulus of elasticity

danshisōshingurui　男子装身具類　haberdashery

dantaihoken　団体保険　group insurance

dantaikōshō　団体交渉　collective bargaining; mass bargaining

dantaikōshōken　団体交渉権　right of collective bargaining

dantaikyōyaku　団体協約　collective agreement; collective contract

dantaiseimeihoken　団体生命保険　group life insurance

dantaishin'yōseimeihoken　団体信用生命保険　group credit life insurance

dantaiteikihoken　団体定期保険　group term insurance

dantaiyōrōhoken　団体養老保険　group endowment insurance

daregimi　だれ気味　[市] dull; idle

dashishiburi　出し渋り　reluctance; holding off; wait-and-see ¶ The *wait-and-see* attitude prevailed for some time.

dashite　出し手　[市] lender; giver ¶ *lender* of call money // *lenders* of call loans // *givers* and takers of Euro-currency

dashitereto 出し手レート offered rate ¶ London Interbank *Offered Rate*, LIBOR

datsukōgyōkashakai 脱工業化社会 post industrial(ized) society

datsuryūsōchi 脱硫装置 desulfurization equipment

datsusararīman 脱サラリーマン corporate refugee

datsuseijukuki 脱成熟期 post-maturing (stage)

datsuzei 脱税 evasion of taxes; tax evasion; tax-dodging; tax default ¶ to reduce wide *tax evasion* to prevent the erosion of tax base // *Tax evasion* costs the Treasury about fr. 200 billion. // to raise additional taxes by clamping down on *tax evasion* // *Tax default* is on the increase.

datsuzeihin 脱税品 smuggled goods

datsuzeisha 脱税者 tax-evader; tax-dodger

dauheikin ダウ平均 Dow-Jones average (of industrials); Dow Jones industrial average ¶ The *Dow Jones industrial average*, up more than 2 points at the outset, lost 2.52 points to 857.93 the worst setback in seven weeks.

dauheikinkabukashisū ダウ平均株価指数 Dow-Jones average index

daujōnzushōhinsōbashisū ダウ・ジョーンズ商品相場指数 Dow-Jones Commodity Index

dauriron ダウ理論 Dow theory

deaichūmon 出合注文 [外] exchange cover

deaisōba 出合相場 [外] cover rate

deau 出合う [市] coming to terms

defure デフレ →デフレーション

defuregyappu デフレ・ギャップ deflationary gap; margin of slack ¶ More public investment is needed to bridge the *deflationary* savings-investment *gap*. // public investment to bridge the *deflationary* savings-investment *gap* // the existence of a considerable *margin of slack* in most countries and sectors

defurekōka デフレ効果 deflationary effect (=impact) ¶ The *deflationary effect* of the oil crisis lingered on. // The *deflationary impact* of the oil price rise was another factor that had contributed to the recession.

defurēshon デフレーション deflation

dekidaka 出来高 production; output; volume; transaction; dealing; turnover; turnout; yield; crop; [市] (trading) volume; turnover ¶ *Turnover* swelled to 18,581,000 shares. // The market was lower in fairly active *turnover*. // *Volume* totaled 4,430,000 shares. // a drop in *volume* // *Volume* came to 25.06 million shares. // Still, daily *trading volume* ran a steady 237 million shares. // *Volume* on the New York Stock Exchange has averaged more than 30 million shares a day this year; in late 1972, daily *turnover* was about half this figure. // [参考] →取引高

dekidakane 出来高値 fixed price; fixing ¶ The French franc was *fixed* unchanged at 32.57 marks. // The dollar was set below its previous *fixing* on Wednesday.

dekidakabarai 出来高払い piece work payment

dekidakabaraichingin 出来高払い賃

金 piece-work rate; piece rate; piece wage ¶ the switch from *piece rates* to fixed wages

dekidakabaraichinginryōritsu 出来高払い賃金料率 piecemeal rate; piece wage rate

dekidakabarainoshigoto 出来高払いの仕事 piece-work

dekidakakyūsei 出来高給制 piece rate plan

dekine 出来値 sale price; quoted price; fixing (price); actual price

demonsutorēshonkōka デモンストレーション効果 demonstration effect

denaori 出直り [市] rally

dengenkaihatsu 電源開発 development of electric power resources

denka 電化 electrification ¶ growing *electrification* of the home

denkikikai 電気機械 electrical machinery (=apparatus; appliances; supplies)

denomi デノミ →デノミネーション

denominēshon デノミネーション redenomination; renaming of monetary units; changing of denomination of monetary units; renewal of monetary units

denpa 伝播 dispersion; spread ¶ The *dispersion* of national inflation rates remained large. // to check the *spread* of the buying spree // →波及; 拡散

denpyō 伝票 slip; voucher; ticket

denpyōkaikei 伝票会計 one-writing system

denryōkuryōkin 電力料金 electricity rates; power rates (=charges)

densankishiyōkōritsu 電算機使用効率 [コン] efficiency of computer

denshikeisanki 電子計算機 [コン] electronic computer; electronic data processing machine; EDPM

denshikeisansoshiki 電子計算組織 electronic data processing system; EDPS

denshinkaisōba 電信買相場 [外] telegraphic transfer buying rate; T.T. buying

denshinkawase 電信為替 telegraphic transfer

denshinryakugo 電信略語 telegraphic code

denshin'urisōba 電信売相場 telegraphic transfer selling rate; T.T. selling

denshiseigyo 電子制御 electronic control

denshishikiseimitsukikai 電子式精密機械(医療用または電気計測用のものに限る) electronic precision instruments (limited to instruments for medical or electrical measurement)

denshizunō 電子頭脳 electronic brain

densōseigyosōchi 伝送制御装置 [コン] transmission control unit

densōtsukekae 電送付替 remittance by teletype

dentatsushudan 伝達手段 vehicle ¶ to choose state enterprises as the principal *vehicle* for industrialization // to provide a *vehicle* for the practical transfer of this knowledge

dentōryōkin 電灯料金 electric light charges

dentōshugi 伝統主義 traditionalism

dentōtekishakai 伝統的社会 traditional society

denwadenpōryōkin 電話・電報料金 telephone and telegram rates (= charges)

deokurekabu 出遅れ株 [市] laggard

depojitorīginkō デポジトリー銀行 [外] depository bank

desaki 出先 outpost

dēta データ data ¶ The April *data* indicate an import value of $967 million. // to collect *data* on the subject // to obtain the recent statistical *data* on foreign trade // The latest year for which sufficiently detailed *data* are available on health and nutrition.

dētabanku データバンク data bank

dētadensō データ伝送 data transmission; data communication

dētashoriki データ処理機 [コン] data processing machine

dētatsūshin データ通信 data communication; data transmission

dētatsūshinmō データ通信網 network of data communication

dētatsūshinsābisu データ通信サービス data transmission service

disuinfurēshon ディスインフレーション disinflation

disukauntosutoa ディスカウント・ストア discount store

dōgaku 動学 dynamics

dōgitekisettoku 道義的説得 moral suasion; moral persuasion ¶ *Moral persuasion* has begun to permeate its effect into national treasuries.

dōgyōsha 同業者 fellow trader

dōgyōshayokin 同業者預金 interbank deposits

dōgyōshukankyōryoku 同業種間協力 intra-group cooperation

dōgyōshukigyōshūdan 同業種企業集団 congeneric (industry group)

dōi 動意 positive attitude; interest; movement ¶ No significant *movements* are expected in inventory investments. // Corporations show considerable *interest* in resuming investment. // There were some signs of *movement* in plant-equipment investment.

dōin 動因 →動機

dōin 動員 mobilization ¶ *mobilization* of capital, or capital *mobilization* // a coherent policy to *mobilize* the savings from remittances into productive investment

doisho 同意書 letter of consent

doitsukakōsai ドイツ貨公債 German mark bond

dōjihassei 同時発生 syndrome; simultaneity ¶ the *syndrome* of inflation worldwide // *simultaneous* inflation the world over

dōjihōteishiki 同次方程式 homogeneous equation

dōjikaisetsushin'yōjō 同時開設信用状 back-to-back credit

dōjiseinokōjun 同時性の公準 homogeneity postulate

dōjishūryōno 同時修了の co-terminous; conterminous

dōjisuiteihō 同時推定法 simultaneous estimation

dojjirain ドッジ・ライン Dodge Line

dojōosen 土壌汚染 soil contamination

dōki 動機 motive; incentive; stimulus; inducement; reason; cause; prompting; incitement; temptation; inspiration ¶ The *motive* for saving lies in general attractiveness of assets. // The acquisition of land is a major *motive* for saving. // Residents of border areas will have *incentives* to diversify their currency balances. // Tax policies provided adequate *incentives* to encourage investment. // The ascending prices offer an *inducement* to investors to hold their notes to maturity. // to reveal hidden *motives* // from mingled *motives* // an action *motivated, stimulated, induced, tempted, prompted,* or *incited* by... // Public demands for cash balances may have been enhanced by precautionary *motives* in the uncertain financial and economic environment.

営業動機　business motive
貨幣保有の動機　motives of holding money
向上の動機　motive of improvement
利潤動機　profit motive
所得動機　income motive
投機的動機　speculative motive
取引動機　transaction motive
予備的動機　precautionary motive
優位動機　advantage motive

dōkō 動向 trend; performance; development; movement; trend; behavior ¶ a satisfactory long-run *trend* // a basic change of *trend* // the downward *trend* in production // widely disparate *trends* // an improving *trend* // The *trend* was arrested. // mixed *trends* // to *trend* strongly downward // to *trend* horizontally // There were marked differences between the *performance* of the various types of production. // the disappointing *performance* of exports // the favorable business *performance* // Overall price *developments* have been stable. // Some downward *movement* in prices has taken place. // the trend in price *movements* // *Movements* in the Scottish economy have broadly paralleled those in the U.K. as a whole. // divergent *trends* in per-

sonal disposable incomes // the *behavior* of business loans by type of borrower // the likely *behavior* of the economy // →動き; 基調

dokuritsuhensū 独立変数 independent variable

dokuritsusaisan 独立採算 self-sustenance

dokuritsusaisanseido 独立採算制度 self-support (=supporting) accounting (system)

dokuritsusaisansekinin 独立採算責任 own profit and loss responsibility

dokuritsutōshi 独立投資 autonomous investment

dokusen 独占 monopoly ¶ The Federal Reserve System has a virtual *monopoly* on the issuance of the nation's currency (with the exception of some authorized issues of coins and notes by the Treasury). // One bank has a virtual *monopoly* over local credit. // Front-runners can exploit their *monopoly* position.

補完独占　complementary monopoly
需要独占　monopsony
買手独占　buyer's monopoly
完全独占　perfect monopoly; absolute monopoly
政府独占　government monopoly
私的独占　private monopoly; private monopolization
自然独占　natural monopoly
双方独占　bilateral monopoly
単独独占　simple monopoly
絶対独占　absolute monopoly

dokusendo 独占度 degree of monopoly

dokusenkakaku 独占価格 monopolistic price

dokusenken 独占権 exclusive

right; exclusive privilege

dokusenkinshihō 独占禁止法 anti-trust law; anti-monopoly law

dokusennogaiaku 独占の害悪 evil of monopoly

dokusenryoku 独占力 monopoly power

dokusenshihon 独占資本 monopolistic capital; monopoly capital

dokusentekijuyō 独占的需要 monopolist demand

dokusentekikyōsō 独占的競争 monopolistic competition

dokusentekikyōsōnōryoku 独占的競争能力 monopolistically competitive capacity

dokusentekishijō 独占的市場 monopolistic market

dōmeihigyōikkibōdōkikentanpoyakkan 同盟罷業一揆暴動危険担保約款 institute strikes, riot and civil commotion clauses

dominokōka ドミノ効果 domino effect ¶ There is little fear of a *domino effect* from any losses that might occur.

donka 鈍化 deceleration; slowing down; edging off (=down); moderation ¶ Growth rate *decelerated*. // Output *edged down* in rate of increase. // Exports *edged off*. // Home building has *moderated* from the feverish pace of last year.

dōrounsō 道路運送 road haulage ¶ Competition from *road haulage* reduced the railways' share of freight.

dorubanare ドル離れ run out of dollars ¶ The immediate result was another run out of dollars. // → ～離れ

dorubōei ドル防衛 defense of the dollar; dollar defense; dollar-

support; dollar-propping; dollar-rescue ¶ The U.S. put together a new *dollar-rescue* package.

dorudakakichō ドル高基調 firm tone of the U.S. dollar

dorudate ドル建て in dollar terms; in terms of dollars; in dollars

dorufuan ドル不安 doubts about the U.S. dollar; market worries about the dollar

doruheika ドル平価 dollar parity

doruheikinhō ドル平均法 dollar average method

dorukinkōkanseiteishi ドル・金交換性停止 suspension of the convertibility of the dollar into gold

dorusetsugenkeikaku ドル節減計画 save-the-dollar program

dorushinnin ドル信認 faith in the dollar; confidence in the dollar

dōryoku 動力 energy; (motive) power; (dynamic; driving) force ¶ the main *force* behind expansion // to reach full *force* // the *forces* making for a further rise // cumulating *forces* in the market

doryokumokuhyō 努力目標 promise of utmost efforts to meet the demand

doryokunotekiryōka 努力の適量化 optimization of effort

dōsan 動産 chattel; movable

dōsanfudōsankanjō 動産不動産勘定 movable and immovable assets accounts

dōsanshintaku 動産信託 movable property in trust

dōsanteitō 動産抵当 chattel mortgage

dosekiseihinkōgyō 土石製品工業 stone and clay products industry

dōshitsutekiseisanbutsu 同質的生産物 homogeneous product

dōshitsutekishakai 同質的社会 homogeneous society

dōshusetsubinotorikae 同種設備の取替え like-for-like replacement

dosūbunpu 度数分布 frequency distribution

dōtaihiritsu 動態比率 dynamic ratio

dōtaikeizai 動態経済 dynamic economy

dōtaitōkei 動態統計 dynamic statistics

dōtekikeikakuhō 動的計画法 dynamic programing; DP

dōtekikessanhyō 動的決算表 dynamic financial statement

dōyō 動揺 turbulence; upheaval; convulsion; turmoil; unrest; commotion; disquiet; disquietude; uncertainty; jolt ¶ the *turbulence* in the foreign exchange market // recurrent *upheavals* in exchange rates // The European snake suffered painful *convulsions* in the wake of the floating of the French franc. // The *turmoil* continued on foreign exchange. // Leading European central banks spent up to $1,000 million to keep the European joint currency snake intact in continued currency market *unrest*. // All of this *commotion* is due to anti-recessionary measures applied consciously. // international monetary *uncertainty* // to prevent giving sudden sharp *jolts* to prices // ［参考］ →混乱

dōzokugaisha 同族会社 family corporation (＝company); closed corporation; private holding company; family-owned corporation

dōzokukankei 同族関係 affinity

E

EC tan'itsutsūka EC単一通貨 single European Community currency

eigyōbi 営業日 business day; workday ¶ Requests will be acted upon on the following *business day*. // The Bahraini business day extends from the closing of the *workday* in Tokyo to the opening in New York, and coincides with office hours in London and Western Europe.

eigyōdōki 営業動機 business motive

eigyōgaihiyō 営業外費用 non-operating expenditure

eigyōgairieki 営業外利益 non-operating profit

eigyōgaishūnyū 営業外収入 non-operating income (＝revenue)

eigyōgaitatemono 営業外建物 building not used in operation (＝operating)

eigyōhi 営業費 business (＝office; working) expenses

eigyōhōkokusho 営業報告書 business report

eigyōjikan 営業時間 business (＝office) hour; hours open; shop hours

eigyōjōto 営業譲渡 transfer of operations; assignment of business; transfer of right

eigyōjōyo 営業剰余 operating surplus

eigyōkamoku 営業科目 line of business; business line

eigyōkatsudō 営業活動 business operations (=activities)

eigyōken 営業権 goodwill ¶ to build *goodwill* // to sell the *goodwill* of the company

eigyōkiban 営業基盤 operational base; infrastructure of business; business infrastructure

eigyōnendo 営業年度 business year

eigyōnissū 営業日数 number of trading days

eigyōrieki 営業利益 business (= operating) profit

eigyōseiseki 営業成績 business result

eigyōseiyokin 営業性預金 demand deposits

eigyōsho 営業所 place of buniness; offlce; business establishment

eigyōshotoku 営業所得 business (=operating) income; business profit

eigyōshotokuzei 営業所得税 business profit income

eigyōshūnyū 営業収入 business (= operating) income (=earning; revenue)

eigyōteishi 営業停止 suspension of business

eigyōyōfudōsanhiritsu 営業用不動産比率 ratio of fixed assets for business to net worth

eigyōyōjūki 営業用什器 office furniture

eigyōyōjunshihongaku 営業用純資本額 net capital

eigyōyōkaoku 営業用家屋 office building

eigyōyosan 営業予算 operating budget

eigyōzei 営業税 business tax

eijite 映じて reflecting; in reflection of ¶ Consumer prices led the upward movement *reflecting* the seasonal advance in food prices. // [参考] The market was boosted by an extension of the rally on Wall Street.

eijūtokō 永住渡航 immigration

eikasai 英貨債 pound sterling bond

eikasaiken 英貨債券 debenture in pound sterling

eikokubyō 英国病 British disease; English sickness

eikyō 影響 influence; effect; consequence; to affect; impact ¶ A beneficial *effect* is being felt in some lines. // The step had a neutralizing *influence* over the monetary phase of the economy. // It may have a serious *consequences*. // The demand was not too adversely *affected*. // to be *influenced* favorably... // The near-term *impact* of these actions will be a reduction in crude oil prices. // to shield production and employment from the *impact* of the major drop in exports // The recession *impacted* the economy. // The most important operational *impact* of their use is on the cash reserve position of member banks. // Net internal demand exerted a depressive *impact* on activity. // The yen's rapid rise had a negative *impact* upon Japan. // The stimulative *impact* of the tax concessions is questioned. // to dampen the adverse *impact* on employment // The recession had a disproportionate *impact* on energy needs. // The debilitating *effects* of the 1974-75 recession were shrugged off in 1976. // to tend to have a significant detrimental *effect* on overall health conditions // to have manifestly detrimental *effects* on developing countries // The upward *influence* came largely from a rise in the volume of contracts, while the downward *influences* were a smaller money supply. // to have neutralizing *influence* over the monetary phase // the psychological *influence* of the Bank rate cut to exercise a restraining *influence* on price developments // to have prompt and pervasive *influences* on markets // to extend a sufficiently moderating *influence* on prices // The *influence* of the public sector together was virtually neutral. // A number of depressive *influences* are at work. // Markets respond to numerous and diverse *influences*. // The ripple *effect* if Chrysler went out of business could throw 600,000 people out of work.

eikyūkōsai 永久公債 permanent debt; funded debt

eikyūsaiken 永久債券 perpetuity (=permanent) bond

einōshikin 営農資金 farming (= cultivation) funds; farm production funds; farming funds

eiranginkō 英蘭銀行 Bank of England

eirijigyō 営利事業 profit-making (=commercial) business

eirikikan 営利機関 profit-making institution ¶ In terms of survival as *profit-making institutions*, they rely primarily on their own management and resourcefulness.

eiriseigenri 営利性原理 principle of profitability

eiseidepāto 衛星デパート suburban store

eiseikonpyūtā 衛星コンピューター satellite computer

eiseitsūka 衛星通貨 satellite currencies

eisenryō 曳船料 tugboat fee

eiyōritsu 栄養率 nutritive ratio

eizengaisha 営繕会社 repairs company

eizokutekikōka 永続的効果 secular boom; sustainable boom

ejjihōjin エッジ法人 ［米］Edge Act corporation; Edge corporation ¶ to establish, under Federal Reserve Act, "*Edge Act corporations*" engaged in foreign banking and financing // Through *Edge corporations,* banks may conduct a deposit and loan business in an out-of-State market.

ejjiwāsushiki エッジワース式 Edgeworth formula

ekikasekiyugasu 液化石油ガス liquefied petroleum gas

ekikinfusannyūkashidashi 益金不算入貸出 non-accrual loan ¶ to put the *loans* on a *non-accrual* basis

ekimu 役務 service ¶ →サービス

ekimubaishō 役務賠償 reparation in service

ekimukeiyaku 役務契約 contract for service; service contract

ekimutokō 役務渡航 travel under service contract

ekkenkōi 越権行為 ultra vires act; unauthorized act; act beyond authority ¶ the right to restrain *ultra vires acts* of corporation

ekonomisuto エコノミスト (professional) economist

ekusuteriaseihin エクステリア製品 outdoor home products

enbaraishōken 円払証券 yen-denominated securities

enbēsukin'yū 円ベース金融 yen-based financing ¶ a new *yen-based* import *financing* system

enbēsutōshi 円ベース投資 yen base investment

enchō 延長 extension; continue; stretching out ¶ to be automatically *extended* each year for a further period of one year. // "A" may *continue* this agreement for five years by twelve months' prior written notice to "B". // The debts were *stretched out* over eight years starting in this year.

endaka 円高 [外] strong yen; higher quotations for the yen; favorable yen exchange rate; higher rate of yen exchange over the central rate; higher yen quotation; exchange rate in favor of yen; appreciation of the yen; yen appreciation ¶ The *Yen* has clearly stabilized at a relatively *high level* against the dollar. // The *higher yen* should hold exports down.

endate 円建て yen-denominated; denominated in yen; in terms of yen; in yen terms

endateyushutsu 円建輸出 yen denominated exports; exports in terms of yen (=in yen terms)

endorusuwappu 円ドル・スワップ yen-dollar swap agreement

endorusuwappukyōtei 円ドル・スワップ協定 yen-dollar swap agreement

enerugīgen エネルギー源 energy source ¶ Coal is the most likely alternative *energy source* when oil starts to get scarce. // conservation and development of non-oil *energy*

sources // longer-lasting and more renewable *energy sources* // intensive development of alternative *energy sources* // to expand alternative *sources* of *energy*

enerugīkeizai エネルギー経済 economy of energy

enerugīkiki エネルギー危機 energy emergency ¶ The deepening *energy emergency* began to pinch in ominous ways.

enerugīshōhi エネルギー消費 energy consumption ¶ Overall *energy consumption* in Sweden is estimated to grow to 540 Twh.

enerugīshōhisenshinkoku エネルギー消費先進国 energy-hungry (=-consuming) advanced (=industrialized) country

engangyogyō 沿岸漁業 coastal fishing

engenkessai 円元決済 yen-yuan settlement

engerukeisū エンゲル係数 Engel's coefficient

engerunohōsoku エンゲルの法則 Engel's law

engurafupaizu 円グラフパイ図 pie(-chart) ¶ Its share of the *pie* shrunk from 25 percent to 22 percent.

enhyōji 円表示 yen-denominated; yen-quoted; in terms yen; in yen terms

enjo 援助 aid; assistance; help; support ¶ technological *assistances* to developing nations // to extend financial *help* to... // to *support* the dollar rate // to seek balance of payments *support* from outside sources // The present flow of foreign capital *assistance* (concessional and nonconcessional) for agriculture in developing countries is estimated at over $5 millions annually. // The World Bank is now the largest supplier of official development *assistance*. // to channel *assistance* to the developing countries // the Sw.Fr. 735 million approved for technical *assistance* and development *aid* // the level of bilateral *aid* provided in concessional terms // DAC *aid* is comprised of financial *aid* (grants and loans), technical *assistance*, and food *aid*. // 70% of OPEC's bilateral *assistance* was committed to five countries. // growth of soft-term external financial *support* to the Third world

外国援助 foreign aid

軍事援助 military aid

紐付き援助 tied aid

開発援助 development aid

enjokoku 援助国 aid providing country; assisting country

enjosochi 援助措置 commitment for aid

enkasai 円貨債 yen bond; yen-denominated bond

enkatsuka 円滑化 smoothing ¶ *smoothing* of trade financing // *smoothing* operations in the foreign exchange market

enkawase 円為替 yen exchange

enkoboshū 縁故募集 private offering ¶ *privately offered* bond issues

enkohakkō 縁故発行 private placement

enkoshawariate 縁故者割当 allotment of new stocks to relatives

enkyoriseigyo 遠距離制御 distant control

enkyoriteigen'unchin 遠距離逓減運賃 tapering freight (rate)

ennō 延納 deferred (=delayed) payment

ennōrishi 延納利子 interest for delayed payment

enpōsōjūkikō 遠方操縦機構 servo-mechanism

ensēru 円セール [外] yen sale

enshakkan 円借款 yen credit

enshakkankyōyo 円借款供与 yen credit supply

enshifuto 円シフト shift of financing operations from dollar import usance to domestic yen; financing operation of Japanese banks to repay borrowings from Euro-money market or foreign banks by raising yen funds in the domestic market; shift to yen; yen shift; yen switch ¶ to encourage (Japanese) importers to *shift* from dollar financing // to yen financing to encourage a *shift* from dollar to yen financing // [参考] to liquidate foreign currency loans from foreign banks and refinance them in yen loans

entai 延滞 arrear; delay; being overdue ¶ Interest *arrears* go back by more than 90 days by then. // Much of the debt has been *overdue* for some months. // to reduce interest *arrears* // to bring interest *arrears* on its foreign debt up to date

entaihibu 延滞日歩 overdue interest per diem

entaikin 延滞金 arrear; back money; arrearage

entaikogitte 延滞小切手 stale check

entainissū 延滞日数 days in arrear(s)

entairishi 延滞利子 overdue interest; interest for delay

entaitsugunaikin 延滞償い金 penalty on delayed delivery

entaiyōkyū 延滞要求 stale demand

entenkan 円転換 Eurodollars' conversion into the yen currency; exchange of Eurodollar funds into yen currency

entenkankisei 円転換規制 regulations on conversion of foreign funds into yen (funds)

enyasu 円安 [外] weak yen; unfavorable yen exchange rate; lower rate of yen exchange against the central rate; lower yen quotation; lower yen; yen depreciation, depreciation of the yen ¶ [参考] The pound has appreciated by over 13% against the yen since the start of the year.

enyōgyogyō 遠洋漁業 deep-sea fishing

enzanjikan 演算時間 [コン] operation time; computing speed

enzansū 演算数 [コン] operand

esukarētājōkō エスカレーター条項 (cost-of-living) escalator clause

esukurōshin'yōjō エスクロー信用状 escrow credit

F

FRB suwapputorikime FRB スワップ取決 swap arrangements between central banks and the Federal Reserve Bank (of New York)

fāmubankingu ファーム・バンキング firm banking

federarufando フェデラル・ファンド [米] Federal funds

federarufandokinri フェデラル・ファンド金利 [米] Federal funds rate

federarufandoshijō フェデラル・ファンド市場 Federal funds market

feroaroiseizōgyō フェロアロイ製造業 ferro-alloy products manufacturing industry

ferunānofukurokōji フェルナーの袋小路 Fellner's impasse

fīdobakkushisutemu フィードバック・システム feedback system

finansharudepāto フィナンシャル・デパート financial department

finansharutaimuzukōgyōkabuka- shisū フィナンシャルタイムズ工業株価指数 Financial Times Index of Industrial Ordinary Shares

finansharutaimuzushōhinsōbashisū フィナンシャルタイムズ商品相場指数 Financial Times Index of Sensitive World Commodity Prices

firippusukyokusen フィリップス曲線 Phillips curve ¶ There has been a perceptible shift in the *Phillips curve.*

fisshāshiki フィッシャー式 [統] Fisher formula

fōmyurapuran フォーミュラ・プラン [米・市] formula plan

fōtoran フォートラン [コン] formula translator; FORTRAN

fuan 不安 uncertainty; unrest; nervousness; loss of confidence ¶ A note of *uncertainty* crept into the thinking of some people. // international monetary *unrest* // international currency *uncertainties* // The market continued *uncertain.* // *un-*

certainty about impending credit restrictions // an indication of continued *nervousness* over the banking situation in the wake of the revelation of difficulties at some banks // the acute *nervousness* of the credit markets // *Nervousness* over the state of the economy triggered short-covering. // marked participants' apparent *loss-of-confidence* in the dollar // [参考] a precarious situation

労働不安　labor unrest

社会不安　social unrest

通貨不安　monetary unrest; unrest over currency

fuankan 不安感　uncertainty; unrest ¶ A note of *uncertainty* crept into the thinking of some people. // emergence of international currency *uncertainties* // There remains *uncertainty* about impending credit restrictions. // to allay some of the businessmen's *uncertainties* about future inflation

fuantei 不安定　instability ¶ Currency *instability* generated the uncertainties about future cost and price levels. // prime causes of exchange rate *instability* // to prevent any fresh outbreaks of exchange rate *instability* // *instability* of economic growth

経済的不安定性　economic instability

fuanteikeizaiseichō 不安定経済成長　unstable (economic) growth

fuanteikinkō 不安定均衡　unstable equilibrium

fuanteikoyō 不安定雇用　unstable employment

fuanteina 不安定な　unstable (＝instable); erratic; precarious ¶ *unstable* balance-of-payments and ex-

change-rate conditions // A total breakdown of the monetary order was responsible for much of the *instability* in the world economy. // to limit *erratic* fluctuations in the floating exchange rates // to curb *erratic* rate movements somewhat // The tax authorities, acting under the pressure of the *precarious* budget situation, speeded up assessment. // The market is subject to temporary *instabilities,* which are self-corrective. // to temper abrupt money market *instability* // the *precarious* nature of the market's confidence in these briefs seen in...

fuanteisei 不安定性　instability; volatility; unsteadiness; unrest; restlessness; vacillation; fragility; disquietude; fugitiveness; being unsettled ¶ Deposit takers have grown used to *volatility* in the dinar market.

物価の不安定性　instability of prices; price instability; inconstant price developments

fuanteishikyō 不安定市況　sensitive market

fuanteiyōso 不安定要素　elements of uncertainty

fubaidōmei 不買同盟　boycott; buyers strike

fubaiundō 不買運動　boycott(movement)

消費者不買運動　consumer boycott ¶ A *consumer boycott* was initiated, which terminated successfully as manufacturers announced a price cut of the order of 20 percent.

fūbāmoratoriamu フーバー・モラトリアム　[米] Hoover Moratorium

fubarai 不払い　non-payment; default; dishonor

fubarai 賦払い installment payment ¶ →割賦

fubaraikin 賦払い金 installment

fubaraikogitte 不払小切手 dishonored check

fubaraitegata 不払手形 dishonored bill

fubaraiyakusokutegata 不払約束手形 dishonored note

fubyōdō 不平等 inequality ¶ *inequality* in income, and of wealth // to reduce and finally eliminate competitive *inequality* between banks and other institutions

fuchō 不調 [市] unsteady; slack; break down; fall through

fudō 浮動 floating; unsteady; erratic; unsettled; wavering; hovering

fūdobyō 風土病 endemic (disease) ¶ Inflation can fairly be called the *endemic disease*.

fudōgyoku 浮動玉 [株] floating supply

fudōjikan 不働時間 idle time

fudōjinkō 浮動人口 floating population

fudōkabu 浮動株 floating stock

fudōkōbairyoku 浮動購買力 floating purchasing power

fudōsan 不動産 immovable; real estate

fudōsanbaibaishūsennin 不動産買売周旋人 real estate broker

fudōsangyō 不動産業 real estate business

fudōsangyōsha 不動産業者 realty dealer; real estate agent; realtor; land-developing company

fudōsanhyōka 不動産評価 appraisal of real estate

fudōsankanri 不動産管理 control of real estate

fudōsankensonzokukikan 不動産権存続期間 quantity of estate

fudōsankin'yū 不動産金融 mortgage credit

fudōsanshintaku 不動産信託 real estate in trust

fudōsanshūeki 不動産収益 profits from immovables

fudōsanteitōkashitsukekin 不動産抵当貸付金 loan secured by real estate

fudōsei 浮動性 volatility ¶ The *volatile* side of the balancing item was negative.

fudōshōken 浮動証券 floater

fufukumōshitate 不服申立て motion for complaint; grievance appeal

fuhenhiyō 不変費用 constant expense

fuhenno 不変の unchanged; no change; constant; steady; still; static; unvarying; flat; level; even; stable; settled; intact; fixed; stationary; standing still; in status quo ¶ The index *levelled* out. // The growth rate was *unchanged* from the previous month.

fuhenshihon 不変資本 constant capital

fuhenshūekikibo 不変収益規模 costant return to scale

fuhōkashidashi 不法貸出 illegal advance

fuhōtorihiki 不法取引 illegal trade ¶ linkage into *illegal trade*

fujitsuhyōji 不実表示 mis-representation; misstatement ¶ to expose widely circulated plausible fraudulent *misrepresenting*

fujo 扶助 assistance; aid
国民扶助 national assistance
公的扶助 public assistance
社会扶助 social assistance

fujukurenrōdō 不熟練労働 unskilled labor

fujuyōgetsu 不需要月　drop-off month

fujuyōki 不需要期　off-demand season ¶ This quarter is an *off-(demand) season* for winter clothing.

fuka 付加　addition; supplement; addendum

fuka 賦課　levy; imposition; assessment

fukachōshū 賦課徴収　assessment and collection

fukadō 不稼働　unoperable; unused; idle

fukafūtai 付加風袋　super-tare

fukagaku 賦課額　amount assessed; amount imposed

fukajōkō 付加条項　rider; amendment; addition; supple-mentary clause; addendum; appendix

fukakachi 付加価値　value added; added value ¶ Industrial *value added* grew by 12% in 1977. // the highly-specialized and high *value-added* sectors of industry

fukakachizei 付加価値税　value-added tax; VAT

fukakachitsūshinmō 付加価値通信網　value-added network; VAN

fukakin 賦課金　dues; charges

fukakōryoku 不可抗力　force majeure; act of God; vis major ¶ Many security arrangements contain *force majeure* exceptions.

fukakōryokujōkō 不可抗力条項　force majeure clause

fukakujitsusei 不確実性　uncertainty ¶ This eliminated an element of *uncertainty* in the economic policy pursued in Denmark. // The demand for money is subject to considerable *uncertainty* in the modern economy. // considerable *uncertainty* inevitably attached to several elements in the forecast // a factor casting *uncertainty* on the whole issue // Conversion into U. S. dollars introduced an additional element of *uncertainty* of the figures. // The future course is always shrouded in *uncertainties*. // In the face of progress, there remains nagging *uncertainty*. // Another damper on the market was *uncertainty* over the future course of Federal Reserve credit policy. // ［参考］It clouds the picture and keeps us from characterizing the economy.

fukakutei 不確定　uncertain; undecided

fukakuteiritsuki 不確定利付き　unfixed interest bearing (securities)

fukanshihei 不換紙幣　inconvertible note; fiat money; paper currency; irredeemable bank note

fukantsūka 不換通貨　inconvertible currency

fukanzenkoggite 不完全小切手　defective check

fukanzenkoyō 不完全雇用　underemployment

fukanzenkōyokinkō 不完全雇用均衡　unemployment equilibrium

fukanzenkoyōseichōritsu 不完全雇用成長率　unemployment rate of growth

fukanzenkyōsō 不完全競争　imperfect competition

fukanzenshūgyō 不完全就業　underemployment

fukappatsu 不活発　inactivity; dullness; lethargy; stagnancy; slackness; sluggishness; slump; torpor; inertia; apathy; depression; quiescence ¶ With all that, the market still seemed to be feeling the *lethargy* that set in last week. // Business stays *lethargic*. // Personal consumption expenditure will stay *dull*.

fukatekikyūfu 付加的給付　fringe benefits

fukatsudōzandaka 不活動残高　inactive balance

fukazei 付加税　supertax; surtax

fukeiki 不景気　inactive business; business slump; recession; depression

fukeizai 不経済　bad economy; poor economy; waste; diseconomy ¶ It is *poor economy* to use electricity in place of heating oil. // It involves a wicked *waste* of precious time and labor. // internal economy and external *diseconomy;* external economies and internal *diseconomies*

外部不経済　external diseconomies

金銭的不経済　pecuniary diseconomies

内部不経済　internal diseconomies

fukine 吹き値　[市] jump in prices; revived quotation

fukineuri 吹き値売り　[市] selling on spurt

fukinkō 不均衡　disequilibrium; imbalance; disparity ¶ external and internal *disequilibria* // The basic *disequilibrium* is being corrected. // to seek to correct structural *imbalances* in production, trade, and prices // the *imbalance* in international payments // *disequilibria* in intercountry money flows // periods of temporary *imbalances* in payments flows // market sensitivity *imbalances* in money flows between countries // to gradually correct U.S. payments *imbalances* caused by capital outflow // to eliminate the *imbalance* between productivity and the level of money incomes // The

economy has accumulated irremediable *imbalances* blocking stable growth. // The redressable *imbalances* that exist are brought under better control. // This reflects the fundamental *imbalance* in the Danish economy, which remain uncorrected. // to overcome some of the most blatant trade *imbalances* // Currency fluctuations increased economic *disparities* among the nine countries. // to redress the enormous U.S. trade *imbalance* with Japan // to rectify the *imbalance* in the external economy // to eliminate or reduce highly disturbing payments *disequilibrium* // [参考] uneven development and lop-sided trade

長期的不均衡　secular disequilibrium

持続的不均衡　persistent disequilibrium

需給不均衡　supply-demand imbalance

過渡の不均衡　cyclical disequilibrium

傾向的不均衡　secular disequilibrium

基礎的不均衡　fundamental disequilibrium

構造的不均衡　structural disequilibrium

社会的不均衡　social imbalance

対外不均衡　external disequilibrium

対内不均衡　internal disequilibrium

fukinkōna 不均衡な　unbalanced ¶ *unbalanced* supply-demand relations

fukinkōseichō 不均衡成長　unbalanced growth (=industrialization)

fukisokuhendō 不規則変動　irregular fluctuation (=variation)

fukkasai 仏貨債　French franc bond

fukkatsu 復活　revival ¶ the so-called *"revival* of monetary policies" around 1950 // a retardation in the spring *revival* of business activity // a *revival* in buying interest // the winter *revival* in oil carryings // Economic activity has *revived.*

fukkatsusesshō 復活折衝(予算の) negotiation for the restoration of reduced funds (=appropriations)

fukkō 復興 rehabilitation ¶ reconstruction and *rehabilitation* of the postwar economy

経済復興 economic rehabilitation

産業復興 industrial rehabilitation

fukōhei 不公平 inequality ¶ action to reduce *inequalities* of income and wealth

fukōseinakyōsō 不公正な競争 unfair competition

fukōseitorihiki 不公正取引 unfair trade

fukōsokuyūshi 不拘束融資 untied loan

fukōtai 富鉱体 bonanza ¶ The market is still no *bonanza* for western exporters. // North Sea oil was hailed as a *bonanza* for the British economy.

fukōyō 不効用 disutility

労動の不効用 disutility of labor

fukugōhensū 複合変数 composite variables ¶ to aggregate various inputs and outputs into a few *composite variables*

fukugōkanzei 複合関税 compound duties

fukugōkeisanki 複合計算機 computer complex

fukugōkigyō 複合企業 conglomerate

fukugōosen 複合汚染 combined pollution

fukugōseisanbutsu 複合生産物 product mix

fukugōyusō 複合輸送 complex transportation

fukugyō 副業 side-work; outside employment; moonlighting; auxiliary occupation; avocation; subsidiary business; side job; side business; side line ¶ to run a mill by *avocation*

fukuhai 復配 resumption of dividend

fukuhon'isei 複本位制 bimetallic standard; double standard; bimetallism

国際複本位 international bimetallism

fukuhon'iseironsha 複本位制論者 bimetallist

fukujitekikōka 副次的効果 side effects

fukujitekirieki 副次的利益 fringe benefits ¶ →諸給与

fukujutakuginkō 副受託銀行 (ADRの) custodian; subdepository (bank)

fukumeitegata 複名手形 double-name paper; two-name paper

fukumi 含み tone; sentiment; atmosphere ¶ The market *tone* became a shade firmer.

fukumikashidashi 含み貸出し off-record loan; off-book loan

fukumishisan 含み資産 latent asset (=property); hidden asset; off-the-book property; hidden property ¶ the *hidden property* potential in a company

fukumishisankabu 含み資産株 hidden asset stock

fukumison 含み損 latent loss

fukumukisoku 服務規則 work rules

fukurihō 複利法 compound interest method

fukurihyō 複利表 table of compound interest

fukurikōsei 福利厚生 welfare

fukusanbutsu 副産物 by-product ¶ a *by-product* from oil refining

fukusayō 副作用 side-effect

fukusen 複占 duopoly

fukushachō 副社長 deputy president; vice-presieent

fukushi 福祉 welfare; well-being ¶ a striking deterioration of our *welfare* state // to safeguard the national economic *welfare*

  経済福祉 economic well being

  公共福祉 public welfare

  社会福祉 social welfare

fukushigatayosan 福祉型予算 welfare-oriented budget

fukushigyappu 福祉ギャップ gap between economic growth and social welfare

fukushikiboki 複式簿記 double-entry bookkeeping

fukushikiueitohōshiki 複式ウエイト方式 compound weight method

fukushikokka 福祉国家 welfare state

fukushikōseijigyō 福祉厚生事業 welfare work

fukushishakai 福祉社会 welfare society; welfare-oriented society ¶ realization of a *welfare society*

fukushishikōgatakeizai 福祉志向型経済 welfare-oriented economy

fukushishisetsu 福祉施設 welfare institution

fukusūkawasesōbasei 複数為替相場制 multiple rates of exchange (system)

fukusūmankiteikiyokin 複数満期定期預金 [米] multiple maturity time deposit

fukusūtsūkakainyūsei 複数通貨介入制 multicurrency intervention (system)

fukusūtsūkasentakukenjōkō 複数通貨選択権条項 multicurrency clause

fukusūtsūkasochi 複数通貨措置 multiple currency practice

fukusūyosanseido 複数予算制度 multiple budget system

fukutanpo 副担保 subsidiary collateral

fukuzatsurōdō 複雑労働 complex labor

fukyō 不況 business depression; business recession; business slump; inactivity; recession ¶ The danger of deep and prolonged *depression* has so far been averted. // a mild economic ailment for building up immunity against a major *depression* // The U.S. is suffering from a serious economic *recession*. // The economy slides deeper into a *recession*. // to move out of a trough of *recession* // The *recession* is now bottoming out. // The *recession* has receded. // The tax cut limited the depth and duration of the *recession*. // to stand in danger of slumping into a prolonged *recession* // The world economy fell into a synchronized *recession*. // to sink into an outright *recession* // to slip into a true *recession* // to extricate the world from the present *recession* // →景気後退

  慢性的不況 chronic depression

  "30年代不況" the Great Depression (in the 30's)

  全面不況 full-blown depression; full-fledged depression

fukyōchiiki 不況地域 depressed region

fukyōgyōshu 不況業種 depressed

industries; recession prone industries

構造不況業種 structurally de-
pressed industries; slump-stricken
branches of business and industry

fukyōji 不況時 recession period;
depression period; bad times

fukyōkan 不況感 recessionary
mood

fukyōkanobukkadaka 不況下の物
価高 stagflation; inflagnation

fukyōkanoinfure 不況下のインフレ
slumpflation

fukyōkaruteru 不況カルテル anti-
depression cartel

fukyōtaisaku 不況対策 remedy for
depression; anti-recession policy;
counter-recession policy measures

fukyū 普及 diffusion; dissemination; popularization; spread; prevalence; omnipresence ¶ the *diffusion*
rate of vacuum cleaners // the widespread *diffusion* of modern commun-
ications and transportation // to
encourage the *diffusion* of information at the local level // the *dissemination* of accurate information on
the economic situation // to achieve
rapid *popularization* of technology //
the *spreading* use of dishwashers //
the general *prevalence* of optimism
among people // to achieve wide
spread popularity // the *popularization* in recent years of monetarist
theories based on a close correlation
between money supply and inflation // an *omnipresence* of TV cam-
eras // [参考] Color TV has now
become in common place in the
country.

fukyūritsu 普及率 diffusion rate;
ownership rate (=ratio) ¶ a high
diffusion rate of color TV sets // a
low *rate of diffusion* of electronic

ovens

fumi 不味 [市] flat; weak; sluggish

fumi 踏み [市] short covering at a
loss; squeeze

fumiage 踏み上げ [市] price advance by short-covering; bear panic

fumiichijun 踏み一巡 [市] temporary end of short-covering operation

fumimono 踏み物 [市] short-covering

funanishōken 船荷証券 bill of lading; B/L

funazumi 船積み shipment; shipping; loading; lading; shiploading

funazumichiiki 船積地域 shipment
area of goods

funazumifunanishōken 船積船荷証
券 shipped B/L; on board B/L

funazumigokin'yū 船積後金融
finance after shipment

funazumihi 船積費 shipping
charges; shipping expenses

funazumijūryō 船積重量 shipping
weight; intake weight

funazumiki 船積期 shipment quarter

funazumikigen 船積期限 fixed
date for loading

funazumikō 船積港 port of shipment; port of loading

funazumimeisaisho 船積明細書
shipping specification

funazumimenjō 船積免状 shipping
permit

funazumimihon 船積見本 shipping sample; outturn sample

funazumiokurijō 船積送状 shipping invoice

funazumirikuagekikan 船積陸揚期
間 lay-days

funazumisashizusho 船積指図書
shipping order; shipping instruction

funazumisho 船積所 shipping

office

funazumishorui 船積書類 shipping documents; shipping papers

funazumitesūryō 船積手数料 shipping commission

funazumitsūchi 船積通知 shipping advice

funazumiyōseki 船積容積 intake measurement; shipping measurement

funazumizengokinyū 船積み前後金融 preshipment or postshipment financing (=credit)

funazumizenkin'yū 船積前金融 finance before shipment

fun'iki 雰囲気 →ムード

funinchochiku 不妊貯蓄 abortive saving

funinkigyō 不妊企業 abortive enterprise

funinkikabu 不人気株 inactive stock

funochochiku 負の貯蓄 dissaving ¶ The Deutsche savings institutions recorded net *dissaving* of Fl. 0.4 milliard in 1974.

funojuntōshi 負の純投資 negative net investment

funokōyō 負の効用 disutility

funoseisan 負の生産 disproduct

funoshotokuzei 負の所得税 negative income tax

funotaizō 負の退蔵 dishoarding

funryōhi 焚料費 bunkering

funshokukanjō 粉飾勘定 window dressing

funshokukessan 粉飾決算 window-dressing settlement (of accounts)

funshokusōsa 粉飾操作 window dressing ¶ seasonal unwinding of inter-bank positions after the traditional year-end *window dress-*

ing of balance sheets

funshokuyokin 粉飾預金 window-dressing deposits

funsō 紛争 dispute ¶ to settle labor *disputes* // to submit the *dispute* to arbitration

furanchaizuchēn フランチャイズ・チェーン franchise chain; FC

fure フレ ［市］ fluctuations (from month to month); (monthly) ups and downs; volatility; variability ¶ a measure of gold price *volatility,* the magnitude of price *variability* of gold // products which exhibit substantial month-to-month *volatility*

furekkusutaimusei フレックス・タイム制 flexi-time system

furenzokusei 不連続性 discontinuity ¶ *discontinuity* in production // *discontinuity* of the index figures // The price index is *discontinued* because of a change in components.

furidashi 振出し drawing; issue

furidashichi 振出地 place of issue

furidashiginkō 振出銀行 drawer (=drawing) bank

furidashihizuke 振出日付 date of issue

furidashinin 振出人 drawer; remitter; issuer

furidasu 振出す draw; issue; write; make

furikae 振替 transfer

furikaechokinkōza 振替貯金口座 transfer savings (account)

furikaedenpyō 振替伝票 transfer slip (=ticket)

furikaekakakusōsa 振替価格操作 price transfer; transfer pricing ¶ The tax haven makes possible the manipulation of *price transfers* on products. // The provisions are designed to curb the use of *transfer pricing* to shift income from high tax to low tax jurisdictions.

furikaekanjō 振替勘定 transfer account

furikaekanōpondo 振替可能ポンド transferable pounds sterling

furikaekanōtsūka 振替可能通貨 transferable currency

furikaekessaihyō 振替決済票 due bill

furikaekessaiseido 振替決済制度 [市] central depository system

furikaekyūjitsu 振替え休日 additional extra national holiday

furikaesashizusho 振替指図書 request of transfer

furikaeshotoku 振替所得 transfer income

furikaeyokin 振替預金 postal transfer savings

furikikan 付利期間 interest-accrual period ¶ *market-based variable rates for six-months interest-accrual periods*

furikō 不履行 non-fulfillment; non-performance; default; breach; delinquency ¶ *debts classified as non-performing* // *rumors that Argentina might default on its debt* // *a delinquent debt* // *possible loan defaults* on U.S. bank loans to foreign borrowers // *evidence of breaches* of customer confidentiality // *Banks are forced to declare some loans non-performing on June 30.*

furikomu 振込む pay in

furikōsha 不履行者 defaulter; delinquent

　債務不履行者 defaulter of an obligation

furikōshasai 不履行社債 defaulted bond

furinahatsumei 不利な発明 unfavorable invention ¶ *unfavorable invention* for capital, or for labor

furisaikōgendo 付利最高限度 maximum limit for interest rates

furō フロー flow; increase or decrease ¶ *The money supply on a flow basis registered a substantial increase.* // *The flow of total domestic credit during the year rose 10 Lit. 39,000 billion, exceeding the figure agreed with the IMF.* // *not to interfere with international trade flows* // *foreign private investment flows among industrialized countries and between them and developing countries* // →流れ

furōkyūfu 不労給付 unearned benefit

furōshotoku 不労所得 unearned income

furōshotokushasō 不労所得者層 rentier class

furukosutogensoku フル・コスト原則 full cost principle

furusōgyō フル操業 working at full capacity; operation at peak (= full) capacity ¶ *Plants are working at full capacity.* // *the factory operating at near-full capacity* // *All major countries were operating at peak capacity.*

furyō 不漁 bad catch

furyōkashitsuke 不良貸付 bad debt (=loan); estimate loss; doubtful; slow loan

furyōsaiken 不良債権 inferior claim; bad debt

furyōsaikenshōkyakushōmeiseido 不良債権償却証明制度 system for depreciation of a bad (=inferior) claim

furyōzaiko 不良在庫 dead stock

fūsa 封鎖 blockade; freeze; restriction ¶ to achieve a total *blockade* of foreign coal imports to Britain in support of a 10-week-old strike
平時封鎖 pacific blockade
経済封鎖 economic blockade
食糧封鎖 hunger blockade

fusae 不冴え bleak; dull; inactive; quiet; no life; stagnancy; sluggishness; lack(ing) luster ¶ Britain faced some *bleak* months. // Farmers turned heavily to more soybeans because of the *bleak* outlook for cotton. // The overall performance of the economy *lacked luster.* // →不活発; 不振

fusai 負債 debt; indebtedness; liabilities; dues; balance of debt; arrearage ¶ to incur fresh *indebtedness* in the form of short-term trade and bank credits // changes in bank *indebtedness*
現金負債 cash liabilities
確定負債 direct liabilities
固定負債 fixed liabilities
未払負債 accrued liabilities; outstanding liabilities
延払負債 deferred liabilities
資本負債 capital liabilities
担保付負債 secured liabilities
当座負債 current liabilities

fusaichōka 負債超過 net liabilities

fusaihiritsu 負債比率 debt-equity ratio

fusaiizondo 負債依存度 leverage ¶ highly *levered* or less *levered* stocks

fusaikaritsu 負債化率 ratio of total liabilities to net worth

fusaikoku 負債国 indebted countries; debtor countries

fusaioyobishihon 負債および資本 liabilities and capital

fusairishi 負債利子 debt interest charges

fusaisanno 不採算の unprofitable; leaving no margin; not on a paying basis

fusaisanten 不採算店 non-profit-making office

fusaishihonhiritsu 負債・資本比率 gearing ratio

fusaishōkyakujunbikin 負債償却準備金 sinking fund; amortization fund

fusaishōninshō 負債承認証 acknowledgement of account; IOU; accounts stated

fūsakanjō 封鎖勘定 blocked account

fūsakeizaitaisei 封鎖経済体制 closed economic system

fūsakogitte 封鎖小切手 blocked check

fusaku 不作 poor harvest; failed harvest; poor crop; bad harvest; bad crop; short crop; failure of crops ¶ widespread *failure* of *harvests* in a number of regions

fūsakuiki 封鎖区域 blockade zone

fūsaseisaku 封鎖政策 blockade policy

fūsasen 封鎖線 blockade line

fūsashiharai 封鎖支払 restricted payment; payment out of blocked accounts

fūsashikin 封鎖資金 blocked funds

fusatsu 賦札 →利札

fūsatsūka 封鎖通貨 blocked currency

fūsayokin 封鎖預金 blocked (deposit) accounts; restricted deposits

fūsayushutsunyūsen 封鎖輸出入船 blockade runner

fuseijiken 不正事件 wrongdoing; scandal; fraud; shenanigans; malpractice; bribery case

fuseikogitte 不正小切手 defective check

fuseino 不勢の inactive; dull; lethargic ¶ → 不活発

fuseiritoku 不正利得 fraudulent gain; undue (＝unfair; unreasonable; unjustified; excessive) profit; unjust enrichment; profiteering

fuseisanteki 不生産的 unproductive; non-productive; dead

fuseisantekijigyō 不生産的事業 unproductive enterprise

fuseisantekikeihi 不生産的経費 unproductive expenditure

fuseisantekirōdō 不生産的労働 unproductive labor

fuseisantekishihon 不生産的資本 unproductive capital; dead capital

fushin 不振 stagnation; lethargy; depression; weakness; slump; inactivity; slack(ness); slackening; inertia ¶ degree of *slack* in the economy // The current business *slack* is not confined to manufacturing. // Any *slackening* in world trade will cut into the rate of export growth. // The *slackening* of activity fits the regular pattern. // The *slump* in job and production confirmed unabated. // to signal an end to the long *slump* of color TV set sales // The danger of a prolonged business *inertia* was averted. // The world steel industry as a whole has emerged from the disastrous *slump* of the past several years. // cyclically *depressed* conditions of labor markets // →不活発

fushinkan 不信感 distrust; mistrust; doubt ¶ growing *distrust* of currencies // to harbor, have, or cherish *distrust* in the U.S. dollar //

to dispel their *mistrust* // to leave no *doubts* of the safety of this investment // growing *distrust* in the dollar // to dispel people's *distrust* in the national currency // traditional worker *distrust* of management // to increase an international sense of *distrust* in the U.S. dollar

fushinki 不振期 period of depressed activity

fushinno 不振の dismal ¶ *dismal* sales performance // ［参考］→不振

fushinshikyō 不振市況 depressed market

fusoku 不足 shortage; deficit; shortfall; lack; dearth; paucity; scarcity; deficiency; deficit; inadequacy; insufficiency ¶ to experience a developing *shortage* of labor // *lack* of experience and confidence // The company *lacks* for funds. // There is a great *dearth* of housing, which poses a serious problem. // the *paucity* of Bahrain's natural resources // the increasing threat of recurrent materials *shortages* as world economies exspand // the drought-induced *shortage* of food // The food *deficit* of the less developed countries as a whole is not insurmountable. // *Shortages* of funds developed and became more acute. // The intense economic activity is accompanied by an increasing *shortage* of labor. // the seasonal summer *shortage* of power supply // whole *shortages* of food // a temporary *shortfall* of oil deliveries to power stations // $200 million of the *shortfall* in revenue

現金不足 short cash

保険権益不足 short insurance interest

陸上不足 short landed
資源不足 resource scarcity
資本不足 capital scarcity
受渡不足 short delivery

fusokugaku 不足額 shortage; deficit; difference

fusokuhoken 不足保険 under-insurance

fusokujitaitaiōkeikaku 不測事態対応計画 contingency plan

fusokunojitai 不測の事態 unforeseen development ¶ Barring *unforeseen developments*, a rise in base lending rates will first materialize around Mid-July.

fusokushōhin 不足商品 scarce (= short) item ¶ a buying spree for *scarce* items

fūsuigaihoken 風水害保険 storm and flood insurance

futai 付帯 incidental; accessory; attendant; collateral; secondary

futaihiyō 付帯費用 incidental expenses

futaijōken 付帯条件 incidental condition; collateral condition

futaika 不胎化 sterilization ¶ the temporary *sterilization* of funds at the Bank // There was a *sterilization* of much of this money in that time deposits in the banking system rose sharply. // *sterilization* of gold, or gold *sterilization*, and of inflowed funds

futaiketsugi 付帯決議 rider; reservation

futaikyūfu 付帯給付 fringe benefits ¶→諸給与

futaiseikyū 付帯請求 accessory claim; attendant claim

futaishōsho 付帯証書 collateral bond

futaisoshō 付帯訴訟 incidental suit; incidental appeal

futan 負担 burden; load; charge; incidence; defrayment ¶ Expenditure on health services will place a considerable added *burden* on the budget. // To reduce the debt service *burden* through longer maturitites // Unwinding unnecessary regulatory *burdens* will take time. // to reduce the burden of tax on profits // The *burden* of taxes and social security contributions levied on companies has increased. // Repayment of the debt imposes a heavy *burden* on the country. // The Bank rate cut reduced the interest payment *burden* of enterprises by ¥400 billion. // The growth in Treasury borrowing adds to the interest *burden* borne by the budget. // to shift a *burden* on to the weaker // to place an unacceptable *burden* on ... // to shift the *burden* of adjustment to the lower income groups // how the *burden* of the interest-rate risk can be moderated, shared, or avoided in future years // to alleviate the social *burdens* of obsolescence // to add to an already *burdensome* load of international debt // to be faced with a relatively onerous external debt *burden* // to achieve a more equitable distribution of the tax *burden* // to impose on public enterprises stringent price controls and other cost *burdens* // to bear the sole *burden* of adjustment

利子負担 interest burden ¶ an increase in the *interest burden* on the country's foreign debt

租税負担 tax burden; tax incidence ¶ Inflation has been responsible for an insidious increase in the *tax burden*.

財政負担 fiscal burden ¶ Aggressive taxation has enlarged the proportion of the total *fiscal burden* borne by individuals.

futanbun 負担分 burden share

futankeigen 負担軽減 reduction of incidence

futankin 負担金 burden charge; share in the expenses

futankinkō 負担均衡 equalization of incidence

futankōheinogensoku 負担公平の原則 principle of burden sharing

futannokōhei 負担の公平 equal shouldering of burdens

futeihyōjun 不定標準 indefinite standard

futeikibin 不定期便 irregular service

futeikikōro 不定期航路 tramp trade; irregular service

futeikisen 不定期船 tramp; tramp steamer; tramp liner

futeikisen'unchinshisū 不定期船運賃指数 freight index of tramps

futeikiyōsen 不定期用船 voyage charter; spot charter

futekiseikessan 不適正決算 presentation of financial conditions deemed inappropriate by a certified public accountant

futō 不当 unjust; wrong; unfair; reckless; undue; improper; exorbitant; unjustifiable; unreasonable ¶ *improper* profits // *exorbitant* prices // *unjustifiable* price hikes // *unreasonable* claims

futōhyōji 不当表示 misleading representation; false labeling

futōjikō 不当事項(予算の) cases of misappropriation of funds

futōkaiko 不当解雇 wrongful dismissal

futōkakōkan 不等価交換 non-equivalent exchange

futōkashitsuke 不当貸付 reckless advance (=loan)

futōkazei 不当課税 unreasonable taxation

futōkeihin 不当景品 unjustifiable premium

futōmei 不透明 [市] inactive; dull

futōnatorihikiseigen 不当な取引制限 undue restriction of business activities; unwarranted restrictions on transactions

futōnedan 不当値段 unreasonable price; exorbitant price; unfair price ¶ →法外な値段

futōrenbai 不当廉売 dumping

futōrenbaikinshihō 不当廉売禁止法 anti-dumping law

futōrenbaizei 不当廉売税 anti-dumping duty

futōritoku 不当利得 excessive profit; profiteering

futōrōdōkōi 不当労働行為 unfair labor practice

futōshishutsu 不当支出 unjust disbursement; misappropriation of funds

futōshiyōryō 埠頭使用料 wharfage; quayage

futōwatashi 埠頭渡し ex-pier; ex-quay; ex-dock

futōzumi 埠頭積み loading from the pier

futsū 普通 normal; regular; common; ordinary; usual; general; universal; average; commonplace; popular; prevailing; prevalent; familiar; medial; plain

futsūginkō 普通銀行 ordinary bank; commercial bank

futsūgodenpō 普通語電報 plain language telegram

futsūhikiuke 普通引受け clean acceptance

futsūhin 普通品 fair average quality

futsūkabu 普通株 common stock; ordinary stock

futsūkashitsuke 普通貸付 general loan; ordinary loan

futsūkawase 普通為替 postal money order

futsūkawasetegata 普通為替手形 clean bill

futsūkogitte 普通小切手 open check

futsūkumiaiin 普通組合員 regular member

futsūmono 普通物 ［証市］ three day's delivery

futsūressha 普通列車 accommodation train; local train

futsuriai 不釣合い disparity ¶ growing *disparity* between workers' efficiency and their remuneration

futsuriaina 不釣合いな disconcerting; disproportionate ¶ Price increases will be *disconcertingly* large. // a *disproportionate* expansion of production relative to growth of demand

futsūsai 普通債 straight bond; non-convertible bond

futsūshūshinhoken 普通終身保険 ordinary whole life insurance

futsūsōko 普通倉庫 free warehouse

futsūtorihiki 普通取引 ［証市］ regular transaction

futsūwaribiki 普通割引 bank discount

futsūyokin 普通預金 ordinary deposit

futsūzeiritsu 普通税率 general tariff

futtei 払底 running-out; exhaustion; dearth; scarcity; shortage; want; famine ¶ The oil *runs out.* // *exhausted* supplies

fuwatari 不渡り dishonor; non-payment

fuwatarikogitte 不渡小切手 dishonored check; past due check; overdue check; protested check

fuwataritegata 不渡手形 dishonored bill

fuyō 扶養 support; maintenance ¶ family *maintenance*, including housing and education

fuyōfukyūkashidashi 不要不急貸出 non-essential and non-urgent lending

fuyōfukyūno 不要不急の non-urgent; inessential; non-essential; non-urgent and non-essential ¶ completely *inessential* goods like bikinis or nailpolish // easy-to-make but unobtainable *inessentials* // *non-essential* and *non-urgent* lending // *non-urgent* projects

fuyōfukyūshikin 不要不急資金 non-urgent funds

fuyōgimu 扶養義務 duty of support

fuyōkazoku 扶養家族 dependent family member; dependent

fuyōkōjo 扶養控除 tax exemption for dependents; deduction for dependents

fuyōsha 扶養者 supporter; sustainer

fuyōshigetsu 不要資月 month of small fund demand; month of sluggish demand for funds ¶ ［参考］ seasonal April mildness of credit demand

fuzaijinushi 不在地主 absentee landlord; absentee land owner

fuzaijinushiseido 不在地主制度 absenteeism

fuzaishoyūken 不在所有権 absentee ownership

fuzaishoyūsha 不在所有者 absentee owner

fuzokuchōsho 付属調書 subsidiary investigation record

fuzokuhin 付属品 accessory

fuzokushorui 付属書類 suppoting documents

fuzuigyōmu 付随業務 contingent business

fuzuihiyō 付随費用 extra charge

fuzuitanpo 付随担保 subsidiary (collateral security)

fuzumi 不積み short shipment

G

GNE sōkikeisanhō GNE 早期計算法 [統] Quick Estimate method; Q.E. method (of GNE calculation)

GNP gyappu GNP ギャップ gross national product gap; degree of utilization of capacity; ratio of actual GNP to potential GNP

gaibuchōtatsu 外部調達 external financing

gaibufukeizai 外部不経済 external diseconomy

gaibufusai 外部負債 external debt

gaibukansa 外部監査 external audit

gaibukeizai 外部経済 external economy

gaibushihon 外部資本 outside capital; borrowed capital

gaibutekiizonkankei 外部的依存関係 external interdependence (of firms)

gaichū 外注 order placed outside; outside order; outward order; outside processing operation

gaichūseihin 外注製品 outside product

gaidansu ガイダンス guidance ¶ the Federal Open Market Committee's instructional *guidance* to the Accounting Manager // All participants would obtain *guidance* from the policy action taken by the Committee. // The supervisory office lays down a *guidance* figure for premium increases for liability insurance. // → 指導

gaidinguraito ガイディング・ライト [英] guiding light ¶ →ガイドライン

gaidoposuto ガイドポスト [米] guidepost ¶ the *guideposts* to assess whether the program is being satisfactorily implemented // →ガイドライン

gaidoposutoseisaku ガイドポスト政策 guidepost policy

gaidorain ガイドライン guide-line ¶ overstepping of the *guidelines* // The Committee's reliance on money market conditions as the Manager's *guideline* gave it no very firm control over the quantity of credit supplied. // to provide explicit *guidelines* for the Manager to follow in foreign currency transactions // The action is consistent with Committee *guidelines*. // to apply *guidelines* to limit the foreign lending by U.S. financial institutions // Salaries could be negotiated in accordance with *guidelines* drawn up by the Government. // Broad *guideline* will be set by the Fed. Govt. // The borrowers specifically commit themselves to new export subsidy *guidelines* agreed within the OECD. // to persuade workers and businessmen to live up to the wage and price *guidelines* // The Cabinet laid down the *guideline* for the Government's budget policy. // to have each basic industry establish price deceleration *guidelines* for itself, which are preferable to government imposed *guidelines* // Most pay settlements are keeping within the *guidelines* laid down by the Government. // pull the growth rate of the monetary aggregates back within the policy *guidelines* laid down earlier // to announce the official *guideline* for money supply growth // to tighten the voluntary wage-price *guideline* // to adjust the *guidelines* for export re-financing // a company's compliance with the Administration's wage and price *guidelines* // companies overstepping the wage *guidelines*.

gaigaitorihiki 外外取引 ［市］ offshore transaction

gaiginkariire 外銀借入れ borrowing from a foreign bank

gaijin 外人 foreigner; alien

gaijingai 外人買い ［証市］ alien stock buying; foreign buying of Japanese company stocks; foreign buying

gaijinhoyūkabusū 外人保有株数 number of stocks possessed by foreigners

gaijinmochikabuhiritsu 外人持株

比率 foreign stockholding ratio; stock holding ratio of foreigners

gaijinmochikabuseigen 外人持株制限 stockholding limit for foreign investors; limit on foreign investors' holdings of stocks

gaika 外貨 foreign currency

gaikaazukekin 外貨預け金 foreign currency deposit

gaikaazukekinrisoku 外貨預け金利息 interest on foreign currency deposits

gaikadatesōba 外貨建相場 rate in foreign currency

gaikahaiseki 外貨排斥 boycott of foreign goods

gaikahoyūdaka 外貨保有高 foreign currency holdings

gaikajunbi 外貨準備 reserves of gold, SDRs and foreign currencies; foreign exchange reserves; external reserves; (gold and foreign) exchange reserve (holdings); foreign reserves ¶ The official figure put India's gold and *foreign exchange reserves* at about Rs. 7.3 billion. // a marked easing of the drain on *exchange reserves* // a net gain of $16 million in *exchange reserve holdings* by the central bank // Certain countries added significantly to their *exchange holdings*. // to slow down the accelerating expansion of the nation's *foreign exchange reserves* // There was a marked easing of the drain on *foreign exchange reserves*. // The Bank of Finland's *foreign exchange reserves,* including gold, declined from Fmk 70.9 billion to Fmk 64.5 billion, equal to about two month's imports. // Israel's *reserve position* and the relationship between *reserves* and foreign currency indebtedness have greatly improved. // Certain countries added significantly to their gold and *foreign exchange holdings.* // *to* replenish its depleted *foreign reserves* by $2 billon this year

適正外貨準備 adequate gold and foreign exchange reserves; optimum reserves of gold and foreign exchange

gaikajunbikinseido 外貨準備金制度 reserve requirement system in foreign currency

gaikajunbizōgen 外貨準備増減 changes in gold and foreign exchange reserves

gaikakakutoku 外貨獲得 acquisition of foreign currencies

gaikakawasetegata 外貨為替手形 bill in foreign currency

gaikakogittehakkōkaitori 外貨小切手発行買取 drawing and buying of checks in foreign currency

gaikakōkan'en 外貨交換円 yen coverted from foreign currency

gaikakōkanzumishōmeisho 外貨交換済証明書 foreign currency conversion certificate

gaikakokusai 外貨国債 government bond in foreign currency

gaikakōsei 外貨攻勢 foreign capital offensive; foreign capital challenge

gaikan 概観 outline; general view; overview; bird's-eye view; picture ¶ an *overview* of the recent monetary developments

gaikapojishon 外貨ポジション foreign currency position

gaikasai 外貨債 foreign currency bond; foreign currecy-denominated debenture; loan denominated in foreign currencies ¶ to float DM-

denominated bonds reaching a value of 100 million marks // *foreign* DM-*denominated loans*

gaikasaiganribaraishikin 外貨債元利払資金 funds for amortization of principal and interest of foreign currency bonds

gaikasaiken 外貨債券 debenture in foreign currency

gaikasaiken 外貨債権 claimable assets in foreign currency

gaikashiteiyokin 外貨指定預金 designated deposit in foreign currency

gaikashōken 外貨証券 foreign (currency) securities

gaikategata 外貨手形 foreign money bill

gaikawariatesei 外貨割当制 foreign exchange allocation system

gaikayokin 外貨預金 foreign currency deposit

gaikayokinkanjō 外貨預金勘定 foreign currency deposit account

gaikayotaku 外貨預託 foreign currency deposit with exchange banks; entrusted foreign currency to exchange banks

gaikayotakusei 外貨預託制 system of entrusting the government's foreign exchange funds to banks handling foreign exchange

gaikinshokuin 外勤職員 field staff

gaikōhanbaiin 外交販売員 salesman

戸別訪問販売員 house-to-house salesman

地方回り外交販売員 traveling salesman

gaikōin 外交員 salesman; sales people; canvasser

gaikokubōeki 外国貿易 foreign trade

gaikokubōekijōsū 外国貿易乗数 foreign trade multiplier

gaikokugaisha 外国会社 foreign company; [米] alien corporation

gaikokuginkō 外国銀行 foreign bank; [米] alien bank

gaikokuhin 外国品 foreign goods

gaikokuhōjin 外国法人 foreign juridical person; foreign corporation; [米] alien corporation

gaikokuhokakufutanpo 外国捕獲不担保 free of capture and seizure

gaikokujinnyūkokuzei 外国人入国税 alien tax

gaikokujintōrokushōmeisho 外国人登録証明書 certificate of alien registration

gaikokujinzaisan 外国人財産 alien property

gaikokukawase 外国為替 foreign exchange

ドル建外国為替 exchange in dollars

円建外国為替 exchange in yen

外貨買入外国為替 foreign currency bills bought

外貨買渡外国為替 foreign currency bills sold

外貨未払外国為替 foreign currency bills payable

外貨取立外国為替 foreign currency bills receivable

邦貨買入外国為替 home currency bills bought

邦貨買渡外国為替 home currency bills sold

邦貨未払外国為替 home currency bills payable

邦貨取立外国為替 home currency bills receivable

未払外国為替 foreign bills payable

取立外国為替 foreign bills receivable

gaikokukawasebaibaimōshikomi 外国為替売買申込 application for purchase and sale of foreign exchange

gaikokukawasedīrā 外国為替ディーラー foreign exchange dealer; cambist

gaikokukawaseginkō 外国為替銀行 foreign exchange bank

gaikokukawasehendōjunbikin 外国為替変動準備金 reserve for foreign exchange fluctuation

gaikokukawasehikiatekashitsuke 外国為替引当貸付 loans against negotiations of usance bills

gaikokukawasehoyūdaka 外国為替保有高 foreign exchange holdings

gaikokukawasekansanhyō 外国為替換算表 foreign exchange conversion table

gaikokukawasekansanritsu 外国為替換算率 foreign exchange conversion rate

gaikokukawasekashitsuke 外国為替貸付 loans in foreign exchange

gaikokukawasekessaishikin 外国為替決済資金 fund for foreign exchange settlement

gaikokukawasekikin 外国為替基金 foreign exchange fund

gaikokukawasekinyūkikan 外国為替金融機関 financial institution for foreign exchange

gaikokukawasekōninginkō 外国為替公認銀行 authorized foreign exchange bank

gaikokukawasekyūshū 外国為替吸収 foreign exchange inducement

gaikokukawasemochidakashūchū-seido 外国為替持高集中制度 system authorizing limited open position

gaikokukawasenakagainin 外国為替仲買人 exchange broker

gaikokukawasenoshūchū 外国為替の集中 concentration (=delivery; surrender) of foreign exchange

gaikokukawasepojishon 外国為替ポジション foreign exchange position

gaikokukawasesaeki 外国為替差益 gain on foreign exchange

gaikokukawasesaitei 外国為替裁定 arbitration of exchange

gaikokukawasesenmonginkō 外国為替専門銀行 specialized foreign exchange bank

gaikokukawaseshijō 外国為替市場 foreign exchange market ¶ The dollar on the Tokyo *foreign exchange market* rose in value. // trading in the *New York exchange market* // The *foreign exchange market* remained calm.

gaikokukawaseshikinshōken 外国為替資金証券 foreign exchange fund bill

gaikokukawaseshūchūseido 外国為替集中制度 foreign exchange holding restriction system; foreign exchange concentration system

gaikokukawasesōba 外国為替相場 foreign exchange rate

gaikokukawasesōsa 外国為替操作 foreign exchange operation

gaikokukawasetegata 外国為替手形 foreign exchange bill (=draft)

gaikokukawasetegatakaitoriseido 外国為替手形買取制度 system for purchase of foreign exchange bills

gaikokukawasetōki 外国為替投機 foreign exchange speculation

gaikokukawasetoriatsukaishiten 外国為替取扱支店 branch handling foreign exchange business

gaikokukawaseun'eishikin 外国為替運営資金 fund for operation of foreign exchange

gaikokukawaseyamishijō 外国為替やみ市場 black bourse

gaikokukawaseyobikin 外国為替予備金 foreign exchange reserves

gaikokukōro 外国航路 overseas shipping service (route)

gaikokukyōdōkaison 外国共同海損 foreign general average

gaikokuniaruoyagaisha 外国にある親会社 foreign-based parent company

gaikokuryokōshashinyōjō 外国旅行者信用状 foreign traveler's letter of credit

gaikokusai 外国債 foreign bond; external bond; foreign issue

gaikokushihon 外国資本 foreign capital; foreign capital investment in Japan

gaikokushisan 外国資産 foreign assets

gaikokushōsha 外国商社 foreign firm; alien firm; foreign house

gaikokusōkin 外国送金 remittance abroad

gaikokusōkintesūryō 外国送金手数料 commission on drafts sold

gaikokutatengari 外国他店借 due to foreign banks

gaikokutatengashi 外国他店貸 due from foreign banks

gaikokutsūkabaibai 外国通貨売買 buying and selling of foreign bank notes and coins

gaikokutsūkaryōgae 外国通貨両替 money exchange

gaikokuyūbinkawase 外国郵便為替 foreign postal money order

gaikōsen 外航船 ocean-going ship; ocean vessel

gaikōsen'unchin 外航船運賃 ocean freight

gaimuin 外務員 fieldman; canvasser

gaisai 外債 foreign bond; foreign debt (=indebtedness); foreign loan; external bond; external debt; external loan; foreign issue ¶ Japan's *foreign bond* flotation policy // to seek sanction for floating *foreign bonds* under the same pattern // New *external bond* offering run at annual rate of $34 billion.

gaisaiboshū 外債募集 flotation of external loan

gaisaiganribaraizaimushintaku-kanjō 外債元利払財務信託勘定 fiscal trust account for payments of principal and interest of external bonded debts

gaisaiganribaraizaimuyokinkanjō 外債元利払財務預金勘定 fiscal deposit accounts for payments of principal and interest of external bonded debts

gaisaihakkōkawarikin 外債発行代り金 proceeds from external bond issuance

gaisairishi 外債利子 interest on external bond

gaisaishōkan 外債償還 redemption of external loan

gaisan 概算 estimate; approximate calculation; estimated amount ¶ the *estimates* of the first quarter balance of payments // The net figure cannot yet to be *estimated.* // The number *approximates* to one thousand.

原価概算 rough cost

gaisanbarai 概算払い payment by rough estimate

gaisanhokenryō 概算保険料 estimated premium

gaisankijitsu 概算期日 approximate due date

gaisansūryō 概算数量 approximate quantity

gaisantaishakutaishōhyō 概算貸借対照表 rough balance sheet

gaiseibumon 外生部門 exogenous sector

gaiseihensū 外生変数 exogenous variable

gaiseiteki 外生的 exogenous

gaiseitekihendo 外生的変動 exogenous change

gaiseitekitōshi 外生的投資 exogenous investment

gaishi 外資 foreign capital; foreign investment ¶ a drive to lure *foreign investment* in the country's booming resource-development industry

gaishidōnyū 外資導入 introduction of foreign capital

gaishikeikigyō 外資系企業 foreign-affiliate; enterprise with foreign capital; foreign-owned corporation

gaishikyūshū 外資吸収 foreign capital inducement

gaishiryūnyū 外資流入 influx (= inflow) of foreign capital

gaishiteikeigaisha 外資提携会社 foreign capital-affiliated company

gaishitoriire 外資取入れ intake of foreign capital; foreign capital intake

gaishiyunyū 外資輸入 importation of foreign capital

gaishoku 外食 eating out; meals out; dining out; away-from-home meal ¶ Americans are spending a large share of their food budget for *eating out.* // There were price rises for some bus journeys and *meals out.* // *dining-out* expenses

gaishokusangyō 外食産業 food service industry; eating-out trade; away-from-home eating trade ¶ The term "*food service*" is used to define businesses or outlets that serve "away-from-home" meals.

gaishokusangyōyōchōrizumishoku-hin 外食産業用調理済食品 pre-cooked foods for distribution to restaurants, etc.

gaiteki 外的 exogenous; extraneous; external ¶ *exogenous* factors // causes *extraneous* to the market // *external* reasons

gakai 瓦解 collapse; crash ¶ a *collapse* of food prices // the *collapse* of the IMF regime // The currency system *collapsed*. // The market *crashed*.

gakumen 額面 face-value; par

gakumendōri 額面通り at par

gakumenhakkō 額面発行 issue at par; issue at face value

gakumenijō 額面以上 above par; at a premium; with premium

gakumenika 額面以下 below par; at a discount; with discount

gakumenkabu 額面株 stocks at par; par value stock

gakumenkakaku 額面価格 face value; par value

gakumenkingaku 額面金額 face amount; principal

gakumenware 額面割れ drop below par

gakusaitekisekkinhō 学際的接近法 interdisciplinery approach

gankin 元金 principal; face amount

gankintōrokushōken 元金登録証券 bond registered only as to principal

ganpon 元本 principal; capital

ganponhoshō 元本保証 principal guaranteed

ganponkakujitsusei 元本確実性 capital certainty

ganri 元利 principal and interest ¶ Companies are way behind on repayments of *principal* and are struggling to pay *interest*.

ganribaraijimu 元利払事務 business relating to servicing of bonds ¶ [参考] The country is able to service its commercial debt properly.

ganrigōkei 元利合計 interest included

ganrikinshiharai 元利金支払 debt service; servicing ¶ The aggregate *debt service* ratio of these 25 countries will rise to 25 per cent of exports. // The growth of the *debt service* burden is inevitable. // the *servicing* capacity of the debtor country // to *service* these obligations in the international markets // Government *debt servicing* will cost more next year than this. // The country will be able to *service* its *debt* to the World Bank. // sufficient foreign exchange to *service* all their foreign debt // the ratio of export earnings to *debt servicing* costs

ganrikintōbunkatsuhensai 元利均等分割返済 level monthly payment of principal and interest

ganrishiharaikin 元利支払金 debt service payment

gantohōshiki ガント方式 Gantt system; task-bonus system

ganzō 贋造 counterfeiting; forgery

ganzōhin 贋造品 counterfeit; sham

ganzōkahei 贋造貨幣 counterfeit; counterfeit coin; forged coin

ganzōsha 贋造者 counterfeiter; forger

ganzōshihei 贋造紙幣 counterfeit;

counterfeit note; forged note

ganzōshōhyō 贋造商標 counterfeited trade mark

ganzōshōken 贋造証券 forged security

gappei 合併 merger; amalgamation; consolidation; fusion; absorption; takeover; purchase; acquisition; buy-out ¶ The number of *mergers* announcements fell sharply. // Bergens Privatbank and Bergens Kreditbank *merged* to form Bergen Bank. // Under the terms of the *merger* Pierson will change its status to a limited liability company. // to *amalgamate* into a single corporation // to be *taken over by* another corporation // to arrange *acquisition* of other companies // There were 123 corporate *acquisitions*. // *Acquisitions* by well-known companies include Pillsbury Co.'s *purchases* of the 113 Steak of Ale restaurants. // Many *buy-outs* now are for cash. // Colgate Palmolive's *buy-out* of Charles A. Eaton Co. // Blacks *took over* a white-owned company. // The company reached a tentative *merger* deal with National Airlines, Inc.

吸収合併 merger; absorption; consolidation take-over; purchase

新設合併 consolidation

垂直的合併 vertical merger ¶ *vertical mergers*, in which a company takes over one of its suppliers or customers

水平合併 horizontal merger ¶ *horizontal mergers* between large companies in the same industry

対等合併 amalgamation on an equal basis

gappeigaisha 合併会社 amalgamated company

gappeisaeki 合併差益 surplus from merged company; profit from amalgamation

gappeitaishakutaishōhyō 合併貸借対照表 consolidated balance sheet

gara 瓦落 [市] crash; sharp drop; heavy slump; dropping at a bound ¶ →がた落ち

garufudoru ガルフ・ドル Gulf dollar ¶ a Gulf dollar lending market

gassanzaimushohyō 合算財務諸表 combined financial statements

gataochi がた落ち [市] slump; setback ¶ The market staged a bad *slump* in the price of railway shares. // The stock market had its worst *setback* of the year as oil shares fell sharply on news of a revolt in Iraq.

gatto ガット General Agreement of Tariff and Trade; GATT

gattotaisei ガット体制 GATT system (=regime)

gattotōkyōsengen ガット東京宣言 Tokyo Declaration of GATT

gejun 下旬 last ten-day period of the month; last ten (or eleven) days of the month; toward month-end; late in the month ¶ in the *last eleven days* of March // for the *last ten-day period* of March // toward March-end

gēmunoriron ゲームの理論 theory of games

gemupuran ゲーム・プラン game plan

genbakantoku 現場監督 site supervisor; site supervisory personnel (= staff)

genbashokuin 現場職員 shopfloor

worker; blue-collar worker; operative; non-clerical staff ¶ *Shopfloor workers* might put the blame on the increasing proportion of "non-productive" workers. // Of the 269,000 employees in the iron and steel industry 213,500 were classed as *operatives* and the remaining 55,000 were administrative, technical and clerical employees.

genbawatashi 現場渡し loco; ex plantation; ex farm; ex factory; ex mill; ex work

genbawatashinedan 現場渡し値段 loco price

genbawatashiokurijō 現場渡し送り状 loco invoice

genbutsu 現物 cash and similar items; spot goods kind; spot

genbutsubaishō 現物賠償 reparations in kind

genbutsukawase 現物為替 spot exchange

genbutsukawasesōba 現物為替相場 spot exchange rate ¶ The *spot* dollar traded for ¥298.00 median.

genbutsukessai 現物決済 spot basis; cash basis ¶ transactions on a *cash basis*

genbutsukōeki 現物交易 barter trade

genbutsukyūyo 現物給与 wage in kind; truck system

genbutsunakagai 現物仲買い spot broker

genbutsunedan 現物値段 spot price

genbutsuni 現物荷 spot cargo

genbutsunōzei 現物納税 tax payment in kind

genbutsushijō 現物市場 cash market; spot market ¶ Dealings in *cash markets* are mostly for immediate

delivery.

genbutsushusshi 現物出資 investment in kind

genbutsushusshidaishōkabu 現物出資代償株 treasury stock

genbutsusōba 現物相場 spot rate; spot quotation

genbutsusokujiwatashiyakujō 現物即時渡約定 spot contract

genbutsutorihiki 現物取引 spot transaction

genbutsuukewatashi 現物受渡し actual delivery

genbutsuwatashi 現物渡し spot delivery

genchichōsa 現地調査 field survey

genchihōjin 現地法人 company incorporated abroad

genchika 現地化 localization

genchikashitsuke 現地貸付 loan in foreign currency extended overseas by a Japanese bank

genchinikkanshi 現地日刊紙 vernacular daily

genchino 現地の vernacular; local ¶ a Japanese *vernacular* daily, or *local* newspaper

genchisagyō 現地作業 field work

gendo 限度 limitation; limit ¶ budgetary *limitations* (=the limitations of the budget) // the highest or maximum *limit* // the lowest or minimum *limit* // to raise (=*increase*) or lower (=reduce) the weight *limit* from... to... // within the prescribed *limits* // to pass, exceed, or overstep the *limits*

過振り限度 limit of overdrawn account

信用限度 credit limit; credit ceiling; credit line

gendoippai 限度一杯 to the limit ¶ House buyers had borrowed *to the* *limit* that their income would allow at the height of the housing price boom.

gendōryoku 原動力 impetus; motive power; driving power; engine ¶ Growth *impetus* continues to come mainly from abroad. // No marked growth *impetus* is expected from the export reaction. // the "trade as the *engine* of growth" thesis

gendoyoyūgaku 限度余裕額 unused portion within the limit; undrawn (=unused) balance ¶ the *unused portion* of the permissible quarterly increase in lending // The *undrawn balance* under these arrangements was SDR 4.8 billion. // an ample *unused margin* // the *unused portion* for a stand-by contract

gengai 現買い outright buying ¶ to *buy dollars outright*

gengaihakkō 限外発行 over-issue of paper currency; excess issue; fiduciary issue

gengetsu 限月 contract month

gengetsuwatashi 限月渡し ［市］ delivery on calendar month basis

genheika 原平価 initial par value

genjitsu 現実 reality; actuality ¶ a review to replace the historical past with current *realities* // to adjust to changing *realities*

genjitsunoshotoku 現実の所得 measured income

genjō 現状 current condition; standing (=existing) situation; present state; plight; position ¶ *current* economic *conditions* // the *standing* business *situation* // the *present state* favorable of external payments // the difficult *plight* and prospects of the low-income developing coun-

tries // the difficulty of diagnosing *existing* economic and financial *conditions* correctly // the *position* and outlook for the auto industry // The international debt *situation* was clarified somewhat. // to assess America's international economic *position* // ［参考］ A reasonably clear picture of U.S. trade flows can be assembled and projected into the future.

genjōijishugi 現状維持主義 preservationism

genka 原価 prime cost; first cost; cost ¶ to sell below *cost,* not at *cost* // at a *cost* of $500 // The price is under first *cost.* // to bring back and cover the *cost*

第一原価　first cost; prime cost
回避可能原価　avoidable cost
期間原価　period cost
工場原価　manufacturing cost
埋没原価　sunk cost
生産原価　cost of production
仕入原価　purchasing cost
真正の原価　bona fide cost

genka 減価 discount; abatement; reduction of price; cut in price; depreciation; devaluation ¶ the dollar is at a considerable *discount* // 15% *discount* from the prescribed price // a 10% *abatement* from the asked price // currency *depreciation* // a *depreciation* of the Chilean money, escudo // a *depreciation* from Cr. $100=US$1 to Cr. $200=US$1 // The *depreciation* of the dollar in terms of the German mark was about 15 per cent. // The riyal *depreciated* to its lower margin vis-à-vis the SDR. // The Jordan dinar *depreciated* slightly in terms of the yen, but its *depreciation* in effective terms was considerably smaller than expected. // the real (price-adjusted) *devaluation* of the dollar between 1969 and March 1973

genkabu 現株 spot share

genkabunseki 原価分析 cost analysis

genkabuohiku 現株を引く to pay for stocks bought

genkabuowatasu 現株を渡す to deliver stocks sold

genkadaka 原価高 high cost

genkahanbai 減価販売 discount sale

genkai 限界 margin; limitation; limit; bounds; threshold ¶ a wide *margin* of free activity // exchange fluctuation *margins* // *limitation* of exchange fluctuation // *limits* of space // *bounds* of knowledge // A currency reached and crossed its *threshold* of divergence fixed at 75%.

genkaidaitairitsu 限界代替率 marginal rate of substitution

genkaigenka 限界原価 marginal cost

genkaijōken 限界条件 marginal conditions

genkaikakumei 限界革命 marginal revolution

genkaikigyōka 限界企業家 marginal entrepreneur

genkaikōyō 限界効用 marginal utility

genkainōdo 限界濃度 limiting concentration

genkainōritsu 限界能率 marginal efficiency

genkaiondo 限界温度 critical temperature

genkairitsu 限界率 marginal rate ¶ to cut the top *marginal rate* on earned income to 60% // to slash

these confiscatory top *marginal* tax *rates* // the *marginal rate* of interest

genkaiseisanhi 限界生産費 marginal cost of production

genkaiseisanryoku 限界生産力 marginal productivity

genkaishōhiseikō 限界消費性向 marginal propensity to consume

genkaisokudo 限界速度 critical speed

genkakachi 原価価値 cost value

genkakanjō 原価勘定 cost account

genkakanjō 減価勘定 depreciation account

genkakeisan 原価計算 cost accounting; costing

genkakirisage 原価切下げ cost reduction; cut in cost

genkamotochō 原価元帳 cost ledger

genkasagaku 原価差額 over-absorbed cost; under-absorbed cost

genkashōkyaku 減価償却 depreciation

genkashōkyakuhi 減価償却費 depreciation expense; depreciations

genkashōkyakuhikiatekin 減価償却引当金 depreciation reserve; accumulated depreciations; depreciation allowance

genkashōkyakuritsu 減価償却率 ratio of depreciation

genkashōkyakushisan 減価償却資産 depreciable assets

genkashōkyakutsumitatekin 減価償却積立金 depreciation reserve

genkashugi 原価主義 cost method

genkin 現金 cash; ready money ¶ *cash* on hand // *cash* holding // to sell only for *cash* // to pay in *cash* // *cash* position

小口現金 petty cash

手許現金 ready money; cash on hand; vault cash; till cash

genkinbaibai 現金売買 cash-sale; cash transaction

genkinbarai 現金払い cash payment; payment in cash

genkinbaraihaitōkin 現金払配当金 cash bonus; cash dividend

genkinbaraihōshiki 現金払方式 pay-as-you-go (plan) ¶ to conduct its trade on a *pay-as-you-go* basis

genkinbaraiwaribiki 現金払割引 cash discount ¶ a 5% *cash discount* // to make or allow 5% *discount* for *cash*

genkinbusoku 現金不足 short of cash

genkinchūmon 現金注文 cash with order; c.w.o.

genkingai 現金買い cash purchase

genkingakari 現金係 cashier

genkinhanbai 現金販売 cash sale

genkinhikikae 現金引換え cash on delivery; c.o.d.

genkinhikikaewatashi 現金引換渡し cash and carry

genkinhiritsu 現金比率 cash ratio

genkinjidōshiharaiki 現金自動支払機 automatic cash paying machine (=dispenser)

genkinjunbi 現金準備 cash reserve; reserve cash; (cash) reserve requirement ¶ Non-member banks hold part of their *cash reserves* in vault but hold the major part in the form of demand deposits with correspondents. // Commercial banks' currency holdings and their deposit accounts with the Federal Reserve Banks serve as the *reserve cash* against the checking and other deposit accounts the community at large holds with these banks. // The *cash reserve requirements* imposed are far less severe than imposed on member banks. // Part of the *reserve requirements* may be met in holdings of federal, state and local government securities. // Both reserve city and country member banks are required to keep the same minimum ratio of *cash reserves* to time deposits, 3 percent for saving deposits and 5 percent for other time deposits. // Open market purchases of eligible financial claims create new *reserve cash* for the commercial banks and sales of such claims absorb *reserve cash* from them.

genkinjunbiritsu 現金準備率 cash (reserve) ratio

genkinjuyō 現金需要 cash need; demand for cash ¶ Around $280 million was raised to help meet the city's *cash needs.* // business *needs of cash* at term-end

genkinka 現金化 cashing; realization; encashment ¶ to *cash* a check // These bonds can be *cashed* quickly.

genkinkaitenhindo 現金回転頻度 quantity (=frequency) of receipt and payment of bank notes

genkinkankakachi 現金換価価値 actual cash value

genkinkessai 現金決済 cash settlement

genkinkōmoku 現金項目 cash item ¶ *cash items* in process of collection

genkinkyaku 現金客 cash customer

genkinkyūyo 現金給与 wages and salaries in cash

genkinryūshutsu 現金流出 cash drain

genkinsakumotsu 現金作物 cash crop

genkinshiharaiki 現金支払機 cash dipenser; CD

genkinshikishiwake 現金式仕訳 cash-journal method

genkinshisan 現金資産 cash assets

genkinshiwakechō 現金仕訳帳 cash journal

genkinshōkan 現金償還 cash redemption

genkinshūchūkessaikanjō 現金集中決済勘定 cash-concentration account

genkinshugi 現金主義 [会] cash basis

genkinshūnyū 現金収入 cash income; money income ¶ The government attempts to restrain the growth of *money incomes*.

genkinsuitōbo 現金出納簿 cash book

genkintegata 現金手形 cash note

genkintemotoaridaka 現金手許有高 cash in (=on) hand

genkintentōwatashi 現金店頭渡し cash and carry

genkintorihiki 現金取引 transaction for cash; bargain for cash

genkintoritateyūbin 現金取立郵便 cash on delivery post

genkintsūka 現金通貨 cash; cash currency ¶ *cash currency* in circulation at month-end

genkinuri 現金売り sale for cash; sale on cash

genkin'yokin 現金・預金 cash on hand and in banks

genkin'yusō 現金輸送 shipment of paper currency and coin ¶ incoming and outgoing *shipments of currency and coin* to and from the F.R. Bank of New York // Requests for *ship-ments of currency and coin* will be acted upon on the day of receipt.

genkin'yusōsha 現金輸送車 bank transport truck

genkin'yusōten 現金輸送点 specie point

genkinzandaka 現金残高 cash holdings; cash balance

genmō 減耗 depletion; attrition ¶ the *attrition* of bank capital through inflation

genmōshisan 減耗資産 wasting assets; depleting assets

gennenryō 原燃料 raw materials and mineral fuels

genpai 減配 reduction of a dividend; reduction of ration; dividend cut; cut in dividends

genpin 現品 goods in stock; stock on hand; actual article

genpinhikikaebarai 現品引換払い cash on delivery; c.o.d.

genpinkyūyosei 現品給与制 wage in kind; truck system

genryō 減量 fat-slicing; weight-reducing; scaling-down

genryōdoryoku 減量努力 effort for reduction of fixed costs

genryōsūryōhyōjun 原料数量標準 [会] material quantity standard

genryōtan 原料炭 coking coal

gensaikikin 減債基金 sinking-fund; amortization fund

gensaikikinhoken 減債基金保険 sinking-fund insurance

gensaitsumitatekin 減債積立金 sinking-fund reserve

gensakishijō 現先市場 gensaki market; bond repurchase market

gensan 減産 production cutback; curtailment of production; production restraints

gensanchihyōji 原産地表示 mark

of origin

gensanchishōmeisho　原産地証明書
certificate of origin

gensankoku　原産国　country of origin; place of origin

gensei　減勢　slowdown; slackening; moderation; deceleration ¶ Output *slumped* to an annual rate of 2.1 million tons. // *moderation* in the growth *slackening* of expansion // rise at a *decelerated* rate // a *deceleration* of the increase in production // a marked *deceleration* in imports attributed to a slowdown in economic activity // [参考]some erosion of the rate of increase

genseidēta　原生データ　［コン］ source data

gensen　源泉　source ¶ *Sources* of financing are drying up, requiring replenishment. // Energy products are a fruitful *source* of fiscal revenues. // One potential *source* of renewable energy is ethyl alcohol. // Cocoa is the foremost *source* of foreign exchange and a major source of tax revenue of Ghana. // Remittances represent a considerable potential *source* for saving and investment. // *sources* and uses of funds // the growth of existing *sources* of finance, supplemented by new funds // a potential *source* of new resources for agricultural development // the disruption of traditional or non-institutional *sources* of farm credit

gensenbunrikazei　源泉分離課税
separate tax withheld at source

gensenbunrisentakukazei　源泉分離選択課税　tax withheld on taxpayer's option

gensenchōshū　源泉徴収　withhold-ing; withholding at source; collection at source; stoppage at source

gensenchōshūhyō　源泉徴収票　(tax) withholding certificate

gensenkazei　源泉課税　tax assessment at source; stoppage at source; pay-as-you-earn (plan); pay-as-you-go (plan)

gensensentakukazei　源泉選択課税
optional assessment

genshi　原資　source of revenue; fiscal resource

genshi　減資　reduction of capital; capital decrease

genshihaikibutsu　原子廃棄物　atomic waste

genshikaisha　減資会社　company with reduced capital

genshinenryō　原子燃料　nuclear fuel

genshin'yōjō　原信用状　original credit

genshipuroguramu　原始プログラム　［コン］source program

genshiro　原子炉　atomic reactor

genshirontekibukkashisūron　原子論的物価指数論　atomistic approach to price indexes (=indices)

genshiryoku　原子力　nuclear energy; atomic energy

genshiryokuenerugī　原子力エネルギー　atomic energy

genshiryokuenjin　原子力エンジン　atomic engine

genshiryokuhatsuden　原子力発電　atomic power generation

genshiryokuhoken　原子力保険　atomic energy insurance

genshiryokukaihatsuriyōchōkikeikaku　原子力開発利用長期計画　long-term plan for the development and utilization of atomic power

genshiryokukonbināto　原子力コン

ビナート nuclear-combinart

genshiryokusangyōgurūpu 原子力産業グループ atomic power industrial group

genshiryokuseitetsu 原子力製鉄 nuclear energy iron making process

genshisaeki 減資差益 gains from stock retirement

genshō 現象 phenomenon ¶ The cooling-off *phenomenon* has been marked. // Economics is the science that treats *phenomena* from the standpoint of price. // It was a passing *phenomenon*.

genshō 減少 decrease; decline; reduction; contraction; shrinkage; abridgment; subtraction; lessening; diminution; abatement; curtailment; cut; cutback; loss; run-down; dip ¶ a sharp *decrease* in population to the 10 million mark // a city *diminishing* gradually in population // Population *lessened* by one million. // The year-to-year deficit was *reduced* to about 3.5 percent. // The rate of growth sharply *abated*. // a marked *contraction* of sales // production *curtailments* // drastic inventory *cutbacks* // the *abatement* of domestic demand // The rate *abated* sharply. // to show little inclination to *abate* // The *contraction* in output spread to all lines. // a shift from expansion to *contraction* // economic *contraction* // *cuts* in output // A slackening in trade will *cut* into the rate of export growth. // a *decrease* of similar magnitude in imports // the *diminution* in the rate of growth // The severity of inflation *diminished*. // a concomitant *reduction* in output // There was no perceptible *reduction* of pressure in

demand. // inventory *reduction* // The deficit was *reduced* to $213 million. // It was the largest published *loss* in the reserves in a single month. // There was a very rapid *run-down* in foreign exchange reserves. // a slight *dip* of output // Sales *dipped* a bit. // →下落; 下降

gensō 現送 cash sending; transport of bank notes (and coins)

gensoku 減速 deceleration; slow-down ¶ The *deceleration* of production was particularly marked in some of the industry groups. // Expansion of bank loans *decelerated*. // a *slow-down* in economic activity // Prices are *slowing down* in the rate of increase. // to *decelerate* their upward course

gensokukeizai "減速経済" "decelerating economy"; "slowed down" economy

gensokuzai 減速材 moderator

gensōten 現送点 specie point; gold export point

gentai 減退 waning; dwindling; ebb; pull-off ¶ The necessity of anti-inflation instruments has *waned*. // Business is at its lowest *ebb*. // Final demand has been on the *ebb*. // international trade which has *dwindled* amid a stagnant worldwide economy // The *pull-off* in activity promises to be less marked than is usual. // [参考] The economy is losing some of its steam.

gentan'i 原単位 basic unit; unit of output ¶ Businesses are economizing on raw material inputs per *unit of output*.

genteihendōsōba 限定変動相場 "wider band"

gen'uri 現売り outright selling

gen'yu 原油 crude oil; crude

genzaidaka 現在高 amount outstanding; amount in hand; stock in (=on) hand; holdings

genzairyō 原材料 raw materials ¶ to import abundant industrial *raw materials* to beat prospective scarcity // *raw-materials* inventories // steel-making *raw materials*

genzairyōchozōhin 原材料・貯蔵品 raw materials and stocks

genzairyōshōhishisū 原材料消費指数 consumption index of raw materials

genzairyōzaikoritsu 原材料在庫率 raw-material inventory ratio to production

genzairyōzaikoshisū 原材料在庫指数 inventory index of raw materials

genzei 減税 tax reduction; tax cut; tax abatement; tax relief; tax slash ¶ The recovery of investment was accelerated by means of a temporary *tax abatement.*

genzeihōan 減税法案 tax-slash bill; bill for tax reduction

geppu 月賦 monthly installment; monthly payment

geppuhanbaihō 月賦販売法 hire-purchase plan; installment system

geppuhoken 月賦保険 installment insurance; installment policy

geppukōnyū 月賦購入 hire purchase; credit purchase

geppuriyō 月賦利用 utilization of monthly installment credit

geraku 下落 decline; drop; dip; fall; falling off; slide; shortfall; setback; drifting-down; down-drift; downturn; down-swing; lowering; sag; slip off; recession; [市] losing ground; loss ¶ The dollar's *decline* was less ac-

centuated vis-à-vis the yen. // The dollar's *slide* this week (0.6% in a single day) resembles the familiar routes of sterling and the lira. // The dollar went on *sliding.* // Grain futures *drifted* mostly *lower* on the Chicago Board of Trade in response to commission house selling. // The stock market *lost* more *ground.* // The market regained much of the *ground lost* in the previous month. // The market recouped some of the *losses* to close little above the day's low. // Some *losses* were cut as trading progressed. // → 下降; 減少; 物価

gerakusakudō 下落策動 [市] gunning a stock

gesshorai 月初来 from the month's opening level ¶ an increase by 12 percent *from the month's opening level*

getchūheikinzandaka 月中平均残高 average daily figure of monthly balance; daily average of monthly balance

getsumatsu 月末 end of the month; month-end ¶ the balance at *the end of* March, or the balance at March-*end* or *end*-March balance

getsumatsubarai 月末払い month-end settlement; month-end payment

getsumatsuheikinzandaka 月末平均残高 average month-end balance

getsumatsuseiri 月末整理 [市] month-end liquidation

getsumatsushikin 月末資金 month-end funds

getsumatsuwatashi 月末渡し month-end delivery

getsureihōkoku 月例報告 monthly (economic) report

genkashōkyakukikin 減価償却基金

depreciation fund

gibusonnogyakusetsu ギブソンの逆説 Gibson paradox

gijinsetsu 擬人説 personification theory

gijutsu 技術 technology; technic; technique; art; knowhow

gijutsuenjo 技術援助 technical aid; technological assistance

gijutsuenjokeiyaku 技術援助契約 technological assistance contract

gijutsuhōteishiki 技術方程式 technical equation; technological equation

gijutsuiten 技術移転 transfer of technology

gijutsukakusa 技術格差 technological difference; technology gap

gijutsukakushin 技術革新 technological innovation (=renovation) ¶ An important technological *innovation* was introduced.

gijutsukeihanbaiin 技術系販売員 sales engineer

gijutsukō 技術工 artificer; artisan

gijutsukomon 技術顧問 technical adviser

gijutsukyōiku 技術教育 technical training

gijutsukyōryoku 技術協力 technical cooperation; technological cooperation

gijutsunojizenhyōka 技術の事前評価 technological assessment

gijutsunosaitenken 技術の再点検 technological (re)assessment

gijutsushashūdan 技術者集団 technostructure

gijutsushidō 技術指導 technical guidance

gijutsushinpo 技術進歩 technological progress; technological advance

gijutsuteikei 技術提携 technological tie-up; technical tieup

gijutsuteikyōkin'yū 技術提供金融 finance of technological assistance

gijutsutekidokusen 技術的独占 technical monopoly

gijutsutekishitsugyō 技術的失業 technological unemployment

gijutsuyushutsu 技術輸出 export of technique (=technology)

gikaitekijūshōshugi 議会的重商主義 parliamentary mercantilism

giketsuken 議決権 right to vote; voting power; vote ¶ the *right to vote* given the individual stockholder—one vote regardless of the member of shares owned // the majority interest entitled to 760 *votes* to be cast // to acquire the *power* to *vote* the stock // to *vote* shares with cumulative *voting* for the election of directors to best advantage // to cast his *vote* at the Annual Meeting

giketsukenshintakushōsho 議決権信託証書 voting trust (certificate)

gimu 義務 obligation ¶ to impose additional payments *obligations* on member governments // the compliance of member countries with their *obligations* relating to exchange rate policies // the *obligations* assumed by members of the Fund under the Articles of Agreement // to accept the *obligations* of Article VIII of the Fund Agreement // to eliminate all *obligation* to use gold in transactions with the Fund // to oversee the accomplishment of each member with *obligations* under Section l of Article IV of the Fund's Articles of Agreement // Members undertake a general *obli-*

gation to collaborate with the Fund. // The Fund worries the observance by each member of its *obligations*. // the abrogation of *obligations* to use gold in payments between the Fund and member countries

gimufutankeiyaku 義務負担契約 onerous contract

gimufutantsukizaisan 義務負担付財産 onerous property

gimukyōiku 義務教育 compulsory education

gimutekikaimodoshi 義務的買戻し obligatory repurchase

ginkō 銀行 bank

地方銀行 regional bank; local bank; country bank; provincial bank

貯蓄銀行 savings bank

普通銀行 ordinary bank

発券銀行 bank of issue

発行銀行 issuing bank; opening bank

引受銀行 accepting bank

買取銀行 negotiating bank

勧業銀行 hypothec bank

勘定保持銀行 carrying bank

勘定保有銀行 depository bank

為替銀行 exchange bank

金匠銀行 goldsmith bank

興業銀行 industrial bank

組合銀行 member bank

親銀行 parent bank

姉妹銀行 affiliated bank

シンジケート銀行 syndicate bank

信託銀行 trust bank; trust and banking company

相互銀行 mutual loan and savings bank

総合銀行 universal bank

提携銀行 associated bank

取引銀行 correspondent bank; banker

都市銀行 city bank; large city-based commercial bank

通知銀行 advising bank; notifying bank

全国銀行 all banks

ginkōdan 銀行団 banking syndicate; syndicate of banks group of banks

ginkōdepāto 銀行デパート multifunctional banking institution

ginkōeigyōjikan 銀行営業時間 bank hours; banking hours

ginkōeigyōshikin 銀行営業資金 banking funds; bank capital

ginkōgyō 銀行業 banking; banking business

ginkōgyōmunohimitsusei 銀行業務の秘密性 banking secrecy

ginkōgyōsei 銀行行政 banking supervision; banking administration

ginkōhatan 銀行破綻 bank failure

ginkōhikiukeshin'yōjō 銀行引受信用状 banker's acceptance credit

ginkōhikiuketegata 銀行引受手形 bank acceptance; banker's acceptance

ginkōjunbikin 銀行準備金 bank reserves

ginkōkai 銀行界 banking community

ginkōkanjō 銀行勘定 bank account

ginkōkanjōchōseihyō 銀行勘定調整表 bank reconciliation

ginkōkanshijō 銀行間市場 interbank market ¶ to place funds in the *interbank market* // six-month Eurocurrency deposits in the London *interbank market*

ginkōkantorihiki 銀行間取引 interbank transaction

ginkōkantorihikisōba 銀行間取引相場 interbank rate ¶ the London *interbank* offered *rate* (LIBOR)

ginkōkariirekin 銀行借入金 borrowing from a bank; bank borrowing(s)

ginkōkashidashi 銀行貸出 bank loans and discounts; bank loans; bank lendings; bank credit (of the banking system) ¶ In April commercial *bank loans and discounts* fell slightly. // The aggregate *loans of the national banking system* rose over $5 million to a total of $29.3 billion. // Outstanding *credit of the banking system* increased by 21 per cent from January to August. // →銀行信用

ginkōkeibihō 銀行警備法 ［米］Bank Protection Act

ginkōken 銀行券 bank note
廃棄銀行券 bank note unfit for reuse; bank notes to be destroyed; unfit note; withdrawn note

ginkōkenhakkōdaka 銀行券発行高 bank note issue; bank notes issued; bank notes in circulation; bank notes outstanding ¶ The *bank note issue* outstanding in September, on a daily average balance basis increased 3.3 per cent over the month. // *Bank notes in circulation* increased by ¥178 billion.

ginkōkentaiyōnensū 銀行券耐用年数 lifecycle of bank notes

ginkōkogitte 銀行小切手 bank check

ginkōkurīnbiru 銀行クリーンビル banker's clean bill

ginkōkyōkō 銀行恐慌 bank crisis

ginkōmochikabugaisha 銀行持株会社 bank holding company

ginkōnoginkō 銀行の銀行 bank of banks; banker's bank ¶ to function as the '*bank of banks*' or the '*banker's bank*'

ginkōnokōdōgenri 銀行の行動原理 basic principle of banking behavior

ginkōsaikōsei 銀行再構成 reorganization and integration of banks

ginkōsanchakubarai 銀行参着払い bank demand draft; bank d.d.

ginkōshiharaijunbi 銀行支払準備 bank reserve

ginkōshihonshugi 銀行資本主義 banker capitalism

ginkōshin'yō 銀行信用 credit of the banking system; bank credit; bank loan; bank lending; bank advance; bank loans and discounts; bank advances and discounts ¶ *Bank credit* was constricted substantially. // Expansion in *bank advances* was stopped, and even reversed. // An upsurge in *bank lending* has yet to come. // The growth of *bank credit* featured a sharp expansion of loans. // final deficits financed by *banking system credit* // ceilings on the growth of net domestic *credit of the banking system* // Seasonally adjusted and at annual rates, *bank credits* outstanding to companies and individuals rose by over 12.5% but *bank credits* to public authorities fell by DM 800 million. // those who already have access to *bank credit* // →銀行貸出

ginkōshin'yōjō 銀行信用状 bank(er's) credit; bank letter of credit

ginkōshūhengyōmu 銀行周辺業務 subsidiary banking business

ginkōsoshiki 銀行組織 banking system ¶ surplus reserves in the *banking system* // the reserve deficit of the *banking system* // The *banking system* as a whole expanded its credit operations by Mex.$6,710 million. // Credit demands have been pressing on the *banking system*. // a rudimentary *banking system* inadequate to its task

ginkōtegata 銀行手形 banker's bill; bank bill

ginkōtesūryō 銀行手数料 bank charge; bank commission

ginkōtorihikiyakujōsho 銀行取引約定書 agreement on bank transactions

ginkōtoritsuke 銀行取付 run on banks ¶ Bank failures precipitated *runs on banks*. // The *bank* suffered a *run on* its deposits.

ginkōtōsan 銀行倒産 bank failure

ginkōtsūchō 銀行通帳 bank-book; pass-book

ginkōwaribiki 銀行割引 bank discount

ginkōwaribikibuai 銀行割引歩合 bank discount rate

ginkōyokin 銀行預金 bank deposit; deposit with (=at, in) bank; bank balance ¶ *Deposits at* commercial *banks* across the nation increased slightly over the year before. // There has been considerable withdrawal of *deposits* from commercial *banks*.

ginshōken 銀証券 silver certificate

gisei 擬制 fiction

giseishihon 擬制資本 fictitious capital; watered capital; dilution of capital

giseishisan 擬制資産 fictitious asset

giseiuketorinin 擬制受取人 fictitious payee (=recipient)

gisōshitsugyō 偽装失業 hidden unemployment; disguised unemployment; unemployment in disguise

gizō 偽造 forgery; counterfeit; fabrication

gizōkabuken 偽造株券 forged stock

gizōkahei 偽造貨幣 counterfeit; forged coin

gizōken 偽造券 counterfeit; forged note

gizōkinka 偽造金貨 phony gold coin

gizōkogitte 偽造小切手 forged check

gizōshihei 偽造紙幣 counterfeit note

gizōshōken 偽造証券 forged certificate

gizōtegata 偽造手形 forged bill

goba 後場 [市] afternoon market; afternoon session; second call

gōbengaisha 合弁会社 joint concern; joint venture; joint venture company

gōbenjigyō 合弁事業 joint venture

gōdō 合同 combination; merger; amalgamation; union; absorption; combine; trust ¶ reorganization of parts of industry into vertically integrated industrial *combines*

gōdōjigyō 合同事業 joint venture; joint undertaking; combine

gōdokanri 合同管理 joint management; joint control

gōdōkeiei 合同経営 joint management

gōdōkigyō 合同企業 joint enterprise

gōhan 合板 plywood

gōi 合意 accord; agreement; concord; consensus ¶ They are in general *accord* with the government views. // to protest with one *accord* // A collective *agreement* was reached and signed. // The present members then *agreed* by *consensus* on an instruction regarding market operatons. // The presidents participating reached a *consensus* on overall monetary policy objectives. // There is now a broad *consensus* on this principle. // a broad *consensus* emerged that... // A degree of social *consensus* is required on the achievement of these resource allocation shifts. // There was broad *consensus* in favor of an expansive policy. // It was essential to obtain a broader *consensus* about the measures chosen. // [参考] a lack of unanimity in defining the money stock in the broader sense // to evalue common views on a new realistic concept of the world economic system

gōisho 合意書 pact; concordat

gōkakuhinshitsu 合格品質 acceptable quality

gōkakuhinshitsusuijun 合格品質水準 acceptable quality level

gokanenkeikaku 5カ年計画 five-year program (=plan)

gokei 互恵 reciprocity

gokeibōekikyōtei 互恵貿易協定 reciprocal trade agreement

gokeijōyaku 互恵条約 reciprocal treaty

gokeikanzei 互恵関税 reciprocal duties; bargaining duties

gokeikanzeiritsu 互恵関税率 reciprocal tariff

gokeishugi 互恵主義 reciprocity principle; reciprocity (basis) ¶ Only with *reciprocity* will domestic producers be able to obtain entry into other markets. // to engage in international negotiations on a *reciprocal basis*

gokeitsūshōkyōteihō 互恵通商協定法 [米] Reciprocal Trade Agree-

ments Act

gokuchōonsokuryokyakuki 極超音速旅客機 hypersonic transport; HST

gōmeigaisha 合名会社 unlimited partnership

gomipaipuyusōshisutemu ごみパイプ輸送システム refuse pneumatic converging system

gomisensō ごみ戦争 garbage war

gomuseihinkōgyō ゴム製品工業 rubber products industry

gorakusangyō 娯楽産業 entertainment industry

gōrika 合理化 rationalization
　配給合理化 rationalization of rationing
　経常合理化 rationalization of management
　産業合理化 rationalization of industry; industrial rationalization
　生産合理化 rationalization of production
　消費合理化 rationalization of consumption

gōrikakaruteru 合理化カルテル rationalization cartel

gōrikashikin 合理化資金 funds for rationalization

gōrikasochi 合理化措置 rationalization measure

gōrikatōshi 合理化投資 rationalization investment

gōritekikōdō 合理的行動 rational behavior

gōruden'awāhōsō ゴールデンアワー放送 prime-time broadcasting

gōrudorasshu ゴールド・ラッシュ gold stampede; gold rush ¶ emergency measures to halt the great *gold stampede*

gōrudorasshutaisaku ゴールド・ラッシュ対策 emergency measures

to halt the great gold stampede

gōrudotoranshe ゴールド・トランシェ gold tranche

gosa 誤差 error ¶ standard *error* of estimate

遠近誤差 longitudinal error
不変誤差 constant error
偶発誤差 accidental error
平均誤差 average error
観測誤差 observation error
公算誤差 probable error
左右誤差 lateral error
周期誤差 periodical error
相殺誤差 compensating error
組織的誤差 systematic error
定誤差 systematic error

gosadatsurō 誤差脱漏 [外] errors and omissions; balancing item

gosahōsoku 誤差法則 law of error; theory of error

gosan 誤算 miscalculation ¶ to make *miscalculations* in policy-making // many *miscalculations* made about the next movement of the market

gōseigomuasufaruto 合成ゴム・アスファルト synthetic rubber asphalt

gōseihikaku 合成皮革 synthetic leather

gōseiparupu 合成パルプ synthetic pulp

gōseisen'i 合成繊維 synthetic fibers

gōseishi 合成紙 artificial paper

gōseishu 合成酒 compound "sake"

gōsen'orimono 合繊織物 synthetic fabrics

gōshi 合資 joint stock; partnership

gōshigaisha 合資会社 limited partnership

gōtōkeihōsōchi 強盗警報装置 robbery alarm system

gūhatsuibutsu 偶発遺物 contingent remainder

gūhatsujikō 偶発事項 contingencies

gūhatsusaimu 偶発債務 contingent liability

gūhatsusaimutsumitatekin 偶発債務積立金 contingent reserve

gunju 軍需 munitions; military stores; war supplies

gunjugaisha 軍需会社 munitions company

gunjuhoshō 軍需補償 indemnities to munitions plants; indemnities to war industries

gunjukabu 軍需株 munitions shares; munitions

gunjukōgyō 軍需工業 munitions industry

gunjukōjō 軍需工場 munitions factory

gunjushizai 軍需資材 war materials; war supplies; munitions

gunjutegata 軍需手形 munitions bill

gunkankeiuketori 軍関係受取 military-related receipt; receipt of foreign military expenditure

gunpyō 軍票 military payment certificate; m.p.c.; military note; military scrip

gurafuhyōji グラフ表示 graphical representation

gureshamunohōsoku グレシャムの法則 Gresham's law

gurīnbakku グリーンバック greenbacks

gurinijjihyōjunji グリニッジ標準時 Greenwich (mean) time; GMT

gūzensei 偶然性 randomness ¶ *randomness* of human behavior

gūzentekihendō 偶然的変動 accidental movement

gūzentekirieki 偶然的利益 windfall profit; unexpected gain

gyakubari 逆張り ［市］ resistance

gyakuchō 逆調 ［外］ adverse balance of trade; unfavorable trade balance; import excess

gyakudominoriron 逆ドミノ理論 domino theory in reverse

gyakuhibu 逆日歩 negative interest per diem

gyakukinri 逆金利 negative interest

gyakunoyuzuriuke 逆の譲り受け inverted take-over

gyakusashine 逆指値 ［市］counter-bid

gyakusashinechūmon 逆指値注文 ［市］ stop-loss order

gyakusenbetsu 逆選別 selection of bank by companies

gyakuten 逆転 adverse change; reversal ¶ External payments *reversed* their balance to register a surplus.

gyakutokka 逆特化 unfavorable specialization

gyakuyunyū 逆輸入 re-import

gyakuzaya 逆鞘 negative interest rate margin; negative spread; back spread; negative interest rate spread ¶ The *spread* between the prime rate and the Bank rate became *negative.*

gyappu ギャップ gap; rift; chasm ¶ to bridge the widening *gap* between private saving and desirable levels of investment // The *gap* between the highest and average incomes has narrowed consistently since the war. // European capital markets could fill the financing *gap* left by New York. // The *gap* between earnings growth and retail price inflation was closing fast and is now likely to have been eliminated altogether. // The *rift* between investment and saving increased. // The *gap* between economic and social welfare has been reduced. // to bridge the *chasm* between the rich and the poor countries

デフレ・ギャップ deflationary gap

ドル・ギャップ dollar gap

福祉ギャップ gap between economic growth and welfare

GNP ギャップ GNP gap

インフレ・ギャップ inflationary gap

情報ギャップ information gap

需要ギャップ demand gap

gyarantitokō ギャランティ渡航 guaranteed trip (＝travel)

gyarappuseronchōsa ギャラップ世論調査 Gallup poll (＝survey)

gyogyō 漁業 fishery; fishing industry

沿岸漁業 inshore fishery; coastal fishing

遠洋漁業 deep-sea fishery; pelagic fishing

河川漁業 river fishery

近海漁業 offshore fishery

湖水漁業 lake fishery

区画漁業 demarcated fishery

専用漁業 exclusive right fishery

定置漁業 fixed net fishery

gyogyōkaisha 漁業会社 fishery company

gyogyōkikai 漁業機械 fishing machines

gyogyōkumiai 漁業組合 fishery guild; fishermen's association

gyogyōkyōdōkumiai 漁業協同組合 fishery cooperative

gyōinjiki 行印字機 ［コン］ line printer

gyōkai 業界 business world; business circles; business quarters

gyokairui 魚介類 fish and shellfish

gyokakudaka 漁獲高 (fish) catch

gyoku 玉 [市] account; bargain
買い玉 long account; bull account
売り玉 short account; bear account

gyokukankei 玉関係 [市] technical
position

gyokuohazusu 玉を外す [市] to
close out

gyokuseiri 玉整理 [市] evening-up
of accounts; technical correction;
liquidation of speculative accounts

gyōkyō 業況 business activity;
business conditions; business situation

gyōkyōchōsa 業況調査 business
research; business survey

gyōkyōhandan 業況判断 (judgment on) business outlook

gyōmu 業務 business (activities;
operations) ¶ the size and character
of *business* of the enterprise // to
expand the *business* concerning foreign exchange of local branches // to
engage in the conduct of securities
business // The newly formed company is fully launched in *business*. //
Non-bank could enter the banking
business more easily than banks
could begin non-bank *activities*. // to
conduct actual *business* rather than
liaison work // to participate and be
engaged in the investment banking
business and the *business* of deposits
and making loans // The World
Bank has resumed lending *operations* in Portugal with a $36 million
loan for power development. // the
first foreign bank launching branch
operations in Spain // commercial
banks transacting international *business* // to carry out banking *opera-

tions with foreign clients

預金貸出業務 business of accepting
deposits and making loans

gyōmuchōsei 業務調整 operational coordination

gyōmujōnojiko 業務上の事故 on-
the-job accident

gyōmukakuchō 業務拡張 extension of business; business expansion

gyōmukanri 業務管理 business
management

gyōmukansa 業務監査 operating
audit

gyōmukeikaku 業務計画 operational programing

gyōmunisshi 業務日誌 business
diary; log

gyōmunogōhōsei 業務の合法性
rightness of business performed

gyōmunotayōka 業務の多様化 diversification of lines of business

gyōmusaigai 業務災害 industrial
accident

gyōmusaikōsekininsha 業務最高責
任者 chief operation officer

gyōmushidō 業務指導 operational
guidance

gyōmutantōshain 業務担当社員
active partner; managing partner

gyōmuteikei 業務提携 business
tie-up (contract)

gyōmutokō 業務渡航 business
travel(=trip) ¶ Higher allowances
may be granted to those *traveling* on
business.

gyōmuyōhaikyū 業務用配給 ration for business use

gyōsei 行政 administration

gyōseikaikaku 行政改革 reform
(=reshaping) of the administrative
structure; administrative reform

gyōseikan 行政官 administrator;
executive

gyōseikanchō 行政官庁 administrative authorities

gyōseiken 行政権 administrative power

gyōseikikan 行政機関 administrative organ

gyōseikikankansoka 行政機関簡素化 simplification of the administrative system

gyōseikyōtsūhi 行政共通費 (common) administrative expenses

gyōseiseiri 行政整理 administrative readjustment

gyōseishidō 行政指導 administrative guidance ¶ to induce *administrative guidance* in setting the 'standard' prices for petroleum products // *administrative guidance* policy of holding down exports by strengthening *administrative guidance*

gyōseishobun 行政処分 administrative action

gyōseisochi 行政措置 administrative measure (=action)

gyōseki 業績 business result; business performance; corporate performance ¶ *Corporate performance* in the past business term showed some deterioration. // ［参考］ to outperform other banks or stay where they are now ranked
　今期業績 (business) results of the current term

gyōsekihōkoku 業績報告 business report

gyōsekikentō 業績検討 business result analysis

gyōshafutankinri 業者負担金利 interest burden for end-borrowers

gyōshu 業種 type of industry; category (=sector) of industry; industrial (=business) line; branch of industry; industrial branch; type of business; industry group ¶ Production expanded in all *branches of industry*. // in the main *branches of industry* // Some *lines of business* performed better than others. // The strong *sectors in business* offset the areas of weakness. // Tighter credit conditions affected unevenly different sectors of the economy and different *types of businesses*. // to classify bank lendings by *industry group* // Prospects vary from *line* to *line*.

gyōshubetsubunrui 業種別分類 industrial classification; classification by industry; breakdown by industry group; industry-to-industry (=industry-wise) breakdown

gyōshubetsuchingin 業種別賃金 prevailing wages, classified by industry

gyōtai 業態 form of business organization; business category; business status ¶ the emerging of the private bank into four *categories*, namely, industrial, agricultural, construction and commercial // the confusion over the various forms of banking *status*

gyōtaichōsa 業態調査 business (conditions) survey; inquiry into business status

H

haaku 把握 grasp; grip ¶ to *grasp* the whole picture of business activity // the economy in the *grip* of inflation // to loosen the *grip* of inflation and stagnation // The industrial sector is caught in the *grip* of rising costs. // The Fed relaxed its *grip* on the money supply. // tightening the Old Lady's *grip* on the banking system // The government shows no sign of relaxing its monetary *grip*.

hachijōkokuenoikō 8条国への移行 assumption of Article VIII status in the International Monetary Fund ¶ →IMF 8 条国

hadakanedan 裸値段 net price

hadakanigawase 裸荷為替 documentary clean bill

hadakasōba 裸相場 ex interest quotation; flat quotation; flat

hadakatorihiki 裸取引 ex interest transaction

hadakayōsen 裸用船 bare-boat charter

hadō 波動 wave; movement; fluctuation; cycle ¶ The *cycle* is stretching out peak to peak.

　大波動 major swing; wild fluctuation; long wave (of the business cycle)

　小波動 minor swing; short wave (of the business cycle)

　短期波動 short wave (of the business cycle

hadōchōsel 波動調整 rolling readjustment

hadōkansū 波動関数 wave function

hadome 歯止め brake; ratchet ¶ A *brake* was applied to the rise in prices. // The Fed began applying the monetary *brake* in earnest. // to push down harder on the monetary *brake* for... // to apply a *brake* in suppressing rising production // Food is acting as a *brake* inflation. // The measure operated as a *ratchet* in the upward direction. // Such an attempt will *ratchet* the economy to an even higher rate of inflation.

hadomekōka 歯止め効果 ratchet affect

haibun 配分 allocation; distribution; division; share ¶ Priority in the *allocation* of investment funds was accorded to basic industries. // A *flow* of capital facilitates against the *allocation* of resources. // The *allocation* of benefits and risks was properly balanced. // the unjust *allocation* of financial burdens // The *distribution* this year between bonds and borrowings will depend largely on the differentials between short and long-term interest rates. // even (=equitable) *distribution* of national income // to reduce the disparity in income *distribution* // uncontrolled and uneven *distribution* of increases in world liquidity // automatic funds *allocation* system // priority *allocation* of labor // efficient allocation of resources // *allocation* of sample sizes // the problem of *allocating* inherently limited resources to a variety of uses // to *allocate* the resources of our economy to their best use // the disproportionate *division* of wealth between producing provinces // ［参考］the maldistribution of gold among nations // the present misallocation of resources to be corrected // a small piece of the budgetary pie

不適正配分　misallocation
比例配分　proportional allocation
傾斜的配分　priority allocation
最適配分　optimum allocation
資源配分　resource allocation

haichi 配置　layout
事務所内配置　office layout
工場内配置　plant layout

haichitenkan 配置転換　redeployment; relocation ¶ to facilitate the necessary *redeployment* of activities by stimulating investment

haiekitarenagashi 廃液たれ流し waste discharge

haigaishisō 排外思想　chauvinism; xenophobia ¶ unseemly manifestations of economic *chauvinism*

haigasunōdokisei 排ガス濃度規制 regulation of emission concentration

haihanjishō 排反事象　mutually exclusive event

haika 廃貨　demonetization
金の廃貨　demonetization of gold

haikei 背景　background; backdrop ¶ against the *background* of a strengthened economic controls // Against a *background* of the rising oil prices the fears which have been lurking in the *background* have come to the front in the credit markets. // against a *backdrop* of general oversupply // against this dismal *back-*

drop in the bond market

haikibutsu 廃棄物　waste
原子力廃棄物　atomic waste
放射性廃棄物　radioactive waste
化学廃棄物　chemical waste
核廃棄物　nuclear waste
公害廃棄物　pollution waste
工場廃棄物　industrial waste
固形廃棄物　solid waste
産業廃棄物　industrial waste

haikibutsusaijunkan 廃棄物再循環 recycling of waste

haikiginkōken 廃棄銀行券　unfit bank note; bank note unfit for circulation

haikyū 配給　rationing; allocation ¶ credit *rationing* // *allocation* of resources // gasoline *rationing* // petroleum *allocation* // a mandatory *rationing* of heating oil
業務用配給　ration for business use
繰上配給　advance ration
強制的配給　mandatory rationing

haikyūkikō 配給機構　distributive machinery; marketing system

haikyūkippu 配給切符　ration coupon; ration ticket

haikyūmai 配給米　rationed rice

haikyūtōsei 配給統制　distribution control

haikyūtsūchō 配給通帳　ration pass-book

haipāmāketto ハイパーマーケット hypermarket

haipurasuchikku 廃プラスチック plastic waste

haishi 廃止　removal;　　abolition; abolishment; lifting; cancel(lation); annulment; revocation; repeal; rescission; rescinding; dismantling ¶ Curbs have been *removed* in three steps. // Price controls had been *lifted* by August. // The law was *abolished.* // India has been *dismantling* the very high duties to reduce the cost of imports. // Duties have already been *abolished* or cut sharply on edible oils.

haishōshōken 廃消証券 canceled bond

haisuikijun 排水基準 effluent standard

haisuikōji 排水工事 drainage work

haitatekikeizaisuiiki 排他的経済水域 economic zone

haiteku ハイテク high-technology ¶ capital-intensive and *high-technology* industries — such as petrochemicals, aircraft, and nuclear power

haitō 配当 dividend; apportionment; allotment
物件配当 property dividend
中間配当 interim dividend
現金配当 cash dividend
株式配当 stock dividend
仮配当 interim dividend
記念配当 commemorative dividend; memorial dividend
未収益配当 unearned dividend
無配当 non-dividend
蛸配当 bogus dividend; fictitious dividend
特別配当 special dividend; extra dividend; plum; bonus
通常配当 regular dividend
積置配当 cumulative dividend
優先配当 preferred dividend
予想配当 prospective dividend; probable dividend

haitōbunrikazei 配当分離課税 separated taxation on dividend income

haitōheikinjunbikin 配当平均準備金 dividend equalization fund

haitōininjō 配当委任状 proxy for receiving dividend

haitōjunbitsumitatekin 配当準備積立金 dividend reserve; dividend equalization reserve

haitōkanjō 配当勘定 dividend account

haitōkanōjōyokin 配当可能剰余金 divisible surplus

haitōkanōrieki 配当可能利益 profit available for dividend

haitōken 配当券 dividend check

haitōkin 配当金 dividend ¶ a *dividend* declared May 20, payable July 1 to shareholders of record June 10
普通株配当金 dividend on common stock
経過配当金 accrued dividend
未払配当金 dividend payable
受取配当金 dividend received
優先株配当金 dividend on preferred stock

haitōochi 配当落ち ex-dividend; dividend off

haitōritsu 配当率 rate of dividend; dividend rate

haitōseikō 配当性向 dividend propensity; payout ratio

haitōtsuki 配当付き cum dividend; dividend on

haiyubōru 廃油ボール tar balls; globular-shaped mixture of oil waste, sludge, and plankton

haiyushori 廃油処理 waste oil disposal

hajimene 始め値 ［市］ opening quotation; opening price

hakabu 端株 odd-lot shares; fractional lot; broken lot

hakabuchūmon 端株注文 fractional order

hakabuseiri 端株整理 broken lot consolidation

hakabutorihiki 端株取引 odd-lot trading (=transaction)

hakabutorihikisha 端株取引者 odd-lotters ¶ the *odd lotters*, as bokers, stock speculators and other stock market professionals are often called

hakaitekikyōsō 破壊的競争 destructive competition

hakaru 量る measure; weigh; gauge; sound; reckon; compute; estimate

hakeguchi 捌口 (market) outlet; vent ¶ to find *outlets* for goods // Sales at durable goods *outlets* remained at advanced levels. // a *vent* for the payments surplus // [参考] to look for a market for the products

haken 覇権 hegemony ¶ The monetary *hegemony* of the U.S. declined.// to hold the *hegemony* in a league // the past Spanish *hegemony* in Latin America

haki 破棄 repudiation
国債破棄 repudiation of public debt

hakkai 発会 first session of the month
大発会 first session of the year

hakkenginkō 発券銀行 issue bank; bank of issue

hakkō 発行 issuance; flotation; launching; putting into circulation ¶ the *issuance* of bank notes, checks and bills, and bonds // *flotation* of a loan or bond // to put new notes *into circulation* // The firm intends to *float* Euro-dollar, notes and bonds. // Credit Commercial is *issuing* $25 million of floating rate notes on the Euro-market. // *launching* of an 8% loan of the Federal Railways at an *issue* price of 99.50% and with a life of five years // [参考] The offering consists of 5-year notes and 10-year bonds.

超過発行 excess issue (over withdrawal); over-issue

額面発行 issue at par; issue at face value

限外発行 over-issue

時価発行 issue at market price

準備発行 issue against securities

借換発行 refunding issue; conversion issue

無準備発行 fiduciary issue

hakkōbitorihiki 発行日取引 [証市] "when issued" transaction

hakkōbitorihikikashitsuke 発行日取引貸付 [証市] loan for when-issued transaction

hakkōchō 発行超 net issue (of bank notes); excess issue (of bank notes) (over withdrawal)

hakkōdan 発行団 issue syndicate

hakkōgaku 発行額 amount of issue ¶ The *amount of* the six-year Euro-bond *issue* has heen increased from Can.$25 to 35 million.

hakkōgendo 発行限度 issue limit

hakkōginkō 発行銀行 issuing bank; opening bank of (a letter of credit)

hakkōginkōken 発行銀行券 bank notes issued

hakkōgyōsha 発行業者 [米] issuing house

hakkōhoshō 発行保証 reserve for (bank note) issue

hakkōirainin 発行依頼人 applicant; opener (of a letter of credit)

hakkōjimu 発行事務 issue business

hakkōjōken 発行条件 terms of issue; conditions of issue; issue terms

hakkōjunbi 発行準備(通貨の) legal backing ¶ *legal backing* for Federal Reserve notes in circulation

hakkōkakaku 発行価格 issue price; par (value); offering price ¶ The *issue price* has been fixed at 100¼

%. // to be set at *par* // It traded at a ¼ point discount to its yet-to-be-fixed *issue price.*

hakkōmotoginkōken 発行元銀行券 bank note to be issued; fit note (for circulation)

hakkōsharimawari 発行者利回り issuer's cost

hakkōshijō 発行市場 financing market; (bond) issue market; primary market; investment market ¶ [参考] The new issue sector held up better than the secondary market.

hakkōshūnyūkin 発行収入金 proceeds of issue; revenue of the loan ¶ The net *proceeds* from the bonds will be advanced to the Development Bank to be used for loan to private electric power companies. // The *revenue of the loan* will be used for financing investment in the electricity sector.

hakkōyoryoku 発行余力 issue margin

hakkōzei 発行税 issue tax

hakkōzumishihon 発行済み資本 outstanding capital

hakō 跛行 uneven; limping; ill-balance; disharmony ¶ an *uneven* rise in activity between different lines of industry // a *limping* business boom // a rise at *ill-balanced* pace between major sectors // *ill-balanced* pace of consumers' performance // The *uneven* economic development was responsible for the lag in the deceleration of hourly wages. // the slow and *uneven* recovery of the world economy from the severe 1974-75 recession // *limping* growth rates of manufacturing // the post-oil-crisis climate of *limping* world economies

hakōhon'isei 跛行本位制 limping standard system

hakōkeiki 跛行景気 limping boom; spotty prosperity ¶ A *limping boom* tendency has begun to emerge viewed as to type of industry or specific region.

hakōsōba 跛行相場 irregular market

hakozuhyō 箱図表 box diagram

hakuri 薄利 narrow margin; small profit

hakuritabai 薄利多売 small profits and big turnover; small profits and quick returns; S.P.Q.R.; quick sales at small profits; quick-returns policy

hakushi 白紙 carte-blanche; blank (card)

hakushiininjō 白紙委任状 blank power of attorney

hakushitegata 白紙手形 inchoate instrument

hakusho 白書 white paper; white book

中小企業白書 White Paper on Small and Medium Enterprises; White Paper on Small Business

漁業白書 White Paper on Fisheries

経済白書 Economic White Paper

建設白書 White Paper on National Land Construction

公害白書 White Paper on Public Environmental Hazards

国民生活白書 White Paper on the People's Livelihood; White Paper on the People's Living Conditions; White Paper on the National Living Environment; White paper on the National Living Conditions

通商白書 White Paper on Trade and Commerce

hakyū 波及 transmission; transfer;

spread; contagion; spilling-over; ripple ¶ intenational *transmission* of inflation // *transmission* of monetary policy to bank behavior and interest rates // The contraction in business profit *spread* to all segments of the economy. // to prevent *contagion* from one firm's failure from causing problems for other firms // to be completely immune to *contagion* from difficulties of other banks // Monetary impulses are *transmitted* between countries. // to check the *spread* of the buying spree // *spreading* use of dish-washers // *spread* of tight-money policy effects // Faster monetary growth might *spill over* into higher prices. // A drop in the dollar in, say, Hong Kong *rippled* rapidly throughout the world.

hakyūkeiro 波及経路 transmission mechanism ¶ The *transmission mechanism* does not run via investment exclusively. // the alternative *transmission mechanism* from monetary variables to growth // a complex chain of intermediate *transmission mechanisms*

金融波及経路 financial transmission mechanism

実体経済波及経路 real transmission mechanism

hakyūkōka 波及効果 multiplied effect; propagating effect; transmitted effect; ripple effect; repercussion effect ¶ Monetary *effects* are *transmitted* to economic growth. // *Ripple effects* throughout the economy could throw many workers out of work. // The *ripple effect* if Chrysler went out of business could throw 600,000 people out of work.

hanagatakabu 花形株 popular stock; leading share; favorite stock; prime stocks; blue chips; blue-chip issues

hanbai 販売 sale; selling; marketing

抱合せ販売 tie-in sale

現金販売 sale for cash

月賦販売 (monthly) installment sale; hire-purchase

委託販売 consignment sale; sale on consignment

巡回販売 route sale

割賦販売 installment sale; sale in installments

共同販売 joint sale

強制販売 forced sale

見本販売 sale by sample

延払販売 sale for account

廉価販売 bargain sale

試供品(=試用)販売 appoval sale; sale on approval

信用販売 sale on credit; sale on account

相互委託販売 reciprocal consignment

大量販売 mass sale

取次販売 sale on commission

hanbaidaikin 販売代金 sales proceeds; proceeds from sale

hanbaidairiten 販売代理店 selling agent

hanbaidaka 販売高 sales (amount; volume) ¶ Wholesale *sales* have been rising more than twice as fast as retail *sales*. // Biannual *sales* of the firm increased in dollar terms but were about level in physical volume.

hanbaidan 販売団 placement group; selling group

hanbaidokusen 販売独占 sellers' monopoly

hanbaieki 販売益 sale profit

hanbaigijutsu 販売技術 salesmanship

hanbaihi 販売費 selling expenses

hanbaihiyosan 販売費予算 selling expense budget

hanbaiitakushōhin 販売委託商品 consigned goods out for sale

hanbaiiyoku 販売意欲 eagerness to sell

hanbaikakaku 販売価格 selling price

hanbaikanri 販売管理 sales management

hanbaikeiro 販売経路 marketing route; marketing channel

hanbaikinō 販売機能 selling function

hanbaikin'yūgaisha 販売金融会社 sales finance company

hanbaikitenkōkoku 販売基点広告 selling point advertisement

hanbaikumiai 販売組合 sales association; cooperative marketing society

hanbaimitsumori 販売見積り sales estimate

hanbaimō 販売網 sales network; marketing network ¶ arrangement and expansion of the *sales network* // consolidation and enlargement of *marketing networks*

hanbaimōnoseibikakujū 販売網の整備拡充 arrangement and expansion of sales network

hanbaimoto 販売元 distributor; selling agency

hanbaimotochō 販売元帳 sales ledger

hanbaiseisaku 販売政策 salesmanship; marketing policy

hanbaisen 販売戦 sales war

hanbaishigekisaku 販売刺激策 sales incentive

hanbaishinjikēto 販売シンジケート selling syndicate

hanbaishiwakechō 販売仕訳帳 sales journal

hanbaisokushin 販売促進 sales promotion

hanbaiteikei 販売提携 sales tie-up

hanbaiten 販売店 outlet ¶ Sales at auto *outlets* declined. // Sales at durable goods *outlets* remained at advanced levels.

hanbaitenkeiyaku 販売店契約 distributorship agreement

hanbaiyosoku 販売予測 sales forecasting

hanbō 繁忙 [市] busy

hanbōkan 繁忙感 difficulty in raising funds; sense of tightness; business feeling of a tight fund position

handan 判断 judgment; discernment ¶ to require a careful *judgment* // to form a *judgment* on... // to avoid hasty *judgment* // in entrepreneurs' *discernment* // with adequate investigation and the exercise of informed *judgment* // [参考] Business views the economic climate more positively than it did last autumn.

handō 反動 reaction; repercussion ¶ to fear the balance of payments *repercussions* of any appreciation of their currencies

handōdaka 反動高 reactionary advance; rebound ¶ The market *advanced reactionary* to the sharp setback of the previous month.

handōgen 反動減 reactionary fall; downturn

handōyasu 反動安 reactionary fall; reactionary slump ¶ The price *fell reactionary* to the sharp rise in the previous week.

han'ei 繁栄 prosperity; affluence; exhilaration ¶ to enjoy a full measure of *prosperity* // to be lagged in the advance of *prosperity* // Economic *prosperity* was raised to new levels. // The economy is set on a course leading to new peaks of *prosperity* and power. // stable and broadly based *prosperity* // a situation of *affluence* // to be in *affluence* // Economic *prosperity* is broadly based. // The state of the world might be summed up as troubled *prosperity*. // the artificial business *prosperity* produced by the war // full *prosperity* without inflation

    長期繁栄 secular exhilaration

    一時的繁栄 temporary exhilaration

han'i 範囲 scope; limits; gamut; range ¶ The Euro-currency market is outside the traditional *scope* of monetary policy. // The *gamut* of inflation rates is wider than ever. // a broad-*ranging* anti-inflation package // in a wide-*ranging* tax reform bill // to increase the *scope* for mutually profitable entrepreneurial initiative

han'ishokumukyū 範囲職務給 range wage rate for job; range rate

hanjukurenkō 半熟練工 semi-skilled worker

hanjukurenrōdōsha 半熟練労働者 semi-skilled labor(er)

hanki 半期 half-term; half-year term; half year

    上半期 first half of the year; first half-year; first half

    四半期 quarter (of the year)

    下半期 second half of the year; second half-year; second half; latter half of the year; latter half-year; latter half

hankihaitō 半期配当 semi-annual dividend

hankikessai 半期決済 half-yearly settlement

hankikessan 半期決算 half-yearly closing of accounts; semi-annual accounting; semi-annual settlement of accounts

hankino 半期の semi-annual; half-yearly; biannual.

hankōgyōkoku 半工業国 semi-industrial country

hankōgyōshugi 反工業主義 anti-industrialism

hankyō 反響 repercussion ¶ The *repercussion* of this policy action is being felt in many sectors.

hankyōkō 半恐慌 semi-panic

hannichimono 半日物 half-day loan

hannō 反応 reaction; response ¶ The market *overreacted* to the trade deficit news. // The market could *respond* very well to any glad tidings either political or economic.

hanpatsu 反発 rebound; rally; reaction ¶ There was a cyclical *rebound* in the export volume. // London stages its biggest *rally* for 13 months. // Coffee has slumped again, after a year's turn *rally*. // a vigorous early *rally* // Coppers opened dull but later *rallied*. // The session was relieved by a solid *rally* among aircrafts. // a rise *reactionary* to the fall on the previous day // to rise in *reaction* to the sharp drop of the last week // →回復

hanpatsudaka 反発高 abrupt rise; reactionary rise

hanro 販路 market; outlet; débouché; channel ¶ a market deterioration in the sales *outlets* of many companies // Sales abroad provide an important *outlet* for many firms. // to find substitute *outlets* for their exports // to switch production from external to domestic *outlets*

hanrokaitaku 販路開拓 cultivation of the market

hanrokakuchō 販路拡張 extension of the market

hanrosōshitsu 販路喪失 loss of the market

hansatsu 藩札 clan note

hanseihin 半製品 semi-finished goods; semi-manufacture; semi-manufactured goods; half-finished goods; partly finished goods

hanshitsugyō 半失業 partial unemployment; hidden unemployment

hanten 反転 reverse; reversal; reverting; turnaround ¶ a *reversal* of the recent downtrend in prices // The balance *reverted* to a surplus. // A critical *reversal* of business occurs. // The exact *reverse* was the case. // financial *reverse* // The balance registered a deficit *reversing* the past performance. // Prices in the stock market, after a number of *reverses* in October and September, advanced sharply in the second week of November. // the *reversal* of the capital account from a surplus of $1.5 billion to a deficit of $500 million // a partial *reversal* of the 1976 outflow of short-term capital // Argentina achieved a dramatic *turnaround* in its balance of payments.

hantō 反騰 reactionary rise; corrective rise; rally; rebound ¶ a *corrective rise* after a sharp fall // a *rally* in commodity market prices // The stock market *rallied*. // The stock market *rally* runs out of

steam. // The *rebound* of exports from effects of the strike is impressive. // A sharp interest rate *rebound* occurred over the past year. // Sales *rebounded* from their fall in August. // →反発; 回復

han'yagyō 半夜業 half-night work; half-night operation

kan'yōdenshikeisansoshiki 汎用電子計算組織 ［コン］ general purpose electronic computer

hanzadōmei ハンザ同盟 Hanseatic League

harai 払い payment; defrayment; discharge; quittance; acquittance; settlement; clearance; liquidation; repayment; pay; reimbursement; retribution; expenditure; expense; outlay ¶ ［参考］ to honor a bill // to strike a balance // to settle, balance, or square accounts with... // to be even with... // to wipe off old scores 分割払い payment in installments 現金払い cash payment; payment in cash 一覧払い payment at sight 持参人払い payment on demand 前金払い payment in advance 参着払い payment on demand 書類引換払い payment against document; p.a.d. 手形払い payment by bill 全額払い payment in full

haraichō 払超 net payments of long-term capital; deficit in long-term capital; deficit on long-term capital balance

haraidashi 払出し payment; paying out; out-payment; disbursement

haraidashiginkō 払出銀行 paying bank

haraidashishōhyō 払出証票 voucher for disbursement

haraikomi 払込み payment; installment
- 一時払込み payment in lump sum; lump sum payment
- 未払込み unpaid
- 全額払込み payment in full

haraikomiijō 払込み以上 ［証市］ above par

haraikomiika 払込み以下 ［証市］ below par

haraikomikin 払込金 subscription ¶ *subscriptions* to the loan

haraikomisaikoku 払込催告 call

haraikomishihon 払込資本 paid-up (=in) capital; capital stock paid in

haraikomitsuki 払込付 ［証市］ cum call

haraikomiyūshikashitsuke 払込融資貸付 loan of subscription payment funds

haraikomizumi 払込済み fully paid up; paid-up

haraikomizumihoken 払込済保険 paid-up insurance

haraikomizumihokenshōken 払込済保険証券 paid-up insurance policy

haraikomizumikabuken 払込済株券 paid-up share

haraikomizumishin'yōjō 払込済信用状 paid credit

haraimodoshi 払戻し repayment; refund; reimbursement; rebate

haraimodoshirisoku 払戻利息 refunded interest

haraimodoshizei 払戻し税 drawback; tax rebate

haraisugi 払過ぎ overpayment; payment in excess

haran 波乱 wide fluctuation of quotations; uneven market; wild fluctuation; violent fluctuation ¶ ［参考］ The dollar was choppy early Wednesday.

haranshijō 波乱市場 uneven market

hasan 破産 bankruptcy; failure; insolvency ¶ to go into *bankruptcy* // to be on the verge of *bankruptcy* // to go *bankrupt* // many *bankruptcies*
- 国家破産 state bankruptcy
- 強制破産 forced liquidation; involuntary liquidation
- 任意破産 voluntary bankruptcy
- 詐欺破産 fraudulent bankruptcy

hasanginko 破産銀行 failed bank

hasanhyō 破産表 black list

hasankanzainin 破産管財人 bankruptcy administrator; receiver in bankruptcy; trustee

hasankanzaininninmeisho 破産管財人任命書 receiving order

hasanmeirei 破産命令 adjudication order

hasansaibansho 破産裁判所 bankruptcy court

hasansaiken 破産債権 claims in bankruptcy

hasansaikensha 破産債権者 bankruptcy creditor

hasansaimu 破産債務 debts provable in bankruptcy

hasansaimusha 破産債務者 bankruptcy debtor

hasanseisannin 破産清算人 accountant in bankruptcy

hasansenkoku 破産宣告 declaration of bankruptcy; adjudication of bankruptcy

hasansha 破産者 bankrupt; insolvent

hasanshinsei 破産申請 petition in bankruptcy

hasanzaidan 破産財団 bankrupt's estate

haseishotoku 派生所得 derivative

income

haseitekiyokin 派生的預金 derivative deposit

hashira 柱 pillar; leg ¶ Exports will again become one of the *pillars* of economic development. // Their exports rest on four *legs*—cars, television, ferrous metals, and textiles.

kasseishugi 発生主義 [会] accrued (=accrual) basis

hasū 端数 fraction; odd-lot

hasūbubun 端数部分 fractional part; fraction

hasūchūmon 端数注文 fractional order; odd-lot order

hasūkabu 端数株 fractional lot (shares)

hasūkirisute 端数切捨て fractions omitted

hasūseiri 端数整理 rounding (of fractions) ¶ Components may not add to totals due to *rounding*. // the arithmetic mean, *rounded* upwards to the nearest $\frac{1}{8}$ of 1 percent

hatanrotei 破綻露呈 being on the verge of bankruptcy

hatarakichūdoku 働き中毒 work-a-holic

兎小屋の働き中毒 *work-a-holics* living in rabit hutchets

hataume 旗埋め [市] short covering; bear covering

hatauri 旗売り [市] short selling ¶ to *sell short* (=go *short*)

hataurisuji 旗売り筋 short sellers

hatchū 発注 placing of order ¶ The caution shown by business toward *placing orders* for capital goods is receding.

hatchūgaku 発注額 orders placed; order booking ¶ *orders placed* for machinery

hatchūnaijisho 発注内示書 letter of intent

hatchūsaiteigenkaiten 発注最低限界点 minimum ordering point

hatsuden 発電 (electric) power generation

超電導発電 superconducting power generation

潮力発電 tidal power generation

原子力発電 atomic power generation

火力発電 steam power generation; thermal power generation

火山発電 hot rock power generation

温度差発電 gradient power generation

水力発電 hydraulic power generation; hydroelectric power generation; water power generation

太陽光発電 photovoltaic power generation

太陽熱発電 solar thermal power generation

hatsutorihiki 初取引 [市] New Year session; initial session

hatten 発展 evolution; development ¶ to follow the social and economic *evolution* of the nation // *evolution* from the oldest to the most modern type // to attain a high state of *development* // Stalled *development* in the Third World became more severe. // to trace the 1975 *evolution* of the market on a quarter-by-quarter basis // The main forces shaping the *development* of the market underwent a radical change. // Today, the international monetary system is no longer *evolving*, it is emerging. // to join the mainstream of national *development* (social, economic, institutional, and environmental) // [参考] →開発

hattentekikinkō 発展的均衡 progressive equilibrium

hattentojōkoku 発展途上国 developing countries (=nations)

hausubiru ハウス・ビル house bill

hayabamai 早場米 early crop rice; early rice crop

hayadashiryō 早出料 dispatch money

hayasu 囃す welcome; be encouraged; be stimulated ¶ Oils rose *welcoming* the news of higher oil prices.

hayauketegata 早受手形 bill for premature delivery

hayaukewatashi 早受渡し premature delivery of futures

hazakaiki 端境期 between season; terminal gap period; off-crop season; pre-harvest season ¶ to import rice to make up for a *preharvest* shortage in August and September // [参考] the traditional lean months of December and Junuary

hazumi 弾み momentum ¶ →加速度

hedoro ヘドロ sludge; industrial waste; colloidal sediment

heigetsusuijun 平月水準 level of the monthly average

heijunka 平準化 leveling; standardization; evening-out flattening ¶ *leveling* of income in different areas // There is in evidence a trend toward the *leveling* of wages. // some progress toward a *leveling* off of differential inflation // *standardization* of wages // a prospective *evening-out* of growth rates between the United States and other countries

heika 平価 par; parity
 ドル平価 dollar parity
 比較平価 relative parity

 法定平価 mint par
 実際平価 real parity
 仮想平価 hypothetical parity
 為替平価 exchange parity; par value of exchange
 金平価 gold parity; gold par value
 購買力平価 purchasing power parity
 公定平価 parity of official exchange rate
 理論平価 theoretical parity
 商業平価 commercial parity

heikaijō 平価以上 above par

heikaika 平価以下 below par

heikakaikin 平価解禁(金の) lifting of gold embargo at par

heikakiriage 平価切上げ (upward) revaluation; upvaluation ¶ a de facto revaluation of the U.S. dollar // a *revaluation* of the Chilean peso by 5 percent *revaluation* of the Deutsche mark // India *revalued* the rupee *upward* by about 2.5 percent against the pound sterling, the second *revaluation* this week as the pound slid on international markets. // A substanatial *upvaluation* lowers the prices of imports expressed in marks.

heikakirisage 平価切下げ downward revaluation; devaluation; depreciation ¶ Ten *devaluations* sank the Chilean money to a level of 1,000 pesos to the U.S. dollar. // The Uruguayan Central Bank announced a further *devaluation* of the Uruguayan peso, and the new rate vis-à-vis the U.S. dollar is now pesos 2.89–2.92. // The Argentine peso has been *devalued* by 3.27 percent in reaction to the U.S. dollar, in the fourth *devaluation* of 1976. // In accordance with the central bank's policy of step-by-step *devaluations*, the Argentine peso was adjusted *downwards* again.

heikakirisagekyōsō 平価切下げ競争 devaluation race; competitive revaluation

heikanohenkō 平価の変更 change in par value

heikanohyōji 平価の表示 expression of par values

heikanoichiritsuhenkō 平価の一律変更 uniform changes in par values

heikin 平均 average ¶ *Averages* are based on the number of trading days in the week. // The figures are seven-day *averages* and include both bank and non-bank dealers. // three months moving *average* // Taking the *average* of 1975, for example, it was only 7.9% greater than the *average* of 1974. // to be already 5.4% above the 1975 *average* // A continuous above-*average* industrial growth is expected.

調和平均　harmonic average
平方平均　square average
移動平均　moving average
加重平均　weighted average
加重算術平均　weighted arithmetic average
幾何平均　geometric average
算術平均　arithmetic average
3か月移動平均　three months moving average
相加平均　arithmetic average
単純平均　simple average; arithmetic average

heikinchi 平均値 mean (value); average

heikinchingin 平均賃金 average wage

heikinchinritsu 平均賃率 average labor rate

heikinharaikomishihon 平均払込資本 average paid-up capital

heikinhensa 平均偏差 mean deviation; average deviation

heikinhokenryō 平均保険料 average premium

heikinjumyō 平均寿命 average life expectancy

heikinkabuka 平均株価 stock price average

heikinkabukasaiyōmeigara 平均株価採用銘柄 stock (issue) used in the average

heikinkikenritsu 平均危険率 average risk

heikinkinri 平均金利 average interest rate

貸出約定平均金利　average interest rate on total contracted (=contractual; agreed) loans

全国銀行貸出約定平均金利　average contracted interest rates on loans and discounts of all banks

heikinmihon 平均見本 average sample

heikinnedan 平均値段 mean value; average price

heikinrijunritsu 平均利潤率 average rate of profit

heikinrimawari 平均利回り average yield

heikinshiharaikijitsu 平均支払期日 equaled time of payment

heikintaiyōji 平均太陽時 mean solar time

heikin'yomei 平均余命 life expectancy ¶ *Life expectancy* has increased in the low-income countries from 36 years to 44 between 1960 and 1975.

heikōkōi 平行行為 parallel act; parallelism

heikōsōsa 平衡操作 exchange

equalization operation

heikōyunyū 並行輸入 parallel import; non-exclusive import-distribution system; paralleled import

heikōyūshi 並行融資 parallel financing ¶ the organization of *parallel financing* from export credit sources for different goods and services

heinensaku 平年作 average crop; normal crop

heiromēkā 平炉メーカー open-hearth furnace steel makers

heisashikitanpotsukishasai 閉鎖式担保付社債 closed mortgage bond

heishin 併進 increase in tandem; parallel inceases ¶ The number of job offers and that of job seekers *increased in tandem.* // *parallel increases* in deposits and loans

heiwariyō 平和利用 peaceful utilization (of atomic power)

heizantōkei 平残統計 statistics on the average outstanding balance

hejji ヘッジ hedge; hedging ¶ The yen holds firm against continental currencies as a *hedge* currency for dollar buying. // participation of the major banks in the so-called "grey" or "unofficial" foreign exchange forward cover *"hedge"* business operating outside of the banking system

インフレヘッジ inflationary hedge; hedge against inflation

買いヘッジ long hedge

片道ヘッジ one-sided hedge

売りヘッジ short hedge

予想のヘッジ anticipatory hedge

henchō 変調 anomaly ¶ The *anomalies* between the yield patterns on the market rates and the banks' dealing rates provided profitable bill arbitrage opportu-

nities.

hendanryokusei 偏弾力性 partial elasticity

hendō 変動 fluctuation; variation; change; oscillation; swing ¶ *Fluctuations* in the mobility rate were sharpest for durable goods lines, and somewhat less acute for nondurables lines. // During Christmas week were there more pronounced *fluctuations* of day-to-day money rates. // Day-to-day money rates mostly *oscillated* slightly above the discount rate with some minor swings. // limited market intervention to smooth out exchange rate *fluctuations* // An incipient loss of confidence may lead to exchange-market *fluctuations* of a kind described as erratic or disorderly. // Britain's trade figures *fluctuated* widely between deficit and surplus. // The rate then *fluctuated* narrowly around this level throughout most of July. // to smooth out unduly sharp and at times excessive exchange rate *movements* generated by a lack of confidence // The capacity utilization rate showed no improvement apart from seasonal or fortuitous *variations*. // Production *oscillated* alternately rising and falling 10%. // Price *swings* on world markets are severe. // [参考] Rates moved erratically. // Rates remained within a narrow band, and ended little changed.

長期趨勢変動 secular trend

不規則変動 irregular variation

為替変動 exchange fluctuation; fluctuation of exchange rate

景気変動 business fluctuation

経済変動 economic fluctuation

季節(的)変動 seasonal variation; seasonal fluctuation

暦日変動 calendar variation

市価変動 (market) price fluctuation; fluctuation of (market) prices

相場変動 fluctuation of quotations

hendōhaba 変動幅 fluctuation margin; margin of fluctuation; band of fluctuation ¶ the width of *margins* on each side of the numeraire // to retain the present *margins* of the "snake" and not to prefer wider *margins* // Around these exchange rates *fluctuation margins* of +1−5% will be established. // [参考] to allow sterling to move by 6% either side of a central rate against each other member's currency

hendōhabajōkagen 変動幅上下限 upper limit rate and lower limit rate of fluctuation

hendōhabakakudai 変動幅拡大 widening of the margins of exchange rate fluctuations; widening of the band

hendōhi 変動費 variable expense; variable cost

hendōki 変動期 state of fiux; period of instability

hendōrishi 変動利子 variable rate (of interest); (interest of) floating rate ¶ a 15-year retractable *floating rate* note (FRN)

hendōritsu 変動率 rate of variability

hendōritsukisai 変動利付債 floating rate note; FRN

hendōritsukiteikiyokinshōsho 変動利付定期預金証書 floating rate certificate of deposit; FRCD

hendōshotoku 変動所得 transitory income, fluctuating income

hendōsōbasei 変動相場制 floating

exchange rate system ¶ to adopt a *system of* floating exchange rates for the dollar // to institute a *flotation* of the S.Franc // the introduction of the *floating system* for the yen // [参考] to float the yen against the dollar // to temporary suspend the limits on the yen exchange rate fluctuation margins // to annul the limitation on dealing margins for the yen

完全変動相場制 free floating exchange rate system

"汚い"変動相場制 "dirty" float

制限付変動相場制 managed float; managed floating exchange rate system; closely-policed float

hendōtekiyūkōriekiritsu 変動的有効利益率 fluctuating effective rate of return

hendōyosan 変動予算 variable budget

hengakushōhin 変額商品 equity prodct

henkan 返還 reversion; return ¶ the *reversion* (=*return*) of Okinawa to Japan

henkō 偏向 bias; distortion; tilt; inclination ¶ to redress the traditional urban *bias* of the financial system in developing countries // Withholding income tax at source tends to create a de facto tax *bias* against employees. // Comparisons of wages are *biased* by the payment of bonuses. // to *distort* incentives in favor of capital-intensive ventures // Lending shows a heavy *bias* in favor of energy projects. // There is now a deeply embedded inflationary *bias* built into the U.S. ecnomoy. // to pursue policies that would not be *biased* against the service sector //

Rising world trade will impart a inflationary *bias* to the international monetary system. // The male-female earnings differential is probably the result of antifemale *bias*. // to encourage an undue *bias* towards capital-intensive investment // an institutional *bias* toward larger producers // to offset the anti-export *bias* of prevailing policies // undesirable distributional *biases* // to support the strong labor-saving *bias* of investment policies // to *tilt* the European monetary system in favor of creditor countries // ［参考］The distribution of wealth is more lopsided in France than anywhere else in the EEC.

henkyōkaihatsu　辺境開発　frontier development

henpin'uketorijōkentsukiotoshiuri
返品受取条件付卸売り　sale and return; sale or return

hensa　偏差　deviation

hensai　返済　repayment; refunding; reimbursement; retirement; pay-back ¶ debt *repayments* totaling $3.6 million // to be free to *repay* the loan completely or in part after 8 years // *reimbursement* to a bondholder of federal income tax paid by the bondholder or to *reimburse* the bondholder for federal income tax, or to *refund* to the bondholder income tax to be paid // to *retire* a loan // to *repay* debts // to *repay* the Fund within an outside range of three to five years // The development loan has 15 years to *pay back* $2 billion at only 6.25% interest. // the *repayment* ahead of schedule of a balance-of-payments financing loan // their faultless *repayment* record since the

war

hensaikigen　返済期限　repayment term

hensainōryoku　返済能力　debt service capacity ¶ the country's debt and its debt service in proper proportion to its rising *debt service capacity*

henshin　変身　metamorphosis; metaphor; transformation ¶ a *metamorphosis* of the economy from mass consumption to resource saving // a *transformation* of the economy from mass consumption to resource saving // a process of *metamorphosis* as the banks convert themselves from quasi-banks to full bank status

hensū　変数　variable ¶ The rate of growth from year to year is a very unstable *variable*.
ダミー変数　dummy variable
独立変数　independent variable
外生変数　exogenous variable
被説明変数　explained variable
従属変数　dependent variable
目的変数　objective variable
内生変数　endogenous variable
先決変数　predetermined variable
説明変数　explanatory variable

henzai　偏在　maldistribution; uneven distribution ¶ to cushion an erratic shift in *maldistribution* of bank reserves between regions // an *uneven distribution* of supluses and deficits among countries

henzai　遍在　omnipresence; universality

henzōkahei　変造貨幣　altered coin

henzōken　変造券　altered note; raised note

hetakabu　へた株　potential stock; unissued share

hibakariakinai　日計り商い　daylight trading

hibu 日歩 interest rate of (the daily formula in) sen per ¥100; per diem rate; interest per diem ¶ at 0.05 yen *per diem* // 2 sen *per diem* for ¥100 ($0.02 \times 365 = 7.2\%$ per annum)

延滞日歩 daily interest in arrears

逆日歩 backwardation; negative interest per diem

hibuhoken 日歩保険 day insurance

hidanryokuteki 非弾力的 inelastic

hidōjihoteishiki 非同時方程式 non-homogeneous equation

hidōmeishokoku 非同盟諸国 non-aligned nations

hieikyūtekishigen 非永久的資源 non-permanent resources

hieirijigyō 非営利事業 non-profit-making business; non-commercial business

hieirikikan 非営利機関 non-profit-making institution

hieirizaidan 非営利財団 non-profit foundation

hiekomi 冷え込み cool(ing)-off; cool(ing)-down ¶ a *cool-off* of business sentiment // a *cooling-off* economic activity // The economy has been *cooling off*. // to *cool down* over-heated economic activity

hienjokoku 被援助国 (aid) recipient country; aided country

higake 日掛け daily installment

higakechokin 日掛貯金 daily installment savings

higinkōkin'yūkikan 非銀行金融機関 nonbank financial institution ¶ the lending and investing activities of both the banks and the *nonbank financial institutions*

higyō 罷業 strike; walkout; stay-in; slowdown; sabotage; go-slow; sit-in; sit-down; work stoppage ¶ 85 percent of the fire fighters *walked out* //

Stoppages by relatively few workers in sky sectors have resulted in paralysis. // →ストライキ

地域罷業 local (spot) strike; spot strike

同情罷業 sympathetic strike

総罷業 general strike

higyōiinkai 罷業委員会 strike committee

higyōken 罷業権 right to strike

higyōkikin 罷業基金 strike fund

higyōshirei 罷業指令 strike order

higyōyaburi 罷業破り strike breaker; fink; scab

hihakaiyomitorikiokusōchi 非破壊読取記憶装置 ［コン］ non-destructive read-out memory

hihei 疲弊 exhaustion; prostration ¶ The war caused financial *exhaustion* of the nation. // Widespread security speculation *prostrated* the economy, by severely curtailing purchasing power.

hihobukken 被保物件 insurable interest

hihōjingaisha 非法人会社 unincorporated company

hihokensha 被保険者 insured; insurant

hiidōsei 非移動性 immobility ¶ *immobility* of capital and of labor

hijiyūkagyōshuhyō 非自由化業種表 negative list

hijiyūkayunyūhinmoku 非自由化輸入品目 non-liberalized import item

hijōjitaisengen 非常事態宣言 proclamation of a state of emergency

hijōjōkabushiki 非上場株式 unlisted stock

hijōkinjūyaku 非常勤重役 absentee director

hijōseigen 非常制限 control in emergencies

hika 比価 parity
金銀比価 parity of gold and silver

hikaeme 控え目 reticence ¶ Industrialists' *reticence* to invest helped to fuel the recession.

hikaemeno 控え目の reserved; conservative; restrained ¶ to take a more *reserved* stance towards economic growth // *conservative* estimates // *restrained* consumption

hikaheiyōkin 非貨幣用金 nonmonetary gold

hikaku 比較 comparison ¶ an economic *comparison* between the merits of equipment-based and labor-based construction methods // A cross-country *comparison* of unemployment rates reflects the variance in monetary policy. // The April increase, on a year-to-year *comparison* basis, was 36.4 percent. // a 26.4 percent increase on an annual *comparison* // *comparison* of two proportions in independent samples // intermarket *comparisons* of intramarket husband-wife earnings differences // Wage rates show an appreciable deceleration by *comparison* with last year.

hikakuchingin 比較賃金 relative wage

hikakudōgaku 比較動学 comparative dynamics

hikakugenka 比較原価 comparative cost

hikakugosa 比較誤差 relative error

hikakuhyō 比較表 comparison table

hikakuji 比較時 time of comparison; period of comparison; current period

hikakuseigaku 比較静学 comparative statics

hikakuseihinkōgyō 皮革製品工業 leather products industry

hikakuseisanhisetsu 比較生産費説 theory of comparative costs

hikakuseisansei 比較生産性 comparative productivity

hikakuson'ekikeisansho 比較損益計算書 comparative profit and loss statement

hikakutekiretsui 比較的劣位 comparative disadvantage

hikakutekiyūi 比較的優位 comparative advantage (=superiority)

hikakuyūinogenri 比較優位の原理 principle of comparative advantage

hikan 悲観 pessimism ¶ to reinforce growing *pessimism* among businessmen about the prospects for...

hikanron 悲観論 pessimism ¶ *Pessimism* over economic prospects continues to wane, albeit only gradually. // The prolonged recession overcasts the future with *pessimism.* // to reject the *pessimism* of vertical technical limits to growth // Pronounced *pessimism* about the movement of interest rates was spreading.

hikanzeishōheki 非関税障壁 nontariff barrier

hikaritokage 光と陰 light and shade; bright and somber sides ¶ The economy had its *bright and somber sides.* // The general economic picture in Italy at present is a mixture of *light and shadow*, though with a preponderance of disquieting aspect.

hikaseginin 日稼人 day-laborer; free (=casual) laborer

hikazeiatsukai 非課税扱い (tax)

exemption

hikazeichochiku 非課税貯蓄 tax exemption savings

hikazeihōjin 非課税法人 tax free corporation

hikazeino 非課税の tax free; no tax; tax exempt

hikazeishotoku 非課税所得 non-taxable income

hike 引け [市] last quotation; closing; close of the session
安値引け closing lower
高値引け closing higher

hikeaji 引け味 [市] closing tone

hikeatokehai 引け跡気配 [市] after-session undertone; street price

hikedaka 引け高 [市] higher quotation at the close

hikegiwa 引け際 [市] at the close of the market

hikegosōba 引け後相場 street price

hikene 引け値 [市] closing quotation; close; finish; closing price ¶ *Closing prices* were at the day's best. // [参考] The market closed lower.

hikeyasu 引け安 [市] lower closing quotation

hikiagechōka 引揚超過 excess withdrawal (in the public-to-Government balance)

hikiageru 引上げる →上げる

hikiageshakokkosaiken 引揚者国庫債券 Repatriation Treasury Bond

hikiagetsūka 引揚げ通貨 money drawn from circulation

hikiai 引合い enquiry (=inquiry); negotiation

hikiatekin 引当金 reserve ¶ Banks are allowed to make tax-free *provision* for rescheduling and new money they supply to problem coun-

tries.

減価償却引当金 reserve for depreciation

補充引当金 replacement reserve

貸倒引当金 reserve for and debts; provision for loan losses

納税引当金 reserve for taxes

修繕引当金 reserve for repairs

退職給与引当金 reserve for retirement allowances

棚卸資産評価引当金 inventory reserve

hikidashi 引出し drawing (down) ¶ *drawings* on the Federal Reserve System // the use of U.S. *drawing* rights on the IMF // *drawing down* on the deposit account // *drawings* on the Federal Reserve system // The loan is repayable in five equal semi-annual installments from the eighth anniversary of the *drawing-down* of funds. ¶ Credit card companies allow customers to *draw* out cash up to their full credit limits.

hikikaekōryoku 引換効力 exchange ability

hikikaeni 引換えに in exchange for; against; on delivery

hikimodoshi 引戻し [市] rally

hikinobashi 引伸ばし spreading-out ¶ the *spreading-out* of expenditure over 10 years

hikin'yūtorihiki 非金融取引 non-financial transactions

hikin'yūtorihikishūshi 非金融取引収支 balance on non-monetary transactions

hikinzoku 卑金属 base metal

hikinzokukōbutsuseihin 非金属鉱物製品 non-metallic mineral manufactures

hikisage 引下げ reduction; lowering; lessening; dwindling; cut;

depreciation; decrease; cut; cutback; curtailment; cutting down; bringing down; pulling down; paring down

物価引下げ　price reduction

賃金引下げ　wage cut; reduction in wage

hikishimari 引締り　firmness; firming-up; hardening tendency; stringency; ［市］ hardened (market); hardening ¶ The tone underlying the financial market is one of *stringency*. // to alleviate monetary and credit *stringency* // From looking at the rates there has been a bit of *tightening* in the money market.

hikishimarikichō 引締り基調　basic trend (=tone) of monetary stringency; tightness in financial positions; taut tone of the financial market ¶ The *basic trend* in the market was *taut*. // The *market* has been basically *tight*. // The *tone* underlying the market was one of *stringency*.

hikishime 引締め　restraint; stringency; tight rein; tightening; squeeze; reining; constraint; restriction ¶ credit *restraint* policy // monetary *restraint* // previous periods of credit *stringency* // to keep a *tight rein* on bank lendings // to *tighten* the *rein on* financing // The Fed *tightened* up further on credit and money. // The growth of domestic demand has been sharply *reined* back. // Consumer spending will bear the brunt of the *squeeze*. // All countries started *reining* in their mony supplies. // The authorities imposed even more *constraints* on the money and financial markets. // The economy responds slowly to the traditional fiscal and monetary *restraints*. // The bank continued to

exhort commercial banks to observe *restraint* in lending. // The general credit policy of the Federal Reserve System was modified in the direction of *restraint*. // ［参考］ The Federal Reserve became less accommodative in meeting the demand for bank reserves. // The Fed began applying the monetary brakes in earnest.

hikishimekōseisaku 引締め政策　restrictive (policy) measures; contractionary policy measures ¶ to introduce strong, *contractionary* fiscal and credit *measures*

hikishimekyōka 引締め強化　tighter rein; additional (monetary) restraint ¶ The supply of cash reserves to the banking system was kept under a *tighter rein*.

hikishimeseisakukaijo 引締め政策解除　relaxation of monetary restraint; lifting of tight money policy; putting an end to the restrictive monetary policy

hikishimeseisakukyōka 引締め政策強化　further restraint of monetary policy; tightening of restrictive monetary policy; intensifying of tight money policy

hikishimesochi 引締め措置　restraint measures ¶ Budgetary *restraint measures* have been introduced as a component of stabilization programs.

hikiuke 引受け　acceptance; ［証市］ firm commitment; purchase; underwriting; taking up; undertaking; subscription; security; guaranty ¶ *underwriting* of government bonds by the Bank of Japan

買取引受　firm comitment underwriting

協議引受　negotiated underwriting; private negotiation

残額引受　stand-by underwriting

hikiukedan 引受団　syndicate; underwriting group; consortium ¶ A Swiss bank *consortium* has underwritten a Norwegian Government bond issue SwF50 million, offered for public subscription at par. // The Deutsche Bank heads the *underwriting consortium* for the seven-year loan for DM100 million launched by the European Investment Bank.

hikiukedannaikeiyaku 引受団内契約　agreement among underwriters

hikiukegaisha 引受会社　underwriter; underwriting company; ［英］ acceptance corporation

hikiukeginkō 引受銀行　accepting bank

hikiukegyōsha 引受業者　investment banker; underwriter; ［英］ accepting house

hikiukegyōshakankeiyaku 引受業者間契約　agreement among underwriters; purchase group agreement; agreement among prospective purchasers

hikiukekanji 引受幹事　［証市］ managing underwriter; manager of underwriting syndicate

hikiukekeiyaku 引受契約　underwriting agreement; purchase agreement (＝contract)

hikiukekyozetsu 引受拒絶　protest; dishonor; non-acceptance

hikiukekyozetsushōsho 引受拒絶証書　protest for non-acceptance

hikiukenin 引受人(手形の)　acceptor

hikiukeritsu 引受率　acceptance rate

hikiukeseikyūtegata 引受請求手形　bill for acceptance

hikiukeshijō 引受市場　acceptance market

hikiukeshinjikēto 引受シンジケート　acceptance syndicate; underwriting syndicate; underwriting (＝purchase) group

hikiukeshōsha 引受商社　［英］ accepting house

hikiukesōba 引受相場　acceptance rate

hikiuketegata 引受手形　acceptance; ［会］ trade acceptances payable

貿易引受手形　trade acceptance

銀行引受手形　bank(er's) acceptance

hikiuketegatashijō 引受手形市場　acceptance market

hikiuketeiji 引受呈示　presentation for acceptance

hikiuketesūryō 引受手数料　underwriting commission; underwriting fee; underwriting spread; underwriting discount

hikiukeuridashi 引受売出し　sale (of securities) on an underwriting basis

hikiukeuridashigyōmu 引受売出業務　［証市］ business of underwriter

hikiukewatashi 引受渡し　document against acceptance

hikiukewatashikawase 引受渡為替　documents against acceptance; D/A bill

hikiukewatashinigawase 引受渡荷為替　documentary acceptance bill

hikiukeyōkyūteiji 引受要求呈示　presentation for acceptance

hikiwatashi 引渡し　delivery; transfer

hikiwatashibarai 引渡払い　cash on delivery; pay delivery

hikiwatashijōkō 引渡条項 terms (and conditions) of delivery

hikiwatashijūryō 引渡重量 delivery weight

hikiwatashishōken 引渡証券 delivery bill

hikiwatashitsūkokusho 引渡通告書 delivery notice

hikiwatashiyūyokin 引渡し猶予金 [英・市] backwardation

hikiwatashizumi 引渡済み delivered

hikiyurumikehai 引緩み気配 signs of an easing situation

hikiyurumu 引緩む ease; weaken; relax

hikōgyōseihin 非工業製品 non-manufactured products; non-manufactured goods

hikōkaigaisha 非公開会社 closed company (=corporation)

hikōkaikabu 非公開株 private-owned company's share

hikōkansei 非交換性 inconvertibility

hikyojūsha 非居住者 non-resident

hikyojūshagaikayokinkanjō 非居住者外貨預金勘定 non-resident foreign currency account

hikyojūshahakkōendatesai 非居住者発行円建債 bonds in yen issued by non-residents

hikyojūshajiyūenkanjō 非居住者自由円勘定 non-resident yen deposit account

himitsusei 秘密性 secrecy ¶ a policy of *secrecy* characteristic of the industry // to preserve the banking *secrecy*

himitsutorihiki 秘密取引 under-the-counter trading

himo 紐 string ¶ Communist aid has always had more *strings* attached to it than Western aid.

himotsukienjo 紐付き援助 tied aid; aid with strings attached ¶ Virtually all communist *aid* is closely *tied* to the purchase of donor country goods. // [参考] to accept the business world's money, even if it comes with ideological strings

himotsukiyūshi 紐付き融資 tied loan; conditional loan; project loan

hinanchi 避難地 refuge; haven ¶ →避難所; 安息地

hinanjo 避難所 haven; refuge ¶ a safe *haven* for international capital // the dollar's reputation as a *haven* currency // to buy dollars as a *refuge* currency // Money is on the run, mostly headed into Switzerland, traditional *refuge* of flight capital. // funds seeking a *refuge* from dollar denominated assets // Some investors may look on gold as the ultimate safe *haven*. // The dollar is a safe *haven* for their funds.

hin'i 品位 fineness; purity; alloy (= metallic) composition

hinkon 貧困 poverty; indigence ¶ to diminish the size of the population falling into the "*poverty* trap" // to combat the widespread *poverty* afficting rural societies // to alleviate *poverty* of the masses in the basic needs // The Federally set "*poverty* level" for a nonfarm family of four is $6,191 a year. // Some 40% of Latin Americans were below the *poverty* line and 19% living in absolute *indigence*.

hinkonka 貧困化 impoverishment
　相対的貧困化 relative impoverishment
　絶対的貧困化 absolute impoverishment

hinkonkazoku 貧困家族 families living in poverty

hinkonnoakujunkan 貧困の悪循環 vicious circle of poverty

hinkonsen 貧困線 poverty line ¶ The *poverty line* can go up and the larger number of poor people be made to look. // The official *poverty line* has risen in real terms. // The member of people whose family income was below the *poverty line* rose from 1.4 million to a staggering 2.3 million.

hinkonsha 貧困者 the poor; humble people
隠れた貧困者 invisible poor
強壮体貧困者 rate-bodied poor
絶対的貧困者 absolute poor

hinminkyūsai 貧民救済 poor relief

hinmoku 品目 article; commodity item

hinmokuunchin 品目運賃 commodity rate

hinōritsu 非能率 inefficiency ¶ Import-substitution policies may permit technical and managerial *inefficiency* to prevail in industries. // waste and *inefficiency in government*

hinpu 貧富 the poor and the rich; wealth and poverty ¶ a great difference between *the poor and the rich* // the juxtaposition (= coexistence) *of present wealth* and great *poverty*

hinshitsufuryō 品質不良 inferior quality

hinshitsukijun 品質基準 quality standards

hinshitsukyōsō 品質競争 quality competition

hinshitsushōmei 品質証明 guarantee of quality; quality certificate

hinshitsuteika 品質低下 adulteration

hippaku 逼迫 tightening; tension; stress; strain; tautness; stringency; crunch ¶ The market remains in a highly *tense* state. // The market *stresses* and *strains* have diminished. // There is no marked abatement of market *strains*. // The market has been considerably *taut*. // The step resulted for a time in greater-than-desired *stringency* in the money market. // The *tensions* in the economy are largely attributable to structural factors. // There are *strains* on resources at both the producer and consumer ends. // Many industries are approaching output levels that *strained* their capacities. // The *strain* between supply and demand remained unchanged. // The money market is experiencing the usual year-end *strains*. // to alleviate protracted international balance-of-payments *strains* // The *strained* reserve positions of banks alleviated. // Long-term financing is under serious *strains*. // The domestic capacity was *strained* by the expansion in aggregate demand. // *Tensions* began to re-emerge, particularly in Italy. // The Eurocurrency market was to under liquidity *strains*. // signs of an easing *tension* // to relax *tensions* in the market // The Treasury faced on cash *crunch*.
金融逼迫 monetary stringency; tight money; credit crunch

hippakukenen 逼迫懸念 worry of credit availability; uncertainty about credit availability; apprehension over tight money

hiraki 開き difference; margin; spread;

discrepancy ¶ the rising *spread* between the Canadian and United States interest rates // The *spread* narrowed. // the *spread* at ½ per cent // The coupon rate carries a 1-¹/₈% *spread* above Eurodollar rates. // the usually large *spread* between the prime rate of the commercial banks and the rate on commercial paper // a widening of *spreads* (in...)

hireidaihyōsei 比例代表制 proportional representation

hireijunbisei 比例準備制 proportional reserve system

hireijunbiseido 比例準備制度 proportional reserve system

hireikazeihō 比例課税法 proportional tax law

hireikazeiritsu 比例課税率 proportional tax rate

hireiwariate 比例割当 proportional allocation

hireiwariateseido 比例割当制度 percentage quota system; PQS

hiritsu 比率 ratio; rate; percentage; per cent(um); share; proportion ¶ the *ratio* of input to output, or the input-output *ratio* // to look at government wages as a *per cent* of total wages in the economy // to be paid for at the *rate* of 102 *per centum* of the par of the bonds // to add to their aid programs each year a small *percentage* of their incremental GNP // Total borrowing by all sectors rose as a *percentage* of GNP. // The *share* of bilateral grants in total disbursements rose to 49%. // Official development assistance as a *share* of GNP rose to 0.33%. // About 5% of the gross national product, close to the peak

shares in the 1872-73 period. // the total as a *share* of GNP // to reduce Federal spending as a *proportion* of GNP // [参考] the number of times earnings cover debt interest charges // the coverage of fixed charges over a period of time

構成比率 distribution ratio; percentage distribution; percentage composition

対級比率 inter-class ratio

hiritsusasatsuhō 比率査察法 ratio study

hiryūdōteki 非流動的 illiquid ¶ Recent Japanese borrowing will be tightly held and fairly *illiquid* as a result.

hisaiseishigen 非再生資源 non-renewable resource; exhaustible resource; depletable resource

hisan'yuhattentojōkoku 非産油発展途上国 non-oil producing developing countries

hisan'yukaihatsutojōkoku 非産油開発途上国 less developed oil consuming country

hiseigengyōshu 非制限業種 non-restricted industry

hiseisanteki 非生産的 unproductive; non-productive

hiseisantekijigyō 非生産的事業 non-productive enterprise

hisenkei 非線型 non-linear

hisetsumeihensū 被説明変数 explained variable

hishijōseishōken 非市場性証券 nonmarketable issue

hishimukesōkinkawaseshiharai 被仕向送金為替支払 [外] payment of remittance from abroad

hitaikyūshōhizai 非耐久消費財 non-durable consumer goods

hitaishō 非対称 asymmetry ¶ the

phenomenon of the *asymmetry* between the upward and downward elasticity of prices

hitaishōbasukettohōshiki 非対称バスケット方式 ［外］adjustable basket technique

hitaishōbunpu 非対称分布 asymmetrical distribution

hiteikeihōshiki 非提携方式 non-tie-up system

hitetsukinzokukō 非鉄金属鉱 non-ferrous metal ores

hitetsukinzokukōgyō 非鉄金属工業 non-ferrous metals and products industry

hitodebusoku 人手不足 shortage of labor; labor shortage

hitoiki 一息 lull; marking time; taking a rest

hitokabuataririeki 一株当り利益 per share profit; profit per share

hitokabukabunushi 一株株主 one-share shareholder

hitoriatariheikin 一人当り平均 average per capita; per capita average

hitsujuhin 必需品 necessities; necessaries; requisites; essential goods ¶ the provision of basic *necessities*, such as food and housing
生活必需品 necessaries of life; daily necessaries; daily necessities

hitsuyōbusshi 必要物資 requisite materials

hitsuyōjōken 必要条件 necessary condition; requisite condition; sine qua non ¶ $6 billion is a *sine qua non* of overall payments equilibrium. // the *sine qua non* of the good life

hitsuyōshikinnokyōkyū 必要資金の供給 supply of necessary funds

hiuragakinin 被裏書人 endorsee

hiyashisugi 冷やし過ぎ(景気の) overkill; over-correction

hiyatoirōdōsha 日雇労働者 day worker; day laborer

hiyō 費(用) expense; expenditure; cost; outlay; spending
代替費用 alternative cost
営業費用 working expenses
不変費用 constant cost
福利厚生費 welfare expenses
限界単位費用 marginal unit cost
減価償却費 depreciation expense
補足的費用 supplementary cost
一般管理費 general administrative expenses
事務費 office expenses
人件費 personnel expenses
実質費用 real cost
可変費用 variable expenses
家計費 household expenses
間接費 indirect expenses
経営費 managing expenses
経常費用 current expenses
機会費用 opportunity cost
固定費用 constant expenses
交通費 transport expenses
摩滅消耗費 wear and tear expenses
臨時費用 incidental expense; non-recurring expense
生活費 living expenses
製造費 manufacturing expenses
接待費 entertainment expenses
社債発行費用 bond expenses
使用者費用 user cost
主要費用 prime cost
創業費 promotion expenses
操業費 running expenses
運営費 working expenses
要素費用 factor cost
雑費 miscellaneous expenses; sundry expenses

hiyōben'ekibunseki 費用便益分析 cost-benefit analysis; cost-performance analysis

hiyōben'ekihiritsu 費用便益比率
cost-benefit ratio

hiyōkansū 費用関数　cost function

hiyōseisanryokuhiritsu 費用・生産
力比率　cost-productivity ratio

hiyōtaikōkabunsekiyosanhōshiki
費用対効果分析予算方式　planning-
programing budgeting system;
PPBS

hizenrintekikoyōshugi 非善隣的雇
用主義　beggar-my(=thy)-neighbor
employment argument

hizuke 日付け　date; dating
後日付け　postdating; postdate
前日付け　antedating; antedate

hizukegorokujūnichibarai 日付後
六十日払い　60 days after date; 60
day's date

hizukegoteikibaraitegata 日付後
定期払手形　bill payable at a fixed
period after sight

hizumi 歪み　distortion; skewness ¶
interest rate *distortions* // repeated
distortions of national life the timing, pace, and scope of removing
price *distortions* // to remove *distortions* in manufacturing // to correct
distortions in the money market due
to the substantial rise of some rates
relative to bank rate // the extent to
which imbalances have created *distortions* in the economy // to correct
the *distortion* of the interest rate
structure // *distortions* in the money
market // to minimize the *distortions*
arising from inflation // inflationary
distortions during the transition
period // the conventional *distortions*
that develop in the economy prior to
recessions // to *distort* resource allocation // Currency fluctuations
distort the trend in commodity

prices. // to *skew* the geographical
distribution of transactions to certain areas of the world economy //
The distribution of land was *skewed*.

hoanrin 保安林　protection forest

hōchijō 報知状　advices

hōchisaku 放置策　do-nothing policy

hodohodono ほどほどの　moderate;
modest ¶ a shift in the policy stance
from one of *moderate* restraint to
that of *modest* easing of monetary
conditions

hōfukukanzei 報復関税　retaliatory duties; retaliatory taxes

hōginkaigaiten 邦銀海外店　overseas branches of Japanese banks

hogo 保護　protection; safeguard-
ing; shelter; safeguard ¶ the most
elementary *safeguards* for the investor // to progressively dismantle tariff and quota *protection* and other
administrative obstacles to imports // Land has almost always
fared well as a form of *protection*
against inflation. // the *protection*-of-
assets motivation for land acquisition // to *protect* the currency from
external vicissitudes // the disadvantage of removing *protection* from
local suppliers of intermediate products // reduction of import-replacement *protection*
環境保護　environmental protection
幼稚産業保護　infant industry protection

hogoazukari 保護預り　deposit for
safekeeping; safe deposit; safekeeping deposit; safe custody

hogobōeki 保護貿易　protective
trade; sheltered trade

hogobōekihō 保護貿易法　protectionist legislation

hogobōekironja 保護貿易論者 protectionist

hogobōekiseido 保護貿易制度 protective system

hogobōekiseisaku 保護貿易政策 protective trade policy; defensive trade policy ¶ to see renewed clamour for *defensive* trade *policies*

hogobōekiseisakusochi 保護貿易政策措置 protectionist policy (measures) ¶ the dismantling of *protectionist measures* which hinder world trade

hogobōekishugi 保護貿易主義 (trade) protectionism ¶ A new threat of *protectionism* is gathering momentum in the developed world. // to beat back the forces of *protectionism* // to roll back a surge of trade *protectionism* that has been gathering momentum // a rise in *protectionism* in the western countries in the form of import quotas // to pledge to abstain from *protectionism* // under the umbrella of spreading *protectionism* // to relapse into open or concealed *protectionism* // to contain or arrest the drift towards *protectionism* // howls of pain and cries for *protectionism* in the U. S. concerning Japanese competition // Deliberate exchange rate policy would lead to a resurgence of *protectionism*. // recourse to *protectionism* in trade and payments // to yield to the temptation to resort to commercial *protectionism* // These goods have been singled out for the most enthusiastic pieces of *protectionism*. // The perceptible increase in *protectionism* arises from the disappointing by slow economic recovery. // to combat the rising tide of *protectionism* sentiment // ［参考］ to reject a *protectionist* course for world trade

hogokaitsuke 保護買付け protective buying

hogokaiunseisaku 保護海運政策 protective shipping policy

hogokanzei 保護関税 protective duty

hogokanzeiritsu 保護関税率 protective tariff

hogosangyō 保護産業 protected industry; sheltered industry

hogoseisaku 保護政策 protective policy; protectionist policy

hogoshugi 保護主義 protectionism ¶ a return to *protectionism* // → 保護貿易主義

hōhōshudan 方法手段 practical ways and means; modalities; practices and procedures ¶ to devise a body of *practices and procedures* to guide the implementation of the broad principles

hōjinchochiku 法人貯蓄 corporate saving

hōjindantai 法人団体 corporate body

hōjinkabunushi 法人株主 corporate shareholder

hōjinkaitsuke 法人買付け institution buying

hōjinken 法人権 corporate rights

hōjinkigyōtōkei 法人企業統計 financial statements of incorporated businesses

hōjinritokuzei 法人利得税 corporation profit tax

hōjinshotoku 法人所得 income from incorporated enterprises; corporate income

hōjin'uri 法人売り institution selling

hōjin'yokin 法人預金 corporation

deposits; corporate deposits; company-sector bank deposits

hojobo 補助簿 subsidiary record

hojogaisha 補助会社 subsidized company

hojokabu 補助株 subsidiary ledger

hojokahei 補助貨幣 subsidiary coin

hojokin 補助金 subsidy; grant; bounty; subvention; incentive ¶ to ask and receive heavy government *subsidies* // a *bounty* granted by the government on exports // job-saving *subventions* to faltering industries // expenditure *incentives* consisting of payments by government to enterprises to certain percentages of the cost of fixed assets and so forth

国庫補助金 government subsidy; state bounty

hojokōro 補助航路 subsidized line

hojomotochō 補助元帳 subsidiary ledger

hojoseisaku 補助政策 subsidizing policy

hojoteki 補助的 auxiliary; supplemental (=~tary); ancillary; subsidiary ¶ Selective credit controls usually are regarded as *ancillary* or *supplementary* to general credit controls. // *subsidiary* or *auxiliary* coins

hojū 補充 replenishment; rebuilding; filling up ¶ Contributions are augmented through periodic *replenishments*. // a *rebuilding* of inventories // fill-ins to *fill up* temporary vacancies

hōka 邦貨 Japanese currency; the (Japanese) yen

hōka 法貨 legal tender

無限法貨 unlimited legal tender

有限法貨 limited legal tender

hōkabaraikōsai 法貨払公債 legal tender bond

hōkadatekawasesōba 邦貨建為替相場 yen rate

hōkai 崩壊 collapse; debacle; crumbling; havoc; breakdown ¶ the *debacle* of the currency markets // the *collapse* of the dollar in European currency markets // Debtor nation's renunciation of their debts would wreak *havoc* in financial markets. // the *breakdown* of the Bretton Woods system // to avoid a widening circle of *collapse* through the contagion of fear // the *collapsed* Bretton Woods regime // Britain's financial system has trembled on the brink of *collapse*. // The building society was close to *collapse*. // to fare without anything remotely resembling the dollar *collapse* of 1978 // The bond market *crumbled*.

hōkakawasetegata 邦貨為替手形 bill in domestic currency

hōkakokusai 邦貨国債 government bonds in domestic currency

hokan 保管 custody; safekeeping

hokanhi 保管費 warehousing and carrying charges

hokanhin 保管品 article in custody

hokankin 保管金 money in custody

hokannin 保管人 custodian; keeper

hokanrin 保管林 managed forest

hokanryō 保管料 storage; charge for custody

hokansōko 保管倉庫 storage warehouse

hokantekishin'yō 補完的信用 supplementing credit; supplementary credit

hokantekiyūshiseido 補完的融資制度 Supplementary Financing Facility of the IMF

hokan'yūkashōken 保管有価証券 securities deposited from others

hōkategata 邦貨手形 yen bill; bill in home currency

hōkatsuhoken 包括保険 blanket insurance

hōkatsuhokenshōken 包括保険証券 floating policy

hōkatsukeishōnin 包括継承人 general successor

hōkatsukyoka 包括許可 blanket license; open general license; O.G.L.

hōkatsuyunyū 包括輸入 import on an escrow basis

hōkatsuyunyūkyokasei 包括輸入許可制 open general license system

hōkatsuzaisan 包括財産 floating property

hoken 保険 insurance; assurance
¶ to carry *insurance* to protect themselves against unpredictable hazards // Blanket *insurance* covers a number of properties under one policy.
重複保険 double insurance
超過保険 excess insurance
長期傷害保険 non-cancellable accident and health insurance
徴集保険 assessment insurance
団体保険 group insurance
団体生命保険 group life insurance
団体傷害保険 group accident insurance
動産保険 property insurance
営業保険 proprietary insurance
営利保険 commercial insurance; proprietary insurance
延長保険 extended insurance
不動産保険 immovable insurance
賦課式保険 assessment insurance
風水害保険 wind, storm and flood insurance
廃疾保険 insurance against invalidity (=disability)
遺族年金保険 survivorship annuity insurance
医療保険 medical insurance
事業生命保険 business life insurance
自家保険 self-insurance
地震保険 earthquake insurance
海上保険 marine insurance
簡易保険 postal insurance
間接的損害保険 consequential loss insurance
火災保険 fire insurance
継続保険 renewable insurance
健康保険 health insurance
危険保険 risk-covering insurance
個人傷害保険 individual accident insurance
国営保険 state insurance
航空保険 aviation insurance
国民保険 national insurance
個人保険 personal insurance
国家保険 state insurance
公共責任保険 public liability insurance
混合保険 joint insurance
厚生年金保険 welfare pension insurance; employees' pension insurance
洪水保険 flood insurance
空輸貨物保険 air cargo insurance
共同保険 co-insurance
共済保険 fraternal insurance
強制保険 forced insurance
給料積立保険 salary saving insurance
無配当保険 non-participating insurance
年金保険 insurance against annuity
農業保険 farm insurance
利益保険 loss of profits insurance; profits insurance
利潤喪失保険 profit loss insurance

労働生命保険 industrial life insurance

労働者災害補償保険 workmen's compensation insurance

老齢遺族保険 old-age and survivorship insurance

旅行者傷害保険 traveler's accident insurance

災害保険 accident insurance

再保険 re-insurance

再取得保険 replacement value insurance

作物保険 crop insurance

産業保険 industrial insurance

製品責任保険 products liability insurance

生命保険 life insurance

生存保険 pure endowment insurance

責任保険 liability insurance

社会保険 social insurance

社会医療保険 socialized medical insurance

疾病保険 insurance against sickness

失業保険 unemployment insurance; jobless insurance

信用保険 credit insurance

終身生命保険 whole life insurance

総合超過損害再保険 aggregate excess of loss reinsurance; stop loss reinsurance; excess of loss ratio reinsurance

相互保険 mutual insurance

損害保険 non-life insurance

据置年金保険 deferred annuity insurance

建物保険 building insurance

定期保険 term insurance

抵当保険 mortgage insurance

盗難保険 burglary insurance

取換費保険 replacement insurance

運送保険 transport insurance; transit insurance; transportation insurance

雇人保険 fidelity guarantee insurance

養老保険 endowment insurance; old-age insurance

財産保険 property insurance

全部保険 full insurance

全損害保険 all-in insurance

hokenburōkā 保険ブローカー insurance broker

hokendairinin 保険代理人 insurance agent

hokengaisha 保険会社 insurance company

hokengijutsu 保険技術 insurance technics

hokengyōsha 保険業者 insurer; underwriter

hokenhaitō 保険配当 insurance dividend

hokenhyōkagaku 保険評価額 policy valuation; agreed value

hokenkakaku 保険価格 insurance value; insurable value

hokenkakekin 保険掛金 insurance premium

hokenkanjō 保険勘定 insurance account

hokenkanyūsha 保険加入者 insured

hokenkeiyaku 保険契約 insurance contract

hokenkeiyakunomokuteki 保険契約者の目的 subject matter of insurance

hokenkeiyakusha 保険契約者 policy holder; insurant

hokenken'ekibusoku 保険権益不足 short insurance interest

hokenkikan 保険期間 term insured

hokenkin 保険金 insurance claim;

insurance benefit; insurance money
¶ gains or losses on *insurance
claims* on shipments

hokenkingaku 保険金額 insurance amount; insured amount; sum insured

hokenkinsaeki 保険金差益 gains on insurance claims

hokenkinsason 保険金差損 losses on insurance claims

hokenkinshiharai 保険金支払 payment of insurance claim

hokenkin'uketorinin 保険金受取人 beneficiary

hokenmōshikomisho 保険申込書 insurance slip

hokenryō 保険料 premium
　営業保険料 gross premium; loaded premium
　正味保険料 net premium
　割増保険料 extra premium

hokenryōdōmei 保険料同盟 tariff association

hokenryōharaimodoshi 保険料払戻し return premium; surrender value

hokenryōharaimodoshitsukihoken 保険料払戻付保険 insurance with return premium

hokenryōjidōkashitsuke 保険料自動貸付 automatic premium loan

hokenryōkōjo 保険料控除 insurance premium deduction

hokenryōritsu 保険料率 rate of premium; insurance rate
　表定保険料率 tariff rate

hokenryōruikahoken 保険料累加保険 increasing premium plan

hokensaiteisekininjōkō 保険最低責任条項 insurance memorandum

hokenseisannin 保険清算人 insurance adjuster

hokensha 保険者 insurer; under-

writer

hokenshōken 保険証券 insurance policy

hokenshōkenkashitsuke 保険証券貸付 policy loan

hokenshōmeisho 保険証明書 certificate of insurance

hokentōkeigishi 保険統計技師 actuary

hokkinin 発起人 promoter; founder; projector; originator

hokkininkabu 発起人株 promoter's share

hokkininkai 発起人会 meeting of promoters

hokkininritoku 発起人利得 promoter's premium

hōkō 方向 direction; orientation; trend ¶ confused prospects of the immediate *direction* of U.S. interest rates // the stance and general *orientation* of economic policies // to await some clues on the *direction* of U.S. interest rates // new developments to spur a major move in either *direction* // uncertainty about the *direction* of U.S. Federal Reserve policy // The dollar's *trend* remains unclear. // Traders await *direction* from the U.S. dollar. // The *direction* of the Bank will be in retail areas and in the use of new technology.

hōkoku 報告 report; return; paper; advice; information
　調査報告 survey report; memoir
　中間報告 progress report; interim report
　営業報告 business report
　月(次)報(告) monthly report; monthly
　経過報告 progress report; followup report
　年(次)報(告) annual report; annual

最終報告 final report

四半期報告 quarterly report; quarterly

hōkokusho 報告書 report; return; account; record; statement

調整報告書 reconciliation statement

hokuyōgyogyō 北洋漁業 northern-sea fisheries

hōkyu 補給 subsidization; replenishment; supply ¶ the *subsidization* of such items as the interest rates on loans and utility rates

hōkyū 俸給 salaries and wages

hokyūki 補給機 fueling plane

hokyūkichi 補給基地 supply base

hokyūkin 補給金 subsidy; grant

hokyūkonnan 補給困難 difficulties of replenishment; supply difficulties; supply constraints

hōkyūseikatsusha 俸給生活者 salaried man; salary man; salariat(e)

hokyūsen 補給船 supply ship

hokyūsen 補給線 supply line; feeder line

hōkyūshiharaikogitte 俸給支払い小切手 pay check

hōkyūshoteate 俸給・諸手当 salaries and allowances

hōman 放漫 laxity ¶ the financial *laxity* of the public administration // The "*lax* financial practices" evident in New York City's encountered with bankruptcy.

hōmankashidashi 放漫貸出 reckless lending

hōmankeiei 放漫経営 lax business policy; sloppy management; free-spending management; irresponsible management

hōmatsugaisha 泡沫会社 mushroom company; bubble (company)

hōmonhanbai 訪問販売 call sales

honegumi 骨組 framework; skele-

ton; structure; girder; general plan; outline ¶ The monetary system can respond to changing circumstances within an agreed legal *framework*.

honegumizai 骨組材 frame timber

hōnen 豊年 year of good harvest; year of abundance; bumper year; plentiful year; rich year

hongentekiyokin 本源的預金 primary deposit

hongokusōkan 本国送還 repatriation ¶ the *repatriation* by foreigners of their investments in Japanese stock // Exported capital is being *repatriated*. // the amnesty allowing illegally exported capital to be *repatriated* without penalization

hongyō 本業 main business (＝occupation)

hon'i 本位 standard ¶ [参考] paper money anchored to one commodity like gold

複本位 double standard; bimetallism

銀本位 silver standard

合成本位 symmetallism

跛行金本位 limping gold standard

管理金本位 managed gold standard

為替本位 exchange standard

金本位 gold standard

金地金本位 gold bullion standard

金貨本位 gold coin standard; gold currency standard

金核本位 gold kernel standard

金為替本位 gold exchange standard

金属本位 metallic standard

交代本位 alternative standard

国際金本位 international gold standard

紙幣本位 paper standard

単本位 monometallic standard; single standard

多数通貨本位 multiple currency stan-

dard
hon'ikahei 本位貨幣 standard coin; standard money

honkakuka 本格化 taking hold; beginning to take full effect; in full effect; on the right track; producing result; in real earnest; well (=firmly) under way; in full scale; becoming full-fledged; firmly based; getting into stride; fully in progress ¶ Policy effects are *taking hold* in the economy. // Trade liberalization was placed *on the right track*. // a *full scale* tight-money policy maneuver // to apply monetary brakes *in earnest* // The recovery now is *firmly underway*. // The exchange rate decline occurred in a situation where domestic inflation had *taken* a firm *hold*. // Economic recovery is now *fully under way*. // The tightening of controls on capital inflows began to *take hold*. // Expansion is now *firmly based* and will proceed at a satisfactory pace. // The new big coal operations *got into* their *stride*. // Inventory adjustment was *fully in progress*.

honkakuteki 本格的 full-scale; full; in earnest ¶ The U.S. economic recovery could easily bloom into a *full-scale* boom. // All are still far from anything that could be touted as *full* prosperity. // The Fed began applying the monetary brakes *in earnest*.

honkakutekihikishime 本格的引締め tightened monetary restraint; earnest tightening of monetary policy

honkakutekikadō 本格的稼働 full-scale operation, full-fledged operation; operation on a full scale

honnaori 本直り ［市］ rally

honpōshihon 本邦資本 domestic capital (assets); Japan's capital invested abroad

honpōshōken 本邦証券 domestic securities

honpōtsūkano IMF tōrokuheika 本邦通貨の IMF 登録平価 IMF par value for the yen

honsen 本船 carrying vessel

honsenwatashi 本船渡し free on board; f.o.b.

honsenzumifunanishōken 本船積船荷証券 on board; B/L

honshahoshō 本社保証 guarantee by the parent company

honshitenkanjō 本支店勘定 inter-office account; in-house account

hontegata 本手形 prime security

honten 本店 main office; head office

hontenshūchūshori 本店集中処理 centralized processing system

hon'yosan 本予算 main budget; principal estimates

hōraku 崩落 ［市］ slump; crash; breakdown; collapse

hōreiihan 法令違反 contravention to the law

hōsaku 豊作 good harvest; rich harvest; abundant harvest; heavy crop; bumper crop ¶ ［参考］ a large rice crop

hoseitekitorihiki 補正的取引 compensatory transaction

hoseiyosan 補正予算 supplementary budget; additional estimates ¶ The Diet approved a *supplementary* General Account *budget* of ¥68 billion for the current fiscal year.

hōsentsumitorihiritsu 邦船積取比率 ratio of cargo carried by Japanese flag ships; percentage of Japa-

hōshanōryūshutsu 放射能流出 radiation exposure

hōshiki 方式 modality ¶ the specific *modalities* for a new facility

hōshin 方針 principle ¶ the most important guiding *principle* in compiling this budget // the broad *principles* guiding the fiscal policy // the *principles* underlying our policy actions // to make it its *principle* to...

hoshō 保証 guarantee; security; guaranty; suretyship; assurance; warranty ¶ to require a cash margin as *security* for the performance of the contract // the specific assets pledged as *security* for a bond issue // official *assurances* to depositors that their deposits are safe 連帯保証 joint (and several) liability on guarantee

hoshō 補償 compensation; indemnification reparation 輸出補償 export indemnity

hōshō 報奨 compensation; reward; incentive; bonus; bounty ¶ in *compensation* for // as a *reward* (for)

hōshō 報償 compensation; consideration; remuneration; reward ¶ in *compensation* (for) // in *consideration* of // in *reward* for services

hoshōbōeki 補償貿易 compensation trade

hōshōbusshi 報奨物資 bonus goods; compensatory goods; incentive goods

hoshōchingin 保証賃金 guaranteed wage

hoshōgaisha 保証会社 surety company

hoshōjō 保証状 letter of guarantee; guaranty; bond of indemnity

hoshōjō 補償状 letter of indemnity

荷物引取補償状 letter of indemnity for withdrawal of the goods

hoshōjōbarai 保証状払い(国債の) payment against bond of indemnity

hoshōjunbi 保証準備 securities for fiduciary (bank note) issue

hoshōjunbitsumitatekin 保証準備積立金 guarantee fund

hoshōkabu 保証株 guaranteed stock

hoshōkashitsuke 保証貸付け cash credit

hoshōkashitsukekin 保証貸付金 loan with third party's guarantee

hoshōkin 保証金 guaranty money; surety money; deposits received

hoshōkin 補償金 indemnity; compensation

hōshōkin 報奨金 cash bonus; cash reward; bounty ¶ a government *bounty* granted on exports, or a *bounty* for export

hōshōkin 報償金 [市] consideration money

hōshōkinseido 報奨金制度 bonus plan

hoshōkogitte 保証小切手 certified check

hoshōnin 保証人 guarantor; guarantee; surety; security; certifier

hōshōryōtei 報奨料定 merit rating

hoshōsaiken 保証債券 guaranteed bond

hoshōsaimu 保証債務 obligations of guarantee; liabilities for guarantees; cautionary obligations

hoshōsaimumikaeri 保証債務見返り customers' liabilities on guarantees

hoshōsaimunohoshō 保証債務の保証 guarantee of guaranteed obligation

hoshōsashiireyūkashōken 保証差入れ有価証券 deposits of securities on contracts

hoshōseichōritsu 保証成長率 warranted rate of growth

hōshōseido 報奨制度 bounty system; compensation system; incentive system

hoshōshihon 保証資本 guaranteed capital

hoshōshōdakudaka 保証承諾高 guarantee arrangement accepted

hoshōshōken 保証証券 guaranty bond

hoshōshūnyū 保証収入 guaranteed income ¶ The recipients of a *guaranteed income* worked fewer hours than families without a *guaranteed income*.

hoshōtesūryō 保証手数料 guarantee commission

hoshōyūshi 補償融資 compensatory financing

hoshu 保守 keeping up; maintenance ¶ to *keep up*, or *maintain*, their premises and equipment

hōshū 報酬 recompense; compensation; consideration; remuneration; reward; honorarium; fee; emoluments; pay; return ¶ in *compensation* for, or in *consideration* of ... // to work for *pay* // to *pay* them for their labor // issuing stock for inadequate *consideration* // to improve skilled labor *remuneration* // *remunerations* for officers // to pay 1,000 dollars in *reward* for services // special quota as a *reward* for export
非金銭的報酬 non-pecuniary reward
金銭的報酬 pecuniary reward

hōshūoyobikyūyo 報酬および給与 emoluments, salaries and allowances

hoshushūzenhi 保守修繕費 repairs

and maintenance expenses

hōshutsu 放出 release

hōshutsubusshi 放出物資 released goods, released commodities

hosokuteki 補足的 complementary ¶ a tool *complementary* to the orthodox control devices // ［参考］→ 補助的

hosokuyūshi 補足融資 supplementary finance

hōsōnizukurikikai 包装・荷造機械 packaging and packing machinery

hosonuno 細布 sheeting

hōsuiki 豊水期 high-water season

hōteidairinin 法定代理人 legal representative

hōteifuyōryō 法定扶養料 legal sustenance allowance

hōteiheika 法定平価 mint par of exchange

hōteijunbi 法定準備 statutory reserve; legal reserve

hōteikajitsu 法定果実 legal fruits

hōteikakaku 法定価格 legal price

hōteikigen 法定期限 legal term

hōteikōkennin 法定後見人 statutory guardian

hōteino 法定の legal; statutory

hōteiriritsu 法定利率 legal rate of interest

hōteirisoku 法定利息 legal interest

hōteishiki 方程式 equation
微分方程式 differential equation
現金残高方程式 cash balance equation
技術方程式 technical equation
関数方程式 functional equation
行動方程式 behavior equation
積分方程式 integral equation
定義方程式 definitional equation
定差方程式 differential equation

hōteishōken 法定証券 legal bond

hōteisōzokunin 法定相続人 heir-at-law

hōteiteisokusū 法定定足数 quorum

hōteitsūka 法定通貨 legal tender ¶ The 500-peso and 1,000-peso notes of the National Bank of Cuba will cease to be *legal tender* and will be demonetized.

hōteitsumitatekin 法定積立金 legal reserve

hōteiyokinjunbiritsu 法定預金準備率 required reserve ratio against deposits

hōteiyūyo 法定猶予 legal delay; days of grace

hōteizeiritsu 法定税率 statutory tariff

hōtekikachikijun 法的価値基準 legal standard (of value)

hōtekikisei 法的規制 mandatory control

hōwa 飽和 saturation ¶ For quite a range of other durables the expansion in sales has been such that a near-*saturation* point has been reached. // Domestic demand for coal is much nearer *saturation* then demand for oil. // A transient *saturation* of the market for durables coincided with a declining investment propensity. // a *saturated* home market for electrical appliances

hōwasuijun 飽和水準 saturation level

hōwaten 飽和点 saturation point

hoyūryō 保有量 reserve ¶ Mexico's natural gas *reserves* are huge.

hoyūdaka 保有高 holding ¶ a decline of SDR 132 million *holdings* in the SDR holdings of industrial countries // a net gain of $16 million in exchange reserve *holdings* by the central bank // regulations concerning equity *holdings* in foreign countries // limits on foreign investors' *holdings* of stocks

hoyūkatsudō 保有活動 holding activity

hoyūkinhenkyaku 保有金返却 restitution ¶ One sixth of the Fund's gold holdings would be *restituted* at the old official price to all Fund members.

hoyūshōken 保有証券 securities holdings; investment portfolio

hoyūson'eki 保有損益 holding gains and losses

hozei 保税 bond

hozeichiiki 保税地域 bonded area

hozeichiikienohannyū 保税地域への搬入 transportation into a bonded area

hozeikaisōnegai 保税回送願い application for transportation in bond

hozeikamotsu 保税貨物 goods in bond; bonded goods

hozeikamotsuunsōnin 保税貨物運送人 licensed truckman

hozeikōjō 保税工場 bonded factory; bonded manufacturing warehouse

hozeinaimihontoridashinegai 保税内見本取出し願い application for specially opening bonded warehouse

hozeinyūkoryō 保税入庫料 bond fee

hozeisōko 保税倉庫 bonded warehouse; bonded store

仮設保税倉庫 temporary bonded warehouse

hozeisōkoazukarishōken 保税倉庫預り証券 bonded warehouse warrant

hozeisōkoutsushinegai 保税倉庫移し願い application for transfer in bond

hozeisōkowatashi 保税倉庫渡し ex bond warehouse; in bond

hozeitokubetsukaikannegai 保税特別開関願い application for specially opening the bonded warehouse

hozeiuwaya 保税上屋 bonded shed

hozeiyushutsumenjō 保税輸出免状 bond note

hozōseikō 保蔵性向 propensity to hoard

hyakkaten 百貨店 department store セルフ・サービス百貨店 self-service department store; SSDS

hyakkatenkyōkai 百貨店協会 association of department stores

hyakkaten'uriagedaka 百貨店売上高 sales of department stores; all department store sales

hyakuenhakudōka 100円白銅貨 100 yen cupro-nickel coin

hyōban 評判 reputation ¶ firms of well-established *reputation* // high *reputation* for business sagacity

hyōhon 標本 sample; specimen ¶ They are not a broad enough *sample* to be representative of the stock market.

hyōhonbunpu 標本分布 sampling distribution

hyōhonchōsahō 標本調査法 sampling method; sampling survey method

hyōhonchūshutsu 標本抽出 sampling ¶ →抽出

hyōhongosa 標本誤差 sampling error

hyōji 表示 denomination; terms; expression; statement ¶ bank notes of higher *denominations* // yen-*denominated* bonds // notes *denominated* in the U.S. dollar // prices in dollar *terms* // the value in *terms* of

U.S. dollars // a loan *expressed* in yen // payment media *stated* in foreign money (=currencies)

悪意不実表示 fraudulent misrepresentation

不実表示 misrepresentation

善意不実表示 innocent misrepresentation

hyōjiseido 表示制度 certification mark system

hyōjun 標準 standard ¶ Italy's inflation is still unacceptably high by European *standards*. // to guarantee any producer a market at a price that is virtually *standard* for all // a substantial share even by spendthrift European *standards*

hyōjunbasukettohōshiki 標準バスケット方式 [外] standard basket; method of valuation of the SDR based on a basket of currencies

hyōjundō 標準銅 standard copper

hyōjundoryōkō 標準度量衡 standard weights or measures

hyōjungaikessaihōhō 標準外決済方法 non-standard method of settlement

hyōjungin 標準銀 standard silver

hyōjunhensa 標準偏差 standard deviation

hyōjunji 標準時 standard time; Greenwich mean Time; G.M.T.

hyōjunkabu 標準株 standard stocks; barometer stocks

hyōjunkakaku 標準価格 standard price; benchmark price

hyōjunkakakumai 標準価格米 standard price rice

hyōjunkakakuseido 標準価格制度 standard price system

hyōjunkeieikanrihōshiki 標準経営管理方式 management operating system; MOS

hyōjunkeiyaku 標準契約 standard contract

hyōjunkessaihōhō 標準決済方法 standard method of settlement

hyōjunkikaku 標準規格 standard specification

hyōjunkin 標準金 standard gold

hyōjunkinri 標準金利 standard money rate; benchmark rate

hyōjunkō 標準鋼 standard steel

hyōjunmihon 標準見本 standard sample

hyōjunnedan 標準値段 standard price

hyōjunrōdōjikan 標準労働時間 standard working hours

hyōjunryōritsu 標準料率 standard rate

hyōjunsagyōryō 標準作業量 standard work volume

hyōjunseikatsuhi 標準生活費 standard living cost; standard cost of living; average cost of living

hyōjun'yojō 標準余剰 standard rate of interest

hyōka 評価 assessment; appraisal; (e)valuation; rating ¶ a general *assessment* of the economy in 1976 // to provide a qualitative *assessment* of the strengths and weaknesses of the existing... // detailed *assessments* of the socioeconomic costs and benefits of different approaches to health care // an overpessimistic *appraisal* of the external accounts // a proper *evaluation* of the true value of the dollar // the more optimistic *appraisals* of prospects of the coming year // wages on job *evaluation* // U.S. dollar reserves at market-related *valuations* // Any *evaluation* of the international outlook for the dollar can best begin with an *assessment* of

the inflationary problem at home. // a slide in the dollar's external *valuation* // the comparatively fovorable *assessment* of future prospects for the world economy emerging at the IMF-World Bank Annual Meeting // The more information would be desirable to permit a more thorough *assessment* of borrowers' condition. // the regular monthly *assessment* of the economic situation // the relationship between ex ante project *appraisal* and ex post project *evaluation* // a somewhat less optimistic *appreciation* of stocks of finished goods by businessmen // the public's poor *rating* of Carter's work on energy problems

帳簿評価 book evaluation

技術評価 technology assessment

法定評価 legal valuation

過大評価 overvaluation ¶ The Swiss franc was *overvalued* vis-à-vis by DM.

環境影響評価 environmental impact assessment

環境評価 environmental assessment

過少評価 undervaluation ¶ The DM was *undervalued* vis-à-vis the SF.

課税価格評価 appraisal of dutiable value

資産評価 valuation of assets

資材評価 valuation of goods

損害評価 valuation of damage

財産評価 property valuation

hyōkaeki 評価益 profit accrued from valuation; appraisal profit; appraisal surplus

hyōkagae 評価替え revaluation; reassessment; reappraisal

hyōkagaku 評価額 assessed amount

(=value); assessment; appraised amount; amount assessed; amount appraised ¶ The *assessment* levied by the Deposit Insurance Corporation for this insurance is $^1/_{12}$ of 1% per aunum on total deposits.

hyōkakakaku 評価価格 estimated value; appraised value

hyōkakamoku 評価科目 valuation items

hyōkakanjō 評価勘定 valuation accounts

hyōkakijun 評価基準 standard of appraisal; appraisal standard; criterion of assessment; assessment criterion

hyōkanin 評価人 appraiser; as-

sessor

hyōkason 評価損 loss resulted from valuation; appraisal loss

hyōkendairi 表見代理 apparent agency

hyōmenka 表面化 surfacing; manifestation; coming to the fore; becoming perceptible ¶ Tension inherent in the situation is likely to *manifest* itself.

hyōmenkinri 表面金利 nominal interest rate; coupon rate

hyōmennoitandakahei 表面の傷んだ貨幣 defaced coin

hyomenriritsu 表面利率 nominal interest rate; coupon rate

hyōryō 秤量 weighing

I

IMF hachijōkoku IMF 8 条国 Article VIII nation of the IMF ¶ Denmark is the twenty-ninth member of the Fund to assume *Article VIII* status. // The number of countries that have accepted the obligations of *Article VIII* of the Fund Agreement increased to 35 with the addition of Ecuador.

IMF kokusaishūshitōkei IMF 国際収支統計 balance of payments statistics based on the IMF standard; balance-of-payments statistics by IMF formula

IMF kyōtei IMF 協定 Articles of Agreement of the International Monetary Fund; IMF Agreement

IMI nijukkakokuiinkai IMF 20カ国委員令 IMF's Committee of Twenty; C-20

IMF taisei IMF 体制 International Monetary Fund structure; IMF system; IMF regime ¶ the monetary system under the *IMF regime*

IMF tokubetsuhikidashiken IMF 特別引出権 → 特別引出権

ībunkīru イーブン・キール even keel ¶ to put the economy on an *even keel* // policy on an *even keel*

ībunkīruseisaku イーブン・キール政策 [米] "even keel" policy ¶ No change in reserve percentages is to become effective in the *"even keel"* period. // Federal Reserve *"even keel" policy* presents a twofold problem for overall monetary policy. // The economy has moved along on an *"even keel"* during the summer months.

ichi 市 market; fair ¶ An agri-

cultural *fair* is opened (=held). // →
市場

見本市　trade fair

闇市　black market; black mart

野菜市　vegetable market; market
for vegetables

ichibi　市日　market day

ichibu　一部　part; portion; section

ichibuhikiuke　一部引受け　partial
acceptance

ichibuhoken　一部保険　under-insurance

ichibuhyōketsu　一部評決　partial
verdict

ichibuitaku　一部委託　partial abandonment

ichibujōto　一部譲渡　partial assignment

ichibujunbihakkōsei　一部準備発行
制　partial reserve system

ichibushiharai　一部支払い　partial
payment

ichibutsuikkanohōsoku　一物一価の
法則　law of indifference (of price)

ichibutsumidashi　一部積出し　partial shipment

ichibuuragaki　一部裏書　partial endorsement

ichibuwariate　一部割当　partial allotment

ichibuyōsen　一部用船　part cargo
charter

ichidandaka　一段高　further rise;
jump in the uptrend

ichien'yokin　1円預金　1-yen deposit ¶ the *"¥1 deposit"* drive
designed to disrupt bank operations

ichijienerugī　一次エネルギー　primary energies

ichijiharaikomi　一時払込み　lump
sum payment; payment in lump
sum

ichijihenkan　一次変換　linear
transformation

ichijikaiko　一時解雇　temporary
release from work; temporary discharge; temporary dismissal; lay-off
¶ →レイオフ制

ichijikariirekin　一時借入金　temporary borrowing

ichijikashitsuke　一時貸付　temporary lending; ways and means
advance

ichijikikoku　一時帰国　travel to
mother country for temporary visit

ichijikikyū　一時帰休　lay-off; part-
pay work furlough ¶ employees on
part-pay furloughs // employees who
are *laid off* // →レイオフ制

ichijisanpin　一次産品　primary
commodity; primary product

ichijisanpinsōgōkeikaku　一次産品
総合計画　integrated program for
primary commodities

ichijiseisan　一次生産　primary production

ichijishotoku　一時所得　occasional
income

ichijitatekae　一時立替　temporary
advance

ichijiteki　一時的　transitory; transient; short-lived; temporary; passing; impermanent ¶ to be due to
transient factors, not reflecting more
basic economic factors // a *short-
lived, passing* boom // only *temporary, impermanent* stabilization

ichijitekihantō　一時的反騰　short-
lived rally; temporary rally; brief
rally ¶ Following a *short-lived rally*,
the franc leveled off against other
European currencies.

ichijitekihendōsōbasei　一時的変動
相場制　system of temporary floating exchange rates

ichijitekijunbishisan 一次的準備資
産　primary reserve

ichijitekishudan 一時的手段　stop-
gap; palliative ¶ Another conve-
nient *palliative* is to shift the burden
on to the State.

ichijitekitsunagi 一時的つなぎ　stop-
gap; makeshift ¶ steps taken as
stopgap measures // purely temporary *makeshift*

ichijunmoyō 一巡模様　[市] lull ¶
After the June-July *lull* the expansion has resumed.

ichimaiiwa 一枚岩　monolith ¶
Activity of some conglomerates
makes them look not *monolith*. //
the *monolithic* Japan Inc.

ichinenmonowaribikisai 一年もの
割引債　one-year discount debenture

ichiranbarai 一覧払い　payable at
sight (＝on demand) ¶ to *pay* a draft
at sight (＝*on demand*)

ichiranbaraitegata 一覧払手形
sight bill; demand bill (＝draft)

ichiranbaraitegatakaisōba 一覧払
手形買相場　at sight buying rate

ichiranbaraitegatashin'yōjō 一覧
手形信用状　sight L/C

**ichiranbaraiyunyūtegatakessaisō-
ba** 一覧払輸入手形決済相場　ac-
ceptance rate

ichiranbraikawase 一覧払為替
sight bill; demand draft

ichirango～nichibarai 一覧後～日
払い　～days after sight ¶ at nine-
ty *days'* (＝three months') *sight* // payable ninety *days after sight*

ichirangoteiikibaraitegata 一覧後
定期払手形　bill payable at sight
after a fixed period

ichiryū 一流　first class; first rate;
top grade leading; top-notch ¶ rates

for *top-grade* commercial paper

**ichiryūginkōhikiuketegatawaribi-
kiritsu** 一流銀行引受手形割引率
[米] bankers acceptance rate (＝BA
rate)

ichiryūkabu 一流株　leader; blue
chip

ichiryūkigyōmukekashidashikinri
一流企業向貸出金利　[米] prime
(loan) rate

ichiryūmēkā 一流メーカー　first
class manufacturer; first class producer

ichiryūshasai 一流社債　prime corporate bond

ichiryūshōken 一流証券　gilt-edged
security

ichiryūshōnin 一流商人　leading
merchant

ichiryūtegata 一流手形　gilt-edged
bill; prime bill; sound bill

idō 移動　movement; shift ¶ large
and abrupt *movements* of deposits //
to bring about free *movement*
throughout the common market for
capital, goods, and persons // a
massive *movement* of short-term
funds out of Mexico // to encourage
intersectoral labor *shifts*

idōheikin 移動平均　moving average ¶ on the three month *moving
average*

idōheikingenkahō 移動平均原価法
moving average cost method

idōheikinhō 移動平均法　moving
average method

idōheikinsen 移動平均線　moving
average

idōkaoku 移動家屋　mobile home

idōsei 移動性　mobility
　労働力の移動性　mobility of labor;
　　labor mobility
　生産要素の移動性　mobility of fac-

tors

資本の移動性　mobility of capital

ifu 委付　abandonment ¶ to *abandon* a cargo

ifujōkō 委付条項　abandonment clause

ifutsūchi 委付通知　notice of abandonment

igainorijun 意外の利潤　windfall profit ¶ to reap a *windfall profit* from deflation

igainoritoku 意外の利得　windfall (gain; profit) ¶ to stand to collect a *windfall* by selling shares at a profit // the *windfall* rise in income of the export sector caused by devaluation // Any excess profits thus earned are treated as *windfall gains.* // profits in the nature of a *windfall profit* brought by inflation

igainosonshitsu 意外の損失　windfall lose

igimōshitate 異議申立て　raising of an objection

ihankōi 違反行為　act on contravention; violation ¶ to be charged with padding accounts in *violation* of the securities transaction law

iine 言い値　asked price; seller's price

iji 維持　maintenance; support; sustenance; upkeep ¶ for the *maintenance* of price stability // to *upkeep* expenses // to *support* the stable yen // Equilibrium was *sustained* at any rate.

ijihi 維持費　cost of maintenance; upkeep (=maintenance) expense; maintenance cost ¶ Heating and other *maintenance costs* in the South are modest. // The *cost of maintaining* a high standard of living for a family of four in the New York is

33% higher than in Nashville.

ijōdaka 異常高 [市] unusual advance; abnormally high price

ijūrōdōsha 移住労働者　expatriate worker; migrant worker

ikigaibōeki 域外貿易　off-shore trade

ikigaichōtatsu 域外調達　off-shore purchase; off-shore procurement

ikigaitorihiki 域外取引　off-shore transaction

ikinaibōeki 域内貿易　intra-trade within the area

ikinonagai 息の長い　long-standing; long-enduring; long-term on a lasting (=durable) basis ¶ to maintain the *long-standing* prosperity // to enjoy a *long-enduring* expansion // *long-term* endeavors // exchange rate policy co-ordinated on a *lasting basis* // economic expansion on a *durable basis* // [参考] the necessary condition for a steady continuation of the recovery

ikioi 勢い　momentum ¶ to brake the *momentum* that pushed prices up by 9.25% last year

ikkanmēkā 一貫メーカー　through-process manufacturer

ikkansagyō 一貫作業　through process; continuous operation; integrated work

ikkanseinonaitōkeiryō 一貫性のない統計量　inconsistent statistic

ikkasei 一過性　passing; temporary; short-lived ¶ [参考] Some of the slowdown is due to soon-to-be-reversed seasonal factors.

ikkodatejūtaku 一戸建て住宅　site-built single-family homes (=house; housing unit); single-family houses built on lots

ikkōittei 一高一低　wavering; erratic; variable; irregular; unsettled; hoverig ¶ The market was *irregular* the rest of the day. // Gold shares were *erratic* but mainly lower on balance. // The international oils moved up after some *wavering*. // The industrial index is *hovering* near the 1,000 mark.

ikō 移行 transition; shift ¶ the year of *transition* from contraction to recovery // a drastic *shift* in policy from a restrictive to easy stance // to achieve or smooth *transition* from cyclical recovery to long-run expansion // The smooth *transition* to a moderate stimulative monetary posture was accomplished. // The labor scene is witnessing a gradual step-by-step *transition* from an unsustainable to a much more sustainable situation. // a *shift* in the policy posture from expansionary to restrictive one // a noticeable *shift* in business opinions from all-out optimism to cautious optimism // to allow a dollar for dollar *shift* of riching farm prices to the final // The three-year base period was *shifted* toward to 1973-74. // the achievement of a smooth *transition* from cyclical recovery to longer-run expansion // a *shift* of labor from low-wage to high-wage occupations // ［参考］ Most funds flowing out of the dollar found their way to the yen.

ikō 意向 ［市］ interest
買い意向 buying interest
下げ意向 selling interest

ikōjō 意向状 letter of intent

imiaruteiri 意味ある定埋 meaningful theorem

iminrōdōryoku 移民労働力 mi-

grant labor; expatriate manpower ¶ reliance on foreign migrant labor // the *expatriate manpower* requirements of the country // the volume of *migrant labor* working in this country

iminrōdōsha 移民労働者 expatriate worker; migrant laborer ¶ *Migrant workers* outnumber the indigenous labor force by large margins. // ［参考］ The major part of this foreign labor worked in unskilled office and manual jobs.

imishakudo 意味尺度 semantic differential

imonoyōsentetu 鋳物用銑鉄 foundry iron; foundry pig iron

indekusēshon インデクセーション indexation

infesshon インフェッション infession; inflationary recession

infuragunēshon インフラグネーション inflagnation; stagflation

infureatsuryoku インフレ圧力 inflationary force; inflationary pressure ¶ *Inflationary forces* were being brought under control. // The *inflationary pressures* in Sweden, particularly those on the labor market, have receded somewhat this year. // to reduce fiscal *inflationary pressures* // to release new *inflationary pressures*

infurefuankan インフレ不安感 inflationary jitter

infuregekka インフレ激化 aggravation of the inflationary trend; tailspinning of the inflationary spiral

infuregyappu インフレ・ギャップ inflationary gap

infurehejji インフレ・ヘッジ hedge against inflation; protection against inflation; inflationary hedge ¶ A house is the best *hedge against inflation.*

infurehejjidōki インフレ・ヘッジ動機 inflation hedging motive

infurekakusa インフレ格差 inflation differential; difference in inflation ¶ the existing *inflation differentials* between countries

infurekanofukyō インフレ下の不況 inflationary recession; infession

infurekanshikikan インフレ監視機関 inflation watching agency

infurekeihō インフレ警報 inflation alert

infurekeikō インフレ傾向 inflationary trend (tendency)

infurekitai インフレ期待 inflationary expectations ¶ Higher interest rates are a reflection of higher *inflationary expectations.* // to risk relaunching *inflationary expectations* // *Inflationary expectations* dominated the thinking of businessmen. // a diminution of *inflationary expectations* associated with the showing in the advance of prices // *Inflationary expectations* have not yet been entirely dispelled. // *Inflationary expectations* can be reduced. // The price effects of entrenched *inflationary expectations* pushed the inflation rate higher. // the persistence of deeply embedded *inflationary expectations* // *Expectations of inflation* became widespread.

infurekokufuku インフレ克服 defeat of inflation; beating inflation; alleviate (=arrest; check; combat; contain; control; curb; cure; fight; put down; reduce; quell; tackle; tame; or to give an end to) inflation ¶ In the *defeat of inflation* mone-

tary policy has an essential role to play. // *Beating inflation* is the only way to a healthier situation. // *Inflation* was *beaten.* // ［参考］The inflationary flare-up of 1979-80 seems finally to be getting under control.

infurekyoyōdo インフレ許容度 degree of tolerance of inflation

infuremiainochin'age インフレ見合いの賃上げ inflation-compensating pay raise

infuremondai インフレ問題 inflation problem

infuremūdo インフレ・ムード inflationary mood ¶ to hold down the *inflationary mood*

infurenakihan'ei "インフレなき繁栄" "full prosperity without inflation" (by Nixon)

infurenakikaifuku インフレなき回復 recovery without inflation ¶ The real choice is between *recovery without inflation* and no recovery at all. // a choice between *recovery* with or *without inflation*

infurenakiseichō インフレなき成長 non-inflationary growth; growth without inflation ¶ to promote the maximum degree of *non-inflationary growth* or sound *inflation-free growth*

infurenenritsu インフレ年率 annual inflation rate; annual rate of inflation

infurenobyōgen インフレの病源 virus of inflation

infurenochinsei インフレの鎮静 abatement of inflation; lessening of inflation; subsidence of rampant inflation ¶ *Inflation* has now *subsided.*

infurenodenpa インフレの伝播 spread of inflation; transmission of inflation

infurenogen'in インフレの原因
cause of inflation

infurenokonzetsu インフレの根絶
eradication of inflation

infurenomitōshi インフレの見通し
inflation outlook

infurenosainen インフレの再燃 rekindling of inflation; reignition of
inflation; recurrence of inflation;
another outburst of inflation; new
wave (=bout) of inflation; resurgence of inflation; releasing of new
inflationary pressures; resumption of
inflation; sparking off a new round
of inflation ¶ to minimize the
chances of *rekindling inflationary
fires* // We will not accept *another
outburst of inflation.* // to avoid a
new wave of inflation // A *resurgence
of inflation* can be avoided. // to run
a serious risk of *releasing new
inflationary pressures* // a *resumption
of* the *inflationary* trend // The creation of new money sparked off a
new bout of inflation. // to release a
new wave of inflation

infurenoshinkō インフレ進行 acceleration of inflation

infurenoshūsoku インフレの収束
solution of inflation; putting an end
to inflation; ceasing inflation, disinflation; ending (=elimination; stemming) inflation ¶ The hope of *ending inflation* was destroyed. //
Monetary policy substantially
contributed to the *elimination of
inflation.* // the primary objective of
stemming inflation

infurenoyokusei インフレの抑制
containing (=curbing; checking
inflation; reduction of inflation) ¶
Monetary policy made a consider-

able contribution to the *containment
of inflation.* // to take the necesssry
measures to *contain inflation* early
enough // to aim at the progressive
reduction of inflation

infurerieki インフレ利益 inflation
profit; inflationary gains ¶ A source
of *inflationary gains* is the debtor's
gain from the inflation-eroded value
of currency. // ［参考］ profits more
in the nature of a windfall profit
brought by inflation

infureritsu インフレ率 inflation
rate; rate of inflation ¶ The *rate of
inflation* had been going down. //
The *inflation rate* in 1973 worked out
at 6.8 per cent. // Switzerland had an
inflation rate of 10% as it had on
average in 1974. // The cheapening
of the greenback may add 3/4% to
this year's U.S. *inflation rate.* // to
bring about an enduring reduction in
the *rate of inflation* // The decline in
the dollar added 1% to the U.S.
inflation rate. // These figures under-
state the true *inflation rate.* // The
underlying *rate of inflation* was
lower than it has turned out to be. //
to tug down to *inflation rate* // There
was a further easing of *inflation
rates* in the U.S. // to hold the overall
inflation rate for the year between 5
and 6 percent // ［参考］ a marked
acceleration of inflationary tension // Inflation is running at more
than a 1 percent monthly clip. //
Inflation can be geared down gradually.

infureshinri インフレ心理 inflationary mentality; inflationary psychology; inflationary sentiment;
inflationary expectation; apprehension over inflation ¶ evidence of

inflationary psychology avound the world // further evidence of a diminution of *inflationary psychology* around the world // the more extreme manifestations of the *inflationary psychology* that gripped Canada was calm. // *Inflation psychology* was whetted by doubts as to fiscal policy. // to prevent the re-emergence of an *inflationary mentality*. // A deep-seated *inflationary mentality* took years to eradicate. // an opportunity to make a clear break in the *inflationary psychology* habits in Britain, Italy, etc.

infurēshon インフレーション infla-tion ¶ The third quarter was a period of substantial *inflation*. // The economy is undergoing a sub-stantial degree of *inflation*. // In many countries *inflation* has gather-ed momentum. // *Inflation* is coming under control. // The specter of a reignited 1973-74-type *inflation* is beginning to worry many members of the Association. // to spark off a new round of *inflation* // the degree to which *inflation* has become im-bedded in the U.S. economy // *Inflation* returned to double figures. // Countries are undergoing rapid *inflation* at such varying rates. // an unrealistic exchange rate, a threat of *inflation* for other countries // to curb *inflation*, which is getting out of control // *Inflation* measured by the cost-of-living index has been halved from 9 to 4.5%. // to hold *inflation* down in single figures // Year-on-year *inflation* fell from 17% to 7%. // *Inflation* was still waiting elsewhere.

悪性インフレ malignant inflation; vicious inflation; virulent inflation; inflation spiral ¶ *Inflation* has become ever more *virulent*. // The floating of the currency ex-acerbated *spiraling inflation*.

賃金インフレ wage-push inflation

超インフレーション hyperinflation

調整インフレ adjustment inflation; controlled inflation

二桁のインフレ double-digit infla-tion; two-digit inflation; double-figure inflation ¶ *Inflation* hit *double figures*.

激しいインフレ high rate inflation; boiling inflation; rampant infla-tion; raging inflation

半インフレ semi-inflation

異常なインフレ exceptional infla-tion; horrendous inflation

需要インフレ demand-pull infla-tion; demand inflation

開放型インフレ open inflation

隠れたインフレ hidden inflation

軽度のインフレ moderate inflation

広範化したインフレ generalized in-flation

国内インフレ domestic inflation; inflation at home

高(=昂)進するインフレ ever-ac-celerating inflation

コスト・プッシュ・インフレ cost-push inflation; cost inflation

駆走するインフレ galloping infla-tion

狂乱インフレ rampant inflation; raging inflation; snarling inflation

急進(的)インフレ galloping infla-tion

慢性的インフレ chronic inflation

野放しのインフレ unbridled infla-tion; runaway inflation

利潤インフレ profit inflation

世界(的)インフレ world inflation;

worldwide inflation; global inflation

石油インフレ　oil(-induced) inflation

戦時インフレ　wartime inflation

潜在的インフレ　potential inflation

紙幣インフレ　paper money inflation

しのびよるインフレ　creeping inflation

真正インフレ　true inflation

信用インフレ　credit inflation

消費インフレ　consumption inflation

商品インフレ　commodity inflation

天井知らずのインフレ　sky's-the-limit inflation; runaway inflation

抑圧的インフレ　repressive inflation; depressed inflation

絶対的インフレ　absolute inflation

infureshūseikaikei インフレ修正会計　accounting for inflation

infureshūsokusaku インフレ収束策　policy actions to solve inflation; policy measures to overcome inflation

infuretaisaku インフレ対策　anti-inflation(ary) policy; counter-inflation(ary) measure; step to curb inflation; measure to combat inflation; policy measure to fight against inflation

共通インフレ対策　unified counter-measures against inflation; concerted anti-inflationary measures

infureteate インフレ手当　anti-inflation allowance

infuretofukyōnoitabasami インフレと不況の板ばさみ　dilemma between inflation and recession; combination of inflation and recession

infuretonotatakai インフレとの闘い　battle against inflation; war on inflation; fight against inflation; com-

bating inflation; attack (=war) on inflation ¶ to switch tactics in the *attack on inflation.* // *Attacking inflation* through higher interest rates worked slowly and took persistence and time to wring inflation out. // the administration's three-pronged *attack on inflation* — high interest rates, wage-price guidelines and budget cuts // policies in *waging* this *war on inflation*

infureyōin インフレ要因　inflation-inspiring factor

ingajunkanbunseki 因果循環分析　recursive analysis

ingajunkanteishiki 因果循環定式　recursive formula

ingakankei 因果関係　causality; causal relationship (=connection; sequence) ¶ *Causality* is unidirectional from money to prices. // Unidirectional *causality* runs from nominal incomes to money. // In the high ranges of a money growth *causality* runs from money to real growth.

ingaritsu 因果律　law of causality

inin 委任　trust; commission; mandate; delegation; authorization; commitment ¶ a formal *mandate* for the country's attempt at a $300 Euroloan // Thailand has awarded the *mandate* for a 200 million U.S. dollar loan to a group of six banks. // to win a *mandate* from the bank to arrange a short-term offshore note issue

ininjō 委任状　power (=letter) of attorney; procuration; proxy; mandate form

株式譲渡委任状　stock-power

ininseido 委任制度　mandate system

ininsha 委任者 mandator

inpakutorōn インパクト・ローン impact loan; untied loan

inpakutorōntoriire インパクト・ローン取入れ intake (=taking-in) of the private untied loan

inrandodepo インランド・デポ inland depot

insaidārepōto インサイダー・レポート insider report

insutantoshokuhin インスタント食品 ready-to-serve foods

intābankutorihiki インターバンク取引 [外]inter-bank exchange dealings

intaizōbusshi 隠退蔵物資 concealed and hoarded goods

interiashōhin インテリア商品 interior goods

intoku 隠匿 hoard; conceal; cache ¶ a *cache* of sugar under tatami // a *cache* of gold // *cached* food // sugar in a *cache*

inzūkensa 員数検査 numerical examination

ippanchingin 一般賃金 prevailing wage ¶ *prevailing wages,* by industry and occupation

ippanjigyōhōjin 一般事業法人 ordinary industrial corporation

ippanjōkō 一般条項 entire understanding; integration

ippankaikei 一般会計 General Account ¶ The Treasury accounts with the public registered a net receipt of ¥1,227 billion on the *general account.*

ippankanjō 一般勘定 [外] General Account (of SDRs)

ippankanrihi 一般管理費 (general) administrative expenses; administrative costs

ippankariiretorikime 一般借入取決

General Agreements to Borrow; GAB

ippankashitsuke 一般貸付 ordinary loan

ippankeihihiritsu 一般経費比率 ratio of total expenses to current income

ippankikai 一般機械 non-electric(al) machinery

ippankinkōriron 一般均衡理論 general equilibrium theory

ippankin'yūkikan 一般金融機関 ordinary financial institution

ippankyōsho 一般教書 （米大統領）State of the Union Message (of the President)

ippannyūsatsu 一般入札 public bid

ippanryūdōseikōka 一般流動性効果 general liquidity effect

ippanseifufusairishi 一般政府負債利子 interest on the general government debt

ippanseifukanjō 一般政府勘定 general government account

ippansenbikikogitte 一般線引小切手 general crossed check

ippanshihonzai 一般資本財 capital goods excluding transport equipment

ippantaishū 一般大衆 general public

ippantegata 一般手形 ordinary bill

ippantokkeikanzei 一般特恵関税 general prefence duties

ippantsūkaseiyokin 一般通貨性預金 private monetary deposits

ippan'yokintaisakujunbi 一般預金対策準備 reserve available to support private nonbank deposits; R.P.D.

ippanzaisei 一般財政 general treasury funds

ipponka 一本化 unification ¶ *unification* of interest rates, or to unify (the rates of interest)

ippuku 一服 pause; lull ¶ a *pause* in economic activity

ireru 入れる [市] stimulated by; buoyed by; influenced by; reflecting; taking advantage of; as news came of... ¶ The market backed away moderately *as news came of* higher interest rates. // *Buoyed by* this news, the franc moved up sharply. // [参考] The dollar has peaked foremost to news of...

iryōshoku 医療食 medical foods

ishikettei 意思決定 decision making ¶ capital accumulation with decentralized *decision making* // The Board has autonomy in its day-to-day *decision making*. // Unions demand for greater involvement in corporate *decision-making*. // the centralization of *decision-making* in many spheres of social activity // The president's overly personalized *decision-making*. // to broaden senior management participation in the *decisionmaking* process // to build a cohesive *decisionmaking* team at the top management level // [参考] clean and unambiguous management options

ishiketteikikan 意思決定機関 decision-making machinery; decision-making organ

ishiki 意識 consciousness; sensitivity ¶ to raise the *consciousness* of businessmen to the sales and potential profits // the interest rate *sensitivity* of borrowers

ishitsusei 異質性 heterogeneity

ishitsutekikyōsō 異質的競争 heteropoly; heterogeneous competition

ishōken 意匠権 design right

ishokujū 衣食住 food, shelter and clothing; food, clothes and shelter

ishutsu 移出 export to an overseas territory

isogigai 急ぎ買い frenzied buying

isseidaka 一斉高 all-round advance; all-round rise; general rise

isseinokaike 一斉の買気 all-round buying; unanimous buying

isseiyasu 一斉安 all-round fall; all-round decline; general slump

isshin'ittai 一進一退 [市](bobbing) up and down; indecisive fluctuation ¶ to enter a phase of *indecisive fluctuations* // Stock, bond and commodity prices *bobbed up and down* in no clear pattern.

isuwari 居据り [市] stationary; static

itaku 委託 trust; charge; commission; delegation; consignment; mandate

itakubaibai 委託売買 sale on consignment; selling on a consignment basis

itakubaibaigyōmu 委託売買業務 [市] business of broker; brokerage business; agency transaction

itakuhanbai 委託販売 consignment sale; sale on commission

itakuhanbaibōeki 委託販売貿易 consignment deal

itakuhanbaikeiyaku 委託販売契約 consignment sale contract

itakuhanbaimishūnyūkin 委託販売未収入金 [会] account due on consignments-out

itakuhanbaisekisōhin 委託販売積送品 consignment

itakuhikiukenin 委託引受人 trustee; consignee

itakuhin 委託品 consignment goods;

venture

制限委託品 consignment with limit

itakuhin'okurijō 委託品送状 consignment invoice

itakukakōkamotsu 委託加工貨物 processing deal

itakukakōbōekikeiyaku 委託加工貿易契約 processing deal contract

itakukakōkamotsu 委託加工貨物 goods for processing on consignment

itakunin 委託人 trustor; consignor

itakushōkokin 委託証拠金 consignment guarantee money; [市] margin; cash or security guarantee deposit required for trading in stock on margin

itakutesūryō 委託手数料 consignment fee; commission

itakuyunyū 委託輸入 consignment import

itchishihyō 一致指標 coincident indicator; coinciding indicator; coincidence indicator

iten 移転 transfer ¶ a new framework for orderly response *transfers* from the rich to the poor nations // to *transfer* funds directly from the sayer-lender to the borrower-investor

itenkatoku 移転稼得 transfer earnings

iten'osengen 移転汚染源 mobile source of pollution

itenshishutsu 移転支出 transfer payments

itenshotoku 移転所得 transfer income

itenshūshi 移転収支 transfers; transfer payments; transfer account ¶ *Transfers* in the current balance showed a deficit of $44 million. // the surplus on *transfer account*

itentekishishutsu 移転的支出 transfer expenditure

itoshinaizaikotōshi 意図しない在庫投資 unintended inventory investment; unplanned inventory investment

itoshitazaikotōshi 意図した在庫投資 intended inventory investment; planned inventory investment

ittehanbai 一手販売 sole agency; exclusive agency; sole agent ¶ contract for *sole agency* // to accept the *sole agency* of a U.S. company in Japan

ittehanbaiken 一手販売権 franchise (rights)

ittehanbaiten 一手販売店 sole agent ¶ a *sole agent* in Japan of a company for the sale of books published by that company

iyakenage 嫌気投げ [市] discouraged sale; stoploss selling; selling by tired longs

iyakenuke 嫌気抜け [市] disappointment selling

iyakeshite 嫌気して on negative reaction to...; discouraged by...

iyakuhinmatawanōyaku 医薬品または農薬 (動物医薬品にかかわるものを含む) drugs or agricultural chemicals (including quasi-drugs for animals)

iyakukin 違約金 penalty; forfeit

iyoku 意欲 motivation; willingness; intension ¶ to have an important effect on savings *motivation* in an economy // to affect entrepreneurial *motivation* as well as the aggregate *motivation* of workers // business *willingness* to invest, or business investment *intentions*

企業投資意欲 business investment intention

個人消費意欲 personal spending intention

izō 遺贈 bequest

izokukokkosaiken 遺族国庫債券 War-bereaved Family Treasury Bond

izon 依存 reliance; dependence ¶ *reliance* of business upon outside financial sources // rate of *reliance* on bond issues of budget revenues // The Netherlands has an export *dependency* second only to that of Luxenburg. // the country's *dependence* on imports

izonritsu 依存率 rate of dependence ¶ the high *rate of dependence* of budget revenues on government bond issues

J

J kābu J カーブ J-curve ¶ A similar *J-curve* phenomenon may occur in capital markets, clearly demonstrated.

jakudenkiki 弱電機器 light electrical appliances

jakushōkigyō 弱小企業 twilight industry

jakushōkin'yūkikan 弱小金融機関 fringe banks

japanfando ジャパン・ファンド ［市］ The Japan Fund, Inc.

jiai 地合 market tone; tone; trend undertone; sentiment ¶ The *market tone* eased considerably. // The *market* is in a strong *tone*. // The *tone* of the commodity *market* was a shade firmer. // The *tone* of the money *market* remained steadily firm. // A firm *tone* was evident in the stock *market*. // The *tone* in the *market* was firm. // The *market trend* has been weak. // A bullish *tone* continued in the *market*. // →基調

jiba 地場 local dealers; local merchants; professionals

jidan 示談 composition; compromise ¶ The debtor enters into a *composition* with only one class of creditors, his unsecured creditors. // The *composition* agreement became operative as the required number of creditors agreed. // The debtor submits the terms of a proposed *compromise*.

jidōanteikinō 自動安定機能 built-in flexibility; built-in stabilizer; automatic stabilizer

jidōchōseijōkō 自動調整条項 escalator (clause)

jidōchōseisayō 自動調整作用 function of automatic adjustment; automatic self-correcting mechanism

jidōfurikaeseido 自動振替制度 pre-authorized direct debit system; automatic transfer system

jidōfurikomiseido 自動振込制度 direct credit system for payroll payment

jidōhanbaiki 自動販売機 automatic vending machine

jidōhikidashiken 自動引出権 automatic drawing rights

jidōjinkōzunōkontorōru 自動人工頭脳コントロール automatic cybernetic control

jidōkakōbutsukōkansōchi 自動加工物交換装置 auto-pallet changer

jidōkeizokuteikiyokin 自動継続定期預金 automatic interest compouding time deposit; automatic renewal time deposit

jidōkōgukōkansōchi 自動工具交換装置 automatic tool change; ATC

jidōsakuzuki 自動作図機 ［コン］ plotter

jidōsei 自動性 automaticity ¶ to be consistent with greater *automaticity* of international resource transfers // an element of *automaticity* built into the resource transfer system

jidōshahaigasukiseikijun 自動車排ガス規制基準 standards of regulations for automotive emissions; automobile gas emission control standards; automobile exhaust emission control standard

jidōshōninseido 自動承認制度 automatic approval system

jidōsōko 自動倉庫 automated warehouse

立体自動倉庫 automated rack-type warehouse

jidōyokin'ukeharaiki 自動預金受払機 teller machine

jidōyunyūwariateseido 自動輸入割当制度 automatic import quota system

jieigyō 自営業 family-operated business; independent business

jieigyōsha 自営業者 individual proprietor; selfemployed (person)

jigane 地金 bullion ¶ purchase, sale, and recasting of silver *bullion*

鋳込地金 ingot metal

雑金地金 miscellaneous gold bullion

雑種地金 miscellanecous silver bullion

jiganehōteikakaku 地金法定価格 mint price of bullion

jiganekanjō 地金勘定 bullion account

jiganenakagainin 地金仲買人 bullion broker

jiganesōba 地金相場 bullion quotation

jigohizuketegata 事後日付け手形 post-dated bill

jigokakutokuzaisanjōkō 爾後獲得財産条項 after-acquired property clause

jigyō 事業 undertaking; enterprise; work; task; business; industry

営利事業 profit-making business

非営利事業 non-profit–making business

自営事業 independent enterprise

継続事業 going business

jigyōhi 事業費 working expenses; operating expenses

jigyōjō 事業場 place of business; working place

jigyōka 事業家 businessmen; industrialist; entrepreneur; enterpriser

jigyōkai 事業界 business circles; industrial world; industrial society

jigyōkakuchōtsumitatekin 事業拡張積立金 reserve for business expansion

jigyōkeikaku 事業計画 project ¶ to draw up, initiate, and carry out a new *project* of land development

jigyōkōsai 事業公債 industrial bond

jigyōnendo 事業年度 business year; accounting period

jigyōnushinomochibun 事業主の持分 proprietor's equity

jigyōsai 事業債 industrial debenture; industrial loan; industrial bond

jigyōshikin 事業資金 business funds

jigyōshūnyū 事業収入 business return (=income)

jigyōzei 事業税 business tax

jihatsuteki 自発的 own accord ¶ production cutbacks of their *own accord*

jihatsutekichochiku 自発的貯蓄 voluntary saving

jihatsutckiidō 自発的移動(資本の) autonomous movement (of capital)

jihatsutekikaimodoshi 自発的買戻 し voluntary repurchase

jijitsujōno 事実上の de facto ¶ It was *de facto* downward revaluation, or virtual devaluation of the dollar.

jijitsujōnoheikakiriagekirisage 事実上の平価切上げ・切下げ de facto revaluation and devaluation; virtual revaluation and devaluation ¶ in the event of a *de facto* or de jure *revaluation* of the DM // In Britain, the *de facto devaluation* now amounts to 9 percent against the U.S. dollars.

jijō 事情 circumstances; conditions ¶ the possibility of tumultous *conditions* in world oil markets

jijodoryoku 自助努力 self-help; self-supporting efforts ¶ need for *self-help* on the part of the recipient nations // *self-supporting* efforts of the beneficiary countries // need for more *self-efforts*

jika 自家 owner-occupied home; (privately) owned house; private home. ¶ Private individuals have placed more orders for the building of *owner-occupied homes.*

jika 時価 current price; ruling price market price; fair price

jikahakkō 時価発行 issue at mar-

ket price

jikan'atarikyūyo 時間当り給与 compensation per man-hour; hourly wage ¶ →時間単位給

jikan'atarishūnyū 時間当り収入 hourly earnings ¶ average *hourly earnings* of production workers in manufacturing // The increase in payrolls is attributed to *hourly earnings.*

jikangai 時間外 overtime ¶ *overtime* hours worked, in addition to paid time of the workweek

jikangaichingin 時間外賃金 overtime pay

jikangairōdōjikan 時間外労働時間 overtime workhours; overtime hours worked

jikangaiteateshikyūritsu 時間外手当支給率 overtime premium (rate)

jikanōgyō 自家農業 family farm

jikantan'ikyū 時間単位給 per-hour wage; hourly wage; time (work) wage ¶ average *hourly wages* and annual wages of hourly paid employees

jikantekisaitei 時間的裁定 arbitrage in time

jikanwarichingin 時間割賃金 hourly wage ¶ a decline in real *hourly wages* // →時間単位給

jikashōhi 自家消費 self-consumption

jikashōhyō 自家商標 private brand

jikatenkan 時価転換 conversion at market price

jikatenkanshasai 時価転換社債 debenture convertible at market price

jikeiretsubunseki 時系列分析 time series analysis

jikeiretsudēta 時系列データ time-series data

jikeiretsuhyo 時系列表 time series table

jiki 次期 next term (=period); immediately following period; ensuing term

jikibō 直貿 direct foreign trade by manufacturers

jikiekurikoshi 次期へ繰越し ［会］ carried foward

jikihaitō 次期配当 dividend for the next term

jikiinkumojiyomitorisōchi 磁気インク文字読取装置 ［コン］ magnetic ink character recognition; MICR

jikikādosōchi 磁気カード装置 ［コン］ magnetic card unit

jikikanjō 次期勘定 ensuing account

jikikessan 次期決算 next closing of account

jikikiokusōchi 磁気記憶装置 ［コン］ magnetic core memory

jikikurikoshidaka 次期繰越高 amount carried forward

jikimono 直物 spot ¶ The *spot* U.S. dollar traded for ￥298,000 median.

jikimonokawase 直物為替 spot exchange

jikimonomochidaka 直物持高 actual position; spot position

jikimonosōba 直物相場 spot rate ¶ The *spot rate* (of the sterling) was bid up to the $2.58 level. // The *spot rate* shot up against the dollar to 11 ¾ percent above its par value.

jikimonotorihiki 直物取引 ［外］ spot operation (=dealing; transaction)

jikisakidōrēto 直先同レート flat rate

jikisakigai 直先買 buying (of the U.S. dollar) both for spot and forward delivery

jikisakisōgōmochidaka 直先総合持高 ［外］ overall position

jikisakisupureddo 直先スプレッド ［外］ forward margin; forward scale

jikitēpusōchi 磁気テープ装置 ［コン］ magnetic tape unit; magnetic tape handler

jikitori 直取 payment by cash

jikiurisakigaitorihiki 直売先買取引 ［外］ sale of spot against purchase of forward exchange; swap; changing over; spot-forward transaction

jikiwatashi 直渡し immediate delivery; spot delivery; prompt delivery

jikiwatashinedan 直渡値段 price for immediate delivery

jikizumi 直積み prompt delivery

jikkentekikeikenron 実験的経験論 experimental empiricism

jikkō 実行 (予約の) delivery

jikkōbi 実行日 value date ¶ the *value date* when the account of the customer will be debited or credited

jikkōkakaku 実行価格 exercise price ¶ The *exercise price* for equity warrants attached to this Eurobond is 326 yen per share, representing a 3.16% premium above the 316 yen closing share price in Tokyo today.

jikkōkakaku 実効価格 effective price

jikkōkikan 実行機関 execution organ

jikkōkinri 実効金利 effective interest rate

jikkoōchi 実行落ち (予約の) winding-up

jikkōsōba 実効相場 ［外］ effective rate ¶ a reduction in the guilder's *effective* exchange *rate* // a substantial appreciation of the average *effective* exchange *rate* of the lira

jikkōtorihiki 実効取引 effective sale

jikkōyosan 実行予算 working budget

jikō 時効 prescription ¶ The *prescription* was required, or completed, after interruptions.

消滅時効 extinctive prescription; negative prescription.

jikoatetegata 自己宛手形 self-addressed bill; house bill

jikobaibaigyōmu 自己売買業務 [市] business of dealer; dealing business; principal transaction

jikochōseikikō 自己調整機構 self-regulating mechanism

jikokabu 自己株 treasury stock

jikokin'yū 自己金融 self-financing; internal financing ¶ The scope for *self-fnancing* of business investments was reduced. // The *self-financing* possibilities of enterprises were improved. // Corporate *self-financing* was strengthened.

jikokin'yūhiritsu 自己金融比率 self-finance ratio

jikokisei 自己規制 self-regulation ¶ to agree on the industry's better *self-regulation*, seeing no need for formal government regulation // the effectiveness of the industry's *self-regulatory* efforts // [参考] to allow the industry to police

jikokoyō 自己雇用 self-employment

jikokutsūkadatesōba 自国通貨建相場 rate in home money; indirect rate

jikōnochūdan 時効の中断 interruption of prescription

jikōnokansei 時効の完成 completion of prescription

jikosashizutegata 自己指図手形

self-order bill

jikosekinintaisei 自己責任体制 rule of self-discipline ¶ to leave it to a *rule of self-discipline* of the concerned circles

jikoshihon 自己資本 owned capital; net worth; proprietary capital

jikoshihonhiritsu 自己資本比率 ratio of net worth (to deposits of a bank); self-owned capital ratio

jikoshihonriekiritsu 自己資本利益率 ratio of profits to net worth

jikoshikin 自己資金 funds on hand

jikoshinkoku 自己申告 self-return; self-assessment

jikōyūzansu 自行ユーザンス usance extended by the bank's own funds

jiku 軸 axis ¶ A line deviating toward the vertical *axis* indicates growing inequality.

jikyū 自給 self-supply [参考] →自給自足

jikyūjisoku 自給自足 self-sufficiency; self-support; autarchy ¶ The United States continues its drive for *self-sufficiency* in energy. // Egypt was, to an unusual extent, a *self-sufficing* country.

jikyūjisokukeizai 自給自足経済 self-sufficient economy

jikyūkiokusōchi 持久記憶装置 [コン] non-volatile storage

jikyūritsu 自給率 self-supply ratio; self-sufficiency rate

jikyūro 自給炉 self-feeding furnace

jimoto 地元 local ¶ *local* capital // *local* banks // *local* industries

jimu 事務 office work; clerical work; business

jimubunshō 事務分掌 division of duties

jimukaizen 事務改善 improvement

of business operation; streamlining
of business systems (and operating
procedures)

jimukanri 事務管理 office management

jimukeihi 事務経費 business expenses

jimukiki 事務機器 office machinery

jimukikō 事務機構 business system

jimureberusesshō 事務レベル折衝 working-level negotiations (=talks; consultations)

jimuryōchōsa 事務量調査 survey on work volume; work volume survey

jimuryōjōhōshisutemu 事務量情報システム ［コン］work volume information system

jimusho 事務所 (business) office ¶ Five banks of U.S. origin established fully operative *offices* in Spain.

jimushokeihi 事務所経費 (運輸にかかわるものを除く) management fees (excluding those to transportation); office expenses

jimushokuin 事務職員 clerical staff

jimushori 事務処理 business processings

jimusoshiki 事務組織 system of duties

jin'aishūshūshorishisetsu じんあい収集処理施設 garbage collection and disposal system

jinetsuenerugī 地熱エネルギー geothermal energy

jin'ikōsaku 人為工作 artificial manipulation

jin'inhojū 人員補充 recruiting; recruitment

jin'inkōsei 人員構成 personnel composition

jin'inseiri 人員整理 personal cutback; personnel discharge; work-

force adjustment; personnel reduction; elimination of surplus workers; discharge of extra workers ¶ ［参考］to lop 100,000 workers off payrolls // to pare employment rolls

jin'isōba 人為相場 artificial price; manipulated quotation; forced quotation

jin'isōsa 人為操作 manipulation ¶ to forbid transactions of a *manipulative*, deceptive, or fraudulent character // to eliminate fraud, *manipulation* and other abuses in security trading

jin'iteki 人為的 artificial; manipulated

jin'itōki 人為騰貴 jacking-up; rig

jin'itōta 人為陶汰 artificial selection

jinji 人事 personnel administration

jinjikiroku 人事記録 personnel records

jinjikōka 人事考課 assessment of performance; performance rating; merit evaluation

jinjikōryū 人事交流 personnel interchange; swapping employees

jinkenhi 人件費 personnel expenses; salaries and wages

jinkenhitaijun'uriagedakahiritsu 人件費対純売上高比率 ratio of labor cost to net sales

jinkenshi 人絹糸 rayon filament yarn

jinkensonchōnoshakai 人権尊重の社会 society where human dignity prevails; society where human rights are respected

jinkō 人口 population ¶ large jumps in *population* over a five- to twelve-year construction period after which the *population* settles to a lower level // Rapid rates of *popu-*

lation increase in relatively scarcely *populated* areas. // to encourage the trend toward concentration rather than dispersion of urban *population* // the free migration of surplus *populations*

浮動人口　floating population
現在人口　population de facto
非農業人口　non-farming population
常住人口　usual population; permanent population
過剰人口　over-population
農業人口　farming population
労働人口　working population; labor force population; economically active population
老人人口　aging population
適正人口　optimum population
有業人口　occupied population
幽霊人口　fraudulently-registered population

jinkōatsuryoku 人口圧力 population pressure
jinkōbakuhatsu 人口爆発 population explosion
jinkōchōsa 人工調査 census
jinkōdōtai 人口動態 movement of population
jinkōdōtaitōkei 人口動態統計 dynamic statistics of population; vital statistics
jinkōgenshō 人口減少 decrease in population; depopulation
jinkōkajō 人口過剰 overpopulation
jinkōkanmiryō 人工甘味料 artificial sweetener
jinkōkaso 人口過疎 underpopulation; depopulation
jinkōkōgai 人口公害 popullution
jinkōmisshūchitai 人口密集地帯 densely populated section
jinkōmitsudo 人口密度 population density
jinkōmondai 人口問題 population problem (=issue)
jinkōnenreikōsei 人口年齢構成 age composition of population
jinkōniku 人工肉 man-made meat; artificial meat
jinkōnogenri 人口の原理 principles of population
jinkōsaihaibun 人口再配分 population redistribution
jinkōsensasu 人口センサス population census
jinkōshokuryōmondai 人口食糧問題 population-food problem
jinkōshūchūdo 人口集中度 (degree of) concentration of population
jinkōtōkei 人口統計 vital statistics; demography ¶ A reason for it is to be found in *demographic* developments. // Labor market conditions change largely because of *demographic* trends.
jinkōtōkeigakuteki 人口統計学的 demographic ¶ Because of relatively unfavorable *demographic* trends residential construction will decline. // *Demographic* trends point to a rise in the unemployment rate. // The reasons are neither economic nor political, but *demographic*. // the current *demographic* changes in Japan—an aging of the population // *demographic* characteristics such as family size // Europe is no longer stuck in the *demographic* transition of population growth.
jinkōyokusei 人口抑制 population control
jinkōzōka 人口増加 increase in population; growth of population
jinkōzunō 人工頭脳 artificial brains
jinkōzunōgaku 人工頭脳学 cyber-

netics

jinminkōsha 人民公社 ［中国］ people's commune

jintekishigen 人的資源 manpower; human resources ¶ contribution of *manpower* to the economy // demand for and supply of *manpower*

jintekishigenkaihatsu 人的資源開発 manpower development

jintekishihon 人的資本 human capital ¶ Husbands as a group possess larger stocks of *human capital* — education, training, experience, and the like — than do wives.

jintekishihontekimusubitsuki 人的・資本の結びつき tie-up in terms of personnel and capital

jintekishotokubunpu 人的所得分布 personal income distribution

jintōzei 人頭税 head tax

jinzaiginkō 人材銀行 talent bank

jireikenkyū 事例研究 case study

jiridaka じり高 gradual advance; edging upward; forging upward; gradual rise; gradual increase; tending upward; inching up ¶ Rates on Treasury coupon issue *inched upward* through mid-December.

jirihin じり貧 sagging; gradual decline; gradual contraction; tail-spinning

jirikikōsei 自力更生 self-reliance ¶ the strong political desire of developing countries for greater *self-reliance*

jiritsuchōsei 自律調整 autonomous adjustment (of business activity)

jiritsukeieinōka 自立経営農家 economically viable farm

jiritsukeizai 自立経済 self-sustaining economy; self-supporting economy; self-sustained economy; self-supported economy

jiritsuteki 自律的 autonomous ¶ *autonomous* expenditure // the economy on the road to *autonomous* recovery

jiriyasu じり安 gradual decline; recession; sagging; continuous decline; edging down

jiro ジロ giro; postal giro

jisa 時差 difference in time

jisakunō 自作農 landed farmer; owner-cultivator; owner farmer

jisakunōijisōsetsushikinkashitsuke 自作農維持創設資金貸付 loan to create and maintain owner-farmer

jisakunōsōsetsuiji 自作農創設維持 creation and maintenance of landed farmers

jisannin 持参人 bearer

jisanninbaraikogitte 持参人払小切手 check to bearer

jisashukkin 時差出勤 staggered office hours; staggered work hours; staggered hours; staggered work schedule

jisasōkan 時差相関 tming relationship; lead-lag correlation

jisei 自制 self-discipline; self-restraint; self-control ¶ agreement to apply *self-discipline* in agricultural export subsidies // ［参考］ restrictive practices of labor unions

jishakabu 自社株 corporation's own stock

jishuchōsei 自主調整 voluntary adjustment

jishukaisan 自主解散 voluntary liquidation

jishukanriundō 自主管理運動 self-control action

jishukisei 自主規制 self-restriction; self-imposed restriction; voluntary restriction (＝restraint); self-imposed controls; voluntary (=non-mandatory) regulation; self-regulation ¶ The Reagan Administration will press Japan to continue *voluntary restraints* on car exports into the U.S. but at a slightly relaxed level.

jishukiseikinri 自主規制金利 voluntarily regulated interest rate

jishukiseisochi 自主規制措置 voluntary restrictive measure

jishuku 自粛 self-regulation; self-discipline ¶ to enforce a firm *self-discipline* in banking acivity // →自主規制; 自制

jishukumōshiawasegendo 自粛申合せ限度 voluntary maximum limit

jishuseisan 自主清算 voluntary liquidation

jishusōtan 自主操短 self-curtailment of (factory) operation; voluntary operation cutback

jishutekishihon'idō 自主的資本移動 autonomous capital movements

jishutekisōgyōtanshuku 自主的操業短縮 self-active curtailment (of factory operation); self-curtailment of (factory) operation; voluntary operation curtailment (=cutback)

jishuunyō 自主運用 in-house management

jisoku 自足 self-sufficiency ¶ Australia is 70% *self-sufficient* in oil. // →自給自足

jissei 実勢 prevailing trend

jisseikawaserēto 実勢為替レート real rate (of exchange)

jisseirēto 実勢レート effective rate; (current) market rate

jisseiyokin 実勢預金 bank deposits on a net basis; deposits deducting checks and bills in process of collection and Government foreign currency deposits

jisseki 実績 result; performance; outturn; actuality; actual; past record ¶ marked discrepancies between expectations and *results* // The fact that the target coincided with the *result* was more or less fortuitous. // The discrepancy between forecasts and *results* has been great. // The *performance* of the individual components deviated sharply from the initial projections. // Textile machinery's declining export *performance* has continued. // Trade *performance* in metal manufacturing generally improved. // The decline in the international *performance* of British industry was repeated. // to cause an export *performance* well below potential // the *realized* investment as compared with investment plans // the *actual outturn* for the month // *actualities* better than prospects // *actuals* for the first six months, not seasonally adjusted

営業実績 results of business; business results; performance of business operation; results of operations

過去の実績 historical performance ¶ distribution of quotas based on *historical performance*

jissekichi 実績値 actual value

jissekiwariate 実績割当 allotment according to past records

jisshi 実施 implementation; enforcement ¶ *implementation* of the recommendations // measures taken to *implement* the official views // a strict *enforcement* of a law

jisshitsu 実質 in real terms; real ¶ GNP *in real terms* // *real* GNP

jisshitsuchingin 実質賃金 real wage; cash earning; actual wage ¶ *real wages* compared with nominal wages // *actual wages* against prospective wages

jisshitsukokuminsōshishutsu 実質国民総支出 gross national expenditures at constant prices

jisshitsuseichōritsu 実質成長率 growth rate in real terms; real growth rate

jisshitsushotoku 実質所得 real income

jisshitsutekikirisage 実質的切下げ substantial exchange devaluation; de facto downward revaluation; virtual devaluation

jisshitsuyokin 実質預金 real deposits; deposits deducted by checks and bills in process of collection

jisshitsuzandakakōka 実質残高効果 real balance effect

jissū 実数 real number; absolute figure

jitchichōsa 実地調査 field investigation

jitchikensa 実地検査 field examination; (on-the-) spot checks ¶ government *spot checks* in oil stockpiles // a *field examination* of investment activity

jitchikenshū 実地研修 practical on-the-job training

jitsubutsu 実物 substance; genuine article; original; spot; actual; 〜 in kind

jitsubutsukeihi 実物経費 expense in kind

jitsubutsukyūyo 実物給与 wage in kind; truck

jitsubutsunonagare 実物の流れ real flow

jitsubutsushijō 実物市場 spot market

jitsubutsutekiippankinkō 実物的一般均衡 real general equilibrium

jitsubutsutorihiki 実物取引 spot transaction; cash transation

jitsubutsutōshi 実物投資 real investment ¶ business investment in *real* assets

jitsubutsuzei 実物税 tax in kind

jitsugenkanōkakaku 実現可能価格 realizable value

jitsugenrieki 実現利益 realized profit

jitsugenshitatōshi 実現した投資 realized investment

jitsugyō 実業 business; industry

jitsugyōdantai 実業団体 business organization

jitsugyōgakkō 実業学校 vocational school; technical school

jitsugyōka 実業家 businessman; industrialist; entrepreneur

jitsugyōkai 実業界 business circles; business world; industrial circles

jitsugyōkyōiku 実業教育 business training; vocational education; technical education

jitsugyōshisatsudan 実業視察団 industrial inspection party; business mission; commercial mission

jitsujikanshisutemu 実時間システム [コン] real time system

jitsujikanshori 実時間処理 [コン] real time processing

jitsuju 実需 actual demand; real demand; demand for consumption; actual requirements; consumptive demand; commercial demand; commercial needs; physical demand

jitsujugai 実需買い covering of actual requirements; buying for consumption; [市] commercial buying ¶ fairly active trading on *commercial* *buying*

jitsujuniyorusakimonotorihiki 実需による先物取引 commercial forward transaction

jitsujusuji 実需筋 consumers; consumptive interests; actual users; industrial users; [市] commercial operators; commercial buyers

jitsujusujikaimono 実需筋買物 commercial demand

jitsuyōsei 実用性 practical utility ¶ to be of little *practical utility*

jitsuyōshin'anken 実用新案権 utility model right

jitsuyōshugi 実用主義 pragmatism

jittai 実態 realities; actualities
経済の実態 realities (=actualities) of the economy; economic realities (=actualities) ¶ →実体経済

jittaichōsa 実態調査 fact-finding (survey)

jittaikahei 実体貨幣 commodity money

jittaikeizai 実体経済 real phases (=side) of the economy; real economy; economic activities; real economic activity; markets for goods and services ¶ impacts of policy actions on *economic activity* // The levels of *economic activity* are influenced by changes in credit conditions. // The impact of policy is felt more directly in financial market than in *over-all goods and services.* // the links between the financial and *real sides of the economy*

jittaikeizaikeisu 実体経済計数 data concerning real variables

jiyū 自由 freedom; liberty ¶ The member is accorded wide *freedom* in the choice of its exchange arrangements.
契約の自由 freedom of contract
結社の自由 freedom of association
選択の自由 freedom of choice
市場参入の自由 freedom of entry
通商の自由 freedom of trade

jiyūbōeki 自由貿易 free trade

jiyūbōekichiiki 自由貿易地域 free trade area

jiyūbōekihyō 自由貿易表 free list

jiyūbōekishugisha 自由貿易主義者 free-trader

jiyūbōekitaisei 自由貿易体制 free trade system

jiyūchūzō 自由鋳造 free coinage

jiyūeigyō 自由営業 free business; non-restricted trade

jiyūenkanjō 自由円勘定 free yen account

jiyūenyokin 自由円預金 non-resident free yen deposit

jiyūfurikaesei 自由振替性 transferability

jiyūgyō 自由業 profession; liberal profession

jiyūhanbai 自由販売 free sale

jiyūhōninshugi 自由放任主義 "laissez faire"; "laisser faire" ¶ to automatically allow the *laisser faire* approach of the financial sector to continue // to occupy the most extreme *laissez-faire* position

jiyūjunbi 自由準備 free reserve

jiyūka 自由化 liberalization; decontrol; freeing; deregulation; lifting control ¶ *liberalization* of capital transaction, interest rate, and trade and exchange // Trade and exchange *liberalization* is proceeding. // The authorities *liberalized* substantially the regulations governing payments to foreign performers. // The *deregulation* of natural gas prices in Canada is designed to increase demand. // Full interest rate *decontrol* would jeoperdize small banks. // Interest rates were *freed* from governmental regulation. // The program of *lifting controls* on the entry of foreign business into Japan. // [参考] a search for economic disarmament to release industry from government clutches

貿易自由化 liberalization of trade

為替自由化 liberalization of exchange transactions

金利自由化 liberalization of interest rates

資本取引の自由化 liberalization of capital transactions

jiyūkagimu 自由化義務 liberalization obligation ¶ derogation from *liberalization obligations*

jiyūkagimunomenjo 自由化義務の免除 derogation from liberalization obligations

jiyūkahinmokuhyō 自由化品目表 liberalization list

jiyūkanoryūho 自由化の留保 retention against liberalization

jiyūkaritsu 自由化率 liberalization rate (＝ratio) ¶ The *liberalization rate* of trade and exchange is now 97 percent. // The *liberalization ratio*, on a 1959 customs clearance basis, has been raised from 89 percent to 90 percent.

jiyūkasochi 自由化措置 measure for liberalization; liberalization measure

jiyūkawasesōbasei 自由為替相場制 free exchange rate system

jiyūkeizai 自由経済 free economy

jiyūkinshijō 自由金市場 free gold market

jiyūkō 自由港 free port

jiyūkōkaishijō 自由公開市場 free and open market

jiyūkōkansei 自由交換性 free convertibility

jiyūkōkōken 自由航行権 freedom of the sea

jiyūku 自由区 free district; free zone

jiyūkusōko 自由区倉庫 free warehouse

jiyūkyōsō 自由競争 free competition; open competition ¶ to want to escape supervision in the interest of *free competition*

jiyūkyōsōnogensoku 自由競争の原則 principle of free competition

jiyūkyōsōshugi 自由競争主義 "laissez faire"

jiyūrōdōsha 自由労働者 free laborer; casual laborer

jiyūsannyū 自由参入 free entry

jiyūshiharai 自由支払 free payment

jiyūshijō 自由市場 free market

jiyūshutsuryōki 自由出猟期 open season

jiyūyokin 自由預金 free deposit

jizenbunseki 事前分析 ex-ante analysis

jizenhizuke 事前日付 antedate

jizenhizukekogitte 事前日付小切手 antedated check

jizenkyōgi 事前協議 prior consultation; preliminary talk

jizenkyōgisei 事前協議制 prior consultation system

jizenninka 事前認可 prior permission

jizentsūkoku 事前通告 advance notice ¶ [参考] to give the debtor three days' notice in writing by registered mail

jizenwariate 事前割当 pre-allocation

jizokutekifukinkō 持続的不均衡 persistent imbalance

jizokutekiseichō 持続的成長 sustainable growth

jōbudantai 上部団体 parent organization

jōbusoshiki 上部組織 superstructure ¶ to raise a larger *superstructure* of money and credit money on the some stock of gold

jōchōkensa 冗長検査 redundancy check

jōgaishijō 場外市場 outside market; street market; curb market; negotiated market

jōgaishōken 場外証券 unlisted securities

jōgaitorihiki 場外取引 outside dealing; off-mart transaction; dealing on the curb; transaction outside stock exchanges

jōgensōba 上限相場 upper limit rate

jōhi 冗費 extravagant expense; useless expense; superfluous expenses; unnecessary expense; frills and fads ¶ to cut down *extravagant expenses* // to cut out the *frills and fads* of government spending // to pare down the *frills and fads* of expenses

jōhō 情報 information ¶ to improve the availability and quality of financial and economic *information* on major borrowing countries // Little *information* is readily accessible on public sector employment. // accurate, timely, and meaningful *information* on aggregate economic performance essential for the assessment of a country's creditworthiness // The *information* available shows that... // widespread dissemination of *information* among the public with respect to... // a collection of the available factual *information* covering all major sectors of the economy // to contain descriptive and statistical *information* for 118 countries // to furnish or obtain *information* concerning... // a useful piece of *information* as to... // amount and value of *information* // perfection of market *information* 内部情報 inside information

jōhōgen 情報源 information source

jōhōgyappu 情報ギャップ inflation gap

jōhōkashakai 情報化社会 information society; post industrial society

jōhōkeihōten 上方警報点 upper warning point

jōhōkensaku 情報検索 information retrieval

jōhōkōkaihō 情報公開法 [米] Freedom of Information Act (of 1966)

jōhōnochikusekitokensaku 情報の蓄積と検索 information storage and retrieval

jōhōryō 情報量 amount of information

jōhōshinjikēto 情報シンジケート information syndicate

jōhōshori 情報処理 information processing

jōhōshorisangyō 情報処理産業(ソフトウエアにかかわるものを含む) information processing (including the computer software industry)

jōhōshoritaikei 情報処理体系 information (management) system

jōhōshūshū 情報収集 data gathering

jōhōshūshūmō 情報収集網 intelligence-gathering network

jōhōteikyōsha 情報提供者 information provider

jōjijūgyōsha 常時従業者 regular employees

jōjō 上場 putting on the market; listing; quoting on the exchange (= bourse) ¶ The bonds will be *quoted on the* Luxemburg *Bourse.*

jōjōhaishikijun 上場廃止基準 de-listing standards

jōjōkabu 上場株 listed stock; listed share

非上場株 unlisted stock; outside share

jōjōmeigara 上場銘柄 listed (stock) issue; listed (commodity) brand ¶ Gainers maintained a 4 to 3 lead over losers among New York *stock* exchange-*listed* issues.

jōjōshinsakijun 上場審査基準 listing standards; listing requirements

jōjōteishi 上場停止 striking off from the list; de-listing ¶ The stock exchange started proceedings to *de-list* the company's stocks. // The shares will be officially *delisted* in November.

jōjūjinkō 常住人口 usual population; population de jure; permanent population

jōjun 上旬 first ten days of the month; first ten-day period of the month; early part of the month

jōkagen 上・下限 (為替相場の) upper and lower margins ¶ The riyal appreciated to its *upper margin* vis-à-vis the SDR. // The *upper margin* for the riyal was exceeded on several occasions. // Iran and Saudi Arabia permitted their currencies to move up from the *lower* to the *upper margins* of the bank bands around the SDR and then pegged them to those *upper margins.*

jōkamachi 城下町 castle town ¶ *castle towns* built up around a single industry

jōkeiki 上景気 boom; brisk market

jōken 条件 condition; term; stipulation; provision; proviso; qualification; terms and conditions; setting; environment; circumstance ¶ the *provision* of financing on attractive *terms* // the vagaries of climatic *conditions* for agricultural products // the continuing development of the orderly underlying *conditions* that are necessary for financial and economic stability // the existence of *conditions* favoring borrowers in international markets // to ease the *terms* on loans // The *terms* will be made as soft as possible. // The *terms* on medium-term international banking credits show spreads declining and maturities lengthening. // Outstanding credits have been directly refinanced on better *terms*. // to compete on equal *terms* with business abroad // to fix the *terms* and conditions of the contract // full satisfaction of *terms and conditions* of the contract // The *terms and conditions* of the Confederation's new, private placement of SF500 million were announced. // Borrowers obtained improved *terms* as regards maturities of loans. // to calculate the difference between old, high-interest terms and the current cheaper *terms* // a hardening of the *terms* of borrowing // the tempering of loan *terms* // [参考] other thing being equal (=ceteris paribus)

売買条件 terms of sale; terms of transaction

不利な条件 unfavorable terms

付帯条件 condition collateral

現金払条件　cash terms

発行条件　terms of issue; issue terms

必須条件　sine qua non; essential condition

一般条件　general terms and conditions

契約条件　terms and conditions of contract; contract terms

決済条件　terms of settlement

交易条件　terms of trade; trade terms

労働条件　labor conditions; working conditions

支払条件　terms of payment; payment terms

停止条件　condition precedent

取引条件　terms of trade; trade terms; terms of business transaction

受渡条件　terms of delivery

有利な条件　advantageous terms

jōkenhenkō 条件変更　alteration of condition

jōkenteiji 条件提示　bidding ¶ brisk and highly competitive *bidding* for the 15 billion dollar debt // Many banks submitted *bids* to provide the whole debt package.

jōkentsuki 条件付　conditional; foul; limited

jōkentsukibaibai 条件付売買　conditional sale

jōkentsukifunanisashizusho 条件付船荷指図書　conditional shipping order; foul shipping order

jōkentsukifunanishōken 条件付船荷証券　conditional bill of lading

jōkentsukihikiuke 条件付引受　conditional acceptance

jōkentsukikanwa 条件付緩和　qualified relaxation

jōkentsukikeiyaku 条件付契約　conditional contract

jōkentsukininka 条件付認可　conditional validation

jōkentsukiryūdōsei 条件付流動性　conditional liquidity

jōkentsukishōnin 条件付承認　conditional approval

jōkentsukiuragaki 条件付裏書　conditional endorsement

jōkin'yakuin 常勤役員　full-time executive

jōkō 条項　clause

ドル条項　dollar clause

延長条項　extension clause

留保条項　saving clause

jōkōbaiasu 上向バイアス　upward bias

jōmukai 常務会　board of managing directors

jōmutorishimariyaku 常務取締役　managing director

jōnai 場内　[市] inside the floor; inside the room

jōsei 情勢　atmosphere; climate ¶ In an *atmosphere* of growing confidence that inflation would be kept under control, interest rates would begin declining. // The general *climate* in industry remains expansionary. // [参考] →環境

jōshin 上伸　rise; pickup; advance; boost; uplift // → 上昇

jōshō 上昇　rise; pickup; advance; boost; uplift; upswing; upsurge; uptrend; upturn; upgrade; moving up(ward); boom; increase; gain ¶ The 1975 *rise* in prices matched *advancing* costs. // Costs *rose* relative to prices. // The incipient *pickup* gathers steam. // Some *pickup* in output has occurred. // a broadly based *advance* in employment // After *advancing* on a broad front in manufacturing, business activity slackened in major sectors. // Prices were *uplifted*. // a strong *upswing* in business activity // An *upsurge* in consumption has yet to come. // The index *surged upward*. // The broad *uptrend* in production slackened. // a business *upturn* // Employment has been on an *upgrade* from lows early this year. // The index has been *moving upward*. // The rate was *moved up* by 0.5 percent. // The recovery got into full *upswing*. // unallayed fears of a fresh *surge* of prices // A rapid-fire of series of *boosts* in price of crude oil *boomed* oil shares. // The August *rise* in the index of wholesale prices is equivalent to an *increase* of 21% on an annual basis. // The dollar finished with pared *gains*. // The market average *gained* 13.6 points from Friday's close to 10,389.53.

jōshōgendo 上昇限度 ceiling

jōshōkaku 上昇角 climbing angle

jōshōritsu 上昇率 rate of increase ¶ the *rate of* average price *increases* across the economy // to *increase* at a distinctly below-average *rate*.

jōshōryoku 上昇力 climbing power; boost; up-pressure ¶ The main *boost* to import prices came from petroleum products.

jōsū 乗数 multiplier
　複合乗数　compound multiplier
　行列乗数　matrix multiplier
　雇用乗数　employment multiplier
　単純乗数　simple multiplier
　投資乗数　investment multiplier

jōsū 常数 constant
　可変常数　variable constant

jōsūriron 乗数理論 theory of multiplier

jōto 譲渡 alienation; assignment ¶ *alienation* of property // proper *assignment* executed either on the certificate itself or on a separate paper // *Assignment* increased transfer of resources to the weaker nations.

jōtokanōshin'yōjō 譲渡可能信用状 transferrable credit

jōtokanōteikiyokinshōsho 譲渡可能定期預金証書 negotiable certificate of deposit; CD; NCD ¶ Japanese banks issued yen-based *negotiable certificates of deposit* totaling Yen 296 billion in July. // Foreign banks having branches in Japan issued ¥61.4 billion of *CDs*.

jōtorijun 譲渡利潤 profit upon alienation

jōtoseigen 譲渡制限 restriction of trasfer (=assignment)

jōtoseiyokin 譲渡性預金 → 譲渡可能定期預金証書

jōtoshōsho 譲渡証書 deed of conveyance

jōtotesūryō 譲渡手数料 assignment charge; assignment fee

jōtouragaki 譲渡裏書 endorsement to tranfer

jōyo 剰余 surplus; residue; balance
　営業剰余　operating surplus
　振当剰余　appropriated surplus
　拠出剰余　contributed surplus
　正味剰余　net surplus
　収益剰余　earned surplus
　総剰余　total surplus

jōyoekikin 剰余益金 surplus profit

jōyokachi 剰余価値 surplus value

jōyokin 剰余金 surplus funds
　減資剰余金　surplus from capital reduction
　評価剰余金　appraisal surplus
　再評価剰余金　surplus from revalua-

tion

失権株式剰余金 surplus from forfeited stock

償還剰余金 surplus from stock redemption

前期繰越利益剰余金 surplus at beginning of the period

jōyokinkanjō 剰余金勘定 surplus account

jōyokinkeikakusho 剰余金計画書 statement of income and retained earnings; statement of earnings and earnings invested in business

jōyokinkeisansho 剰余金計算書 surplus statement

jōyokinshobun 剰余金処分 appropriation of surplus

jōyokinshūsei 剰余金修正 surplus adjustment

jōyōrōdōryoku 常用労働力 full-time labor force

jōyōrōdōsha 常用労働者 regular worker

jōyōrōdōshachinginshisū 常用労働者賃金指数 wage index of regular workers

jōyoseisan 剰余生産 surplus production

jōyotsumitatekin 剰余積立金 surplus reserves

juchū 受注 acceptance of order; receipt of order; order (received) ¶ Incoming *orders* perked up somewhat. // New *orders* placed for machines forged ahead. // machine *orders* placed with industry // The Finnish shipyards are finding their *order* books looking increasingly slender as they look forward to the second half-year. // the flow of new *orders received* by durable goods manufacturers // Export *orders* fared worse than home *orders*. //

Export *order* books are more satisfactory than domestic *order* books. // the latest statistics on *orders* booked by industry in May // the inflow of *orders* from the home markets and from overseas // The intake of export *orders* declined. // The *order* situation has improved. // Machinery and construction *order* bookings rose. // There have been a slight improvement in total *order* books, a more marked recovery in export *order* books. // to worry about weak *order* books

juchūdaka 受注高 amount of orders received; amount of orders accepted; value of orders; business on (=in) hand ¶ Shipyards have enough *business on hand*. // The *value of orders* booked by the engineering industry was just under 5% higher than in 1975.

juchūryō 受注量 order volume; order books ¶ There is now a total *order volume* stretching 8.5 months ahead. // *Order books* are becoming shorter. // At month-end industry had an *order book* ensuring work for 7.9 months. // →受注

juchūsho 受注書 acknowledgment of order

juchūzan 受注残 unfilled orders; backlog of orders; order backlog; order stock; work on (=in) hand ¶ At June-end industry's *order backlog* at current prices shaved an increase of 8% over the year. // The end-May *order backlog* was 5% higher than a year earlier, with the export share of the total *backlog* dropping from 47 to 46%. // *Order backlogs* are melting away. // The *backlog* of *unfilled orders* moved up. // The value of *work on hand* at month-end was put at Fr. 12.5 billion. // Average *work on hand* in the industry was equal to 7.3 months' output at the end of March.

judakuzumishōken 受諾済証券 accepted bond; assented bond

jūdenkikai 重電機械 heavy(-duty) electrical machinery

juekisha 受益者 beneficiary

juekishafutangensoku 受益者負担原則 benefit(-received) principle (of taxation); benefit theory

juekishafutanryōkin 受益者負担料金 beneficial rates; remunerative rates

juekishafutansetsu 受益者負担説 benefit theory

juekishōken 受益証券 beneficiary certificate ¶ acquisition of publicly offered *beneficiary certificates*

jūenseidōka 10円青銅貨 10 yen bronze coin

jugurānonami ジュグラーの波 Juglar cycle; Juglar's wave

jūgyōin 従業員 employee; worker

jūgyōinmochikabuseido 従業員持株制度 employee's ownership; employee stock ownership; employee stock ownership plan; ESOP; stock ownership by workers ¶ a great proliferation of *ESOP*'s in 1977 and 1978 // *ESOP*'s are spreading.

jūjitsu 充実 consolidation; replenishment; enhancement; repletion ¶ to *consolidate* social overhead capital // to *replenish* social welfare // to *enhance* national welfare // realization of a qualitative *repletion* rather than quantitative expansion

jūka 従価 ad valorem ¶ 20% *ad valorem* import deposits

jūkagakukōgyōhin 重化学工業品

heavy industrial and chemical products

jūkazei 従価税 ad valorem duty

jukenshihon 授権資本 authorized capital

jukkakokuzōshōkaigi 10ヵ国蔵相会議 The Ministers and Governors of the Group of Ten (Countries participating in the General Agreement to Borrow)

jūkōgyō 重工業 heavy industries

jūkōgyōyakuhin 重工業薬品 heavy chemicals

jukuren 熟練 skill; practice; expertise; experience ¶ the shortage of *skilled,* both entrepreneurial and technical // scarcity of *specific skills* acquired in formal training

jukurenkō 熟練工 skilled worker

jukurenrōdō 熟練労働 skilled labor

jūkyo 住居 dwelling; residence; house; home ¶ →住宅

jūkyohi 住居費 housing expenses; dwelling expenses

jūkyoteate 住居手当 housing allowance

jukyūchōsei 需給調整 regulation of supply and demand; adjustment of the supply and demand situation; control of the relation between supply and demand

jukyūfukinkō 需給不均衡 supply-demand imbalance ¶ The *imbalance* between *supply* and *demand* has increased. // the disproportion between, or the *imbalance* between *supply* and *demand* // [参考] Supplies remain seriously out of balance with commercial requirement.

jukyūgyappu 需給ギャップ demand gap; supply-demand gap in GNP

jukyūkankei 需給関係 relation between supply and demand; supply and demand situation; supply-demand picture; supply-demand equation ¶ The *supply-demand picture* for newsprint depicts a development. // The latest *supply-demand equation* looks bearish.

jukyūshikaku 受給資格 qualification of recipient

jukyūsuisan 需給推算 estimated supply and demand

jukyūtōsei 需給統制 control of supply and demand

jūnansei 柔軟性 resilience ¶ The Norwegian economy has shown a remarkable *resilience* to external shocks and disequilibrating influences.

junbi 準備 reserve; provision ¶ a *reserve* against loss // in *reserve* for payment // International *reserves* of the Philippines stood at $2.15 billion, up by $268 million from the end of 1979. // The minimum cash *reserves* for demand deposits are set at 15%. // to spread the country's *reserves* in the many currencies as possible to cushion itself against the impact of exchange fluctuations // to diversify exchange *reserves*, not holding *reserves* in only one foreign currency // Import capability of four months is generally considered a reasonable norm for foreign exchange *reserves*. // The number of months of imports covered by gross *reserves* declined from 2.1 in 1974 to 1.5 in 1978. // Guyana's international *reserves* were virtually depleted. // a 20 percent *reserve* required against demand deposits, or the ratio of 20 percent of *reserves* to

demand deposits // A member bank at which $100 is deposited needs to hold $20 in *reserve* at the Reserve Bank. // to draw on *reserves* held in dollars // Those *reserves* have nearly run out, so they will be on a shorter leash.

超過準備 excess reserve

第一線準備 first-line reserves

第二線準備 secondary reserves; second-line reserves

ドル準備 dollar reserve

外貨準備 foreign currency reserve; gold and foreign exchange reserves

現金準備 cash reserve

銀行支払準備 bank reserves

平均準備 average reserve

法定準備 legal reserve

自由準備 free reserve

金ドル準備 gold dollar reserves

流動性準備 liquid reserves

正貨準備 specie reserve

支払準備 payment reserve; cash reserve

適正外貨準備 adequate gold and exchange reserves

通貨準備 monetary reserve

預金準備 deposit reserve

junbiginkō 準備銀行 reserve bank

junbikikin 準備(基)金 reserve fund; reserve; provision ¶ tax-date and other seasonal pressures draining *reserves* // a special *provision* for international exposure of the bank // contractual savings scheme like *provident fund* schemes and annuities // to *provide* a *reserve fund* for maintenance and replacement charges // An investment *reserve fund* should be set up out of company profits.

営業準備金 operating reserve

銀行支払準備金　bank reserve
配当平均準備金　reserve for equalization of dividend
非常準備金　emergency reserve
法定準備金　legal reserve
保険準備金　insurance reserve
資本準備金　capital reserve
償還準備金　call provision
初回準備金　initial reserve
償却準備金　reserve for equalization of redemption
投資準備金　investment reserve

junbikinshijō　準備金市場　[米]Federal funds market

junbiritsu　準備率　reserve (requirement) ratio; ratio of reserve requirement; required reserve percentages; reserve requirements ¶ to fix and change the *ratios of* cash *reserves* to deposits // The *required reserve percentage* against deposits was cut by 0.25 percent. // Federal Reserve authority to vary the *required reserve percentages* for commercial banks is a relatively new tool of reserve banking. // The range of Federal Reserve discretion over *reserve percentages* and the *percentage requirements* in effect in December are shown in the table. // The Fed considers restructuring and reducing member banks' *reserve requirements*. // The *ratio of reserve requirement*, or *reserve requirement ratio* against demand deposits was increased by 0.25 percent.

junbiritsusettei　準備率設定　establishment of the reserve ratio

junbishihyōseido　準備指標制度　[外]　system of reserve indicators

junbishisan　準備資産　reserve asset ¶ The special drawing right is the principal *reserve asset* in the international monetary system. // a *reserve asset* replacing part of their excessive dollar reserves

junbishudan　準備手段　reserve media

junbitsūka　準備通貨　reserve currency

junbitsūkakoku　準備通貨国　reserve center

junbiyokin　準備預金　reserve deposit; reserve requirement ¶ to impose *reserve requirements* on the deposits and similar liabilities of branches of foreign banks // to subject branches to *reserve requirements* but exempt subsidiary banks

junbiyokinfusoku　準備預金不足　reserve deposit deficiency; lack of full compliance with the legal reserve requirements ¶ Commercial banks pay as much as 30 percent to cover *reserve deficiencies* and thus avoid the still higher 35 percent penalty imposed on banks failing to meet their 20 percent reserve requirement.

junbiyokinkataikin　準備預金過怠金　penalty for reserve deposit deficiency

junbiyokinseido　準備預金制度　reserve deposit requirement system

junchōna　順調な　fair; sound; favorable; satisfactory; increasing steadily; rising continuously

jundokusen　準独占　quasi-monopoly; near-monopoly ¶ a *quasi-monopolistic* business privilege granted by charter

jun'eki　純益　net receipt; net profit ¶ Tourist *receipts* are expected to *net* over $1 billion. // transactions have *netted* a handsome *profit* for the company.

jun'ekishobunkanjō 純益処分勘定 appropriation account

junfusai 純負債 net liability; net debt; net obligation

jungenka 純原価 net cost

junhokenryō 純保険料 net premium

jun'i 順位 priority

junjonoarubunrui 順序のある分類 ordered classification

junjōyokin 純剰余金 net surplus

junjunbi 純準備 net reserve

junkaihanbai 巡回販売 route sale

junkaishin'yōjō 巡回信用状 circular credit

junkan 循環 cycle; circulation; rotation; circle; circular flow ¶ the working capital *cycle*, or *circular flow* of working capital // to break the traditional *cycle* of rapid growth followed by high inflation and a rapid loss of competitiveness // The construction *cycle* is now in decline. // Italy may finally break out of its inflation-recession *cycle*. // The *cycle* is stretching out peak to peak. // to iron out some of mature economies' investment *cycle's* peaks and troughs // boom-and-bust commodity *cycles* // separate and uncoordinated national economic *cycles* of growth and contraction // the virtuous *circle* of an appreciating currency going hand in hand with lower wage increases // to break the vicious wage-price *circle* // The business *cycle* entered a new phase. // The recovery phase of the business *cycle* has started. // The expansive phase of the present business *cycle* continued. // a nadir of an inventory *cycle* // *rotation* buying of stocks

悪循環 vicious circle; vicious cycle

¶ →p.3

長期的技術革新循環 Kondratieff cycle

中期的投資循環 Juglar cycle

自由(な)循環 free cycle

純粋再投資循環 pure reinvestment cycle

軽微な不況循環 mild depression cycle

景気循環 business cycle; trade cycle ¶ →p.229

建築循環 building cycle

好循環 virtuous circle

矩形的循環 rectangular cycle

極限循環 limit cycle

二次の再投資循環 secondary reinvestment cycle

再投資循環 reinvestment cycle

成長率循環 Kuznets cycle

生態循環 ecological cycle

小循環 minor cycle

主循環 major cycle

太陽黒点・天候循環 sun-spot cycle

短期的在庫循環 Kitchin cycle

投資循環 investment cycle

在庫循環 inventory cycle

善循環 virtuous cycle ¶ →p.593

junkandaka 循環高 circular rise

junkangai 循環買 circular buying; rotation buying

junkanhendō 循環変動 cyclical fluctuation

junkanhendōchōsei 循環変動調整 cyclical adjustment

junkanhendōchōseizuminoseisan 循環変動調整済の生産 cyclically neutral level of output

junkanronpō 循環論法 reasoning in a circle

junkanshin'yōjō 循環信用状 revolving credit

junkantekihendō 循環的変動 cyclical fluctuation; cyclical variation

junkantekikakakushinshukusei 循環的価格伸縮性 cyclical price-flexibility

junkantekishitsugyō 循環的失業 cyclical unemployment

junkantekiteikoyō 循環的低雇用 cyclical underemployment

junkawase 順為替 exchange bill payable; demand draft

junkeiyosan 純計予算 net budget

junkin 純金 pure gold; fine gold

junkinyūshisan 純金融資産 net financial assets

junkōgyōkoku 準工業国 semi-industrial country

junkokuminfukushi 純国民福祉 net national welfare; NNW

junkoteikawasesōbasei 準固定為替相場制 system of quasi-fixed exchange rate

junkyohō 準拠法 applicable law; governing law ¶ This agreement must be *governed* by the *laws* of Japan.

junpō 旬報 ten-day report

junpōtōsō 順法闘争 work-to-rule struggle; go-slow campaign; law-abiding labor offensive ¶ Hospital workers will begin a *work to rule* from next Monday.

junrimawari 純利回り net return; net yield

junrisoku 純利息 net interest

junruisekihaibungaku 純累積配分額 net cumulative allocation (of SDRs)

junryō 純量 net weight

junryūdōseishūshi 純流動性収支 net liquidity balance

junseifukikan 準政府機関 quasi-governmental organization; quasi-public organization ¶ governments or *quasi-public organizations* in various countries

junshōhinkōekijōken 純商品交易条件 net barter terms of trade

junshūekihiritsu 純収益比率 ratio of total expenses to total revenues

junson'eki 純損益 net profit or loss

juntakuna 潤沢な adequate; comfortable; sufficient; ample

juntsūka 準通貨 quasi-money

junzaya 順鞘 regular spread

jūryōyōsekishōmeisho 重量容積証明書 list of weight and measurement

jushi 需資 financing requirement; demand for credit; credit demand; fund demand ¶ Corporate *credit requirements* mounted toward the year-end. // →資金需要

jūshi 重視 priority ¶ a lowering of the *priority* that has been accorded by the US authorities to the reduction of inflation in a medium-term contact

jushingyōmu 受信業務 debit business

jushinnōryoku 受信能力 debt ability; credit worthiness

jūsōkankeisū 重相関係数 multiple correlation coefficient

jusshinhō 10進法 decimal notation; decimal numeration

jusshinhōka 10進法化 decimalization

jusshinhōkaheisei 10進法貨幣制 decimal coinage

jusshinhōtsūka 10進法通貨 decimal currency

jūtaku 住宅 dwelling (unit); residence; house; home ¶ Starts of single-detached *dwellings* declined 22 percent while multiple unit *dwellings* were up 19 percent. // Sales of new single-family *houses* fell 4.9%. //

New one-family *home* sales totaled 229,000. // private purchases of *dwellings* whether purchased for tenant or owner occupancy // the number of newly-built *dwelling units*

一戸建住宅 one-unit home; single family home

jūtakuchiku 住宅地区 residential quarter

jutakuchochikuginkō 受託貯蓄銀行 [英] trustee saving bank

jūtakuchochikukojoseido 住宅貯蓄控除制度 tax exemption system on housing savings

jutakugaisha 受託会社 trustee

jutakuginkō 受託銀行 depository bank; commissioned bank

jutakugyōmu 受託業務（銀行の）automated customer services

jūtakukanrenkigyō 住宅関連企業 housing-allied enterprise

jūtakukashitsuke 住宅貸付 housing credit; housing loan

jutakukeieishasō 受託経営者層 trusteeship zone

jutakukeiyakujunsoku 受託契約準則 entrustment contract regulations

jūtakukensetsu 住宅建設 residential construction; house-building; dwelling construction; housing; housing construction

jūtakukensetsuchakkōsū 住宅建設着工数 housing starts ¶ *Housing starts* are still running at boisterous annual rate of nearly 2m. // The number of *housing starts* rose to 19,846 in October.

jūtakukensetsushikin 住宅建設資金 residential construction funds; housing funds

jutakukikan 受託機関 depository

jūtakukin'yū 住宅金融 financing

of housing; housing finance

jūtakukin'yūgaisha 住宅金融会社 (private) housing finance company; mortgage banker

jūtakukin'yūgyō 住宅金融業 mortgage banking

jūtakukōdan 住宅公団 housing corporation

jūtakunan 住宅難 housing shortage

jūtakusaiken 住宅債券 housing bond

jūtakusangyō 住宅産業 housing industry

jutakusha 受託者 fiduciary; trustee ¶ business as *trustee* of bonds and debentures

jutakushasaiken 受託者債券 trustees' certificate

jutakushasekinin 受託者責任 fiduciary responsibility

jūtakushikinkashitsuke 住宅資金貸付 housing mortgage loan

jūtakushin'yō 住宅信用 housing credit

jūtakushin'yōhokanseido 住宅信用補完制度 housing loan insurance system

jūtakusōgōhoken 住宅総合保険 dwelling-house comprehensive insurance

jūtakutaisakuhi 住宅対策費 housing expenses

jūtakuteate 住宅手当 housing allowance

jūtakuteitōkashitsuke 住宅抵当貸付 home mortgage loan

jūtakutōshi 住宅投資 housing investment; residential investment

jūtakuyūshi 住宅融資 housing loan ¶ *housing loan* insurance // [参考] The country's largest housing lender raised its prime rate for mortgages to 12%.

jūten 重点 emphasis; focus; importance; priority; stress; accent; weight ¶ the *priority* of social regeneration to political reform // to place, lay, cast, put, throw, give, special, forcible, strong, or main, or *emphasis* on... // Less *stress* has been given marketability and more to stability. // to lay particular *stress* on... // Success needs to be assessed with a *focus* on cost. // The *emphasis* of lending will be more on quality than on quantity. // Particular *stress* was laid on the planned measures. // The banking law place heavy *emphasis* on the objective of financial stability. // Financial policies laid special *emphasis* on economic growth objectives. // the shifting *emphasis* in Federal spending toward grants during the 1970's // More *weight* is given in tax cuts. // ［参考］ Cabinet makes economic recovery its main thrust.

超重点 high priority
非重点 low priority

jūtensangyō 重点産業 priority industry; key industry

jūtenshugi 重点主義 priority principle

jūtenwariate 重点割当 priority rationing; priority allocation

jūtōkin 充当金 appropriation; money appropriated; money earmarked ¶ a State *appropriation* of $20 billion for the project // There is no budgetary *appropriation* to private projects. // a sum *appropriated* from the national treasury

jūyakutasūketsuhō 重役多数決法 jury-of-executive-opinion method

juyō 需要 demand; requirement; need ¶ There is an acute, brisk, heavy, pressing, strong, or great *demand* of iron ores for steelmaking from abroad. // The poor, limited, moderate, or small *demand* for flour from abroad was easily met, supplied, satisfied, or fulfilled. // The *demand* for credit continued to gather strength. // The slackening in credit *demand* has intensified. // The failure of *demand* has intensified. // The growth in *demand* has been substantial. // *Demand* conditions are vigorous. // The increased *demand* from both home and abroad has begun to make itself felt in production. // March normally sees the beginning of an upsurge in the *demands* of bank credit. // The sagging *demand* was clearly manifested. // The *demand* situation softened. // The strain between supply and *demand* on the money market remained taut. // Shrinking *demand* for raw materials suggests a slack in production. // Corporate credit *requirements* mounted. // Long-term *need* is for further expansion. // Excess *demand* must be eliminated. // spillover of domestic *demand* into imports // excess global *demand* // to contain *demand* to some extent // to meet and satisfy borrowing *requirements* of business // recession-softened *demand*

超過需要 excess demand
中間需要 wholesalers' demand; intermediate demand
弾力的需要 elastic demand
派生需要 derived demand
非弾力的需要 inelastic demand
保有需要 reservation demand
実需（要） actual demand; genuine

demand; ¶ →p.156

海外需要 foreign demand; external demand; demand from abroad

開発需要 development demand; development requirement

借入需要 credit demand; borrowing requirement; demand for bank loans ¶ The *demand for bank loans* has been strong and has been strengthened markedly in recent weeks.

仮需要 speculative demand; fictitious demand; imaginary demand

結合需要 joint demand

国民総需要 gross national demand

国内需要 domestic demand; demand at home; internal demand; home demand

季節需要 seasonal demand

繰延べ需要 backlog of demand

競争的需要 competitive demand

急需要 spot needs

思惑需要 speculative demand

労働需要 labor demand

累積需要 cumulative demand; pent-up demand

留保需要 reserved demand; pent-up demand

最終需要 final demand ¶ *Final demand,* taken in the aggregate and as measured by the aggregate of consumer buying, business investment in plant and equipment, expenditure for housing, net exports, and government purchases was well maintained.

選択需要 alternative demand

潜在需要 latent demand

資金需要 demand for funds; fund demand; financial requirement; demand for credit; credit demand ¶ →p.444

消費(者)需要 consumer demand; consumption demand

相互需要 reciprocal demand

総需要 gross demand; aggregate demand; total demand

退蔵需要 hoarding demand

取換え需要 replacement demand

予備的需要 precautionary demand

有効需要 effective demand

ずれ込み需要 demand carry-over; demand carried forward

juyōatsuryoku 需要圧力 demand pressure ¶ *Demand pressures* emanating from abroad weakened.

juyōchōka 需要超過 excess of demand over supply

juyōdanryoku 需要弾力 elasticity of demand

juyōdokusen 需要独占 buyer's monopoly; monopsony

juyōdokusensha 需要独占者 monopsonist

juyōdonka 需要鈍化 sales resistance

juyōkakaku 需要価格 demand price

juyōkanki 需要喚起 demand boosting

juyōkansū 需要関数 demand function

juyōkata 需要過多 excessive demand

juyōki 需要期 demand season ¶ The *demand season* is on for fruit.

juyōkōmoku 需要項目 demand component; demand element ¶ Other *components* of domestic *demand* decelerated. // The major *element* of *demand* is private investment. // Exports will constitute the most buoyant *component of demand*.

juyōkōzō 需要構造 demand structure

juyōkyōkyūnohōsoku 需要供給の法則 law of demand and supply

juyōkyōkyūnokakakudanryokusei 需要供給の価格弾力性 price elasticities of demand and supply

juyōnohasei 需要の派生 derivation of demand

juyōnohazakaiki 需要の端境期 off-demand season ¶ This quarter is an *off-demand season* for winter clothing. // to be *off season* for clothing

juyōnokanki 需要の喚起 demand boosting

juyōnokōsadanryokusei 需要の交差弾力性 cross elasticity of demand

juyōnosattō 需要の殺到 rush of demand

juyōsakugen 需要削減 demand retrenchment

juyōseisaku 需要政策 (restrictive) demand management

juyōsha 需要者 consumer; customer ¶ industrial *consumers*

juyōshifuto 需要シフト shift in demand; change in demand structure

juyōtasen 需要多占 oligopsony

juyōtasensha 需要多占者 oligopsonist

juyōtokyōkyū 需要と供給 supply and demand ¶ The relation between *supply and demand* eased. //

an improvement in the relationship between *supply and demand* for copper // The disequilibrium between *supply and demand* caused a rise in prices. // The latest *supply-demand* equation looks bearish. // to leave *supply and demand* forces free to determine the market price // The forces of *supply and demand* do not have free play. // *Supply and demand* of oil are now back to balance. // The best guess is an uneasy *supply-demand* balance. // a structural and regional mismatch between labor *supply and demand*

juyōusu 需要薄 diminished demand

juyōyokuseiseisaku 需要抑制政策 demand management policy; general demand-repressing policies; policy (measures) for management of total (=aggregate) demand

juyōyokuseisochi 需要抑制措置 demand-curbing (policy) measure; restrictive demand management (policy) measure; demand squeeze; demand deflation

juyōyosoku 需要予測 demand forecast

juyōzōdai 需要増大 increased demand

jūzokugaisha 従属会社 subsidiary (company); subordinate company

K

kabātorihiki カバー取引 [外] covering transaction

kabin 過敏 [市] nervous

kabuhai 株配 stock dividend

kabuka 株価 stock (=share) price (=quotation) ¶ *Prices* wilted on unfavorable news from Washington. // [参考] The stock market churned ahead. // Oils made big gains. // The stock market is inordinately high following a long advance.

修正平均株価 revised average stock price

単純平均株価 simple average stock price

kabukashisū 株価指数 stock price index; share index ¶ The Financial Times *index* of 30 industrials closed at 340.6, up 5.6. // The exchange's composite *index* of all its listed common stocks was up 0.24 at 48.19. // The Financial Times 30 *share index* closed at record 712.5. // Most index constituents actually drifted slightly lower.

kabukashūekiritsu 株価収益率 price earnings ratio; PER; share price earning ratio

kabukashūekiritsubaisū 株価収益率倍数 price earnings multiple

kabukasōsa 株価操作 stock manipulation; manipulation of stock price

kabuken 株券 share-(=stock-)certificate

仮株券 scrip; certificate

記名株券 inscribed stock certificate

無記名株券 stock certificate to bearer; bearer certificate

割当株券 allotment certificate

kabukenjōtoininjō 株券譲渡委任状 stock power

kabukenjōtoshō 株券譲渡証 stock receipt

kabukenkōkan 株券交換 interchange of share certificate

kabukenmeigikakikae 株券名義書換 transfer of a share-certificate

kabukenmeigikakikaeteishi 株券名義書換停止 transfer books closed

kabukenmeigikakikaeteishikaijo 株券名義書換停止解除 transfer books open

kabukikō 下部機構 infrastructure; substructure ¶ *infrastructure* of business, or business *infrastructure* // The *infranstructure* horse must come before the industrialization cart. // to develop the *infrastructure* for tourism // to provide basic urban *infrastructure*-including water supply, human waste disposal, drainage, footpaths and roads // investment in inland transportation *infrastructure*

社会下部機構 social infrastructure

kabunushi 株主 stockholder; shareholder ¶ A *stockholder* becomes a *shareholder* as soon as his subscription is received *by the corporation*. // the big 30 *stock holders* // to become a *shareholder* in a company

普通株主 ordinary shareholder

小株主 small shareholder

大株主 large shareholder

少数株主 minority shareholders

多数株主 majority shareholders

優先株主 preference shareholder

kabunushianteikōsaku 株主安定工作 stockholder stabilization; stable stockholder operation

kabunushigiketsuken 株主議決権 voting right of stockholder

kabunushihaitō 株主配当 share (=stock) dividend

kabunushikanjō 株主勘定 capital stock and surplus account

kabunushiken 株主権 stockholder's right

kabunushimeibo 株主名簿 share-(=stock-)holders' list; share register

kabunushishihon 株主資本 capital stock; owner's capital

kabunushisōkai 株主総会 general

meeting of shareholders

kabunushiwariate 株主割当 allotment to shareholders ¶ direct *allotment* of new shares *to* the present *shareholders* at par value // New stock issues are mostly conducted by *allotment to* the present *shareholders*.

kabunushiyūsenbonyū 株主優先募入 privileged allocation of issuance to stockholders

kaburi 過振り overdraft; overdrawing ¶ an *overdraft of* 100,000 yen // This check *overdraws* the account.

kaburigendo 過振限度 limit of overdrawn account

kabushiki 株(式) stock; share (of capital stock) ¶ to issue *stocks* // to allot *shares* // to place *stocks* for public subscription // to buy *shares of stock* in a company // to take *stock* in a company // to purchase *stock* from another stockholder // the owner of ten *shares*, without nominal or par value, of the capital *stock* of the Corporation // A subscription to capital *stock* is an offer to purchase *shares* in a corporation. // The ownership of a corporation is divided into *shares* of *capital stock* evidenced by certificates held by shareholders.

売買確定株 firm stock

場株 listed stock on the local market

防衛株 defensive stock

中型株 middle-sized stock

注目株 watched stock

第一優先株 first preferred stock

出遅れ株 laggard

浮動株 floating stock

普通株 ordinary stock; common stock

外国非上場株 foreign stocks unlisted

現株 spot share; spot

議決権株 voting stock

端株 odd lot; fractional share

花形株 active stock; leading stock

発起人株 founder's share

一流株 pivotal stock; standard stock

実株 real stock; spot share; spot

上場株 listed stock ¶ to *list* the *stock* on the Tokyo Stock Exchange First Section

譲渡指定株 assigned stock

重役株 management stock

借株 borrowing stock; borrowed stock

借株残株 balance of stock loans

貸株 lending stock

経営参加株 stock purchased for participation in management

権利株 potential stock

子株 new stock

公募株 publicly subscribed stock

公開株 outstanding stock; publicly held stock; introduced stock

小型株 small-sized stock

国際株 international stock

競争力ある株 competitive stock

孫株 neo-new stock

名儀株 dummy stock

未払込株 part-paid stock

無額面株 non-par stock

無議決権株 non-voting stock

無償株式抱合せ公募付半額増資株 50% capital increase partially through share dividend and partially by public subscription

値嵩株 high-priced; fancy stock; blue chip

人気株 popular stock

大型株 giant-capital stock

大型低位株 low-priced giant-capital stock

親株 old stock

利益後受株 deferred stock

成長株 growth stock

市場経由株 stock purchased on the market

資格株 qualification share

失権株 unclaimed stock

品薄株 scarce stock; rare stock

資産株 income stock; asset issue

仕手株 speculative stock

賞与株 bonus stock

主力株 prime stock; leader

高値株 high flier

店頭株 counter stock

優先株 preferred stock; preference stock

幽霊株 bogus stock

雑株 miscellaneous stocks

全額払込株 paid-up stock; fully-paid stock

kabushikibaibaieki 株式売買益 capital gain

kabushikibonyūkotowarijō 株式募入断り状 letter of regret

kabushikiboshūkaishi 株式募集開始 subscription book open

kabushikiboshūshimekiri 株式募集締切 subscription book closed

kabushikibunkatsu 株式分割 stock split; split-up

kabushikigaisha 株式会社 joint-stock company

kabushikigakumen 株式額面 par; par value of the share

kabushikigappei 株式合併 reverse split of stock; share consolidation

kabushikigenzaigaku 株式現在額 capital stock outstanding

kabushikigōshigaisha 株式合資会社 joint stock limited partnership

kabushikihaibunhō 株式配分法 stocksharing system

kabushikihaitōkin 株式配当金 dividend on stock; stock dividend ¶ to declare *stock dividends* of 20 percent per annum // to maintain its *dividend* at 15 percent

kabushikihakkō 株式発行 stock issue ¶ a *stock issue* at the current price

kabushikihakkōgaku 株式発行額 capital stock issued

kabushikihakkōsaikōgendo 株式発行最高限度 capital stock authorized; authorized capital

kabushikihoyū 株式保有 stock (= share; equity) holding ¶ regulations concerning *equity holdings* in foreign companies // Firms are permitted to retain up to 51 percent of their foreign *equity holdings*.

kabushikihoyūritsu 株式保有率 holding ratio for a company's stock; share holding ratio

kabushikijiko 株式事故 share trouble

kabushikikaitorikentsukishasai 株式買取権付社債 bond with stock purchase warrant

kabushikikaitoriopushon 株式買取オプション stock purchase option

kabushikikanjō 株式勘定 share account

kabushikikōkaikaitsuke 株式公開買付 take-over bid

kabushikikyōkō 株式恐慌 stock exchange panic

kabushikimihakkōgaku 株式未発行額 capital stock unissued

kabushikiminshuka 株式民主化 stock democratization

kabushikimochiai 株式持合い interlocking stockholding

kabushikimochibunkachi 株式持分価値 stock equity

kabushikimōshikomi 株式申込み subscription for shares; stock subscription

kabushikimōshikomikin 株式申込金 application money for stock

kabushikimōshikominin 株式申込人 subscriber for shares

kabushikimōshikomisho 株式申込書 subscription blank; application form for stocks

kabushikimotochō 株式元帳 stock ledger

kabushikinakagainin 株式仲買人 stock broker; broker; stock-jobber

kabushikinojikahakkō 株式の時価発行 increase in capital at the market price; stock issue at the current price

kabushikinokokizamimushōkōfu 株式の小刻み無償交付 small partial share dividend

kabushikinotōgō 株式の統合 consolidation of stocks; reverse split of shares

kabushikiōbo 株式応募 subscription for shares; stock subscription

kabushikisaiteitorihiki 株式裁定取引 stock arbitrage

kabushikiseisanjo 株式清算所 stock exchange clearing house

kabushikishihon 株式資本 share-capital; equity capital

kabushikishijō 株式市場 stock (= share) market ¶ The *stock market* turned upward Friday with a moderate afternoon rally. // The *market* was higher at the start. // In the *share market* investors appear to be taking a sanguine view of future economic prospects. // Enterprises took advantage of the buoyant *share market* to sell new shares at high issue prices.

kabushikishintakushōsho 株式信託証書 stock interest certificate

kabushikishutoku 株式取得 acquisition of stock

kabushikisōbadenshinki 株式相場電信機 telegraphic stock printer

kabushikisōbahyō 株式相場表 stock list

kabushikisōbahyōtēpu 株式相場表テープ ticker-tape

kabushikitōki 株式投機 stock speculation; speculation in stocks; speculation on the stock market ¶ to *speculate in stocks*

kabushikitorihikidaka 株式取引高 stock dealings; trading; volume ¶ *Volume* picked up slightly to 16,280,000 shares. // As *trading* slackened, industrials led a down-trend. // a drop in *volume* // Industrial shares jumped up in heavy *trading*.

kabushikitorihikiin 株式取引員 broker agent

kabushikitorihikijo 株式取引所 stock exchange ¶ 1,800 issues are traded on the New York *Stock Exchange*. // The international oils moved up on the London *Stock Exchange* Friday.

kabushikitorihikijokōhō 株式取引所公報 stock exchange daily official list

kabushikitorihikijokaiinken 株式取引所会員権 stock exchange seat

kabushikitorihikijokyūjitsu 株式取引所休日 stock exchange holiday

kabushikitorihikijoseisanka 株式取引所清算課 stock exchange clearing house

kabushikitorihikijokashitsuke 株式取引所貸付 stock exchange loan

kabushikitōshi 株式投資 stock investment; investment in stocks; equity investment

kabushikitōshishintaku 株式投資信託 stock investment trust

kabushikiuridashikakaku 株式売出価格 offering price

kabushikiwariate 株式割当 allotment (of shares)

kabushikiwariatekyozetsusho 株式割当拒絶書 letter of regret

kabushikiwariateshōsho 株式割当証書 allotment certificate

kabushikiwariatetsūchi 株式割当通知 share allotment letter

kabusoshiki 下部組織 infrastructure ¶ social *infrastructure* // *infrastructural* investment

kachi 価値 value; worth ¶ to raise the *value* of the yen relative to the dollar over the long term // Money is a measure of *value* as well as a store of *value*.

物的価値 material value
超過余剰価値 extra-surplus value
付加価値 value added; added value
派生価値 derived value
比較価値 comparative value
実際価値 actual value
実質価値 real value
実在価値 intrinsic value
剰余価値 surplus value
貨幣価値 monetary value; value of money
経済価値 economic value; commercial value
希少価値 scarcity value
交換価値 value in exchange; exchange value
客観価値 objective value
名目価値 nominal value
最適価値 optimum value
正常価値 normal value

資本還元価値 capitalized value
市場価値 market value
使用価値 value in use; utility value
商品価値 commercial value; commodity value;
相対価値 relative value
相対的余剰価値 relative surplus value
主観価値 subjective value
適正価値 reasonable value
残存価値 residue value

kachihandan 価値判断 evaluation; valuation; appraisal; judgment of value

kachihozōshudan 価値保蔵(＝保存)手段 means of store of value ¶ [参考] Money is a store of value.

kachihyōjishudan 価値表示手段 measure of value

kachihyōjun 価値標準 standard of value

kachikan 価値観 sense of values; ordering of values ¶ a change in the *sense of values* // the forced re-*ordering of values*

kachikijun 価値基準 standard of value

kachishakudo 価値尺度 measure of value ¶ the inadequacy of gold as a stable *measure of value*

kachōkin 課徴金 charges; imposition; surcharge

kadai 課題 task ¶ Trade policy faces two broad *tasks* which are linked together. // It rendered the *task* of economic policy singularly difficult. // to assess the *task* of adjustment that lies ahead

kadaihyōka 過大評価 overestimate; overvaluation

kadaishihon 過大資本 overcapitalization

kadaizōshi 過大増資 stock watering

kaden 家電 electric home appliances; household electrical appliances

kadō 稼働 operation ¶ The factory began *operations.* // The plant is in full *operation.* The economy is *operating* at a high level, and close to capacity. // Steel mill *operations* were 42 percent of capacity. // The percentage of plant capacity being *operated* increased. // Plant and machinery are *operating* at full stretch.

全面稼働 full operation; operation to full capacity ¶ The industry is *operating* to near-*full capacity.*

kadōnōryoku 稼働能力 operation capacity

kādopanchishisutemu カード・パンチ・システム ［コン］ punched card system; PCS

kadōritsu 稼働率 rate of operation; degree of capacity utilization; operation rate; operating level ¶ The modest growth in production has as yet produced no noteworthy increase in the *degree of capacity utilization.* // Although the highest since 81.7 percent in the quarter of 1914, that was still well below the 92 percent or better *operation* levels in 1973. // In June industry was operating at 80.5 *percent of capacity* by the Federal Reserve measure, up slightly from 80.3 percent in May. // *Capacity utilization* remains at relatively low levels.

kadōritsushisū 稼働率指数 capacity utilization index; index of operating ratio

kaeriniunchin 帰り荷運賃 homeward freight

kafusoku 過不足 overs and shorts; excess and deficiency; shortages or overages; shortages and gluts; shortage and surfeit (＝overage) ¶ the automatic corrections of *shortages and gluts* by misleading market signals // *Shortages and surfeits* of reserves will result in appreciation and depreciations of the dollar.

kagakuseihin 化学製品 chemicals; chemical products

kagakutekikanrihō 科学的管理法 scientific management

kagensōba 下限相場 ［外］ lower limit rate

kageri かげり dark spots; dark shadow; darkening signs; downward trends; gray spot; signs of a decline; shading; recession shadow; partial business slowdown; partial overcasting phenomena; gloom ¶ The economic *gloom* deepened.

kahei 貨幣 money; coin; note; currency

物品貨幣 material money

鋳造貨幣 coined money; coin

代表貨幣 representative money

封鎖貨幣 blocked money

贋造貨幣 counterfeit coin; false coin

銀行貨幣 bank money

合法貨幣 lawful money

引揚貨幣 coin withdrawn from circulation

卑金属貨幣 base-metallic coin

補助貨幣 subsidiary coin; auxiliary coin

本位貨幣 standard coin

法定貨幣 legal money

実物貨幣 commodity money

確定貨幣 definitive money

計算貨幣 money of account

緊急貨幣 emergency currency

金属貨幣　metallic money
小切手貨幣　checkbook money
国家貨幣　state money
摩滅貨幣　defaced coin
名目貨幣　token (money); fiat money
労働貨幣　labor note
信用貨幣　faith money; credit money
商品貨幣　commodity money

kaheibērukan　貨幣ベール観　veil of money; theory of dichotomy

kaheibunseki　貨幣分析　monetary analysis

kaheichūzōhi　貨幣鋳造費　coinage; brassage

kaheichūzōken　貨幣鋳造権　right of coinage

kaheichūzōrisa　貨幣鋳造利差　seigniorage (gain)

kaheidakanken　貨幣兌換券　coin certificate

kaheidōmei　貨幣同盟　monetary union

kaheiganzōsha　貨幣贋造者　(unlawful) coiner; counterfeiter

kaheigensō　貨幣現送　money shipment; transport of money (= bank notes and coins)

kaheikachi　貨幣価値　value of money ¶ The *value of money* will be preserved. // Their belief in the future *value of money* was undermined. // maintenance of the *value of money*

kaheikyū　貨幣給　money wage

kaheinojuyō　貨幣の需要　demand for money

kaheinokōsa　貨幣の公差　remedy and allowance of money; tolerance

kaheinoshotokusokudo　貨幣の所得速度　income velocity of money

kaheinotaigaikachi　貨幣の対外価値　external purchasing power of money

kaheirishi　貨幣利子　monetary interest

kaheisaiteitorihiki　貨幣裁定取引　money arbitrage

kaheisakkaku　貨幣錯覚　money illusion

kaheiseido　貨幣制度　monetary system

kaheiseidonokannōsei　貨幣制度の感応性　responsiveness of monetary system

kaheishihon　貨幣資本　money capital

kaheisūryōsetsu　貨幣数量説　quantity theory of money

kaheisūryōtekibunseki　貨幣数量的分析　quantitative analysis of money

kaheitan'i　貨幣単位　unit of money; monetary unit

kaheiyōkin　貨幣用金　monetary gold

kahenkinri　可変金利　floating rate (of interest)

kahentōshizei　可変投資税　variable investment tax

kahogo　過保護　over-protection ¶ *over-protection* of some specific industry

kahōkōchokusei　下方硬直性　downward rigidity

kahōshūsei　下方修正　downward revision ¶ The increase was smaller than the *downward-revised* 3.8% increase. // [参考] This experience led authorities to scale down their estimates of the rate of increase in the capacity over time.

kaiageshōkan　買上償還　retirement by purchase

kaiaori　買煽り　[市] rig; boost; bull; scour; scramble ¶ to *rig* the market // to *bull* the market // to *boost* the market // to *scour* markets for sugar // a *scramble* for scarce goods

kaiaorisuji 買煽筋 ［市］riggers

kaiasari 買漁り hurried buying; rushed buying; buying (=shopping) spree; panic buying; buying craze; "lead time" buying; early buying; frenzied buying ¶ An inflationary psychology stimulated *hurried buying.* // a collective *buying spree* for scarce materials and components // *"lead time" purchases* of petroleum materials before the prospective rise in oil prices // *buying early* to beat inflation // *Frenzied buying* by speculators pushed gold to a new high. // The *buying spree* has dissipated. // People are at the height of the *buying spree.* // A *shopping spree* came to an end. // to touch off *panic buying* among people // →買急ぎ

kaibikae 買控え withholding purchases; reluctance in buying; holding down of purchase; restrained buying; conservative buying (attitude); wait-and-see buying attitude ¶ Consumers *held down their purchases* of articles of luxury. // *conservative* stock *purchases*

kaichō 会長 chairman of the board of directors

kaichūmon 買注文 buying order; bid; ［市］buy order

kaidame 買溜め hoarding; hoarding purchase ¶ *hoarding* of heating oil to beat inflation

kaifuku 回復 recovery; revival; resumption; revitalizing; rebound; recuperation; restoration; reattainment; resurgence; regaining; recouping; rally; convalescence ¶ Production *recovered* from the low point reached in June. // The ground lost in September was *recovered* in Octo-

ber. // The *revival* in buying interest points to something more basic. // A slow *resumption* of real growth was recorded. // Growth *resumed.* // Consumer spending was *revitalized.* // Steps have been taken to *revitalize* business activity. // A *rebound* in the economy has become visible. // Convertibility was *recuperated* for the currency. // *recuperation* of convertibility // the *restoration* of a better performance // The balance of payments was *restored* to equilibrium. // Business *reattained* vital activity after comparative absence of expansion. // Output registered a marked *resurgence.* // External payments *regained* a surplus balance. // These losses have by now been *recouped.* // Profit-taking blunted the sharp *rally* of the past two sessions. // to experience no more than a slow and uncertain *convalescence* // →反騰

kaifukukatei 回復過程 recovery phase (=period) of the business cycle; recovery process ¶ The economy is entering into a *recovery phase* of the business cycle. // Canada was entering the *recovery period of the business cycle* with a high continuing rate of inflation.

kaifukutojōkoku 回復途上国 convalescent countries ¶ the *convalescent countries* such as France and Italy

kaigai 海外 foreign countries; overseas countries; foreign; overseas; abroad; offshore ¶ economic trends in *foreign countries* // in *overseas* markets // to come from *abroad* // ［参考］the financial surplus of the rest-of-the-world sector

kaigaiginkō 海外銀行 overseas

bank

kaigaijigyō 海外事業 overseas business ¶ financing for *overseas business*

kaigaijigyōsho 海外事業所 field office abroad

kaigaikanjō 海外勘定 external transactions account

kaigaikarakojin'enoiten 海外から個人への移転 current transfers from rest of the world to persons

kaigaikeiki 海外景気 overseas business conditions

kaigaikeizai 海外経済 foreign economic situation; overseas economies; economic conditions abroad

kaigaikinri 海外金利 overseas interest rate; interest rate abroad; money rate overseas

kaigaikōjōkensetsu 海外工場建設 factory construction abroad

kaigainiokerugaikataishaku 海外における外貨貸借 extending foreign currency credit to non-residents

kaigainitaisurusaikennojunzō 海外に対する債権の純増 net lending to rest of the world

kaigairyokō 海外旅行 tourism; foreign travel; overseas trip ¶ expenses for *foreign travels* // earnings from *tourism*

kaigaishakkankarimiaigashi 海外借款借見合貸 customer's liabilities on loans due to foreign banks

kaigaishijō 海外市場 overseas market ¶ to open up *overseas markets* for... // competitive powers on *overseas markets*

kaigaishutsuryō 海外出漁 fishery in foreign waters

kaigaisōba 海外相場 rate in overseas market; quotation on overseas markets

kaigaitanshi 海外短資 foreign short-term capital

kaigaitōshi 海外投資 (direct) investment overeas ¶ Japanese enterprises making *direct investment* in *overseas* markets

kaigaitōshiganponhoken 海外投資元本保険 external investment principal insurance

kaigaitōshikin'yū 海外投資金融 financing of overseas investment and overseas enterprise

kaigaitōshikōdōkijun 海外投資行動基準 guidelines for investment activities in developing countries

kaigaiyojō 海外余剰 external surplus

kaigyoku 買玉 [市] bull account; long account

kaihatsu 開発 development; exploitation ¶ more efficient and rationalized *development* of industry

長期開発 secular development; long-term development

地域開発 regional development

人的資源開発 manpower development; human resource development

経済開発 economic development

経済社会開発 economic and social development

社会開発 social development

総合開発 multi-purpose development

土地開発 land development

都市開発 urban development

kaihatsuchōsashikinkyōkyū 開発調査資金供給 providing funds for development research

kaihatsuenjo 開発援助 development aid; development assistance ¶ to devote 0.15 percent of national product to *development aid* // a substantial increase in the *development assistance*

kaihatsujigyōkashitsuke 開発事業貸付 loan on development project

kaihatsukakusa 開発格差 development gap

kaihatsukeikaku 開発計画 development project; development plan

kaihatsukin'yū 開発金融 development finance

kaihatsunotamenokokusaitōshi 開発のための国際投資 international investment for the development

kaihatsuriyō 開発利用 exploitation; development ¶ The inadequate *exploitation* of local resources is prevalent in the provision of welfare services. // the costs of resource *exploitation* // a way of *exploitating* economies of modern mechanized cultivation in export crop production // The margin available for passing on price increases might be unduly *exploited* in some sectors. // *Development* is now more balanced and more sound.

kaihatsushikinkashitsuke 開発資金貸付 lending of development funds

kaihatsutojōkoku 開発途上国 developing countries (=nations)

kaihatsutojōkokuenjo 開発途上国援助 aid to developing countries

kaihatsuyunyūhōshiki 開発輸入方式 develop-and-import scheme

kaihi 回避 ward off; fend off; forestall ¶ The flow of foreign exchange has been successfully *warded off*. // to *forestall* possible heavy selling of dollars

kaihō 開放 opening(-up) ¶ the pro-

gressive *opening-up* of the economy to foreign competition // a wider *opening* of its markets particularly for manufactured goods // the *opening* of the Japanese market to foreign goods // a greater *opening* in Japan for foreign goods // [参考] fair access in the Japanese market for U.S. goods and services

kaihōgatatanpo 開放型担保 open-end mortgage

kaihōsei 開放性 openness ¶ proof of Japan's new *openness* to international banking

kaihōtaikei 開放体系 open system

kaihōtaisei 開放体制 open system; open regime ¶ a fairly *open* and liberalized trade *regime*

kaihōteki 開放的 open; liberal; free ¶ more *open* trade policies // Access to markets is relatively *liberal*. // to *open* its economy to competition from overseas // to *open* up Tokyo's capital markets to more foreign investment

kaiinken 会員権 →加盟権

kaiiregaikokukawase 買入外国為替 foreign exchange bought; [会] bills bought

kaiiregurūpu 買入グループ [証市] purchase group

kaiirekakaku 買入価格 purchase price; buying price; purchasing price

kaiiresaimuhiritsu 買入債務比率 payables to sales ratio; payable turnover

kaiireshikin 買入資金 funds for purchase; purchase funds

kaiireshōkan 買入償還 purchasing redemption

kaiireshōkyaku 買入消却 retirement by purchase

kaiiretaishōsaiken 買入対象債券

instruments for (the Bank of Japan's) buying operation

kaiisogi 買急ぎ scouring; scurrying; over-ordering; buying craze; scare buying ¶ to *scour* for sugar to beat inflation // to *scurry* from store to store // Customers are *over-ordering* for simply hoarding. // The *buying craze* on smaller cars has become frenetic because of rising gasoline prices. // ［参考］Consumers are increasingly buying the advance of needs. // to foster a buy-now philosophy // a significant switch away from the recent "buy in advance syndrome" // →買漁り

kaiji 開示 disclosure ¶ → 公開
完全開示　full disclosure
継続開示　continuous disclosure

kaijinogensoku 開示の原則 disclosure philosophy

kaijōhoken 海上保険 marine insurance; maritime insurance

kaijōhokenshōken 海上保険証券 marine insurance policy

kaijōkiken 海上危険 ordinary marine risk

kaikakekin 買掛金 accounts payable

kaikakesaimu 買掛債務 accounts payable

kaikaku 改革 reorganization; reform; restructuring; reshaping ¶ a sweeping *reorganization* of the banking system proposed by President Nixon // the steps toward international monetary *reform* // a far-reaching *reform* of the tax system // the first stage in the evolutionary *reform* of the international monetary system // a long road of discussions about monetary *reform* // The process of international monetary *reform* has been under way for more than a decade. // a financial *reform* bill aimed at *restructuring* the U.S. banking system // We began to see the reward for fundamental *reform*. // banking system *restructuring* // to *reshape* the financial order into a pattern reflecting the realities // the financial *restructuring* of industrial firms // the separate and uncoordinated *reform* of the world trade and monetary system // a greater voice in *reshaping* the world monetary and trade systems // to undertake bold policy *reforms* and institutional *restructuring* // the implementation of the wide-ranging program of economic *reforms* that was drawn up last year

kaikawase 買為替 buying exchange; exchange bought; bills bought

kaikei 会計 accounting
部門別会計　departmental accounting
発生主義会計　accrual accounting
インフレ修正会計　accounting for inflation
一般会計　general account
企業会計　business accounting
国民会計　national accounting
社会会計　social accounting
特別会計　special account
財務会計　financial accounting

kaikeibo 会計簿 account-book

kaikeigakari 会計係 accountant; treasurer

kaikeigensoku 会計原則 accounting principles
一般に認められた会計原則　generally accepted accounting principles

kaikeigyōmu 会計業務 accountancy

kaikeihōkoku 会計報告 financial report

kaikeikansa 会計監査 auditing; audit

継続会計監査 continuous audit

期末会計監査 completed audit

kaikeikansanin 会計監査人 independent auditor

kaikeikensa 会計検査 auditing; audit

kaikeikensakan 会計検査官 auditor

kaikeikijun 会計基準 accounting standards

一般に認められた会計基準 generally accepted accounting standards

kaikeikikan 会計期間 accounting period

kaikeinendo 会計年度 fiscal year; financial year; accounting year ¶ the budget for *fiscal* 1956 // in the *financial year* of 1977 // of the 1978 *fiscal year*

kaikeishi 会計士 chartered accountant; public accountant

公認会計士 certified public accountant; CPA

特許会計士 chartered accountant

kaikeishorihōshin 会計処理方針 accounting policies ¶ a summary of significant *accounting policies* // disclosure of *accounting policies*

kaikeitan'i 会計単位 accounting unit

kaiki 回帰 regression ¶ The *regression* expressing the relation of growth to intermediation is... // One hundred and eight *regressions* of the complete model were run using different values for x. // to *regress* the rate of income growth directly

upon monetary variables

放物線回帰 parabolic regression

級間回帰 between classes regression

級内回帰 within classes regression

kaiki 買気 buying interest; buying sentiment; buying disposition; [市] bullish sentiment; bullish support ¶ The market lost *bullish support.* // The market was higher supported by *bullish sentiment.* // Some retail *buying interest* is seen in short materials.

一斉の買気 unanimous (=allround) buying

kaikibunsekihō 回帰分析法 regression analysis method

逐次重回帰分析 stepwise multiple regression analysis

kaikihōteishiki 回帰方程式 regression equation

kaikikeisū 回帰係数 regression coefficient

kaikiōsei 買気旺盛 aggressive buying

kaikisen 回帰線 regression line

kaikiusu 買気薄 [市] lack of (buying) interest ¶ Prices wilted under two main factors; profit-taking and sheer *lack of interest.*

kaiko 解雇 dismissal; discharge ¶ The pace of *dismissal* has accelerated.

不名誉な解雇 dishonorable discharge

一時解雇 temporary discharge

kaikokin 解雇金 dismissal wage; severance wage; terminal wage

kaikoritsu 解雇率 discharge rate; quit rate

kaikototenbō 回顧と展望 retrospect and prospect ¶ *retrospects* of 1980 and 1981 *prospects*

kaikotsūchisho 解雇通知書 dismissal notice

kaikyū 階級 class
知識階級 educated class
知的職業階級 professional class
中産階級 middle class
不生産的階級 unproductive class
地主階級 landed class; proprietary class
上流階級 upper class
下層階級 lower class
金利生活者階級 rentier class
無産階級 propertyless class
労働階級 working class; laboring class
社会階級 social class
有閑階級 leisure class
有産階級 propertied class; proprietary class

kaimawarihin 買回り品 shopping goods

kaimochi 買持ち overbought position; long position ¶ Dealers go *long* of exchange expecting a rise in the market. // The bank acquired a net *long* forward exchange *position*.

kaimodoshi 買戻し repurchase; redemption; bear-covering; short-covering ¶ open market transactions involving *repurchase* agreements // selling operation under *repurchase* agreement
特約に基づく買戻し contractual repurchase

kaimodoshigimu 買戻義務 repurchase obligation

kaimodoshijōkentsukibaikyaku 買戻条件付売却 [米] matched sale-purchase transaction (=operation) ¶ The Account Manager employs *matched sale-purchase transactions* with dealers. // The dealers must borrow the funds they will use to enter into *matched sale-purchase agreements*. // The yield dealers receive on the *matched sale-purchase operation* produces a small spread over the cost of funds borrowed.

kaimodoshijōkentsukibaikyakutegatawaribikiryō 買戻条件付売却手形割引料 discount on bills sold on condition of repurchase

kaimodoshijōkentsukiurioperēshon 買戻条件付売りオペレーション selling operation under repurchase agreement

kaimodoshikeiyaku 買戻契約 repurchase agreement ¶ They do not include purchases or sales of securities under *repurchase agreements,* repurchase (i.e., resale), or similar contracts. // securities held under *repurchase agreement* // *purchases under agreements* to resell

kaimodoshiken 買戻権 right of redemption; right of repurchase

kaimodoshinedan 買戻値段 call price; repurchase price

kaimodoshinin 買戻人 redeemer

kaimodoshisekiyu 買戻石油 buy-back oil

kaimōshikomi 買申込み [市] buying offer

kainin 懐妊 gestation ¶ Italy's long-*gestating* economic recovery plan saw the light of day.

kaininki 買い人気 [市] interest; speculative interest ¶ high *speculative interest* among traders and the public

kaininkikan 懐妊期間 gestation period; gestation lag ¶ The *gestation* period for investment is long. // The expansion of capacity was constrained by normal *gestation lags*. // the long *gestation period* of regulations governing the financial reorganization of companies

kainushinokikenfutangensoku 買主の危険負担原則 "caveat emptor" (philosophy)

kainyū 介入 intervention ¶ the Bank's *intervention* in the market in support of the dollar // The Bank has recently *intervened* in the foreign exchange market to support the US dollar. // arrangements among the European central banks for mutual *intervention* // *intervention* operations on the spot foreign exchange market // direct *intervention* // The $1,119 million fall resulted from the Bank's *direct intervention* on the foreign markets. // to make exchange-market *interventions* in support of other members' currencies // policy of foreign exchange market *intervention* to smooth out erratic exchange rate fluctuations // to exclude the possibility of *interventions* taking place before the *intervention* limits have been reached, i.e. "intra-marginal *interventions*." // The Minister called on the Bank to *intervene* more actively in the foreign exchange market. // In March *intervention* sales totalled $550 million. // to coordinate dollar *interventions* to avoid simultaneous reverse *interventions* // to effect, and then discontinue, its massive exchange-market *interventions* // protracted large-scale *intervention* in one direction in the exchange market // dollar *interventions* to be supplemented by more *intervention* in non-dollar currencies

kainyūgai 介入買い intervention purchase

kainyūsōsa 介入操作 intervention operation ¶ dollar balances acquired in official *intervention operations* // *intervention operations* on the spot foreign exchange market

kainyūsuijun 介入水準 intervention level ¶ The Bank decides on its *intervention levels* daily.

kainyūten 介入点 intervention point ¶ the upper or lower market *intervention point* // to set upper and lower *intervention points* against the dollar

kainyūtenjōkagen 介入点上下限 upper or lower market intervention point

kainyūtsūka 介入通貨 intervention currency ¶ to maintain the US dollar as an *intervention currency*

kainyūuri 介入売り intervention sale

kaioperēshon 買いオペレーション buying operation ¶ *buying operation* in securities vis-à-vis securities dealers

売戻条件付買いオペ（レーション） buying operation under repurchase agreement

kairi 乖離 divergence; deviation ¶ the *divergence* of an individual currency from the movement of the weighted average of all member currencies // discernible upward and forward *deviations* from the planned rate of monetary growth // the margin of *deviation* from the trend line // *deviations* of M_1 from its average rate of growth // *deviation* away from the intended path // *divergences* in inflation rates // a marked *divergence* of trend between the domestic and overseas prices

kairigendo 乖離限度 threshold of divergence; divergence threshold ¶ The Belgian franc crossed its *threshold of divergence* against the European currency unit.

kairishihyō 乖離指標 divergence indicator

kairiten 乖離点 threshold of divergence

kaisakudō 買策動 bull campaign

kaisankachi 解散価値 break-up value

kaisasae 買支え support buying; support operation; price-bolstering purchase ¶ to engage in *support buying* of the US dollar // to *support* the US dollar on the Tokyo exchange market // Jimmy Carter's save-the-dollar programs of *price-bolstering purchases* and high interest rates

kaisasaechūmon 買支え注文 supporting order

kaisei 改正 modification; amendment ¶ The proposed *modifications* are extensive and are assembled under twenty headings in the report. // The *amendment* does not represent a total, revision of the Articles of Agreement.

kaisha 会社 corporation; company; firm; concern; house; partnership ¶ Japanese *companies,* centering on steel *firms* // business results of major *corporations* // foreign affiliated trading *firms* // business *concerns* incorporated overseas

別働会社 shell company; holding company

同族会社 family company

合名会社 ordinary partnership

合資会社 limited partnership

非上場会社 unlisted company

泡沫会社 bubble company

上場会社 listed company

従属会社 subordinate company

株式会社 joint stock company

活況会社 going company

関連(=関係)会社 affiliated company; affiliate

系列会社 affiliated company; affiliate; related company; subsidiary company; subsidiary

金融会社 finance company

子会社 subsidiary company; subsidiary

個人会社 sole corporation

抹消会社 defunct company

持株会社 holding company

親会社 parent company; holding company

信託会社 trust company

相互保険会社 mutual insurance company

証券会社 securities company (= house)

証券金融会社 securities finance company

特許会社 chartered company

有限会社 limited liability company

kaishaboki 会社簿記 corporation book keeping

kaishagatatōshin 会社型投信 corporation type investment trust

kaishakaikei 会社会計 corporation accounting

kaishakanshijō 会社間市場 inter-company market

kaishakin'yū 会社金融 corporation finance; corporate finance

kaishakōsei 会社更生 corporation reorganization

kaishasoshiki 会社組織 company organization

kaishasuji 会社筋 [市] insiders

kaishasujikaranojōhō 会社筋から

の情報 insider information

kaishatoshi 会社都市 company town

kaishiburi 買渋り consumer resistance

kaishime 買占め corner; cornering ¶ to form a *corner* in land // the big firm's *cornering* of the market in stocks and real estate

kaishimenin 買占人 cornerman; rigger; monopolist

kaishimerengō 買占連合 ring

kaishimeshōryaku 買占商略 [市] bull speculation

kaishū 回収 recovery; collection; call; retirement; recall; calling-in; withdrawal; retraction ¶ bank notes *withdrawn* from circulation // *collection* of bills // to *collect* sales proceeds // *calling* back of lendings // to *retire* bonds // *calling-in* by the Bank of Japan of loans with commercial banks // a 15-year *retractable* floating rate note // After five years, investors can *retract* the issue (of 50 million dollars which pays 1/4 par over six-month London Eurodollar deposit rates, and the borrower can *recall* it, at par). // Commercial loans are *retired* within a brief period.

貸倒れ回収 recovery of bad debt

欠損回収 recovery of loss

売掛金回収 collection of bills; bill collection

kaishūfunōmikomi 回収不能見込 estimated loss ¶ *estimated loss* on loans

kaishūgimon 回収疑問 doubtful ¶ *doubtful* loans

kaishūjimu 回収事務 collection business

kaishūjōken 回収条件 collection terms of sales proceeds

kaishūsen 回収船 recovery ship

kaishūshōken 回収証券 retired bond

kaishutsudō 買出動 [市] buying drive ¶ to conduct a *buying drive*

kaisō 階層 group; class; bracket; span; stratum; range; level; ladder ¶ The pivot of housing demand shifted to the low-*bracket* income *stratum*. // people in higher income *strata* // employees at the upper end of the salary *range* // the number of employees below different salary *levels* // migrants at the bottom of the social *ladder*

所得階層 income bracket; income group ¶ people in the lower-, middle-, and higher-*income brackets* // upper *income groups*

年齢層 age-span; age bracket; age group ¶ career earnings over the *age-span* 30-50 // people in the *age-group* 35-45

kaisōba 買相場 buying rate; [市] bull market ¶ The official limits of the *buying* and selling *rates* for U.S. dollars (spot) are set at ¥362.70 (upper limit) and ¥357.30 (lower limit), per US$1.

kaison 海損 marine loss; average ¶ a general *average* // a particular *average*

kaisugi 買過ぎ overbuying; loading up; overbought ¶ to be in an *overbought* position

kaisugisōba 買過ぎ相場 overbought market

kaisuinotansuika 海水の淡水化 desalination of sea water

kaisusumi 買進み active buying; aggressive buying; persistent buying

kaitakushashikin'yūzūseido 開拓者資金融通制度 settler's fund

system

kaite 買手 purchaser; buyer; vendee; customer; client

kaitefutan 買手負担 buyer's risk

kaitei 改訂 revision ¶ The amendment does not represent on total *revision* of the Articles of Agreement. // The proposed *revision* is an amendment of the existing Articles and does not constitute a new treaty.

kaiteikeisū 改定計数 revised figure; revised data

kaiteiyudenkussakusōchi 海底油田掘削装置 off-shore drilling rig

kaitekikijun 快適基準 standard of comfort

kaitekinaseikatsu 快適な生活 amenities ¶ differences in the *amenities* available in different parts of the country

kaitekinaseikatsuoitonamukenri 快適な生活を営む権利 amenity right

kaiten 回転 turnover ¶ to *turn over* each unit of our money foster // inventory *turnover* period

kaitenkikin 回転基金 revolving fund

kaitennissu 回転日数 turnover period

kaitenritsu 回転率 turnover (ratio) ¶ The merchandise *turnover* is 5 times a year, or the total stock is sold out or turned over every 72 days (360 divided by 5). // the concern the more frequent *turnover* // The inventory is *turned over* approximately every 60 days, or 6 times a year.

支払勘定回転率 turnover ratio of accounts payable

資本回転率 turnover ratio of capital

使用総資本回転率 turnover ratio of total liabilities

商品回転率 merchandise turnover

棚卸資産回転率 turnover ratio of inventory; inventory turnover

kaitenshin'yōjō 回転信用状 revolving (letter of) credit

kaiteshijō 買手市場 buyer's market

kaitōkigentsukiofā 回答期限付きオファー firm offer

kaitonae 買唱え bid; bidding

kaitori 買取り buying; purchase; acquisition; take-over ¶ A bank plans to *buy* a controlling interest in another bank. // The bank bids to *buy* a 51% stake in a Swiss bank. // to plan to *take over* another bank

kaitorigaikokukawase 買取外国為替 foreign exchange bills bought

kaitoriginkō 買取銀行 negotiating bank

kaitorishikinhoshō 買取資金補償 reimbursement

kaitsukekenshōsho 買付権証書 (subscription) warrant ¶ to issue 100,000 three-month Euro-Treasury *warrants* to buy the old Treasury long bond

kaitsukeshikin 買付資金 purchase funds

kaitsunagi 買いつなぎ hedge; hedging ¶ →ヘッジ

kaiukekenshōsho 買受権証書 subscription warrant; stock (purchase) warrant

kaiume 買埋め ［市］ short-covering; repurchase

kaiundōmei 海運同盟 shipping conference; ship(ping) ring

kaiungaisha 海運会社 shipping company

kaiunshijō 海運市場 shipping

market

kaiuntorihikisho 海運取引所 shipping exchange

kaiyakuharaimodoshikin 解約払戻金 surrender value

kaiyakuhenkankakaku 解約返還価格 surrender value

kaiyakukin 解約金 cancellation money

kaiyakukōjokin 解約控除金 surrender charge

kaiyakukokuchikikan 解約告知期間 term for prior notice for cancellation

kaiyōkaihatsu 海洋開発 ocean development; offshore and ocean development

kaiyōsangyō 海洋産業 ocean industry

kaiyōshigen 海洋資源 ocean resources

kaizen 改善 improvement; favorable swing; betterment ¶ to show *improvement* in profits over the previous year of some 12 percent // a *favorable swing* of business activity // a sigificant *betterment* of business administration

事務改善 better business

生活改善 better living

kaizō 改造 remodeling ¶ *remodeling* of the Japanese

kajitsu 果実 fruit; income; return ¶ the principals and *fruit* of foreign investment // the monthly *income* of a trust company from investment in real estate

kajō 過剰 excess; surplus; overabundance; glut; plethora; overhang ¶ *excess* liquidity // *surplus* funds in the market // the market *glutted* with oil products // a situation of liquidity *glut* // a *plethora* of special subsidies and governmental intervention //a situation of liquidity *glut* // The recession-induced world oil *glut* is shrinking. // Temporary global *glut* of crude oil kept a lid on prices. // to bring a sharp end to the oil *glut* // The much-talked-about oil *glut* proved to be short-lived. // the market *glutted* with oil products // The dollar *overhang* is expected to expand. // The *overhang* of stocks accumulated will drag on production. // →過重

揚荷過剰 overdischarge

供給過剰 oversupply

生産過剰 overproduction

船腹過剰 overtonnage

資本過剰 overcapitalization

積荷過剰 overburden

在荷過剰 overstock

kajōchochiku 過剰貯蓄 oversaving

kajōhikishime 過剰引締め overbraking

kajōjin'in 過剰人員 excess workers; surplus work force ¶ Major companies are carrying *excess workers*. // The situation of *excess workers* was most serious in manufacturing industries.

kajōjunbi 過剰準備 excessive reserves

kajōjuyō 過剰需要 excessive demand

kajōkoyō 過剰雇用 surplus labor; overmanning; labor redundancy; excess employment; overemployment ¶ Managements face the problem of *surplus labor* retained within enterprises. // to be hanging on to the *overmanning* in order to keep jobs // to reduce costs by eliminating *overmanning* // Much of British industry is currently *overmanned*. // *Labor redundancy* assumed serious proportions as a cyclical issue.

企業内過剰雇用　surplus labor retained within enterprises

kajōnimotsu 過剰荷物　overloaded cargo

kajōryūdōsei 過剰流動性　excess liquidity

kajōseisan 過剰生産　overproduction

kajōsetsubi 過剰設備　excess capacity; overcapacity (situation); surplus capacity ¶ Industry has been plagued by idle *surplus* plant *capacity*.

kajōshōhin 過剰商品　surplus commodity

kajōtōshi 過剰投資　over-investment

kajōzaiko 過剰在庫　inventory glut; overhang of stocks ¶ Manufacturers are realizing the threat of an *inventory glut*. // The accumulated *overhang of stocks* is a drag on output levels.

kajū 加重　weighting ¶ the trade-*weighted* average value of the U.S. dollar

kajū 過重　excess(ive); surplus; superfluous; overabundant; extra ¶ *excess* liquidity // to curb an *excessive* increase in loans // *overabundant* oil supplies // *superfluous* corporate liquidity // to mop up *extra* funds from the market // →過剰

kajūheikin 加重平均　weighted arithmetic average (=mean)

kajūheikingenkahō 加重平均原価法 ［会］ weighted average cost method

kajūheikinkabuka 加重平均株価　weighted stock price average

kajūidōheikin 加重移動平均　weighted moving average ¶ This series is a *weighted* 4-term *moving average* (with weights 1, 2, 2, 1) placed at the terminal month of the span.

kajūmatawakajitsuinryō 果汁また は果実飲料　fruits juice or fruit beverages

kajūshisū 加重指数　weighted index

kajūtōkajizokusōonryō 加重等価 持続騒音量　weight equivalent continuous perceived noise level; WECPNL

kajūzaiko 過重在庫　excess inventory; surplus stock ¶ to reduce *excess inventories* // a large *surplus stock* of unsold TV sets

kakaku 価格　price; value ¶ The average world crude oil *price*, measured in 1983 dollars, dipped to 26 dollars a barrel in 1986. // Wheat *prices* climbed 20% to over \$3 a bushel. // Coffee *prices* continued to drift. // Grain *prices* have been held in check and the *prices* of some grains have even declined. // Crude futures and cash *prices* surged beyond product *prices*, but are likely to go lower over the short term. // *Prices* in the stock market advanced sharply. // *Prices* of these products displayed remarkable strength. // Exports increased by 5 percent both in volume and in *value* (terms).

賃貸価格　rental value

帳簿価格　book value

超過需要価格　excess demand price

長期均衡価格　long-run equilibrium price

長期供給価格　long-period supply price

長期正常価格　long-term normal

price

独占価格　monopoly price

概算価格　approximate value

額面価格　par value; par

現物価格　spot price

発行価格　issue price

表記価格　declared price

評定価格　appraised value

表示価格　list price; posted price

一時的均衡価格　temporary equilibrium price

実効価格　effective price

実質価格　real price

自由価格　free price; black market price

解約価格　surrender value

管理価格　managed price; administered price

寡占価格　oligopoly price

可処分価格　disposal value

課税価格　assessment value

計算価格　accounting price

均一価格　uniform price

均衡価格　equilibrium price

禁止的価格　prohibitive price

購買価格　purchase price; buying price; purchased value

硬直価格　rigid price

公開価格　open price

公正市場価格　fair market price

行使価格　practice price

公定価格　official price

小売価格　retail price

許可価格　approved price

供給価格　supply price

協定価格　conventional price; stipulated price

名目価格　nominal price

見積価格　estimated price

黙認価格　permitted price

二重価格　dual price

卸売価格　wholesale price

パリティ価格　parity price

再販価格　resale price

最高価格　ceiling price; maximum price

最終価格　final price

最低価格　floor price; minimum price

最適価格　optimum price

先物価格　futures price

参入阻止価格　entry-preventing price

政治価格　political price

正常価格　normal price

正常優位価格　normal advantage price

生産者価格　producer price

潜在価格　shadow price

消費者価格　cousumer price

指導価格　guide-line price; guide price; government-set guidepost price

自然価格　natural price

支持価格　support price; maintenance price

市場価格　market price; marketable price

相対価格　relative price

短期供給価格　short-period supply price

短期正常価格　short-term normal price

短期的均衡価格　short-term equilibrium price; market price

適正価格　fair price; reasonable price; just price

届出価格　reported price

統制価格　controlled price; fixed price

売出価格　offering price

有効予想価格　expected effective price

全国市街地価格　city land price

絶対価格　absolute price

kakakubakuhatsu 価格爆発　price

explosion ¶ The oil *price explosion* subjected the payments pattern to enormous strains.

kakakubunseki 価格分析 price analysis

kakakuchōseihokyūkin 価格調整補給金 price-control compensation

kakakudanryokusei 価格弾力性 price-elasticity; elasticity of price ¶ The *price elasticity* of U.S. demand for foreign imports is high. // U.S. exports have a low price elasticity of foreign demand. // *Price elasticities* in foreign trade have proved to be low. // a high *price elasticity* against exports

kakakuhannō 価格反応 price responsiveness

kakakuhendō 価格変動 price fluctuation; price variation; change in prices; price swing; price movement ¶ factors for *price variations* // *Prices* have *fluctuated* narrowly. // *Fluctuations in prices* were sharpest for imported raw materials, and somewhat less acute for domestic products. // *Changes in prices* have been slight. // prime products subject to wide *price swings* // Erratic *price swings* may occur. // *Price swings* on world markets are severe. // to protect farmers from the wide *fluctuations of* world *prices* // volatile gold *price movements*, both in absolute and percentage terms markedly higher than before

kakakuhendōjōkō 価格変動条項 fluctuation clause; escalator clause

kakakuhendōjunbikin 価格変動準備金 price fluctuation reserve; reserve for price fluctuation

kakakuhendōshūsei 価格変動修正 adjustment for price fluctuations (= variances)

kakakuhyō 価格表 price-list

kakakuijikōi 価格維持行為 price maintenance efforts

kakakujōshōkitai 価格上昇期待 expectation for price rises

kakakukanshi 価格監視 price surveillance; price supervision ¶ A new Federal decree on *price supervision* will come into force, to reduce unjustified prices for all types of products.

kakakukeiki 価格景気 cost(-push) inflation; price(-induced) inflation

kakakukeisei 価格形成 formation of price; price formation; pricing ¶ There is great freedom in the *pricing* behavior of sheltered industries. // formulation of general principles of a *pricing* policy for commodity export // to *price* goods out of the market

kakakukettei 価格決定 pricing; price determination ¶ to receive the price set by the crude oil *pricing* arrangement announced last year

kakakukikō 価格機構 price mechanism ¶ proper functioning of the *price mechanism*

kakakukōchokusei 価格硬直性 price rigidity

kakakukōka 価格効果 effects of prices

kakakukōtei 価格公定 official price fixing; valorization

kakakukyōsō 価格競争 price competition

kakakukyōtei 価格協定 price-fixing agreement; price cartel

kakakunoparamētākinō 価格のパラメーター機能 parametric function of prices

kakakunoshēre 価格のシェーレ

Schere; price scissors

kakakusabetsuka 価格差別化 price discrimination

kakakusaekikin 価格差益金 profit from the difference between new and old official prices

kakakusaikōgendo 価格最高限度 price ceiling ¶ *Price ceilings* will be imposed on the wine and beer consumed in restaurants.

kakakusendōsei 価格先導性 price leadership

kakakusendōsha 価格先導者 price leader

kakakushiji 価格支持 price support

kakakushijiseido 価格支持制度 price support(ing) system

kakakushikō 価格志向 orientation toward price raises

kakakushinshukusei 価格伸縮性 price flexibility

kakakusōsa 価格操作 price rigging; manipulation of the market

kakakutai 価格帯 price range

kakakutaikei 価格体系 price structure ¶ to lessen distortions in the *price structure* of petroleum products instead of increasing them

kakakutōketsu 価格凍結 price freeze; freeze on prices; freezing of prices ¶ to introduce a *freeze on* all *prices* // to lift the *price freeze* // The government announced a temporary *freeze of* all *prices* with retroactive effect from Sept. 1.

kakakutōsei 価格統制 price control

kakakutōseikaijo 価格統制解除 price decontrol

kake 掛 credit; trust ¶ to buy goods on *credit* // to purchase for *credit* // to sell and buy on *trust*

kakegaenonaichikyū かけがえのない地球 "only one earth"; "one precious earth"

kakegaenonaishigen かけがえのない資源 irreplaceable resources

kakegai 掛買い credit purchase

kakei 家計 household; household account; household economy; family budget; household budget; domestic economy; family finance; housekeeping ¶ workers' *households* // Rising prices of food have strained the *budgets* of many *households*. // Honolulu requires substantially higher *family budgets*. // the typical U.S. urban *family budget*

kakeibo 家計簿 household account book; housekeeping (account) book

kakeiboki 家計簿記 family bookkeeping

kakeibumon 家計部門 household sector

kakeichōsa 家計調査 family income and expenditure survey; family budget inquiry; means test; family budget statistics

kakeichōsafutaichōsa 家計調査付帯調査 supplementary inquiry about the family income and expenditure survey

kakeihi 家計費 household expenses; housekeeping expenses

kakeikanri 家計管理 home management

kakeishōhi 家計消費 household consumption ¶ *Household consumption* is the main support of business activity.

kakeishotoku 家計所得 family income

kakekanjō 掛勘定 credit account

kakekin 掛金 installment

kakekomi 駆け込み getting under

the wire; jumping on the bandwagon at the last minute ¶ to *get under the wire* before the ban // Soybean futures tumbled on the Chicago Board of Trade in a wave of *last-minute* selling. // to *jump on the* wage-hike *bandwagon at the last minute* // *last-minute* price hikes

kakekomishinsei 駆け込み申請 rushed application for license; application made getting under the wire; flux of last-minute applications

kakeme 掛目(担保の) loan-to-value ratio; loan(able) value; collateral value ¶ The *loanable value* of listed securities was increased to 25% of the market value. // reductions in *loan-to-value ratios* on home mortgages

kakene 掛け値 ［市］ overbid

kakesutehoken 掛け捨て保険 term insurance

kaketsunagi 掛けつなぎ hedge ¶ a scheme providing a *hedge* against inflation // →ヘッジ

kakeuri 掛売り credit sale; sale on account; sale on credit

kakeurijōken 掛売条件 credit terms

kakeurikanjō 掛売勘定 credit account

kakeurinedan 掛売値段 credit price

kakeuriseido 掛売制度 credit system

kakeuritokuisaki 掛売得意先 credit customer

kakiaitegata 書き合い手形 accommodation bill; kite

kakikae 書換え rewriting; transfer; renewal

kakikaedaichō 書換台帳 transfer book

kakikaekeizoku 書換継続 renewal

kakikaekinyūchō 書換記入帳 transfer register

kakikaeteishi 書換停止 transfer book closed

kakine "垣根" distinction; boundary ¶ to set the *boundaries* for foreign banks

kakinenotekkyo "垣根" の撤去 elimination of distinctions ¶ the *elimination of distinctions* between commercial banks and savings and loan institutions // ［参考］ The banks are moving into the territory reserved in the past only for securities companies. // to give banks new powers to compete on equal footing with unregulated competitors which provide bank-like services and many products currently off limits to banks // The exact fields of service institutions, and the lines of demarcation between them, are not clear cut. // a gradual homogenizing of the entire financial sector // Limiting legislation is removed and new ways to avoid restrictive barriers are found. // to blur the distinction between loan and bond markets

kakki 活気 vigor; mettle; dynamism; vitality ¶ the *vigor* of consumer markets // the *vigor* of economic recovery // The *mettle* of the market has been severely tested. // the loss of *dynamism* in world trade // *Dynamism* for future growth has to come from its large agricultural sector. // The economy is showing a good deal of *vitality*.

kakkidatta 活気立った ［市］ excited; vigorous

kakkokutsūka 各国通貨(キーカレンシー以外の) national currency;

local currency

kakkyō 活況 boom

一時的活況 boom-and-bust; passing boom

kakō 下降 decline; downdrift; down-swing; downturn; drop; fall; sag; slip; setback; moving down (ward); descent ¶ a disastrous *decline* in sales of the past few years // Output *declined* slightly. // Production continued its gradual *downdrift*. // Business continued on the *downswing*. // The sideways movement is giving way to a moderate *downturn*. // Average prices all *dropped* 1 or 2 percent. // The price *fall* was quite general. // The market *sagged*. // The price *slipped* below its peak 1925 level. // moderating *setbacks* of the market // The production index moved *downward*. // Output accelerated its *downward* course. // Price movements continued to be *downward*. // The market's *descent* has steepened and accelerated in recent sessions.

kakō 加工 processing ¶ agro-*processing* units engaged in the *processing* of agricultural inputs

kakōhi 加工費 processing fee

kakōkeikō 下降傾向 downward trend; down-trend ¶ the *down-trend* in the building sector // The *downward trend* was less pronounced. // The stock-sales ratio continued *downward*.

kakōkyokumen 下降局面 downward phase of the business cycle; declining phase of the business cycle ¶ The *phase of business decline* ended with the first quarter of 1976.

kakonodēta 過去のデータ historical data

kakōsen 下降線 downhill course ¶ The index followed a *downhill course*.

kakōshokuhin 加工食品 processed food

kakuchōkeiro 拡張経路 expansion path

kakuchōkōji 拡張工事 expansion works

kakuchōtōshi 拡張投資 expansion investment

kakudai 拡大 expansion; enlargement; spread; growth ¶ The economy enjoyed *expansion* at a rate which is sufficiently temperate to be sustainable. // The economy has experienced a long *expansion*, albeit at an uneven rate. // the highly synchronized *expansion* in the world economy of 1972-73 // to achieve our objective of orderly and sustained *expansion* // the vigorously proceeding economic *expansion* on a widenig front // The record-long economic *expansion* rolls on. // to enjoy long-enduring *expansion* // the uncontrolled *expansion* of the Euro-currency market // an only moderate *expansion* of production // the *enlarged* European Communities // to check the *spread* of scare buying // to *spread* reserves across a range of currencies // the steady monetary *growth* // to restore more satisfactory *growth* of activity // an obstacle to stronger *growth* of aggregate demand in Germany

kakudaiatsuryoku 拡大圧力 expansionary force

kakudaihendōhaba 拡大変動幅 → ワイダー・バンド

kakudaikazoku 拡大家族 expanded family

kakudaikeizai 拡大経済 expanding economy; expansive economy

kakudaikichō 拡大基調 expansive keynote // ［参考］→基調

kakudaikinkō 拡大均衡 expanding equilibrium

kakudaisaiseisan 拡大再生産 reproduction on an expanded scale; expanded reproduction

kakudaiseisaku 拡大政策 expansive policy; expansionary policy; expansionist policy

kakudaiteki 拡大的 expansionary; expansive ¶ domestic *expansionary* force // further *expansionary* impulses // *expansive* forces in the economy // more *expansionary* fiscal policy

kakuhaikibutsu 核廃棄物 nuclear waste

kakuhōchi 確報値 → 確定計数

kakujū 拡充 enrichment ¶ The plan emphasizes the *enrichment* of social welfare programs.

kakukazoku 核家族 nuclear family

kakumei 革命 revolution
価格革命 price revolution
経営者革命 managerial revolution
ケインズ革命 Keynesian revolution
金融革命 financial revolution
農業革命 agricultural revolution
流通革命 distribution revolution
産業革命 industrial revolution
商業革命 commercial revolution
所得革命 income revolution
材料革命 material revolution

kakūmeigiyokin 架空名義預金 deposit in an assumed (= fictitious) name

kakunenryō 核燃料 nuclear fuel

kakunin 確認 confirmation ¶ to receive a *confirmation* of his sale, specifying the transaction date // a telephonic *confirmation* of the transaction given the customer

kakuninshin'yōjō 確認信用状 confirmed credit

kakuran'yōin 攪乱要因 disturbing factor ¶ The most *disturbing factor* in the commodity market was a buying spree to beat inflation.

kakuretakakakuhikiage 隠れた価格引上げ hidden price increase

kakuretate 隠れた手 hidden hand; invisible hand

kakūrieki 仮空利益 paper profit; fictitious profit

kakuritsu 確率 probability

kakusa 格差 differential; difference; gap; spread; variation; variety; disparity; unevenness ¶ *gap* narrowed to a very small *differential* // *Differences* also persist among industrial countries in respect of exchange rate policy. // interest rate *differentials* // the wide *gap* between the supply and demand // Sales *varied* greatly between localities. // The unexplained male-female wage *differential* shrank. // adjustments of wage *differentials* to desired structural shifts in the economy // to reduce the growth *differential* vis-à-vis the U.S. // The inflationary *differential* is large, ranging from almost 3% in Germany to 8-11% in the larger EEC countries. // the widening interest rate *differentials* in favor of the U.S. // The latest data to hand suggest an even greater *disparity*. // to make for *uneven* wage levels // *divergence* with respect to inflation and interest rates

kakusakintōka 格差均等化 equalizing divergences

kakusan 拡散 proliferation; diffusion ¶ to avoid a *proliferation* of trade restrictions or other policies // to minimize the risk of nuclear *proliferation*

kakusanshisū 拡散指数 diffusion index ¶ The *diffusion index* (composite, 25 key indicators) last December declined by 14.7 percentage points to 41.3 per cent, the first decline below the 50 per cent line in six months.

kakushin 革新 innovation; renovation

技術革新 technological innovation

kakushin 確信 confidence; assurance ¶ consumers' confidence in improved conditions within the next twelve months // the loss of *confidence* in the value of money // There are good grounds for *confidence* that... // The recent uplift in production increased *confidence*. // Moderation in monetary policy bolstered *confidence* in the economic future. // This will pose threat to consumer and business *confidence*. // Renewed *confidence* in the future has replaced doubts about the economic outlook. // The degree to which *confidence* in the future value of money had been shaken. // Steady growth should increase investor *confidence* in the British economy. // Public *confidence* in the economic outlook has been blighted by the virulent rise of prices. // It constitutes eloquent proof of the *confidence* placed in the solidity of the natural economy. // There is little *confidence* in a boom developing. // →コンフィデンス

kakushinedan 隠し値段 reserve price

kakushizaigen 隠し財源 hidden treasury reserves

kakushizaisan 隠し財産 hidden property ¶ a study of the *hidden property* potential in the company

kakushūshūkyūfutsukasei 隔週週休2日制 five-day week on an alternate week basis; a five-day workweek every other week

kakuteibibaraitegata 確定日払手形 bill payable at a fixed date

kakuteibiwatashi 確定日渡し ［外］ fixed-date delivery

kakuteichūmon 確定注文 firm order

kakuteikeisū 確定計数 final figure

kakuteishinkoku 確定申告 final declaration (＝return)

kakuzuke 格付け (credit) rating; grading ¶ Many borrowers with less than prime *credit ratings* found it difficult to borrow at all in securities markets. // The debenture was granted the *rating* of "AAA," which means the highest quality by all standards. // The average yields on new issues of Aaa-*rated* utilities rose. // the *rating* of bond issues // the debenture issue *rated* A, or *rated* as most trustworthy // bonds of high *ratings* // a number of issues including a $150 million Aa-*rated* offering by a finance company // notes and bonds *rated* Aa by Moody's and A by Standard & Poor's // the yields on comparably *rated* industrial issues // Moody's Investors Service Inc. assigned a AAA *rating* to this issue of notes. // The Bank's obligations carry a Triple A *rating* at the three principal bond *rating* services in the U.S. // Moody's downgraded its *rating* of the company. // borrowers having no *ratings* by Moody's or Standard & Poor's

kakuzukekikan 格付機関 rating agency

kakyō 華僑 overseas Chinese; Chinese living abroad

kakyūkanrisō 下級管理層 lower supervisory management zone

kameiginkō 加盟銀行 member bank

手形交換所加盟銀行 member bank of the clearing house

連邦準備制度加盟銀行 member bank of the Federal Reserve System

kameiken 加盟権 membership ¶ The World Bank aims at universality of *membership*, both among its potential contributors and among its recipients. // the willingness of banks to drop their *membership* in the Federal Reserve System

kamihanki 上半期 first half (of the year); first half-year (period)

kamikakōhin 紙加工品 paper products

kamitsuchiiki 過密地域 densely-populated area; overcongested region (=area)

kamitsujōtai 過密状態 overcrowding

kamitsukasotaisaku 過密過疎対策 countermeasures against excessive concentration of population

kamitsutoshi 過密都市 over-populated city

kamotsu 貨物 cargo; freight; goods; merchandise

付保貨物 insured cargo

不燃焼貨物 non-inflammable cargo

重量貨物 heavy weight cargo

甲板貨物 deck cargo

軽量貨物 light cargo

裁量貨物 measurement cargo

船室貨物 under-deck cargo

損害貨物 damaged cargo

kamotsudaikinnomaeukekin 貨物代金の前受金 prepaid value of goods

kamotsueki 貨物駅 goods station; freight station

kamotsufukusō 貨物輻輳 congestion of cargoes (=freights)

kamotsuhikikaesho 貨物引換書 way bill

kamotsuhikiwatashisashizu 貨物引渡指図 freighter release

kamotsuhikōki 貨物飛行機 air freighter

kamotsuhokanshō 貨物保管証 warehouse receipt

kamotsujōkō 貨物条項 cargo clause

kamotsusen 貨物船 cargo-boat (=ship; steamer); freight ship; freighter

kamotsushūnyū 貨物収入 goods earnings; freight earnings

kamotsutsūchisho 貨物通知書 railway acknowledgment

kamotsutsumioroshisōchi 貨物積降装置 cargo gear

kamotsuunchin 貨物運賃 freight; freight tariff; freight rate

kamotsuunsō 貨物運送 freight traffic ¶ Rail *freight traffic* dropped a sizable 6%.

kamotsuunsōjō 貨物運送状 consignment note

kamotsuunsōkeiyaku 貨物運送契約 freight engagement

kamotsuunsōten 貨物運送店 goods agent; freight agent

kamotsuuwaya 貨物上屋 shed station; depot

kanaikigyō 家内企業 family enterprise

kanaikōgyō 家内工業 domestic-cottage industry

kanbenkeisanhō 簡便計算法 shortened computation

kanbutsu 換物 conversion of money into goods

kanendosaishutsu 過年度歳出 expense belonging to the preceding fiscal year

kanetsu 過熱 overheating ¶ to cool down the *overheated* economy // The symptoms of *overheating* in the economy are apparent. // The economy is becoming *overheated* with worse inflation still ahead. // to reduce *overheated* loan demand

kanetsukeizai 過熱経済 overheated economy; overexuberant economy

kanezumari 金詰り tightness of money; monetary stringency; monetary stress and strain; money crunch

kangen 還元 refund; return; rebate; passing on ¶ to make *refund* to customers // tax *rebate* to tax payers // Importers *return* to consumers part of the benefits they received from the dollar's sharp fall. // *passing-on* of some additional benefit to its depositors by increasing its deposit rates // *passing on* to consumers exchange profits gained by industries from the yen's appreciation against the dollar // The reduction in the cost of money is *passed* along to the borrower. // to *pass on* some additional benefit to its depositors by increasing its deposit rates

kangyōekioyobikangyōshūnyū 官業益及び官業収入 receipts from Government enterprises and properties

kan'ichōsa 簡易調査 brief investigation

kan'iseimeihoken 簡易生命保険 postal life insurance

kanji 幹事 supervisor; manager; secretary; leader

kanjiginkō 幹事銀行(シンジケートの) managing bank (of a syndicate); manager ¶ a *syndicate* led by Credit Lyonnais

共同幹事(銀行) co-manager

主幹事(銀行) lead manager

kanjitesūryō 幹事手数料 management fee

kanjō 勘定 account; calculation; computation; counting; reckoning; payment of bill; settlement of account ¶ to open, maintain, and close a current *account* with a bank // to *reckon* gains and losses

売買一任勘定 [市] discretionary account

重複勘定 overlapping account

中間勘定 interim account

営業勘定 operating account

振子勘定 swing account

現金勘定 cash account

現金預金勘定 cash and deposits with bank account

控勘定 memorandum account

非居住者(自由)円預金勘定 non-resident (free) yen account

本支店勘定 inter-office account

一般政府勘定 general government account

為替平衡勘定 exchange equalization account

仮勘定 temporary account; suspense account

借方勘定 debit account

貸方勘定 credit account

貸付金勘定　loans to customers account

活勘定　active account; working account

経常勘定　current account

個人勘定　households and private non-profit institutions account

国民資本勘定　national capital account

共同勘定　joint account

休止勘定　dormant account; sleeping account

見合勘定　per contra account

未決済勘定　outstanding account

作業勘定　operation account

債権勘定　account receivable

債務勘定　account payable

整理勘定　adjustment account

清算勘定　open account

先方勘定　their account

シャドウ勘定　shadow account

支払勘定　account payable

支払済勘定　settled account

資本(金)勘定　capital account

資金循環勘定　flow of funds account

新規勘定　new account

損益勘定　profit and loss account

当方勘定　our account

当座勘定　current account

売掛金勘定　charge account

残金勘定　account in arrear

雑勘定　sundry account

続行勘定　running account

kanjōbi　勘定日　pay-day; settlement day

kanjōchigai　勘定違い　miscalculation

kanjōgakari　勘定係　accountant

kanjōjiri　勘定尻　balance of account

　為替尻　balance of exchange; balance of clearing

　決済尻　balance of clearing

交互計算尻　balance of mutual accounts

交換尻　balance of exchange

kanjōkamoku　勘定科目　title of account

kanjōkamokubangōhyōjihō　勘定科目番号表示法　account number plan

kanjōkōmoku　勘定項目　item of account

kanjōsho　勘定書　bill ¶ a *bill* for books // a *bill* from a restaurant // to pay a *bill* // to settle a *bill* // to collect a *bill*

kanjōshutai　勘定主体　accounting entity

kanjōsoshiki　勘定組織　account system; accounting system

kanjōtaikei　勘定体系　accounting system

kanjōtori　勘定取り　bill collector

kanka　換価　realization; conversion into cash; cashing ¶ *realization* sales // to *cash* a check

kankafunōshisan　換価不能資産　unrealizable assets

kankei　関係　connection; bearing; interest; concern; participation; involvement; influence; relationship; relation; association; link(age); tie ¶ The theoretical treatment of the influence of inflation upon growth arrives at a positive *relationship*. // No significant *relationship* was found between the rate of income growth and the instability of income growth. // The concurrent *relation* between growth and inflation was examined. // Current inflation is significantly negatively *related* to growth. // a loosening *relationship* between the yen-dollar rate and U.S. interest rates // to enhance the existing close business *relationship* // to deal with the intricacies of modern international economic *relations* // Past research suggests a strong *association* between trade strategies and growth rates. // to imply a causal *linkage*, a significant positive *relationship* between the two // the economy's behavioral *relationships* and their *linkages* to financial flows // the scope of production *linkage* between their export and domestic sectors // the close economic and financial *ties* between many European countries

取引関係 business relations; commercial relations (＝relationship)

kankeigaisha 関係会社 concern interested; affiliated company; affiliate

kankeigaishakariirekin 関係会社借入金 ［会］borrowings from affiliates

kankeigaishakashitsukekin 関係会社貸付金 ［会］loans to affiliates

kankeigaishashasai 関係会社社債 bonds of affiliates

kankeigaishashusshikin 関係会社出資金 investment in affiliates

kankeigaishaurikakekin 関係会社売掛金 ［会］receivables from affiliates

kankeigaishayūkashōken 関係会社有価証券 ［会］securities of affiliates

kankeikanchō 関係官庁 authorities concerned

kankeisha 関係者 parties concerned; interested parties ¶ To *whom concerned*.

kankeishorui 関係書類 relative documents ¶ →添付書類

kankeitōkyoku 関係当局 competent authorities

kankinsakumotsu 換金作物 cash crop

kankin'uri 換金売り realization sales; realization selling

kankō 慣行 (customary) practice; habit ¶ generally recognized trade *practices* followed with respect to...// to harmonize company accounting *practice* // Traders restored or adopted international export-import *practices*.

雇用慣行 employment practice
商業慣行 business practice

kankokusōtan 勧告操短 curtailed operation on government advice

kankōryokō 観光旅行 tourism; tourist trip

kankōtokō 観光渡航 sightseeing travel (＝trip); pleasure travel (＝trip)

kankōtokōnomochidashigaikaseigen 観光渡航の持出し外貨制限 limit of foreign currency allocations to nationals making overseas pleasure trip

kankyō 環境 environment; circumstance; setting; milieu; climate; surroundings ¶ an affluent living *environment* // Banks operate in a less hospitable economic *environment* than the previous decade. // Monetary policy can only provide an *environment* conducive to the unwinding of these problems. // in poor economic *circumstances* // the domestic *setting* for market developments // The economic and social *milieu* of private businesses is now less comfortable than a while back. // to foster a financial *climate* conducive to a satisfactory recovery // This would imply a considerably more restrictive monetary *climate*. // The social *milieu* and policy environment are supportive. // the export shortfall due to unfavorable *climatic* conditions in the market for the export commodities // a marked cooling-off in the economic *climate* // to help establish an economic *climate* which is conducive to private-sector growth // to cultivate a congenial business *climate* // to provide the *setting* for or resumption of economic growth // typical low-income family in an urban *setting*

海岸線環境 coastline environment

海洋環境 marine environment

金融環境 financial environment; banking environment

労働環境 labor environment; work environment

生活環境 life environment

生活適性環境 livable environment

社会環境 social environment; community setting

自然環境 natural environment

kankyōasesumento 環境アセスメント environmental (impact) assessment

kankyōeisei 環境衛生 environmental sanitation

kankyōhakai 環境破壊 environmental destruction; environmental disruption; environmental debacle ¶ an age of *environmental disruption* and social-economic disorganization at both national and international level

kankyōhogo 環境保護 protection of the environment; environment(al) protection (=safeguard) ¶ to impose upon the economy rules for *protection of the environment*

kankyōhogokyoku 環境保護局 [米] Environmental Protection Agency

kankyōhozen 環境保全 environment conservation; environment protection; environmental safeguard; environmental preservation

kankyōjōka 環境浄化 environmental clean-up

kankyōkaikaku 環境改革 environmental reform

kankyōkaizen 環境改善 environmental improvement

kankyōkaizenjigyo 環境改善事業 environmental services

kankyōken 環境権 environmental right

kankyōkiki 環境危機 environmental crisis

kankyōkōjō 環境向上 environmental enhancement

kankyōkosuto 環境コスト pollution prevention cost

kankyōnokiki 環境の危機 environmental peril

kankyōnoshitsu 環境の質 environmental quality

kankyōosen 環境汚染 environmental pollution; environmental contamination; pollution; environmental spoilation ¶ *Environmental spoilation* is an international cancer, eroding hard-won economic gains.

kankyōran'yō 環境濫用 environmental abuse

kankyōsaigai 環境災害 environmental disaster

kankyōteika 環境低下 environmental degradation; environmental deterioration ¶ a project causing severe or irreversible *environmental deterioration*

kanman 緩慢 slow; slack; sluggish; dilatory; tardy; laggard; moderate

¶ The pace of recovery was *slow*. // *slackening* of activity // *sluggish* increase in income // *sluggishness* of consumer demand // U.S. economic growth is in fact *moderating*.

kanmon 関門 resistance level; barrier

kannōdo 感応度 responsiveness ¶ to estimate the *responsiveness* of both demand and saving to changes in income and relative prices

kannōsei 感応性 responsiveness ¶ the *responsiveness* of demand to changes in price

kanōsei 可能性 likelihood ¶ There is every *likelihood* that production would increase further.

kanpu 還付 restoration; repayment; refunding; rebate

kanpukin 還付金 repayment money; refund; rebate

kanrensangyō 関連産業 allied industry; related industry

kanren 〜関連 -related ¶ export-*related* issues // defense-*related* stocks // auto and *related* industries // import-*related* activities

kanrenzai 関連財 related goods
公共投資関連財 public investment related goods

kanri 管理 administration; management; control; stewardship ¶ *administration* of monetary policy // fiscal *administration* // *administrated* prices // business *management* // foreign trade *controls* // *control* over financial transactions // the management's *stewardship* of corporate affairs // to ease, not tighten, foreign exchange and trade *controls* // Imposing and removing *controls* will scarcely change the speed of inflation. // Fiscal policy will have to

be brought under closer *control*. // The bank has to retain its *control* over the domestic money supply. // The rising deficit prompts tighter *controls* on foreign borrowing. // diminishing of the wage and price *controls*, which will be phased out by the year-end // mandatory, not voluntary, interest *controls*

貿易管理 trade control
部門管理 department management
分権の管理 decentralized control
物財管理 material control
帳票管理 business forms control
中間管理 middle management
営業管理 business control
複合管理 multiple control
現金管理 cash management
群管理 group control
業務管理 business management
行政管理 administration control
販売管理 sales management
品質管理 quality control
事後原価管理 post cost control
時間管理 time management
事務管理 clerical work control
需要管理 demand management
科学的管理 scientific management
課業管理 task management
下級管理 lower management
為替管理 exchange control
経営管理 management control
研究管理 administration of research activities
機能式管理 functional management
購買管理 purchase control
工場管理 factory management
工程管理 process control
共同管理 joint control
供給管理 supply management
成行管理 drifting management
人間関係管理 human relations pro-

gram

作業管理 labor control

債務管理 debt management

政府管理 government control

生産管理 production management; production control

資産管理 assets management

食糧管理 staple-food management

商品管理 merchandise control

利潤利益管理 profit management

労働(力)管理 manpower control

労働者の生産管理 labor's control of production

労務管理 labor management; personnel administration

単一管理 single control

通貨管理 monetary control

有価証券管理 securities administration

在庫管理 inventory control; stock control

財務管理 financial management

kanrigijutsu 管理技術 managerial technique

kanrihendōsōba 管理変動相場 managed floating (exchange rate)

kanrihi 管理費 administrative cost; management expenses; supervision expenses ¶ The *administrative costs* of loans to large producers are about 3 to 4 percent of outstanding loans.

kanrikaikei 管理会計 managerial accounting

kanrikakaku 管理価格 administrated price

kanrikeizai 管理経済 governed economy

kanrinin 管理人 administrator; manager; supervisor; superintendent; custodian

kanrinōryoku 管理能力 administrative ability

kanrisaiken 管理債権 bad claim

kanrisekinin 管理責任 stewardship (responsibility)

経営者管理責任 managed stewardship (responsibility)

kanrishakunrenkeikaku 管理者訓練計画 management training program; MTP

kanrishoku 管理職 controller; manager; management

kanrishokunō 管理職能 management function

kanrisō 管理層 management

部門管理層 division management (zone)

中間管理層 middle (zone of) management

下級管理層 lower (zone of) management

最高管理層 top management

kanrisoshiki 管理組織 organization for management

kanritsūka 管理通貨 managed currency

kanrizu 管理図 control chart

kanryū 還流 reflux; reflow; return-flow; withdrawal ¶ quick *reflux* of bank notes // substantial *return-flows* of short-term capital // net *withdrawals* of bank notes

kanryū 環流 recycle; recycling; unwinding; reversal; channeling back; return current ¶ Arab bankers *recycled* directly only a tiny proportion of this amount back to borrowers on international capital markets. // *recycling* of oil-money // There was a *"recycling"* problem; a problem of re-distributing the flows forthcoming from the OPEC countries. // to facilitate the *recycling* of OPEC surpluses to countries in need of external financing // an *unwind-*

ing of the earlier capital outflows // a *reversal* of leads and lags of current payments // *recycling* the deposits withdrawn back into the property markets // to offset the temporary withdrawal of funds by *channelling back* to the money market the Government's free Bundesbank balances

kansahōjin 監査法人 incorporated accounting firm

kansahōkoku 監査報告 opinion of independent accountants; audit report; auditor's report

kansakijun 監査基準 auditing standards

一般に認められた監査基準 generally accepted auditing standards

kansan 換算 conversion; translation; change ¶ to *convert* the yen into the dollar as ¥308＝$1 // *translation* of foreign currencies at rates of exchange prevailing at dates of acquisition // The dollar figure is arrived at by *converting* the (Hungarian) forint total at the official commercial rate of exchange prevailing on 31/12/75. // *converted* back to the old basis (1971＝100), the understood at 155.65 // ［参考］ In coal-equivalent terms, commercial energy was only about 25 percent of total consumption.

kansan 閑散 ［市］ quiet; thin; inactive ¶ Trading was *thin* and *quiet* for most of the day reflecting Tokyo's local holiday.

kansan'enkagaku 換算円価額 yen equivalent

kansanhyō 換算表 exchange table; conversion table

相場換算表 stock conversion table

kansan'insū 換算因数 conversion factor

kansanki 閑散期 off-season

kansannaibukyōchōkankei 官産内部協調関係 government-business (＝co-operative) relationship

kansanritsu 換算率 rate of exchange; exchange rate; conversion rate

kansanshikyō 閑散市況 slack market; small turnover; diminishing (trade) volume

kansashōmei 監査証明 audit certification

kansatsushiryō 観察資料 observational data

kansayaku 監査役 (corporate) auditor

常任監査役 standing auditor

kanseihin 完成品 manufactured goods; finished goods; manufactured products ¶ *finished-goods* inventories with manufacturers

kansetsubaibai 間接売買 indirect sales

kansetsubōeki 間接貿易 indirect trade

kansetsuboshū 間接募集 indirect offering of new securities

kansetsuhakkō 間接発行 offer for sale

kansetsuhi 間接費 indirect cost; indirect expense; overhead charge; overhead cost; oncost

kansetsuhibunpai 間接費分配 distribution of overhead cost

kansetsuhikappuritsu 間接費割賦率 application rate of overhead cost

kansetsukawase 間接為替 indirect exchange

kansetsurimawari 間接利回り indirect yield

kansetsusongaihoken 間接損害保

険 consequential damage insurance

kansetsutōshi 間接投資 indirect investment; portfolio investment

kansetsuyoyaku 間接予約 indirect contract

kansetsuzei 間接税 indirect tax

kanshi 監視 surveillance; monitoring; overseeing; oversight ¶ to be vigilant and resolute in pursuit of *surveillance* of exchange rates // to bring under strict *surveillance* // The Fund shall exercise firm *surveillance* over the exchange rate policies of members. // to promote better international *surveillance* of international liquidity // principles and procedures for firm *surveillance* over exchange rate policies // to exercise firm *surveillance* over // the central debt office responsible for *monitoring* debt transactions // More difficult to *monitor* is the growth of short-term financing arrangements. // financial centers where *monitoring* is lax // The Fund shall *oversee* the international monetary system in order to.... // the *oversight* and *surveillance* authority of the Reserve Bank over government securities dealers

kanshisōchi 監視装置 surveillance system

kanshō 干渉 intervention; intrusion ¶ Growing public *intervention* is required in the running of individual industries. // minimal *intrusion* of government in the free economic system //an under *intrusion* on the banking secrecy // →介入

kanshoku 閑職 sinecure

kanshokusha 閑職者 sinecurist

kanshōsayō 緩衝作用 buffer action

kanshōzaiko 緩衝在庫 buffer stock ¶ drawing on the previously accumulated *buffer stock*

kanshū 慣習 (usual) practice; custom; customary practice ¶ according to the established local banking *practice*

国際取引慣習 customary practice in international commercial transaction

商慣習 customary practice in business

kanshū 還収 withdrawal (of bank notes from circulation)

kanshūchō 還収超 net withdrawal; excess withdrawal (over issue); net return ¶ an *excess withdrawal* of bank notes of ¥6 billion over issue

kanshūkasetsu 慣習仮説 habit hypothesis

kansoka 簡素化 streamlining; simplification

kansoku 観測 observation ¶ Available *observations* within the relevant time period are considered.

kansokugosa 観測誤差 observational error

kansū 関数 function

貯蓄関数 saving function

同企業内生産関数 intra-firm production function

反応関数 reaction function

異企業内生産関数 inter-firm production function

需要関数 demand function

貨幣需要関数 demand function for money

効用関数 utility function

供給関数 supply function

目的関数 objective function

生産関数 production function

社会価値関数 social value function

社会的厚生関数 social welfare

function

総需要関数 aggregate demand function

総供給関数 aggregate supply function

投資関数 investment function

kansūrontekibukkashisūron 関数論的物価指数論 functional approach to price indices

kanteikakaku 鑑定価格 appraised value

kanteinin 鑑定人 appraiser

kantoku 監督 supervision ¶ *supervision* of the Federal Reserve over banks // close or less exacting *supervision* // Effective *supervision* over the banking systems has been greatly tightened. // the stricter prudential *supervision* over deposit-taking companies

kantokukanchō 監督官庁 regulatory authorities

kantokukanrisō 監督管理層 supervisory management (zone)

kantokukikan 監督機関 supervisory authority

kantokusha 監督者 supervisor

第一線監督者 first line supervisor

kantokushakunren 監督者訓練 training within industry for supervisor

kantokutōkyoku 監督当局 supervisory authorities ¶ Banks are chartered and regulated by *supervisory authorities* under the jurisdiction of the state governments. // high examination standards among the federal and state *supervisory authorities*

kantorīrisuku カントリーリスク country risk; sovereign risk; exposure ¶ to analize *sovereign risk*, which is seen as split up into two components; the probability of

default and the expected loss rate // Types of lendings include *sovereign risk* loans, non-*sovereign risk* loans, trade and project finance, and others. // The bank's loan *exposure* in five Latin American countries represents 7-8 percent of its £48 billion of total assets. // The bank's problem debt *exposure* represents more than twice equity base of £1.56 billion. // the special provision for international *exposure*

kanwa 緩和 temper; ease; easing-off; alleviate; relax; moderate; mitigate; soften; cushion ¶ measures to *temper* the tightening of monetary conditions // to continue on the *ease* // a perception of *easing* tensions in the Middle East to *alleviate* the strained cash position of banks // a *relaxation* of the credit restrictions // The growth of imports *moderated*. // Expansion proceeded at a more *moderate* rate. // *Easing* strains and *moderating* setbacks are at hand. // Pressures in the money market have been *mitigated*. // The commodity market *softened*. // to *cushion* the business recession // an *easing* tension // a *moderate* economic recovery // monetary *relaxation* // The *easing-off* in bank lending and money growth had widely been expected.

金融引締めの大幅緩和 substantial loose of (credit) reins; drastic monetary relaxation

kanwazai 緩和剤 palliative ¶ Protectionism is tempting as a very short-term *palliative*.

kan'yōdo 寛容度 tolerance; latitude ¶ the degree of *tolerance* of the expansion of monetary aggregates // the *latitude* for price increase // the *tolerance* limit of price rises // *tolerance* for inflation

kan'yū 勧誘 solicitation; invitation; canvassing ¶ New issues are sold through *solicitations* by salespeople in the employ of investment banking firms. // to *invite* to a syndicated loan // to *canvass* for a new product

kanyūdētatsūshinsābisu 加入データ通信サービス public data communication service

kanzainin 管財人 receiver; administrator

kanzaininsaiken 管財人債券 receivers' certificate

kanzei 関税 customs duty; duty; tariff ¶ to impose stiff *duties* on imports // goods subject to a *custom duty* // an across-the-board *tariff* cut // *duty*-free and *dutiable* imports // the present low average levels of *tariffs* // Substantial progress has been achieved during past *tariff* negotiations. // *tariff* negotiations

便益関税 beneficial duty
地方特恵関税 regional preferential tariff
ダンピング防止関税 anti-dumping duty
弾力関税 elastic duty
複関税 bi-line tariff
複数関税 double tariff; multiple-column tariff
複合関税 compound tariff
互恵関税 reciprocal tariff
報復関税 retaliatory duty
保護関税 protective duty
維持関税 preserving tariff
自主関税 autonomous tariff

自由貿易関税 free trade tariff
従価関税 ad valorem tariff
従量関税 specific tariff
滑準関税 sliding (scale) duty
緊急関税 emergency tariff
禁止関税 prohibitive duty
季節関税 seasonal duty
混合関税 mixed tariff
高率関税 high duty
固定関税 statutory tariff; general tariff
共通関税 common tariff
協定関税 conventional duties
差別関税 discriminative (=discriminatory; discriminating) duty; differential tariff
三重関税 treble tariff
選択関税 alternative duty
奢侈品関税 luxury tariff
相殺関税 compensatory duty
スライド関税 sliding (scale) duty
対抗関税 counter duty
単一関税 single(-line) tariff; uni(-line) tariff; single-column tariff
特恵関税 preferential tariff
輸入関税 import duty
輸出関税 export duty

kanzeidaishōjōkyoritsu 関税代償譲許率 tariff compensatory concession rate

kanzeidōmei 関税同盟 tariff customs union

kanzeiharaimodoshiseido 関税払い戻し制度 draw-back system

kanzeihyōka 関税評価 valuation for customs clearance; customs valuation

kanzeiikkatsuhikisagekōshō 関税一括引き下げ交渉 negotiations for a linear tariff reduction

kanzeijōkyo 関税譲許 concession of tariff

kanzeijōkyohyō 関税譲許表

schedules of concessions

kanzeijōkyoritsu 関税譲許率 tariff concession rate

kanzeijōyaku 関税条約 tariff treaty

kanzeikaisei 関税改正 tariff reform

kanzeikōshō 関税交渉 tariff negotiation

kanzeikyūsen 関税休戦 tariff truce

kanzeimibarai 関税未払い duty unpaid

kanzeioyobibōekinikansuruippankyōtei 関税及び貿易に関する一般協定 General Agreement on Tariffs and Trade; GATT

kanzeiritsu 関税率 tariff
固定関税率 autonomous tariff
協定関税率 coventional tariff

kanzeiritsuhyō 関税率表 customs tariff schedules

kanzeisakibarai 関税先払い duty forward

kanzeisensō 関税戦争 tariff war

kanzeishiharaizumi 関税支払済み duty paid

kanzeishinsakan 関税審査官 duty appraiser

kanzeishōheki 関税障壁 tariff wall; tariff barrier ¶ →障壁

kanzeiteiritsuhō 関税定率法 tariff law

kanzeiwariate 関税割当 tariff quota

kanzendokusen 完全独占 perfect monopoly; complete monopoly

kanzenjidōka 完全自動化 (full) automation

kanzenjōhō 完全情報 complete information

kanzenkasen 完全寡占 perfect oligopoly

kanzenkinhon'iseido 完全金本位制度 full gold standard; gold specie standard

kanzenkoyō 完全雇用 full employment ¶ The United States economy began to approach the *full-employment* zone.

kanzenkyōsō 完全競争 perfect competition ¶ to maintain *perfect competition* in the textile market

kanzenshitsugyō 完全失業 wholly unemployed ¶ The seasonally adjusted number of normally capable persons *wholly unemployed* rose.

kanzensōgyō 完全操業 full operation; operation to full capacity

kanzentōrokushōken 完全登録証券 fully registered bond

kappatsuna 活発な brisk; active; vigorous; buoyant; energetic; animated; brighter ¶ The *brisk* expansion of consumption was backed by the increase in income. // *active* corporate investment // to continue with increasing *vigor* // the lack of *buoyancy* in housing demand // Production showed great *animation*.

kappatsushikyō 活発市況 active (＝brisk) market; animated market

kappubarai 割賦払い installment (payment); payment in installment ¶ to buy in *installments* // payable by monthly equal *installments* of $25

kappubaraikin 割賦払金 installment ¶ The loan is repayable in five equal semi-annual *installments* from the eighth anniversary of the drawing-down of funds.

kappuhanbai 割賦販売 installment sale

kappuhanbaihō 割賦販売法 →分割払方式

kappuhensai 割賦返済 installment payment ¶ to *pay installments* when they become due

kappukin 割賦金 allotment; share

kappushiire 割賦仕入 installment purchase

karakeiki 空景気 borrowed boom; artificial boom (=prosperity)

karategata から手形 fictitious bill

karatorihiki から取引 fictitious transaction

karauri 空売り［市］ short sale (= selling)

karaurisuji 空売り筋［市］ short sellers

kari 仮 temporary; provisional; interim; transient; transitory; improvised; informal; suspense; ad referendum

karieigyō 仮営業 temporary business (operation)

kariire 借入 borrowing; credit taking ¶ *borrowings* from banks and affiliates // Businesses' haste *borrowing* tightened the money market. // Bold business expansion was financed by *borrowings*. // The increased *borrowing* from banks was largely seasonal, stemming from corporate tax payments. // The larger-than-usual amount of tax *borrowing* brought total loan volume to the August level. // Member bank *borrowings* from the Federal Reserve Banks expanded by $198 million. // March generally ushers in a surge of new bank *borrowing*. // The loan agreement for the $1 milliard Euromarket *borrowing* by Spain was signed. // *borrowing* to cover the cost of imports // ［参考］to float a loan of $2 million to obtain a loan from the bank // The banking system's recourse to the central bank rose by F.fr. 2,200 million.

kariiregendo 借入限度 borrowing limit ¶ Many of the deficit nations are approaching their *borrowing limit.*

kariirejunbi 借入準備 borrowed reserve

kariirejuyō 借入需要 credit demand; loan demand; borrowing demand; financing requirement; financing demand; borrower requirement; borrowing need ¶ Corporate *demands for credit* increased substantially, and continued brisk. // Business *credit demand* mounted toward the year-end. // 880 *credit demands*, totaling $14 billion, were submitted to this bank. // Overall *loan demand* at commercial banks slackened. // *Loan demand* weakened somewhat, but remains still heavy and intense. // Business *loan demand* subsided and is no longer so pressing. // Businesses' *borrowing* requirement mounted, but the public sector *borrowing requirement* (PSBR) dropped sharply. // The Exchequer *borrowing requirement* is estimated to equal about 13% of GNP. // The greater share of *borrower demands* is directed toward banks. // the additional liquidity to meet the financing of the government's *borrowing needs* // *Demands for financing* in the international markets reflect the needs of the oil-importing countries. // to feel a pressing *need* to obtain *financing* // The government's *borrowing requirement* has been steadily reduced. // Corporate *borrowing needs* will overburden the market. // to respond to the insistent *demand* of the public for consumer *credit* // Business *loan demands* are wilting. // seasonally expanded corporate *financing requirements* // *credit demand* for equipment funds // active *credit requirements* of smaller business for expansive business purposes // a decline in *financing demands* // Many oil-importing countries need a pressing *need* to obtain *financing*.

kariirekin 借入金 borrowed money; loan; debt; [会] loan payable 一時借入金 floating debt

kariirekinkanjō 借入金勘定 loan account

kariirekinkinri 借入金金利 interest on borrowings

kariirenōryoku 借入能力 capacity to borrow; borrowing capacity; borrowing potential; potentiality of borrowing ¶ to have little *capacity to borrow* abroad on commercial terms // The company's *potentiality of* overseas *borrowing* is great.

kariiresaimu 借入債務 borrowed indebtedness; debt obligation ¶ to pay off its *borrowed indebtedness* to banks // to serve their existing *debt obligations*

kariiresakikakudai 借入先拡大 diversification of channels for raising fresh funds

kariireshihon 借入資本 outside capital; borrowed capital

kariireyoyaku 借入予約 stand-by arrangement

kariireyūkashōken 借入有価証券 securities borrowing; borrowed securities; securities borrowed

kariisogi 借急ぎ haste in borrowing

karijuyō 仮需要 anticipatory demand; anticipatory buying (order) ¶ The mark's appreciation set off a wave of *anticipatory orders* for German goods from abroad. // *anticipatory buying* prompted by rising raw material prices

karikabuken 仮株券 scrip

karikabunitaisuruyūshinobairitsu 借株に対する融資の倍率 ratio of money loans to stock loans ¶ The *ratio of money loans to stock loans* stands at 15-16-fold.

karikabuzandaka 借株残高 balance of stock loans ¶ The *balance of stock loans* has stood at 40 million shares.

karikae 借換え conversion; refunding; reborrowing; refinance; renewal ¶ to *refund* the existing bonds // to *renew* a loan // to *convert* a bond into another // The Treasury should *refund* some of its debt by issuing perpetual obligations. // The Government can continue to meet part of its maturing obligations by *reborrowing*. // to liquidate outstanding foreign currency loans from foreign banks and *refinance* them in yen loans 現金借換え cash refunding 期限前借換え advance refunding 満期借換え refunding at maturity

karikaehakkō 借換発行 conversion issue

karikaesaiken 借換債券 refunding bond

karikaeteitōtsukishasai 借換抵当付社債 funding mortgage bond

karikanjō 仮勘定 suspense account

karikata 借方 debit; debtor; debit side ¶ to *debit* an account // to enter or place to the *debit* of an account

karikataginkō 借方銀行 debtor bank

karikatahyō 借方票 debit note (= ticket; slip); debtor note

karikatakanjō 借方勘定 debtor account

karikataran 借方欄 debtor side

karikatazandaka 借方残高 debit balance; debtor balance

karikeisansho 仮計算書 provisional statement of account

karikeiyaku 仮契約 provisional contract; ad referendum contract

karikijitsu 仮期日 provisional due date

karikisoku 仮規則 provisional rules

karikoshi 借越し outstanding debt; overdrawing; overdraft

karikoshikanjō 借越勘定 overdrawn account

karikoshinisuru 借越にする letting a debt stand over; leaving a debt outstanding

karikyōtei 仮協定 provisional agreement

karimitsumori 仮見積り preliminary estimate

karimokuromisho 仮目論見書 preliminary prospectus; red herring (prospectus)

kariokiba 仮置場 free depot

karisashiosae 仮差押え provisional seizure

karishikkō 仮執行 provisional execution

karishobun 仮処分 provisional disposition

karishōken 仮証券 scrip certificate; interim certificate

karishūzen 仮修繕 temporary repairs

kariukekin 借受金 suspense receipt; advance received on contract; deposit received; abvance on subscription

kariukenin 借受人 lessee; borrower; hirer; lease-holder

karuteru カルテル cartel ¶ to form a recession *cartel* to tide over the protracted shipbuilding slump // a *cartel* organized to promote rationalization // to scrap the price *cartel* formed last year // to develop a *cartelized* attitude towards business

貿易カルテル trade cartel

地域カルテル regional cartel

中小企業カルテル smaller enterprise cartel

不況(防止)カルテル anti-depression cartel

合理化カルテル rationalization cartel

価格カルテル price cartel

国際カルテル international cartel

karuteruka カルテル化 cartelization

kasadakahin 嵩高品 bulky goods

kasaihoken 火災保険 fire insurance

kasaihokengaisha 火災保険会社 fire insurance company

kasaihokengyōsha 火災保険業者 fire underwriter

kasaihokenkeiyaku 火災保険契約 fire insurance contract

kasaihokenkensa 火災保険検査 fire insurance surveying

kasaihokenkyōteiritsu 火災保険協定率 fire insurance tariff

kasaihokenryōkin 火災保険料金 fire insurance rate

kasaihokenshōken 火災保険証券 fire insurance policy

kaseigaku 家政学 domestic science; home economics

kasen 寡占 oligopoly; non-isolated selling

完全寡占 perfect oligopoly

共謀寡占 collusion oligopoly

双方寡占 bilateral oligopoly

kasengyogyō 河川漁業 river fishery

kasenkakaku 寡占価格 oligopoly price

kasenkeizai 寡占経済 oligopolistic economy

kasensangyō 寡占産業 oligopoly industry

kasenshiki 河川敷 river area

kasentaisei 寡占体制 oligopolistic system

kasentekikyōsō 寡占的競争 oligopolistic competition

kasentekishihai 寡占的支配 oligopolistic control ¶ to induce *oligopolistic control* to businesses in each national market // The *oligopolistic control* of supply is possible to maintain prices by reducing output.

kashi 貸し loan; lending; advance

現地貸し loans and overdrafts outside Japan

保証貸し loan on personal guarantee

信用貸し unsecured loan; fiduciary loan; credit loan; personal loan

担保貸し collateral loan

抵当貸し mortgage loan

当座貸し call loan; demand loan; sight loan; day-to-day loan

預金貸し deposit loan

kashichi 貸地 land to let; lot to let; land for rent; lot for rent

kashichin 貸賃 rent; hire

kashidaore 貸倒れ bad debt; dead loan; lending loss; loan loss ¶ The World Bank has not had any *losses* on its *loans*.

kashidaorehikiatekin 貸倒引当金 reserve (= provision) for uncollectible account

kashidaorehoken 貸倒保険 bad debt insurance

kashidaorejunbikin 貸倒準備金 bad debt reserve; reserve (=provision) for possible loan losses

kashidaorekinshōkyaku 貸倒金償却 bad debt written off

kashidaoresonshitsu 貸倒損失 bad debt loss

kashidaoreyosō 貸倒予想 doubtful debt

kashidashi 貸出 loan; advance; lending; discount and advance ¶ The Bank's cumulative *lending* rose to 889 *loans* amounting to almost $8.7 billion. // The *loans* granted by the Development Bank included two *loans* to Brazil for $74 million and $50 million and one of $105 million to Guatemala. // Disbursed and outstanding *loans* held by the World Bank at the end of 1975 amounted to over $12.6 billion, and a further $9.4 billion of committed loans had not yet been disbursed. // The banks have been accommodating a growing volume of *loans*. // The expansion of *loans* extended to foreign countries moderated. // Commercial bank *loans* and discounts fell slightly.

不当貸出 illegal advance

非常貸出 emergency advance

放漫貸出 reckless advances (= lending)

国内貸出 loans and overdrafts in Japan

kashidashidaka 貸出高 amount of loans; advances; lendings; loan volume ¶ the highest annual *loan volume* in the Bank's history

kashidashigendogaku 貸出限度額 maximum limit on lendings; credit ceiling; loan limit; lending limit ¶ The *ceiling on lending* commitments, known as the *credit ceiling*, was raised by a total of 8% in the course of 1975. // to determine their *loan limits* for particular countries // *Credit ceilings* are established for each bank in the form of facilities for overdraft and rediscount from the central bank. // The Bank introduced *credit ceilings*. // The *credit ceiling* was raised by 8%. // to rediscount loans beyond the *credit ceiling*

kashidashigendogakutekiyōseido 貸出限度額適用制度 credit ceiling system

kashidashihōshin 貸出方針 lending policy ¶ Many banks expressed restrictive *lending policies*. // Banks continued to pursue their accommodative *lending policy*.

kashidashijōken 貸出条件 terms and conditions of loan ¶ ［参考］ to offer a more favorable spread of loan terms and rates than at present

kashidashijōkenmeijihō 貸出条件明示法 ［米］ Truth in Lending Act of 1968

kashidashijōkenmeijinohōsoku 貸出条件明示の法則 Truth in Lending; rules of disclosure as to credit charges and repayment terms

kashidashikettei 貸出決定 loan decision; loan commitment

kashidashikinri 貸出金利 interest rate on loans; loan rate; lending rate

kashidashikōsei 貸出構成 loan composition

kashidashikyōso 貸出競争 lending race; loan competition ¶ Banks are urged to halt the present *lending race*. // to avoid the already severe *competition* among banks for *loans*

kashidashinokaishū 貸出の回収 recovery of loans; call-in of loans

kashidashinokarikaekeizoku 貸出の借越継続 renewal and extension of loans

kashidashinosaimufurikō 貸出の債務不履行 default on loan

kashidashinoyakusoku 貸出の約束 loan commitment

kashidashinoyokusei 貸出の抑制 restriction of bank lending

kashidashiriritsu 貸出利率 loan (interest) rate; lending rate; (interest) rate on loans

kashidashirisuku 貸出リスク (loan; debt) exposure ¶ The bank's loan *exposure* in five Latin American countries represents 7-8 percent of total assets. // the special provision for international *exposure* // →リスク

kashidashiseisaku 貸出政策 lending policy ¶ to consistently pursue a moderately restrictive *lending policy* // The principal measure of the *lending policy* is to change the Bank rate.

kashidashishijō 貸出市場 lending market ¶ Foreign banks' dominance on the world's *lending markets* remained unchallenged. // Iraq plays no role on international *lending markets*. // a Gulf dollar *lending market*

kashidashishikin 貸出資金 loanable resources ¶ to ease the World Bank's *loanable resources* in the most efficient way possible and to leverage them the maximum

kashidashishinsa 貸出審査 examination of loan application; screening of application for loan

kashidashishisei 貸出姿勢 lending posture ¶ to assume an accommodative or restrictive *lending posture*

kashidashiwaku 貸出枠 limit of credit; credit ceiling

kashidashiyakujōheikinkinri 貸出約定平均金利 average contractual (=contracted; agreed) interest rate on bank loans ¶ *Average contracted interest rates* for loans by city banks fell by 0.071 percentage points to 5.682% per annum.

kashidashiyoryoku 貸出余力 loanable (=lendable) funds

kashidashiyoyaku 貸出予約 loan commitment ¶ New mortgage *commitments* by savings and loan associations have risen strongly.

kashidashizandaka 貸出残高 loans (=lendings) outstanding; outstanding loans and discounts

業種別貸出残高 outstanding loans and discounts by industry

担保別貸出残高 outstanding loans and discounts by kind of collateral

kashidashizōkagakukisei 貸出増加額規制 regulation on bank's lendings; regulatory control on bank lending increase; measures to check the increase in city bank lendings; ceiling on bank credit expansion; quantitative limits on the increase in bank lending; norms for credit expansion (= growth); window guidance frameworks; unofficial ceilings for net additional lending; credit ceiling ¶ The Bank of Japan tightened its *unofficial control over* commercial banks' *net additional lend-*

ing in the July-September quarter. // [参考] The ceilings on the growth of credit will not be removed this year. // Authorized expansion in lending subject to the ceilings for this year as a whole is 1 percentage point less than in last year. // to scrap the sacrosanct system of credit growth ceilings

kashidashizōkagakukiseitaishōgaikin'yūkikan 貸出増加額規制対象外金融機関 financial institutions outside the purview of loan regulation by the Bank of Japan

kashidashizōkagakukiseitaishōkin'yūkikan 貸出増加額規制対象金融機関 banks coming under the purview of loan regulation by the Bank of Japan

kashijimusho 貸事務所 office to let; office for rent

kashikabu 貸株 lending stock

kashikabushijō 貸株市場 stock loan market

kashikata 貸方 credit; creditor; credit side ¶ to *credit* an account // to enter or place to the *credit* of an account // France's *creditor* position in the IMF fell by Fr. fr.8 million to Fr. fr. 4.077 billion.

kashikataginkō 貸方銀行 creditor balance

kashikingyō 貸金業 money lender; money lending business

kashikinko 貸金庫 safe deposit box

kashikoshi 貸越し outstanding account; overdrawn account ¶ an *account* remaining *outstanding,* or due but unpaid

当座貸越し overdraft

kashikoshikyokudogaku 貸越極度額 maximum limit of overdraft

kashinushi 貸主 creditor; lessor; landlord

kashidashisakikibobetsubunrui 貸出先規模別分類 size-of-borrower distribution ¶ The *size-of-borrower distribution* of member bank loans has shifted appreciably.

kashitenokiken 貸手の危険 lender's risk

kashitsuke 貸付 loan; advance; lending ¶ to extend a *loan* on bills // to make an *advance* // →貸付金
　長期貸付 long-term loan
　不動産貸付 loan on real estate
　銀行貸付 bank loan
　保証付貸付 loan with third party's guarantee
　一時貸付 temporary loan
　株券貸付 stock loan
　既往貸付 outstanding loan
　工場貸付 loan on plant
　極度貸付 line of credit; credit line
　証券担保貸付 〔英〕 Lombard loan
　証書貸付 loan on deed
　短期貸付 short-term loan
　手形貸付 loan on bill
　定期貸付 time loan
　当座貸付 call loan; day-to-day loan; demand loan
　翌日払い貸付 overnight loan; overnight money

kashitsukebuai 貸付歩合 → 貸付金利子

kashitsukegakari 貸付係 loan-teller

kashitsukejōken 貸付条件 terms and conditions of loan

kashitsukekachi 貸付価値 loan value

kashitsukekanjō 貸付勘定 loan account

kashitsukekeiyaku 貸付契約 loan contract ¶ The European Investment Bank signed 77 *loan contracts* for a total of 1,006.5 million units of account.

kashitsukekeiyakusho 貸付契約書 loan agreement; loan contract

kashitsukekin 貸付金 loan; advance; lending ¶ →貸付
　不動産抵当貸付金 loan secured by real estate
　債権担保貸付金 loan secured by account receivable
　政府貸付金 loan to Government
　財団抵当貸付金 loan secured by floating mortgage

kashitsukekinrishi 貸付金利子 interest on (=of) loans (=advances)

kashitsukekinrisokuwarimodoshi 貸付金利息割戻し interest on loans rebated

kashitsukekinsaikenshutoku 貸付金債権取得 acquisition of claimable assets arising from loans; acquisition of claims in the form of loans

kashitsukemotochō 貸付元帳 loan ledger

kashitsukenomōshikomi 貸付の申込み loan application ¶ to receive and screen *applications for loan*

kashitsukerishiritsu 貸付利子率 lending rate; loan interest rate

kashitsukeseido 貸付制度 lending facility ¶ the establishment of a new intermediate *lending facility* in the World Bank known as the Third Window

kashitsukeshihon 貸付資本 loan capital

kashitsukeshijō 貸付市場 loan market; lending market; credit market

kashitsukeshikin 貸付資金 loanable funds; lendable funds

kashitsukeshintaku 貸付信託
loan in trust; loan trust

kashitsukeshōdaku 貸付承諾
credit commitment ¶ to publicize
Euro-currency *credit commitments*

kashitsukeyakujō 貸付約定
(terms and conditions of) loan agreement

kashitsukeyakujōryō 貸付約定料
(loan) commitment fee

kashitsukeyūkashōken 貸付有価証
券 loan receivable in securities;
securities lent

kashitsukezandaka 貸付残高
debit balance

kashiwatashi 貸渡し trust receipt
¶ *trust receipt* of collateral
goods

kashiya 貸家 house to let; house
for rent

kashobunshotoku 可処分所得
disposable income; spendable earnings ¶ to devote a quarter of their
disposable income to the repayment
of debt // Gross national *disposable
income* at constant market prices
went up by 4.5% between 1978 and
1979. // Real *spendable earnings* of
workers rose by 0.2%, seasonally
adjusted, in March. // Private real
disposable income remained unchanged from the previous year. // The
personal saving rate is in the range
of 5% of *disposable* personal *income*. // On a seasonally adjusted
basis, real *spendable earnings* fell by
0.4% in June.
実質個人可処分所得 real personal
disposable income; R.P.D.I.

kashōchochiku 過少貯蓄 under-
saving

kashōhyōka 過少評価 undervaluation; underestimation ¶ The

Canadian dollar remains *undervalued* against the U.S. dollar.

kashōkoyō 過少雇用 underemployment
循環的過少雇用 cyclical underem-
ployment
構造的過少雇用 structural under-
employment
潜在的過少雇用 disguised underemployment

kashōriyō 過少利用 under-
utilization

kashōryūdōsei 過少流動性 insufficient liquidity

kashōseisan 過少生産 underproduction

kashōsetsubi 過少設備 under-
capacity

kashōshiharai 過少支払い under-
payment

kashōshōhi 過少消費 under-
consumption

kashōtōshi 過少投資 under-
investment ¶ *under-investment* in
education

kasochiiki 過疎地域 area of depleting population; underpopulated area

kasoka 過疎化 population drain;
depopulation

kasoku 加速 acceleration ¶ The
acceleration in corporate tax payments is complete. // The current
inflation is steadily *accelerating*. //
The *acceleration* to January of the
tax increase scheduled for September. // to *accelerate* the schedule from
the currently proposed next March
to this autumn // to halt the *accelerating* inflationary trends

kasokudo 加速度 momentum ¶
Inflation gathered much *momentum*. // Expansionary forces lost
some of their *momentum*. // The rise

gained further *momentum*. // Recovery in activity gathered further *momentum*. // Prices rose at the *momentum* of the export drive. // The *momentum* of sales continued. // Production expanded on the *momentum* of business boom. // The decline reached its maximum *momentum*. // Yields maintained their upward *momentum*.

kasokudogenri 加速度原理 acceleration principle

kasokudoinshi 加速度因子 accelerator

(非)線型加速度因子 (non-)linear accelerator

伸縮的加速度因子 flexible accelerator

kasokushōkyaku 加速償却 accelerated depreciation

kasokuteki 加速的 accelerating; increasing; progressive ¶ Income acted as an *accelerating* factor in price rises. // Prices rose at an *accelerating* rate. // Output decreased *increasingly* fast. // Shipments gained at *progressively* rising pace. // The situation became *increasingly* difficult. // The pace of upswing of economic activity *accelerated*.

kasokutekigenkashōkyaku 加速的減価償却 accelerated depreciation

kasseiodei 活性汚泥 activated sludge

kassuiki 渇水期 dry season; low-water season

katabōeki 片貿易 one-sided trade; lopsided trade

katagawari 肩替り tranfer; refinancing; taking over ¶ *taking-over* of debts by the company

katagawarinin 肩替人 transferee

kataikin 過怠金 penalty money

katamichihejjingu 片道ヘッジング one-sided hedging

katamichiyōki 片道容器 one-way package

katei 仮定 assumption ¶ *assumption* of independence in analysis of variance

katei 家庭 household; family; home ¶ per farm *household* cash income for 1975 // *family* income // electrical *household* appliances

katei 過程 process ¶ National bank notes are in *process* of retirement. // stages in the *process* of production, or manufacturing *process* // to shorten the present adjustment *process* // the product of an evolutionary *process* covering more than a century // The reallocation of resources is a slow and often costly *process*. // a cautious tidying-up *process* following the huge foreign exchange inflows // an economic adjustment *process,* or a *process* of economic adjustment

蓄積過程 accumulative process

調整過程 adjustment process

利潤形成過程 profit-making process

累積過程 accumulative process; cumulative process

再投資過程 plow-back process

成長過程 growth process ¶ to bring the poor into the growth *process*

生産過程 production process

kateikeizai 家庭経済 domestic economy; household economy

kateisaihōsangyō 家庭裁縫産業 home sewing industry

kateiyōdenkikiki 家庭用電気機器 electric(al) household machinery and equipment; electric home appliances

kateiyōhin 家庭用品 household appliances; household furnishings; house articles

kato 過渡 transition ¶ The nation's current wave of stinginess is *transitional.*

katoki 過渡期 transitional period; transit period; period of transition

katokuchōsa 稼得調査 earnings test

katokunōryoku 稼得能力 earning power

katokusha 稼得者 earner

katōkyōsei 過当矯正 overcorrection; overkill

katōkyōsō 過当競争 undue competition; overcompetition

katōtōki 過当投機 over-speculation

katsudō 活動 activity ¶ It is another gentle rise in *activity,* but still a rise. // *Activity* in manufacturing continued below normal. // Business *activity* slackened in some major sectors. // Expansion reached the level of *activity* desired. // *Activity* approached the crest. // The over-all measures of *activity* moved broadly sideways. // The main support to the intense economic *activity* came from equipment investment. // *Activity* in the construction industry rose more strongly. // By any measure, growth of foreign banking *activity* is not abating. // The Bank accelerated its *activities* to counter the problem of unemployment. // The issuing *activity* in the Eurobond market is relatively unregulated. // the various areas of financial *activity* — commercial banking, deposit-taking, securities, commodities, insurance, and a new secondary

market for long-term assets // Overall (bond) issuing *activity* turned out high. // The Bank continued to expand its *activities* in 1978. // Financial *activities* with foreign countries will increase. // Business investment *activity* was brisk. // The over-all measures of *activity* moved broadly sideways. // a downturn or a prolonged pause in *activity* // The revival of *activity* led to increase in output.

katsudōgenkin 活動現金 active money

katsudōkanjō 活動勘定 active account

katsudōshihon 活動資本 active capital

katsudōshisan 活動資産 active asset

katsudōsuijun 活動水準 activity level ¶ The *activity level* in the manufacturing sector is closely linked to *activity levels* in the rest of the economy.

katsudōyokin 活動預金 active deposit

katsudōzandaka 活動残高 active balance

katuryoku 活力 →活気

kawarazu 変らず no change; unchanged; no alteration; static ¶ The spot dollar opened virtually *unchanged* from the pre-holiday closing of ¥240 flat.

kawarikin 代り金 proceeds ¶ sizable export *proceeds* // *proceeds* from exports // yen *proceeds* from sales of goods to Japan // Export *proceeds* must be surrendered within 10 days from the date of acquisition. // Inflows of export *proceeds* eased the financial environment.

kawaseburōkā 為替ブローカー [外] foreign exchange broker ¶ More than 90 percent of all transactions are conducted through the intermediary of *foreign exchange brokers.*

kawasefuridashinin 為替振出人 drawer; sender

kawasegyōmu 為替業務 exchange business

kawasehanbaigyō 為替販売業 retail dealer in exchange

kawaseheika 為替平価 par value of exchange

kawaseheikōkanjō 為替平衡勘定 [英] foreign exchange equalization account

kawasehendōhaba 為替変動幅 exchange rate fluctuation margin (= range); exchange rate band ¶ to permit a temporary widening of the *exchange rate fluctuation margins* // wider *margins of exchange rates* // The *fluctuation margin* limitation on the yen *exchange rate* was suspended temporarily. // The available *margins* of up to 2.25 per cent on each side of parity must not be violated. // to operate intervention policies within a wide *margin* of 4.5 percent either side of par // Their currencies are permitted to move up from the lower to the upper *margins* of the bands around the SDR. // It gave the Bank welcome scope to resume foreign exchange interventions for smoothing out violent, excessive *rate fluctuations.*

kawasehendōhoken 為替変動保険 foreign exchange fluctuation insurance

kawasehikiukesōba 為替引受相場 accepting rate of exchange

kawasekainyū 為替介入 exchange intervention

kawasekanshō 為替干渉 exchange intervention

kawasemarī 為替マリー exchange marry

kawasemarīeki 為替マリー益 exchange marriage profit

kawasemochidaka 為替持高 exchange position; overall balance of foreign exchange

kawasenakagainin 為替仲買人 exchange broker

kawasenodeai 為替の出合い exchange cover

kawasenohendō 為替の変動 exchange fluctuation

kawasepojishon 為替ポジション →為替持高

kawaserēto 為替レート rate of exchange; exchange rate ¶ →為替相場 複数為替レート plural exchange rate 一本建為替レート single exchange rate

kawaserisuku 為替リスク exchange risk ¶ safeguards against *exchange risks*

kawaseshijō 為替市場 exchange market ¶ closure and reopening of *exchange markets* // uncertainty on the *exchange markets* // The yen was quoted on the Tokyo foreign *exchange market* at 339=U.S.$1, or some 6% above the old official rate of 360.

kawasesōba 為替相場 exchange rate; rate of exchange; exchange quotation ¶ The new *exchange rate* for the US dollar against the rouble will be $1.55=R1. // This is the lowest *exchange rate* over quoted for the US dollar against the rouble. //

The pound *exchange rate* passed through in psychological barrier of two dollars to the pound. // The yen's *rate* on the dollar had already risen by about 4 percent to under ¥295.

長期為替相場 long exchange rate

複数建て為替相場 plural exchange rate

現実的為替相場 actual rate of exchange

一本建て為替相場 single exchange rate

自由変動為替相場 floating exchange rate

固定為替相場 fixed exchange rate

屈伸為替相場 flexible exchange rate

目標為替相場 target rate of exchange

理論的為替相場 theoretical rate of exchange

参考為替相場 reference rate of exchange

信用状付為替相場 credit rate of exchange

対米為替相場 exchange rate on New York; exchange between Tokyo and New York

多数為替相場 multiple exchange rate

kawasetegata 為替手形 bill of exchange; draft

代金取立為替手形 sales bill of exchange

複券為替手形 set of bills (of exchange)

銀行為替手形 bank bill

裸為替手形 clean bill

内国為替手形 domestic bill of exchange; domestic draft

荷為替手形 bill of lading

商業為替手形 merchant bill

証券付為替手形 stock draft

単券為替手形 solo bill

要求払為替手形 demand draft; demand bill

輸入為替手形 import draft; import bill

kawasetegatahikiuke 為替手形引受け acceptance of a bill (=draft); to honor a bill; to protect a bill

kawasetegatanoshiharaikyohi 為替手形の支払拒否 to dishonor a bill; to protest a bill

kawasetegatanoteiji 為替手形の提示 presentation of bill

kawasetesūryō 為替手数料 charge for remittance

kawasetōki 為替投機 exchange speculation

kawasetorihiki 為替取引 exchange dealing; exchange transaction

銀行間為替取引 inter-bank exchange dealing

kawasetorikime 為替取決 exchange arrangement ¶ to maintain orderly *exchange arrangements*

kawasetorikumi 為替取組 [外] negotiation of export bills

kawasetorikumitsūchi 為替取組通知 remittance instruction

kawasetōzagashi 為替当座貸 [外] overdrafts for export bills

kawaseyamisōba 為替闇相場 dark exchange

kawaseyoyaku 為替予約 exchange (forward) contract

kawaseyoyakunojikkō 為替予約の実行 delivery

kazaidōgu 家財道具 household effects; goods and chattels

kazanhatsuden 火山発電 hot rock power generation

kazei 課税 taxation; assessment ¶

The *taxation* of the country was levied in commodities and service.

分離課税 separated assessment; separate taxation

源泉課税 taxation at source; stoppage at source

逆累進課税 regressive taxation

二重課税 double taxation

累進課税 progressive taxation

累退課税 regressive taxation

総合課税 general assessment; consolidated assessment; general taxation

kazeibukken 課税物件 taxation article; object of taxation

kazeigenbo 課税原簿 assessment roll

kazeihan'i 課税範囲 scope of assessment

kazeihin 課税品 article subject to taxation; taxable goods; dutiable goods; customable goods

kazeihyōjun 課税標準 basis of assessment

kazeikakaku 課税価格 value of assessment

kazeikijun 課税基準 basis of assessment

kazeimitsumorikakaku 課税見積価格 ratable value

kazeinendo 課税年度 taxable year

kazeinohōshigensoku 課税の奉仕原則 cost-of-service principle

kazeiritsu 課税率 tax rate; tariff

kazeisaiteigaku 課税最低額 minimum taxable ceiling; lowest taxable limit

kazeisanpin 課税産品 taxed product

kazeishotoku 課税所得 assessable (=taxable) income ¶ Interest is a deductible expense from *taxable income*. ¶ to raise the proportion of

total foreign sales deductible from *taxable income* to 20%

kazokujūgyōin 家族従業員 family employee; family worker

kazokukibonōjō 家族規模農場 family-sized farm

kazokuteate 家族手当 family allowance

kehai 気配 ［市］tone of the market; atmosphere of the market; quote; quotation ¶ The *tone of the market* was firm. // The *market tone* remained steady. // The market maintained a buoyant *tone*. // *Quotes in the market* were higher at the start but turned lower.

買気配 asked price; bid(ding) quotation

売気配 bid price

ヤリ気配 ask(ed) quotation

kehaijō 気配状 ［証市］stock-list

kehaisōba 気配相場 indication ¶ Dealers are *indicating* silver three months at 575 to 577 pence per troy ounce.

keiei 経営 operation; administration; management; to run; to conduct ¶ business *operation* // *administration* of a company // business *management* of a company // to *run* a business

科学的経営法 scientific management

個人経営 private enterprise

集団経営 corporate enterprise

多角経営 multilateral management

keieibunseki 経営分析 business analysis

keieidairinin 経営代理人 managing agent

keieigaishisan 経営外資産 non-operating assets

計量経営学 business econometrics

keieigōrika 経営合理化 improvement (=modernization) of business operations; betterment of business management; managerial and operational rationalization of business

keieihi 経営費 operating expenses; working expenses; overhead charges

keieihiritsu 経営比率 operating ratios

keieijin 経営陣 executives

keieijissen 経営実践 business practice

keieijōhōshisutemu 経営情報システム management information system; MIS

keieikaizen 経営改善 administrative improvement; managerial betterment

keieikanri 経営管理 business management

keieikeikaku 経営計画 management plan

keieiken 経営権 right of administration; right of management; franchise rights

keieikiban 経営基盤 management foundation

keieikonsarutanto 経営コンサルタント management consultant

keieikōritsu 経営効率 efficiency of management

keieikyōgikai 経営協議会 management council; managerial joint committee

keieinodōgu 経営の道具 managerial tool

keieiritchi 経営立地 management location

keieisaikōsekininsha 経営最高責任者 chief operating officer; COO

keieisanka 経営参加 participation in management; management participation; management involvement ¶ to *participate in the management* of a corporation // stock purchased for *participation in management* // The lack of home-based banking expertise requires a certain amount of *management involvement* from foreign nationals. // ［参考］to allow foreign investors access to the management of enterprises // to take part in running and managing enterprises

keieiseiseki 経営成績 results of (business) operations

keieisha 経営者 operator; administrator; manager; management

keieishakakumei 経営者革命 managerial revolution

keieishashihai 経営者支配 management control

keieishi 経営士 management consultant

keieishihyō 経営指標 management index

keieishuwan 経営手腕 administrative ability

keieisō 経営層 zones of management

keieitōkei 経営統計 business statistics

keigen 軽減 attenuation; moderation; blunting; diminution; easing; relaxation; abatement; mitigation; subsidence ¶ Pressures in the market *attenuated.* // Inflationary pressures were somewhat *eased.* // The price declines *blunted.* // Cost pressures continued *unabated.* // The growth of imports *moderated.* // The major expansive influence of budgetary expenditures *subsided.*

keigenzeiritsu 軽減税率 reduced rate

keihi 経費 expense; expenditure;

outlay; spending; cost ¶ housing *expenses* // increase in government *expenditure* // *expenditures* on public works // housing *expenses* // increase in government *expenditure*

営業外経費 non-operating expense

営業経費 operating expense

販売経費 selling expense

事後経費 after cost

実物経費 expense in kind

金購入経費 expenses involved in buying gold

臨時経費 non-recurring expense

割当経費 expenses quota

keihikessan 経費決算 closing of expenditure accounts

keihikessanhōkoku 経費決算報告 report on expenses

keihinoshiharai 経費の支払 payment of expenditures

keihinsutanpu 景品スタンプ (trade) stamp

keihiritsu 経費率 (銀行の) ratio of general expenses to deposits

keihisetsugen 経費節減 curtailment of expenditures; reduction of expenditures; financial retrenchment

keihiwariate 経費割当 expenses quota

keihiyosan 経費予算 expenses budget

keihōten 警報点 warning point ¶ →警戒点

上方警報点 upper warning point

下方警報点 lower warning point

keihyō 計表 tabular statements; tabulation; tables

keihyōhon'isei 計表本位制 tabular standard system

keijōgai 経常外 non-recurring

keijōgaison'eki 経常外損益 non-recurring profit and loss

keijōgenka 経常減価 normal depreciation

keijōhi 経常費 current expenses; working expenses; running expenses; ordinary expenses; overhead charges

keijōhojokin 経常補助金 current subsidies

keijōjunbi 経常準備 working reserve

keijōkaigaiyojō 経常海外余剰 surplus of the nation on current account

keijōkakaku 経常価格 current price

keijōrieki 経常利益 recurring profit ¶ to score record pre-tax *recurring* profits in the latest business year

keijōsainyū 経常歳入 ordinary (annual) revenue

keijōsaishutsu 経常歳出 ordinary (annual) expenditure

keijōshiharai 経常支払 current payments

keijōshishutsu 経常支出 current expenditure

keijōshishutsutaikeijōshūnyūhiritsu 経常支出対経常収入比率 ratio of current expenses to current income

keijōshushijiri 経常収支尻 current balance; current account balance; current transactions; balance on current account

keijōshushiritsu 経常収支率 ratio of current income to current expenses

keijōtekiun'eihi 経常的運営費 running expenses of management

keijōtorihiki 経常取引 current transaction

keijōyosan 経常予算 ordinary budget

keikabunseki 経過分析 process

analysis

keikahaitō 経過配当 accrued dividend

keikahokenshōken 経過保険証券 lapsed policy

keikai 警戒 vigilance; caution; prudence; heed; care; wariness ¶ to employ, exercise, take, use, observe due *caution* // to act with *prudence* // to be *wary* of prospective inflation // to exercise extreme *vigilance* against inflation // The greatest *caution* must be used not to... // policy actions with *prudence* // to pay much *heed* to price developments // to require watchful *care* and *vigilance* // investor *caution* in advance of the weekend // An atmosphere of *caution* persisted in market. // a more *cautious* attitude toward high prices // Investors proceeded *cautiously*.

高値警戒 cautiousness of higher prices ¶ The market marked time as buyers were *cautious of higher prices*.

keikaichūritsugatayosan 警戒中立型予算 cautious-neutral budget

keikaigimi 警戒気味 hesitancy ¶ to be *hesitant* in buying // The *hesitant* tone persisted in July. // The *hesitancy* largely disappeared.

keikaininki 警戒人気 cautious atmosphere; atmosphere of caution; cautious mood; cautiousness ¶ A *cautious atmosphere* persisted in the market. // A *cautious mood* prevailed on the stock market. // The market is in a *cautious mood* for fear of another dip in stock prices. // The market underwent its second straight weekly decline in a *cautious mood*. // *Cautiousness* on

higher prices prevailed. // The *cautiousness* of the preceding month persisted. // The market became *cautious* on higher prices.

keikaishingō 警戒信号 amber lights ¶ The *amber lights* began to flash. // *Amber lights* are winking in Japan's economy. // [参考] reddish yellow light // The signal moves to orange.

keikaisuijun 警戒水準 warning level ¶ The Belgian franc fell below its early *warning level*.

keikaiteki 警戒的 [市] cautious

keikaitekichūritsu 警戒的中立 more cautious than neutral; cautious neutrality

keikaitekichūritsuyosan 警戒的中立予算 broadly neutral with a bias, if any, on the side of caution; reasonably conservative budget (by Nixon)

keikaitekirakkan 警戒的楽観 cautious optimism; guarded optimism ¶ Business opinions shifted from all-out optimism to *cautious optimism*. // The Bank of France is *cautiously optimistic* about the future trend of business activity.

keikaiten 警戒点 warning point ¶ The "lower" *warning point* would be midway between the low point and the base level for reserves.

keikajikan 経過時間 lapsed time

keikakanjō 経過勘定 deferred and accrued accounts

keikaku 計画 project; plan; program; scheme; design ¶ business investment *plans* // a development *project* // an eight-point *program* of price stabilization // to curtail the scope of the *program* // construction on a five years' *scheme* in contemplation // a policy *designed* to stimulate business // Appropriate borrower involvement in the genesis and preparation of *project*, and adequate responsiveness of *project* design to local conditions are important determinants of project success. // soundly conceived and efficiently executed *programs* // President Reagan's budget *plan projects* a deficit of 181 billion dollars. // The performance of the individual components deviated sharply from the initial *projections*. // A major consideration in economic *planning* is the existence of foreign exchange constraints. // The growth in consumption deviated markedly from the *projections* in the long-term *program*. // Carter's spending *plan* for the fiscal year would increase outlays by 3.1%. // to incorporate some of the ideas in the *plan* tabled in Parliament // The investment initially *scheduled* for iron and steel for the year was somewhat delayed and the *planned program* could be carried out in full.

開発計画　development project

管理者訓練計画　management training program; MTP

経済計画　economic planning

机上計画　blue-print; desk plan

国土計画　national land planning

租税還付計画　negative tax plan

耐乏生活計画　austerity program

多目的計画　multi-purpose project

都市計画　city planning; town planning

財政計画　financial program

keikakukeizai 計画経済 planned economy ¶ countries with centrally *planned economies*

keikakusha 計画者 projector; promotor; planner

keikakutekikekkin 計画的欠勤 absenteeism

keikakutekitōshi 計画的投資 planned investment

keikakuyūshi 計画融資 project-based lending; project loan

keikanissū 経過日数 lapsed (time in) days; number of days elapsed

keikarishi 経過利子 accrued interest

keikashisan 経過資産 deferred assets

keikasochi 経過措置 interim measure; transitional measure

keiken 経験 experience ¶ in the light of precedent and *experience* // The upsurge in sales in May was a repeat of the April *experience*. // the diversity in individual industry *experience* // judging from past *experience* // to have a bitter, hard or painful *experience* // to be little or much *experienced* in handling inflation // *Experience* demonstrates that this is not always the case.

keikenshugiteki 経験主義的 empirical ¶ To what extent are the hypotheses *empirically* verified? // trends to confirm *empirical* evidence // The *empirical* evidence supports the hypothesis. // There seems to be no *empirical* regularity about the manner in which reserves are determined. // *Empirical* examinations of Fund stabilization programs found that...

keikentekichishiki 経験的知識 empirical knowledge

keikentekijisshō 経験的実証 empirical evidence ¶ The *empirical evidence* for the period reviewed supports the hypothesis.

keiki 契機 momentum; strength; support ¶ Prices rose at the *momentum* of the expert drive. // Production expanded on the *momentum* of business boom. // with this as a *momentum* // on the *momentum* of business boom // on the *strength* of this // *Supported* by this, ...

keiki 景気 business activity; business; business conditions; business situation; business picture; business climate ¶ National *business activity* increased fairly sharply. // *Business* shows a distinct improvement. // The country's *business conditions* improved. // The *business situation* is disturbing. // Honduran *business activity* continued below-normal. // *Business activity* continued high in 1975. // General *business activity* was characterized by mixed trends. // There has been some decline in domestic *business activity* from last year's peak. // *Business conditions* recovered from a period of readjustments. // There has been a perceptible ralaxation in the German *economic situation.*

空景気 artificial boom; borrowed boom; artificial prosperity; borrowed prosperity

にわか景気 flush; boom

投資主導型景気 business boom led (=spearheaded) by investment

keikiatamauchi 景気頭打ち business slackening; slackened business activity

keikichinsei 景気鎮静 moderation (=slowdown) of business activity; cooling-off; calming-down

keikichōsei 景気調整 cyclical adjustment (of business activity); business adjustment ¶ The recent *adjustment* has led to a distinct slackening of activity.

keikidōkōchōsa 景気動向調査 survey of business trends; business survey

keikidōkōshihyō 景気動向指標 diffusion index

keikidōkōshisū 景気動向指数 →拡散指数

keikidōkōsōgōkeiretsushisū 景気動向総合系列指数 over-all weighted index of key economic indicators

keikifushin 景気不振 business depression; business stagnation; business slump; business slack; subdued business; lull in business activity; torpor ¶ The danger of deep and prolonged *depression* has been averted. // A recession is a mild economic ailment to build up immunity against a major *depression.* // to fall into *stagnation* // to ward off a *lull* // the near-*stagnation* in activity // the *slump* in the acute industry // Business activity *slackened.* // [参考] The hesitant tone in the economy persisted // The signs of the economic contraction are evident. // The January lull was only a temporary interruption in the business expansion. // →不況

keikifuyōsaku 景気浮揚策 reflation; reflationary measure; business propping

keikigentai 景気減退 business recession; deceleration; weakness; slowdown ¶ The economy is in for a *recession,* not a depression. // The signs of the *recession* became more evident. // The Japanese economy slipped into *recession, recession*-Japanese style. // The turning-point of the stubborn *recession* has been reached. // The U.S. economy is recovering from the 1973-75 *recession*. // The economy has passed through the worst of the *recession*.

keikihandan 景気判断 judgment of business situation (=activity)

keikiheijunkaseisaku 景気平準化政策 counter-cyclical (policy) measure

keikihendō 景気変動 business fluctuation; fluctuation in business activity; cyclical fluctuation in business activity

keikijōshō 景気上昇 business (= economic) upswing; business upturn; business pickup; business boom; business prosperity ¶ The normal cyclical *upswing in business* activity began. // Deflationary measures killed the incipient *economic upswing*. // the *upturns* in *business* activity // an *upward* phase of the *business* cycle // The economy will *turn up* promptly. // signs of the hoped-for *business pickup* // The *boom* reached full force. // The *boom* gathered further momentum. // the third *boom* year after a recession // [参考] activity in *moving up* instead of down

keikijunkan 景気循環 business cycle; [英] trade cycle ¶ The *business cycle* entered a new phase. // The economy swung into the recovery phase of the *business cycle.* // in the expanding phase of the *business cycle* // A *cyclical reversal* of *business* occurred. // to analyze the *cyclical* position in the EEC countries // France will be entering the ascending phase of the *business cycle.* // The expansive phase of the present *business cycle* would continue for

another quarter. // *Cyclical* ups and downs of the economy unmistakably intensified. // We witness a dissynchronized world *business cycle.*

keikijunkanheijunkasaku 景気循環平準化策 →景気対策

keikikaifuku 景気回復 business recovery; revival of business activity ¶ A moderate *recovery* has begun. // Some signs of emerging *recovery* became visible. // *Economic recovery* is cumulating. // the *revival of activity* from the winter recession low // a retardation in the spring *revival of business activity* // [参考] to resume the upturn course // to reverse the downward trend // to pass its lowest point

keikikanetsu 景気過熱 overheating; business (=economic) overheating; overheating of business activity ¶ to cool down the *overheated economy*

keikikansoku 景気観測 business outlook; business prospects; business forecast ¶ The *outlook* for domestic *business* activity remains promising. // *Prospects* for the current year point to no marked change in the trends of *business* activity. // There is every *prospect* that... // *prospects* for the short-run future // Medium-term *forecasts* are pessimistic. // Signs indicate favorable *prospects for business* activity. // [参考] The economic climate is difficult to forecast.

keikikeikokushihyō 景気警告指標 business (early) warning indicator

keikikōtai 景気後退 business recession; business downturn; business dip; business setback; decline in business activity ¶ The economy was still in the grip of a *recession*. // The economy experienced its mildest *recession*. // to gauge the severity of the current *recession* // Industry bounced back from the *recession* lows of February. // The *business downturn* was mild. // to suffer a slight *setback* // to combat a *downturn in* general *business activity* // whether or not such a *recession*, if it occurs, is short and shallow or deep and protracted // The *business downturn* will prove shorter and shallower than many now expect.

keikikyokumen 景気局面 state of business conditions; phase of the business cycle ¶ The economy entered a downward *phase of the business cycle*. // The business cycle entered a new *phase*. // EEC countries find themselves in the expanding *phase of the business cycle*. // The economy is embarking on a new *phase* that may be called pause, readjustment or even recession.

上昇局面	upward phase
回復局面	revival phase
下降局面	downward phase
拡大局面	expansion phase
後退局面	recession phase
収縮局面	contraction phase

keikinohiekomi 景気の冷え込み cooling-down; cooling-off ¶ a *cooling-down* of the economy // Business sentiment is *cooling off*.

keikinotani 景気の谷 trough; bottom; nadir ¶ The recession has passed its *trough*. // to decline to the *trough* month of February // The decline appears to have touched *bottom* in July. // February was probably the *nadir* of an inventory cycle. // The commercial and indus-

trial loan totals remain well below the level recorded at the *trough* of the business cycle in March 1975. // [参考] Business loan demand has been weak in 15 months since the low point of the recession.

keikinouwamuki 景気の上向き upturn of business activity; business upturn; upswing in business activity ¶ Any hopes of *upturn in the economy* have been dispersed. // Signs of a *business upturn* were becoming increasingly evident. // The *business upswing* strengthened. // [参考] The recession passed its lower turning point. // The downward trend was reversed. // A recovery began from the slackening of domestic activity. // Business trends are taking a turn for the better. // Business activity revived.

keikinoyama 景気の山 peak; zenith ¶ some decline from last year's *peak* // to surpass the *peak* reached in 1973 // in the *zenith* of its prosperity

keikiseisaku 景気政策 countercyclical (policy) measure; anticyclical (policy) measure ¶ →景気対策

keikishigeki 景気刺激 stimulation of business activity; encouragement of economic activity; pump-priming ¶ The removal of credit restrictions will *stimulate the economy* to resume a higher growth path. // The government is doing its best to *stimulate business* by stepping up its public works expenditure. // the *stimulative* fiscal actions proposed by the President // The *stimulating* factors in the domestic business picture were... // to make much use of taxpayers' money for the purpose of *pump-priming* // the need for a *prime-the-pump* policy

keikishigekisaku 景気刺激策　economic stimulus; stimulatory (policy) measure; program to encourage economic expansion; measure to stimulate the economy; stimulative (economic policy) measure; (package of) business stimulation measures; anti-recession measure; ¶ The active *stimulatory measures* kept imports at a high level. // These developments are partly explained by the *stimulatory fiscal measures* taken in June. // *Stimulative policies* continued to offset slack export demand. // a package of further *measures to stimulate* domestic demand and employment // Three rounds of *anti-recession measures* were implemented from September to October. // Washington has been making ready the most massive fiscal *stimulus* to combat recession.

keikishihyō 景気指標　business indicator; business barometer ¶ The leading *business indicators* predict immediate business recovery. // The overall 25-line *business indicator* for April stood at 64.6 per cent, indicating the nation's business activities were now on an uptrend. // Recent *business indicators,* though confirming the downturn has leveled off, would seem to suggest that the prospective upswing may be delayed.

keikisokoire 景気底入れ　bottoming-out of the recession; moving out of a trough of recession of the economy

keikitaisaku 景気対策　anticyclical measures; countercyclical (=contracyclical) measures; policy conceived to counter the cyclical variation of economic activity ¶ to pursue pro-cyclical rather than *counter-cyclical* policies

keikiteitai 景気停滞　stagnant business condition; business stagnation; business slack; lull; slackness ¶ The current *business stagnancy* is not confined to manufacturing industries. // There were unmistakable signs of a *slackening* in *business activity.* // [参考] The hesitant tone persisted.

keikitekoire 景気てこ入れ　bottoming-out of business activity; reflation; business stimulation; reactivation of business activity ¶ *reflationary* policy // *stimulative* (policy) measure

keikiyokusei 景気抑制　restraint on excessive business expansion

keikiyokuseigatayosan 景気抑制型予算　restrictive budget

keikiyokuseisaku 景気抑制策　business-restraining policy

keikiyosoku 景気予測　business outlook; economic prospect; business forecasting ¶ The government *economic outlook* for fiscal 1977 was released. // The *outlook* for imports remain promising. // Important developments have significantly improved the *outlook* for greater stability in prices. // The *prospects* for the economy are now brighter than they were in January. // The exact timing of a change in the economic climate is difficult to *forecast.* // There is every *prospect* that business activity will rise. // The *prospects* will be favorable. // [参考] We can look to the future with more confident expectation. // →展望

keikizuku 景気づく rally; pick up; buoy (up)

keikō 傾向 trend; tendency; inclination; streak; lurch; bias; trait ¶ *Trends* in the world economy were already veering toward "stagflation" or even "slumpflation." // The confluence of these *trends* explains much of the recent uneasiness about banking. // to let the incipient rising *trend* of interest rates continue unchecked // to try to reverse this fifteen-year *trend* of deficit spending and expanding money supplies // The agricultural sector has generally escaped the liberalizing *trend*. // Divergent *tendencies* were apparent in the trade. // Following a three-session losing *streak*, prices rebounded. // to correct the long-run inflationary *bias* in the U.S. economy // There appeared to be a *tendency* on the part of many retailers to curtail inventories. // This recessionary *tendency* was mild, especially in relation to the increase in output. // Certain seasonal *tendencies* have again come to the fore. // The *trend* of prices have been much less favorable this year than in the previous year. // Output resumed its upward *trend*. // The steep upward movement of wages shows as yet little *inclination* to abate. // Wholesalers are *inclined* to decumulate their stocks. // Economic *trends* in 1975 were marked by rapid inflation. // State enterprises *tend* to be inward-looking. // Private enterprise in France is endowed with a national *trait* of

being more prudent than innovative.

keikōgyōhin 軽工業品 light industry products

keikoku 警告 caveat; warning ¶ There are still some *caveats* to these estimates.

keikyō 景況 business condition; business climate; business picture ¶ *Business conditions* in October were better than for many years. // The fall season produced a drastic change in the *business climate*. // In an otherwise gloomy *picture*, the only encouraging factor is the price trend. // →景気

keikyōkan 景況感 perceptions of the state of the economy ¶ *Perceptions of the state of the economy* on the part of both individual corporations and households continued to deteriorate.

keinzushugi ケインズ主義 Keynesianism

keirekikanriseido 経歴管理制度 career program

keiretsu 系列 business affiliation; series ¶ break in *series* due to change in coverage of the figures

keiretsugaisha 系列会社 related company; affiliated company

keiretsukin'yū 系列金融 financing to affiliated companies

keirikijun 経理基準 accounting code

keirishi 計理士 accountant

keiryōbunseki 計量分析 econometric analysis

keiryōka 計量化 quantification; measurement; assessment ¶ A *quantification* of monetary aims of policy should not be adopted as an easy option. // difficulties in the definition and *quantification* of potential GNP

keiryōkeizaimoderubunseki 計量
経済モデル分析 econometric model
analysis

keisankahei 計算貨幣 accounting
money

keisankakaku 計算価格 accounting price

keisanki 計算機 computer
計数型自動計算機 automatic
digital computer
計数計算機 digital computer

keisansho 計算書 statement

keisantan'i 計算単位 unit of
account; numéraire ¶ Iceland
intends to raise a loan of 12 million
units of account. // The SDR is the
numéraire of the new system. //
GNP estimates in US dollars or
some other *numéraire* are calculated.

keiseiki 形成期 formative period

keisen ケイ線 ［市］ chart

keisen'ya ケイ線屋 ［市］ chart
reader; technician

keishakōka 傾斜効果 gap tilt
effect

keishaseisanhōshiki 傾斜生産方式
priority production (system)

keishatekirōdōryokuhaichi 傾斜
的労働力配置 priority allocation of
labor

keisū 係数 coefficient ¶ The
coefficient for monetary instability
was not significant.
エンゲル係数 Engel's coefficient
期待係数 coefficient of expectation
資本係数 capital coefficient
挺率係数 leverage coefficient

keisūdēta 計数データ enumeration
data

keisūkanri 計数管理 management
through figures

keitōgaiazukekin 系統外預け金
deposit with outside organization

keitōgaikikan 系統外機関 outside
organization

keitōkashidashi 系統貸出 loans to
affiliated organization

keitōkikan 系統機関 affiliated
organization; subordinate organization

keitokikan'azukekin 系統機関預け
金 deposit with affiliated organization

keiyaku 契約 contract; agreement;
bargain ¶ a written *contract* (=
contract in writing) under seal //
under a *contract* between two
parties dated today it is provided, in
effect, that... // to stipulate by *contract* that... // No money passes
between the parties to the exchange
contract until the date of consumma-
tion of the *contract*. // to exchange
written *contracts* // to fix up and
fulfill an *agreement* // to conclude an
annual wage *bargain* // to enter into
some form of "gentlemen's *agreement*" with... on the matter
売買契約 sales contract
分割契約 several contract
不法契約 illegal contract; unlawful
contract
片務契約 unilateral contract
非方式契約 informal contract
本船渡契約 f.o.b. contract
方式契約 formal contract
条件付契約 conditional contract
空売契約 short-selling contract
仮契約 provisional contract; covering note
口頭契約 verbal agreement; oral
agreement
求償貿易契約 compensating deal
contract; barter contract

無条件契約　absolute contract
沖渡契約　free overside contract
連帯契約　joint contract
略式契約　simple contract
先物契約　forward contract; futures contract
正式契約　formal contract
書面契約　written agreement; contract in writing
双務契約　bilateral contract
適法契約　legal contract; lawful contract
有償契約　onerous contract
暫定契約　open contract

keiyakubēsu 契約ベース contract basis ¶ the money value of plant exports on a *contract basis*

keiyakuchingin 契約賃金 contractual wage

keiyakufurikō 契約不履行 default (on a contract); non-fulfillment; evasion; inobservance ¶ When a buyer *defaults* on an overseas contract, the amount of the exporter's claim is paid by the gurantee scheme based on the sterling rate ruling at the time of *default*. // ［参考］ to fail to fulfill (＝neglect; evade; disregard) the contract

keiyakugatatōshin 契約型投信 contractual type investment trust

keiyakugimu 契約義務 commitment

keiyakuhenkō 契約変更 alteration of a contract

keiyakuhizuke 契約日付 contract date

keiyakuhōki 契約放棄 cancellation of a contract; denunciation (＝retraction; breakage) of a contract ¶ to *cancel* (＝*denounce; retract; break) the contract*

keiyakuhoshōkin 契約保証金 contract money

keiyakuihan 契約違反 breach of a contract (＝agreement); infraction of contract; violation of a contract; infringement; transgression ¶ to *breach* (＝*violate; infringe; transgress) the contract* // To commit or knowingly permit a material *breach of* the *Agreement* is not cured within thirty days from the notice of the breach // late payments and other *contract infractions* specified

keiyakuimin 契約移民 indentured immigrant

keiyakujōken 契約条件 terms and conditions of a contract; contract terms

keiyakukaijo 契約解除 annulment (＝rescission; cancellation) of a contract ¶ to *annul* (＝*rescind*) a contract

keiyakukakaku 契約価格 contract price

keiyakukigen 契約期限 period of a contract ¶ a contract of five years // on a three-year contract

keiyakukikan 契約期間 term of contract

keiyakukōshin 契約更新 renewal of a contract ¶ to *renew the contract* before its expiry

keiyakunoenchō 契約の延長 extension of a contract ¶ to *extend the contract* for another year

keiyakunojiyū 契約の自由 freedom of contract

keiyakunomanki 契約の満期 expiration of a contract; expiry of a contract ¶ to agree on an extension of the contract before its *expiration*

keiyakurikō 契約履行 fulfillment of a contract ¶ to *fulfill* (＝perform; observe) *the contract*

keiyakurikōhoshō 契約履行保証 performance bond

keiyakurōdō 契約労働 contract labor

keiyakusha 契約者 contractor; contracting party; parties to a contract

keiyakushahaitō 契約者配当 bonus

keiyakushūketsu 契約終結 termination of a contract ¶ The *contract* was *terminated* (=the *contract terminated*).

keiyakushūsei 契約修正 modification of a contract ¶ to *modify* the *contract* // introduce *modifications* in the *contract*

keiyakuteiketsu 契約締結 conclusion of a contract ¶ to *conclude* (= make; draw up; sign) a contract

keizai 経済 economy ¶ national *economy* // domestic *economy* // world *economy* // The Australian *economy* was progressing. // Northern Ireland's frail *economy* is lurching into deep trouble. // The *economy* is in for a recession. // The *economies* of all major industrial countries have experienced no growth or slow growth. // The *economy* suffered a set back. // The performance of the world *economy* was less than satisfactory. // an *economy* of time and effort // to effect considerable economy in the use of oil // *economies* of scale
安定経済 stable economy
厚みのある経済 solid economy
バーター経済 barter economy
ブロック経済 bloc economy
地域経済 regional economy
中央計画経済 centrally planned economy

大規模工業の経済 economies of large scale industry
大規模生産の経済 economies of large scale production
脱工業化経済 post-industry economy
伝統指向型経済 tradition-directed economy
動態経済 dynamic economy
エネルギー経済 economy of energy
複合経済 plural economy
封鎖経済 closed economy
外部経済 external economies
現物経済 spot economy
減速経済 decelerating economy; lower-growth economy
平時経済 peacetime economy
豊富経済 economy of abundance
自立経済 self-reliant economy
自由経済 free economy
自給(自足)経済 self-sufficient economy; subsistence economy
実践経済 practical economy
開放経済 open economy
快楽の経済 pleasure economy
拡大経済 expansive economy
過熱経済 overheated economy; over-exuberant economy
完全雇用経済 fully employed economy
家庭経済 household economy
計画経済 planned economy
希少経済 economy of scarcity
高圧経済 high-pressure economy
高賃金経済 high-wage economy
広域経済 great sphere economy
交換経済 exchange economy
国家計画経済 state planned economy
国民経済 national economy
国内経済 internal economy, domestic economy
国際経済 international economy

高密度経済　high-density economy

混合経済　mixed economy

弧立経済　isolated economy

規模の経済　economies of scale

金融経済　monetary economy

民間投資主導型経済　economy led by private investment

未来経済　futures economy

内部経済　internal economies

二重構造経済　dual economy

農業経済　agrarian economy; agricultural economy

農家経済　farm economy

農村経済　rural economy

先物経済　futures economy

産業経済　industrial economy

成熟経済　mature economy

静態経済　static economy

生存経済　subsistence economy

世界経済　world economy; global economy

戦時経済　wartime economy

市場経済　market economy

資源節約型経済　resource-saving economy

自然経済　natural economy

象徴経済　symbol economy

消費経済　economy of consumption

商品経済　commodity economy

手工業経済　handicraft economy

水産経済　marine economy

竹馬経済　economy "on stilts"

低圧経済　low-pressure economy

低賃金経済　low-wage economy

低成長経済　low-growth economy

飛地経済　enclave economy

統制経済　controlled economy

病める経済　sick (=ailing) economy

keizaianteiseisaku　経済安定政策　(economic) stabilization policy

keizaianzenhoshō　経済安全保障　economic security

keizaibunseki　経済分析　economic analysis

keizaichitsujo　経済秩序　economic order ¶ disequilibria in the *economic order*

keizaichōsa　経済調査　economic research; economic intelligence ¶ to initiate other research, including *research* related to the regional *economies* // The Board of Governors coordinates the *economic intelligence* function of all the Reserve banks.

keizaidōkō　経済動向　economic developments; economic trends; economic performance ¶ *economic developments* at home and abroad // the recent *trends* in the domestic economy // As regards domestic *economic developments,* the conjuncture today also presents a better *picture* than it did this time last year. // The economy continued to be characterized by mixed *trends.* // the financial and real *performance* of the *economy* // some important differences in recent *economic performance* between the U.S. and Germany

keizaienjo　経済援助　economic aid

keizaienjoseisaku　経済援助政策　economic support measures

keizaifukkō　経済復興　economic recovery; economic rehabilitation; economic revival (=revitalization) ¶ to attain a quick and remarkable *economic recovery* // to *revitalize* the Swedish economy

keizaifūsa　経済封鎖　economic blockade

keizaigaikō　経済外交　economic diplomacy

keizaigaitekikyōsei　経済外的強制　non-economic compulsion

keizaigenshō 経済現象 economic phenomenon ¶ It is one of the postwar *economic phenomena.* // an *economic phenomenon* peculiar to that country

keizaigensoku 経済原則 economic principle

keizaihakusho 経済白書 [英] Economic Survey; [日] White Paper on Economy; economic white paper ¶ *Economic White Paper* for fiscal 1975 // *"Economic Survey of Japan"*

keizaihatchūryō 経済発注量 economic order quantity; EOQ

keizaijin 経済人 economic man

keizaijōkyō 経済状況 economic conditions; economic contours ¶ The *contours* of the *economic* geography are in constant and dynamic movement. // →経済情勢

keizaijōsei 経済情勢 economic situation; economic conditions; economic climate; economic developments; economic atmosphere; economic picture; economic activity ¶ There has been a perceptible relaxation in the German *economic conditions.* // General *economic conditions* in 1984 compare favorably with those in 1983. // to establish the sound underlying domestic *economic conditions* // The *picture* is by no means clear, but there have been several favorable *developments.* // The domestic *economic situation* has not changed much. // There were evidences of some improvement in the *economic climate.* // The stimulating factors in the domestic *economic picture* were... // [参考] to reflect the economic realities of the present world in the structure // →景気

keizaijunkan 経済循環 process of reproduction; circular flow of economic system

keizaikai 経済界 economic world; economic community; business circles ¶ In the *business community* more of a wait-and-see attitude is prevalent. // The *business community* became a little more cautious. // the *economic circles* of the United States // an optimistic sentiment prevailing throughout the *economic world* // All in *economic circles* are requested to maintain strict financial discipline.

keizaikaifuku 経済回復 economic recovery; economic revival

keizaikaihatsukatei 経済開発過程 process of economic development ¶ a country in the *process of economic development*

keizaikaihatsukeikaku 経済開発計画 economic development program

keizaikaikaku 経済改革 economic reform; economic reformation ¶ to introduce a wide-ranging *economic reform* // The *economic reforms* have been under way for some years. // to carry out radical *reforms in the economy* // a sweeping *reformation* of the present *economic constitution*

keizaikakudai 経済拡大 economic expansion; economic gain ¶ The *economic expansion* was tending to slow down, though it was still proceeding at a considerable pace. // The business *(= economic) expansion* was proceeding vigorously. // the 1975 business *(= economic) expansion* in the United States // the vigorous *expansion* of *economic* activity // to make impressive *eco-*

nomic gains // The *economic expansion* proceeded with rigor. // The vigorous *expansion* of the *economy* continued, based on a buoyant domestic demand. // a solid and sustainable *expansion* of the *economy* // The scope of the *economic expansion* has narrowed and its pace has slackened. // The interruption of the *expansionary* trend of the *economy* has now lasted nearly two years. // The record-long *economic expansion* rolls on but with a new tone of moderation and a mood of doubt. // Economic activity revived after comparative absence of *expansion*.

keizaikakuryōkaigi 経済閣僚会議 meeting of Cabinet ministers in charge of economic affairs; Cabinet Committee of Economic Ministers

keizaikankeikakuryō 経済関係閣僚 economic affairs ministers

keizaikankyō 経済環境 economic environment; economic climate; economic conditions ¶ the severity of the international *economic environment* surrounding Japan // Inflation of 25% a year was a passing storm, not a permanent change in the *economic climate.* // to create an *economic environment* that is balanced and vigorous

keizaikansoku 経済観測 economic forecasting ¶ ［参考］→展望

keizaikansokushihyō 経済観測指標 economic barometer

keizaikatsudō 経済活動 economic activity; economic performance; economic life ¶ *Economic activity* continues strong. // The slow-down in *economic activity* intensified. // The total *economic activity* increased fairly sharply. // *economic*

activity to continue its upward course // a very sharp upturn in *economic activity* // The sluggishness in *economic activity* is deepening. // *Economic activity* started to accelerate. // The slowdown in *economic activity* intensified. // to be able to raise the competitive *performance of their economies* // to measure the overall *economic performance* // a slackening in *economic activity* // *Economic activity* moved into new high ground. // The *performance of the* world *economy* was less than satisfactory. // The growth *performance of the economy* exceeded the medium-term average. // *Economic activity* increases or decreases; expands or contracts; rises or falls.

keizaikatsudōjinkō 経済活動人口 economically active population

keizaikeikaku 経済計画 economic plan(ning) ¶ an important bearing on the consistency and sustainability of an overall *economic* growth *plan* // A major consideration in *economic planning* is the existence of foreign exchange constraints.

keizaikeisatsu 経済警察 economic police

keizaikiban 経済基盤 economic foundation; foundation of the economy; economic base; (economic) infrastructure ¶ to strengthen the *foundation of the economy* // to lay the strong *foundation* of the *economy* // The yard is Ulster's *economic* base.

keizaikishidō 経済騎士道 economic chivalry

keizaikōi 経済行為 economic behavior; economic action

keizaikōka 経済効果 economic

result ¶ Changes in interest rates can have more clearly definable *economic results.*

keizaikōritsu 経済効率 economic efficiency

keizaikyōkō 経済恐慌 economic crisis ¶ to tide the *economy* over a serious *crisis* // The nation tided over a violent *economic crisis.* // The nation is in a grave *economic crisis.*

keizaikyōryoku 経済協力 economic cooperation ¶ the necessity of closer and harmonious international *economic cooperation* // to promote industrial nations' willing *economic cooperation* given to developing nations // to give or obtain systematized *economic cooperation* // international *economic cooperation* of industrial nations 多国間経済協力 multi-(national) economic co-operation

keizaikyōryokuhakusho 経済協力白書 [日] "Actual Condition and Problems of Economic Cooperation"; white paper on economic co-operation

keizaikyōsō 経済競争 economic competition

keizaimitōshi 経済見通し →展望

keizaimondai 経済問題 economic issue; economic problem ¶ General accord was reached on all major *economic issues.* // to provide the answers to the country's domestic *economic problems* // Inflation overtook unemployment as "*economic problem* number one."

keizainohihei 経済の疲弊 economic prostration

keizainokadai 経済の課題 tasks of the economy ¶ main *tasks of the* world *economy* during the coming year

keizainokōketsuatsushō 経済の"高血圧症" economic equivalent of "high blood pressure"

keizainokōritsuka 経済の効率化 promotion of economic efficiency

keizainokōzōhendō 経済の構造変動 structural changes in the economy

keizainonijūkōzō 経済の二重構造 dual structure of the economy

keizainoōgataka 経済の大型化 expanding scale of economic activity

keizainorōkagenshō 経済の老化現象 gradual withering of the economy; aging of the economy

keizainosābisuka 経済のサービス化 service-orientation of the economy

keizairieki 経済利益 economic benefit

keizairinri 経済倫理 economic ethics; economic morality

keizairosen 経済路線 (economic) path; course; track ¶ The economy is back on an upward *path.* // The economy will gain a satisfactory long-run trend *path.* // the *path* the economy is currently traversing // The economy is set on a *course* leading through new frontiers to new peaks of prosperity. // to resume its upward *course* // to get the world back on a more stable *economic track* // to keep the economy on a *path* of steady growth // →軌道

keizaisaikenseibi 経済再建整備 economic reconstruction and readjustment

keizaiseichō 経済成長 economic growth ¶ The *growth* performance of the *economy* is favorable. // to achieve the highest sustainable *economic growth* // Nominal *economic* *growth* showed a vigorous rise of 24.5 per cent over the year. // as extraordinary discrepancy in *economic growth* between nominal and real terms // Signs point to vigorous *economic growth.* // The scope of *economic growth* narrowed. // It was necessary to aim at more balanced and lasting *economic growth.* // to foster orderly *economic growth* with reasonable price stability // a framework that sustained sound *economic growth* // to seek to enhance *economic growth* through outward looking economic policies // Events point to a period of reduced *economic growth* in the industrial countries.

keizaiseichōhenchōshugi 経済成長偏重主義 growthmanship

keizaiseichōritsu 経済成長率 rate of economic growth; economic growth rate ¶ to lower the presently high *rate of economic growth* // to attain a real *economic growth rate* of 5.5 percent // The *economic growth rate* rose both in nominal and real terms. // the *rate of* real *economic growth*

keizaiseijuku 経済成熟 economic maturity

keizaiseikatsu 経済生活 economic life ¶ unbridled political intervention in *economic life*

keizaiseirigaku 経済生理学 economic physiology

keizaiseisai 経済制裁 economic sanction

keizaiseisaku 経済政策 economic policy ¶ to formulate, enforce, and pursue an *economic policy* designed to stabilize prices // Some modification of *economic policy* was called for under the circum-

stances. // to draw up a basic *economic policy* for the next year aiming more vigorously at expansion // to design, modify, and implement; to tighten or ease; and to direct and shift the *economic policy* to a policy objective // restrictive or expansionary *economic policies* // The stance of *economic policy* became restrictive but was relaxed later. // National *economic policy* in 1985 will focus on the twin goals of reducing unemployment and restraining price inflation. // abundant possibilities for inconsistencies or conflicts among nations in the conduct of their *economic policies*

keizaiseisakuhoken 経済政策保険 economic policy insurance

keizaisenjutsu 経済戦術 economic tactics

keizaisenryaku 経済戦略 economic strategy ¶ to implement a new *economic strategy* for tackling the country's economic ills

keizaisensō 経済戦争 economic war; economic warfare

keizaisetogiwaseisaku 経済瀬戸際政策 economic brinkmanship

keizaishakaihattenkeikaku 経済社会発展計画 economic and social development program

keizaishakaikaihatsu 経済社会開発 economic and social development

keizaishihyō 経済指標 economic indicator ¶ Among the microeconomic indicators, profitability and financial soundness are important. // →バロメーター

keizaishippei 経済疾病 economic ill; economic malaise ¶ A variety of perceptions, concerns, and proposed solutions for the world's *economic* *ills* were offered. // solutions to the deepening European *malaise* of unemployment and stagnation // The Middle East is beset by *economic ills*. // the remedies for this particular *economic ill* // a new economic strategy for tackling British *economic ills*

keizaishukushō 経済縮小 economic contraction

keizaishunōkaigi 経済首脳会議 economic summit

keizaishutai 経済主体 economic agent; economic unit

keizaisokudo 経済速度 economical speed ¶ The most *economical speed* of driving a car is 60 kilometers per hour.

keizaisoshiki 経済組織 economic organization (=system; mechanisn) ¶ the institutional setting and *organization* of the *economy* // a more effectively, and more equitably, organized international *economic system*

keizaisuiiki 経済水域 coastal (= littoral) states, economic zone; economic sea zone ¶ rigidly exclusive 200-mile *economic sea zone* // The *economic sea zone* will be set at 200 nautical miles from the shores of *littoral states*. // Establishment of national *economic sea zones* would mean, inter alia, a higher cost of maritime tranportation.

keizaitaikoku 経済大国 economic big power; major economic power (of the world); economic superpower; economic giant ¶ Japan is one of the world's financial and *economic giants*.

keizaitaisei 経済体制 economic system ¶ to maintain an open-

market oriented *economic system*

keizaitaishitsu 経済体質 economic institution

keizaiteki 経済的 economical ¶ to be *economical* of time and money // to be *economical* in the use of petroleum products

keizaitekiatsuryoku 経済的圧力 economic pressures

keizaitekichii 経済的地位 economic position ¶ Workers attempt to increase their *economic position* relative to management.

keizaitekichinpuka 経済的陳腐化 economic obsolescence

keizaitekidōki 経済的動機 economic motive

keizaitekigenjitsu 経済的現実 economic reality ¶ Given the complexity of *economic reality,* monetary policy is subject to a number of limitations.

keizaitekihōfuku 経済的報復 economic reprisal ¶ a move the workers interpret as a direct *economic reprisal* against Protestant intransigence.

keizaitekijiyū 経済的自由 economic freedom; free enterprise

keizaitekikabukōzō 経済的下部構造 economic infrastructure

keizaitekikiketsu 経済的帰結 economic consequence

keizaitekikiseichū 経済的寄生虫 economic parasite

keizaitekikokuminshugi 経済的国民主義 economic nationalism

keizaitekikokusaishugi 経済的国際主義 economic internationalism

keizaitekikōsei 経済的厚生 economic welfare

keizaitekikunan 経済的苦難 economic distress; economic suffering;

economic woe; economic hardship

keizaitekikutsū 経済的苦痛 economic malaise (=ills) ¶ to pull the industrial countries out of their *malaise* // →経済疾病

keizaitekimasatsu 経済(的)摩擦 economic friction

keizaitekiseijuku 経済的成熟 economic maturity

keizaitekiseisai 経済的制裁 economic sanction; punitive economic measure ¶ the application of *economic sanctions* in Ulster // The Government is enforcing *punitive economic measures.*

keizaitekishinkaichi 経済的新開地 economic frontier

keizaitetsugaku 経済哲学 economic philosophy ¶ the diversity of *economic philosophies* governing the management of these economies

keizaitōgō 経済統合 economic integration ¶ to undermine international *economic integration*

keizaitōitsu 経済統一 economic unity

keizaiun'ei 経済運営 economic management; management of the economy; operation of the economy ¶ the *management of* both the domestic and the external *economy*

keizaiyosoku 経済予測 economic outlook; economic prediction; economic prospects ¶→展望

keizaizai 経済財 economic goods

keizokuhi 継続費 continued expenses; continuing expenditure; expenses for continued projects

keizokujigyō 継続事業 continued project; project already undertaken ¶ [参考] to finish up half-completed projects

keizokukeisan 継続計算 running

account

keizokukigyō 継続企業 going concern ¶ A *going concern* will not have to reduce its debt as it grows.

keizokukigyōkachi 継続企業価値 going concern value

keizokukikan 継続期間 duration

keizokutōshi 継続投資 investment project already undertaken

kekkan 欠陥 deficiency; defect ¶ to exacerbate, not overcome, the structural *deficiencies* inherent in the economies of the LDCs.

kekkansha 欠陥車 defective car; faulty car

kekkinritsu 欠勤率 absenteeism rate

kekkintaigyō 欠勤怠業 absenteeism

ken 圏 bloc; area

   ドル圏 dollar bloc

   経済圏 economic bloc

   硬貨圏 hard currency area

   小売商圏 retail trade area

   軟貨圏 soft currency area

   ポンド圏 pound bloc

   商圏 trade area

kenchikuchakkōsū 建築着工(数) construction starts; building constructions started

   住宅建築新規着工 new housing starts

kenchikujuchū 建築受注 construction awards

kenchikukyoka 建築許可 building permit ¶ *Building permits* rose in June, reaching their highest level in eighteen months.

kenchikuzairyō 建築材料 building materials

kenchō 堅調 steady; higher; firm; solid; constant; steadfast; unwavering ¶ The market was *higher* at the start, turned mixed and moved *higher* in the afternoon. // The commodity market remained *firm*. // Interest rates will hold *firm*.

ken'eiginkōseido 兼営銀行制度 mixed banking system

kenen 懸念 concern; apprehension; anxiety; fear; misgiving ¶ some signs warranting *concern* // Some *apprehensions* were caused as to... // a cause for *concern* // a matter of serious *concern* // to feel *concern* about the future of... // There is mounting *concern* about international debts, prompted partly by... // *anxiety* about future inflation persisting in the market // The high *anxiety* coursing through the world's financial markets will subside. // *Apprehension* over government anti-inflation policies hit the London Stock Exchange. // to arouse widespread, considerable *anxiety* about the future // The strong popular *fear* of futher price inflation has been dissipated. // to dispel *misgivings* about the bleak business outlook // A rapid rise in prices became the subject of increasing *concern*. // heightened fears of all-round rise in prices

kengen 権限 power; authority ¶ Adequate *powers* for this purpose were conferred on the Board of Governors. // The bill provides for *power* to impose a price stop. // to *authorize* the filing of a financing statement on his behalf // to be countersigned by duly *authorized* officials // Presidential use of such *authority* is still considered a possibility rather than a probability.

kengen 権原 title

kengen'ijō 権限委譲 delegation of authority (＝power)

kengenka 顕現化 manifest; materialize; surface; become visible ¶ Difficulties *manifested* in high rates of inflation. // Supply constraints *materialized*. // Effects on prices began to *surface*.

kengennoijō 権限の委譲 delegation of authority

kengensho 権限書 power of attorney

kengyō 兼業 side-line (business); side-job; subsidiary business; by-business; additional operation; bywork

kengyōnōka 兼業農家 side-work farmer

kenjitsukeiei 堅実経営 sound management practice

kenkashu 券・貨種 denomination ¶ coins of higher *denominations* // US dollar-*denominated* notes

kenkōhoken 健康保険 health insurance

kenkōshokuhin 健康食品 health food

kenkyūkaihatsu 研究開発 research and development; R&D ¶ Firms are doing routine *R&D* to strengthen product lines. // to undertake and carry on *R&D*

kenkyūkaihatsuhi 研究開発費 research and development (＝R&D) expenditure (＝spending) ¶ In the United States, federal *R and D spending* began to recover under President Carter.

kenkyūkaihatsutōshi 研究開発投資 investment in research and development; R&D investment; R&D management expenditure

kenkyūkaihatukeikaku 研究開発計

画　research and development project; R&D project (= program) ¶ *R&D project* were undertaken and yielded higher net expected gains. // the acceptability of potential *R&D projects* // to seek an *R&D program* to maximize the present expected value of project

kenkyūkanri 研究管理　administration of research activities

kenmengaku 券面額　face amount; face value; par value

kenmenshurui 券面種類　denomination ¶ yen-*denominated* notes // bonds *denominated* in U.S. dollars // notes in small and large *denominations*

kenmu 兼務　concurrent office

kennintorishimariyakusei 兼任取締役制　interlocking directorate

kenpeiritsu 建ぺい率　building coverage

kenri 権利　right; claim; title; privilege; option ¶ a *right* to property // the proprietary *rights* of others // a *claim* of damages // compensation *claims* // to acquire *title* to land // to obtain exclusive *privilege* of reproducing the article // to have the *option* of doing or not // to confer the sole *rights* on certain commodities and to use certain articles // to encroach upon, or infringe, others, patent *rights* // to establish and register the *right* of pledge

代表権　right of representation
団体交渉権　right of collective bargaining
罷業権　right to strike
意匠権　design right
実用新案権　utility model right
株主引受け権　subscription right
株主権　stockholder's right

貨幣鋳造権　right of coinage
買戻し権　right of repurchase (= redemption)
経営権　right of administration; right of management
既得権　vested right
求償権　right of demanding compensation
日照権　right to enjoy sunshine
労働権　right to work
労働全収権　right to the whole produce of labor
請求権　right to claim
質権　right of pledge
紙幣発行権　right of (sole) issue
商標権　right of trade-mark
少数株主権　minority stockholder right
所有権　proprietay right
主権　sovereignty
土地収用権　right of eminent domain
特許権　patent right
優先権　preferential right
財産所有権　property right

kenrikabu 権利株　potential shares

kenrikin 権利金　premium

kenrikōshi 権利行使　exercise of right, use of right; making claim ¶ to claim and exercise their rights // to use the *right* to refuse the acceptance of...

kenrikyōyū 権利享有　enjoyment of rights ¶ to hold and *enjoy* prior *rights* to the land

kenriochi 権利落ち　[証市] ex new; ex warrants; ex rights

kenrishingai 権利侵害　encroachment of right; infringement of right ¶ to *encroach upon* others' *rights* // to *infringe* foreigners' extraterritorial *rights*

kenrishōken 権利証券　document

of title

kenrishutoku 権利取得 obtainment of right; acquisition of right ¶ to *obtain* fishing *rights* // to *acquire a right* to... // [参考] to be given the sole right of reproduction // to be granted certain rights

kenriteishi 権利停止 suspension of right

kenritsuki 権利付き [証市] cum rights; with warrants; rights-on

kenryōshōmeisho 検量証明書 survey report

kensa 検査 inspection; check; examination ¶ standards for *inspection* // different criteria for the *examination* of... // to *check* the number against the invoice for accuracy // the Ministry of Finance's *inspecion* of a bank

kensanarabiniyōryōsokutei 検査並びに容量測定 inspection and measurement

kensashōmeisho 検査証明書 certificate of inspection

kenseiseido 牽制制度 check-and-balance system ¶ the *check-and-balance* between an executive and a judiciary

kensetsuhi 建設費 construction expenses; cost of construction

kensetsuhikanjō 建設費勘定 construction account

kensetsujimusho 建設事務所 building office

kensetsukairyōhi 建設改良費 expenses for construction and improvement

kensetsukarikanjō 建設仮勘定 construction account; construction in process

kensetsukōji 建設工事 construction works; civil works ¶ large *civil*

works such as dams, major highways, and ports

kensetsukōjijuchūgaku 建設工事受注額 orders received for construction

kensetsukōsai 建設公債 construction bond

kensetsumaewatashikin 建設前渡金 contract deposits paid

kensetsurisoku 建設利息 interest during construction

kensetsushizai 建設資材 construction supplies; construction materials

kenshōhanbai 懸賞販売 sale with contest prizes as a premium

kenshū 研修 training ¶ to receive a brief *training* course in the elements of investment and the principles of security selling // to be well equipped by *training* to furnish advice // special *training* programs, both theoretical and on-the-job, developed for the site supervisory staff

職場外研修 off-the-job training
職場内研修 on-the-job training

kensūin 検数員 tallyman

kensūryō 検数料 tally fee

ken'yaku 倹約 frugality; thrift ¶ A new atmosphere of *frugality* in public spending became widespread.

kenzai 建材 housing material ¶ noninflammable, not inflammable *housing material*

kenzenginkōshugi 健全銀行主義 sound banking principle

kenzenseichō 健全成長 sound growth

kenzenseijunsoku 健全性準則 standards of soundness

kenzentōshi 健全投資 sound investment

kenzenzaisei 健全財政 sound finance; balanced budget

kenzenzaiseishugi 健全財政主義 sound finance (=fiscal) policy

kessai 血債 blood debt ¶ the *blood-debt* issue // *blood-debt* agreements

kessai 決済 settlement; liquidation ¶ prompt *settlement* of bills // to pay a sum in *settlement* of an account // term-end *settlements* of business accounts // to *liquidate* accounts, damages, or debts
貸借決済 settlement of account

kessaichi 決済地 place of settlement

kessaihōhō 決済方法 means of settlement
標準外決済方法 non-standard means of settlement
標準決済方法 standard means of settlement

kessaijōken 決済条件 settlement terms of business transactions

kessaikanjō 決済勘定 transactions account

kessaikanrenshikin 決済関連資金 transaction-related funds

kessaikyōtei 血債協定 blood debt agreement

kessaishikin 決済資金 settlement funds

kessaishikinkashidashi 決済資金貸出 loan for settlements of term-end business accounts

kessaitorikime 決済取決 arrangement of settlement

kessaitsūka 決済通貨 currency of settlement; settlement money

kessaiwaribiki 決済割引 settlement discount

kessan 決算 closing of accounts; settlement of accounts; liquidation; settled accounts

粉飾決算 window-dressing settlement

半期決算 half-yearly settlement; biannual settlement; semi-annual settlement (of accounts)

期末決算 term-end settlement of accounts; settlement of term-end business accounts

やりくり決算 makeshift settlement

kessanbi 決算日 settling day; closing day; date of settlement

kessanhōkoku 決算報告 statement of accounts

kessanjōkyō 決算状況 sales and profits for the business term

kessankaishagyōseki 決算会社業績 corporate business results ¶ *corporate business results* for the March-end terms

kessankakaku 決算価格 settlement price

kessanki 決算期 (six- month, or 12-month) accounting term; settlement term ¶ the March *settlement term* (=the *settlement term* ending in March) // the Oct. 1976—Mar. 1977 *accounting term*

kessanshikin 決算資金 business fund demand for account-settlements; funds to be paid after term-end settlement of accounts

kessanshiwake 決算仕訳 closing entries

kesson 欠損 deficit; loss ¶ to have a *deficit* of $40,000 // to show a heavy *deficit* amounting to $40,000 // to record a net *loss* of $12,000 for the current term // The company chalked up huge but undisclosed *losses*. // After four *loss*-making years, the company made £7 m. profit in 1978.

kessongaku 欠損額 deficiency; amount of loss ¶ to make good the estimated *deficiency* of £2,000 // the *amount of net loss* for the term totaling $12,000 // →欠損

kessonhotentsumitatekin 欠損填積立金 reserve for losses

kessonkinshorikeisansho 欠損金処理計算書 deficit disposition statement

kesu 消す reverse; cancel; erase ¶ Much of this advance was *reversed* by early November. // A good part of the gain was *cancelled*. // The gain in earnings was mostly *erased*.

keta 桁 figure; digit; place; ［コン］column ¶ a double-*figure* advance // a two-*digit* rate of growth // income counted by the seven *figures* // Data shown here have been rounded to fewer *digits* than those shown elsewhere.

ketsuin 欠員 (job) vacancy ¶ to fill the *vacancy* from within

ketsuinfuhojū 欠員不補充 leaving vacancies unfilled; letting vacancies go unfilled

kettei 決定 determination ¶ to assess the *determination* developing country trade by industrial country demand
賃金決定 wage determination
価格決定 price determination
所得決定 income determination

ketteikeisū 決定系数 ［統］coefficient of determination

ketteiyōin 決定要因 determinant ¶ The main *determinant* of economic development is the petroleum industries. // to theorize about long-term growth *determinants*

kiban 基盤 foundation; basis; base; footing ¶ to further strengthen than the already firm *foundation* of the economy // to strengthen demand on

a broad geographical *basis* // to expand the productive *base* of the economy // to put Swedish companies on a similar *footing* to those in other industrialized countries

kibishii 厳しい harsh; strict; severe; rigid; rigorous; stern; hard ¶ *harsh* reality // *harsh* economic developments here and abroad // *strict* enforcement of *severe* restrictions // to tide over the rigor of *severe* inflation

kibo 規模 size; scale; scope ¶ Public expenditure grew to a *size* out of proportion with the real resources of the country. // small capital inflows relative to the economic *size* of these countries // The *size* of the Eurocurrency market continued to grow. // to take up the issues of the built environment on a global *scale* // to mobilize resources on a broad *scale* // a corporation which is national in *scope* // businesses of large and small *scale*, or large and small *scale* enterprises // production on a commercial *scale* // The activity of small-*sized* firms abroad was only on a modest *scale*.
生産規模 scale of production
選好規模 scale of preference

kibokakudaitōshi 規模拡大投資 scale expansion investment

kibonikansurushūeki 規模に関する収益 return to scale ¶ a fall in the degree of *return to scale*

kibonokeizaiseifukeizaisei 規模の経済性・不経済性 economies and diseconomies of scale ¶ *Economies of scale* are generated within industries. // the *economies of scale* associated with increasing urban size // One would expect *disecono-*

mies of scale to occur within each industry.

kibonorieki 規模の利益 economies of scale; profit from scale; scale merit; increasing returns to scale ¶ The rate of income growth may be influenced by *economies of scale.* // to acquire much *scale merit* // the *merits of* the large *scale* of business // the existence of *economies of scale* in productive activities which cannot be efficiently exploited by the private sector

kibōrieki 希望利益 expected profit; imaginary profit

kibōriekihoken 希望利益保険 expected profit insurance

kichō 基調 basic tone; underlying tone; trend; undertone; note; keynote ¶ High levels in business activity set the *keynote* in all sectors of the economy. // The hesitant *tone* that developed in the economy persisted. // The *underlying tone* of the market was a shade firmer. // The dollar's *undertone* remained firm. // The market *undertone* is a shade firmer. // Period rates found little followthrough to last week's easier *trend.* // Widely disparate *trends* took place in manufacturing in the past year. // Bank deposits resumed their upward *trend.* // Labor market conditions ended the year on a positive *note.* // The monetary growth target must accurately reflect the *underlying* monetary *trend.* // The *basic* unemployment *trend* is still static despite the rise in the last two months. // The market continued on a dull and soft *note* throughout the week. // Open market operations began the year on an expansive

note. // January began on a worrisome *note*, with no significant improvement in the dollar. // The year started on a very strong *note.*

kichōtetsuzuki 記帳手続 booking procedure

kidō 軌道 railroad; track; tramway; orbit; path ¶ to place the economy on the right *track*, to the sustainable growth // getting our growth rates back down to the normal *path* that is set by productivity and labor force increases // The economy will be held to a gradual and sustained growth *path.* // to put international trade back on the right *track*, and keep it there // Most industrial countries are on a parallel cyclical *track.* // to put the economy back on the *rails* // [参考] The recovery of production was consolidated by the mid-year.

kigachingin 飢餓賃金 starvation wage

kigayushutsu 飢餓輸出 hunger export

kigen 期限 term; time limit; maturity; due date; tenure; deadline; repayment period ¶ to fix the *term* of payment // to extend the *tenure* of office // promissory notes falling *due* // bonds of long *maturities* // with a *maturity* of three years or less // less than ten years *maturity* // to pay at *maturity* // to reach *maturity* // to extend the *deadline* for payment of the other half by nine months to March 15, 1985 // The *maturities* of most new Eurocurrency bank credits were in five to seven-year range, and few extended up to ten years. // *Repayment periods* have been stretched out to range from 12 to 35 years with grace *periods* of rarely less than three years. // [参考] a bill due next month // near-term bonds // →期日

kigen'enchō 期限延長 extension of maturity

kigenhenkin 期限返金 repayment at maturity

kigenkeika 期限経過 overdue ¶ to be *overdue* // an *overdue* payment

kigenkeikakanjō 期限経過勘定 overdue account

kigenkeikakashitsuke 期限経過貸付 overdue loan

kigenkeikakogitte 期限経過小切手 overdue check

kigenkeikategata 期限経過手形 overdue bill; postdue bill

kigenmanryō 期限満了 expiry; expiration; termination ¶ on the *expiry* of the five years' term // at the *expiration* of the agreement // on the *termination* of the present contract

kigennorieki 期限の利益 benefit of period of grace

kigentsukikawase 期限付為替 after sight bill; usance bill

kigentsukisanjūnichitegatasōba 期限付30日手形相場 30 days buying rate

kigentsukitegata 期限付手形 time bill; usance bill

kigentsukiyunyūtegata 期限付輸入手形 import usance bill

kigentsukiyushutsutegataseido 期限付輸出手形制度 export usance bill (system)

kigenzenhenkin 期限前返金 prematuruty payment; prepayment ¶ Amounts *prepaid* will be subject to ½ pct prepayment premium.

kigyō 企業 undertaking; (business) enterprise; corporation; concern; corporate business; business; partnership; firm ¶ to inaugurate and manage an industrial *enterprise* // private and state *enterprises* already undertaken // to succeed in a business *enterprise* // *corporate business* management

超国家企業 transnational corporation

弱小企業 twilight business

住宅関連企業 housing-allied enterprises

家内企業 family enterprise

継続企業 going concern

企業家経営企業 entrepreneurial firm

後発企業 newcomer

公共企業 public corporation

国営企業 state enterprise

協同組合企業 cooperative firm

休止企業 discontinued business

労働者自主管理企業 labor-managed firm

多国籍企業 maltinational corporation

統合企業 partnership

kigyō 起業 promotion; organization ¶ to *promote* a business // to *organize* a business // to *organize* a company

kigyōbaishū 企業買収 acquisition; purchase (of a corporation)

kigyōbetsukumiai 企業別組合 enterprise labor union

kigyōchochiku 企業貯蓄 business savings

kigyōdōkō 企業動向 business behavior

kigyōgenzei 企業減税 tax cut for business and enterprise

kigyōgōdō 企業合同 merger; amalgamation; trust

kigyōgōrika 企業合理化 managerial and operational rationalization; rationalization of enterprise; modernization of business

kigyōhi 起業費 initial expenses

kigyōimēji 企業イメージ corporate identity

kigyōka 企業化 production on a commercial basis; industrialization ¶ to *produce on a commercial basis* // to *industrialize* the product

kigyōka 企業家 entrepreneur; industrialist; businessman

kigyōkahandan 企業家判断 entrepreneurs' discernment

kigyōkaikeigensoku 企業会計原則 business (=corporate) accounting principles

kigyōkanchinginkōzō 企業間賃金構造 external wage structure

kigyōkanfusai 企業間負債 inter-company indebtedness

kigyōkanokekki 企業家の血気 "animal spirit" (of entrepreneurs)

kigyōkanshin'yō 企業間信用 inter-trade credit; inter-company credit; inter-enterprise commercial credit; company credit; trade credit; intra-industry credit (=borrowing and lending); inter-firm credit ¶ [参考] export contracts on a supplier credit basis financed in foreign currency

kigyōkariire 企業借入 business borrowing; corporate borrowing; enterprise borrowing

kigyōkaseishin 企業家精神 entrepreneur (=entrepreneurial) daring

kigyōkashidashi 企業貸出 business lending; business loan

kigyōkashinri 企業家心理 business sentiment

kigyōkeiei 企業経営 corporate (= business) management; business

administration ¶ *Corporate managements* saw their rate of returns to diminish. // Japanese *business managements* experienced high earnings.

kigyōkeiretsuka 企業系列化 interlocking of enterprises

kigyōkeitai 企業形態 form of business organization; type of business enterprise

kigyōketsugō 企業結合 business combination

kigyōkibobetsukeieibunseki 企業規模別経営分析 activity (=business) analysis according to scale of enterprise

kigyōkin'yū 企業金融 business credit; corporate financing; business finance

kigyōkin'yūjōhōsābisu 企業金融情報サービス firm banking service

kigyōkōdō 企業行動 behavior of enterprises

kigyōkōsai 企業公債 industrial loan; industrial bond

kigyōmaindo 企業マインド business confidence; business sentiment ¶ On a scale of zero to 100, the measure of *business confidence* declined to 41. // *Business confidence* dwindled to its lowest level ever reached. // 企業心理

kigyōnaibuchōtatsu 企業内部調達 financing from internal reserves ¶ to raise necessary *funds from internal reserves*

kigyōnaiyōkaiji 企業内容開示 disclosure ¶ →公開

kigyōnenkin 企業年金 private enterprise's annuity

kigyōnetsu 企業熱 mania for enterprise; boom in enterprise ¶ There is quite a *mania for enterprise.*

kigyōnoishikettei 企業の意思決定 business decision making

kigyōnonijūkōzō 企業の二重構造 dual structure of enterprise

kigyōnoshakaitekisekinin 企業の社会的責任 social responsibility of enterprises

kigyōrengō 企業連合 cartel; combination
垂直的連合 vertical combination
水平的連合 horizontal combination

kigyōrieki 企業利益 business income (=profit) ¶ →企業収益

kigyōsaikōsei 企業再構成 business reorganization

kigyōseibi 企業整備 industrial reorganization; industrial adjustment

kigyōseikō 企業性向 business behavior

kigyōsharijun 企業者利潤 entrepreneurial income; entrepreneurs' profit

kigyōshin 企業心 entrepreneur (= enterprise; enterprising) spirit

kigyōshindan 企業診断 management consulting

kigyōshinri 企業心理 business sentiment; business psychology; business confidence; psychological climate; business expectations ¶ *Business expectations* are weak. // *Business sentiments* are now at their lowest ebb. // The *business psychology* is quite pessimistic. // *Business confidence* has been increased by an uplift in sales. // The *psychological climate* is somewhat optimistic.

kigyōshūdan 企業集団 industrial group

kigyōshūeki 企業収益 business profit; corporate earnings; business earnings; entrepreneurial earnings ¶ An increase in export contributed to the improvement of the *corporate profit*. // serious distortions in the structure of *corporate profits* by boosting nominal profits // pre-tax *corporate profits* increased by an average of 9.8% a year // *corporate profit* margins narrowed, not expanded // The *corporate profit* position improved. // There were signs of an improvement in *entrepreneurial earnings*.

kigyōshūnyūtanpokōsai 企業収入担保公債 industrial revenue bond; IRB

kigyōtai 企業体 business entity

kigyōtaishitsu 企業体質 business structure; constitution of business; business quality; corporate structure; constitution of enterprise ¶ to improve the *corporate structure* which had shaped under high growth // the *constitutional* improvement of *enterprises* // [参考] An excessive outflow of funds from business reduced their financial fitness.

kigyōteikei 企業提携 business tie-up

kigyōtemotoryūdōsei 企業手許流動性 fund position of corporation; business liquidity ¶ *Corporate fund positions* have generally tightened. // *Business liquidity* has increased.

kigyōtōkei 企業統計 business statistics

kigyōtōsan 企業倒産 business insolvency; business failure; bankruptcy ¶ the number of cases of *bankruptcy* // The influence of *business failure* is spreading.

kigyōtoshi 企業投資 business investment ¶ to encourage flagging *business investment* in plant and equipment // Planned *investment* by U.S. *business* is expected to reach $37 billion, compared with total realized *investment* of $35 billion a year before.

kigyōyokin 企業預金 business deposit

kigyōyosan 企業予算 business budget

kigyōyosoku 企業予測 business forecast

kigyōyūchi 企業誘致 attraction of enterprises ¶ to *attract enterprises* to the city

kigyōzaiko 企業在庫 business inventory

kigyōzaimu 企業財務 business (= corporate) finance ¶ to correct the distorted *business finances*

kihakuka 希薄化 dilution ¶ An aging of the population is *diluting* the lifetime employment system.

kihakukabōshijōkō 希薄化防止条項 anti-dilution clause

kihatsusai 既発債 already-issued bond; outstanding bond

kihatsusairimawari 既発債利回り yield of already-issued bond

kihonbuai 基本歩合 base rate; basic rate ¶ The *base rates* for rediscount and advances by the Bank of Italy were increased from 10.5% to 12%.

kihonbunrui 基本分類 basic group (ing)

kihonkikan 基本期間 basic (= base) period

kihonkyū 基本給 base pay; base wage; basic wage; basic salary ¶ a bonus equal to some multiple of a month's *base pay*

kihonryōritsu 基本料率 basic rate

kijikamono 期近物 [市] transaction of near delivery; near futures;

[証市] near-dated issue; short-dates ¶ [参考] certificates with less than three months to run

kijikasai 期近債 securities of near maturity; near-term securities

kijikurēto 基軸レート pivot(al) rate

kijikutsūka 基軸通貨 key currency

kijitsu 期日 date; appointed day; time limit; maturity; due date; expiration; (date of) maturity; date ¶ to restructure the *maturity* of external debt through long-term placements // bonds with outstanding *maturities* of less than five years and one month // Particular *maturities* must be met punctually. // → 期限

先物期日 appointed date
指定期日 futures date

kijitsukosei 期日構成 maturity strcuture

kijitsumadeni 期日迄に by the appointed time (=day); when the bill (=check) falls due

kijitsushiteiyokin 期日指定預金 maturity-designated deposit

kijitsutorihiki 期日取引 collection at maturity

kijitsuzenhenkin 期日前返金 pre-maturity payment

kijitsuzenjikkō 期日前実行(予約の) [外] premature delivery; premature drawing

kijun 基準 criterion; standard; base; basis; benchmark; guideline; norm ¶ The specific performance *criteria* must be commonly used. // failure to observe a performance *criterion* // New or amended *criteria* are established. // Money is a *standard* of deferred payment. // compliance with generally applicable environmental, fuel efficiency or safety *standards* // government mandated product *standards* that serve as barriers to trade // to monitor and co-ordinate *standards* of conduct for foreign banking units // Japan's low growth is normal growth by international *standards*. // The downturn promises to be quite modest by historical *standards*. // to apply consistent *standards* throughout the industry // the long-term prime rate as a major *benchmark* in the traditionally fixed formation of various interest rates // the measurement of production on a *basis* common to all sectors // Government finance statistics are generally *based* on the flow during the period. // The deficit on current account on a transactions *basis* was not reflected in the cash-basis figures. // Canadian banks U.S. dollar *base* lending rates—the rates of which they make loans denominated in U.S. dollars // The indicators have now been *rebased* on 1975 =100. // Inflation was contained below the statutory *benchmark* of 10%. // to set medium-term guidelines or *benchmarks* to help discipline our own day-to-day policy decisions

平均物価基準　tabular standard
評価基準　standard of appraisal
上場基準　listing standard
国際基準　international standard
労働基準　labor standard
水質基準　water quality standard
優良基準　standard to evaluate good financial standing of securities company

kijun 規準 norm ¶ The British truck unions have now accepted a *norm* of about 4 ½ percent for the next round of wage increases. // This is far above the 1 percent *norm* which is usually applied in this context and fitted in well with the customary method calculating the *normative* financial deficit. // The financial deficit returned to its *normative* value. // the differential between the actual current deficit and the *normative* structural deficit // ［参考］→基準

行動規準　norms of behavior ¶ the member's conformity with the *norms of behavior* explicitly laid down in the Articles of Agreement // the general *norms* for exchange rate *behavior* spelled out in principles

kijunbi 基準日 base date; basis date ¶ the 12-year-old *base date* for calculation of the index // The *basis date* for the growth was brought forward to 31/12/78 from 31/3/77.

kijunchingin 基準賃金 standard wage; basic pay

kijungaikokukawasesōba 基準外国為替相場 basic rate of exchange

kijunhyōjungenka 基準標準原価 basic standard cost

kijunjikajūsōtaihōsanshiki 基準時加重相対法算式 →ラスパイレス式

kijunjikoteiueito 基準時固定ウエイト fixed weight at the base period

kijunjitanaoroshihyōkahō 基準時棚卸評価法 base stock method

kijunkakaku 基準価格 constant prices ¶ gross national product at *constant prices* // Total output at *constant prices* went down.

kijunkashitsukebuai 基準貸付歩合 base lending rate ¶ a rise in its *base lending rate* from 10 to 11 ½%

kijunkikan 基準期間 benchmark

period; base period ¶ as measured from the *benchmark* (=*base*) *period* of 1970 to 1975

kijunkinri 基準金利 basic money rate; ［英］ Base Rate

kijunnakane 基準仲値 basic mean rate

kijunnen 基準年 base year ¶ The *base year* of the new index is 1980. // Real output on a 1975=100 *base* fell at a 4.2% annual rate.

kijunrēto 基準レート central rate

kijunshakudo 基準尺度 yardstick; numeraire ¶ an accurate *yardstick* for measuring... // SDR as an international monetary *numeraire*

kijunwaribikibuai 基準割引歩合 basic rediscount rate; central bank rate; base rate ¶ to raise or reduce the *basic rediscount rate* by some percentage points // The *base rates* for *rediscounts* and advances applied by the Bank of Italy were lowered from 11.5 to 10.5%.

kijunzaiko 基準在庫 basic inventory

kijutsutōkei 記述統計 descriptive statistics

kikaheikin 幾何平均 geometric average (=mean)

kikai 機会 opportunity ¶ to provide profitable bill arbitrage *opportunities* // The 1974-75 recession reduced lending *opportunities* among manufacturing industries. // to allow foreigners increased investment *opportunities* in the country // America offers relatively attractive investment *opportunities*. // to enhance trade *opportunities* // the surge toward more equitable economic *opportunity* // Investment *opportunities* are tending to become less

numerous.

交換機会 exchange opportunity

就業機会 job opportunity; employment opportunity

投資機会 investment opportunity

雇用機会 employment opportunity; job opportunity

kikaigo 機械語 ［コン］ machine language

kikaijuchūgaku 機械受注額 orders received for machinery

kikaika 機械化 mechanization; computerization ¶ *mechanization* of the sorting and counting of bank notes // to *computerize* the processing of checks

農業機械化 farm mechanization

kikaikanōgyō 機械化農業 mechanized farming

kikaikintō 機会均等 equal opportunity; equality of opportunities ¶ *equality of opportunity* among men, both within nations and between nations // the standpoint of offering *equality of* economic *opportunity*

kikaikinzukukōgyō 機械金属工業 engineering and metalworking industry

kikaikōgyō 機械工業 machinery industry

kikaikōsei 機械構成 ［コン］ configuration

kikaiyoryuku 機械余力 surplus capability of the system

kikaku 規格 specification

標準規格 standard specification

kikakukeikakuyosanseido 企画・計画・予算制度 planning-programing-budgeting system; P.P.B.S.

kikan 期間 life; term; time span; period of time duration; currency; maturity ¶ notes with a five to six-year *life* // Domestic bond issues with a minimum ten-year *term*. // The shorter leading index is relevant over a 6-month *time span*. // Hire-purchase loans are restricted to two years' *duration* for cars. // the *life* of the new contract which runs until 1981 // to stretch *maturities* further to lengthen the average *maturity* of commercial debt // The *maturity* of certificates of deposit was increased to a minimum of one year from six months. // The loan will have a *currency* of five years. // to have a *maturity* of ten years // a loan with a *life* of three years // a five years' *duration* // A franchise may be limited as to *duration,* it may be perpetual, or may be of intermediate *duration*. // →期限

kikanbunseki 期間分析 period analysis

kikangai 機関買い ［市］ buying by institutional investors; institutional stock purchases; equity purchases by institutions ¶ heavy *buying by institutional investors* among traders and the public

kikankōsei 期間構成 maturity structure; maturity distribution; maturity breakdown; term structure ¶ a *maturity distribution* of international bank lending // the *maturity structure* of these countries external indebtedness // programs to improve the *maturity structure* of external debt // a shortening of the debt *maturity structure* // to reform the *term structure* of interest rates

kikansangyō 基幹産業 key industry; basic industy

kikansharon 機関車論 locomotive theory

kikantōshika 機関投資家 insti-

tutional investor

kikeikahokenryō 既経過保険料 earned premium

kiken 危険 danger; peril; risk; hazard ¶ There can be no real banking without *risk*. // Some of the theoretical aspects of *risk* are studied. // to take the *risks* into account when joining a loan syndication // protection of depositors from the *danger* of loss due to bank failures // to be wary of incurring the *risks* that attend investment // interest-rate *risk,* purchasing-power *risk*, and financial *risk* // The *risk* that stronger demand expansion would rekindle general inflationary pressure would seem rather small. // The *risks* emanating from the expansion of the money supply should not be underrated. // the *risks* which money-supply figures implied for the future // to avert environmental *risks* // to seek a higher rate of returns by assuming larger market *risk* // Export credit insurance may cover both the commercial *risks* and the political *risks*. // ［参考］ The country is exposed to financial stability. // →リスク

不履行危険　default risk
不良危険　bad risk
外部危険　external hazard
海上危険　marine risk
買手持ち危険　buyer's risk
貸出危険　loan exposure
個有危険　inherent risk
荷主持ち危険　consigner's risk
陸上危険　shore risk
戦時危険　war risk
自然的危険　physical risk
売手持ち危険　seller's risk
優良危険　good risk

kikenbunsan 危険分散 distribution of risks; diversification of risks; diffusion of risks ¶ [参考] One should not "put all his eggs in one basket": the old adage reflecting the value of diversification.

kikenfutan 危険負担 risk-bearing; risk-taking

全危険負担 against all risks; all risks; A.R.

kikenfutanshihon 危険負担資本 risk capital

kikenhiyō 危険費用 risk cost

kikenhoken 危険保険 risk-covering insurance

kikenkaijisho 危険開示書 risk disclosure statement

kikenkanri 危険管理 risk management

kikenshingō 危険信号 danger signal; signal of danger ¶ to flash (= hoist; make) a *signal of danger*

kikenshisan 危険資産 risky assets

kikenteate 危険手当 danger money

kikenten 危険点 peril point; danger point ¶ Reserves were approaching the *peril point*. // Inflationary tendencies developed to the *danger point*.

kiken'uchibu 危険打歩 risk premium

kiki 危機 crisis ¶ A deepening poverty *crisis* is facing several African countries. // to prevent a regular recurrence of debt *crises* every four to five years // to tide the country over a balance of payments *crisis* precipitated by the international oil glut // Effective management is crucial to avoiding debt servicing *crises*. // Floating spared the world a series of exchange rate *crises*. // A

liquidity *crisis* of corporation was overcome. // An atmosphere of *crisis* was produced. // The sense of *crisis* pervaded the economic circles. // An air of *crisis* is spreading across the U.S. // to tide over an acute food *crisis* // The energy *crisis* is a *crisis* of plenty and not of scarcity. // [参考] to alleviate the financial plight

ドル危機 dollar crisis

資本主義の一般的危機 general crisis of capitalism

環境危機 environmental crisis

ポンド危機 pound crisis

kikikan 危機感 crisis atmosphere; sense of crisis; air of crisis ¶ A *crisis atmosphere* pervades the economic circles. // An *atmosphere of crisis* was produced. // The *sense of impending crisis* may spread. // to reawaken a *sense of looming crisis* // An *air of crisis* is spreading across the U.S.

kikin 基金 fund ¶ to establish and operate a *fund* for economic development assistance // a government-*funded* research body

kikinzoku 貴金属 precious metals

kikō 機構 system ¶ to maintain an open-market oriented economic *system*

kikōkaikaku 機構改革 (structural) reorganization; reform; restructuring; institutional innovation ¶ to carry out a drastic *reorganization of the structure* of the existing institution // a *reform* of the international currency system // *Institutional reform* can be successful if pursued with vision, tenacity, and strong political backing. // to achieve a substantial *restructuring* of industry

kikuzure 気崩れ [市] bearish

flurry; slump; depression; demoralization ¶ Trading slackened by a *bearish flurry.* // Stocks *slumped* on unfavorable news from Washington. // The market slackened as international oils became *depressed.*

kikyū 帰休 lay-off; part-pay furlough; compulsory temporary leave ¶ the recent abatement of heavy *lay-offs* in aircraft // In some sectors production workers were *laid off.* // *Lay-offs* reached a peak of 31 workers per 1,000. // The *lay-off* rate in January was 12 workers per 1,000. // Companies are *laying off* fewer workers. // recalls of *laid-off* employees // The company is bringing back about 1,500 *laid-off* workers. // Over 2,000 workers were *laid off.* // →レイオフ制

無期限帰休 indefinite lay-off

kimatsu 期末 end of the term; term-end ¶ at the *end of the* current *term.* // the balance *at term-end* // *the term-end* figure

kimatsuhyōka 期末評価 term-end valuation

kimatsukanjō 期末勘定 term-end account

kimatsukessan 期末決算 term-end settlement of accounts

kimatsuseiri 期末整理 adjustments at the term-end

kimatsutanaoroshidaka 期末棚卸高 final inventory

kimatsuyōin 期末要因 term-end factor

kimatsuzandaka 期末残高 balance at the term-end; the term-end balance ¶ The *balance at the end of the term* stood at ¥123 million. // *the balance at the end of the* March *term*

kimayoi 気迷い [市] hesitant; unsettled; vacillating; uncertain; trendless ¶ Investor sentiment continues to *vacillate* between a pessimistic long-term view and a brighter interim scenario. // a period of *uncertain* trading with dealers unsure about the direction of the dollar // [参考] The market is a little nervous, with no one being quite sure what to do about the market. // →気迷い人気

kimayoigimi 気迷い気味 [市] wavering; hovering ¶ The international oils moved up after some *wavering.* // [参考] The market showed no definite trend.

kimayoininki 気迷い人気 [市] sentiment of hesitation; uncertainty; incertitude market; sick market ¶ The *sentiment of hesitation* prevailed on the market. // This news brought *uncertainty* to the market. // The market continued *uncertain.* // [参考] →気迷い

kimeihenkō 記名変更 change of inscribed owner

kimeikabu 記名株 name share; registered stock; inscribed stock

kimeikōsai 記名公債 registered bond; inscribed bond

kimeinatsuin 記名捺印 signature and seal ¶ to put their *signatures and seals* // a note bearing the *signature and seal* of...

kimeishikiuragaki 記名式裏書 special endorsement

kimeishōken 記名証券 inscribed (=nonbearer) bond

kimeiuragaki 記名裏書 special endorsement

kimi 気味 tinge; flavor ¶ in an atmosphere *tinged* with anxiety // securities with a speculative *flavor* //

[参考] to be somewhat tight // Share prices ended mixed with a slight upward bias. // The market tone was a shade firmer. // with a slight tendency to trend lower

kimiyoi 気味よい ［市］ buoyant

kin 金 gold
非貨幣用金 non-monetary gold
貨幣用金 monetary gold

kinchō 緊張 tension ¶ to relax *tensions* between the two countries on economic issues

kinchozōshisetsu 金貯蔵施設 gold-storage facility

kindaika 近代化 modernization ¶ to *modernize* existing capacity (= facilities) // industial *modernization* projects
設備近代化 modernization of equipment
流通近代化 modernization in the structure of distribution

kindakan 金兌換 conversion to gold

kinfuran 金フラン gold franc

kinfutaika 金不胎化 gold sterilization

kingaku 金額 money value; amount ¶ clearance and settlement of the *money values* of securities delivered

kingakuhyōjitan'i 金額表示単位 denominator

kingensōten 金現送点 gold point; specie point

kinhaijoseisaku 金排除政策 gold exclusion policy

kinheika 金平価 gold parity

kinhenzai 金偏在 maldistribution of gold

kinhoyūdaka 金保有高 gold holdings; holdings of gold

kin'itsukyoshutsusei 均一拠出制

flat rate of contribution

kin'itsuryōkin 均一料金 flat rate

kinjichiriron 近似値理論 theory of approximation

kinjigane 金地金 gold bullion

kinjiganehon'isei 金地金本位制 gold bullion standard

kinjikahei 近似貨幣 near-money

kinjitsuwatashi 近日渡し ［市］ near delivery

kinjunbi 金準備 gold cover; gold reserve ¶ The bank is subject to a legal *gold cover* requirement.

kinjunbiritsu 金準備率 gold reserve ratio to total monetary reserves

kinka 金貨 gold coin

kinkabaraikōsai 金貨払い公債 gold loan; gold bond

kinkachihoshōjōkō 金価値保証条項 gold value clause

kinkai 金塊 gold ingot; gold bullion

kinkaikin 金解禁 lifting of the gold embargo

kinkakakuhikiage 金価格引上げ raising of official gold price

kinkawase 金為替 gold exchange

kinkenchochiku 勤倹貯蓄 thrift and saving

kinkenseiji 金権政治 money politics

kinkō 均衡 balance; equilibrium ¶ to bring the country's current-account surplus into line with international *equilibrium* // Interntional reserve flows *equilibrate* money supply to money demand. // A new *equilibrium* was reached. // to bring the current account closer to *equilibrium* // The balance of payments is more or less in *equilibrium*. // Chemical exports and imports were in near *equilibrium*. // to bring supply and demand for funds into *equilibrium* // A new and sounder *equilibrium* was achieved in the world foreign exchange market. // to achieve bilateral *equilibrium* with every trading partner // to interfere with the area's ecological *balance* // not to change the delicate *balance* of global politico-economic power which they have built and maintained // The federal budget will remain in *balance*. // Final accounts will be *balanced*.

安定均衡 stable equilibrium

不安定均衡 unstable equilibrium

不完全雇用均衡 underemployment equilibrium

動態均衡 dynamic equilibrium

発展的均衡 progressive equilibrium

移動均衡 moving equilibrium; shifting equilibrium

一時的均衡 temporary equilibrium

一般的経済均衡 general economic equilibrium

異時的均衡 inter-temporal equilibrium

需給の均衡 balance of (=between) supply and demand; equilibrium of supply and demand ¶ to maintain the *balance between supply and demand* // The *imbalance between supply and demand* increased. // [参考] the lessening of the disproportion between supply and demand // Supplies remain seriously out of balance with commercial requirements. // A renewed acceleration of demand might compromise equilibrium.

価格均衡 price equilibrium

完全均衡 full equilibrium

完全雇用均衡 full employment equilibrium

牽制均衡 checks and balances

期待均衡 expectation equilibrium

交換均衡 exchange equilibrium

国内均衡 internal equilibrium

構造的均衡 structural equilibrium

競争的均衡 competitive equilibrium

債券市場均衡 bond market equilibrium

静態均衡 static equilibrium

商品市場均衡 commodity market equilibrium

瞬間的均衡 momentary equilibrium

多元均衡 multiple equilibrium

対外均衡 external equilibrium

対内均衡 internal equilibrium

退歩的均衡 retrogressive equilibrium

多数均衡 plural equilibrium

多数市場均衡 multi-market equilibrium

定常均衡 stationary equilibrium

低水準均衡 low level equilibrium

kinkōhakaiteki 均衡破壊的 disequilibrating ¶ *disequilibrating* movements of funds

kinkōhakaitekishihon'idō 均衡破壊的資本移動 disequilibrating movements of funds

kinkōkansei 金交換性 convertibilitiy into gold ¶ to temporarily suspend the full *convertibility into gold* of dollars

kinkōkatekishihon'idō 均衡化的資本移動 equilibrium movements of funds

kinkōkawasesōba 均衡為替相場 equilibrium rate of exchange; par exchange rate

kinkōrēto 均衡レート equilibrium rate

kinkōrishiritsu 均衡利子率 equilibrium rate of interest

kinkōseichō 均衡成長 balanced growth

kinkōseichōritsu 均衡成長率 equilibrium rate of growth

kinkōteikakaku 金公定価格 official price of gold

kinkōtekihatten 均衡的発展 balanced expansion ¶ to place the economy on the track of *balanced expansion*

kinkōyosan 均衡予算 balanced budget ¶ The stage is set for a *balanced* Federal budget as early as next financial year.

kinkōzaisei 均衡財政 balanced finance

kinkōzaiseishugi 均衡財政主義 balanced finance policy

kinkyūchōsei 緊急調整 emergency adjustment

kinkyūjitai 緊急事態 state of emergency; exigency ¶ to remain in a *state of emergency* for oil // to declare the *state of emergency* // The *exigencies* of World War II led to the creation of many new agencies.

kinkyūsochi 緊急措置 emergency measures ¶ ［参考］ measures which need to be taken with special urgency

kinkyūtsūka 緊急通貨 emergency currency

kinkyūyunyū 緊急輸入 emergency import ¶ part of Japan's $4 billion *emergency-imports* package planned for this fiscal year to help reduce the soaring trade surplus // products on the *emergency-imports* list

kinkyūyunyūseigenjōkō 緊急輸入制限条項 safe-guard clause

kinkyūyūshi 緊急融資 emergency loan

kinmuhyōteiseido 勤務評定制度 efficiency rating (system); job evaluating; efficiency rating; job rating; performance approval

kinmujikan 勤務時間 working hours; work hours; office hours; business hours; company time ¶ visitors during *working hours* // personal work on *company time*

kinmyaku 金脈 gold vein; "financial background"; "financial sources"; "monetary connections"

kinnijūkakakusei 金二重価格制 two-tier (system for) gold price

kinnogōkinjigane 金の合金地金 alloyed gold bullion

kinnohaika 金の廃貨 demonetization of gold

kinnoita 金の板 gold plate

kinnokōteikakakuhaishi 金の公定価格廃止 abolition of the official price of gold

kinnonobebō 金の延べ棒 gold bar

kinnosakimonoyoyaku 金の先物予約 gold-futures contract

kinnousuita 金の薄板 gold wafer

kinō 機能 function; utility; operation; working; mechanism ¶ segregation of the *functions* of brokers and dealers under consideration // Credit performs the same cardinal *function* as money, serving as a means of payment. // It threatened the effective *functioning* of the existing economic and social institutions. // a smoothly *functioning* international economy // Both the finacial and relative factors *functioned* as a restraining influence. // the banking system's credit *operations* // to cease to have practical *utility* // intensive knowledge of the *workings* of the industry and the market // to allow the expenditure-reducing *mechanism* of an exchange depreciation (or expenditure-increasing *mechanism* of an exchange appreciation) to take place

kinōbunseki 機能分析 functional analysis

kinoriusu 気乗り薄 ［市］ reluctant

kinpaku 緊迫 stress; strain; tension; pressure; tautness; tightness ¶ to generate unbearable *strains* on domestic financial conditions // to take much of the *strain* off the Swiss franc // efforts to take the *strain* off the dollar // A reawakening of consumer appetites could cause immediate *strains* on prices. // Rolls-Royce was virtually exempt from the *stress* and *strain* of industrial battle. // Australia has emerged from earlier difficult periods of economic *stress*. // the seasonal *strain* of tax payments // the *strain* between supply and demand on market // a *taut* tone of the market // the *tight* labor market // *Pressures* subsided somewhat.

kinpūrukaigi 金プール会議 gold pool conference

kinpūrukameikoku 金プール加盟国 gold pool member (country)

kinri 金利 interest rate; rate of interest; money rate ¶ Most *interest rates* exhibited a rising trend. // *Interest rates* have turned upward. // *Interest rates* charged by large city banks on prime loans to business have lagged behind changes in open market *rates*. // Drawings on the oil facilities carried market-related *interest rates* that were higher than those charged on the use of the Fund's own resources. // *Interest rates* fluctuated over a fairly wide range. // The *interest rate* spiral slackened. // The disparity between British and foreign *rates of interest* became untenable. // Short-term *money rates* tended to stiffen. // *Interest rates* declined cosiderably. // to reduce, cut, or decrease *money rates* // to increase or raise *interest rates* // →利子

長中期金利 long and medium-term interest rates

標準金利 standard interest rate

表面金利 nominal rate of interest; nominal interest rate; coupon rate

借入金金利 interest rate on borrowing

協定金利 conventional money rate; voluntarily agreed rate

マイナスの金利 negative interest

最良企業向け貸出金利 interest charged on biggest and most creditworthy borrowers

最優遇金利 prime rate; ［英］blue-chip rate

市中金利 market interest rates; open market rates; money market rates ¶ → p. 428

消費者金利 consumer credit rate

短期金利 short-term interest rate

約定金利 contracted interest rate; contractual interest rate

kinrichōsei 金利調整 adjustment of interest rates; interest rate adjustment

kinridōkō 金利動向 movement of interest rates; interest rate movement

kinrifutan 金利負担 interest payment burden; interest cost; burden of interest

kinrifutannōryoku 金利負担能力

interest coverage

kinriheikōzei 金利平衡税 ［米］ interest equalization tax

kinrihikiage 金利引上げ raising (=increase; hike) of interest rate

kinrihikisage 金利引下げ lowering (=reduction) of interest rate; cut in interest rate

kinrihyōka 金利評価 interest parity

kinrikikō 金利機構 interest rate mechanism ¶ a more flexible *interest rate mechanism* to ensure a more effective distribution of available funds // more effective working of the *interest rate mechanism*

kinrikinō 金利機能 function of interest rate

kinrinkyūbōkaseisaku 近隣窮乏化政策 "Beggar-my-(=thy)-neighbor policy ¶ The world's major trading nations renewed their pledge not to pursue *"beggar-my-neighbor"* economic policies. // to avoid *"beggar-thy-neighbor"* policies which can very easily arise // Some have been accused of conducting *beggar-my-neighbor* policies through currency dumping. // Resort to *"beggar-my-neighbor" policies* is so far notable mostly by its absence. // It could set off a *beggar-thy-neighbor* currency war. // to adjust exchange rates to economic realities through *beggar-thy-neighbor* competitive depreciation

kinrinkyūbōtekikoyōshugi 近隣窮乏的雇用主義 beggar-my-(=thy)-neighbor employment argument

kinrinojiyūka 金利の自由化 liberalization of interest rates

kinrinotsuizuihikisage 金利の追随引下げ lowering of interest rate

following the market trend

kinrisa 金利差 interest differential; interest spread; interest discrepancy; margin ¶ *Interest differentials* could not be the main factor in these capital movements; for instance *interest rate spreads* then were actually narrowing. // *Spreads* between lending and deposit rates widened sharply. // *Interest rate differentials* remain wide. // The *differential* between Japanese and foreign *interest rates* is quite large. // *Interest rate differentials* favor at present investments in dollar assets. // Increases in U.S. short-term interest rates virtually eliminated the *interest differential* favoring Canada. // the *differential* between domestic and foreign *interest rates* // *Spreads* above the Japanese prime rate are fairly uniform and the *differentiation* by borrower is markedly narrower than on the Euro-credit market. // Lending rate *spreads* on new medium-term Euro-loans to borrowers with high credit standing dropped to less than 1% over LIBOR. // The minimum *spread* for high ranking borrowers narrowed to ½%. // a general compression of the range of average *spreads* for borrowers of different credit standing // a further squeeze of effective *spreads*, including fees // On the loan carrying a rate of 0.5% above LIBOR, the banks make a decent *spread*. // the narrow *margin* between interest rates on short-term instruments and capital-market yields // The *interest differential* remains in the dollar's favor.

kinrisaiteitorihiki 金利裁定取引 interest arbitrage

kinriseikatsusha 金利生活者 rentier

kinriseisaku 金利政策 interest rate policy

kinrisensō 金利戦争 interest rate war ¶ [参考] international disarmament of *interest rates*

kinrishigekikōka 金利刺激効果 interest incentive effect

kinrisuijun 金利水準 level of interest rate; interest rate level ¶ to bring the discount rate into better alignment of the reduced *level of* short-term *rates* // a sharp fall in the international *interest level*

kinritaikei 金利体系 structure (= formation) of interest rates; interest rate structure; interest rate spectrum; money rate structure; interest rate pattern ¶ rearrangement of the *interest rate structure* // the traditionally fixed *formation* of various Japanese *interest rates* // a rise in the whole *spectrum of interest rates* // a change in the *interest rate structure* // to normalize the *interest rate structure* // under the old *interest rate structure*, short-term credits well set at 11.5% and medium-term credits at 14% // a sustained fall in the Austrian *interest rate structure* in order to stimulate investment // Short-term rates are running above long-term rates in a reversal of the normal *interest pattern.*

kinrōiyoku 勤労意欲 will to work; willingness to work

kinrōkaikyū 勤労階級 wage-earning class

kinrōsha 勤労者 wage-earner; worker

kinrōshamochiiekensetsusuishin-seido 勤労者持家建設推進制度

system for the promotion of wage earner's private home construction

kinrōshasetai 勤労者世帯 worker household; worker's family; working family

kinrōshazaisankeiseisokushinseido 勤労者財産形成促進制度 system for the promotion of wage earner's property accumulation

kinrōshazaisankeiseichochikusei-do 勤労者財産形成貯蓄制度 tax exemption system on wage earner's property accumulation

kinrōshotoku 勤労所得 earned income

kinrōtaishū 勤労大衆 working masses

kinryūshutsu 金流出 drain (= outflow; efflux) of gold

kinryūshutsunyū 金流出入 gold movement; influx (=inflow) and efflux (=outflow) of gold

kinseihin 禁制品 contraband; smuggled goods

kinsenkō 金選好 gold preference; preference for gold

kinsensaikenshintaku 金銭債権信託 monetary claim in trust

kinsenshintaku 金銭信託 money trust; money in trust

kinsentekifujo 金銭的扶助 pecuniary assistance (=aid)

kinshi 禁止 ban ¶ introduction of the *ban* on sales of Swiss securities to non-residents // the *ban* imposed on the spending of local branches by foreign banks // a lifting of the *ban* on new direct foreign branching // the lifting or relaxation of the *ban* on the sale of Swiss securities to non-residents

kinshitekikakaku 禁止的価格 prohibitive price

kinshōken 金証券 gold certificate

kinshoyūkinshi 金所有禁止 ban on gold-ownership; ban on private ownership of gold

kinshuku 緊縮 retrenchment; shrinkage; contraction; constriction; tightening; austerity ¶ The psychological effects of the New York City crisis caused State and local governments to *tighten* their budgets. // fiscal *retrenchment* // *retrenchment* policy // a marked *shrinkage* of personal consumption // The *contraction* in output spread to all segments of manufacturing. // a moderately *contractive* influence on economic activity // Oil supply has been *constricted* substantially. // The government announced wide-ranging *austerity* measures in a bid to cut consumer spending. // *Austerity* measures introduced last week will have a swift effect.

kinshukuseisakusochi 緊縮政策措置 austerity measure ¶ The selective *austerity measures* are wisely chosen. // wide-ranging *austerity measures* in a bid to cut consumer spending

kinshukuzaiseiyosan 緊縮財政予算 tight budget; retrenchment budget; restrictive budget management; budget drawn up in a spirit of austerity; fiscal retrenchment; austere budgetary and fiscal policies; austere budget; austerity budget; lean(er) budget; stern budget ¶ the coming battle over Reagan's *tight budget* // to introduce *fiscal retrenchment* // The United States will maintain *austere budgetary* and fiscal policies to control inflation. // to introduce an *austere budget* designed

to reduce living standards // Portugal's National Assembly approved a severe *austerity budget* which the Government claimed would cut imports by 16%. // In no sense was the Nixon budget an *'austerity' budget.* // to put greater reliance on a *leaner budget* in order to tug down the inflation rate // Carter's *lean, austere budget* // [参考] Tight budgetary control is maintained // The Cabinet adopted an austere stance for the 1982 budget.

kinshusshi 金出資 subscription in gold

kintaizō 金退蔵 gold hoarding

kintanposhakkan 金担保借款 gold collateral loan

kin'uchibu 金打歩 gold premium

kin'yakkan 金約款 gold clause

kin'yu 禁輸 ban (on export or import); embargo

kin'yū 金融 financing; finance; banking; financial accommodation ¶ tightening corporate *finance* // to *finance* consumer needs // for *financing* unsold stocks // the *financing* of the current deficits of the oil importing countries // the *banking* system // the restricted amount of *finance* available through official channels // The international availability of bank *finance* is great. // customers seeking conditional *finance* from official sources // to obtain all the essential *financing* from the money and capital markets // Spending will be *financed* from tax income of DM 111.2 billion. // to be *financed* by tapping the savings of the non-bank public

赤字金融 deficit finance; finance for

deficit

備蓄金融	stockpile finance
直接金融	direct finance
外部金融	external finance
自己金融	self-finance
株式金融	equity financing
開発金融	development finance
間接金融	indirect finance
寡頭金融	oligarchy finance
系列金融	finance to affiliated companies
健全金融	sound finance
企業金融	corporate finance; business finance
内部金融	internal finance
農業金融	agricultural finance
債権金融	debt financing
政策金融	guidance policy finance
商業金融	commercial finance
所得造出金融	income-creating finance
証券金融	securities finance
滞貨金融	finance for dead stock
裏口金融	back-door finance
売掛金融	accounts-receivable finance
輸入金融	import finance
輸出金融	export finance
在庫金融	inventory finance

kinyū 記入 entry into a book; record

kin'yūchitsujo 金融秩序 monetary order ¶ a major element on the road to a new world *monetary order*

kinyūchō 記入帳 record; register; book

kin'yūchōsetsu 金融調節 monetary and credit control; monetary regulation; monetary adjustment

kin'yūchōsetsushudan 金融調節手段 monetary measure; monetary instrument; monetary tool; monetary device; credit control instrument

instrument of monetary regulation ¶ to diversify the *instruments of monetary control* // The lending policy is used as a principal *instrument of monetary regulation.*

kin'yūchūkaikikan 金融仲介機関 financial intermediary ¶ to make more use of regional *financial intermediaries* to channel funds to them // Thirty states and Puerto Rico now act as *financial intermediaries* through a variety of agencies, authorities, and public corporations. // States have begun large-scale operations of state instrumentalities as *financial intermediaries.*

kin'yūchūshinchi 金融中心地 money market center; financial center; banking center ¶ the emergence of the main *centers* of international *banking*

kin'yūdan 金融団 financial syndicate; consortium

kin'yūenjo 金融援助 financial aid (=assistance; support) ¶ to provide (=extend; offer; give; render) its continued *financial assistance* // to seek the Fund's *financial support* // to *support financially* a country's economic program

kin'yūfutan 金融負担 financing burden ¶ The size of the U.S. deficit lightened the *financing burdens* of other deficit countires.

kin'yūgaitorihiki 金融外取引 non-financial transaction

kin'yūgyō 金融業 banking business; financial operations

kin'yūgyōsha 金融業者 financier; money-lender; banker

kin'yūhikishime 金融引締め monetary (=crdedit) restraint; monetary

(=credit) squeeze; money (=monetary) tightening; stringency ¶ the thrust of *monetary restraint* reductions in the availability of credit // The *monetary squeeze* was tightened further. // a repetition of the severe *credit squeeze* of 1972 // The *credit squeeze* was further tightened. // a prolonged, intensified, and more general *credit squeeze* // to put on a vigorous credit squeeze // Several *monetary restraints* were adopted. // *tightening of monetary* conditions // *restrictive credit* policy // selective *credit restraint* in the climate of excess demand for loanable funds // [参考] The Federal Reserve was willing to step hard on the monetary brake at times. // The FRB is easing its credit grip.

kin'yūhikishimenoshintō 金融引締めの浸透 permeation of tight money policy; spread of monetary stringency

kin'yūhikishimeseisaku 金融引締め政策 tight money policy; monetary restraint; restrictive monetary polioy

kin'yuhin 禁輸品 article under the embargo; contraband

kin'yūhippaku 金融逼迫 monetary stringency; tightening of financial positions

kin'yūhiyō 金融費用 financial cost; financial expense ¶ The relation of *financial costs* to the total borrowed capital is consistently lower than the rate of returns.

kin'yū hiyōtai jun'uriagedaka hiritsu 金融費用対純売上高比率 ratio of financial cost to net sales

kin'yūjijōchōsa 金融事情調査 research on the monetary situation

kin'yūjishuken 金融自主権 monetary sovereignty

kin'yūjōsei 金融情勢 financial conditions; monetary conditions ¶ The undertone of the *monetary conditions* began to relax.

kin'yūkai 金融界 financial circles; financial society; banking community // at the pinnacle of the *financial community* // the virtual unanimity of the *banking community* on the topic

kin'yūkakudai 金融拡大 monetary expansion; monetary growth ¶ the steady winding-down of *monetary growth*

kin'yūkanjō 金融勘定 [外] balance of monetary movements

kin'yūkankyō 金融環境 financial environment; financial circumstances; banking environment ¶ There is in the current *financial environment* a stubborn structural problem. // The financial markets are in a much different, and in recent years much more difficult and volatile, *environment.* // The current *circumstances* surrounding *banking* operations are not very comfortable.

kin'yūkanwa 金融緩和 monetary (=credit) ralaxation; monetary ease; monetary expansion ¶ Pressure is building for a *relaxation of the credit* restrictions. // *easing of monetary* conditions // *easy money* policy

kin'yūkanwakitai 金融緩和期待 expectation of monetary relaxation

kin'yūkanwaseisaku 金融緩和政策 relaxation of tight money policy; easy money policy

kin'yūkanwasochi 金融緩和措置 measure for monetary ease

kin'yūkatsudō 金融活動 financing (=financial) activities; financial operations; banking activities ¶ The credit market encompasses a wide range of specialized *financing activities*.

kin'yūkikan 金融機関 financial (= credit) institution; credit (=lending) agency ¶ lendings of *financial institutions* // *financial institutions* for small business // agricultural *financial institutions* // other types of *lending agencies,* both private and public, than commercial banks // private and government *financial institutions* for small business // lendings of (=from; by) agricultural *financial institutions* // elimination of differences in the field of operations of various *financial institutions*

長期金融機関 financial institution for long-term credit

中小企業金融機関 financial institution for small business

外国為替金融機関 financial institution for foreign exchange

国際金融機関 international financial institution

農林漁業金融機関 financial institution for agriculture, forestry and fisheries

政府金融機関 government financial institution; governmental financial agency

専門金融機関 specialized credit institution; specialized financial institution

kin'yūkikandōshitsuka 金融機関同質化 elimination of differences in the field of operations of financial institutions; assimilation of financial institutions

kin'yūkikankariirekin 金融機関借

入金 borrowed money from (other) financial institutions

kin'yūkikankashitsukekin 金融機関貸付金 loan to (other) financial institutions

kin'yūkikō 金融機構 financial machinery; financial system; banking machinery; financial structure ¶ to strengthen and improve the nation's *financial machinery* // The Arab States are reluctant to develop the necessary *banking machinery* to make the best use of their disposable oil revenues. // The *financial structure* of the Fund is broadly built on the quotas of its members.

kin'yūkinpaku 金融緊迫 financial strain and stress ¶ *financial strains and stresses* at the year-end

kin'yūkisei 金融規制 financial regulation; credit control

kin'yūkōsoku 金融梗塞 stringency; credit crunch; money crunch

kin'yukōzō 金融構造 financial structure; monetary structure; banking system ¶ A sound *financial structure* is one essential ingredient of a growing economy. // the removal of abnormal features in the Japanese *monetary structure*

kin'yūkyōkō 金融恐慌 financial crisis; financial panic

kin'yūkyōtei 金融協定 financial agreement

kin'yūmekanizumu 金融メカニズム financial mechanism ¶ the gains in efficiency of the economy's *financial mechanism* from such activities

kin'yūmoderu 金融モデル financial model

kin'yūnan 金融難 financial difficulty; financial embarassment ¶ *financially embarassed* purchasers

kin'yūnojiyūka 金融の自由化 financial liberalization

kin'yūnokisetsusei 金融の季節性 financial seasonableness

kin'yūrenkanhiritsu 金融連関比率 financial interrelation ratio

kin'yūsābisu 金融サービス banking facilities; financial services ¶ an adequate spread of *banking facilities* in rural areas

kin'yūsai 金融債 bank debenture; bank bond ¶ *Bank bonds* made up an even larger proportion than usual of total bond sales. // Sales of the *bonds of* specialized *banks* and other *bank bonds* were small.

kin'yūsaihakkōdaka 金融債発行高 bank debentures issued

kin'yūsaiken 金融債権 financial claim ¶ The money market deals in standardized *financial claims* of very short maturity. // holdings of marketable *financial claims*

kin'yūsaimu 金融債務 financial obligation ¶ to fail to honor its *financial obligations* towards its customers

kin'yūsakimonoshōhin 金融先物商品 financial futures instrument

kin'yūseido 金融制度 financial system; banking system ¶ Each policy instrument has been shaped to adjust to financial, structural, or technological changes in the U.S. *financial system.*

kin'yūseijōka 金融正常化 financial normalization

kin'yūseisaku 金融政策 monetary policy; financial policy; monetary and credit policy ¶ The *monetary policy* turned restrictive. // the development of the *monetary policy* // the pursuit of a vigorous and well articulated *monetary policy* // The scope for operating *monetary policy* is limited. // Control of monetary aggregates is an essential aspect of *monetary policy*. // The call-money market will become a more important arena for the conduct of *monetary policy*. // to pursue (=follow) an excessively lenient monetary policy // *Monetary and credit policy* has been adapted to a severe anti-inflationary program. // *Monetary policy* should be less than fully accommodating. // the formation and execution of *monetary policy* to affect financial conditions // A restrictive or expansionary *monetary policy*, which is directed toward stabilization of prices, is adopted. // to implement restrictive *monetary policy* // The firming of *monetary policy* of late has not yet taken complete hold, and will take time to work through the economy. // *Monetary policy*, conceived and managed by the National Bank under the control of and in agreement with the Government, is implemented essentially through the financial agents, more particularly the banks.

kin'yūseisakunofukkatsu 金融政策の復活 revival of monetary policies

kin'yūseisakunokōchokuka 金融政策の硬直化 hardening of credit policies; arteriosclerosis of monetary policy

kin'yūseisakunoun'eimokuhyō 金融政策の運営目標 (monetary policy) operating target; intermediate target (of monetary policy)

kin'yūseisakushudan 金融政策手段 monetary policy instrument (=

device; tool; weapon)

kin'yūseisakutaido 金融政策態度 monetary policy stance; monetary policy posture ¶ to assume and maintain a restrictive *stance in monetary policy* actions // The *monetary policy posture* continues restrictive.

kin'yūsensō 金融戦争 financial war

kin'yūsetsudo 金融節度 monetary discipline; financial discipline ¶ Major countries were prone to disregard the *financial discipline*.

kin'yūshienkyōtei 金融支援協定 financial support (facility) agreement; "Safety Net" agreement

kin'yūshihon 金融資本 financial capital

kin'yūshijō 金融市場 financial market; money and credit market; credit markets; money and capital market; banking market ¶ The *financial market* was quite taut. // Stringent conditions prevailed in the *money and credit market*. // The *financial market* became more restrictive. // *Financial markets* were buffeted by international disturbances. // the relaxation of domestic *credit markets* based on external factors // Developments in the *money and capital markets* during the current recovery contrast sharply with those observed in past cyclical upswings. // International *banking markets* will remain liquid.

長期金融市場 long-term credit market

短期金融市場 short-term credit market; money market

kin'yūshijōenokainyū 金融市場への介入 money market intervention

¶ The Bank of France suspended certain of the *money-market interventions*.

kin'yūshijōnoun'ei 金融市場の運営 money-market management ¶ *Money-market management* was directed towards defending the franc.

kin'yūshijōshōken 金融市場証券 money market securities; money market instruments

kin'yūshijōshōsho 金融市場証書 money market certificate; MMC

kin'yūshisan 金融資産 financial asset; financial portfolio ¶ increase in financial assets of the personal sector // Accumulation of *financial assets* increased. // The outstanding *financial assets* grew 5.5 folds.

kin'yūshisanfusaizandakahyō 金融資産負債残高表 financial assets and liabilities accounts

kin'yūshisansenkō 金融資産選好 preference of financial assets

kin'yūshohin 禁輸商品 embargo goods

kin'yūshudan 金融手段 financial ways and means; financing vehicle ¶ the more common use of floating rate notes as a *financing vehicle*

kin'yushutsu 金輸出 export of gold; shipment of gold

kin'yushutsukaikin 金輸出解禁 repeal (=lifting) of gold embargo

kin'yushutsukinshi 金輸出禁止 gold ban; gold embargo

kin'yushutsuten 金輸出点 gold export point

kin'yūsoshiki 金融組織 financial structure

kin'yūtekiryūtsū 金融的流通 financial circulation

kin'yūtekishudan 金融的手段 →金融調節手段

kin'yūtorihiki 金融取引 financial transaction

kin'yūtorihikihyō 金融取引表 financial transaction accounts

kin'yūzaiseikeisū 金融財政計数 data concerning monetary and financial variables

kinzokunensūbetsushikyūritsu 勤続年数別支給率 payment rate based on years of service

kinzokuseihinkōgyō 金属製品工業 fabricated metal industry

kiōkashidashi 既往貸出 outstanding loan

kiokukōdo 記憶コード ［コン］ mnemonic code

kiokushori 記憶処理 book-keeping

kiokusōchi 記憶装置 ［コン］ memory storage; store

緩衝記憶装置 buffer storage
固定記憶装置 fixed memory; read-only memory

kiokuyōryō 記憶容量 ［コン］ memory capacity

kiōsaikō 既往最高 all-time high; new high; record high; (new) peak; historical high ¶ to record an *all-time high* // to mark a *new high* // to reach a *record high*

kiōshiharaikurinobekessaijuyō 既往支払繰延べ決済需要 credit demand for the settlement of deferred payments

kirisute 切捨て（債券の） write-off (=-down); cancellation; discharge ¶ → 帳消し

kiroku 記録 record ¶ to keep a *record* of... // authentic *records* show that... // *Records* fail to show that... // to make a *record* of... // to break the previous *record* of... // to be on or off *record* // The August deficit was the biggest on *record*, exceeding the previous high of \$1.44 billion registered in January of last year.

kirokuteki 記録的 (new) record (high, low, rise; etc.) ¶ to establish a *new* output *record* of 2 million units // to *record a new high* of 62 percent // to mark a *record high* of 12 tons // output reached on all-time *record* figure of 100 tons // one of the sharpest movements on *record* // on near-*record* deficit // Production marked the biggest decline on *record*.

kisai 起債 flotation of loan; issue of bond; issuance; flotation; launching of loan; placement ¶ the *issuance* of industrial bonds // increased *flotations* of bank debentures // to *issue* (= *float*) *a loan* // The government has approved the *flotation* of Finland's national bonds in Japan, the first foreign bond *flotation* in Japan since 1973. // Japan banned the *issue of* yen-quoted foreign *bonds* in Japan in November 1973. // The seven-year *loan* for DM 100 million *launched* by the European Investment Bank has been raised to DM 200 million. // the terms and conditions of the confederation's new, private *placement* of SF 500 million // The aggregate of bonds and private *placements* made throughout the region rose to \$5.7 billion last year.

kisaichōsei 起債調整 co-ordination of bond issues

kisaigaku 起債額 amount issued

kisaimaegashi 起債前貸 temporary loan before bond flotation

kisairyōnochōsei 起債量の調整 volume control of the bond market

kisaishijō 起債市場 bond (flotation) market; issue market; capital market; investment market

kisaitasseiritsu 起債達成率 achievement ratio of bond flotation; bond flotation ratio

kisanbi 起算日 initial date in reckoning

kisei 規制 control; regulation; restriction; regimentation ¶ The New Zealand Goverment imposed a new round of interest rate *controls* on institutions. // the *restrictions* placed on the growth of lending in lire // More rigorous hire-purchase *restrictions* have been introduced. // *regulations* deriving from current legislation concerning the eligibility for benefits // to watch that monetary policy *regulations* are being observed // to lay down and enforce strict foreign exchange *control* regulations // removal of tight *regulations* on oil supply // The central bank should run tight *control* of the credit supply. // pressure for *regimentation of* economic activity

量的規制　quantitative restriction
質的規制　qualitative restriction
有事規制　emergency regulation

kiseikaijo 規制解除 deregulation; lifting of regulations; decontrol ¶ *deregulation* of Euroyen loans // Japan should *deregulate* its interbank wholesale markets. // ［参考］ →自由化

kiseikinri 規制金利 regulated interest rate

kiseisochi 規制措置 regulatory measure; regulatory action ¶ The general welfare should guide any *regulatory measures* and actions.

kiseiyoi 気勢よい ［市］ spirited

kisetsu 季節 season ¶ to have the busiest *season* // during the high *season* // in the off *season* // to be out of *season* // The opening weeks of the fall *season* have not produced any striking changes in the business climate. // The vacation *season* is drawing to a close. // The prices have recovered from a sharp fall at the beginning of the selling *season* in August. // the approach of the favorable *season* of the year

kisetsuchōsei 季節調整 seasonal adjustment ¶ the price index after *seasonal adjustment* // the *seasonally adjusted* price index // → 季節変動調整

kisetsuchōseizuminenritsu 季節調整済年率 seasonally adjusted annual rate

kisetsuhendō 季節変動 seasonal variation ¶ The index of industrial production corrected for *seasonal variations*, stood at 146.2. // The underlying rate of production, after adjustment for *seasonal variations*, was slightly above the February level. // Without adjustment for *seasonal variations*, there was a 2% increase over the quarter.

kisetsuhendōchōsei 季節変動調整 seasonal adjustment; correction for seasonal variation; seasonal allowance; seasonal fluctuation ¶ With *seasonal adjustment*, exports fell 5.5%. // The balance was adverse, after *seasonal adjustment* by $80 million. // Unemployment rose to a *seasonally adjusted* 4.8%. // The wholesale price index increased at an annual rate of 5.2% in May on a *seasonally adjusted* basis.

kisetsuhendōchōseizumi 季節変動調整済 adjusted to seasonal variations; seasonally adjusted

kisetsuhendōchōseizumikeisū 季節変動調整済計数 seasonally adjusted figure; figure after seasonal adjustment

kisetsuhin 季節品 seasonal goods

kisetsujukyū 季節需給 seasonal supply and demand

kisetsurōdōryoku 季節労働力 seasonal migrant labor

kisetsuryūnyūrōdōryoku 季節流入労働力 seasonal migrant labor

kisetsusei 季節性 seasonality ¶ to recognize the limitations and *seasonality* in labor supply

kisetsushikin 季節資金 seasonal funds

kisetsushisū 季節指数 seasonal index

kisetsushōhin 季節商品 seasonal commodities; seasonal goods; seasonal item ¶ Liquidators mark additional discounts on such *seasonal items* as greeting cards, chocolate, Easter eggs and summer furniture.

kisetsutai 季節帯 seasonal zone

kisetsuteki 季節的 seasonal ¶ to show a less than *seasonal* decline // Personal consumption in real terms, adjusted for *seasonal* strain of tax payments will occur. // after allowing for normal *seasonal* variations // to decline, following usual *seasonal* patterns // more than a spring *seasonal* upsurge // to enter a *seasonal* outpayments // Demand deposits moved down *seasonally*. // the *seasonally* adjusted rate of unemployment // in excess of those *seasonally* expected // The decline was smaller than warranted by *seasonal* factors. // The increased borrowing was largely *seasonal* in

nature. // The banks had a large *seasonal* loss in demand deposits. // While demand deposits moved down *seasonally*, time deposits increased contraseasonally.

kisetsutekihendō 季節的変動 seasonal change; seasonal variation; seasonal movements ¶ These figures are not adjusted for *seasonal movements*. // →季節変動

kisetsutekijuyō 季節的需要 seasonal demand

kisetsutekishitsugyō 季節的失業 seasonal unemployment

kishingō 黄信号 amber lights ¶ The *amber lights* began to flash, making a warning of looming inflation.

kishohiyō 期初費用 front-end fee

kishōkachi 希少価値 rarity value; scarcity value ¶ bonds which carry *rarity value* in the market

kishōsei 希少性 scarcity
人為の希少性 contrived scarcity
資源の希少性 scarcity of resources

kishōshigen 希少資源 scarce resources

kishōtsūka 希少通貨 scarce currency

kishōzaika 希少財貨 scarcity goods; scarce goods

kishu 期首 beginning of period

kishukōshin 機種更新 model change

kishushikakarihin 期首仕掛品 initial goods in process; initial work in process

kishutanaoroshidaka 期首棚卸高 initial inventory; opening inventory

kishuzandaka 期首残高 balance at the beginning of the period

kiso 基礎 base; basis; foundation; ground; grounding; groundwork;

footing; pedestal ¶ a *base* for business operations // comparison on a monthly average *basis* // to lay the *foundations* of industry // a firm *foundation* for the subsequent expansion // a well-*grounded* theory // a firm *grounding* in theory // generalization *based* upon sufficient data // the *base* period for... // to solidify the *foundation* of... // a belief *founded* in experience // There are good *grounds* to believe it. // to prepare the *ground* for... // This is time for laying the *groundwork* for a new mode of economic developments. // The *groundwork* has been laid for an evolution of somewhat longer-run relationships among wages, productivity, profits and interest rates. // The recovery is now on a solid *footing*. // to place the public finances on a healthier *footing* // an adequate self-sustaining growth *footing*

kisobumon 基礎部門 subsistence sector

kisokōjo 基準控除 basic exemption

kison 毀損 mutilation; damage; injury

kisonkigyō 既存企業 existing company

kisonkogitte 毀損小切手 mutilated check

kisosangyō 基礎産業 basic industry; key industry

kisotekifukinkō 基礎的不均衡 [外] fundamental disequilibrium; basic disequilibrium; basic imbalance ¶ to correct, or prevent the emergence of, a *fundamental disequilibrium*

kisotekijōken 基礎的条件 fundamentals ¶ encouraging performance of the economic *fundamentals* // Confidence in Japan's economic *fundamentals* continued to mount. // a price increase as determined by market *fundamentals*

kisotekishūshi 基礎的収支 [外] basic balance (of payments); current balance and long-term capital balance

kitai 期待 expectation ¶ Price *expectations* in an economy that is highly dependent on foreign trade tend to be excessive. // to kindle and sustain favorable *expectations* regarding exchange rate developments
長期期待 long-term expectation
短期期待 short-term expectation

kitairieki 期待利益 expected profit ¶ to maximize the discounted *expected profits*

kitaisonshitsu 期待損失 expected loss

kitaisuru 期待する expect; anticipate; hope; prospect; look forward to ¶ as might be *expected* to occur // *Expectations* a year ago ranged from 8 to 10 percent. // to foment unrealistic *expectations* // Inflationary *expectations* are spreading. // A gain in imports was caused mainly by *anticipations* of shortages. // There is little *hope* of an immediate recovery. // There is *prospect* of price stability unless unexpected changes take place. // The economy can now *look forward to* a period of sound growth from a firm base. // inflationary *expectations* // There was little *expectation* of a business recovery. // Performance has not come up to *expectations*. // the high *expectations* held by the optimists // the government's anti-inflation strategies aimed at dampening inflationary *expectations*

kitaiusu 期待薄 remote possibility; remote probability ¶ relatively *remote possibility* of any early recovery // ［参考］An early restoration is held by most to be improbable.

kitaiyōin 期待要因 expectational factor; expectational influence ¶ Interest rates are influenced by *expectational factors.* // One of the most important *expectational influences* has been attitudes toward inflation.

kitchinnonami キッチンの波 Kitchin cycle; Kitchin's wave

kitokuken 既得権 vested right; vested interests; acquired right

kitsumeni きつめに on a more restrictive (=stronger; severer) basis ¶ to enforce the discount-window operation *on a stronger basis* than before // to pursue monetary policy *on a severer basis* than in the previous quarter // ［参考］monetary fiscal policy of a posture of modest restraint

kittetegata 切手手形 checks and bills ¶ *checks and bills* in the process of collection

kittetegatahoyūritsu 切手手形保有率 ratio of checks and bills to total deposits

kiun 気運 tendency; mood ¶ There is a growing *tendency* on the part of many entrepreneurs to increase fixed investments. // The *tendency* toward a further price increase became more pronounced as oil imports tapered off. // A wait-and-see *mood* pushed down the Dow-Jones average.

kiyodo 寄与度 contribution; share ¶ The tax haven sector contributes a relatively important *share* to the country's GNP. // The *share* of demand satisfied by imported products will rise.

kiyoritsu 寄与率 percentage contribution; contribution ratio; proportionate contribution ¶ Its *percentage contribution* to the slowdown of the uptrend increased.

kizashi 兆し sign; symptom; signal; indication; augury; foreboding change; glimmering; hint ¶ There are disquieting *signs* indicating a crisis. // visible *signs* of emerging recovery // *Signs* are that the market will remain bearish. // few *signs* of an early slowdown // Some danger *signs* were yet to be removed. // Another *sign* of strength is that... // The first *signs* of improvement were discernible. // *Signs* of an incipient downturn in economic activity were evident as far back as 1973. // Increasingly convincing *signs* that the economy has already turned up are obvious. // The spread of protection is *symptomatic* of the problems of structural adjustment. // seemingly conflicting *signals* from the fundamental factors which shape the market // The most promising *indication* is that... // There are widespread *indications* in consumer markets that the economy will advance. // It is of good *augury* for the future of the firm. // *Glimmerings* of an advance are apparent in some countries. // not-so-robust growth in nonfarm payroll being interpreted as a *hint* of a possible slowdown // The first limited *signs* of the modest economic recovery are becoming apparent. // Some positive *signs* are on the horizon. // Boom *symptoms* still predominate. // [参考] A worsening ahead in the Iran-Iraq conflict bodes badly for currencies. // Higher nominal rates, when combined with lower inflation, portend higher real rates.

kizokurishi 帰属利子 imputed interest ¶ *interest imputable* to...

kizonshisan 既存資産 existing asset ¶ speculative investment in *existing assets* such as land and stocks

koama 小甘 [市] easy

kōatsukahei 高圧貨幣 high-powered money

kōatsukeizai 高圧経済 high pressure economy

kōbai 公売 public auction; forced sale

kōbaibu 購買部 purchasing agent

kōbaidōkichōsa 購買動機調査 motivation research

kōbaiiyoku 購買意欲 buying intention; incentive for buying; buying inclination; buying interest; willingness to buy ¶ the July survey of consumer *buying intentions* // The *buying intentions* of consumers questioned in surveys indicated a continuing strong upsurge of cars and homes.

kōbaikumiai 購買組合 consumers' purchase cooperative association

kōbairyoku 購買力 purchasing (= buying) power (=strength) ¶ The weakness of the dollar has eroded the international *purchasing power* of oil exporters' receipts. // *Purchasing power* was skimmed off by means of a 30% value added tax on luxury goods. // Giant stores drain *purchasing power* from town centers. // to fix the *purchasing power* of each unit of the currency to an absolute standard // The trade deficit is sucking the *purchasing power* out of the country. // a changing level of the *purchasing power* of money // an adequate wage representing a fairly even and stable *purchasing power* // The stagnation depressed the *purchasing power* of the dollar. // treasury injections of *purchasing power* // The *power* of labor to *purchase* goods will not be changed. // the *buying power* of the wages of American workers after adjustment for inflation but before taxes // The *buying power* of their pay checks shrinks by 11%. // a moderate loss in households' *buying power* // the stagnation of its internal *buying strength* // to safeguard households' *buying power* // a moderate loss in its internal *buying strength*

浮動購買力 floating purchasing power

大衆購買力 mass purchasing power

通貨購買力 purchasing power of money

kōbairyokuchūnyū 購買力注入 injection of purchasing power ¶ repeated *injections of purchasing power* from tax reductions or higher public expenditure

kōbairyokuheika 購買力平価 purchasing power parity ¶ The biggest gains in GDP per head, calculated at current *purchasing power parities* were experienced by Belgium and France.

kōbairyokuheikakawasesōba 購買力平価為替相場 purchasing power

parity exchange rate

kōbairyokukyūshū 購買力吸収 absorption of purchasing power ¶ to *absorb* (=siphon; mop up; suck) *purchasing power*

kobetsukyoka 個別許可 licensing on a case-by-case basis

kobetsushinsa 個別審査 case-by-case screening; examination on an individual basis ¶ to *screen* loan applications on a *case-by-case* basis

kōbo 公募 public placement; public offering; public subscription ¶ Nearly two-thirds of the capital-market loans were *placed publicly*. // dollar denominated *public placements* in Tokyo

予約公募 offer by subscription

kōbohakkō 公募発行 public subscription; public placement; public offering ¶ the first *public offering* of the common stock of the company // a *publicly offered* stock // to *offer* debentures for *public subscription* // *publicly offered* loan // to offer a loan for *public subscription* // ［参考］to place the loan on the market

非公募発行 direct placement; private placement

kōbokabu 公募株 publicly subscribed share

kōbōsen 攻防線 barrier ¶ The Dow-Jones industrial average pierced the 500 *barrier*.

心理的攻防線 psychological barrier

kobudagurasukansū コブ・ダグラス関数 Cobb-Douglas function

kōbutsuseinenryō 鉱物性燃料 mineral fuels

kōchakujōtai 膠着状態 ［市］quiescent market

kōchi 耕地 cultivated land; arable land

kōchō 好調 favorable; improving; buoyant ¶ The trend of prices is less *favorable* this year than in 1975. // The payments position has been *improving* appreciably. // Production retains the *buoyancy* characteristic of recent years.

kōchokuka 硬直化 hardening; arteriosclerosis; rigidity ¶ *hardening* of credit policies // *arteriosclerosis* of monetary policy // downward *rigidity* of prices // *rigidity* of currency

kōchokukakaku 硬直価格 rigid price; sticky price

kōchokusei 硬直性 rigidity; inflexibility; stickiness ¶ to deal with structural *rigidities* in the job market // *inflexibility* of public finance and budget preparation // Deep seated structural and institutional *rigidities* limit the mobility of resources. // to eliminate the *rigidities* and impediments to resource mobility // the *rigidity* that can be observed in the fiscal deficits of many countries // built-in *rigidities* in the goods and labor markets // countries with *inflexible* nominal wages // a gradual elimination, or reduction, of the *stickiness* of domestic prices // the downward *rigidity* of prices

賃金の硬直性 wage rigidity; rigidity of wages

上方硬直性 upward rigidity

下方硬直性 downward rigidity

価格硬直性 price rigidity; rigidity of prices

構造的硬直性 structural rigidity

kodaikōkoku 誇大広告 exaggerated advertisement; excessive advertisement; bait advertisement; fraudulent advertizing

kōdan 公団 public corporation

kodashi 小出し piecemeal ¶ The bank has taken steps to increase its credit operations on a *piecemeal* basis.

kōdō 行動 behavior ¶ *behavior* of consumers, or consumer *behavior* // The moderate *behavior* of consumers has been reflected in a more sober tone in the commodity market. // Consumer *behavior* was highly unpredictable. // The difference between bank credit and demand deposits is afforded by the *behavior* of time deposits. // Less encouraging was the *behavior* of construction activity. // The *behavior* of prices cannot by itself be used to diagnose the state of demand. // The *behavior* of lumber prices, rising sharply and then leveling off, has reflected a seasonal fluctuation in demand and supply. // Special factors impinged on the *behavior* of prices. // speculative crazes or other "bandwagon forms" of *behavior* // Expectations of inflation have become more deeply set in thinking and *behavior*. // freedom in the pricing *behavior* // Further action by the Fed depended on how the market *behaved*. // Exchange rates *behaved* very differently among countries.
合理的行動 rational behavior
目的行動 purposeful behavior
企業行動 business behavior
極大化行動 maximization behavior
最適化行動 optimizing behavior
選好行動 preferential behavior
シンボル行動 symbolic behavior
消費者行動 consumer behavior

kōdogijutsu 高度技術 advanced technology; high technology sophisticated technology ¶ industries *technologically* very *sophisticated* and require highly skilled manpower

kōdogijutsusangyō 高度技術産業 high-technology industry

kōdoka 高度化 advancement; improvement; sophistication ¶ technical *sophistication* of many final products // highly *sophisticated* social systems // highly *sophisticated* financial systems // a *highly developed* industry // the *advancement* of technology // products of high technology and *sophistication*

kōdōkagaku 行動科学 behavioral science

kōdoseichō 高度成長 high (economic) growth; high rate of growth; high growth rate ¶ Economic *growth* is *higher* than should be maintained.

kōeijigyo 公営事業 public enterprise

kōeishichiya 公営質屋 public pawn shop

kōeitobaku 公営賭博 public gambling

kōeki 公益 public interest; public utilities; public services; common; good public good; public benefit ¶ to investigate whether this merger act against the *public interest* or not // Regulatory burdens add to costs without commensurate *public benefits*.

kōeki 交易 trade ¶ to open, promote, stimulate, and expand *trade* with America

kōekidantai 公益団体 public utility corporation; public service corporation

kōekihōjin 公益法人 juridical person for public interests; non-profit foundation

kōekijōken 交易条件 terms of trade; trade terms ¶ The *terms of trade* turned in favor of France. // The *terms of trade* deteriorated. // Sweden's *terms of trade* remained stable, // index of *trade terms* // large adverse changes of developing countries' *terms of trade* // a deterioration of 18 per cent in Kenya's external *terms of trade* // to redress an oil-induced *terms-of-trade* loss // substantial *terms-of-trade* gains reflecting the favorable movement of oil prices

商品交易条件 commodity terms of trade

要素交易条件 factoral terms of trade

kōekijōkenshisū 交易条件指数 index of terms of trade

kōekikabu 公益株 [証市] public utilities (stocks)

kōekikaisha 公益会社 public utility company; public service company

kōekishadan 公益社団 public utility association

kōekiyūsen 公益優先 public interests first; priority of public interest; preference of public interest; the public interests over the private ¶ the principle of "*public interests first*"

kōekizaidan 公益財団 public utility foundation

kōfu 交付 delivery; grant

kōfukin 交付金 grant; subsidy; bounty; grant-in-aid ¶ budgetary *grants-in-aid,* or *grants-in-aid* to regional budgets

kōfukokusai 交付国債 government compensation bond; grant bond

kōfukushi 高福祉 high state of welfare

kōfukushikōfutan 高福祉・高負担 higher welfare benefits even at higher costs; higher social benefits at higher costs

kōfusha 交付者 deliverer; grantor; donator

kōgai 公害 pollution; public nuisance; public hazard

情報公害 information pollution

騒音公害 sonic pollution

kōgaibōshi 公害防止 prevention of public nuisances

kōgaibōshisōchi 公害防止装置 antipollution appliance; antipollution device; antipollution preventive device

kōgaibōshiyōyūshi 公害防止用融資 antipollution loan

kōgaifukkyū 鉱害復旧 rehabilitation of mine damage

kōgaijokyosōchi 公害除去装置 antipollution appliances; antipollution devices; antipollution equipment and machinery

kōgaikanrenkabu 公害関連株 issues of companies manufacturing equipment for prevention of public nuisances

kōgaikanrentōshi 公害関連投資 antipollution investment

kōgaikyojūsha 郊外居住者 suburbanite

kogaisha 子会社 subsidiary (company) ¶ the company's wholly-owned Japanese *subsidiary* // to permit U.S. companies to set up wholly-owned *subsidiaries*

部分所有子会社 partially-owned subsidiary

非連結子会社 unconsolidated subsidiary

連結子会社 consolidated subsidiary

全部所有子会社 wholly-owned subsidiary

全額出資子会社 wholly-owned subsidiary

kogaishaginkō 子会社銀行 subsidiary bank

kogaishahaitōkin 子会社配当金 dividend from subsidiary

kogaishakabushikitōshi 子会社株式投資 stock investment to subsidiary

kogaishakashitsukekin 子会社貸付金 loan to subsidiary

kōgaiyushutsu 公害輸出 pollution export

kōgaizai 公害罪 crime relating to environmental pollution

kōgakukiki 光学機器 optical instruments

kōgakumojiyomitorisōchi 光学文字読取装置 [コン] optical character recognition; OCR

kōgakushotokusō 高額所得層 high income brackets

kōgakutekikenchi 光学的検知 optical detection

kōgakuyomitorisōchi 光学読取装置 [コン] optical mark recognition; OMR

kogatakabu 小型株 small-sized stocks

kogatanorisesshon 小型のリセッション mini-recession

kōge 高下 fluctuation; rise and fall; up and down; seesaw ¶ Price *fluctuations* were slight. // *Fluctuations* were sharpest for the international oils. // Prices *fluctuated* narrowly around horizontal trends. // to show continual *ups and downs, rises and falls* // Prices are steady *up and down* the line. // The US dollar con-

tinued to marginally *seesaw* against the yen. // [参考] The dollar was choppy in early Wednesday. // Stock, bond, and commodity prices bobbed and downed in no clear pattern.

kōgenkeiki 高原景気 leveling out (of business activity) on a high plateau

kogetsuki 焦付き [市] quiescent; inactive; quiet; still

kogetsukigashi 焦付き貸し uncollectible loan; doubtful loan; frozen loan; bad debt

kogetsukisaiken 焦付き債権 frozen credit; bad debt

kogetsukishikin 焦付き資金 locked-up capital

kogetsukishin'yōgashi 焦付き信用貸し frozen credit

kogetsukishojo 焦付き商状 stiff market

kogitte 小切手 check (=cheque) ¶ to draw a *check* on a bank // a *check* drawn to one's order // to issue a *check* for $100

遅延小切手 stale check

符号付小切手 marked check

複本小切手 duplicated check

紛失小切手 lost check

普通小切手 open check; uncrossed check

不渡り小切手 dishonored check

原本小切手 original check

銀行小切手 banker's check; bank check

偽造小切手 forged check

変造小切手 raised check

保証小切手 certified check

持参人払小切手 check to bearer

国際小切手 international check

横線小切手 crossed check

旅行(者)小切手 traveler's check

先日付小切手 post-dated check; foredated check

政府小切手　government check

指図人払小切手　check to order

支払保証小切手　certified check

支払拒絶小切手　protested check

他所払小切手　domiciled check

透字小切手　perforated check

特定線引小切手　special crossed check

kogittechō　小切手帳　check book

kogittefuridashinin　小切手振出人　check drawer

kogittesashizunin　小切手指図人　check holder

kogitteshiharainin　小切手支払人　check drawee

kogitteyokin　小切手預金　［米］checking account; ［英］cheque-deposit

kōgokeisanjiri　交互計算尻　balance of mutual accounts

kōgokeisankanjō　交互計算勘定　mutual current account

koguchi　小口　small lot

koguchiatsukai　小口扱い　small-lot consignment

koguchichūmon　小口注文　small-lot order; petty order

koguchigenkin　小口現金　petty cash

koguchigenkinsuitōbo　小口現金出納簿　petty cash-book

koguchihoken　小口保険　petty insurance

koguchikashidashi　小口貸出し　petty loan; lending in small lot; small-lot loan

koguchikin'yū　小口金融　retail banking ¶ the Bank's thrust in *retail banking* at the expense of other activities

koguchikin'yūkikan　小口金融機関　retail bank

koguchisuji　小口筋　［市］small-lot traders; pikers; little fellows

koguchitōzayokin　小口当座預金　petty current deposit

koguchiuri　小口売り　small-lot sale

koguchiyochokin　小口預貯金　petty savings

kōgyō　工業　industry; manufacturing industry

紡績・紡織・工業　spinning and weaving industry

重要工業　key industries

家内工業　domestic industry; home industry

製造工業　manufacturing industry

雑工業　miscellaneous industries

kōgyō　鉱業　mining; mining industry

kōgyō　興行　entertainment; performance

kōgyōboki　工業簿記　industrial bookkeeping

kōgyōchi　鉱業地　mining area; diggings

kōgyōchitai　工業地帯　industrial district

kōgyōchūshinchi　工業中心地　industrial center

kōgyōdanchi　工業団地　industrial complex ¶ to establish *industrial complexes*

kōgyōen　工業塩　industrial salt

kōgyōgakkō　工業学校　industrial technical school

kōgyōgasorin　工業ガソリン　industrial naphtha

kōgyōkabu　工業株　industrial shares; industrials

kōgyōkabu　鉱業株　mining shares; minings

kōgyōkagaku　工業化学　industrial chemistry

kōgyōkai　工業界　industrial world;

industrial circles

kōgyōkaikei 鉱業会計 mining accounting

kōgyōkaisha 鉱業会社 mining company

kōgyōkashakai 工業化社会 industrial society ¶ a diverse and well organized *industrial society* as in the United States

kōgyōkeiei 工業経営 industrial management; industrial operation

kōgyōken 鉱業権 mining concession; mining right

kōgyōkikai 鉱業機械 mining machinery

kōgyōkoku 工業国 industrialized country ¶ the market-economy *industrialized countries* — the OECD countries — of the West

kōgyōkumiai 工業組合 industrial guild; industrial association

kōgyōkurabu 工業倶楽部 industrial club

kōgyōkyōiku 工業教育 industrial technical education

kōgyōkyōkō 工業恐慌 industrial crisis

kōgyōkyokubuka 工業局部化 localization of industry

kōgyōnetsuyōgenshiro 工業熱用原子炉 industrial heat reactor

kōgyōritchi 工業立地 industrial orientation; industrial location

kōgyōrodōkumiai 鉱業労働組合 miners' union; mine workers' union

kōgyōsaihaichi 工業再配置 relocation of industries

kōgyōseihin 工業製品 manufactured products (=goods); products of manufacturing industries; manufacturing (industry) products; manufacture

kōgyōseihinseisanshabukkashisū

工業製品生産者物価指数 producer price index for manufactured products

kōgyōseisaku 工業政策 industrial policy

kōgyōseisan 工業生産 industrial production; industrial output; production of manufacturing industries ¶ The growth of *industrial production* edged downward. // *Industrial output* entered its usual summer slowdown. // The weakness of demand resulted in diminished levels of *industrial output.* // ［参考］ Sluggish industrial performance is hampering economic development.

kōgyōseisanbutsu 鉱業生産物 mining products

kōgyōsensasu 工業センサス census of manufactures; census of manufacturing industries

kōgyōshikenjo 工業試験場 industrial experimental station

kōgyōshōken 工業証券 industrial securities

kōgyōshoyūken 工業所有権 industrial property right; industrial property

kōgyōshūsekido 工業集積度 degree of industrial accumulation

kōgyōtegata 工業手形 industrial bill; industrial paper

kōgyōtōkeihyō 工業統計表 census of manufactures

kōgyōtoshi 工業都市 industrial city

kōgyōyakuhin 工業薬品 industrial chemicals

kohaba 小幅 narrow range; small margin ¶ Prices remain in a *narrow range.* // Prices fluctuated *narrowly.* // The U.S. unit ranged *narrowly* between 232.80 and 233.20 yen. //

Prices remained within *narrow* limits. // Price movements were *small.* // The value remained higher, but by a *reduced margin,* than a year before.

kohabamushō 小幅無償 ［証市］ fractional capital increase on a gratis basis

kohabatōraku 小幅騰落 fluctuation of a narrow range ¶ Indexes of wholesale and consumer prices have *fluctuated narrowly* around horizontal trends.

kohabaugoki 小幅動き move within narrow limits; narrow move ¶ Prices *moved within narrow limits.* // The index *moved narrowly.*

kōhaikabu 後配株 deferred stock (＝share)

kōhan 鋼板 (steel) sheets and plates

kōhanseido 公販制度 open selling system

kōhatsu 後発 latecomer ¶ *latecomers* in this line of business // The world's *latecomers* to industrialization can catch up with their forerunners.

kōhatsuhattentojōkoku 後発発展途上国 least less developed countries; LLDC

kōhei 公平 equity; equality; fairness; impartiality ¶ the degree of horizontal and vertical *equity,* within as well as between income groups, of taxation // to give *equitable* treatment to all workers // to place investors on a more *equal* footing with respect to *equality* of opportunity, insuring a fair and orderly market and adhering to just and *equitable* principles of trade

kōhin'ikō 高品位鉱 high grade ores

kōhōkatsudō 広報活動 publicity campaign; public relations; P.R. ¶ to launch an extensive *publicity campaign* to galvanize consumer action

kōhōsenden 広報宣伝 public information and propaganda

kōhōsendenkatsudo 広報宣伝活動 public information and propaganda

kōikikeizai 広域経済 great sphere economy

kōikikeizaiken 広域経済圏 economic bloc

kōin 工員 →現場職員

kōishō 後遺症 after-effect ¶ The sharp oil price rise since the oil crisis had still various *after-effects* on the economy.

kojikakaku 公示価格 posted price ¶ *posted prices* and realized prices of crude oil

kojikkarishōjō 小じっかり商状 slight steadiness ¶ The market was *slightly steady,* // The market then *steadied slightly.*

kojimari 小締り slight tightening; slight tightness

kojinbumon 個人部門 personal sector

kojinchochiku 個人貯蓄 personal savings

kojingyōshu 個人業主 simple proprietorship; sole proprietor

kojingyōshushotoku 個人業主所得 income from unincorporated enterprises

kojinhaitōshotoku 個人配当所得 personal dividend income

kojinjigyō 個人事業 proprietorship; unincorporated enterprise

kojinjigyōshuhōshū 個人事業主報酬 remuneration to proprietor

kojinkabunushi 個人株主 individual stockholder

kojinkanjō 個人勘定 households and private nonprofit institutions account

kojinkanzoyō 個人間贈与 donation between individuals

kojinkaranokaigaienoiten 個人からの海外への移転 current tranfers from persons to the rest of the world

kojinkaraseifuenoiten 個人から政府への移転 current tranfers from persons to the Government

kojinkashitsuke 個人貸付 personal loan

kojinkeieino 個人経営の owner-managed; private-managed

kojinkōshō 個人交渉 individual bargaining

kojinkyūyōchingin 個人給与・賃金 personal salaries and wages

kojinmochiiekashitsuke 個人持家貸付 loan for individual house-owner

kojinmochikabuhiritsu 個人持株比率 ratio of individual stock ownership

kojinrishishotoku 個人利子所得 personal interest income

kojinshishutsu 個人支出 personal expenditure

kojinshōhi 個人消費 personal consumption

kojinshōhishishutsu 個人消費支出 personal consumption expenditure

kojinshotoku 個人所得 personal income

kojintaishakuryōshotoku 個人貸借料所得 personal rental income

kojintegata 個人手形 private bill; personal bill

kojintekizaisan 個人的財産 personal effects

kojintōshika 個人投資家 individ-

ual investor

kojin'yokin 個人預金 private deposit; personal deposit

kojinzaisanshotoku 個人財産所得 personal income from property

kōjiukeoikeiyaku 工事請負契約 contract for construction work; construction contract

kōjo 控除 subtraction; deduction
勤労控除 earned income exemption
基礎控除 legal exemption from income tax

kojō 工場 factory; plant; mill; work; workshop; manufactory
試験工場 pilot factory; pilot plant

kōjōapāto 工場アパート apartment plant

kōjōchō 工場長 factory superintendent

kōjogaku 控除額 amount deducted

kōjōhaikibutsu 工場廃棄物 industrial waste

kōjōhaisui 工場廃水 industrial waste water; plant

kōjōheisa 工場閉鎖 lockout; closure; plant shutdown; plant closure ¶ the number of reports of *plant closures* and lay-off // West German employers threaten continued *lockouts* of striking metal workers. // A *lockout* was declared against 19,000 metal workers. // to *lock out* workers // to *close* down a factory // More *shutdowns* are scheduled, including a Rolls-Royes components factory. // Several factories have already *closed*.

kōjōkakaku 恒常価格 constant price

kōjōkanri 工場管理 factory management

kōjōkantoku 工場監督 factory manager; labor foreman; supervisor

kōjōkensetsuyōchi 工場建設用地 factory site

kōjōnaihaichi 工場内配置 plant layout

kōjōnushi 工場主 mill owner; factory owner; a factory proprietor and operator

kōjōritchi 工場立地 factory (= plant) site ¶ the difficulty of securing new plant sites

kōjōshihonka 工場資本家 factory capitalist

kōjōshotokukasetsu 恒常所得仮説 permanent income hypothesis

kōjōshukka 工場出荷 factory shipment

kōjōteki 恒常的 chronic; perennial; secular; permanent; constant ¶ the *chronic* over-borrowed position of Japanese business // the *perennial* U.S. balance-of-payments deficit // A deficit payments position has become *chronic* with the U.S.

kōjōtekichiseido 工場適地制度 system for regional allocation of factories

kōjōtekiseichōkeiro 恒常的成長経路 steady-state growth path

kōjōwatashi 工場渡し ex factory; ex mill; ex works

kōjōzaidan 工場財団 industrial foundation; factory foundation

kōjōzaika 工場在荷 mill stock; stocks with factories

kōjōzaiko 工場在庫 factory stock

kōjun'isaiken 後順位債券 junior bond

kōjun'iteitō 後順位抵当 junior mortgage

kōka 考課 merits evaluation; performance appraisal; efficiency rating merits valuation

kōka 効果 effect; impact; result ¶ The *effects* began to come through in 1984. // *Effects* are taking hold. // The step worked out its full *effect*. // to take full *effect*. // The step is producing good *results*. // a dampening *effect* on the rise in prices // magnified *effects* due to the increased power of international transmission mechanism // A Bank rate cut was decided, *effective* July 22. // The *effects* on the economy are spreading. // The contractive, or contractionary *effect* of the measure on the money supply is visible, or apparent. // The industry experienced no ill *effects* from decreasing output. // The step has not yet any far-reaching *effect* upon the market. // *effects* inadvertently caused by policies that have other objectives // to reduce or remove the trade-restricting or distorting *effects* of non-tariff measures // to offset the demand reducing *effects* of the oil situation // The recovery in output will have or negative, not positive, *effect* on the balance of payments as the year proceeds. // Accelerated depreciation tends to be more cost-*effective* than tax credits in stimulating capital outlays. // to reduce the transmission of price *effects* from one country to another // The final *impact* of a flexible monetary policy is more often pro-cyclical than anti-cyclical. // The *effects* of the measures take a relatively long time to emerge.

分裂効果 polarization effect

鎮静効果 calming effect

デフレ効果 deflationary effect

永続的効果 permanent effect

フィードバック効果 feedback

effect
逆流効果　backwash effect
ギャップ効果　gap tilt effect
波及効果　multiplied effect; ripple effect; spill over effect; spread effect; repercussion effect; propagating effect
歯止め効果　ratchet effect
反作用効果　repercussion effect
発表効果　statement effect; announcement effect
保護効果　protection effect
補完的効果　complementary effect
補正効果　compensation effect
情報効果　information effect
需要効果　demand(-inducing) effect
乗数(＝相乗)効果　multiplier effect
価格効果　price effect
拡張効果　expansion effect
告知効果　announcement effect; statement effect
規模の効果　scale effect
無形の効果　intangible effect
能力効果　capacity effect
ピグー効果　Pigou(vian) effect
累積効果　cumulative effect
再配分効果　redistribution effect
産業効果　industry effect
産出量効果　output effect
誘い水(＝呼び水)効果　pump-priming effect
生産力効果　productivity effect
心理的効果　psychological effect
浸透効果　trickling-down effect
市場破壊効果　maket-destroying effect
市場造出効果　market-creating effect
資産効果　wealth effect
所期の効果　desired effect
所得効果　income effect
収入効果　revenue effect
修正効果　ameliorative effect

即時的効果　impact effect
挺率効果　leverage effect
閉込め効果　lock-in effect
有形の効果　tangible effect
kōka 硬貨　hard money; hard currency; coin
kokabu 小株　new share
kokabuochi 子株落ち　cx new; ex allotment
kokabutsuki 子株付き　cum new
kōkagakusumoggu 光化学スモッグ　photochemical smog
kōkahakyūkeiro 効果波及経路　(effect) transmission mechanism
kōkahiyōbunseki 効果費用分析　benefit cost analysis
kōkai 公海　international waters; open sea; high seas
kōkai 公開　disclosure; [証市]public offering; marketing ¶ The Code calls for *disclosure* of information on the policies of intra-group pricing of multinational companies. // to make greater *disclosure* of bank examination reports to their customers // improper payment *disclosures* // failure to fully *disclose* material facts regarding its financial operations // an agreement calling for *disclosure* to the Bank of foreign exchange deals exceeding $5 million // The SEC's replacement cost *disclosures* were intended to give investors a better picture of companies' financial situations. // The SEC's replacing-cost *disclosure* is not required of small companies. // Large publicly-held companies have to *disclose* the cost of replacing inventories and plant. // to achieve full and fair *disclosure* of all pertinent and material facts relating to any corporate security issue // →開

示

kōkaihanbaiseido 公開販売制度
open selling system; open sales system

kōkaijō 公開状 open letter

kōkaikabu 公開株 outstanding share; publicly held stock; introduced stock

kōkaikaitsuke 公開買付［証市］
takeover (bid)

kōkaikakakuseido 公開価格制度
open price system

kōkaikikan 公開期間 open period

kōkainyūsatsu 公開入札 public bid(ding)

kōkaisei 公開性 disclosure; openness; freedom ¶ the proper limit of *openness* in government // *freedom* of information // →公開

kōkaiseinogensoku 公開性の原則
principle of disclosure

kōkaishijō 公開市場 open market; market overt ¶ Federal Reserve purchases or sales of securities in the *open market* // *open market* transactions

kōkaishijōsōsa 公開市場操作 open market operation ¶ The efficient conduct of *open market operations* requires a well performing Government securities market. // *operations* in short-term securities // The Federal Reserve extended the area of its *open market operations* to longer term securities. // the market for Treasury bills as a vehicle for *open market operations* to guide short-term money rates

kōkaiyōsen 航海用船 voyage charter; spot charter

kōkaken 硬貨圏 hard currency area

kōkamason 硬貨磨損 abrasion of

coin; wearing of coin ¶ ［参考］ worn coins; wornout coin

kōkan 交換 conversion; exchange; interchange; clearing ¶ the *conversion* of notes into gold // the *conversion* from notes to gold // to *exchange* this yen note for those American coins // to *exchange* dollars into yen // to *exchange* views with others // Goods delivered in *exchange* for money. // an *exchange* of bills // an *interchange* of views // *clearing* of bills // Money is a medium of *exchange*.

物々交換 barter; give-and-take ¶ to *barter* rum for slaves

不等価交換 unequivalent exchange

利益交換 reciprocity of benefits

手形交換 bill clearing

等価交換 equivalent exchange

kōkanataikyūshōhizai 高価な耐久消費財 high-priced durable consumer goods

kōkanhiritsu 交換比率 ratio of exchange

kōkanjiri 交換尻 clearing balance

kōkanjirikessai 交換尻決済 settlement of clearing balance

kōkanjokameiginkō 交換所加盟銀行 ［英］ clearing bank ¶ a London *clearing bank,* or a member bank of London Clearing House

kōkankachi 交換価値 value in exchange; exchange value ¶ a further appreciable reduction in the *exchange value* of the Canadian dollar in terms of the countries of Canada's principal trading partners // The *exchange value* of the U.S. dollar against the SDR was 1.03919.

kōkankanōkōsai 交換可能公債
convertible bond

kōkankanōtsūka 交換可能通貨

convertible currency

kōkankessai 交換決済 clearing (of bills); bill clearing

kōkankogitte 交換小切手 clearing bill

kōkanmochidashitegata 交換持出手形 credit exchange

kōkanmochikaeritegata 交換持帰手形 debit exchange

kōkansei 交換性 convertibility ¶ the suspension of gold *convertibility* for the dollar in August 1971 // The Venezuelan authorities have maintained full and unrestricted *convertibility* of the national currency. // The restoration of *convertibility* to a wide range of leading currencies in the 1950s.
非交換性 inconvertibility
制限付交換性 limited convertibility
対外交換性 external convertibility

kōkanten 交換点 convertibility point

kōkanzai 交換財 exchange goods

kōkanzandakahyō 交換残高表 clearing-house balance (ticket)

kokeihaikibutsu 固形廃棄物 solid waste

kōkeiki 好景気 prosperity; good times; boom ¶ The economy is enjoying *prosperity*. // when times are *good* // a *boom* in certain industries // *Boom* symptoms still predominate. // The *boom* passed its upper turning point. // →好況

kōkeikijidai 好景気時代 prosperous days; good times; boom period

kōkeikishikyō 好景気市況 booming market

kōkenshikin 購繭資金 cocoon purchasing funds

kōki 後期 latter term; second half; latter half-year

kōkigyō 公企業 public enterprise

kōkihaitō 後期配当 dividend for the second half

kōkikessan 後期決算 settlement of accounts for the latter half (year)

kōkin 公金 public money; official money; government funds

kōkinrijidai 高金利時代 era of high interest rates

kōkinriseisaku 高金利政策 dear money policy; high interest rate policy

kōkinrishikin 高金利資金 dear money

kōkin'yokin 公金預金 official deposit

kokizamichōseisaku 小刻み調整策 piecemeal approach; [外] crawling pegs; changes if necessary in the parity rate of a currency at certain fixed intervals

kokizamimushō 小刻み無償 [証市] fractional free issue; fractional free distribution

kokizamisōba 小刻み相場 split quotations

kokko 国庫 national treasury; Treasury; [英] Exchequer

kokkofutan 国庫負担 national treasury charge

kokkogenbo 国庫原簿 ledger of Treasury funds

kokkohojo 国庫補助 government subsidy; State aid

kokkohojokin 国庫補助金 state bounty

kokkokeisankamoku 国庫計算科目 sub-items of Treasury account

kokkokin 国庫金 Treasury funds; national treasury money

kokkokinfurikae 国庫金振替 transfer of Treasury funds

kokkokinfurikomiseikyū 国庫金振

込請求 application for Treasury paying-in

kokkokin'inō 国庫金移納 transfer of Treasury funds to the Government

kokkokinkumikae 国庫金組替 conversion of Treasury funds

kokkokinmiseiri 国庫金未整理 Treasury suspense account

kokkokinsōkin 国庫金送金 Treasury remittance

kokkokin'ukeharai 国庫金受払 receipt and payment of Treasury funds

kokkokin'yoyūkinkurikae 国庫金余裕金繰替 temporary transfer of Treasury surplus

kokkonaikawase 国庫内為替 intra-Treasury remittance

kokkonōfukin 国庫納付金 payment earmarked to the Government

kokkosaiken 国庫債券 Treasury bond; Treasury note; [英] Exchequer bond

国際開発協会通貨代用国庫債券 Note in Substitution for currency of the International Development Association

農地被買収者国庫債券 Non-Interest Treasury Bond for Expropriated Land Owners

kokkosaimufutankōi 国庫債務負担行為 contract authorization; acts incurring liabilities on the Treasury; contract resulting in Treasury obligation

kokkosainyūsaishutsu 国庫歳入歳出 revenue and expenditure of Treasury

kokkoshiben 国庫支弁 defrayment out of the Treasury

kokkoshishutsukin 国庫支出金 national treasury disbursement

kokkoshūnyū 国庫収入 Treasury receipt

kokkosōkin'annai 国庫送金案内 Treasury remittance order

kokkosōkin'irai 国庫送金依頼 request for Treasury remittance

kokkosōkinkawase 国庫送金為替 remittance by Treasury order

kokkosōkinkessai 国庫送金決済 Treasury remittance settlement

kokkosōkinseikyū 国庫送金請求 application for Treasury remittance

kokkoyokin 国庫預金 Treasury deposit

kokkoyoyūkinfurikae 国庫余裕金振替 Treasury surplus temporarily tranferred

kokkoyoyūkin'un'yō 国庫余裕金運用 employment of Treasury surplus

kokkyōzeichōsei 国境税調整 border tax adjustment

kōko 公庫 finance corporation; loan corporation

kōkōgyōseisan 鉱工業生産 mining and manufacturing production; industrial production

kōkōgyōseisanshisū 鉱工業生産指数 mining and manufacturing production index; index of industrial production

kōkokubaitai 広告媒体 advertising medium

kōkokudairiten 広告代理店 advertising agency; publicity agency

kōkokuhi 広告費 advertising outlays; advertisement expenditures; advertising expenditures; outlays for advertisement

kōkokusenden 広告宣伝 advertising; advertisement; publicity; public notice ¶ to *advertise* products for sale // *advertisement* charges // expenses for *advertisement*

kokuchikōka 告知効果 announcement effect; statement effect

kokuchitekikōkoku 告知的広告 informative advertising

kokudokaihatsu 国土開発 national development

kokudokeikaku 国土計画 national land planning

kokueibōeki 国営貿易 state trading

kokueisangyō 国営産業 state(-run) industry

kokueki 国益 national interest

kokufu 国富 national wealth

kokufukusuru 克服する defeat; surmount; tide over; overcome ¶ *defeat* of inflation // to *defeat* inflation // to *surmount* the spiraling inflation // to *tide* the economy *over* the monetary upheavals // [参考] to breast itself to the crisis

kōkūhoken 航空保険 aviation insurance

kokuji 告示 notification
大蔵省告示第○号 [日] Notification (Ministry of Finance Ordinance No...)

kokujisaikōkinri 告示最高金利 published ceiling interest rate

kōkūkamotsu 航空貨物 air cargo

kōkūkamotsuunsōjō 航空貨物運送状 air way bill; air consignment note

kōkūkiosenbutsu 航空機汚染物 aircraft pollutant; airliner pollutant

kōkūkonsaikamotsu 航空混載貨物 consolidated air cargo

kokumin 国民 nation; people ¶ to guide the *nation* through the economic upheaval // the awakening *nations* of the East // an exporting *nation* // industrialized *nations* // cooperation among the *nations* of the world // to arouse the *people* to the importance of fiscal retrenchment // to bring the *peoples* of the Pacific together into better understanding // the general or common run of *people*

kokuminbunpaibun 国民分配分 national dividend

kokuminchochiku 国民貯蓄 national savings

kokuminfukushi 国民福祉 national welfare; nation's welfare; welfare ¶ amelioration of *welfare* // step-up *national welfare* buildup // expansion of *welfare* facilities

kokuminfukushishihyō 国民福祉指標 net national welfare; NNW

kokuminhoken 国民保険 national insurance

kokuminjunseisan 国民純生産 net national product; NNP

kokuminkeizai 国民経済 national economy; nation's economy

kokuminkeizaikeisan 国民経済計算 national economic accounting; national economic budget; nation's economic budget

kokuminkeizaikeisantaikei 国民経済計算体系 system of national accounts; SNA

kokuminkenkōhoken 国民健康保険 national health insurance

kokuminnenkin 国民年金 national pension (for the self-employed)

kokuminseikatsu 国民生活 national life; people's life ¶ stabilization and improvement of the *national life* // improvement of the quality of the *people's life*

kokuminseikatsudaiichishugi 国民生活第一主義 "people's living standard first" principle

kokuminseikatsuyūsen 国民生活優先 "priority for the people's livelihood"

kokuminshihon 国民資本 national capital

kokuminshihonkanjō 国民資本勘定 national capital account

kokuminshotoku 国民所得 national income

分配国民所得 disposable national income; national income distributed

実質国民所得 real national income; national income in real terms

貨幣国民所得 money national income

名目国民所得 nominal national income; national income in nominal terms

産業源泉別国民所得 national income by industrial origin

生産国民所得 productive national income; national income produced

市場価格表示国民所得 national income at market prices

要素価格表示国民所得 national income at factor prices

kokuminshotokubunpaikanjō 国民所得分配勘定 distribution account of national income

kokuminshotokubunseki 国民所得分析 national income analysis

kokuminshotokuhyōjunhōshiki 国民所得標準方式 system of national accounting (of the United Nations); SNA

kokuminshotokukanjō 国民所得勘定 national income account

kokuminshotokukeisan 国民所得計算 national income accounting

kokuminshotokunokokusaitan'i 国民所得の国際単位 international unit of national income; IU

kokuminshotokutōkei 国民所得統計 national income statistics

kokuminsōseisan 国民総生産 gross national product; GNP

kokuminsōshisan 国民総資産 gross national wealth

kokuminsōshishutsu 国民総支出 gross national expenditure; GNE

kokumintaishakutaishōhyō 国民貸借対照表 national balance sheet; Balance-Sheet Account for the Nation

kokumintekigōi 国民的合意 national consensus

kokumintōhyō 国民投票 referendum; plebiscite

kokumin'yūsen 国民優先 national preference

kokumotsuseisan 穀物生産 grain production

kokunaikokusaikinkō 国内・国際均衡 internal and external equilibrium (=equilibria)

kokunaishin'yōjō 国内信用状 local credit; domestic (letter) credit

kokunaishin'yōzōkagaku 国内信用増加額 domestic credit expansion; D.C.E.

kokunaisōseisan 国内総生産 gross domestic product; GDP ¶ Between 1959 and 1974, the manufacturing sector's real *gross domestic production* rose at an average annual rate of about 13 percent. // The manufacturing sector's share in total *GDP* rose from 23 per cent in 1968 to 35 per cent in 1984.

kokunaisōshihonkeisei 国内総資本形成 gross domestic capital formation

kokunaitaigaikinkō 国内対外均衡 domestic and international equilibria

kokurenbuntankin 国連分担金 United Nations assessments

kokurenkaihatsunojūnenkeikaku 国連開発の10年計画 United Nations Development Decade Program

kokurenkaitenkikin 国連回転基金 United Nations Revolving Fund

kokurenkeizaitokubetsusōkai 国連経済特別総会 Special Session of U.N. General Assembly for Development and International Cooperation

kokurenkokuminshotokuhyōjunhō shiki 国連国民所得標準方式 system of national account of United Nations; SNA

kokurenningenkankyōkaigi 国連人間環境会議 United Nations conference on the human environment

kokurenningenkyojūkaigi 国連人間居住会議 United Nations conference on human settlements

kokurenshigensōkai 国連資源総会 special session of the United Nations general assembly (in 1974)

kokuritsuginkō 国立銀行 state bank; national bank

kokusai 国債 national debt; government bond; government indebtedness; government obligation; State loan ¶ The *national debt* was about $42,000,000, including interest in default. // In its first overseas *loan* issue since World War II, the Government of Japan floated, on February 18, 1959, $30 million *bonds* on the New York market. // to offer $5 million of 3-year *bonds* // The New Zealand Government issued in London a $5 million *loan*, 1978-82, at 96½, and bearing interest at 5¼ percent. // The Finance Ministry floated a 15-year *State loan* of F.1,500 million, which is priced at

par and carries a coupon of 8%. // launching of a new *state bond* issue, the seventh *state loan* issued by way of tender

長期国債 long-term government securities

外貨国債 government bond in foreign currency

交付国債 delivery bond

短期国債 short-term government securities

特別減税国債 special tax reduction bond

kokusaibaibai 国債売買 purchase and sale of government bonds

kokusaibaibaitesūryō 国債売買手数料 commission for purchase and sale of government bonds

kokusaibaikyakueki 国債売却益 profit from sale of government bonds

kokusaibōeki 国際貿易 international trade

kokusaiboshūhikiukedan 国債募集引受団 (international) syndicate; consortium ¶ A *syndicate* of banks and securities companies was formed to underwrite the loan. // a *consortium* headed (=led) by Credit Lyonnais

kokusaibungyō 国際分業 international division of labor; international specialization

kokusaichūkeibōeki 国際中継貿易 international intermediary trade

kokusaidairiten 国債代理店 agency for government bonds

kokusaidaiyōshōsho 国債代用証書 substitute certificate for government bonds

kokusaidokusen 国際独占 international monopoly

kokusaifukkōkaihatsuginkōtsūka-

daiyōkokkosaiken 国際復興開発銀行通貨代用国庫債券 note in substitution for currency of the International Bank for Reconstruction and Development

kokusaifukkōkaihatsuginkōkashi-tsukekin 国際復興開発銀行貸付金 loan to the International Bank for Reconstruction and Development

kokusaifukuhon'isei 国際複本位制 international bimetallism

kokusaiganrikinshiharaitoriatsu-kaiten 国債元利金支払取扱店 paying agency for government bonds

kokusaigengaku 国債減額 cut in government bond issue

kokusaigenzaidaka 国債現在高 outstanding bonds

kokusaiginkōkankin'yūdētatsū-shinkyōkai 国際銀行間金融データ通信協会 Society for Worldwide Interbank Financial Telecommunication; SWIFT

kokusaigyōmu 国際業務 international business; international operations ¶ Many commercial banks became over-extended in their *international operations*

kokusaihaki 国際破棄 repudiation of national debt

kokusaihakkōdaka 国債発行高 government bond issue

kokusaihika 国際比価 international parity

kokusaihikaku 国際比較 country-by-country comparison; intercountry comparison; cross-country comparison ¶ *cross-country comparisons* of balance-of-payments performance // *comparisons across countries* for a given period

kokusaihikiuke 国債引受 under-writing of government securities

kokusaihikiukedan 国際引受団 international syndicate; international consortium international underwring group

kokusaihōkikanshū 国際法規・慣習 international laws and practices

kokusaihyōjundō 国際標準銅 international standard copper

kokusaiizondo 国債依存度 rate of reliance on bond issues; rate of dependence of budget revenue on government bond issues; percentage of the national bond issue in the total general account revenues ¶ ［参考］ to end dependence on the floating of bonds to cover the budget deficit which now accounts for nearly 40 percent of total budget financing

kokusaika 国際化 internationalization ¶ Japan's economy amidst *internationalization* // to *internationalize* the use of the yen // the constantly increasing *internationalization* of banking business // the *internationalization* of corporate business activities by means of foreign direct investment

kokusaikabuken 国際株券 international stock

kokusaikachi 国際価値 international value

kokusaikaikeikijunnikansurushui-sho 国際会計基準に関する趣意書 preface to statements of international accounting standards

kokusaikanri 国債管理 national debt management ¶ Britain's *debt management* strategy which involves stretching out the country's external debt repayments.

kokusaikanriseisaku 国債管理政策 debt management policy

kokusaikaruteru 国際カルテル international cartel

kokusaikawase 国際為替 international exchange

kokusaikeisatsugun 国際警察軍 international police forces

kokusaikeizaikyōkai 国際経済協会 international economic cooperation

kokusaikeizaikyōryokukaigi 国際経済協力会議 Conference on International Economic Cooperation

kokusaikessaitsūka 国際決済通貨 international settlement currencies; money for international settlement

kokusaikikan'enobuntankin 国際機関への分担金 contribution to an international institution

kokusaikikō 国際機構 international organization

kokusaikinkō 国際均衡 international equilibrium

kokusaikin'yū 国際金融 international finance (=banking)

kokusaikin'yūkikanshusshi 国際金融機関出資 subscription to international financial instiutions

kokusaikin'yūseido 国際金融制度 international financial system ¶ the integration of the developing countries in a sound *international financial system*

kokusaikin'yushijō 国際金融市場 international monetary market; IMM; international financial (=banking) market; international money market

kokusaikogitte 国際小切手 international check

kokusaikōgyōkaigi 国際工業会議 World Engineering Congress

kokusaikōhō 国際公法 international public law

kokusaikyōsōryoku 国際競争力 →競争力

kokusaimeigara 国際銘柄 [証市] internationally-known issue

kokusaimihon'ichi 国際見本市 international trade fair

kokusainyūsatsu 国際入札 international bidding; international tender

kokusaiōbo 国債応募 subscription to government securities

kokusairibaraiteishi 国債利払停止 suspension of interest payment on government bonds

kokusairisoku 国債利息 interest on government securities

kokusairōdōkaigi 国際労働会議 international labor convention

kokusairyūdōsei 国際流動性 international liquidity

kokusaisaimu 国際債務 international indebtedness

kokusaiseirikikin 国債整理基金 national debt consolidation fund

kokusaishihō 国際私法 international private law

kokusaishihongōdō 国際資本合同 (international) consortium ¶ to establish a *consortium* bank with three participating banks // An *international consortium* of banks signed a credit agreement for $600 million with the international investment bank. // A *consortium* of international banks granted the Spanish National Institute of Industry a five year loan of $30 million.

kokusaishihon'idō 国際資本移動 international flow of capital; international capital movement ¶ *international* long-term and short-term *capital movements*

kokusaishihonshijō 国際資本市場 international capital market

kokusaishijōkakaku 国際市場価格 world market price; international market price

kokusaishisan'un'yō 国際資産運用 international asset management

kokusaishōhin 国際商品 internationally traded commodities; international merchandise; world market commodities ¶ The wholesale price index (in terms of U.S. dollars) of 37 basic *commodities traded* internationally increased.

kokusaishōhinkyōtei 国際商品協定 international commodity agreement

kokusaishōka 国債消化 absorption of government bonds; digestion of government bonds ¶ [参考] receptive conditions for sales of government paper outside the banking system

kokusaishōkanshūhō 国際商慣習法 international commercial custom

kokusaishōken 国債証券 government bond certificate

kokusaishōken 国際証券 international securities

kokusaishūshi 国際収支 balance of payments; balance of international payments; international balance of payments; international balance of accounts; balance of external payments; external payments balance ¶ The present configuration of the U.S. *balance of payments* is not an aberration. // The *balance of payments* remained in equilibrium; was close to equilibrium; continued to be favorable; turned in Mexico's favor; had improved sufficiently to yield accretions to exchange reserves; or was in surplus by $22 billion. // The over-all *balance of payments* position was strong and continues in comfortable surplus in 1975. // Singapore reduced its adverse *balance* from $M619 million to $M384 million. // The deterioration in the goods and services account of the *balance of payments* has accelerated during the year. // The United Arab Republic is experiencing *balance of payments* difficulties. // [参考] Denmark's net foreign exchange position vis-à-vis the hard currency area strengthened. // Japan's trade and overall payments have continued to burgeon. // the restoration of viability to a payments position // payments difficulties due to developments in the rest of the world // to produce a sustainable external position

kokusaishūshichōseikatei 国際収支調整過程 adjustment process of the balance of payments

kokusaishūshijiri 国際収支尻 balance of payments; external account ¶ The Dutch currents-account *balance of payment* was moving back from deficit towards equilibrium with the prospect of a modest surplus in 1981. // Britain's swing from deficit to surplus of the current account of its *balance of payments.* // to reduce the U.S. current-account *balance-of-payments* deficit // a marked improvement in the *external account* compared with last year

kokusaishūshikōzō 国際収支構造 balance of payments structure

kokusaishūshinotenjō 国際収支の天井 ceiling of international payments capacity; balance-of-payments constraint (on growth) set by the ability of exports to expand ¶ The *"ceiling" of* Japan's *interna-*

tional payments capacity has been raised.

kokusaishūshisetsudo 国際収支節度 balance of payments discipline

kokusaishūshitōkei 国際収支統計 balance of payments statistics

kokusaitaishaku 国際貸借 international debits and credits; international indebtedness

kokusaitan'i 国際単位 international unit

kokusaitanpotegatawaribiki 国際担保手形割引 discount of bills with government bonds as collateral

kokusaitekiseisai 国際的制裁 international sanction

kokusaitekishōjitorihiki 国際的商事取引 international commercial transaction

kokusaitoriatsukaitesūryō 国債取扱手数料 commission for government bond business; commission for government securities business

kokusaitorihiki 国際取引 international commerce; trans-border commerce

kokusaitorihikikanshū 国際取引慣習 international commercial usage; international commercial practice; customary practice in international commercial transaction

kokusaitōrokubo 国債登録簿 register of government bonds

kokusaitoshi 国際都市 cosmopolitan city

kokusaitōshi 国際投資 international investment

kokusaitōshiginkō 国際投資銀行 international investment bank

kokusaitōshin 国際投信 international investment trust; off-shore mutual funds

kokusaitsūka 国際通貨 interna-

tional currency; international money

kokusaitsūkachōsei 国際通貨調整 international currency realignment; international realignment of currencies

kokusaitsūkafuan 国際通貨不安 international currency anxiety (= uneasiness; uncertainty; disturbance; upheaval; turbulence; unrest); international monetary turmoil ¶ The *unrest* on the *international currency* scene resulted in an inflow of DM 7 milliard.

kokusaitsūkakaigi 国際通貨会議 international monetary conference

kokusaitsūkakikinhoyūenkakitakusho 国際通貨基金保有円貨寄託所 depository for the IMF holdings of Japanese yen

kokusaitsūkakikinkashitsukekin 国際通貨基金貸付金 loan to the International Monetary Fund

kokusaitsūkakikintsūkadaiyōshōken 国際通貨基金通貨代用証券 note in substitution for currency of the International Monetary Fund

kokusaitsūkakikō 国際通貨機構 international monetary organization ¶ its fundamental role as the worldwide *international monetary organization* with the aim of maintaining a one-world international monetary system

kokusaitsūkamondai 国際通貨問題 international monetary problems

kokusaitsūkaseido 国際通貨制度 international (=world) monetary (= currency) system ¶ the world-wide organization with the aim of maintaining a one-world *international monetary system*

kokusaitsūkataisei 国際通貨体制 international monetary system ¶ a successful evaluation of the *international monetary system*

kokusaitsūshō 国際通商 international commerce

kokusaiun'yōshikin 国債運用資金 fund for operation of government bonds

kokusaiwaribikiryō 国債割引料 discount on government securities

kokusan'enerugī 国産エネルギー home-grown energy

kokusanhin 国産品 domestically made goods; domestic goods; home-made articles

kokusanhiritsu 国産比率 domestic content; local content

kokuseichōsa 国勢調査 national census; population census

kokusōchitai 穀倉地帯 farm belt; granary

kokuteizeiritsu 国定税率 national tariff; autonomous tariff

kokuyūkaginkō 国有化銀行 state-owned bank; nationalized bank

kokuyūkasangyō 国有化産業 state-owned industry, nationalized industry ¶ to cut back spending by national and local governments and *state-owned industry*

kokuyūkinkoseido 国有金庫制度 national cash chest system

kokuyūzaisan 国有財産 national assets

kokuzeifukazei 国税付加税 surtax on national tax

kokuzeishikinshiharaimeireikan 国税資金支払命令官 national tax fund disbursing official

kokuzeishūnōkanri 国税収納官吏 national tax receiving official

kokuzeishūnōmeireikan 国税収納命令官 national tax collector

kokyaku 顧客 clientele; customer; client ¶ the *clientele* of banks, or *customers* of banks // the *client* banks of the central bank // bankers furnish references about their *customers,* their means, standing and respectability // to lose regular *customers*

kokyakumochikabuseido 顧客持株制度 customer ownership system

kokyakunohimitsu 顧客の秘密 customer confidentiality ¶ the lack of evidence of breaches of *customer confidentiality*

kōkyō 好況 boom; period of prosperity; euphoria ¶ The *boom* in Sweden continues. // three years of *boom* // the third *boom* year after the recession // The *boom* reached full force. // pronounced *boom* conditions // to *boom* to a full measure of *prosperity* // a year of economic *prosperity* // business *boom* spearheaded by investment // The ten *euphoric* years of world trade from 1963 to 1973. // →好景気

永続的好況　secular boom
一時的好況　temporary boom

kōkyōbumon 公共部門 public sector

kōkyōbumonkariirejuyō 公共部門借入需要 public sector borrowing requirement; PSBR ¶ The United Kingdom will limit the *public sector borrowing requirement (PSBR)* to £8.5 billion. // The *public sector borrowing requirement* has shot up to nearly 13% of nominal GNP. // The *public-sector borrowing requirement* will rise to £10 billion. // A *PSBR* of £5 bilion for 1979-80 could be achieved by increasing tobacco and alcohol duties. // The government's objective is to reduce the *public-sector borrowing requirement (PSBR)* without deflating the economy.

kōkyōbumonshudōgatakēzai 公共部門主導型経済 economy led by public sector

kōkyōdantai 公共団体 public body; public entity
地方公共団体 local public authorities; local public body; local public entity; municipality

kōkyōfukushi 公共福祉 public welfare

kōkyōhōjin 公共法人 public service corporation

kōkyōjigyō 公共事業 public utilities; public works; public enterprise; public service

kōkyōjigyōdantai 公共事業団体 public utility corporation

kōkyōjigyōkankeihi 公共事業関係費 public works expenses

kōkyōjigyōkeikaku 公共事業計画 public works projects

kōkyōkigyō 公共企業 public corporation; public utility company; public enterprise

kōkyōkoyōkeikaku 公共雇用計画 public-employment program ¶ The addition to *public-employment program* workers totaled 250,000.

kōkyōryōkin 公共料金 public utility rates; public utilities charges ¶ to fix the *rates* which *utilities* can charge for ...

kōkyōsābisu 公共サービス public services ¶ Most poor people have limited access to such *public services* as education, healthcare, and water supplies.

kōkyōseiryōkin 公共性料金 publicly fixed rates

kōkyōshijō 好況市場 [市] active market

kōkyōshisetsu 公共施設 public utility

kōkyōshishutsu 公共支出 public expenditure

kōkyōtekiyokubō 公共的欲望 public want

kōkyōtōshi 公共投資 public investment; investment in public utilities

kōkyōtōshishudōgatakeizai 公共投資主導型経済 economy led by social overhead capital

kōkyōzai 公共財 public goods

kōkyōzaisan 公共財産 public property

kōkyūhin 高級品 products of high technology and sophistication

kōkyūimin 恒久移民 permanent migration

kōkyūshōhizai 高級消費財 luxurious consumer goods

komai 古米 long stored rice

komāsharupēpā コマーシャル・ペーパー commercial paper

kōmitsudokeizaishakai 高密度経済社会 high-density economy and society

kōmitsudoshūsekikairo 高密度集積回路 large-scale integration

komoditifurōbunseki コモディティ・フロー分析 commodity flow analysis

komodoshi 小戻し [市] slight (= moderate) recovery; some rally ¶ Steels led a *slight* market *recovery* in heavy trading. // There was *some recovery* of share prices. // The recession showed some improvement relieved by a *slight rally* among aircrafts. // Coppers *rallied slightly*. // The market *recovered moderately*. // [参考] Oils recouped some of the losses.

kōmoku 項目 item; component ¶ The largest *item* in the budget is net payment to the states and local authorities. // Other *components* of domestic demand decelerated. // Exports of goods and services were the only dynamic *component* of overall real demand. // major demand *components* // to aid new cost *components* to enterprises' profitability planning

komyunitirirēshon コミュニティ・リレーション community relations; CR

konbināto コンビナート giant interlocking production complex; industrial combine; complex; ¶ a petrochemical *complex* // *combined* (=linked) business operation of related corporations

konbinēshondīru コンビネーション・ディール combination deal

konbiniensufūzu コンビニエンス・フーズ convenience foods

konbiniensusutoa コンビニエンス・ストア convenience store; CVS

kondorachefunonami コンドラチェフの波 Kondratieff cycle; Kondratieff's wave

kōnetsuhi 光熱費 fuel and light expenses; fuel and lighting costs

konfidensu コンフィデンス confidence ¶ Consumer surveys have indicated some improvement in *confidence*. // Stock prices, another indicator of *confidence*, have continued to rise briskly. // The bond market became firmer since investors regained *confidence* following this government step. // The market passed through a crisis of *confidence*. // The *confidence* of investors is being strengthened by the downward trend of interest rates abroad. // The mounting *confidence* of the business community appears to have given new impetus to stockbuilding. // Business *confidence* as well as people's *confidence* was shaken. // *Confidence* in the markets has improved greatly. // more cautious attitudes toward expanding commitments after the mid-year crisis in *confidence* // a considerable restoration of *confidence* in the markets // a return of *confidence* in international markets // the savers' *confidence* in the financial institutions // It would pose a threat to consumer and business *confidence*.

kongōkanzei 混合関税 mixed tariff

kongōsenryaku 混合戦略 mixed strategy

konguromāchanto コングロマーチャント conglo-merchant

konguromaritto コングロマリット conglomerate

kōninkaikeishi 公認会計士 certified public accountant; CPA

koninkaikeishinoikensho 公認会計士の意見書 opinion of independent certified public accountants

konomi 好み taste; predilection ¶ diversification of consumer's *tastes* // The 1920's witnessed a radical change in the public *taste* for securities. // to respond to popular *tastes* // the highly sophisticated public *tastes* // the growing *predilection* of borrowers for low-interest, yen syndicated loans

konpyūtāriyōgijutsu コンピューター利用技術 development of software for computers

konpyūtāsensō コンピューター戦争

computerized war

konran 混乱 confusion; chaos; erratic state; disturbance; dislocation; disorder ¶ The world sugar trade has been thrown into *confusion by* recent contracts for massive Philippine sugar sales to big American refiners. // The country's economy is in a state of *chaos.* // Sugar trade is in *chaos.* // to be in an *erratic state* // The economic *dislocation* caused by the war became apparent. // international currency *disturbances* // The period of exchange-market *disorder* ended. // The value of sterling, falling to an unjustified level, caused *disorderly* market conditions. // Inflation will end in some major economic, social and political *disorders* so severe as to compel solutions. // [参考] The international economy was beset by severe payments imbalances. // →動揺

konsarutingusērusu コンサルティング・セールス consulting sales

konsorukōsai コンソル公債 [英] Consols; Consolidated Fund; Consolidated Annuity

kontenasen コンテナ船 container ship

kontenayusō コンテナ輸送 containerized transportation

kōnyūkeikaku 購入計画 plan for purchase ¶ Consumers have scaled down their *plans for purchase* of new cars.

konzetsu 根絶 eradication ¶ Inflation was progressively reduced and finally *eradicated*.

kōreika 高齢化 aging ¶ The *aging* of the intra-enterprise workforce proceeds. // the progressing *aging* of Japanese labor force composition

kōreishimin 高齢市民 senior citizen

koresonmonetaria コレソン・モネタリア monetary correction

kōri 高利 high interest rate; high rate of interest; usury

kōrigashi 高利貸し usurer; usurious man ¶ the anti-*usury* law

kōrimawari 好利回り good yield

kōritsu 効率 efficiency ¶ to increase the efficiency of funds
   限界効率 marginal efficiency
   保証効率 guaranteed efficiency
   経営効率 management efficiency
   経済効率 economic efficiency
   資金効率 efficiency of fund operation
   相対効率 relative efficiency

kōritsukishasai 高利付社債 high-interest-bearing debenture

kōritsutekiyō 高率適用 supplementary interest charge; higher interest charge on banks

kōritsutekiyōgendogaku 高率適用限度額 limit of application of higher interest rates

koroainokakaku 頃合いの価格 moderate price; reasonable price

korogashi ころがし roll-over ¶ Euro-currency loans are largely financed on a *roll-over* basis. // to refinance the extensions of the maturities of Euro-credits on a *roll-over* basis // The loan is on a three-month *roll-over,* rather than the usual six months. // to ask creditors to *roll over* about $2.6 billion in short-term debts // Much of short-term bank credit is *rolled over* indefinitely.

korogashirōn ころがしローン roll-over lending ¶ 5 year roll-over lending on mortgage

kōromēkā 高炉メーカー blast furnace steel maker

koronbokeikaku コロンボ計画 Colombo Plan

kōru コール call loan; call money; money at call

月越物コール overmonth; overmonth-end loan

無条件物コール unconditional; unconditional call loan

翌日物コール overnight; overnight loan

kōrudeaizandaka コール出合残高 call transactions made; call turnover made

kōruhibu コール日歩 call rate; perdiem rate for call loan

koruhōzu コルホーズ kolk(h)oz

kōrumanē コール・マネー call money; call loan ¶ to borrow or lend *call money* (=a call loan)

kōrurēto コール・レート call-money rate; call (loan) rate ¶ to raise *call-money rates* by 0.125% for overnight money and 4.25% for unconditional money with immediate effect // *rates* on *call money* (= call loans)*

koruresukanjō コルレス勘定 correspondent account

koruresukankei コルレス関係 correspondent relation(ship)

koruresukeiyaku コルレス契約 correspondent contract (=arrangement) ¶ A bank allowed to make a *correspondent contract.*

海外コルレス overseas correspondents

国内コルレス domestic correspondents (in Japan)

korusetto コルセット ［英］ ¶ The Chancellor brought back the so-called "*corset*" to limit the ability of banks to raise fresh money. // Banks are squeezed financially by the *corset*. // The banks increased their lending by 6.5% without splitting the *corset*. // Credit cards are outside the scope of the *corset* controls.

kōrushijō コール市場 call market; call loan market; call money market

kōrutoriire コール取入れ seeking funds on the call money market

kōryū 交流 exchange; interchange; intercourse

文化交流 cultural exchange

人事交流 personnel interchange

経済交流 economic intercourse ¶ advantages of free *economic intercourse*

kōsa 公差 tolerance; permissible limit of tolerance ¶ *tolerance* on the weight

kōsahiritsu 交叉比率 ratio of gross profit to inventory investment

kōsai 公債 public loan; public bond; public debt; State and local government debt; public authorities' debt; (=indebtedness); government debt ¶ Wars breed *public debts.* // The *debt* of the *public authorities* rose to DM 325.2 billion in 1977. // The new *indebtedness* of the federal *authorities* was up by 18% to a total of DM 147.9 billion.

米貨払公債 U.S. dollar bond

英貨払公債 sterling bond

永久公債 perpetual loan; funded debt

五分利公債 5 percent bond; fives

軍事公債 war bond

自由公債 liberty bond

無記名公債 blank bond

無利子公債 passive bond

利付公債 active bond

流動公債 unfunded debt; floating

loan
三分半利公債 3½% bond
整理公債 consolidated bond; consols
担保付公債 secured bond
登録公債 registered bond
有期公債 terminable bond
kōsaihaki 公債破棄 repudiation of public debt
kōsaihakkō 公債発行 issuance of bond; bond flotation; flotation of loan; issuance of government securities; flotation of government bonds ¶ proceeds of *Government securities issues* // The *Government* offered publicly in New York an *issue* of $27.5 million, 5½ percent *bonds* (due in 1980) at 97.75.
kōsaihi 公債費 national debt service expenditure
kōsaihi 交際費 (business) entertainment expenditure; expense account; table money
kōsainokarikae 公債の借換え conversion of loan
kōsairishi 公債利子 interest on government securities ¶ Fund for Payment of *Interest on Government Securities* // [参考] The loan carries an interest coupon of 8 percent per annum.
kōsaiseiri 公債整理 consolidation of public loans
kōsaishijō 公債市場 bond market
kōsaishōkan 公債償還 redemption of bond; redemption of government securities ¶ funds for *redemption of government securities*
kōsaishoyūsha 公債所有者 bondholder
kosakunin 小作人 tenant (farmer); share cropper
kōsakutan'i 耕作単位 tillage unit

kōsei 構成 structure; composition ¶ The debt *structure* of the Bank consists primarily of long-term and intermediate-term obligations. // the age *structure* of the population // a drift in the currency *composition* of the Euro-market // based on the age-sex *composition* of the labor force in 1976 // to explain the commodity *composition* of trade // The major *compositional* change on the expenditures side of the budget. // the faulty asset *structure* of many fringe banks // to give them more flexibility in determing the *composition* of their assets
kōseibōeki 公正貿易 fair trade
kōseichingin 公正賃金 just wage; fair wage
koseichōkigyō 高成長企業 high growth enterprise
kōseihi 構成比 composition ratio; percentage composition (=distribution); component ratio; distribution ratio ¶ the *composition ratio* of employees by industry // the *percentage composition* of products // [参考] The highest representation of nationals was in agriculture.
kōseihinmoku 構成品目 commodities component ¶ The non-food *commodities component* of the index rose more slowly than the average.
kōseikakaku 公正価格 fair price
kōseikanshūkisoku 公正慣習規則 rules of fair practice
kōseikettei 更正決定 reassessment ¶ to *reassess* the tax
kōseikyōsōkiyaku 公正競争規約 fair competition rule
kōseina 好勢な [市] cheerful
kōseinenkinhoken 厚生年金保険 employees pension insurance

kōseishikinkashitsuke 更生資金貸付 rehabilitation loan; resuscitation loan

kōseishisetsu 厚生施設 recreational facilities

kōseishōsho 公正証書 notarial deed

kōseitorihikikanshū 公正取引慣習 fair trade practice

kōseiyōso 構成要素 component; constituent ¶ major *components* of the wholesale price index // The biggest *components* of the rapid rise in consumer prices have been food and fuel. // principal demand *components* // The raw materials *component* of the U.S. wholesale price index has soared nearly 20%. // Other *components* of domestic demand decelerated. // the *component* contributing most to the decline of the index // other *components* depressing the index // Stock prices were the only *component* on the plus side of the index. // Industrial output is the major *constituent* of the overall growth of the economy.

kosenshūshū 古銭収集 numismatics

kōsha 公社 public corporation

kōshasai 公社債 bonds; bonds and debentures; public and corporate bonds; public and corporate loans; government bonds and corporate debentures

kōshasaihikiukenin 公社債引受人 bond underwriter ¶ *Bond Underwriters'* Association

kōshasaijōjōsōba 公社債上場相場 rates of listed bonds

kōshasaishijō 公社債市場 bonds and debentures market; bond market

kōshasaitanpokashitsuke 公社債担保貸付 loan secured by government bonds or corporate debentures

kōshasaitanpokin'yū 公社債担保金融 bond collateral loan

kōshasaitōshishintaku 公社債投資信託 bond investment trust; open-end bond trust; open-end bond investment trust

kōshin 更新 ［外］ renewal (of exchange contract)

kōshin 高進 surge; increase; rise ¶ unallayed fears of a fresh *surge* of inflation

kōshinbi 更新日 rollover date; refix date; reset date

kōshinchiiki 後進地域 underdeveloped area; backward areas

kōshinkoku 後進国 underdeveloped country; nonindustrial country; less-advanced country; developing country

kōshinsei 後進性 backwardness

kōshintōshi 更新投資 replacement investment

kōshitsugyōjidai 高失業時代 heavy unemployment period

kōshō 交渉 bargain(ing); negotiation
団体交渉 collective bargain
個人交渉 individual bargain
統一交渉 multi-employer bargain

kōshōnin 公証人 notary public ¶ attestation of *notary public*

kōshōninnoninshō 公証人の認証 attestation of notary public

kōshōnoba 交渉の場 negotiating forum

koshōtsukifunanishōken 故障付船荷証券 foul B/L

kōshūeiseisābisu 公衆衛生サービス public health service

kōshūeki 高収益 fast profit

kōshūjūran 公衆縦覧 public inspection

kōsōbiru 高層ビル high rise building

kōsōjūtaku 高層住宅 high rise apartment house

kōsokōka 公租公課 taxes and other public charges

kōsokujikan 拘束時間 nominal hours; binding hours

kōsokukiokusōchi 高速記憶装置 [コン] high speed memory; random access memory

kōsokuseiyokin 拘束性預金 derivative deposit

kōsuijun 高水準 high level; high plateau ¶ to level out at a *high level* // Production has been leveling off on a *high plateau.*

kōsuijunjizoku 高水準持続 maintenance of a high level

kosumomoderu コスモ・モデル comprehensive system model

kosuto コスト cost ¶ This wage round will boost Britain's unit labor *cost* further.

kosutodaka コスト高 high cost of production; high production costs ¶ [参考] at an enormous cost // at considerable cost // at a heavy cost

kosutohikisage コスト引下げ reduction (=cut-down; lowering) of cost ¶ to *reduce the cost* of production // to *cut down* the production *costs* // to *lower* operation *costs* // to keep *down* the *cost* of labor

kosutoishiki コスト意識 cost consciousness; awareness of costs; cost-sensitiveness ¶ Increased competition forced banks to become increasingly *cost-conscious.* // Heightened competitive forces compelled

deposit institutions to be more *cost-sensitive.* // Many more consumers are now *aware of the costs* involved in borrowing money. // greater *awareness of* credit *costs*

kōtai 後退 [市]pulling-back ¶ The stock market *pulled back* Monday, yielding to continuing concern over rising interest rates.

kōtaihojūritsu 交替補充率 replacement rate

kōtaikinmuseido 交替勤務制度 shift system ¶ a mill operating on a three-*shift system,* or on three 8-hour *shifts* // to work in *shifts* of eight hours

kotei 固定 fixing; fixation; tie-up; lock-up

kōtei 公定 official; legal; fixed

kōteibuai 公定歩合 official discount rate; official rate; Bank rate ¶ to fix, change, raise, and reduce the *official discount rate* of the central bank // The *official discount rate* of the Bank of Japan was reduced to 6.57 percent, effective Jan. 26. // The cut in the *Bank rate* was designed to correct the discrepancy between the *official* and market *rates.*

kōteibuaiseisaku 公定歩合政策 discount policy; bank rate policy

kōteibunseki 工程分析 process study

kōteichika 公定地価 assessed value of land

koteichōkitekigōritsu 固定長期適合率 ratio of fixed assets to long-term capital

koteifusai 固定負債 fixed liabilities

kōteiheika 公定平価 parity of official exchange rate

koteihi 固定費 fixed cost; fixed

charge

koteihiritsu 固定比率 ratio of fixed assets to net worth; fixed assets ratio

koteikakaku 固定価格 firm price

kōteikakaku 公定価格 official price (ceiling) ¶ abolition of the *official price* of goods

kōteikanri 工程管理 process control

koteikariirekin 固定借入金 fixed debt

koteikawasesōbaseido 固定為替相場制度 ¶ to *peg* their *exchange rates* either to a single currency or to a basket of the currencies of their major trading partners

koteikyū 固定給 fixed wage; fixed salary ¶ the switch from piece rates to *fixed wages*

koteimikomikashidashi 固定見込貸出 substandard; slow; "S" ¶ a loan rated as "S"

koteishihon 固定資本 fixed capital

koteishihontōshi 固定資本投資 fixed capital investment; fixed investment; capital spending ¶ Business *fixed investment* leveled off in 1975. // *Fixed investment* by industry presumably contracted, most markedly in house-building. // *Capital spending* grew steadily and very fast and then weakened progressively.

koteishisan 固定資産 fixed assets

koteishisanbaikyakueki 固定資産売却益 gains from sale of fixed assets

koteishisanbaikyakuson 固定資産売却損 losses from sale of fixed assets

koteishisanhiritsu 固定資産比率 fixed assets ratio; fixed assets to net worth ratio

koteishisanhyōkaeki 固定資産評価益 gains resulting from revaluation of fixed assets

koteishisanhyōkason 固定資産評価損 losses from revaluation of fixed assets

koteishisankaitenritsu 固定資産回転率 fixed assets turnover ratio

koteishisanmotochō 固定資産元帳 plant ledger

koteishisantaichōkishihonhiritsu 固定資産対長期資本比率 ratio of fixed assets to long-term debts

koteishisanzei 固定資産税 real estate tax; municipal property tax

koteishotokusō 固定所得層 fixed-income classes

koteishūnyū 固定収入 fixed income

koteisōba 固定相場 pegged rate of exchange; fixed exchange rate ¶ countries choosing either to *peg* or float their *exchange rate* // to choose as floating or *pegged exchange rate* // whether the *peg* is right—that is, whether they *peg* on the correct currency or package of currencies // Uganda had a formal SDR *peg* with a de facto *peg* to the U.S. dollar, and then changed to a dollar *peg*.

kōteisōba 公定相場 ceiling (official) quotation

koteisōbasei 固定相場制 system of fixed rate of exchange

koteitōshi 固定投資 fixed investment

koteiueito 固定ウエイト fixed weight

基準時固定ウエイト fixed weight at the base period

kōteiwaribikibuai 公定割引歩合 → 公定歩合

koteizeiritsu 固定税率 fixed general tariff

kōtekifujo 公的扶助 public assistance

kōtekikaihatsuenjo 公的開発援助 official development assistance; ODA ¶ The grant element of *ODA* loans remained at the level of 62%.

kōtekikainyū 公的介入 official intervention

kōtekikessaibēsu 公的決済ベース official reserve transaction basis

kōtekikessaishūshi 公的決済収支 ⌊外⌋ balance on official settlement basis

kōtekikinjunbi 公的金準備 official gold reserve

kōten 好転 improvement; turn for the better; favorable turn; favorable swing; amelioration; betterment; recovery ¶ a marked *improvement* in the world economy // Signs of *improvement* appeared. // a *favorable swing* in economic activity // the vigor of the recent economic *recovery* // the steady *recovery* in the economy // marked *betterment* of the payments balance

kōten 後転 backward shifting

kotō 降等 demotion; degradation

kōtō 高騰 (sharp) rise; advance; boom; run-up; soaring; leap; upsurge ¶ the housing price *boom* // Inflationary pressures were mostly associated with *run-up* of oil prices. // Prices *soared* up to 300 percent on a wide range of stocks. // The *leap* in oil prices created fresh difficulties. // Additional high *rises* occurred in oil prices. // A spectacular *boom* hit the Argentine Stock Exchange Monday. // Unemployment began a strong *upward*

surge. // The oil price *surge* began a decade ago. // The price *soars* were concentrated in the durable goods. // The prices of non-food items *soared* at an annual rate of 7%. // Additional *soars* have occurred in prices. // → 急騰

kōtōkeiyaku 口頭契約 verbal agreement

kōtōshijō 高騰市場 soaring market

kōtsūanzenteikiyokin 交通安全定期預金 time deposit with interest covering insurance fee for traffic accident

kōtsūhi 交通費 transportation charge

kōtsūtsūshinhi 交通通信費 communication and transportation expenses

kouri 小売り retail (trading) ¶ Japanese cars *retail* for roughly the same prices in Japan as in the U.S. // a sharp rebound of *retail* sales // the physical volume of goods passing through *retail* channels

kouribukka 小売物価 retail prices ¶ The twelve-month rise in *retail prices* was 7.9%.

kouribukkashisū 小売物価指数 retail price index

kourigyō 小売業 retail business; retail trade

kourigyōsha 小売業者 retailer; retail trader

kourikakakuchōsa 小売価格調査 retail price survey; r.p.s.

kourinedan 小売値段 retail price

kourishijō 小売市場 retail market

kourishō 小売商 retailer; retail trader

kourishōhin 小売商品 retail goods

kourishōken 小売商圏 retail trade

area

kouriuriagedakashisū 小売売上高指数 index of retail sales

kouriwaribiki 小売割引 retail discount

kourizei 小売税 retail excise (tax)

kōwanrōdōsha 港湾労働者 stevedore

kōwanshokeihi 港湾諸経費 port disbursements; port charges

kōwansuto 港湾スト harbor strike; maritime strike; dock strike

kōwantaika 港湾滞貨 port congestion

koyasu 小安 [市] soft; easy; weak ¶ The market opened *soft*. // Metals *softened* as trading slackened. // The market was *weak* at the start. // Prices *weakened*.

koyō 雇用 employment ¶ *Employment* elther gained or held firm. // *Employment* was maintained at a high level. // The fall in *employment* was less than that expected. // Production worker *employment*, or manufacturing *employment*, slipped less than 2%. // to alleviate the *employment* situation through demand management // to create new *employment* for redundant workers in the coal industry // The 100 biggest firms provided *employment* for nearly 1.2 million of the 1.3 million employees of Sweden's 200 largest companies. // The increase in non-farm payroll *employment* moderated. // New workers who entered the *employment* ranks over the past two years must have now gained skills and experience. // [参考] Firms plan to engage additional workers.

超完全雇用 overfull employment; hyper-(=full-) employment

超完全雇用 over-full employment; hyperemployment

永久雇用 permanent employment

不安定雇用 unstable employment

不完全雇用 under-employment

一時雇用 temporary employment

常用雇用 regular employment

完全雇用 full employment

水増し雇用 feather-bedding

生産転換雇用 change-over employment

選択雇用 selective employment

終身雇用 life(-time) employment

kōyō 効用 utility; instrumentality ¶ to be of little practical *utility* // Recently states have begun large-scale operations of state *instrumentalities* as financial intermediaries.

限界効用 marginal utility

形態効用 form utility

全部効用 total utility

koyōchōsei 雇用調整 employment adjustment

koyōdanseichi 雇用弾性値 value of elasticity of employment

koyōimin 雇用移民 migration for employment

koyōjōken 雇用条件 terms and conditions of employment; employment conditions

koyōjōsei 雇用情勢 employment situation ¶ The improvement of the *employment situation* was very slow in coming.

koyōjōsū 雇用乗数 employment multiplier

koyōkankei 雇用関係 employment relationship

koyōkankō 雇用慣行 employment practices

koyōkeieisha 雇用経営者 employed manager; salaried manager

koyōkeitai 雇用形態 system of

employment ¶ The Japanese *system of employment* was both merits and drawbacks.

koyōkeiyaku 雇用契約 employment agreement; contract of employment

koyōkikai 雇用機会 employment opportunity; job opportunity ¶ to provide *employment opportunities* // to provide more equity in the distribution of *employment opportunities* // Reduced industrial *job opportunities* forced farmers back to their fields. // Capital investments will have to rise to create adequate *employment opportunities*. // to encourage the creation of *job opportunities* // to deny *employment opportunities* to teenagers possessing only limited skills // women looking for *employment opportunities* outside the home // *Job opportunities* for adults rose by 2,000 to 18,500.

koyōkikainokintō 雇用機会の均等 equal employment opportunity

koyōkikan 雇用期間 period of employment

koyōnohoshō 雇用の保証 guarantee of employment

koyōritsu 雇用率 employment rate

koyōshashotoku 雇用者所得 employees' income

koyōshisū 雇用指数 employment index

kōyōshugi 効用主義 utilitarianism

koyōsokushinhō 雇用促進法 [米] Job Development Act

koyōsokushinsaku 雇用促進策 employment-promoting measure; employment-generating projects; [参考] enlargement of the employment potential

kōyōteigen 効用逓減 diminishing

utility ¶ the law of *diminishing utility*

kōyōtokō 公用渡航 official trip; official travel

koyurumi 小緩み [市] weak; slack; easy; dull ¶ The tone for business was slightly *weaker* but still basically strong. // As trading *slackened,* industrials led a moderate downtrend. // Monetary conditions *eased.* // Coppers opened *dull* but later rallied with a rise in the price.

kōza 口座 account ¶ to open and maintain a banking *account* with (= at) a bank, and then close it // to deposit money in the *account,* and draw on the *account* // to keep and settle the *account*

振替口座 (postal) transfer account

kōzai 鋼材 steel products; rolled steel

kōzairyō 好材料 [市] favorable news; bullish news; strong indication; good news; strong incentive ¶ Stocks rose on *favorable news* from Washington. // Confidence was bolstered by *favorable news* of Armco's price advance. // a large assortment of *bullish news* // The stock market advanced as *favorable news* came of the lower discount rate. // Stocks rose on *good* economic *news.*

kozaya 小鞘 small spread; narrow spread ¶ a *small spread* of profit // *narrow* interest rate *spreads*

kozayakasegi 小鞘稼ぎ profiting by slight market fluctuations; scalping ¶ to *scalp* stocks, grain, and tickets

kozayanedan 小鞘値段 close price

kozayatori 小鞘取り scalper

kōzō 構造 structure ¶ The commodity and geographical *structure* of Dutch foreign trade was unfavorable. // major changes in the supply *structure* of the economy // the adoption of a three-tier pyramidal *structure* for delivery of health services // The *structure* of corporate profits was distorted by boosting nominal profits. // to regard the interest rate *structure* as the centerpiece of the monetary mechanism // to maintain a realistic *structure* of interest rates // to change the underlying *structure* of the economy // Germany would seem to be a *structural* capital exporter. // Germany's *structurally* entrenched trade surpluses and invisibles deficits. // to arrive at a *structurally* sound budget // a *structural* feature of the economy // in such a lopsided banking *structure* as Hong Kong's // formation of a sound *structure* of rates, or interest rate *structure*

地域構造　regional structure
賃金構造　wage structure
価格構造　price structure
経済構造　economic structure
企業間賃金構造　external wage structure
期間構造　term structure
金融構造　financial structure
給与構造　wage structure; salary structure
二重構造　dual structure
産業間構造　intra-industry structure
産業構造　industrial structure
社会構造　social structure
所得構造　income structure
就業構造　occupational structure; structure of occupation
租税構造　tax structure
kōzōbunseki　構造分析　structural analysis

kōzōfukyōgyōshu　構造不況業種　structurally depressed industries

kōzōhenka　構造変化　structural change ¶ to adjust workers to *structural changes* which result from changing patterns of international trade // *Changes* in the *structure* of domestic demand are expected to be minor. // Petroleum development will *change* the production and export *structure* in favor of raw materials.

kōzōkaikaku　構造改革　structural reconstruction (=reform)

kōzōkaizenkin'yū　構造改善金融　preferential financing for reshaping industrial structure

kōzōseisaku　構造政策　structural (policy) measure

kōzōtekifukinkō　構造的不均衡　structural disequilibrium

kōzōtekifukyō　構造的不況　structural depression

kōzōtekishinshukusei　構造的伸縮性　built-in flexibility

kōzōtekishitsugyō　構造的失業　structural unemployment

kōzōtekiteikoyō　構造的低雇用　structural under-employment

kōzōyōgōhan　構造用合板　plywood for constructive use

kubetsu　区別　distinction ¶ to make a clear *distinction* between long-and short-term credit banks // to wipe away many of the present *distinctions* between commercial banks and thrift institutions

kubun　区分(企業集団等の)　segmentation

kugizuke　釘付け　pegging ¶ to *peg* the price at $74 // crawling *peg* system for par values

kujibikihanbai　くじ引販売　raffle

¶ to sell by a raffle // to raffle off washing machines

kujō 苦情 grievance; complaint ¶ to investigate and adjust *grievances* between the public and members and between members

kujōshorikikan 苦情処理機関 grievance machinery; trouble shooter

kujōshoritetsuzuki 苦情処理手続 grievance procedure

kukakugyogyō 区画漁業 demarcated fishery

kukanseido 苦汗制度 sweating system; sweat shop

kūkōshiyōryō 空港使用料 landing fee

kuku 区々 [市] irregular; patchy; mixed; spotted ¶ The market was *irregular* the rest of the day. // Petroleums closed *irregular* after early firmness. // The market was *mixed* in early trading and closed *patchy*. // The market was *mixed* with a slight upward tendency. // The market was *spotted* throughout the day but the averaging edged ahead.

kukushōjō 区々商状 [市] patchy market

kumiai 組合 association; society; partnership; guild; union; syndicate ¶ to form an *association* of scholars for the advancement of knowledge // to organize and keep up the *society* to be received into and then leave the *society*

同業組合 trade association; guild
御用組合 company union
販売組合 marketing cooperative association; sales cooperative association
従業員組合 workers' union

購買組合 purchasing association
協同組合 cooperative association; cooperative; cooperative society
共済組合 fraternal association; mutual benefit association; benefit association
利用組合 utility cooperative association
労働組合 labor union; trade union
産業組合 cooperative society
生産者組合 producers' association
職業別組合 craft union
消費組合 consumers' cooperative society
消費者組合 consumers' association
商工組合 commercial (and industrial) association
匿名組合 anonymous association
通常組合 ordinary partnership

kumiaiboki 組合簿記 partnership book-keeping

kumiaikatsudō 組合活動 union activities

kumiaikeiyaku 組合契約 partnership agreement; syndicate contract

kumiaikin'yū 組合金融 cooperative financing

kumiaikin'yūkikan 組合金融機関 cooperative type specialized financial institution

kumiaikiyaku 組合規約 articles of partnership; articles of association

kumiaishakaishugi 組合社会主義 guild socialism

kumiaishugi 組合主義 unionism

kumiaiyakuin 組合役員 union executive

kumiawasetorihiki 組合せ取引 combination deal

kumitate 組立て assemblage; assembly

kumitatebumon 組立部門 assembly department

kumitatekōjō 組立工場 assembling plant; assembly plant

kumitatekōtei 組立工程 assembly process

kumitatesagyō 組立作業 assembling work

kumitegata 組手形 set bills

kunren 訓練 training
職場外訓練 off-the-job training
職場内訓練 on-the-job training; training within industry
職業訓練 vocational training; job training

kurabarai 蔵払い rummage sale; haggling; discount sale; sellout

kurashikiryō 倉敷料 storage; fee for warehousing

kuraudinguauto クラウディング・アウト crowding-out ¶ to result in a *crowding-out* of private-sector demand on the capital market // the *crowding-out* of private sector investment by public spending // the problem of *crowding-out* of LDCs on account of increased loan demand in the industrial countries // the worry of the public and private sectors *crowding* each other *out* in the demand for borrowed funds // Developing countries tend to be *crowded out* of the depressed external bond market. // Personal demands are being *crowded out* as corporate requirements mounted. // These government securities may *crowd out* private money demand. // More productive private investment has been *crowded out* over a long period by less productive public sector investment.

kurejittofashiriti クレジット・ファシリティ credit facility

kurejittorain クレジット・ライン line of credit; credit line ¶ to establish a *line of credit* in favor of members, entitling them to draw on the Fund's resources // Our bank will hold a *line of credit* in Euro-dollars in favor of your bank of $50,000.

kurejittotoranshe クレジット・トランシェ credit tranche

kurēmu クレーム （運輸保険にかかわるものを除く） claim (excluding those of transportation and insurance) ¶ A *claim* for compensation was filed, accepted and satisfied. // to *claim* a large sum against a company for damages // *Claims* shall be filed by cable, amicably settled between the parties. // to settle *claims* promptly and fairly

kuriage 繰上げ ahead of schedule; prior to ¶ Payment *ahead of schedule* // repayment *prior to* maturity

kuriageshōkan 繰上償還 advance(d) redemption ¶ There is no provision for *advance redemption*. // [参考] to redeem prior to maturity

kurikaebarai 繰替払い payment made by appropriation from another fund

kurikaebaraitōsuitōkanri 繰替払等出納官吏 accounting official with funds pool

kurikoshi 繰越し transfer; carryover; [会] carried forward; brought forward; brought over ¶ to *carry forward* to the next account // to *bring over* from the last account // orders *carried over* to the next year

kurikoshikanjō 繰越勘定 brought forward account

kurikoshikessonkin 繰越欠損金 loss brought forward

kurikoshikichō 繰越記帳 opening entry

kurikoshikin 繰越金 balance at the beginning of a period

kurikoshimai 繰越米 rice stock brought forward

kurikoshizandaka 繰越残高 opening balance; balance brought forward

kurimodoshi 繰戻し carryback

kurīnbiru クリーンビル clean bill

kurinobe 繰延べ postponement; deferment; carry-over ¶ The government *postponed* the disbursement of appropriations from the national treasury. // a 1-year *deferment* of the tax increases

kurinobefusai 繰延負債 deferred liability

kurinobehibu 繰延日歩 contango; carrying charge

kurinobehiyō 繰延費用 deferred charge

kurinobejigyō 繰延事業 postponed undertaking

kurinobejushi 繰延需資 pent-up demand; backlog of demand; residual demand ¶ the higher funds rate reflecting the *residual demand* from yesterday, the end of the month

kurinobekanjō 繰延勘定 deferred account

kurinobekeiyaku 繰延契約 carrying-over contract

kurinobekessai 繰延決済 delaying settlement

kurinoberisatsu 繰延利札 extended coupon; arrear coupon

kurinobeshiharaikin 繰延支払金 deferred payment

kurinobeshisan 繰延資産 deferred asset

kurinobeshishutsu 繰延支出 budget deferral; deferment; postponement; deferred expenditure ¶ government's decision regarding *budget deferrals* for combating inflation // *deferment* of part of investment projects

kurinobeshūeki 繰延収益 deferred income

kurinobetorihiki 繰延取引 extenuation; contango dealing

kuroji 黒字 surplus; favorable balance; black (ink) figure ¶ the *surplus* in the balance of payments, or the balance-of-payments *surplus* // trade *surplus,* or a *surplus* on trade account // The *balance* of payments *turned* in Mexico's *favor.* // to show a *favorable balance* of $700 million // The trade account ended in *surplus.* // The business was in the *black.* // Britain ran a payments *surplus* of £69 million. // A sharp cut in imports put the trade balance into comfortable *surplus.* // The balance of payments closed with a *surplus* of Lit. 250 billion in May. // The payments balance ended with a sizable *surplus.* // A big visible trade *surplus* in Germany's favor still remains. // reduction, rather than elimination of Germany's structurally entrenched trade *surpluses* // the continued erosion of the trade *surpluses* // The overall balance moved into the *black.* // to register a *black-ink figure* of DM 1.5 milliard // The current account is heavily back into the *black.*

kurojikoku 黒字国 surplus country; creditor(=black-ink figure; surplus trade) nation ¶ the so-called capital *surplus countries*, the capital-*surplus* oil-exporting *countries* of the Middle East, or petroleum surplus developing countries

kurōringupeggu クローリング・ペッグ [外] crawling peg; sliding parity; changes if necessary in the parity rate of a currency at certain fixed intervals

kurosuraisensu クロス・ライセンス cross license contracts; mutual exchange contracts

kurosurēto クロス・レート cross rate

英米クロス・レート sterling-dollar cross rate

kuroutosuji くろうと筋 [市] professional dealers; professionals

kusshinkawasesōba 届伸為替相場 flexible exchange rate

kusshinseigenseido 届伸制限制度 elastic limit system (of bank note issue)

kutsurogimoyō くつろぎ模様 [市] easy

kuzunettsunonami クズネッツの波 Kuznets' cycle; Kuznets' wave

kyakkanshihyō 客観指標 objective indicator

kyakkantekikakuritsu 客観的確率 objective probability

kyakudamari 客溜り customers' room

kyarakutāshōhō キャラクター商法 character business

kyasshuresushakai キャッシュレス社会 cashless society

kyōryoku 協力 cooperation ¶ to further financial *cooperation* and carry out various forms of technical *cooperation* // closer and harmonious international *cooperation* // systematized multi-economic *cooperation*

kyōbai 競売 auction ¶ The total amount accrued from all *auctions*

held so far is $1.58 billion. // a phenomenal reception for Thursday's *auction* of 30-year bonds

せり下げ競売 Dutch auction

kyōbaininmenkyo 競売人免許 auctioneer's license

kyōbaishobun 競売処分 forced sale

kyōchō 協調 co-ordination; concertation ¶ Better world *co-ordination* of economic policies is desired. // in timely *co-ordination* with changes in circumstances // close *co-ordination* of fiscal and monetary policies // a well *co-ordinated* fiscal-monetary policy mix // close economic *coordination* among Arab states // Policy *co-ordination* between the administration and the Federal Reserve became closer. // a *concertation* of national economic policies which are compatible with one another at the international level // A wide *concertation* of policy seems essential. // much closer and more continuous *concertation* of views among governments on the trade issues

kyōchō 強調 emphasis; stress; accentuation; firmness; steadiness; [市] bullish; strong; firm; steady; buoyed ¶ to place an *emphasis* on the problem // to *emphasize* the tasks of monetary policy // to lay particular *stress* on the fact that... // Longstanding difficulties in maintaining stable prices were *accentuated*. // The tone of the money market was generally quite *firm*. // A steadily *firm* tone was evident in the market. // The market became a shade *firmer*. // Prices have *firmed* down. // The dollar remains *buoyed* by a *firm* Federal funds rate. // The *strong* sectors more than offset the areas of weakness.

kyōchōkainyū 協調介入 coordinated intervention

kyōchōkankei 協調関係 cooperative relationship

kyōchōkōdō 協調行動 concerted action ¶ Central banks may take some *concerted action* on the dollar.

kyōchōkyōgi 協調・協議 collaboration and confrontation

kyōchōsenryaku 協調戦略 coordinated strategy

kyōchōyūshi 協調融資 joint-financing; blending credit; co-financing; participation loan; financial participation ¶ The Japanese government assented to *financial participation* in an international venture.

kyōchōyūshikoku 協調融資国 syndication group

kyodaikigyō 巨大企業 big business; business giant

kyodaikoku 巨大国 super power

kyōdōfurōto 共同フロート →共同変動相場

kyōdōhanbai 協同販売 cooperative marketing

kyōdōhendōsōba 共同変動相場 joint float; (European) joint currency float; joint-floating market system; the 'snake (in the tunnel)' arrangement; common float (of European countries); joint floating exchange rate; joint float; bloc float

kyōdōhokensha 共同保険者 co-insurer

kyōdōikkan'yusō 協同一貫輸送 intermodal tranportation

kyōdōjūtaku 共同住宅 corporative housing

kyōdōkaison 共同海損 general average

kyōdōkaitsuke 共同買付 joint buying; joint purchase

kyōdōkanri 共同管理 joint control; joint management; cooperative management

kyōdōkeiei 共同経営 joint management; joint operation

kyōdōkeisan 共同計算 joint accounting

kyōdōkeisansentā 共同計算センター data center; computing center

kyōdōkōi 共同行為 collusive activity; concerted action

kyōdōkōnyū 共同購入 joint buying; joint purchase

kyōdōkumiai 協同組合 cooperative (association; society)
販売協同組合 sales cooperative association; marketing cooperative association
農業協同組合 agricultural cooperative association
生産協同組合 producers' cooperative society

kyōdōshihai 共同支配 joint control

kyōdōshihon 共同資本 joint stock

kyōdōshoyūken 共同所有権 collective ownership

kyōdōshusshi 共同出資 joint capital investment; joint account; joint contribution

kyōdōshusshisha 共同出資者 partner

kyōdōtai 共同体 community
村落共同体 village community
都市共同体 urban community

kyōdōtōshi 共同投資 joint investment

kyōdōukanjō 共同勘定 joint account

kyōdōukeoi 共同請負 joint venture

kyōdōunkō 共同運航 joint service

kyōdōuyūshi 共同融資 co-financing; joint financing; syndicated financing ¶ *cofinancing* involving international lending institutions and private lenders // funds for *joint financing* of mutually agreed projects // *cofinancing* between private sources and official development institutions // governmental and private *co-financing* of development projects with the multilateral development banker

kyōdōyushutsukikan 共同輸出機関 cooperative export organization

kyōgō 競合 clash; conflict ¶ the *clash* between public borrowing and private demand on the capital market // to seek a balance among *conflicting* objectives // [参考] →競争

kyōgyō 協業 cooperation of labor; joint venture ¶ Agreements between the foreign investors and the government on *joint*-refinery *ventures*.

kyōgyōka 協業化 grouping into a cooperative

kyōgyōsūpā 協業スーパー cooperative super market

kyōi 脅威 threat ¶ The *threat* of inflation is of great importance and may move beyond control.

kyōikushikin 教育資金 reserve for education

kyojūseinonintei 居住性の認定 identification of residential status

kyojūsha 居住者 (exchange) resident

kyojūshagaikayokinkanjō 居住者外貨預金勘定 resident foreign currency deposit account

kyojūsuijun 居住水準 housing standard

kyoka 許可 permission; permit; approval; license ¶ The volume of construction *permits* issued picked up.

kyōka 強化 intensify; strengthen ¶ Price pressures continue *intensifying*. // to *intensify* exchange controls // to *strengthen* the management of demand // Some influences *strengthened* prices. // [参考] to make severer // to increase intensity

kyōkai 協会 association; society ¶ labor credit *associations* // building *societies* // to organize a mutual aid *society* under the name of...

kyōkaitsuminijōkō 協会積荷条項 Institute Cargo Clauses

kyokasei 許可制 license system; licensing

包括(輸入)許可制 open general licensing system

輸出許可制 export licensing system

kyōken 強権 power of coercion ¶ The authorities exercised their *power of coercion* in the financial sphere. // *coercion* by making use of their *power* to levy

kyōkentekikisei 強権的規制 mandatory control

kyōkō 恐慌 crisis; panic ¶ to tide the economy over a *crisis* // to come through many *crises* // to forestall any serious financial *crisis* // *Panic* has been averted. // War rumors caused a financial *panic*.

安定恐慌 stabilization crisis

半恐慌 semi-crisis

株式恐慌 stock exchange crisis

経済恐慌 economic crisis

金融恐慌 financial crisis

農業恐慌 agrarian crisis; agricultural crisis

産業恐慌 industrial crisis

世界経済恐慌　world economic crisis

商業恐慌　commercial crisis

kyōkōsōba 恐慌相場　panic price; near-panic market

kyōkōten 恐慌点　panic point

kyokudaichi 極大値　maximum value

kyokudaika 極大化　maximization ¶ modern, risk-taking, profit-*maximizing* and more traditional, risk-averse, sales-*maximizing* entrepreneurs // The income-*maximizing* pair of jobs is the pair that *maximizes* the sum of their wage rates.

厚生極大化　welfare maximization

効用極大化　utility maximization

満足極大化　maximization of satisfaction

利潤極大化　profit maximization

産出量極大化　output maximization

売上高極大化　sales maximization

kyokudaikagenri 極大化原理　principle of maximization

kyokudonokenyaku 極度の倹約　parsimony

kyokudotorihiki 極度取引　agreement on loan facilities up to a given amount

kyokumen 局面　phase; aspect ¶ The international debt situation moved from the crisis *phase* to the adjustment *phase*. // The international economy is entering a *phase* of higher inflation and more sluggish growth. // The American economic recovery is now moving into a more mature *phase*. // the catch-up *aspects* of the economy's performance // real and monetary *aspects* of the economy // various *phases* of the business cycle

上昇局面　upward phase

回復局面　recovery phase; revival

下降局面　downward phase

拡張局面　expansion phase

後退局面　recession phase

収縮局面　contraction phase

kyokusen 曲線　curve

費用曲線　cost curve

需要曲線　demand curve

価格・消費曲線　price-consumption curve

効用曲線　utility curve

屈折需要曲線　kinky demand curve

供給曲線　supply curve

マーシャル曲線　Marshall curve

無差別曲線　indifference curve

ローレンツ曲線　Lorenz curve

kyōkyū 供給　supply; provide; furnish; feed ¶ Beyond meeting seasonal requirements, there was little increase in the money *supply*. // the scarcity of oil *supplies* // an ample *supply* of water power // to amply *provide* industry with raw materials // The company *furnished* electric power to towns and cities in the district. // the imbalance between *supply* and demand // the *supply*-demand picture // *Supplies* remain out of balance with requirements. // a large *supply* of cheap and efficient labor // to cut oil *supply* // petroleums in very short *supply* // to be not well *supplied* in crude oil // to *supply* him with information // to be amply *provided* with raw materials // to be ill *provided* with food // to *feed* grain to the mill // to *feed* industry with fuel // There will be no important disruptions in the *supply* of oil. // indulgence of tight *supply* conditions for domestic goods and services // The outlook for energy *supply* over the short and medium term remained good. // the oil and gas reserves equal to between four and five years' *supply* at current rates of consumption // The completion geared to assuring their immediate oil *supply*. // replacements for costly, dwindling *supplies* of oil and natural gas // to *provide* an elastic *supply* of currency // Available energy *supplies* were limited. // Stocks represent a 50 days *supply*. // ample, not scarce, manufacturing *supplies* // The money *supply* outstanding at June-end was 16 percent higher than a year earlier. // estimated *supply* of necessary industrial funds // a state of over- or short-*supply*

超過供給 excess supply; over-supply

長期供給 long period supply

限界供給 marginal supply

非弾性供給 inelastic supply

費用不変供給 constant-cost supply

費用逓増供給 increasing-cost supply

過剰供給 over-supply

結合供給 joint supply

国民総供給 gross national supply

競争的供給 competitive supply

最終供給 final supply

市場供給 market supply

総供給 aggregate supply; total supply; schedule supply

通貨供給(量) money supply ¶ →マネー・サプライ

豊かな供給 abundant supply; ample supply`

kyōkyūatsuryoku 供給圧力 supply pressure

kyōkyūbusoku 供給不足 short supply; deficiency (=shortfall) of supply ¶ The *supply* is short. // Food is in very *short supply*. // the anticipated *shortfall* in *supply* of funds // to *be deficient in* capital // *supplies* show a *deficiency*. // to make good a *deficiency* of oil *supply*

kyōkyūchōsei 供給調整 supply adjustment

kyōkyūgen 供給源 source of supply

kyōkyūjōnoseiyaku 供給上の制約 supply constraint; supply bottleneck ¶ *Supply constraints* began to appear. // *Constraints* appeared on the *supply* side.

kyōkyūkajō 供給過剰 over-supply; excessive supply; excess supply; glut; sating; satiation ¶ *excessive supply* of funds over demand // The market is *glutted* with petroleums. // There is a *glut* of oil in the market. // a state of *over-supply* // a *glut* of goods in the market // Some *gluts* may develop. // The market is *sated* with new bonds. // Energy will not lurch quickly into *glut*. // The recession-induced world oil *glut* is shrinking. // [参考] Asian supplies will flood the market.

kyōkyūkakaku 供給価格 supply price

kyōkyūnōryoku 供給能力 supply capacity; capacity to supply ¶ a large addition to the *supply capacity* of non-manufacturing industries // ample *supply capacity* to keep pace with growing demand

kyōkyūsha 供給者 supplier; purveyor; provider ¶ The main *providers* of balance of payments financing and the *suppliers* of international reserves to official entities have been the commercial banks.

kyōkyūtsūkaryō 供給通貨量 money

supply ¶ There was little increase in the *money supply* beyond meeting seasonal requiements. // →マネー・サプライ

kyōkyūyoryoku 供給余力 surplus of supply capacity; surplus capacity; excess supply capacity ¶ The economy retained a considerable *surplus of supply capacity*. // the prevailing high lease of *surplus capacity*

kyōmaidaikin 供米代金 payment for rice delivery

kyōmiusu 興味薄 ［市］ uninterested

kyōnen 凶年 bad year

kyōranbukka 狂乱物価 frenzied price inflation; rampant inflation; runaway inflation; a wild price rise

kyōryoku 協力 cooperation; voluntary compliance ¶ to further define areas of *cooperation* to ease Latin America's debt burden

kyōryokukyōchō 協力・協調 cooperation and compromise ¶ concerted action in a spirit of *cooperation and compromise*

kyōsai 共済 mutual aid

kyōsainōgyōkyōdōkumiairengōkai 共済農業協同組合連合会 mutual insurance federation of agricultural cooperatives

kyōseibokin 強制的募金 forced collection

kyōseichochiku 強制貯蓄 compulsory saving

kyōseihasan 強制破産 forced liquidation; involuntary liquidation

kyōseihoken 強制保険 forced insurance

kyōseikaisan 強制解散 compulsory winding-up

kyōseikokuminhokenseido 強制国民健康保険制度 compulsory national health insurance system

kyōseirōdō 強制労働 forced labor

kyōseiryoku 強制力 power of coercion; coercive power ¶ increasing exercise by the public authorities of their power of *coercion* in the financial sphere // The authorities do not exercise *coercion* by making use of their power to levy taxes.

kyōseisetsuyaku 強制節約 forced frugality

kyōseiteki 強制的 mandatory; coercive ¶ a *mandatory* rationing of gasoline and heating oil // *coercive* restraints on credit accommodation for financing stock purchases

kyoshiteki 巨視的 macroscopic; macrocosmic

kyoshitekibunseki 巨視的分析 macro-analysis

kyoshitekikeizaigenshō 巨視的経済現象 macro-economic phenomenon

kyoshutsukin 拠出金 subscription (money); contribution

kyoshutsuseikokuminnenkin 拠出制国民年金 national annuity through premium payment

kyōsō 競争 competition; rivalry; rivalship; vying; race ¶ Ruinous *competition* was avoided by price arrangement. // to touch off a rate-cutting *race* among the major countries // to *compete* against others in price // a keen *competition* for prospective buyers // *competition* from imported goods // to *compete* in the *race* for increased fixed investment // to keep Japanese goods *competitive* in export markets // persistent and heavy *competitive* pressures prompted adjustments in output. // Finland's shipyards face stiff *competition*. // Several industries are hard hit by foreign *competition*. // to resume needed safety without stiffening initiative and *competition* // to enter into *rivalry* with others for customers // They are being challenged by *competing* shipbuiders from all corners of the globe. // They are prepared to quote a more *competitive* price. // This will enable them to *compete* more effectively. // Banks are in *competition* with thousands of specialized thrift institutions for depositors of savings. // The private and public sectors *vie* for funds. // Banks' restrictive operation does not exclude hard *competition* for good customers. // to face a surge of efficient low-cost *competition* from the newly developed countries // the industries most exposed to foreign *competition* // to spur full-scale interbank *competition* // In these sectors *competition* was less keen. // Foreign *competition* remains very stiff on markets abroad, but has slackened on domestic markets. // bitter *rivalry* among banks for customers // *Rivalry* for travellers became stiffer among airlines and railway companies. // Borrowers took advantage of *competitive* pressures among lenders.

同質的競争 homogeneous competition

不完全競争 imperfect competition

不公正競争 unfair competition

異質的競争 heterogeneous competition

実効競争 workable competition; effective competition

自由競争 free competition; open competition

純粋競争 pure competition

価格競争 price competition ¶ Congress considers measures to encourage *price competition* by business.

価格外競争 non-price competition

完全競争 perfect competition

貸出競争 loans race

過当競争 excessive competition; over-competition; super-competition

切下げ競争 competitive devaluation; competitive depreciation ¶ Efforts to gain advantage by *competitive depreciation* were a tragic mirage with benefits to no one. // →競争的切下げ

国内競争 domestic competition

国際競争 international competition

公正な競争 fair competition

殺人的競争 cut-throat competition

生存競争 struggle for existence;

有効競争 effective competition; workable competition

kyōsōgenri 競争原理 elements of competition ¶ to infuse more *elements of competition* in industry

kyōsōhin 競争品 competitive commodity; competitor

kyōsonkyōei 共存共栄 prosperous coexistence

kyōsōnyūsatsu 競争入札 competitive bidding

kyōsōritsu 競争率 (average) competition rate

kyōsōryoku 競争力 competitive abilities; competitive power; competitivity; competitive position; competitiveness; competitive edge; competitive advantage; competitive strength; competitive footing; competitive standing ¶ the increased *competitive abilities* of their products on world markets // Possible currency changes obviously can affect export *competitivity*. // improved international *competitiveness* of industry // the risks of loss of *competitiveness* due to wage cost increases // The external *competitive position* would be eroded. // Switzerland experienced a loss in *competitiveness* of about 27%. // Argentina's *ability* to *compete* is severely hampered by inflation. // *competitive* abilities of the industry's products increased. // New technology gives developing nations a *competitive edge*. // Higher relative costs have blunted the *competitive edge* of Britain's exports against those of its main trading partners. // to give a *competitive edge* in penetrating the local lending market // the *competitive edge* enjoyed by Euro-currency banks over their U.S. counterparts // A *competitive advantage* obtained from an exchange rate change is likely to be eroded. // American banks' capture of market share based upon sound fundamental *competitive strengths* // to gain an unfair *competitive advantage* over other members

価格競争力 price competitiveness ¶ The *price competitiveness* of U.S. goods has improved over the three previous years.

国際競争力 international competitiveness; competitiveness in international markets; competitive position in international markets; international competitive position; international competitive abilities ¶ The strong upward movement of the Swiss Franc was engendering the *inter-national competitiveness* of Swiss industry.

kyōsōshijō 競争市場 competitive marketplace ¶ Choice is left to the free play of a *competitive marketplace*.

kyōsōtaihinkonsha 強壮体貧困者 able-bodied poor

kyōsōtekikirisage 競争的切下げ competitive exchange depreciation; competitive downward revaluation of exchange; competitive exchange devaluation

kyōtakujiyū 供託事由 reason for depositing

kyōtakukin 供託金 deposited money; deposit

kyōtakuyūkashōken 供託有価証券 deposited securities

kyōtei 協定 agreement; arrangement; bargain; (com)pact; concordat; contract ¶ a *concordat* allocating responsibilities among lenders of last resort // →契約

kyōteibōeki 協定貿易 trade by agreement

kyōteichingin 協定賃金 contractual wage ¶ The 3% rise in gross real *contractual wages* produces a net real *contractual wages* of 1.7%.

kyōteigaichingin 協定外賃金 wage drift ¶ The *wage drift* is the consequence of the labor shortage.

kyōteihikiuke 協定引受 negotiated underwriting

kyōteikakaku 協定価格 stipulated price; contract price

kyōteikakakutai 協定価格帯 conventional price range

kyōteikinri 協定金利 conventional money rate; voluntary agreed rate

kyōteizeiritsu 協定税率 conventional tariff

kyoten 拠点 base; foothold ¶ overseas *bases* of business operations // to gain a strong *foothold* in portfolio management business on the Swiss market

kyotenkaihatsuhōshiki 拠点開発方式 principle of the nodal system development

kyōtsūhyōjitan'i 共通表示単位 common denominator

kyōtsūinfuretaisaku 共通インフレ対策 unified counter-measures against inflation

kyōtsūkanzei 共通関税 common tariff

kyōtsūnōgyōseisaku 共通農業政策 Common Agricultural Policy (of EC countries)

kyōtsūtanpo 共通担保 common collateral

kyoyōdo 許容度 →寛容度

kyoyōgendo 許容限度 tolerance limit; allowable maximum (amount) ¶ to keep the money supply within the *tolerance limits* of inflation

kyōyōgorakuhi 教養娯楽費 cultural-amusement expenses

kyoyōgosa 許容誤差 permissible error

kyoyōsuijun 許容水準 permissible level

kyōyūchi 共有地 communization

kyōyūshisan 共有資産 common property

kyōzairyō 強材料 [市] favorable news; strong incentives; bullish influences ¶ The market bulled ahead on *favorable news* from Washington. // The news of lower interest rates was an *strong incentive* to Monday's rally. // More *bullish influences* were the continued rise in rail car-loadings and a boost in living costs.

kyozetsuhannō 拒絶反応 symptoms of rejection

kyozetsushōsho 拒絶証書 protest (for non-acceptance; for non-payment)

kyozetsushōshosakuseimenjo 拒絶証書作成免除 protest waved; no protest

kyūbō 窮乏 narrow circumstances; narrow means

kyūbōka 窮乏化 impoverishment
相対的窮乏化 relative impoverishment
絶対的窮乏化 absolute impoverishment

kyūbōkariron 窮乏化理論 theory of deterioration of conditions of working-class

kyūen 救援 relief; rescue; aid; assistance; help ¶ to provide the bank with *relief* funds, or financial aid, under a *rescue* package to keep the bank afloat // to organize a *rescue* package for a bank on the verge of collapse // to fill the funding gap by a goverment and commercial bank *aid* package

kyūfukin 給付金 benefit; dole ¶ the jobless people drawing the unemployment *benefit*
賃金比例給付 earning-related benefit
医療給付 medical benefit
共同給付 joint benefit
共済給付 friendly benefit
労働不能給付 disability benefit
最低生活費給付 subsistence benefit
失業給付 unemployment benefit
職業転換給付 benefit for change of job
出産給付 maternity benefit

kyūhanraku 急反落 sharp setback; sharp loss; sudden downturn ¶ The market had a *sharp setback* on news of the revolt in Iraq. // Oils with resources in the Middle East took *sharp losses*. // →急落

kyūhin 救貧 antipoverty ¶ the *antipoverty* program and policy

kyūjin 求人 job offers; (unfilled job) vacancies; openings ¶ *Unfilled vacancies* totaled 3,335. // *Job vacancies* numbered 62,000. // the ratio of *job offers* to job seekers // Notified *job vacancies* fell by 6,400, seasonally adjusted, to 211,000. // the seasonally adjusted number of *vacancies* relative to the number of job applicants // *Job vacancies* have been decreasing. // Unfilled *vacancies* have been increasing continuously. 有効求人 effective job openings

kyūjinbairitsu 求人倍率 ratio of (effective) job offers to (effective) job applicants; ratio of (effective) job offers to seekers; opening-to-application ratio ¶ *The ratio of (effective) job offers to (effective) job applicants* dipped slightly. // The *job-offers to job-seekers ratio* in April remained at a seasonally adjusted 0.64, indicating that there were in April 64 job offers for every 100 workers seeking employment. // [参考] The seasonally adjusted ratio of vacancies to job-seekers was 0.65. // the indicator measuring the seasonally adjusted number of job-offers continued to fall

kyūjinjūsokuritsu 求人充足率 ratio of placement to job opening

kyūjinshijō 求人市場 Job market

kyūjinsukauto 求人スカウト head hunter

kyūjitsu 休日(所定の) (normal) day off (=off-day) 銀行休日 bank holiday

kyūjuyōhin 急需要品 spot need

kyūkanchi 休閑地 fallow

kyūkutsu 窮屈 [市] tight; taut

kyūkutsuka 窮屈化 tightening ¶ a marked tightening of monetary conditions

kyūkutsukan 窮屈感(手許の) difficulty in raising funds; sense of tightness; business feeling of a tight fund position ¶ The *sense of tightness* in corporate financing eased.

kyūminjōtai 休眠状態 dormancy ¶ Winter wheat did not emerge from its January-February *dormancy* because of "winterkill".

kyūraku 急落 sharp drop; sharp break; sudden fall; precipitous drop; steep decline; tumble; sagging; plunge; plummet; nosedive ¶ Equity prices on Wall Street *fell sharply*. // *sharp falls* in bond prices precipitated by worries about... // Shares *tumbled* in accelerated falls. // The market underwent its second straight weekly *tumble*. // The market *tumbled* as news came of oil embargo. // The market *sagged*. // The Bank managed to hold sterling's *plunge*. // The lira *plunged* again to 880 against the dollar. // Share prices on the London Stock Exchange *plunged* on news that Wilson plans to step down as Prime Minister. // The French franc *plummeted* to a 22-month low on Europe's money markets.

kyūryō 給料 salary 固定給 fixed salary ¶ →賃金; 給与 初任給 starting (=beginning) salary

kyūryōbi 給料日 pay-day

kyūryōchingin 給料賃金 salaries and wages

kyūsai 救済 →救援

kyūsaijigyō 救済事業 relief works

kyūsaikarikae 旧債借換 refunding of matured bond

kyūsaishikin 救済資金 relief funds

kyūsaisochi 救済措置 relief measure

kyūsaiyūshi 救済融資 relief loan

kyūshō 求償 claim for compensation; barter; give and take

kyūshōbōeki 求償貿易 reciprocal trade; barter trade

kyūshōken 求償権 right of demanding compensation; guarantor's right of indemnity

kyūshoku 求職 application for employment; job application; employment application; job search; job seeking; applications for vacancies ¶ the persistence of excesses of *applications for employment* over vacancies // unemployed workers demoralized by unsuccessful *job searches*

kyūshokubairitsu 求職倍率 application-to-opening ratio; ratio of labor supply to demand

kyūshokusha 求職者 job seeker; job applicant; people seeking work; job hunter; people in search of employment ¶ The number of *job-seekers* for whom work could not be found rose to 137,255. // The number of *people seeking work* fell to 1,455,000. // Of the labor force, totaling 18.9 million, 18.2 million are actually employed, while 0.7 million are *in search of employment*. // The number of *persons in search of employment* rose by 21,000 between April

1975 and April 1976. // The number of Australian unemployed *seeking* full-time *work* eased to an estimated 5.8% of the full-time labor force.

kyūshū 吸収 absorption; siphoning; sponging; soaking; mopping; sucking; drain ¶ Much labor can be productively *absorbed* in the development process // to *absorb* surplus funds on the market // to *absorb* unemployment more slowly but more surely than usual // to inhibit the *absorption* of imports into the economy // to *siphon* off holdings of these currencies that are in excess of their holders' needs // The Bundesbank *sponged* up DM3 billion in liquidity through sales of open-market paper. // The community's existing revenue sources were wholly *sucked* up by farm spending. // The excess liquidity was *mopped* up mainly through the Bank's calling-in of loans. // New bond issues were entirely *absorbed* in the banking system. // Faster growth of the labor force was not *absorbed* by new employment opportunities. // to *siphon* surplus funds *off* the market // The Fed will again *drain* reserves from the banking system. // Take-up of Treasury bills will *drain* 100 million sterling from the market.

kyūshūgappei 吸収合併 take-over; absorption ¶ to *take over* a company // to *absorb* small companies into the corporation // Croda's first big *acquisition* was chemicals producer Keyworth.

kyūshūnōryoku 吸収能力 absorption capacity

kyūsuisisetsu 給水施設 water

works

kyūtō 急騰 precipitous rise; sharp runup; spurt-up; shoot-up; soar; high rise; spurt; boost; boom; zoom ¶ a *spurt* in the market after a period of dullness // A rapid-fire series of *boosts* in prices of crude have *boomed* oil shares. // *Boom* in commodity prices escalated import costs. // the paralleled *boom* in land and property values // →高騰; 急増

kyūtōshōshūseiheikinkabukashisū 旧東証修正平均株価指数 old average stock price index of Tokyo Stock Exchange

kyūyo 給与 compensation; remuneration; salaries and allowances ¶ The swift advance in hourly *compensation* was softened somewhat. // → 賃金

現金給与 money wage

kyūyoiinkai 給与委員会 wages and salaries committee

kyūyojūtaku 給与住宅 issued house

kyūyoshotokukōjo 給与所得控除 earned income exemption

kyūyosuijun 給与水準 pay (= wage) level

kyūyotaikei 給与体系 wage system; salary structure; salary scale ¶ Directors decide upon an appropriate *salary scale*.

kyūzō 急増 large gain; sharp increase; considerable rise; rapid expansion; spurt; boost ¶ The *spurt* in imports is a measure of economic recovery. // the appropriation of money for *boosted* exports // Production was *boosted* in particular by foreign demand. // →高騰; 急騰

M

MOF yotakukin MOF預託金 ［日］ deposit by the Ministry of Finance

mabara まばら ［市］ spotted

māchantobanku マーチャント・バンク ［英］ merchant bank

machiairiron 待合理論 waiting-time theory; queuing theory

madoguchi 窓口 counter; window
　貸付窓口 lending window; discount window
　預金窓口 deposit window

madoguchishidō 窓口指導 policy of lending window; policy of discount window; discount window operation; window operation; ［日］ "window-guidance" ¶ *"window-guidance"* to banks in lending // The Bank of Japan has advised commercial banks of their *"window-guidance"* guidelines for the third quarter of this year, which represent a tightening of unofficial control over their net additional lending. // The Bank of Japan has informed thirteen Japanese city banks of their *window guidance* frameworks for the October-December quarter totalling ¥1,830 billion. // The total *"window guidance"* framework for 63 local banks in the quarter will be cut by 33.5% to ¥1,090 billion from the level recorded a year earlier.

maebarai 前払い payment in advance; prepayment; cash before delivery; c.b.d.
　運賃前払い freight prepaid
　郵税前払い postage prepaid

maebaraihiyō 前払費用 prepaid expenses

maebaraihokenryō 前払保険料 prepaid insurance

maebaraikin 前払金 purchase deposits; prepayment

maebarairisoku 前払利息 prepaid interest

maebaraitesūryō 前払手数料 front-end-fee

maedaoshi 前倒し acceleration ¶ an *acceleration* of the amortization schedule

maegari 前借り borrowing in advance

maegashi 前貸し advance
　船長前貸し advance to captain; prepaid freight

maegashikin 前貸金 advances; amount advanced

maegashitegata 前貸手形 advance bill; advance note
　輸入前貸手形 import advance bill
　輸出前貸手形 export advance bill

maemuki 前向き positive attitude; positive posture; positive stance; positive approach; forward-looking; outward-looking ¶ a *positive approach* to the problem // to assume a *positive posture* in solving the pollution problem; the lack of a *forward-looking* indicator to point to the likely rate of growth of demand // a help for a *forward looking* central-bank policy

maeukekin 前受金 prepayment; advance received; sales deposits ¶

export *prepayment* // *prepayment* for exports

maeukekinhenkanhoshō 前受金返還保証 refundment guarantee; refund bond

maewatashikin 前渡金 advance 買受契約前渡金 advance on purchase contract
小口前渡金 petty cash (advance)
仕入先前渡金 advance to wholesaler; advances to vendor

maewatashikobaraishikin 前渡小払資金 imprest cash

mainasuseichō マイナス成長 negative growth; minus growth; subzero growth ¶ Two-digit inflation and *subzero growth* still exist. // *growth* at an estimated *sub-zero* figure

mainasuyōin マイナス要因 deterrent; minus factor; negative factor; adverse element; depressant ¶ a major *deterrent* in pushing up wholesale prices // The main *depressant* of stock prices was the government's report of an 8.3 percent rise in GNP. // →要因

maindo マインド confidence; expectation; sentiment ¶ Consumer *confidence* continued to falter. // *Confidence* among consumers improved.

maizōryō 埋蔵量 deposit; reserve ¶ to develop iron ore *deposits* in northeast China // The oil *reserves* of these countries are being depleted. // Mexico's undersea oil *deposits* in the Pohai Gulf // the fourth largest coal *reserves* in the world // Japan's oil and gas *reserves*, located both off and onshore, total some 1.3 billion kls.
確認埋蔵量 proven reserve ¶ *Proven reserves* (i.e. those with a 90%

chance of being recovered) are put at 0.739 billion cubic meters.
推定埋蔵量 expected reserves; probable reserves ¶ Additional *expected reserves* (defined as those with a 50% chance of being recovered) are estimated at 815 billion cubic meters.
予想埋蔵量 possible reserves

mājin マージン spread; margin ¶ The coupon rate carries a 1 *percent* spread above the Euro-dollar rate. // a widening of *spreads* in interest rates // The lowest Euro-credit *spreads* shot up to 1 ¼ percent. // A squeeze on domestic interest *spreads* curbed profits from domestic business of banks. // → 格差

makikaeshi 巻き返し roll-back

makimodoshi 巻き戻し unwinding; rewinding ¶ the *unwinding* of earlier, leads and lags of current payments // a partial *unwinding* of short-term swaps and dollar sales resulting from the capital conversion requirement

mamapapasutoā ママ・パパ・ストアー ［米］ mom and pop store

manēsapurai マネー・サプライ money supply; money stock ¶ Growth of the *money supply* (= stock) accelerated. // The active *money supply,* consisting of demand deposits and currency, rose by $1.5 billion. // The credit and *money supply* was inelastic. // The narrowly-defined *money supply* (M_1), or the active *money supply,* consists of demand deposits at banks plus currency in circulation; the broadly-defined *money supply* represents M_1 plus time deposits. // The average *money supply* rose by 2%, seasonally adjusted, in June, giving a year-on-year rise of 11.3%. // to keep the rise in *money supply* to within 6-8% // The *money supply* growth rate is thus approaching the Bank's target range of expansion of 6-9% over the year. // The growth in the nation's basic *money supply* — currency plus checking accounts in commercial banks — came to an abrupt halt in November and have been shrinking. // The central-bank *money stock* rose at an annual rate of 7%. // The *money-stock* level is expected to remain high.

広義のマネーサプライ broadly-defined money supply; M_2, M_3, M_4... ¶ the rise in *money supply* expressed by the M_3 definition // M_3, the widest definition of the *money supply* rose at an annual rate of 12.8%.

狭義のマネーサプライ narrowly-defined money supply; M_1 ¶ The narrow measure of *money supply*, which takes in cash plus demand deposits, expanded at a much revised annual rate of 8.1%.

manetarīsābei マネタリー・サーベイ monetary survey

manki 満期 maturity; due date; expiration of the term; expiry; termination; arrival of the due date ¶ distribution of investment *maturities* // About $20 billion is falling *due* this year. // The extension of the *maturities* of Euro-credits was predominating refinances on a roll-over basis.

mankiharaimodoshikin 満期払戻金 matured repayment

mankihokenkin 満期保険金 matured endowment

mankiikkatsubarai 満期一括払い payment to be made by a lump sum at maturity

mankijitsu 満期日 date of maturity; due date

mankijitsudate 満期日建 maturity basis

mankijitsuhyō 満期日表 maturity list

mankijitsukōsei 満期日構成 maturity structure; debt maturity profile ¶ to improve the *maturity structure* of foreign debt // Country's *debt maturity profile* has become shorter.

mankijitsuoboechō 満期日覚え帳 maturity tickler

mankikogittetegata 満期小切手・手形 matured bills and notes

mankinobunsan 満期の分散 diversity of maturities availability

mankishōkan 満期償還 redemption at maturity

mankizenshōkan 満期前償還 prior redemption

mankizen'urimodoshi 満期前売戻し resale before maturity

manryō 満了 expiration; termination; expiry

契約期間満了 expiry of the term of contract

mansei 慢性 chronic; perpetual ¶ *chronic* inflation // *perpetual* external payments deficit // *perpetuation* of the over-borrowed position of business

manseiteki 慢性的 chronic ¶ The Eisenhower years were years of *chronic* growth stagnation.

manseitekifukyō 慢性的不況 chronic depression

manseitekiinfure 慢性的インフレ chronic inflationary situation; chronic inflation; (deep-)rooted (=inveterated; infixed; implanted) inflation

manshon マンション →アパート

maruchishōhō マルチ商法 multi-level marketing system

maruyūseido マル優制度 [日] non-tax system for small savings; "preferred" savings system ¶ [参考] deposits held through illegal use of tax-free savings accounts

masatsu 摩擦 friction ¶ to ameliorate trade *frictions* with the U.S. // trade-related *frictions* evolving from changes in competitive position among specific industries

māsharuenjo マーシャル援助 Marshall aid

māsharukeikaku マーシャル計画 Marshall Plan: European Recovery Program

māsharunokei マーシャルの K Marshallian *"k"*

mashibaraikin 増払金 additional payment; extrapayment; demurrage

mashishōkokin 増証拠金 additional warrant money; additional cover; additional margin

mashitanpo 増担保 additional security; additional collateral

masukīhō マスキー法 [米] Muskie Act

mattanjuyō 末端需要 ultimate demand; final demand ¶ →最終需要

mattantōshika 末端投資家 end investors

mawashigyoku 回し玉 wash-order; cross order

meberi 目減り loss in weight; decrement; reduction; erosion; attrition ¶ the *erosion* of the value of money by inflation // Workers tried to offset the *erosion* of their paychecks by increased wage demands. // the dramatic *attrition* of

personal financial wealth from inflation // the *erosion* in India's export earnings due to the decline in the rupee value of the dollar // The depreciation of the dollar can *erode* Nigeria's oil revenue in real terms by as much as 40%. // The *reduction* of the value of deposits by inflation was considerable. // [参考] Inflation undermined pay checks and savings.

medamashōhin 目玉商品 loss leader

meigara 銘柄 description; title; issue ¶ various *issues* of the loan

meigarabaibai 銘柄売買 sale by brand; sale on description

meigarahin 銘柄品 brand-named item

meigikakikae 名義書換 transfer of name; name transfer ¶ *Transfer* books are opened and closed. // shares *transferred* to his *name* on the corporation's books

meigikakikaedairinin 名義書換代理人 transfer agent

meimokuchingin 名目賃金 nominal wage; cash earning

meimokufusai 名目負債 nominal liabilities

meimokukahei 名目貨幣 token money

meimokukokuminsōshishutsu 名目国民総支出 gross national expenditures at current prices

meimokunedan 名目値段 nominal price

meimokuno 名目の in nominal terms; at current (market) prices; nominal

meimokurieki 名目利益 nominal profit

meimokuriritsu 名目利率 nominal

rate of interest

meimokuseichōritsu 名目成長率 growth rate in nominal terms; nominal growth rate

meimokushihon 名目資本 nominal capital

meimokushisan 名目資産 nominal assets

meimokushūnyū 名目収入 nominal income

meimokusōba 名目相場 nominal quotation; nominal rate

meimokutetsukekin 名目手付金 nominal consideration

meimokuwaribikiritsu 名目割引率 nominal rate of discount

meirō 明朗 [市] cheerful

meisai 明細 particulars; details

mejā メジャー(石油会社) major international oil companies

mēkāhin メーカー品 brand-named item

menbō 綿紡 cotton spinning

men'eki 免疫 immunity ¶ to be *immune* from the current wage-price spiral // The dollar will not be miraculously *immune* to the vicissitudes of floating *immunity*. // The economy is now *immune* to external influences.

men'ekichidai 免役地代 quit rent

menkyosei 免許制 license system; licensing ¶ [参考] two foreign banks with Australian banking licenses

men'orimono 綿織物 cotton fabrics

mensekijōkō 免責条項 exemption clause; waiver clause; escape clause; [証市] market-out clause ¶ →ウエイバー

mensetsuchōsahō 面接調査法 interview system

menzei 免税 tax exemption; duty

exemption; tax relief ¶ to provide *exemptions* from payroll *taxes* or the equivalent tax credit // *exemptions* from particular *taxes* such as property and registration taxes, and stamp duties // full *tax exemption* for imports of capital goods for modernization // to grant *tax relief* to the lowest income group

menzeigendo 免税限度 duty-free allowance

menzeihin 免税品 duty-free goods; goods exempt from duties; free goods; non-dutiable articles; non-taxable goods

menzeishōken 免税証券 tax-free bond; tax-exempt bond

menzeiten 免税点 exemption; exemption point

menzeitōshi 免税投資 tax-free investment

menzeiyunyūhin 免税輸入品 duty-free imports

meppunshitsushōken 滅紛失証券 destroyed or lost bond

mērudē メール・デー mail days

mērukurejitto メール・クレジット mail credit

mesaki 目先き immediate future; near future →当面

mesakikan 目先観 immediate outlook; outlook in the near future; near-time prospects; immediate prospects ¶ The *immediate prospect* was by no means bad.

mesakinorieki 目先の利益 immediate profit

mesakisōba 目先相場 quotations in the near future; near-term market trend

mesakiyasu 目先安 weak for the immediate future

meyasu 目安 guidance; guidepost;

guideline; benchmark; barometer ¶ The rates below are a *guide* to general levels but don't always represent actual transactions. // ［参考］ →ガイドライン

miaikanjō 見合勘定 (per) contra-account; mate account; corresponding account

mibunpaihōjinrijun 未分配法人利潤 undistributed corporate profit

michakuhinbaibai 未着品売買 sale to arrive

midorinokokuseichōsa 緑の国勢調査 →自然環境保全調査

mihaitōrieki 未配当利益 undivided profit

miharaichingin 未払賃金 wage payable

miharaifusai 未払負債 accrued liability

miharaihaitōkin 未払配当金 dividends unclaimed

miharaikanjō 未払勘定 account payable; outstanding account; call account; unpaid account

miharaikin 未払金 payment arrears; amount in arrears; arrearage; account payable; arrears ¶ short-term external *payment arrears* of Zambia rose to an unprecedented level. // a buildup of *arrears*; on external payments

miharaikomigaku 未払込額 capital stock unpaid

miharaino 未払いの unpaid; overdue; delinquent outstanding; unsettled; payable; unclaimed; in arrear(s) ¶ debtor countries in *arrear* with their external payments // Interest payments became more than 30 days *overdue*. // the number of days and interest *in arrears* // All *delinquent* principal and interest have been brought current.

miharairishi 未払利子 interest payable; overdue interest payment

miharaishihonkin 未払資本金 unpaid capital; uncalled capital

miharaizandaka 未払残高 outstanding balance

miharaizeikin 未払税金 tax payable

mihon 見本 sample; specimen
標準見本 standard sample
商品見本 trade sample

mihonhin 見本品 sample; specimen ¶ *samples* of clothing // *specimen* coins

mihonichi 見本市 trade fair; sample fair

mihonshōken 見本証券 specimen certificate

mihontsūka 見本通貨 specimen currency

mijitsugenrieki 未実現利益 unrealized profit

mijukurengenkairōdōsha 未熟練限界労働者 unskilled marginal worker

mijūsokujuyō 未充足需要 demand backlog ¶ production to catch up on the demand *backlog*

mikaerishikin 見返り資金 counterpart funds

mikaeritanpo 見返り担保 collateral security

mikaeriyushutsu 見返り輸出 collateral export

mikaihatsuno 未開発の undeveloped; underdeveloped; rudimentary; untapped ¶ *underdeveloped* regions with *rudimentary* capital markets and *untapped* natural resources

mikaihatsushigen 未開発資源 untapped resource

mikaishūyokintōsaiken 未回収預

金等債権 uncollected deposit rights

mikakuninshihonryūshutsunyū 未確認資本流出入 unidentified capital outflow and inflow

mikakunintorihiki 未確認取引 unidentified transaction

mikeikahiyō 未経過費用 prepaid expenses; expenses paid in advance

mikeikahokenryō 未経過保険料 unearned premium; unexpired insurance premium

mikeikano 未経過の unearned; unexpired; prepaid

mikeikarishi 未経過利子 unexpired interest

mikeikasaikenhi 未経過債券費 debenture expenses not elapsed

mikeikasaikenwaribikiryō 未経過債券割引料 unamortized discount on non-interest-bearing debentures

mikeikawaribikiryō 未経過割引料 unearned discount

mikessaikawase 未決済為替 outstanding exchange

mikessaikawaseshikinkari 未決済為替資金借 domestic exchange unsettled account, Cr.

mikessaikawaseshikinkashi 未決済為替資金貸 domestic exchange unsettled account, Dr.

mikessaino 未決済の outstanding; unsettled; suspense

mikessankanjō 未決算勘定 open account; suspense account; unsettled account; unbalanced account; outstanding account

mikessanmotochō 未決算元帳 open ledger

mikessanno 未決算の unsettled; unbalanced; open

mikirihin 見切品 clearance goods; bargain

mikirihinbaibai 見切品売買 clear-

ance sale; bargain sale

mikirinedan 見切値段 sacrifice price; sacrificial price; clearance price; bargain price

mikiriuri 見切売り sacrifice sale; bargain sale; clearance sale; rummage sale; sell-off

mikōfushōken 未交付証券 unclaimed bond

mikomi 見込み projection ¶ a *projected* 2.3 billion dollar shortfall in the budget for the coming year // to assemble a picture of trade flows and *project* it into the future // Economic advisors *projected* the second quarter GNP at the lower end of a three to five percent range. // →見通し; 予測

mikomiakinai 見込商内 speculative trading (=transaction); speculation

mikomikakaku 見込み価格 anticipated price

mikomikyaku 見込み客 prospective customer (=client); prospect; potential buyer ¶ to interview *prospects* to obtain orders

mikomirieki 見込み利益 anticipated profit ¶ The issuer is not liable for the loss of the underwriters' *anticipated profits*.

mikomiseisan 見込み生産 market production

mikomiyunyū 見込み輸入 anticipated import

mikoshi 見越し anticipation; expectation ¶ in *anticipation* of a rise in prices // ［参考］ hurried buying to beat inflation

mikoshiakinai 見越商内 →見込商内

mikoshibaibai 見越売買 sales on contingent

mikoshigai 見越買い speculative

buying

mikoshikanjō 見越勘定 accrued account

mikoshiyunyū 見越輸入 speculative imports

minaoshi 見直し reassessment; review; reconsideration; overhaul; reappraisal; ¶ a *reassessment* of the effectiveness of monetary policy measures in force // a *review* of conventional methods // a major *overhaul* of prices should wipe out accumulated losses // to reassess the level of provisions for bad debts // These objectives could be promoted by an *overhaul* of the structure of Federal taxation. // These policy measures would be *re appraised* from time to time. // the decrease in demand from industrial borrowers led to a *reappraisal* of the potential of international banking // to provide a unique opportunity to *review* tariff structures // The government should seriously reassess its food subsidy plans, and *reappraise* the EEC countries' Agricultural Policy.

minaosu 見直す [市] rally; recover; improve

minashison'eki みなし損益 artificial accounting profit or loss

min'eijigyō 民営事業 private undertaking; private enterprise; privately operated business

minirisesshon ミニ・リセッション mini-recession; mild recession; shallow (but prolonged) recession

minkangaishi 民間外資 private foreign capital

minkan'inpakutorōn 民間インパクトローン untied private loan

minkanjūtakukensetsu 民間住宅建設 private residential construction; private housing

minkannenkin 民間年金 private annuity; private pension

minkanno 民間の private; private sector; non-government(al)

minkanshōhi 民間消費 private consumption

minomawarihin 身の回り品 apparel; personal effects

minsei 民生 people's livelihood

minseiyōdenkikiki 民生用電気機器 electric(al) household machines and equipment

minzokujiketsushugi 民族自決主義 national (=racial) self-determination principle

miokuri 見送り marking time; [市] wait-and-see

miriyōno 未利用の unused; underemployed; unemployed; untapped ¶ to expand exports by drawing on *underemployed* resources

miriyōnōryoku 未利用能力 unused capacity ¶ The *unused capacity* of business plant and equipment is measured at 16-17%.

miriyōrōdō 未利用労働 unused labor

miriyōsetsubi 未利用設備 unused (productive) capacity; unutilized (productive) facility; idle capacity

miriyōshigen 未利用資源 unused resources ¶ There are sufficient *unused resources* to provide for further expansion.

miriyōshihon 未利用資本 unsued capital; idle capital

misaichūmon 未済注文 back order; unfilled order; backlog of orders

misaikanjō 未済勘定 unsettled account; outstanding account

misaino 未済の unpaid; unsettled; outstanding

misaishakkin 未済借金 outstanding debt

misejimai 店仕舞い going out of business ¶ The once giant retailer is conducting the *going-out-of-business* sale. // An *out-of-business* sale represents the bargain of a lifetime.

mishobunkesson 未処分欠損 undisposed deficit

mishobunno 未処分の undivided; undisposed

mishobunrieki 未処分利益 undivided profit

mishobunriekijōyokin 未処分利益剰余金 unappropriated profit

mishōkachūmon 未消化注文 unfulfilled order; backlog of (unfulfilled) orders; order backlog ¶→受注残

mishōkakōjidaka 未消化工事高 value of unfinished work (on hand)

mishōkandaka 未償還高 outstanding issues

mishōkankōsai 未償還公債 outstanding loans

mishōkanno 未償還の outstanding; unredeemed

mishōkano 未消化の unabsorbed; undigested; unfulfilled; unexecuted; unsold

mishōkanshōken 未償還証券 outstanding securities

mishōkashōken 未消化証券 undigested securities

mishōkyakukensetsurisoku 未償却建設利息 unamortized interest during construction

mishōkyakuno 未償却の unamortized

mishūhaitō 未収配当 dividend receivable

mishūhokenryō 未収保険料 unearned premium; deferred premium

mishūkin 未収金 accounts receivable

mishūno 未収の accrued; receivable; unearned; deferred

mishūrishi 未収利子 interest receivable

mishūryōkin 未収料金 outstanding fee

mishūshikanjō 未収支勘定 accrued accounts; accruals

mishūshūeki 未収収益 uncollected income; accrued income

misoshikirōdōsha 未組織労働者 unorganized workers; unorganized labor

mitatsukanjō 未達勘定 account in transit

mitatsushōhin 未達商品 goods in transit

miteisūryōkeiyaku 未定数量契約 open-end contract

mitōshi 見通し prospect; outlook; perspective; foresight; projection; prevision; preview; prognosis; vista ¶ Many observers raised their sights on the business *prospect* for the remainder of the year. // The *prospect* is encouraging. // There is every *prospect* for continued expansion in the German economy. // *Prospects* for renewal of business expansion are strengthened by a flow of new orders. // *Prospects* in the longer run are expected by international developments. // The *outlook* for the South African economy remains promising. // Two important factors are progressively enhancing the *outlook* for the Belgian economy. // Important developments have significantly improved the *outlook* for greater stability in our economy. // Unexpected declines in production and trade added a new note of caution to the *outlook*. // This beclouded the business *outlook*. // to get the right *perspective* // to see through the *perspective* of years // The price *prospects* look bleak. // Among manufacturing firms, export *prospects* are being viewed with increasing optimism. // Future *prospects* are judged more favorably. // Most international forecasters remain sceptical about Italian *prospects*. // The immediate *prospects* are by no means bad. // The *propsects* for the coming year are clouded by anxiety about the world economic situation. // the administration's rosier economic *projections* // to lack *foresight* as to... // *Views* in Denmark on the economic situation were not harmonious. // The slowness in fixed asset investment makes the *prognosis* a slow recovery for a considerable time. // a *preview* of the financial statements of a business // [参考] The economy can now look forward to a period of sound growth. // As we look to the future, there is grounds for confidence that... // a forward-looking appraisal of the financial aspects of the business program // →展望；予測

mitōshinan 見通し難 uncertainty about the outlook (=prospects); confused outlook; lack of direction ¶ business *uncertainties* about the long-term implications of the new energy situation for Japan // Dealers remain *confused* about the near term *outlook* for the *lack of direction* for the market. // The exchange markets remained in the grip of *uncertainty* over the *outlook* for

major currencies. // They are resigned to several more months of *uncertainty* over business *prospects*. // [参考] Many participants are uncertain where the market is actually heading.

mitsumata みつまた paper birch

mitsumori 見積り estimate; estimation; assessment; valuation; computation
過大見積り over-estimation
過少見積り under-estimation

mitsumorifūtai 見積風袋 computed fare

mitsumorigenka 見積原価 estimated cost

mitsumorikaitsukekanjōsho 見積買付勘定書 proforma account of purchase

mitsumorikakaku 見積価格 estimated value; assessed value

mitsumorikawasetegata 見積為替手形 proforma bill; proforma draft

mitsumoriokurijō 見積送状 proforma invoice

mitsumorisho 見積書 (written) estimate; tender

mitsumoritaishakutaishōhyō 見積貸借対照表 proforma balance sheet

mitsuyunyū 密輸入 smuggling; contraband cheaper than legal gold. ¶ tenders at near the going *contraband* rate, not the legal one

mitsuyunyūsen 密輸入船 smuggling vessel; smuggler

mitsuyunyūsha 密輸入者 smuggler

mitsuyunyūsōsakan 密輸入捜査官 searcher (for smuggling)

mitsuyushutsu 密輸出 smuggling abroad

mizounokakkyō 未曾有の活況 unprecedented activity (=expansion);

unprecedentedly brisk activity

mizumashi 水増し padding; watering; featherbedding; dilution // *watered* assets // *featherbedding* of employment ¶ to be charged with *padding* accounts and illegally declare dividends // *watering* of assets, and of sotcks

mizumashichingin 水増し賃金 make-up pay

mizumashikabu 水増し株 watered stock

mizumashishisan 水増し資産 feathered assets; watered assets

mizusakiannairyō 水先案内料 pilotage

mizushigenkaihatsu 水資源開発 water resources development

mochiai 保合い quiet; no change; maintained; unchanged; level; leveling-off; leveling-out; static; stationary; steady; flat; even keel ¶ Automotive sales were virtually *flat*. // Rates are holding basically *unchanged*. // The market is on an *even keel*, not going down. // [参考] Equities marked time this week. // The dollar ended little changed at the openlng level. // The other components of the index average combined to show little change. // → 物価

強保合い steady with an upward tendency

弱保合い steady with a downward tendency

mochibun 持分 share; equity; proprietary interest; holding; interest
残余持分 residual interest

mochibunshutoku 持分取得 acquisition of proprietary interest

mochidaka 持高 position; holdings ¶ to square the foreign exchange *position*, by covering the short *position*, or liquidating the long position // → 保有(高)

mochidakachōsei 持高調整 position squaring; book squaring; position unwinding; evening out of position ¶ *unwinding* of long yen *positions* on Chicago's future market // to *even out positions* ahead of the weekend // U.S. dollars rose strongly in active end-of-month *position squaring* by merchant banks.

mochidakakisei 持高規制 [外] regulation on banks' foreign exchange position

mochidakashūchūsei 持高集中制 [外] limited open position system

mochidakasōsa 持高操作 [外] exchange operation

mochiie 持家 owner-occupied home; (privately) owned house; owner-occupied house

mochikabu 持株 shares held; shareholdings; equity share ¶ The *equity share* of Toyo Kogyo in the proposed Toyota-Ford car making venture would be less than 20 percent. // [参考] Ford owns a 25 percent equity in this company.

mochikabugaisha 持株会社 holding company

mochikoshi 持越し over-carrying

mochikoshihi 持越し費 over-carrying cost

mochikoshihin 持越し品 goods carried over; carry-over

mochikoshimai 持越し米 rice stock carried over

mochinaoshi 持直し recovery; improvement; rally; revival; resurgence; rebound ¶ On the *recovery* trading picked up again. // The *recovery* has gathered momentum. // A *recovery* began on a broad base from the slackening of domestic activity. // Economic *recovery* cumulates. // A *rally* on the London stock exchange Tuesday reached most sectors except gold mining shares.

mochinaosu 持直す improve; recover; rally; revive; [市] regain

moderuchenji モデルチェンジ model change-over

moderukōsei モデル構成 model building

modoririsoku 戻り利息 prepaid interest paid back

modoritakane 戻り高値 [市] recovery high

modoriuri 戻り売り [市] selling on a rally

modoshi 戻し return; [市] cutting (=recouping) loss ¶ Some *losses* were *cut*.

modoshikai 戻し買い covering purchase (=contract)

modoshikawase 戻し為替 re-draft; return bill

modoshisōkin 戻し送金 return remittance

modoshiunchin 戻し運賃 return freight; rebate of freight; refund

modoshiuragaki 戻し裏書 re-endorsement

modoshizei 戻し税 drawback; (tax) rebate

mōgeijishōkoshorui モーゲイジ証拠書類 mortgage (securities); mortgage pass-through certificate; mortgage loan certificate; mortgage participation certificate

mogijikken 模擬実験 simulation

mojihyōjisōchi 文字表示装置 [コン] character display unit to withhold *lucrative* govenment contracts from some companies // to direct

products from contract deliveries to more *lucrative* spot sales

mōkaru 儲かる lucrative ¶ to put money out to most *lucrative* borrowers // to gain competitive edge in the *lucrative* Florida market

mokuhyō 目標 target; goal; objective; focus; mark; aim ¶ Of the 13 agricultural projects, 8 achieved or surpassed their production *targets*. // The Soviet Union has scaled down production *targets* for 1976-80. // The draft version of the plan contained a *target* increase of 26-28%. // This *target* range has been lowered gradually over time. // Belgium has not fixed a specific *target* for money supply growth. // The actual output will fall short of the *targets*. // The *target* of one-digit inflation will probably be attained. // The spending ceiling will become a *target* to guide the American lawmarkers as they consider expenditures for federal programs for 1977. // to reconcile these partly conflicting policy *goals* // It would be too ambitious a *goal* for the time being to bring about a stabilization of foreign exchange rates at a specific level. // A permanent *objective* of monetary policy is to maintain the value of the domestic currency. // The Federal Reserve quantified its long-range *objectives* with regard to important monetary aggregates. // The report is to provide a *focus* for informed Congressional debate. // The primary *aim* of the recent series of policy actions is to curb price inflation. // The country *aims* at double exports. // The market operations have been directed toward the *aim* of discouraging sales to the Federal Reserve of short-term securities. // the *aimed*-at expansion in the central-bank money supply // The Finance Ministry's conventional forecasting methods were overshooting the *mark* by more than 8 1/2%. // This *aim* was embodied in the government plan. // to express the monetary *aims* of policy in terms of the target figure // →政策（運営）目標

mokuhyōchi 目標値 targeted value

mokuhyōhensū 目標変数 target variable

mokuhyōken 目標圏 target range; target zone; target band ¶ the figure of M1 growth being just below the high end of the quarterly *target range* // U.S. money supply growth fell below the Fed's five-nine parcent *target range*. // The Bank of Canada's annual growth *target range* set for M1 money supply is 6-10% from the June base. // to aim at real economic growth in the 3-3.5% *target range* // The *target range* for M2 growth was raised from 4-9% to one of 5-10%. // to roll forward the 8-12 range for sterling M3 // The current rate of expansion of the money supply, M1, is a little below the upper limit of the existing *target band*. // British money-supply growth, sterling M3, at mid-October was likely to be below the 8-12% *range*, the *target* originally set for the twelve months ending next April. // the *target zone* of the money supply growth // [参考] The Banking committee was aiming for money-supply growth in the year of 4-6.5% for M1, 6.5-9% for

M2 and 7.5-10% for M3.

mokuhyōsangyō 目標産業 target industries

mokuhyōsōbaken 目標相場圏 target zone of rates ¶ to push the exchange rate below the lower limit of the *target zone* // →目標圏

mokuromi 目論見 plan; scheme; project; intention; design; aim; object; view; program

mokuromisho 目論見書 prospectus ¶ This *prospectus* shall not constitute an offer to sell these securities prior to registration under the securities laws.

　　会社設立目論見書 prospectus of promotion
　　仮目論見書 preliminary prospectus
　　要約目論見書 summary prospectus

mokuseihinkōgyō 木製品工業 wooden products industry

mokuteki 目的 →目標

mokutekichokin 目的貯金 savings with a certain object

mokuzai 木材 timber; lumber

mokuzaikōgyō 木材工業 lumber industry

momiai もみ合い ［市］ hovering; wavering ¶ Prices *hovered* around the ¥4,000-mark. // to *waver* low

momiaishōjō もみ合い商状 slight fluctuation

mondaiten 問題点 problematical point; problem-incurring point; recurring source of controversy; controversial object; problem ¶ to remain a continuing *problem* in many lines // It has been the *subject* of much *controversy*.

moratoriamu モラトリアム moratorium ¶ Farmers lost some $2 billion in sales during last year's *moratorium* on grain sales to the

Soviet Union. // Industrialized countries may have to grant developing countries a *moratorium* on debts totaling $142 million.

morikaesu 盛り返す ［市］ revive; rally; surge up; rebound ¶ →回復

mosaku 摸索 trials and errors; groping

mōshikomi 申込み application; offer; proposal; request; subscription ¶ to achieve greater coordination in the examination and processing of *applications* for aid
買申込み buying offer
売申込み selling offer

mōshikomihoshōkin 申込保証金 deposit; deposit received

mōshikomikin 申込金 subscription money; application money

mōshikomisha 申込者 applicant; subscriber; proposer

mōshikomishōkokin 申込証拠金 advances on subscription

motochō 元帳 ledger; control account

motohikiukegyō 元引受業 underwriting (group)

moyōnagame 模様眺め ［市］ wait-and-see; buyers on the sidelines; watch-and-wait ¶ The *wait-and-see* attitude prevailed among investors for some time. // Many dealers stayed *on the sidelines* ahead of release of money supply figures due out tomorrow. // Trading was quiet with most buyers *sidelined*. // ［参考］ Traders generally held off to see the market direction. // to seek a direction to the market // Many traders and investors took to the sidelines to wait for the next major movement.

moyorihin 最寄り品 convenience goods

mozōkahei 模造貨幣 imitated coin; counterfeit

mozōken 模造券 imitated note; counterfeit (note)

mūdishisū ムーディ指数 Moody index (of commodity prices); Moody's index number

mūdo ムード mood; atmosphere; sentiment; psychology; mentality air; climate ¶ The present more optimistic *mood* of consumers could be destroyed by a new burst of inflation. // Business *mood* will swing to the optimistic side. // a subdued economic *atmosphere* // an inflationary *psychology* spreading over the economy // Hard times foster a merger *mentality*. // The optimistic *mood* of industry has confidence in the future business trend. // The *mood* in the bond market darkened. // There was a marked change of *mood* in the market. // The exuberant *mood* that then emerged in the business community gave rise to waves of speculation. // International banks and bankers are in an expansionary *mood* not a defensive *mood*. // The defensive *moods* of the past 18 months, while still prevalent to some degree, have given way to a *mood* of guarded optimism. // This expansionary *mood* is tempered by concern about banks' capital adequacy. // The past go-go banking *mood* of international bankers has ended. // An *atmosphere* of crisis was produced. // An *air* of crisis is spreading across the U.S. // the importance of a liberal *climate* for international investment flows // a considerably more restrictive monetary *climate* // →気運

mugakumenkabu 無額面株 non-par stock

mugawaseyushutsunyū 無為替輸出入 no-draft export and import

mugenhōka 無限法貨 unlimited legal tender

mugensekinin 無限責任 unlimited liability

mugensekininkaisha 無限責任会社 unlimited liability company

mugensekininkumiai 無限責任組合 unlimited partnership

mugensekininshain 無限責任社員 general partner

mugiketsukenkabu 無議決権株 non-voting stock

muhai 無配 non-dividend-paying

muhaihokenryō 無配保険料 non-participating rate

muhaikabu 無配株 non-dividend payer

muhainisuru 無配にする pass (= omit) dividend ¶ news of cut or *omitted dividends*

muhaitō 無配当 passed dividend ¶ to *pass a dividend*

muhiyōshōkan 無費用償還 repayment without cost

muhizuke 無日付け undated; dateless

muhizukehikiuke 無日付引受け undated acceptance

muhizuketegata 無日付手形 undated bill

mujin'ekishisutemu 無人駅システム unmanned station system

mujingaisha 無尽会社 mutual loan company; ［日］ "mujin" company

mujinhanbai 無人販売 robot selling

mujinkasen 無人化船 unmanned ship

mujinkōjō 無人工場 push button factory

mujinkyūfukin 無尽給付金 mutual installment loan

mujinsōko 無人倉庫 unmanned warehouse

mujinsūpā 無人スーパー automatic supermarket

mujintenpo 無人店舗 robot-retailing store; nonattended store

mujōkenhikidashiken 無条件引出権 ［外］ unconditional drawing right

mujōkenmono 無条件物 unconditional call loan; unconditionals

mujōkenno 無条件の unconditional; unqualified; open

mujōken'operēshon 無条件オペレーション unconditional operation

mujōkenryūdōsei 無条件流動性 unconditional liquidity

mujōkenshin'yōjō 無条件信用状 open credit

mujōkentorihiki 無条件取引 outright dealing (=transaction; operation)

mukachishisan 無価値資産 dead asset

mukainomi 向い呑み ［市］ bucketing

mukakuninshin'yōjō 無確認信用状 unconfirmed credit

mukawaseyushutsunyū 無為替輸出入 export on a consignment base; export (or import) without foreign exchange

mukeibunkazai 無形文化財 intangible cultural property

mukeienjo 無形援助 moral support

mukeikoteishisan 無形固定資産 intangible fixed asset

mukeino 無形の invisible; intangible; immaterial

mukeishihon 無形資本 immaterial capital; intangible (=invisible) capital

mukeishisan 無形資産 intangible (=invisible) asset

mukeizaisan 無形財産 immaterial property; intangible property

mukigen 無期限 perpetual; indefinite ¶ a strike for an *indefinite* period // to postpone *indefinitely*

mukigenkashitsukekin 無期限貸付金 dead loan

mukigenkōsai 無期限公債 perpetual loan

mukigennenkin 無期限年金 perpetual annuity

mukigenshasai 無期限社債 perpetual bond

mukimeiininjō 無記名委任状 blank letter of attorney

mukimeikabu 無記名株 bearer share; uninscribed stock

mukimeikōsai 無記名公債 bearer (government) bond

mukimeino 無記名の unregistered; uninscribed; blank; general

mukimeisaiken 無記名債券 bearer bond (−debenture)

mukimeishasai 無記名社債 bearer (industrial) bond

mukimeishōken 無記名証券 bearer security (=bond)

mukimeitegata 無記名手形 blank letter of bill

mukimeiteikiyokin 無記名定期預金 anonymous time deposit

mukimeitōhyō 無記名投票 secret voting; secret ballot; unsigned vote

mukimeiuragaki 無記名裏書 blank letter of endorsement; general endorsement

mukimeiyokin 無記名預金 unin-scribed deposit

mukiryoku 無気力 listlessness; lifelessness; lethargy ¶ The stock market drifted *listlessly* Wednesday after the failure of its bid to reach a new 1976 high on Tuesday. // There was little in the day's economic news to stir traders out of their *lethargy*. // The dollar traded *listlessly* in a narrow band.

mukōgaienjin 無公害エンジン clean engine

mukōgaikonbināto 無公害コンビナート pollution-free industrial complex

mukōgaisha 無公害車 non-polluting vehicle

mukōno 無効の null and void; invalid; unavailable

mukoshōfunanishōken 無故障船荷証券 clean bill of lading; clean B/L

mukyoshutsunenkin 無拠出年金 non-contributory pension

mukyōsōshūdan 無競争集団 non-competing groups

mukyūekimu 無給役務 unpaid services

muranoaru むらのある [市] patchy; mixed

murishishakkan 無利子借款 interest-free loan

murisoku 無利息 interest-free; flat; passive; non-interest-bearing

murisokukōsai 無利息公債 flat bond; non-interest-bearing bond; passive bond

murisokusaimu 無利息債務 passive debt

murisokushōken 無利息証券 non-interest-bearing securitiy

musabetsu 無差別 non-discrimination; indiscriminate ¶ *non-discriminatory* treatment accorded all nationalities // the generalized *indiscriminate* slowdown in international lending by the banks

museigenhōka 無制限法貨 unlimited legal tender

museigenno 無制限の unlimited; unrestricted; free; liberal; unbridled ¶ to control the hitherto *unbridled* expansion of offshore lending by banks

museigentsūka 無制限通貨 free currency

museikyūhaito 無請求配当 unclaimed dividend

museikyūkabuken 無請求株券 unclaimed stock

museikyūyokin 無請求預金 unclaimed deposit

mushōhaikyū 無償配給 free distribution

mushōinin 無償委任 naked authority

mushōkabu 無償株 gratis share; stock dividend

mushōkeiyaku 無償契約 naked contract

mushōkeizaikyōryoku 無償経済協力 economic grant

mushōkennō 無償権能 naked power

mushōkōfu 無償交付 free distribution; stock dividend

mushōkōi 無償行為 gratuitous act

mushōno 無償の naked; gratis; free of charge; without compensa-tion; without quid pro quo

mushōnokamotsu 無償の貨物 goods without compensation

mushōnokyūjutsuhin 無償の救じゅつ品 goods sent without compensation for relief purpose

mushōshintaku 無償信託 naked trust

mushōtorihiki 無償取引 gratuitous transaction

mushōwariate 無償割当 gratis issue; gratis distribution; gratis allocation

mutanpokariire 無担保借入 clean loan

mutanpokashitsuke 無担保貸付 unsecured advance

mutanpokōsai 無担保公債 unsecured bond

mutanpono 無担保の unsecured; without collateral; naked

mutanposaiken 無担保債券 plain bond; debenture (bond)

mutanposaikensha 無担保債権者 unsecured creditor

mutanposhasai 無担保社債 unsecured debenture; unsecured bond

mutanpowaribikitegata 無担保割引手形 unsecured discount bill

muzairyō 無材料 [市] without new stimulants (=incentives)

muzaya 無鞘 no margin

myūchuarufando ミューチュアル・ファンド [米] mutual fund; investment company

N

naatenin 名宛人 drawee (of a check), addressee (of a letter)

nabezokogata な べ 底 型 gradual U-shaped pattern

nagare 流れ tide; flow ¶ Intervention by the central bank turned the *tide* of trading in the exchange market. // to deprive consumers of a free *flow* of information // the disappointing *flow* of orders // to increase the *flow* of investment for agricultural production in the developing countries // to disturb the smooth *flow* of merchandise // to improve the *flow* of official development assistance to developing countries // long-term financial *flows* in the developing countries

nagaresagyō 流れ作業 conveyor system; assembly line; flow system; line production

nagaresagyōzu 流れ作業図 flow chart

nage 投げ [市] shaking-out; spilling; forced liquidation; sacrific; stop-loss

嫌気投げ turning into stale account

nagemono 投げ物 [市] spilling stock; sacrifice sale

nagemonoshōka 投げ物消化 [市] absorption of spilling stocks

nageni 投荷 jettison; discard; to throw goods overboard (so as to lighten a ship in danger)

nagesōba 投げ相場 sacrifice

nageuri 投売り sacrifce sale; less-than-cost bargain; slaughter sale; dumping; distress sale (=selling)

nageurishōhin 投売り商品 distress goods

naibufukeizai 内部不経済 internal diseconomy

naibukansa 内部監査 internal audit

naibukeiei 内部経営 internal management

naibukensa 内部検査 internal inspection

naibukenseisoshiki 内部牽制組織 internal check system

naiburyūho 内部留保 retained profit; inner reserve; internal reserve

naibushikin 内部資金 internally generated funds

naibutōsei 内部統制 internal control

naibuyōin 内部要因 internal factor

naichishiteiyokin 内地指定預金 designated domestic deposit

naigaiju 内外需 domestic and foreign demand; internal and external demand; demand at home and abroad

naigaikinkō 内外均衡 equilibrium at home and abroad; domestic and international equilibrium; internal and external equilibria

naigaikinrisa 内外金利差 differrential between interest rates at home and abroad; spread between domestic and overseas interest rates; gap between domestic and international interest rates; interest rate differentials between Japan and other countries; differentials between Japanese and overseas interest rates

naiju 内需 domestic demand; home demand

naikinshokuin 内勤職員 back-office force (=staff)

naikokubōeki 内国貿易 inland trade; home trade; domestic trade

naikokukangyōhakurankai 内国勧業博覧会 national industrial fair; national industrial exhibition

naikokukawasekyūshū 内国為替吸収 domestic exchange inducement

naikokumintaigū 内国民待遇 national treatment

naikokuno 内国の home; inland; domestic

naikokusai 内国債 internal loan; domestic bond

naikokuseihin 内国製品 home made goods; domestic manufacture; domestic products

naikokushiharaishudan 内国支払手段 domestic means of payment

naikokushijō 内国市場 home market; domestic market

naikokushōgyō 内国商業 domestic trade; inland trade; home trade

naikokuzei 内国税 internal tax; inland tax

naisai 内債 internal loan; domestic bond

naiseihensū 内生変数 endogenous variable

naiseiri 内整理 winding-up; voluntary liquidation

naiseiteki 内生的 indigenous; endogenous ¶ Kuwait enjoys sufficient *indigenous* banking expertise.

naiseitekitōshi 内生的投資 endogenous investment

naishoku 内職 side job; private occupation; sideline

naizaitekikachi 内在的価値 intrinsic value; intrinsic merit

naizaitekipuremiamu 内在的プレミアム intrinsic premium

nakadarumi 中だるみ respite ¶ After a brief *respite* in the fall, consumption spending has lately shown signs of vigor.

nakagai 仲買 brokerage

nakagaikōsen 仲買口銭 brokerage; commission

nakagaimeigiininjōtsukikabushiki 仲買名義委任状付株式 brokerage proxies

nakagainin 仲買人 broker; commission merchant

保険仲買人	insurance broker
場外仲買人	[市] outside broker
場内仲買人	[市] inside broker
株式仲買人	stock broker
為替仲買人	exchange broker
手形仲買人	bill broker
売込仲買人	sales broker
仕入仲買人	purchase broker
商品仲買人	commodity broker

nakagaiten 仲買店 brokerage house; commission merchant

nakagiri 中限 next-month delivery

nakama 仲間 company; party; partner; associate; fellow-trader

nakamakōsen 仲間口銭 fellow-trader commission

nakamakyōbai 仲間競売 trade sale

nakamanedan 仲間値段 inside (trade) price; trader's price

nakamasōba 仲間相場 fellow-trader price

nakamatorihiki 仲間取引 traders' transaction

nakamawaribiki 仲間割引 trade discount; fellow-trader discount

nakane 仲値 middle price; bid and

asked prices; bid and offered

nakashi 仲仕 stevedore; longshore-man; baggage-man

nakashichin 仲仕賃 stevedorage

nami 波 wave ¶ The third speculative *wave* in the U.S. occurred in the real estate market. // a series of interrelated and partly overlapping *waves* of speculation // a new *wave* of speculation got under way-this time in inventories // The exuberant mood gave rise to *waves* of speculation.

namikawase 並為替 ordinary remittance

namisū 並数 mode

namitegata 並手形 ordinary bill

namitegatatanpokashitsukekinri 並手形担保貸付金利 interest rate on loans secured by bills other than prime commercial bills and specially designated securities

nanbokukaigi 南北会議 'North-South' conference; conference on international economic cooperation

nanbokumondai 南北問題 North-South problems (=issues); problems between north and south

nanchakuriku 軟着陸 soft landing ¶ a *soft landing* on the path of normal growth // a *soft landing* to a more sustainable pace of economic growth // the *soft landing* of the economy from high growth // The United States has brought its cyclical expansion to a *soft landing* at a rate of growth consistent with its long-term growth potential. // to steer the economy into a *soft landing* without creating a recession

nanchō 軟調 weak; soft; downward; dropping; subdued; falling; bearish ¶ The tone of the market

was *weak*. // The *downward* trend that began in June continued into July. // Signs of *weakness* persisted in the market. // The market was *soft* as the sell-off came. // The market *drop* became pronounced.

nanchōshikyō 軟調市況 soft market; stagnant market; sluggish market; bearish market

nanka 軟化 adverse development; weakening; softening; easing ¶ The *softening* of the dollar did not affect the commodity market. // a slight *easing* in the dollar from yesterday's peak levels // Sterling *eased* narrowly against Continental currencies. // *softening* of share prices, or of the stock market // The dollar then *eased* to around 2.74 marks. // The *easing* at the short end extended into the nearer periods, but longer rates were not materially changed. // [参考] The share price melted to 228 from 258 pence for a loss of 30 pence.

nanka 軟貨 soft currency; soft money

nankaihōmatsujiken 南海泡沫事件 South Sea Bubbles

nankakeikō 軟化傾向 weakening tendency; softening

nankaken 軟化圏 soft currency area

nankazairyō 軟化材料 discouraging factor; weakening factor; bearish factor; depressant ¶ Gold resisted the potential *depressant* of the dollar's climb.

nankyoku 難局 impasse; deadlock; stalemate ¶ The world economy has not yet emerged from the structural *impasse*.

nanpa 軟派 [市] bear-interests;

bears

nanpakamotsu 難破貨物 wrecked goods

nanpanourimono 軟派の売物 ［市］ short-selling

nanpashite 軟派仕手 ［市］ bear operator

• **nanpin** 難平 ［市］ averaging

nanpingai 難平買い ［市］ averaging down; buying on a scale

nanpin'uri 難平売り ［市］ averaging up

nanpōzōrin 南方造林 tropical plantation

nanzairyō 軟材料 ［市］ bearish factor

narashite ならして on the average; on an average; as average

narasu ならす average; smoothing; evening; flatten (out) ¶ to *smooth out* peaks and troughs // Intervention operations have been successful in *evening out* erratic exchange rate fluctuations.

nareaibaibai なれ合い売買 wash sale; wash trade; cross trade; accommodation trade; crossed orders; fictitious transaction

nareaitegata なれ合い手形 accommodation bill; kite

nareaitegatafuridashi なれ合い手形振出 kiting; kite-flying

nariagarimono 成り上がり者 parvenu ¶ rise of a rich *parvenu* class

nariyuki 成行き ［市］ at the market

nariyukichūmon 成行注文 carte blanche order; order without limit; market order

nariyukigai 成行買い market order

nariyukisōba 成行相場 current rate

nashikuzushi なし崩し phasing out; invisible relaxation; sapping ¶

to *phase out* credit restraints by virtually increasing money supply through various channels // an *invisible relaxation* of monetary restraints // With demand *sapped*, industry went into a slump.

nashikuzushikanwa なし崩し緩和 gradual relaxation (of monetary restraints); gradual and limited easing (of money)

nashonarugōru ナショナル・ゴール national goal

nashonaruminimamu ナショナル・ミニマム national minimum

nashonarutorasuto ナショナル・トラスト national trust

natsugare 夏枯れ summer slump; summer decline; summer doldrums; summer slack ¶ The *summer decline* in bookings continued into September. // to recover from *summer doldrums* // the traditional *summer slump* in production // Bankers expect the traditional *summer slack* period to arrive late this year.

natsugareki 夏枯れ期 summer dry season; summer slack period

natsuinshōsho 捺印証書 deed 条件付捺印証書 escrow

natsumonouridashi 夏物売出し（布などの）white sale

nawabariarasoinosutoraiki 縄張り争いのストライキ jurisdictional strike

nazudakku ナズダック National Association of Securities Dealers Automated Quotation; NASDAQ

ne 値 price; cost; value

neagarikabu 値上がり株 advances; gainers ¶ *Advances* outnumbered declines by a small margin on the New York stock exchange. // *Gainers* and losers were about equally balanced.

neage 値上げ increase in price; price increase; price raise; price hike; mark-up

電気料金値上げ increase in (electric) power rates

ガス料金値上げ increase in gas rates

neagenojizenshinkokusei 値上げの事前申告制 prior-notification system for price raise

nebiki 値引き reduction (＝cut) in price; price-cutting; discount; abatement of price; allowance ¶ New variations on *price-cutting* methods are being devised. // a rebate in the form of a *discount* on the other article sold // to give a 15% *discount* off the posted prices // to allow 10% *discount* from list prices // to make a *discount* for quantity // The U.S. dollar is at a considerable *discount*. // to make a substantial *abatement* from the price asked // to make a generous *allowance* off the listed price

nebiraki 値開き margin; spread; difference in prices

nebumi 値踏み appraisal; appraisement; valuation; estimation; assessment

nedan 値段 price; cost

現場値段 spot price

現場渡値段 loco price

現物値段 spot price

波止場渡値段 ex-quay price

平均値段 average price

本船渡値段 f.o.b. price

直物値段 spot price

貨車渡値段 on rail price; truck price

基準値段 basic price

小売値段 retail price

繰越値段 making-up price

競争値段 competitive price

持込値段 delivery price

申込値段 offered price

仲間値段 inside (trade) price

成行値段 best obtainable price

卸値段 wholesale price; trade(r's) price

先物値段 futures price

船側渡値段 f.a.s. price

仕入値段 purchase price

品薄値段 scarce price

倉庫渡値段 ex-warehouse price; go-down

諸掛り込値段 all-round price; overhead price

手合せ値段 agreed price; price agreed upon

手頃な値段 reasonable price

到着渡値段 to-arrive price

突込値段 blanket price

吊上値段 lifted price

運賃保険込値段 c.i.f. price

割引値段 reduced price

税引値段 price after tax; price minus tax

税込値段 price before tax; price including tax; pre-tax price

nedanhyō 値段表 price-list

negasakabu 値嵩株 high-priced stocks; blue chip shares; fancy stocks

negiri 値切り haggling ¶ a *haggling* over prices // to *haggle* about the price // So far, *haggling* has been over cuts of about one pound on the 6-pound limit.

negoro 値頃 reasonable price

negorogai 値頃買い bargain hunting at bottom; purchase at low price

nehaba 値幅 range in prices; price range

nekkyōsōba 熱狂相場 feverish market

nekkyōteki 熱狂的 ［市］ feverish

nenheikinshisū 年平均指数 average indexes in calendar (or fiscal) years

nenjihōkoku 年次報告 annual report

nenjikessan 年次決算 annual accounting; annual settlement of accounts; closing of accounts for the year

nenjishinsa 年次審査 annual survey

nenjōshōyōin 年上昇要因 annual improvement factor

nenkanchinginkyōtei 年間賃金協定 annual wage agreement

nenkanhoshōchinginsei 年間保証賃金制 guaranteed annual wage plan

nenkankokyakusū 年間顧客数 annual attendance

nenkin 年金 annuity; pension ¶ to grant or pay an *annuity* // an *annuity* of ¥2 million for life // an ex-official on *pension* // to retire on a *pension* of ¥2 million

母子年金 mother's annuity
長期年金 long-term annuity
不時払年金 contingent annuity
銀行年金 bank annuity
遺族年金 survivorship annuity; pension for war-bereaved families
企業年金 private enterprise annuity
国民年金 national annuity
厚生年金 employees' pension insurance
組合年金 union pension
拠出制国民年金 national annuity through premium payment
無期年金 perpetual annuity

農民年金 farmer's annuity
離農年金 farm retirement annuity
即時払年金 immediate annuity
据置年金 deferred annuity
終身年金 annuity for life; life annuity
養老年金 old-age pension; endowment annuity
郵便年金 postal annuity
有期年金 terminable annuity
漸増年金 increasing annuity
随時払年金 contingent annuity

nenkingenka 年金現価 present value of annuity

nenkinhoken 年金保険 insurance against annuity

nenkinjukyūsha 年金受給者 annuitant; pensioner

nenkinkikin 年金基金 pension fund

nenkinkōsai 年金公債 annuity bond

nenkinkumiai 年金組合 pension trust

nenkinseido 年金制度 pension scheme; pension program; pension plan

nenkinshikin 年金資金 pension funds

nenkinshintaku 年金信託 pension trust

nenkinshōsho 年金証書 annuity certificate

nenkintaikei 年金体系 pension scheme; pension scales

nenkō 年功 seniority; long service; continued service

nenkōchingin 年功賃金 seniority-based wages; wage rates based on seniority

nenkōjoretsu 年功序列 seniority system

nenkōjoretsugatachingin 年功序

列型賃金 seniority order wage (system); pay by "seniority" (system); wage by seniority (system); (system of) pay rising by seniority; seniority-based wage (system); seniority payment (system) ¶ The *seniority payment system* is beginning to be questioned. // the *seniority system* by which *pay* rises with age

nenkōjoretsusei 年功序列制 promotion-by-age system; seniority-oriented promotion-scheme

nenkōkahō 年功加俸 long service allowance; longevity pay; seniority bonus

nenmatsuchōsei 年末調整 year-end adjustment

nenmatsutsūka 年末通貨 bank notes issued at the year-end; bank notes in circulation at the end of the year; bank notes outstanding at the year-end

nenpu 年賦 annual installment; yearly installment

nenpuhoken 年賦保険 installment insurance

nenpushōkan 年賦償還 redemption by yearly installment

nenreikaisō 年齢階層 age group; age span ¶ career earnings over the *age group* 35-65 // within the *age span* 30 to 40 // the higher *age groups*

nenreikōsei 年齢構成 age structure

nenreikyūyosei 年齢給与制 wage-by-age system

nenreishūdan 年齢集団 age growth

nenri 年利 per-annum rate; interest per annum ¶ at 5.0% *p.a.* // a coupon rate at about 9.5 percent *per annum*

nenritsu 年率 annual rate; annualized rate; rate on an annual basis ¶

reckoned on an *annual basis* // to rise at an 8.3 percent *annual rate* measured from December to December // to rise to 0.1 percent at an *annual rate* // to run at an *annual rate* of 19 percent // Inventory opening rose at a blistering *annual rate* of 34 percent. // Monthly statistics are often expressed at an *annual rate*. // The German economy will reach on *annualized* growth *rate* of 3½% in the second half of this year. // Prices rose at an *annualized rate* of 29 percent. // a steady decline in the *annualized rate* of the quarterly current-account deficits // The *annualized* growth *rate* came to 4.5 percent. // Inflation is running at 14% *on an annual basis*. // [参考] Italy's public-sector deficit started expanding at double last year's rate.

nenryō 燃料 fuels; mineral fuels

nensho 念書 letter of comfort; comfort letter; letter of responsibility

nenshō 念証 letter of indemnity on guarantee

nesagarikabu 値下がり株 declines; losers ¶ Advances outnumbered *declines* by a small margin on the New York stock exchange. // Gainers and *losers* were about equally balanced.

nesage 値下げ reduction in price; price reduction; markdown; price cutdown; price cut

nesageundō 値下げ運動 campaign for price reduction; price-cut movement

netsuosen 熱汚染 heat pollution

neugoki 値動き price movements; price developments; price changes; gains or losses ¶ *Price movements* continued to be small. // strong upward *price movements* in machinery // Overall *price developments* have been stable. // erratic *price changes* // Most stocks had *gains or losses* of fractions to around $1 a share. // The market was characterized by only minor *price movements*. // the narrowness of the yen's *movement* against the dollar

neyasukabu 値安株 low priced stocks

nezaya 値鞘 spread; margin

nezuke 値付け maintain a market

nezuyoi 根強い persistent; consistent; stubborn; ingrained; imbedded; deep seated; deep rooted ¶ a *persistent* rise // The rise *persisted*. // Inflationary expectations are not yet deeply *ingrained*. // deeply *imbedded* inflation // Only the *stubborn* 235 percent inflation remains a problem.

niage 荷揚げ discharge; unloading

nibansaku 二番作 aftercrop

nibanteitō 二番抵当 second mortgage

nibanteitōkentsukishōken 二番抵当権付証券 second mortgage bond

nibantenjō 二番天井 double top

nibanzoko 二番底 double bottom ¶ a *"double-bottomed"* recession

nichigen 日限 date; term; timelimit; deadline

nichigin'azukekin 日銀預け金 deposit with the Bank of Japan

nichiginhikiuke 日銀引受(国債の) underwriting by the Bank of Japan

nichiginkariirekin 日銀借入金 borrowed money from the Bank of Japan

nichiginsōkin 日銀送金 Bank of Japan remittance

nichijōgyōmu 日常業務 day-to-

day business; daily routines; routine business

nichiyōhin 日用品 daily necessities; daily necessaries; articles of daily use

nidankaikōnyūhōshiki 二段階購入方式 (house) buying system by two steps

nidori 荷取り load

niekihi 荷役費 stevedorage

niekirōdōsha 荷役労働者 dock worker; longshorer

nigawase 荷為替 documentary draft; documentary bill; documentary paper ¶ to draw a *documentary bill*

nigawasefuridashitsūchijō 荷為替振出通知状 letter of advice

nigawasehikiuketegata 荷為替引受手形 documentary acceptance bill

nigawaseshin'yōjō 荷為替信用状 documentary letter of credit

nigawaseshin'yōjōnikansurutōitsukisokuoyobikanrei 荷為替信用状に関する統一規則および慣例 Uniform Customs and Practice for Documentary Credits (of the International Chamber of Commerce)

nigawasetegata 荷為替手形 documentary bill; commercial bill
引受渡荷為替手形 documents against acceptance bill; D/A
支払渡荷為替手形 documents against payment bill; D/P
輸出(輸入)荷為替手形 documentary export (or import) bill

nigawasetegatafukusho 荷為替手形副書 letter of hypothecation

nigawasetegatatanponimotsuhokanshō 荷為替手形担保荷物保管証 trust receipt

nihonhyōjunsangyōbunrui 日本標

準産業分類 Japan Standard Industrial classifications; JSIC

nihonkogyōseihinkikaku 日本工業製品規格 Japanese Industrial Standard; JIS

nihonrettōkaizō 日本列島改造 Japanese islands' reconstucting; all-out reconstruction of the Japanese islands; structural altering of the Japanese islands; remodeling of the Japanese archipelago

nijisanjiseihin 二次・三次製品 highly processed goods

nijiseihin 二次製品 secondary products

nijūbeika 二重米価 double rice price

nijūkakakusei 二重価格制 dual pricing practice; arbitrary pricing; dual price system; two-tier price system ¶ agreement on a world's *dual price system* for gold, also known as a *two-tier price system*

nijūkawaseshijō 二重為替市場 two-tier foreign exchange market

nijūkazei 二重課税 double taxation

nijūkeisan 二重計算 double counting; double accounting

nijūkeizai 二重経済 dual economy

nijūkinkakakusei 二重金価格制 two-tier gold price system

nijūkin'yū 二重金融 duplication of credit; double financing

nijūkōzō 二重構造 dual(istic) structure; dualism ¶ a *dual system* of state and national banking // the economy of *dual structure* // the *dual structure* of the economy

nijūshakai 二重社会 dual society

nijūsōbasei 二重相場制 ［外］two-tier foreign exchange market; dual foreign exchange market

nijūunchinsei 二重運賃制 dual rate system

nijūzoko 二重底 double bottom ¶ The recession presumably reached the *double bottom*.

nikkeidau 日経ダウ ［日］ the Nikkei Dow-Jones Average

nikkeihyō 日計表 daily trial balance; daily account

nikkyū 日給 daily wage; daily pay; day wage

nikkyūrōdōsha 日給労働者 day laborer

nikokukankyōtei 二国間協定 bilateral agreement

nikōtaisei 二交代制 double shift; two-shift system

nikuseihinseizōgyō 肉製品製造業 （ハム，ソーセージ，ベーコン，食肉，食鳥処理にかかるものに限る） meat products manufacturing industry (limited to enterprises engaged in manufacturing of ham, sausage, and bacon, and processing of meat and poultry meat)

nikusonomikkusu ニクソノミックス Nixonomics

nikutairōdō 肉体労働 manual labor

nikutairōdōsha 肉体労働者 manual worker; manual laborer

nikyokubunka 二極分化 dichotomy; polarization ¶ a rigid "North-South" *dichotomy* creating a *bipolar* concept of world economic dynamics

nimōsaku 二毛作 double cropping

nimotarekan 荷もたれ感 sentiment of overstocking

nimotsuhikitorihoshōsho 荷物引取保証書 letter of guarantee; L/G

nimotsukashiwatashishō 荷物貸渡し証 trust receipt; T/R

ningenkankyōsengen 人間環境宣言 Statement for Human Environmental Quality

ningenkōdōnorandamusei 人間行動のランダム性 randomness of human behavior

ningennogenkashokyakuhi 人間の減価償却費 human depreciation

nin'i 任意 option; voluntariness; discretion

nin'ichūshutsuhō 任意抽出法 random sampling

nin'ihoken 任意保険 voluntary insurance

nin'ikumiai 任意組合 voluntary association

nin'ishōkan 任意償還 optional redemption

nin'ishōkanjōkentsukishoken 任意償還条件保証券 noncallable bond

nin'itaishoku 任意退職 voluntary retirement

nin'itsumitatekin 任意積立金 voluntary reserve

ninka 認可 validation ¶ *validated* applications for foreign capital investment

ninkakijun 認可基準 criteria for validation

ninki 人気 mood; market sentiment ¶ The *mood* in the market was less buoyant than at the turn of the year. // A cautious *mood* prevailed on Wall Street last week. // *Market sentiment* toward the dollar remained very bearish.

ninkikabu 人気株 active stock; favorite; star performer

ninmen'idō 任免・異動 assignment

ninshō 認証 recognition; authentication; identification; validation ¶ criteria for the government's *validation* of export

ninshōdairinin 認証代理人 authenticating agent

nintei 認定 recognition

ninushi 荷主 shipper

ninushikin'yū 荷主金融 shipper's credit

niokurinin 荷送人 shipper

nioroshi 荷卸し discharge

nipponginkōeigyōmaijunhōkoku 日本銀行営業毎旬報告 ten-day report of the Bank of Japan accounts

nipponginkōken 日本銀行券 Bank of Japan note; bank note

nipponginkōkenhakkōdaka 日本銀行券発行高 Bank of Japan notes issued

nirinjidōsha 二輪自動車 motorcycle

niritsuhaihanriron 二律背反理論 antinomy policy

nisedoru にせドル fake dollar bill

nishinhō 2 進法 [コン] binary notation

nishinkajūsshinhō 2 進化 10 進法 [コン] binary-coded decimal notation

nishinsū 2 進数 [コン] binary digit

nisshōken 日照権 right to enjoy sunshine

nisshōkinzandaka 日証金残高 loan balance of Japan Securities Finance Company

nittō 日当 daily pay; day wage; daily allawance; payment per diem ¶ to *pay* $200 *per diem*

niugoki 荷動き cargo movement; railway carloadings

niukefunazumidairigyō 荷受け船積代理業 shipping agent

niukenin 荷受人 consignee

niwakakeiki にわか景気 temporary boom; boom; flush

niwakanarikin にわか成金 neuveau riche; new(ly) rich; upstand millionaire ¶ war-made *neuveaux riches* // a shipping *millionaire* // [参考] a war profiteer

niwasakisōba 庭先相場 loco price

niwasakiwatashi 庭先渡し ex farm; ex yard

niwatashi 荷渡し delivery of goods

niwatashichi 荷渡地 place of delivery

niwatashihi 荷渡費 expense of delivery

niwatashikijitsu 荷渡期日 time of delivery

niwatashisashizusho 荷渡指図書 delivery order

nizukurimokuroku 荷造目録 packing list

nizumi 荷積み stowage

nobanashino 野放しの runaway; unchecked; uncontrolled; unbridled ¶ *runaway* inflation // *unbridled* business expansion and inflation

nobebarai 延払い deferred payment

nobebaraihōshiki 延払方式 deferred payment method

nobebaraishin'yō 延払信用 deferred payment credit ¶ to receive *deferred payment credits* on imports // to extend trade *credits* in the form of *deferred payments*

nobebaraiyushutsu 延払輸出 export on a deferred payment basis; export by deferred payment method

nobesū 延べ数 running number; total number

nobewatashi 延渡し forward delivary

nobinayami 伸び悩み slackening in the rate of growth; sluggish rise; slower growth; leveling-off; slack-

ened growth; sluggishness; stagnancy; faltering; marking time; sparing increase ¶ Output has *marked time*. // The growth of demand *increased* only *sparingly*. // Prices *faltered*. // [参考] The expansion rolls on but with a new one of moderation and a mood of doubt.

nobiritsu 伸び率 rate of increase; growth rate ¶ The *rate of increase* in production slackened, // The *rate of* economic *growth* rose only moderately,

nōburandoshōhin ノーブランド商品 merchandise of the generic brand

nōchikaikaku 農地改革 agrarian (= farm land; agricultural land) reform

nōchikusuisanbutsu 農畜水産物 agricultural, livestock and marine products

nōchishintaku 農地信託 farm land trust

nōchishōken 農地証券 farm bond

nōdokisei 濃度規制 regulation of emission concentration

nōdōtekikōsai 能動的公債 active debt

nōfukigen 納付期限 time-limit of payment

nōfusho 納付書 payment statement

nōgyō 農業 agriculture; agribusiness

牧畜農業 pastoral farming
航空農業 aerial farming
酪農業 dairy farming
零細農業 minute agriculture
生存農業 subsistence farming
粗放農業 extensive agriculture
主穀農業 agriculture specializing in grain cultivation

集約農業 intensive agriculture

多角的農業 multiple agriculture

有畜農業 agriculture with livestock as a major side-line

有機農業 organic farming

nōgyōboki 農業簿記 agricultural book-keeping

nōgyōbutsukakaku 農業物価格 agricultural prices

nōgyōdōtaichōsa 農業動態調査 agricultural census

nōgyōgaishūnyū 農業外収入 income from non-farming business; non-agricultural receipts

nōgyōhaikibutsu 農業廃棄物 agricultural waste

nōgyōjinkō 農業人口 agricultural population

nōgyōkai 農業会 agricultural association

nōgyōkairyōshikinseido 農業改良資金制度 agricultural improvement fund system

nōgyōkakumei 農業革命 agricultural revolution; agrarian revolution

nōgyōkanrensangyō 農業関連産業 agribusiness

nōgyōkansoku 農業観測 agricultural outlook (service)

nōgyōkeiei 農業経営 agronomics

nōgyōkeizai 農業経済 agrarian economy; agricultural economy; agronomy

nōgyōkibanseibihi 農業基盤整備費 expenses for inprovement of conditions for agricultural production

nōgyōkikai 農業機械 farm machinery; agricultural machines

nōgyōkikaika 農業機械化 farm (=agricultural) mechanization

nōgyōkindaikashikinseido 農業近代化資金制度 agricultural modernization fund system

nōgyōkin'yū 農業金融 agricultural financing; farm credit

nōgyōkoku 農業国 agrarian country

nōgyōkōzōseisaku 農業構造政策 policy on agricultural structure

nōgyōkyōdōkumiai 農業協同組合 agricultural cooperative association

nōgyōkyōkō 農業恐慌 agricultural panic(=crisis); farm panic; agrarian crisis

nōgyōkyōsai 農業共済 agricultural insurance

nōgyōkyōsaikin 農業共済金 agricultural mutual aid insurance money

nōgyōparitichōsa 農業パリティ調査 agricultural parity index

nōgyōrōdōsha 農業労働者 farmworker; agrarian laborer; farm hand

nōgyōsaigaihoshōseido 農業災害補償制度 agricultural disaster indemnity system

nōgyōseisanhōjin 農業生産法人 agricultural production corporation

nōgyōsensasu 農業センサス agricultural census

nōgyōshotoku 農業所得 agricultural income

nōgyōshūnyū 農業収入 farming income; agricultural income

nōgyōsōsanshutsugaku 農業総産出額 gross agricultural production

nōgyōtegata 農業手形 agricultural bill

nōgyōtegatakyōsaikikin 農業手形共済基金 mutual aid fund for agricultural bills

nōhanki 農繁期 farmer's busy season; farming season

nōhonshugi 農本主義 physiocracy

nōjichōseihō 農事調整法 [米]Agricultural Adjustment Act; AAA

nōjōrōdōsha 農場労働者 farm hand

nōka 農家 farming household; farming family; farmers' household; farmers' family

兼業農家 side-work farmer; farming households supported by sidelines; agricultural households partly supported by non-farm income

主畜農家 farm household based on (=with priority to) livestock raising

nōkai 納会 closing session of the exchange

nōkakeizaichōsa 農家経済調査 farm household economy survey; survey of receipts and disbursements of farmers

nōkakeizaichōsabutsuzaitōkei 農家経済調査物財統計 commodity statistics of farm household economy

nōkanki 農閑期 farmer's leisure season

nōkigu 農機具 agricultural implements

nokkudaunseisan ノックダウン生産 knockdown production

nōminnenkin 農民年金 farmer's annuity

nomiya 呑屋 [市] bucket shop; bucket-shop operator; outside broker

nondepojitorīginkō ノン・デポジトリー銀行 non-depository bank

nōnyūkokuchisho 納入告知書 notice of payment

noren 暖簾 good will; credit ¶ to build *good will* and to sell the *good will*

noriireken 乗入れ権 traffic right

norikae 乗換え carrying-over; continuation; refunding

norikaetorihiki 乗換取引 swap; changeover

nōringyogyōkin'yūkikan 農林漁業金融機関 financial institutions for agriculture, forestry and fisheries

nōringyogyōshakashitsuke 農林漁業者貸付 lending to agriculture, forestry, and fisheries

nōrinsuisangyō 農林水産業 primary industries related to agriculture, forestry and fisheries

nōrinsuisangyōseisanbutsu 農林水産業生産物 agriculture, forestry, fishing and hunting products

nōritsuchingin 能率賃金 efficiency wages

nōritsukyū 能率給 efficiency wage; payment by results; incentive wage

nōryoku 能力 ability; capacity; capability ¶ Their *ability* to obtain additional external financing in private markets is comparatively limited. // debtor countries' *capacity* to incur further debt // more than average *ability* to compete in overseas markets. // The *ability* to counteract imported inflation in lower developing countries than in industrial countries. // the *ability* of the foreign exchange market to absorb large orders without temporary distortions // the absorptive *capacity* of the capital market // The company's fund-raising *capacity* on the market is great. // a considerable surplus of supply *capacity* // Factories operated at 81.01% of *capacity*. // the level of underutilized *capacity* // working at full *capacity* // operating to near-*capacity* // *capacity* to profits // There remains some unused *capacity*, both in human and material resources. // maximum utilization of human and material *capacity* // production running out of *capacity* // to broaden their countries' borrowing *capacity* in international financial markets // the community's *capacity* to invest // legal and market restrictions on their borrowing *capacity* // The community should acquire funding *capacity* which is used for investments. // The level of under-utilized *capacity* was reduced. // The company is working at full *capacity*. // The race of business expansion has approached *capacity*. // Industry is operating to near-*capacity*. // The company's fund-raising *capacity* on the market is great. // a considerable surplus of supply *capacity* // Productive *capabilities* of Europe and Japan were extensively damaged by World War II. // to aim for a "steady and conspicuous" increase in defense *capability*

超過能力　over-capacity
不足能力　deficient capacity
実際的能力　practical capacity
稼働能力　operating capacity
過剰能力　surplus capacity; excess capacity
管理能力　administrative ability
完全能力　full capacity
経営能力　executive ability
吸収能力　absorption capacity
最適能力　optimum capacity
生産能力　production capacity; productive capacity
製造能力　manufacturing capacity
設備能力　equipment capacity
支払能力　ability to pay
組織能力　organization ability
租税能力　taxable capacity
対外借入能力 ability to borrow overseas
転換能力　ability to transfer

遊休能力　idle capacity

nōryokukyū 能力給　pay according to ability

nōryokusanshutsuryō 能力産出量 capacity output

nōsakumotsukyōkyūheijunka 農作物供給平準化　ever-normal granary

nōsanbutsu 農産物　agricultural commodities; agricultural produce; farm produce; agricultural products
余剰農産物　farm surpluses

nōsanbutsukakakushijijoseikin 農産物価格支持助成金　farm subsidies

nōsanbutsukakakushijiseido 農産物価格支持制度　farm price supports system

nōshukuuran 濃縮ウラン　enriched uranium

nōsonbukkashisū 農村物価指数 price index in rural district

nōsonkyōdōtai 農村共同体　rural community

nottori 乗っ取り　acquisition; purchase; buy-out; take-over ¶ There were 112 foreign *takeovers*. // to arrange *acquisition* of other companies // There were 113 corporate *acquisitions*. // *Acquisitions* by well-known companies include Pillsbury Co.'s *purchase* of the 113 Steak & Ale restaurants. // Many *buy-outs* now are for cash. // Colgate Palmolive's *buy-out* of Charles A. Eaton Co. // Banks are willing to make *buy-out* loans. // Citibank recently helped blacks to *take over* a profitable Chicago, largely white-owned margarine company. // The capital increase in the joint venture disturbed the ownership balance and led to a *take-over* by the foreign firm. // The foreign firm promised not to *takeover* its joint venture partner. // The Sri Lanka Government *took over* the island's largest privately-owned cotton mill. // →合併

nouhau ノウ・ハウ know-how; technical skill; technological information

nōyaku 農薬 agricultural chemicals

nōzeihikiatekin 納税引当金 reserve for taxes

nōzeijunbiyokin 納税準備預金 deposit for tax payments

nōzeikijitsu 納税期日 tax day; date of tax payment

nōzeikumiai 納税組合 taxpayer's association

nōzeisha 納税者 taxpayer

nōzeishanohanran 納税者の反乱 tax revolt

nōzeishōken 納税証券 tax anticipation bill

nōzeishōmeisho 納税証明書 certificate for paid tax

nōzeitsuchisho 納税通知書 notice of tax payment

nozomashiiseichōritsu 望ましい成長率 desirable growth rate

nukeana 抜け穴 loophole ¶ The government must plug *loopholes* in company taxation ¶ Through a tax *loophole* the bonds were able to offer investors a return of 19% tax-free. // to stop tax *loopholes* // →しり抜け

nuketokeai 抜け解合い ［市］ liquidation by mutual consent

nukikensa 抜き検査 random test ¶ to make, or apply, a *random test* // to test at random

nūnsōba ヌーン相場 ［市］ noon market

nyūchō 入超 trade deficit; import surplus; excess of imports over exports

nyūgyoryō 入漁料 fishing fees

nyūka 入荷 arrival of goods; fresh supply of goods

nyūkaikin 入会金 admission fee

nyūkatsūchi 入荷通知 arrival notice

nyūkinzumitsūchisho 入金済通知書 advice of credit; credit advice

nyūkō 入港 entry into port; arrival in port; docking

nyūkōtesūryō 入港手数料 entrance fee

nyūkōtetsuzuki 入港手続 clearance inwards; entry

nyūkōzei 入港税 port dues; harbor dues; keelage

nyūsatsu 入札 tender; bid; competitive bidding ¶ to invite *tenders* for... // to sell by *tender* // to offer notes to a *tender* panel of institutions which have the right to *bid* for the paper // Those 91-day certificates are offered for *tender*. // Members of the Fund may submit *bids* in the public auctions. // the average 91-day rate of Treasury bill *tenders* // Awards will be made to bidders whose *bids* are at or above the lowest accepted price. // Each accepted *bid* will be awarded gold at the *bid* price. // ［参考］ awards to bidders submitting

一般入札 open tender; public bid

強制競争入札 compulsory competitive bidding

最高入札 highest tender; highest bid

指名入札 specified tender; approved tender

追加入札 supplementary bid

nyūsatsubi 入札日 day of tender

nyūsatsuhoshō 入札保証 bid bond

nyusatsuhoshōjō 入札保証状 bid bond

nyūsatsuhoshōkin 入札保証金 tender money

nyūsatsukakaku 入札価格 bidding price; bid price ¶ ［参考］ the minimum acceptable bid

nyūsatsukisoku 入札規則 bidding rules

nyūsatsukōkoku 入札広告 advertisement for tender

nyūsatsurēto 入札レート tender rate

nyūsatsusha 入札者 tenderer; bidder

  最高入札者 highest tenderer

nyūsatsushashimei 入札者指名 specified tender; approved tender

nyūsatsusho 入札書 tender; bid

nyūsatsutetsuzuki 入札手続 bidding procedure

nyūshokuritsu 入職率 accession rate of new workers

nyūshutsuryokuseigyokikō 入出力制御機構 ［コン］ input-output control system; IOCS

O

ōakinai 大商内 ［市］ active turnover; heavy turnover; heavy trading broad market; ¶ The stock market bulled ahead in *heavy trading*.

ōbākiru オーバーキル overkill; overcorrection ¶ Monetary restraints should not produce an *overkill*.

ōbārōn オーバーローン over-loan (ed) position (of commercial banks); over-borrowed situation of commercial banks

ōbike 大引け ［市］ closing; finishing

ōbikenedan 大引け値段 closing (quotation); finish ¶ slightly off its intra-day high to a *closing* 2.525 marks, compared with Friday's 2.513 *finish*

ōbo 応募 subscription ¶ The loan was over-*subscribed*.

oboegakibōeki 覚え書貿易 memorandum trade

ōbosha 応募者 subscriber ¶ *subscribers* to the newly floated loan

ōbosharimawari 応募者利回り yield to subscribers; subscriber's yield

ōboshikin 応募資金 subscribed capital (＝funds)

ōbosōgaku 応募総額 total amount subscribed

ochi 落ち ［市］ ex; off

  抽籤落ち ex drawing; drawing off

  配当落ち ex dividend; dividend off

  権利落ち ex rights; rights off

  利子落ち ex interest; interest off

  新株落ち ex new

ochitsuita 落着いた moderate; sedate ¶ to sustain a fairly *sedate* growth of the economy

ochitsuki 落着き steadying(-down); calming(-down); cooling(-off); settling-down; quieting; tempering; moderation ¶ The economy is *settling down* to a marathon pace after an initial sprint. // a *moderate* stock market reflecting the *tempering* of economic growth

ochitsukikichō 落着き基調　[市]
steady tone; calmness; general tendency towards a calming down; subsidence ¶ The market was in a
steady tone. // The *tone* of the market was one of *calmness.*

ochitsukishikyō 落着き市況　[市]
moderate trading; quiet market;
steady market ¶ The market was
quiet in *moderate trading.*

ōdai 大台 barrier ¶ The Dow-
Jones industrial average pierced the
500 *barrier* marking its new high of
501.76.

ōdanmenbunseki 横断面分析 cross-
section analysis

odeishori 汚泥処理 sludge treatment

odoririsoku 踊り利息 double interest

odoru 躍る　[市] advance; jump;
soar; skyrocket

ōekigensoku 応益原則 benefit principle

ōfukutorihiki 往復取引　[市] round
trip trade

ofurainshori オフライン処理　[コ
ン] off-line processing

ōgatafando 大型ファンド key
industries investment fund; basic
industries investment fund

ōgatagappei 大型合併 large scale
merger; large scale amalgamation

ōgatagijutsu 大型技術 large-scale
technology

ōgatakabu 大型株 large-capital
stock

ōgatakanoriten 大型化の利点 merits of large scale operation; superiority of large scale operation

ōgatapurojekuto 大型プロジェクト
national development program of

industrial technology

ōgatasha 大型車 full-sized car ¶
full-sized gas-guzzlers

ōgonyoku 黄金欲 gold lust; lust for
gold

ōguchi 大口 large-lot ¶ *large-lot*
lendings and deposits

ōguchibaibai 大口売買　[市] block
trade

ōguchichūmon 大口注文 large order

ōguchijuyō 大口需要 large demand

ōguchikaitsuke 大口買付 large
purchase

ōguchikashidashisaki 大口貸出先
prime borrower

ōguchikin'yūkikan 大口金融機関
wholesale bank; money market
bank

ōguchisaiken 大口債券 large bond

ōguchitorihikisaki 大口取引先
prime borrower

ōguchiyokin 大口預金 large deposit

ōhabazōka 大幅増加 large gain;
sharp increase; considerable rise ¶
Output showed a large gain. // Sales
registered a *sharp increase.* // The
consumer price index marked a *considerable rise.* // [参考] to increase by
quite a margin // to expand substantially

oikakeshikihanbaihō 追いかけ式販
売法 follow-up system

oirudarā オイル・ダラー petro-
dollar; oil-dollar ¶ direct *petro-
dollar* intakes on a governmental
basis, or bilateral basis

oirudarākanryū オイル・ダラー還流
oil-dollar recycling; recycling of oil-
dollars

oiruinfure オイル・インフレ oil-induced inflation; oil inflation

oirumanē オイル・マネー oil-money; petro-currency

oirushēru オイル・シェール oil shale

oishō 追い証 [市] re-margin; additional cover; additional margin; more margin ¶ to put up *additional cover* // demand *more margin*

oitsukijuyō 追い付き需要 catch-up demand

oitsukikatei 追い付き過程 catching-up process

oiuchisaku 追い打ち策 follow-up measure

okikae 置換え replacement ¶ →取替え

okikaetōshi 置換え投資 replacement investment

okiwatashi 沖渡し free overside

okizumi 沖積み loading in stream

ōkuradaijinbaibaisōba 大蔵大臣売買相場 [外] buying and selling rates of the Minister of Finance

ōkurashō 大蔵省 Minister of Finance; Finance Ministry; [米] Treasury Department; [英] Exchequer

ōkurashōshōken 大蔵省証券 Treasury bill; TB; Finance Ministry note

ōkurashōshōkenhakkōdaka 大蔵省証券発行高 Treasury bills issued (=outstanding)

ōkurashōshōkenkinri 大蔵省証券金利 Treasury bill rate; TB rate

okure 遅れ lag(ging behind); delay ¶ Foreign demand continues to *lag* behind domestic demand. // It will cause a long *delay* in arrival. // →ラグ

okurijō 送り状 invoice ¶ to make out an *invoice* // to *invoice* the books

現場渡し送り状 loco invoice
本船渡し送り状 f.o.b. invoice
工場渡し送り状 factory invoice
持込渡し送り状 franco invoice
領事査証送り状 consular invoice
船側渡し送り状 f.a.s. invoice
試算送り状 pro forma invoice
運賃込み送り状 c.&f. invoice
輸入送り状 import invoice
輸出送り状 export invoice

okurijōkingaku 送り状金額 invoice amount

okurijōmenkakaku 送り状面価格 invoice cost (=value)

okurijōnedan 送り状値段 invoice price

omiyagekōfukin おみやげ交付金 "pork barrel" ¶ to attract *"pork barrel"* spending projects

omowaku 思惑 speculation ¶ The recent strength in the yen has sparked *speculation* that Japan's discount rate may be cut. // to *speculate* in Japanese yen // to buy it on (a) *speculation* // a *speculative* boom in real estate // There is increasing *speculation* that the dollar's advance could prompt the Bank of England to raise interest rates to protect sterling.

omowakugai 思惑買い speculative buying

omowakugaisuji 思惑買筋 speculative buyers

omowakujuyō 思惑需要 speculative demand

omowakukaininki 思惑買人気 [市] speculative interest ¶ high and widespread *speculative interest* among traders

omowakukibun 思惑気分 speculative mood

omowakushi 思惑師 speculator

omowakushikyō 思惑市況 speculative market

omowakusuji 思惑筋 speculative interests

omowakutorihiki 思惑取引 speculative transaction

omowakutōshi 思惑投資 speculative investment

omowakuuri 思惑売り speculative selling

onhaisui 温排水 thermal effluent

onkei 恩恵 benefit ¶ A broader distribution of the *benefits* of growth was possible.

onkyū 恩給 (governmental) pension ¶ He lives on a *pension*. // He is an old ex-official on *pension*.

onkyūjuryōsha 恩給受領者 pensioner

onkyūkikin 恩給基金 pension fund

onkyūseido 恩給制度 pension system (=scheme; program)

onkyūtanpokashitsuke 恩給担保貸付 loan secured by pensions; loan on pension; loan against pension

onrainshori オンライン処理 [コン] on-line processing

onwanasettoku 温和な説得 peaceful persuasion

operēshontsuisuto オペレーション・ツイスト operation twist

ōpungatatōshishintaku オープン型投資信託 open-end investment trust

ōpunkakaku オープン価格 open price

ōpunpojishon オープン・ポジション open position

opushonkijitsu オプション期日 [外] option date

opushontsukisakimono オプション付先物 [外] option forwards

orikomu 織込む account for;

digest; discount ¶ The figures are already *accounted for* in present rates of the dollar. // The discount rate cut is not yet fully *digested*. // Currency markets appear to have already *discounted* a November U.S. trade deficit to be announced today. // The data are already *discounted* in current dollar levels. // The market has largely *discounted* a half percentage point cut in the official discount rate. // Such a cut is not yet fully *digested*. // Its effect is already *discounted* in the prospects.

oroshiuri 卸売り wholesale trading

oroshiuribukka 卸売物価 wholesale price ¶ *Wholesale prices* increased at a sharply accelerated pace. // The steep fall in *wholesale price* inflation is flattening out.

oroshiuribukkashisū 卸売物価指数 wholesale price index; WPI ¶ The *wholesale price index* climbed steeply at an annual rate of 5 percent.

oroshiurigyōsha 卸売業者 wholesale trader; wholesale dealer; wholesale merchant; wholesaler

oroshiurisenmonshō 卸売専門商 specialty wholesaler

oroshiurishijō 卸売市場 wholesale market

ōryō 横領 embezzlement

ōsa 往査 visiting audit

osen 汚染 pollution; contamination; defilement ¶ air *pollution* // environmental *pollution* // the increasing *pollution* of the Japanese coastal waters // *pollution*-prevention machinery // radioactive *contamination* // *defiled* bank notes // the high non-productive capital investment for *pollution* controls // a factory which *pollutes* the air

土壌汚染　soil pollution

放射能汚染　radioactive pollution

海洋汚染　marine pollution; pollution of the sea; sea pollution

核汚染　nuclear pollution

環境汚染　environmental contamination; environmental pollution

熱汚染　thermal pollution

石油汚染　oil pollution

水質汚染　water pollution

大気汚染　air pollution

都市汚染　urban pollution; city's pollution

ōseina 旺盛な active ¶ the *active* demand for funds // The *active* money supply rose by $ 1.5 billion.

osenbōgyo 汚染防御 pollution defense

osenbōshikijun 汚染防止基準 antipollution standard ¶ the government's strenghtening of *antipollution standards*

osenbutsu 汚染物 pollutant; contaminant

自動車汚染物　vehicle pollutant

航空気汚染物　air-liner pollutant

大気汚染物　air pollutant

osenchiiki 汚染地域 polluted area

osengen 汚染源 pollution source

osenhannin 汚染犯人 polluter ¶ the sharing of risk between the *polluter* and the polluted

osenkisei 汚染規制 pollution control

osenkisonshōken 汚染毀損証券 soiled or multilated bond

ōsenkogitte 横線小切手 crossed check

osenshafutannogensoku 汚染者負担の原則 "polluter pays" principle ¶ additional investments in accordance with the *"polluter pays" principle*

osentaiki 汚染大気 polluted air

oshime 押目 temporary fall; pull back; meandering lower

oshimegai 押目買い ［市］buying on decline

ōshūdōmei 欧州同盟 European Union

ōshūjiyūbōekichiiki 欧州自由貿易地域 European Free Trade Area

ōshūkaishahō 欧州会社法 European company statute

ōshūkeisantan'i 欧州計算単位 European Unit of Account

ōshūkigyō 欧州企業 European enterprise

ōshūtsūkagōseitan'i 欧州通貨合成単位 EURCO

ōshūtsūkaseido 欧州通貨制度 European Monetary System; EMS

ōshūtsūkatan'i 欧州通貨単位 European Currency Unit; ECU

ossoraiinkai オッソラ委員会 Ossola Group

osuishori 汚水処理 sewage collection and treatment

ōteshōsha 大手商社 big trader (= firm; concern)

ōtesuji 大手筋 large operators; big traders; main buyers; leading speculators

ōtōjikan 応答時間 ［コン］response time

ōtomēshonkōjō オートメーション工場 automated factory

ōtomeun'yu オートメ運輸 automation transportation

otorikin おとり金 bait money

otorikōkoku おとり広告 bait advertising

otosu 落す(手形を) honor ¶ to *honor* a bill // *honored* bills // to fail to *honor* the bill

owarine 終り値 ［市］closing quotation; closing price; close; finish ¶ The dollar reached a six-month peak of 2.5290 marks, well above Friday's pre-holiday *close* of 2.5110. // Eurodollar deposit rates ended 1/16 point higher than Friday's pre-holiday *finish*. // On the London stock exchange, the company's shares *closed* at 234 pence down from yesterday's *close*. //

Eurodollar deposit rates ended 1/16 point higher than Friday's pre-holiday *finish*.

oyagaisha 親会社 parent company; holding company; senior company

oyaginkō 親銀行 parent bank

oyakabu 親株 old stock (＝share)

oyakorōn 親子ローン two-generation loan

ōzoko 大底 ［市］rock bottom

P

POW kanjō POW 勘定 POW (＝payment order of withdrawal) account

pabu パブ ［英］public house

paizuhyō パイ図表 pie-chart ¶ a small piece of the budgetary *pie*

pakettotsūshin パケット通信 packet telecommunication

pākinsonnohōsoku パーキンソンの法則 Parkinson's law

paneruchōsa パネル調査 panel research

papamamasutoa パパ・ママ・ストア ［米］mom and pop store

paramētā パラメーター parameter 構造パラメーター structural parameter

paramētākinō パラメーター機能 parametric function (of price)

pararerumāketto パラレル・マーケット parallel market; secondary market

parētonohōsoku パレートの法則 Pareto's law

parettoyusō パレット輸送 palletization

paritihōshiki パリティ方式 parity account

paritikakaku パリティ価格 parity price

paritishisū パリティ指数 parity index

pāsheshiki パーシェ式 ［統］Paasche formula

patān パターン pattern ¶ to follow the seasonal *pattern* // Slackening of activity fits the regular *pattern*. // a cyclical *pattern* in the development of... // the general *pattern* of behavior // to organize after Western *pattern* // The *pattern* of economic developments during the year was shaped largely by the shifts in major components of demand. // the type of expansion *pattern* that emerged as 1976 unfolded // The business *pattern* is more fairly described as a high level plateau than anything else. // There was a marked change in the *pattern* of output in 1975. // structural changes in the *pattern* of production // Production nationally was down from June, which follows the usual *pattern*. // This general *pattern* of behavior was shared to a large extent by all categories of stores. // Cyclical developments in productivity in the United States have conformed to the usual *pattern*. // The country-by-country *pattern* of import growth varied last year. // There were only small changes in the global *pattern* of current payments balances. // the geographical *pattern* of international banking flows // Broad *patterns* in household demand and saving are identified.

pātotaimugyō パート・タイム業 temporary help business; part-time business

pīaru ピーアール public relations; P.R.

pigūkōka ピグー効果 Pigou(vian) effect

pinhane ぴんはね kickback

pointo ポイント point ¶ The retail price index rose by 1.2 *points* over the month.

porishīmikkusu ポリシー・ミックス policy mix; mixture of (fiscal and monetary) policies; fiscal-monetary policy mix ¶ The familiar "growth oriented" *fiscal-monetary mix* has

been applied long enough. // A *policy mix* combining demand restraint with price and fiscal policies is needed. // The *policy mix* between fiscal and monetary policies can check inflationary pressures. // to use a *mix* of fiscal (and monetary) *policies* // the application of a correct *mix* of fiscal and monetary *policies* // The *mix* and thrust of *policies* varied from country to country.

puraibētobiru プライベート・ビル private bill; trade bill

puraimurēto プライム・レート prime (interest) rate (on loans) ¶ The *prime rate*, the interest rate commercial banks charge their most creditworthy corporate customers, has been raised upwards from 7¾% to 9¾%.

purantosen プラント船 floating plant

purantoyushutsu プラント輸出 exports of plants; plant exports

purasuyōin プラス要因 stimulus; positive factor; contributive (=conducive) element

purebisshuhōkoku プレビッシュ報告 Prebisch Report, 1964: "Towards a new trade policy for development"

purehabujūtaku プレハブ住宅 prefabricated house

R

ragu ラグ lag ¶ the *lag* in the workings of monetary policy // There is always some *lag* between the start of the general economic

recovery and an upswing in loan demand at commercial banks. // There is a long and uncertain *lag* between policy formation and execution. // Interest rates may rise only with a *lag*. // to determine the length of the adjustment *lag* using the Almon *lag* technique // Employment usually responds to output with a *lag*. // The time *lags* in response of export and import volume are both long. // an average *lag* of approximately one and a half years in the relationship between money and prices // the *lagged* price response to changes in the monetary aggregates // to add the mean *lag* of one year established in the relationship // The reserve coefficients *lagging* behind the price changes significantly different from zero.

実施ラグ　administrative lag
効果波及ラグ　operational lag
認知ラグ　recognition lag
産出量ラグ　output lag
政策ラグ　policy lag ¶ The existence of *policy lag* in proportional policy makes the system unstable. // The length of *policy lag* in relation to the stability of the system is examined.
支出ラグ　expenditure lag
消費ラグ　consumption lag
収入ラグ　earning lag

raibō ライボー LIBOR; London interbank offered rate

raifusaikurukeikaku ライフ・サイクル計画　life cycle program

raimīn ライミーン LIMEAN; average of the London interbank bid and offered rate

raintosutaffu ラインとスタッフ line and staff

raisensuseisan ライセンス生産 license production

rakkan 楽観 optimism; optimistic view ¶ The *optimism* over economic prospects continues to wane. // Business *optimism* began to fade. // the more *optimistic* appraisals of prospects for the coming year // The *optimists* were still smarting from high expectations still awaiting fulfillment. // The latest survey of business *optimism* reveals a sharp fall in *optimism* about business prospects occurred during the last month. // A sudden wave of *optimism* overtook economists. // No unconditional *optimism* is warranted for the future course of prices. // cautious, or guarded *optimism* // The principal source of my *optimism* lies in increasing demand. // A wave of *optimism* on the economic prospects seemed to seize the western world. // further factors allowing for greater *optimism* about economic prospects // A very *optimistic view* was also being taken as to prospects for the coming year. // Greater *optimism* about business prospects in the next few months prevailed in the export industries. // unrealistic estimates on over-*optimistic* production forecasts by oil companies // Companies are quietly *optimistic* about the next few months.

警戒的楽観　guarded optimism; cautious optimism ¶ In IMF consultations, *guarded optimism* was expressed on prices. // to share his cautious *optimism* // to confound much of *cautious optimism* that ran through the bond market

rakuchō 落調 [市] declining market; downward tendency; sagging market; weakening market

rakunō 酪農 dairy-farming

rakunōjō 酪農場 dairy-farm; milk-ranch

rakunōnōka 酪農農家 dairy-farming household

rakunōseihin 酪農製品 dairy products

rakusatsu 落札 successful bid

rakusatsune 落札値 highest bid price

rakusatsusha 落札者 successful bidder

rakusei 落勢 [市] declining market; bearish market

ranbai 乱売 underselling; panicky selling

ranbuiekyōtei ランブイエ協定 Rambouillet Agreement ¶ to put vigorously into practice the *Rambouillet Agreement*

ranbuiesengen ランブイエ宣言 Rambouillet Declaration ¶ Languages of the *Rambouillet Declaration* were particularly reassuring.

ranbuieshunōkaidan ランブイエ首脳会談 Rambouillet summit

ranchōshi 乱調子 unsteady; erratic; irregular; confused; [市] →乱高下市況

randōruhōkokusho ランドール報告書 [米] Randall Report (of 1954)

rankōge 乱高下 wide fluctuation; erratic fluctuation; violent fluctuation; erratic (=wild) ups and downs ¶ [参考] Stock, bond and commodity prices bobbed and downed in no clear pattern.

rankōgeshikyō 乱高下市況 uneven market; fluctuating market; erratic market

rasupairesushiki ラスパイレス式 [統] Laspeyres formula

ratendarā ラテン・ダラー Latin-dollars

regyurāuei レギュラー・ウエイ [証

市] regular way

regyurēshon Q レギュレーション Q [米] Regulation Q

reienhaisui 冷延廃水 cold rolling waste water

reigaigyōshu 例外業種(対内直接投資自由化の) unaffected industries; exceptional industries (of the liberalization of direct investment in Japan)

reigaikitei 例外規定 escape clause; exceptive clause

reikyakukikan 冷却期間 cooling-off period; cooling time

reiofu レイオフ lay-off ¶ Extensive *lay-offs* that occurred primarily in the automobile industry are spreading in related sectors. // The company is bringing back about 1500 *laid-off* workers. // Small companies are *laying off* surplus workers. // Over 2,000 workers were *laid off*. // The *lay-off* rate in January was 12 workers per 1,000. // →帰休

reisaichokin 零細貯金 petty savings

reisaikigyō 零細企業 small business

reisaishikinkashitsuke 零細資金貸付 petty loan

rejākabu レジャー株 stock related to leisure-time activities; leisure-time stock

rejākatsudō レジャー活動 leisure-time activity

rejāsangyō レジャー産業 leisure industry; leisure-time (activity) industry

rejāyōhin レジャー用品 leisure-time articles; goods for leisure-time activities

rekigetsuwatashi 暦月渡し [外]

delivery on calendar month basis

rekinen 暦年 calendar year; civil year

rekishidēta 歴史データ historical data

rekishitekishinkiroku 歴史的新記録 historical new record; historical record high (or low); unprecedented high (or low)

renbai 廉売 bargain sale; dumping

renbaikyōsō 廉売競争 price war; price competition

renbainedan 廉売値段 bargain price

renbaishijō 廉売市場 bargain market

rendōjimu 連動事務 interlocking business

renkankōka 連関効果 linkage effects

後方連関効果 backward linkage effects

相互連関効果 lateral linkage effects

前方連関効果 forward linkage effects

renketsu 連結 combination; connection; coupling; joint

renketsuseihin 連結製品 co-product

renketsushisū 連結指数 chain-index

renketsuson'ekikeisansho 連結損益計算書 consolidated income statement

renketsutaishakutaishōhyō 連結貸借対照表 consolidated balance sheet

renketsuzaimushohyō 連結財務諸表 consolidated financial statements

renkyū 連休 holiday-studded period

renritsuhōteishiki 連立方程式 multi-equations; simultaneous equations

rensahannō 連鎖反応 chain reactions

renshodairinin 連署代理人 co-authenticating agent

rensatekieikyō 連鎖的影響 chain repercussion; chain reaction

rensaten 連鎖店 chain (store; restaurant); [英] multiple shop ¶ Borel erected a ubiquitous *chain* of restaurants along the highways.

rensatōsan 連鎖倒産 chain-reaction bankruptcies

rentaihoshō 連帯保証 joint and several guarantee; solidarity guarantee

rentaisaimu 連帯債務 joint and several obligation; joint debt

rentaisaimusha 連帯債務者 joint debtor

rentaiyakusokutegata 連帯約束手形 joint promissory note

renzokuatsuenki 連続圧延機 strip mill

熱間連続圧延機 hot strip mill
冷間連続圧延機 cold strip mill

renzokubunseki 連続分析 continuous analysis

renzokuchūzō 連続鋳造 continuous casting system

renzokuno ～連続の straight; consecutive; successive; in a row ¶ the 14th *straight* monthly gain // Sales registered a decline for the second *consecutive* month, though slightly. // This was the eleventh *consecutive* monthly rise in the index. // The index showed a rise for the six *consecutive* months. // The index rose for the eleventh month *in a row* to 97.8 (1975=100) up by 1.2% from

August.

renzokuryōkeisanki 連続量計算機 [コン] analog computer

renzokusei 連続性 continuity; series ¶ a break in *series* due to change in coverage of the reported figures

reonchefuhyō レオンチェフ表 Leontief table

retsugofusai 劣後負債 subordinated debt

retsugono 劣後の subordinated ¶ a *subordinated* bond issue 600 million francs

riage 利上げ interest rate raise; raise in the rate of interest; increase in interest rates

ribarai 利払い interest payment; debt service

ribaraiteishi 利払停止 suspension of interest payment

ridatsu 離脱 desertion; breaking away; extrication; going off; getting out; leave; departure; emerging out ¶ The French franc's *desertion* from the snake was announced. // The Zaire currency *broke away* from gold and the U.S. dollar and was pegged to the SDR of the IMF. // Domestic business will *extricate* itself from the protracted recession. // a floating exchange rate—"*going off* the gold standard" // Business is likely to *get out* of the impact of the inflationary recession this year. // Business investment projects are gradually *departing* from a protracted state of lethargy. // *Departure* of the French franc from the so-called snake seems to be foreordained.

rieki 利益 profit; gain; return; interest; benefit; advantage ¶ to earn (= get; make; gain) a big (=large) *profit* from business // to produce or bring, yield, or net a *profit* to a business // to get both pecuniary and moral *gain* // to make a clear *gain* of $20,000 from business transactions // business showing an adequate *gain*, not a loss // small *profits* and quick *returns* // investment yielding or earning a fair *return* // transactions bringing in small *returns* // to seek and realize a higher *return* on capital investment // to *profit* or *gain* from or by business // The company is expected to chalk up pre-tax recurring *profits* for the current one-year period ending next March. // The consolidated net *profits* of the company in the six-month interim period ended last June recorded a sharp 2.6-fold increase over a year before. // Factory *profit* margins slipped slightly after having rebounded strongly. // For most of corporate America, *profits* in the second quarter of this year have rebounded smartly from the depressed levels of a year ago. // Importers should return to consumers part of the *benefits* they received from the dollar's sharp fall.

帳簿上の利益 paper profit

限界利益 marginal profit

配当可能利益 profit available for dividend

純利益 net profit; pure profit; net profit; clear profit

隠し利益 unreported profit; hidden profit

経常利益 recurring profit; current profit; ordinary profit

期待利益 expected profit

未実現利益 unrealized profit

臨時利益 non-recurring profit

償却前利益 pre-depreciation profit

粗利益 gross profit

総利益 gross profit

予想利益 expected profit; anticipated profit; imaginary profit; paper profit; estimated profit; profit estimate

税引き利益 taxed profit; after-tax profit

税込み利益 profit including tax; before-tax profit

riekibunpaikikō 利益分配機構 profit-sharing scheme

riekidaihyōkoku 利益代表国 protecting power

riekidaiichishugi 利益第一主義 profit-first principle

riekihaba 利益幅 (profit) margin ¶ Factory *profit margins* rebounded from the depressed level in the first quarter. // In terms of profit per dollar of sales, factory *margins* were as much as 27% higher than in the first quarter. // Companies attempt to widen *profit margins*. // Their *profit margin* on each dollar of sales held up fairly well. // Now with sales rebounding, the *margins* translate into zooming total profits.

riekihaitō 利益配当 profit-sharing; distribution of profits; bonus

riekihaitōkabu 利益配当株 participating stock

riekihaitōshasai 利益配当社債 participating bond

riekihaitōshōmeisho 利益配当証明書 certificate of beneficial interest

riekihaitōtsukihokenshōsho 利益配当付保険証書 participating policy

riekihaitōtsukishasai 利益配当付社債 participating bond

riekihaitōyūsenkabu 利益配当優先

株 participating preferred stock

riekihaitōzei 利益配当税 tax on dividends

riekijōyokin 利益剰余金 earned surplus; retained earnings; earnings retained for use in business

riekijōyokin 利益剰余金 earned surplus; retained surplus

riekijōyokinchōsei 利益剰余金調整 surplus reconcilement

riekijōyokinkeisansho 利益剰余金計算書 earned surplus statement

riekijunbikin 利益準備金 revenue reserve

riekikeikaku 利益計画 profit planning

riekikeiri 利益経理 profitability accounting

riekikin 利益金 earning; profit

未処分利益金 undivided profit

処分可能利益金 available profit

riekikintenseichingin 利益均てん制賃金 profit-sharing (wage) plan

riekikōkan 利益交換 reciprocity of benefits

riekinoaru 利益のある lucrative; profitable; gainful ¶ to lend money to more *lucrative* borrowers // a shift to more *profitable* securities // The number of foreigners in *gainful* employment declined.

riekisankashasai 利益参加社債 participating bond

riekishobun 利益処分 distribution of net profit

rifurēshon リフレーション reflation

rigaikankei 利害関係 interest ¶ to have, protect, and advance important *interests* abroad // Japan's commercial *interests* overseas // Their *interests* harmonize.

rigainofuitchi 利害の不一致 conflicting interests; conflicts of interest; diversity of interest ¶ the reconciliation of *conflicting interests* // There is significant internal *diversity of interest* within each group.

rigainori 理外の理 [市] reason transcending reason

rigu リグ (offshore drilling) rig

rigui 利食い profit-taking; realizing; realization; profit-cashing ¶ The dollar was under sporadic *profit-taking* pressure. // Nonferrous metals fell amid *profit-taking*. // to begin *taking profits* on long positions // to take the opportunity to *realize profits*

riguiuri 利食売り profit-taking sale

rihaba 利幅 profit margin ¶ manufacturers' profit margins averaged 5.4% of sales. // Factory *profit margins* slipped slightly after having rebounded strongly. // to rebuild the *profit margins* which have been heavily eroded by the recession and by the rise in wage costs // to keep *margins* low on well-known, advertized products // The price leaves only a narrow *margin* of profit for retailers.

rijun 利潤 profit ¶ The *profit* position of industry deteriorated rapidly. // U.S. shippers carry wheat to the Soviet Union at a *profit*. // →利益

超過利潤　excess profit; super profit
独占利潤　monopoly profit
不労利潤　unearned profit
発起人利潤　prompter's profit
譲渡利潤　profit upon alienation
結合利潤　joint profit
企業者利潤　entrepreneur's profit
最適利潤　best profit
再投資用利潤　plowing-back profit
正常利潤　normal profit

資本利潤　capital profit
税引き前法人利潤　corporate profit before tax

rijun'asshuku 利潤圧縮 reduction of profit (margin); profit squeeze ¶ a general reduction of *profit margins*

rijunbunpai 利潤分配 porfit-sharing

rijunritsuheikinkahōsoku 利潤率平均化法則 law of equi-profit rate

rijuntsuikyū 利潤追求 profit seeking

riken 利権 interests ¶ fear of domination by foreign *interests* that hold a large part of the stock

rikengenyu 利権原油 company equity oil

rikōgimu 履行義務 performance obligation

rikōhoshōjō 履行保証状 performance bond

rikuagedairinin 陸揚代理人 landing agent

rikuagekō 陸揚港 port of discharge; unloading port

rikuun 陸運 land carriage; surface transport

rikuungaisha 陸運会社 land transportation company

rikuunkamotsu 陸運貨物 landborne goods

rimawari 利回り yield; interest; return ¶ *Yields* on high-grade corporate bonds have fluctuated moderately. // Most bond *yeilds* were at levels prevailing early in 1984. // Security *yields* tended upward. // Market *yields* on high-grade corporate bonds fluctuated moderately. // bond *yielding* about 59% to maturity // to invest money in high-*yielding* money-market mutual funds // to switch into higher-

yielding debt intruments

長期利回り long-term yield

直接利回り direct yield

発行者利回り issuer's cost

平均利回り average yield

間接利回り indirect yield

既発債利回り yield on already-issued bond

好利回り good yield; attractive yield

満期利回り yield to maturity

応募者利回り yield to subscribers; subscriber's yield

債券利回り bond yield

最終利回り final yield; yield to maturity

市場利回り market yield

証券利回り securities yield

短期利回り short-term yield

運用利回り yield on investment

予想利回り prospective yield

rimawariritsu 利回率 rate of yield

rimawarisaisan 利回り採算 yield accounting; yield consideration

ringikashidashi 稟議貸出 lending under credit report approved by the head office

ringisho 稟議(書) consultation (for internal approval by circular)

ringyō 林業 forestry

ringyōkin'yū 林業金融 forest credit

rinjihi 臨時費 extraordinary expenses; contingent outlays; incidental expenses; extra expenditures; emergency funds

rinjiyatoi 臨時雇い odd hand

rinkaisaishōdoryoku 臨界最小努力 critical minimum effort

rinkino 臨機の expedient; emergency; stopgap ¶ *expedient* measures without any long-term solution

rinkinosochi 臨機の措置 ex-pedient (measure) ¶ to use *expedients* more suitable for raising seasonal working capital // short-term borrowing *expedients*

rinōkyūfukin 離農給付金 farm retirement pension

rinose 利乗せ pyramiding

rinsaku 輪作 crop rotation; rotation of crops; shift of crops

rinsanbutsu 林産物 forest products

riochi 利落ち ex-interest; interest-off

riochisaiken 利落債券 ex-interest bond

ririku 離陸 (economic) take-off ¶ Some countries entered *"take-off"* in the second quarter of this century.

riritsu 利率 interest rate; rate of interest ¶ an increase by about 1.5 points across the whole spectrum of *interest rates* // to access the capital markets at the finest *rates* possible // The loan bears (=carries) *interest* at (=of) $1\text{-}^1/_8\%$ above London interbank offered *rates* (LIBOR). // The four year floating *rate* CDs carry a flat LIBOR for the first three years, and LIBOR plus 0.125 percentage point in the last year. // →金利

銀行利率 bank rate

表面利率 nominal interest rate

定利率 legal rate of interest

riritsuhikiage 利率引上げ raise of interest rate; increase in interest rate; interest rate increase; interest rate hike

riritsuhikisage 利率引下げ decrease in interest rate; reduction of interest rate; cut in the rate of interest; interest rate reduction

riron 理論 theory; rationale ¶ This reasoning is the *rationale* for reversal of the steps taken by the central bank.

rironseikatsuhi 理論生活費 theoretical cost of living

risage 利下げ lowering of interest rate

risaikuringu リサイクリング recycling ¶ *recycling* of petrodollars; resources *recycling* system // →環流

risatsu 利札 coupon ¶ The *coupon* on the loan is 5½%. // The bond carries a coupon of 5½%. // a 6% *coupon*

risatsubangō 利札番号 coupon number

risatsuhikikaehyō 利札引換票 talon

risatsukenmengaku 利札券面額 face amount of coupon

risatsuochi 利札落ち ex-coupon; coupon-off

risatsutsuki 利札付き cum-coupon; coupon-on

risatsutsukisaiken 利札付債券 coupon bond

rishi 利子 interest ¶ to issue a loan at 6% *interest* // with *interest* at 6% // bearing *interest* at 6% // to compute, reckon, or figure *interest* // A Federal Reserve Bank charges interest at a rate known as the discount rate. // Banks pay interest on deposits at 4 percent. // privilege of non-taxation on *interest* accruing from deposits // an investment yielding high-rate *interest* // The rate of *interest* allowed on postal savings was reduced by 0.3 percent. // [参考] The five-year loan will pay participating banks a spread of 1⅜%. // →金利

延滞利子 interest for delay; overdue interest

負の利子 negative interest

外債利子 interest on external loan

銀行利子 bank interest

実物利子 real interest

確定利子 fixed interest

貸付利子 loan interest; interest on loans; lending rate

経過利子 accrued interest

帰属利子 imputed interest

未払利子 interest payable

社債利子 debenture interest

消費者負債利子 interest on consumer debt

預金利子 deposit interest; interest on deposits; deposit rate

rishifutan 利子負担 interest burden ¶ the *interest burden* on the country's foreign debt

rishiheikōzei 利子平衡税 interest equalization tax

rishihikazeinotokken 利子非課税の特権 privilege of nontaxation on interest accruing from deposits

rishihokyū 利子補給 grant for paying a fixed rate of interest; interest subsidy ¶ that *interest subsidizing* system for shipping firms

rishiritsu 利(子)率 rate of interest; interest rate ¶ →金利

rishiritsukōzō 利子率構造 structure of interest rates; interest rate structure

rishiritsutaikei 利子率体系 term structure of interest rates

rishisekisū 利子積数 interest product

rishishiharaikijitsu 利子支払期日 interest payment date

rishishiharaisashizusho 利子支払指図書 interest warrant

rishishiharaishikin 利子支払資金 (accrued) interest payment fund

rishiumishisan 利子生み資産 interest-bearing asset

rishiyūinkōka 利子誘因効果 interest incentive effect

rishokuritsu 離職率 ratio of separated workers; separation ratio; quit rate ¶ The *quit rate* in manufacturing moved up 1/4 of percentage point, climbing to 2 1/3 percent.

risoku 利息 interest ¶ →金利; 利子
前受利息 interest prepaid

risokuseigenhō 利息制限法 interest restriction law

risōsanshiki 理想算式 [統] Ideal formula; Fisher('s) formula

rīsugimu リース義務 lease obligation; lease commitment

risuku リスク risk ¶ to run dangerous *risks* of economic overheating // Some lenders may recognize country *risk* above bank *risk*. // to reduce the bank's exposure to unnecessary interest rate *risks* // to reduce the period during which the company is at *risk* // to limit their *risks* to prudent levels // to assume large *risk* for larger returns // Investors have a strong aversion to *risks*. // acceptance of *risk* inherent in financial intermediation // Exporters thus have to bear a heavier burden of exchange *risks*. // [参考] the bank's over-exposure to one single borrower // the explosion of bank exposure in several countries since the late 1970s // →危険

risukuchūwaka リスク中和化 risk neutrality

risukufutan リスク負担 risk (exposure)

risukukabā リスク・カバー [外] covering exchange risks; safeguards against exchange risks

rīsusangyō リース産業 leasing industry

rīsushisan リース資産 leased asset

rīsushisankenri リース資産権利 property rights under leases

ritchi 立地 location
工業(＝産業)立地 industrial location; location of industry

ritchijōken 立地条件 geographical conditions

ritchiron 立地論 theory of location

ritoku 利得 profit; gain; return
営業利得 operating gain
不当利得 fraudulent gain
保有利得 holding gain

ritokusha 利得者 gainer; beneficiary
不当利得者 profiteer

ritokuzei 利得税 profits tax
超過利得税 excess profits tax; E.P.T.

ritsuki 利付き interest-bearing; with interest; interest on; cum interest
不確定利付き variable interest-bearing
確定利付き fixed interest-bearing

ritsukigaikasaiken 利付外貨債券 interest-bearing foreign currency bond

ritsukihakkō 利付発行 issuance of interest-bearing securities

ritsukikawasetegata 利付為替手形 interest bill

ritsukikin'yūsai 利付金融債 interest-bearing bank debenture

ritsukikokusai 利付国債 fixed rate government bond

ritsukikōsai 利付公債 active bond; interest-bearing bond

ritsukisaiken 利付債券 interest-bearing bond

不確定利付債券　variable interest-bearing bond; non-fixed interest-bearing bond

確定利付債券　fixed interest-bearing bond

ritsukishōken 利付証券　interest-bearing security

ritsukiyokin 利付預金　interest-bearing deposit

riyō 利用　utilization ¶ The year saw a sharp contraction in the *utilization* of both plant and labor. // the resources available for domestic *utilization*

riyōkanōsei 利用可能性　→アベイラビリティ

riyōkumiai 利用組合　utility co-operative association

rizaya 利鞘　profit margin of interest rate; interest rate spread; (interest) margin; spread ¶ Commitment fees raised the effective *margins* above the contractual *spreads*.

rīzuandoraguzu リーズ・アンド・ラグズ　leading and lagging of payments; leads and lags of payment; leads and lags ¶ a reversal, or rewinding, of *leads and lags of* current *payments* // The yen continued in strong demand partly because of commercial *leads and lags.* // The yen came on offer in the exchanges as importers and exporters unwound earlier *leads and lags of payments* in favor of yen. // The yen held marginally away from its ceiling reflecting a partial unwinding of *leads and lags.* // The *leads and lags* built up in the months prior to the floating of the yen were now being unwound. // Pressure on the lira continued as *leads and lags* remained adverse. // Price develop-

ments have reflected the *leads and lags* in the structure of production. // the reversal of previously adverse commercial *leads and lags*

rōbai 狼狽　［市］nervousness; jitter

rōbaiuri 狼狽売り　［市］blind sale

robōhanbai 路傍販売　curb service

robottokakumei ロボット革命　robotic revolution

rōdō 労働　labor; manpower ¶ to employ young, cheap and plentiful manual *labor* // save much *labor* to others // to command the skilled and trained *labor* of 1,500 hands // to require arduous *labors* // *labor*-management wage bargaining // a shortage of seasoned *manpower*

賃金労働　wage labor

抽象的労働　abstract labor

抽象的人間的労働　abstract human labor

不熟練労働　unskilled labor

不生産的労働　unproductive labor

不定期的労働　casual labor

必要労働　necessary labor

日雇い労働　casual labor

移民労働　immigrant labor

若年労働　young labor

熟練労働　skilled labor

契約労働　contract labor; indentured labor

契約移民労働　contract immigrant labor

季節的労働　seasonal labor

未熟練労働　unskilled labor

未利用労働　unused labor

肉体的労働　manual labor

生産的労働　productive labor

精神的労働　mental labor; brain labor; intellectual labor

商業労働　commercial labor

単純労働　simple labor

低賃金労働　cheap labor; sweated

labor

請負労働　contract labor

幼児労働　child labor

余剰労働　surplus labor

頭脳労働　mental labor; non-manual labor; intellectual labor

rōdōbunpairitsu　労働分配率　labor's relative share

rōdōdaihyō　労働代表　labor delegate

rōdōdaitaitōshi　労働代替投資　investment in substitution for labor

rōdōfuan　労働不安　labor unrest

rōdōhinmin　労働貧民　laboring poor

rōdōhō　労働法　labor laws; labor legislation

rōdōidō　労働異動　labor turnover

rōdōjikan　労働時間　working hours; hours of work; on-the-job hours; hours worked; labor hours; hours of labor ¶ Business extended working hours. // The number of *working hours* lost through labor disputes came to 17,504,000. // American airlines get more *working hours* per day out of their airliners. // to cut the maximum *working* week from 52 to 50 *hours* // As *hours of work* were increasing, so too were average hourly earnings. // Extra time off cut their *on-the-job time* to 38 hours. // The number of *manhours worked* per month declined by 18%.

週労働時間　workweek; working week ¶ The average *workweek* for the private nonfarm economy increased 0.4 hour to 40.3 hours. // demands for a five-hour cut in the *working week* to 35 hours with no loss of pay

rōdōjinkō　労働人口　working population ¶ the incorporation of women in the *working population*

rōdōjōken　労働条件　working conditions; labor conditions ¶ to impose unrealistic *working conditions* derived from practices in high-income countries

rōdōjukyū　労働需給　supply and demand on the labor market; situation in the labor market; labor market conditions; labor market; supply and demand of labor ¶ *Labor market* conditions remained tight. // The *labor market* reflects most clearly the excess demand. // The strains on the *labor market* are growing. // →労働市場

rōdōkahei　労働貨幣　labor note

rōdōkankeihō　労働関係法　labor laws

rōdōken　労働権　right to work

rōdōkihonken　労働基本権　basic legal right of labor

rōdōkijunhō　労働基準法　labor standards law

rōdōkinko　労働金庫　laborers' credit cooperative

rōdōkishaku　労働希釈　dilution of labor

rōdōkizoku　労働貴族　aristocracy of labor; labor aristocrat

rōdōkōsei　労働攻勢　labor offensive ¶ the first wave of spring *labor offensive*

rōdōkosuto　労働コスト　labor cost ¶ *Labor costs* per unit output rose by 2.9 percent because of its large increase in hourly wages.

rōdōkumiai　労働組合　labor union; trade union

地区労働組合　local union

企業別労働組合　company-based union

企業内労働組合　company union

産業別労働組合 vertical union; industrial union

職業別労働組合 horizontal union; craft union

単位(労働)組合 unit labor union

多産業間労働組合 multi-industrial union

rōdōkumiaiyakuin 労働組合役員 union official

rōdōkyōka 労働強化 intensification of labor; intensified labor; stretchout; overwork

rōdōkyōkyū 労働供給 labor supply

rōdōkyōyaku 労働協約 labor agreement; collective agreement; collective contract ¶ Wages and salaries negotiated under *collective* labor *agreements* rose by 6.8% between March 1978 and March 1979.

rōdōnissū 労働日数 working days ¶ The number of *working days* lost by stoppages was 1,755,000.

rōdōnohiidōsei 労働の非移動性 immobility of labor

rōdōnōritsu 労働能率 labor efficiency

rōdōnōryokunonaihinmin 労働能力のない貧民 impotent poor

rōdōnoryūdōsei 労働の流動性 labor liquidity

rōdōnosenmonka 労働の専門化 specialization of labor

rōdōrippo 労働立法 labor legislation

rōdōryoku 労働力 labor force; work force; economically active population ¶ Sweden's 200 lagrest companies raised their *labor force* by 50,000 people to 1.3 million. // 7,000 workers have been chopped from an inflated *work force*. // the widespread influx of working wives into the *labor force* // a huge influx of inexperienced young people, women and part-time workers into the *labor force* // the slower growth, or even a decline, in the *labor force* available to the manufacturing sectors (measured in man-hours) // The white male dominates the *workforce* available to a nation-wide business.

rōdōryokubusoku 労働力不足 shortage of labor; manpower shortage; shortage of workers; labor shortage ¶ *Shortage of labor,* particularly skilled labor, became more acute and widespread. // We face an unusual *shortage* of seasoned *manpower.* // [参考] Young labor is particularly in demand.

rōdōryokujinkō 労働力人口 labor force; working force; manpower ¶ The civilian *labor force* grew rapidly. // new entry, or participation, in the *labor force*, and earlier withdrawal therefrom // the composition of the *labor force* // Employers shed some of their *work force* and lengthen working hours instead. // persistent and acute shortages of indigeneous *manpower*

良質の労働力 high quality man power

余剰労働力 redundant labor force; surplus labor

rōdōryokukaritsu 労働力化率 participation rate ¶ The impact on registered unemployment was offset by a further decline in *participation rates*. // The rise in unemployment was contained by a downturn in *participation rates*.

rōdōryokunoidōsei 労働力の移動性 mobility of manpower; mobility of labor

rōdōsaihaichi 労働再配置 manpower relocation

rōdōseisansei 労働生産性 labor productivity ¶ The cost of wage increases is not based on improved *productivity*. // A rise in contracted wages equals 4% of the increase in *productivity*. // Net output per head is an internationally recognized index of manpower *productivity*. // The steel industry's manpower *productivity* was 7 percent below average.

rōdōseisanseishisū 労働生産性指数 labor productivity index

rōdōsetsuyakutekikikai 労働節約的機械 labor-saving machinery

rōdōsetsuyakutekinōgyōgijutsu 労働節約的農業技術 labor-saving technique of agriculture

rōdōsetsuyakutekitōshi 労働節約的投資 labor-saving investment

rōdōsha 労働者 worker; laborer; operative; workingman; laboring man; labor; labor force; work force; working force ¶ skilled and unskilled production *workers* // both mental, or brain, and manual *workers* // civilian *labor force,* or non-government *work force* // Legislation provides organized *workers* in large companies with the right to parity representation on the policy boards of their companies.
知的労働者 brain worker; white-collar worker
不熟練労働者 unskilled worker
限界労働者 marginal worker
半熟練労働者 semi-skilled worker
日雇い労働者 casual laborer
自由労働者 day-laborer
熟練労働者 skilled worker
契約労働者 contract laborer; indentured laborer
季節労働者 seasonal laborer
工場労働者 factory worker
肉体労働者 blue-collar worker
農業労働者 agricultural laborer
農業賃金労働者 hired agricultural laborer
産業労働者 manufacturing worker; industrial laborer
組織労働者 organized workers
低賃金労働者 sweated laborer
幼児労働者 child laborer
余剰労働者 redundant worker
頭脳労働者 brain worker; white-collar worker

rōdōshainyū 労働者移入 immigration of laborers

rōdōshakaikyū 労働者階級 working class; laboring class; proletariat

rōdōshasaigaihoshō 労働者災害補償 workman's compensation

rōdōshijō 労働市場 labor market; job market ¶ The *labor market* is still characterized by an unusual strain. // The *labor market* eased, mainly in vacancies. // The disappearance of a labor surplus has led to a tightening of the *labor market*. // It could restrict access to the *labor market* for many of the work force. // A worrying shortage of new jobs for young entrants into the *labor market*. // The situation in the *labor market* improved. // influxes into the *labor market* // school-leavers coming onto the *job market* // →労働需要

rōdōshijōenoshinkisannyū 労働市場への新規参入 influx into the labor market

rōdōshūyakudo 労働集約度 labor intensity

rōdōshūyakutekikōgyōhin 労働集

約的工業品 labor intensive industrial products

rōdōsōgi 労働争議 labor dispute → ストライキ

rōdōsōgiassen 労働争議斡旋 reconciliation in a labor dispute

rōdōsōgichōtei 労働争議調停 mediation in a labor dispute

rōdōsōgichūsai 労働争議仲裁 arbitration in a labor dispute

rōdōtōnyūryō 労働投入量 labor input

rōdōundō 労働運動 labor movement; labor campaign; labor drive; labor offensive

rōdōyobigun 労働予備軍 reserve army of labor

rōdōzenshūken 労働全収権 right to the whole produce of labor

rōgoshikin 老後資金 reserve for old age

rōhi 浪費 prodigality; waste; frittering; squandering; lavishment ¶ the oil bonanza ecouraging *prodigality* // deep and complex causes of *prodigality* among oil-rich countries // to avoid *waste* of money, labor, and time // Remittances have been *frittered* away in personal consumption and social ceremonies. // The developing nations are resisting to the *squandering* of their natural resources by advanced nations. // to *squander* its ill-gotten gains on luxury goods

roitāshōhinshisū ロイター商品指数 (English) Reuter index of commodity prices

rōjinjinkō 老人人口 aging population

rokujūninentsūshōkakudaihō 62年通商拡大法 ［米］Trade Expansion Act of 1962

rōkyūsetsubi 老朽設備 obsolete equipment

rōmukanri 労務管理 labor management; personnel administration

rōmukansa 労務監査 personnel audit

ronbādorēto ロンバード・レート Lombard rate; the rate charged for normal advances to banks against securities

rondonginkōkantorihikikinri ロンドン銀行間取引金利 London interbank offered rate; LIBOR

rōreifujo 老齢扶助 old-age assistance

rōreihinkonsha 老齢貧困者 aged poor

rosen 路線 track; path ¶ to leave the economy still on a recession *track* // to place the economy on the right *track* to the sustainable growth // the shift in the growth *track* of the economy to a decelerating one // to run off the stable growth *track* // to put western economies back on the *track* of sustained economic growth // The economy is moving back onto a growth *track*. The Federal revenue continued pursuing a *path* of moderate monetary growth. // to bring monetary growth on to the desired *path* // to keep monetary aggregates roughly on the envisaged growth *path* // The economy is back on an upward *path*, on a less exuberant long-term growth *path*. // Actual developments deviated from the officially envisaged growth *path*. // to be on a strong uphill *path* // ［参考］the U.S. on the way to a solid expansion

安定路線 stable path; steady path
経済路線 economic path

成長路線　growth path

rōshi 労使　management and labor; workers and employer

rōshi 労資　capital and labor

rōshikankei 労使関係　labor-management relations; industrial relations ¶ *Labor-management relations* were fraught with class-conscious "us against them" confrontations. ¶ to improve *industrial relations*

rōshikankei 労資関係　relation between capital and labor ¶ harmonious *relations between capital and labor* // ［参考］to be tackled jointly by both sides on industry

rōshikankeihō 労使関係法　labor-management relations law

rōshikyōchō 労資協調　labor-capital reconciliation; labor-capital collaboration

rōshikyōgi 労使協議　labor-management talk

rōshikyōgisei 労使協議制　joint labor-management conference system

rōshitairitsu 労使対立　labor-management confrontation

rōshutsu 漏出　leakage; waste; loss; dispersion; drain ¶ to lcad to the habitual *leakage* of rural savings into urban credit

現金の漏出　cash drain

rosutouriron ロストウ理論　Rostow's theory

rōzabondo ローザ・ボンド　［米］ Roosa bond

ruibetsu 類別　group; grouping; class; classification ¶ commodity *groups; grouping* by commodity items // *classification* by industry group

ruigenzei 累減税　degressive tax

ruijibuhinkakōhō 類似部品加工法 group technology

ruijihin 類似品　similar; like (article); imitation ¶ to be replaced with *similars* // this or the *like* // Beware of *imitations!*

ruikei 累計　total sum; sum total; aggregate; cumulative total

ruisekiakaji 累積赤字　cumulative deficit; accumulated deficit

ruisekijuyō 累積需要　pent-up demand; cumulate demand; demand carry-overs

ruisekikatei 累積過程　process of accumulation; accumulative process

ruisekitōhyō 累積投票　cumulative voting

ruisekitōshi 累積投資　accumulative investment; accumulated investment

ruishin 累進　graduated; progressive ¶ penalty deposits at *graduated* rates // *progressive* tax rates

ruishinzeiritsu 累進税率　progressive (tax) rates

rusukazokusōkin 留守家族送金　remittance to family overseas ¶ *remittance* by foreign nationals in Japan to their *families overseas*

rūto ルート　channel; route; conduit; regular course ¶ to form a *channel* of communication // *conduits* through which financial resources are *channeled* for, and distributed to, small firms by banks // *channels* of transactions // the *route* in delivering milk

配給ルート　rationing channel

正式ルート　legitimate channel ¶ *legitimate channels* of purchase

ryō 量　(physical) volume (=stock); quantum; quantity ¶ The *physical volume* of exports has risen above the trough of January. // *physical* *stocks* in the retail trade sector actually rose in March. // to obtain a larger *volume* of imports for a given *quantum* of exports

ryō 漁 catch
大漁 good catch
不漁 bad catch

ryōdate 両建 [市] straddling; double option

ryōdatechūmon 両建注文 matched orders

ryōdateyokin 両建預金 compulsory deposit as a condition for loans

ryōgae 両替え exchange of money

ryōgaeryō 両替料 charge for change

ryōgaeshō 両替商 money changer

ryōgaeya 両替屋 exchange house; money changer

ryōhanten 量販店 mass sales store

ryōiki 領域 territory; boundary; arena; sphere; province ¶ Commercial banks are nibbling at the traditional *territory* of the investment banks. // to break into the investment banking *arena* // A number of adjustments in the monetary *sphere* may be necessary. // the World Bank not straying into the economic adjustment loan area which has long been the *province* of the IMF
生産可能(性)領域 production possibility boundary
生産機会領域 production opportunity boundary

ryōjisashōokurijō 領事査証送り状 consular invoice

ryōjisashōryō 領事査証料 consular fee

ryōkai 領海 territorial sea; territorial waters ¶ extensions of *territorial waters* by maritime nations

ryōkin 料金 (service) charge; rate; fee; fare; price ¶ power *charges* or electricity *rates* // public utility *rates* // doctor's consultation *fee* // Train *fares*, rail freight *charges*, inland letter *rates*, telephone *charges*, and cigarette *prices* are fixed by the government.
電力料金 electric power rates
電信電話料金 telegraph and telephone charges
受益者負担料金 remunerative rates
国鉄料金 JNR fares
公共料金 public utility rates
入浴料金 public bath charges; bath house fees
鉄道料金 rail fares
郵便料金 postal rates

ryōkintōseijigyō 料金統制事業 rate-regulated enterprise

ryokōshin'yōjō 旅行信用状 (letter of) traveler's credit

ryokōshōgaihoken 旅行傷害保険 traveler's (personal) accident insurance

ryokukasangyō 緑化産業 green business

ryokyakuunchin 旅客運賃 passenger fee

ryōmoku 量目 weight; quantity

ryōmokubusoku 量目不足 short weight

ryōmokusakushukahei 量目削取貨幣 defaced coin

ryōritsu 料率 →料金

ryōritsuhyō 料率表 tariff

ryōsan 量産 volume production; quantity production ¶ The designers are moving toward *volume production*.

ryōshūsho 領収(書) receipt

ryōtekihaaku 量的把握 →計量

ryōtekikakudai 量的拡大 numerical expansion; quantitative expansion

ryōtekikinyūshihyō 量的金融指標 monetary aggregates ¶ The growth of the *monetary aggregates* remained sluggish.

ryōtekikisei 量的規制 quantitative regulation; quantitative restriction ¶ *quantitative* credit *regulation*

ryōtekiseibutsushigen 量的生物資源 biomass

ryōtekishin'yōkisei 量的信用規制 quantitative credit control (=regulation)

ryūdo 粒度 grain size

ryūdō 流動 floating; liquid; current

ryūdōfusai 流動負債 current liabilities; floating liabilities

ryūdōhiritsu 流動比率 current ratio; liquidity ratio; ratio of current assets to current liabilities ¶ The *liquidity ratio,* i.e. the money supply expressed as a percentage of national income, showed a further decline of 1 percentage point. // The *liquidity ratio* of the companies —measuring their current assets as a percentage of their current liabilities—showed a further improvement.

ryūdōsaiken 流動債権 liquid claim ¶ to acquire or sell the standardized *liquid claims* // transactions in the *liquid claims* of the money market

ryūdōsei 流動性 liquidity; liquidity position ¶ The banks still maintained a comfortable margin of *liquidity* to meet reserve requirements. // The large U.S. dificit has created an abundance of available *liquidity.* // to squeeze money-market *liquidity* in the immediate future // to provide the economy

with abundant *liquidity* // to limit the *liquidity* drain through the new measures to some DM 4 billion // to dampen the *liquidity* impact of a large government budget deficit // to build and augment the amount of onternal *liquidity* // to mop up surplus *liquidity* // *Liquidity* at the disposal of institutional investors seems to be abundant.

銀行流動性 bank liquidity; liquidity of the banking system ¶ *Bank liquidity* increased sharply. // a large volume of surplus *liquidity in the banking system* // The total *liquidity of* German banks is between DM 6 and 7 billion higher than in the previous month. // monetary policy actions to offset the drain on *bank liquidity* due to the market // The *banking system* has continued to be rather *liquid.*

企業流動性 corporate liquidity; business liquidity ¶ The total *business liquidity* in the form of cash and bank balances increased. // The *liquidity* position of *business* was held high.

国際流動性 international liquidity ¶ The risk of a fat too exuberant increase in *international liquidity* is evident. // foreign loans and credits to safeguard the country's *international liquidity* // Denmark's *international liquidity* increased by D.Kr. 5,204 million over the period.

労働の流動性 liquidity of labor; mobility of labor

市場流動性 money-market liquidity ¶ to place government funds commercial banks to help ease *money-market liquidity* // to relieve current tightness in domestic *money-market liquidity*

適正流動性　adequate liquidity

ryūdōseijirenma 流動性ジレンマ liquidity-dilemma

ryūdōseijuyō 流動性需要 need for liquidity

ryūdōseinosōshutsu 流動性の創出 liquidity creation; creation of liquidity

ryūdōseisenkōsetsu 流動性選好説 liquidity preference theory

ryūdōseishisan 流動(性)資産 liquid assets; quick assets; floating assets

ryūdōseishūshi 流動性収支 balance on liquidity basis

ryūdōseiuchibu 流動性打歩 liquidity premium

ryūdōshihon 流動資本 floating capital

ryūdōshikin 流動資金 liquid funds; floating funds

ryūdōshisan 流動資産 current assets; liquid assets; floating assets

ryūdōshizai 流動資材 liquid resources

ryūdōshōken 流動証券 liquid securities

ryūgakutokō 留学渡航 trip for study abroad; travel for study abroad

ryūhojōkō 留保条項 saving clause

ryūhorieki 留保利益 retained earning; retained income; accumulated earning; earning retained for use in the business ¶ the internal growth of capital from *retention* of *earnings*

ryūkōhin 流行品 fashion goods

ryūnyū 流入 inflow; influx ¶ a substantial long-term *inflow* of capital into Brazil // the short-term capital *inflow* increased // to ward off unwanted capital *inflows* // to check massive *inflows* of foreign capital // intervention to soak up currency *inflows*

ryūnyūchō 流入超 excess inflow (over outflow)

ryūnyūshikinnofutaika 流入資金の不胎化 sterilization of inflowed funds ¶ to *sterilize inflowed funds* at the central bank

ryūshutsu 流出 outflow; drain; effluence; efflux; drainage ¶ The regional aggregate of short-term *outflows* of capital did not grow further. // The low rate of operation caused a substantial *drain* on the company's earnings. // a marked easing of the *drain* on foreign *exchange* reserves // to prevent a *drainage* abroad or into private hoards of gold // a *drain* on banks' reserves by half-yearly payment of corporate taxes // the steady *outflow* of Japanese capital to higher yield instruments

ryūshutsuchō 流出超 excess outflow (over inflow)

ryūshutsunyū 流出入 inflow and outflow; influx and efflux

ryūtsū 流通 circulation; distribution ¶ bank notes in *circulation* // to withdraw notes from *circulation* // to *distribute* merchandise // Money in *circulation* dropped some lempira 7 million below the year-ago figure. // The monetary *circulation* expanded. // The net withdrawal of bank notes from *circulation* totaled ¥56 million. // a return of currency from public *circulation* // to put new notes into *circulation* // money *circulated* rapidly, or the velocity of *circulation* was high. // a successive contraction and expansion of the *circulating* medium

金融的流通 financial circulation

産業的流通 industrial circulation

ryūtsūbumon 流通部門 distribution sector

ryūtsūfubentsūka 流通不便通貨 currency unfit for circulation

ryūtsūkeihi 流通経費 distribution cost

ryūtsūkeiro 流通経路 distribution channel

ryūtsūken 流通券 bank notes in circulation

ryūtsūkikō 流通機構 distribution system; marketing system; distibution structure ¶ modernization of the food *distribution structure* // Japan's multilayered, complex *distribution* system // strong rises in the price of beef as it passed through the *distribution* system

ryūtsūkindaika 流通近代化 modernization in the structure of distribution

ryūtsūmājin 流通マージン distributor's (profit) margin

ryūtsūsangyō 流通産業 distributive industry

ryūtsūsentā 流通センター commercial distribution center

ryūtsūshihei 流通紙幣 (bank) notes in circulation; circulating notes

ryūtsūshijō 流通市場 distribution sector; wholesalers and retailers level; trading market; secondary market; circulation market

ryūtsūshōken 流通証券 negotiable instrument

ryūtsūsokudo 流通速度 velocity of circulation (of money) ¶ The *velocity of circulation* has returned to its normal value. // many forces that alter the *velocity of circulation* of our money supply // The slowing-down of the *velocity of money circulation* may be reversed.

所得流通速度 income velocity (of circulation) of money

取引流通速度 transactions velocity of money

ryūtsūtsūka 流通通貨 money in circulation ¶ The *money in circulation* dropped some $7 million below the figure reached one year earlier. // *Money circulated* rapidly.

ryūtsūzaiko 流通在庫 dealers' inventories; distributors' inventory; inventories with distributors; trade inventories

ryūyō 流用 diversion; appropriation; misappropriation ¶ a *diversion* of, or *appropriation* from, another fund // a *misappropriation* of public money

S

SDR SDR Special Drawing Right (of the International Monetary Fund); SDR ¶ the *SDR*, the principal reserve asset in the international monetary system // Total reserves, which comprise the holdings of foreign exchange, gold, and *SDRs* and reserve positions in the Fund, amounted to the equivalent of *SDR* 100.7 billion. // The total use of *SDRs* by participants was *SDR* 826 million. // world export unit values in terms of *SDRs*

SDR torihikikachi SDR 取引価値 valuation of the SDR

sabetsu 差別 discrimination ¶ *discrimination* by employers against females, or employer *discrimination* against females, accounts for a sizable depression in female wage rates. // the drive against racial *discrimination* // non-*discrimination* in trade // Luxury taxes should not *discriminate* between domestic and foreign goods. // to forbid hiring *discrimination* based on age and by sex // age *discrimination* in employment // unfair *discrimination* in recruitment and hiring // to eliminate job *discrimination* as regards women

sabetsukanzei 差別関税 differential duty

sabetsutekidekidakakyūseido 差別的出来高給制度 differential piece-rate plan (=system)

sabetsutekikakakukeisei 差別的価格形成 discriminating pricing

sabetsutekitsūkasochi 差別的通貨措置 discriminatory currency practice (=arrangement) ¶ to avoid *discriminatory currency practices* // to engage in multiple exchange practices or *discriminatory currency arrangements*

sābisu サービス service ¶ These *services* are rendered at actual cost. // These banks obtain mechanical and advisory *services* from big city banks. // A strike paralyzed bank's over-the-counter customer *services*. // The city bank *serves*

gratis as intermediary for its correspondents, or *serves* as agent in placing funds in the interbank market. // a city bank that offers the best package of compensating *services* // A fairly uniform basic level of *services* is provided nationwide. // to market sophisticated international banking *services* to customers // The banking and financial *services* available to the American consumer have been enlarged. // The country now faces a breakdown in public *services* (water, sewerage, rubbish collection). // All banks are eligible to participate in the *services* of the regional reserve banks. // to allow uniform access to Federal Reserve *services* at equal costs

sābisubumon サービス部門 service sector

sābisuekonomī サービス・エコノミー service economy

sābisugyō サービス業 service(-type) industries; services sector

sābisukyōsō サービス競争 better-service competition; competition providing better service

sābisuryōkin サービス料金 service charge

sābisuryōkomi サービス料込み(ホテルなどの) attendance included

sābisuteikyōsha サービス提供者 purveyor of service

sābisuyushutsunyū サービス輸出入 services exports and imports; services trade

sabotāju サボタージュ sabotage ¶ The union continued its struggle by carrying out acts of *sabotage* at work sites. // → 怠業

sabupuroguramu サブプログラム [コン] subprogram; subroutine

sagakushikyū 差額支給(賃金の) makeup pay; makeup payment ¶ to *make up payment* for the increase agreed in the spring wage negotiation

sagaru 下がる fall; drop; go down; decline; move down; recede; depreciate; sag; slip ¶ →下降; 下落; 物価

sageashi 下げ足 downward movement; downward drift; downward trend; downtrend ¶ The market moved *downward* as big blocks of oil shares sold. // Equity prices continued their *downward* drift. // The *downward trend* in prices continued for 8th straight day. // Industrials led a moderate *downtrend*.

sagedomari 下げ止まり leveling out (=off); flattenig-out; bottoming-out; edging lower; ceasing to fall ¶ Prices edged lower. // Production *flattened out*. // Indications are that the fall in the balance-of-payment position is *leveling*. // Business activity appeared to be *bottoming out*. // The *fall* in activity may *cease* shortly. // Prices *ceased to fall*. // [参考] The dollar may have reached a plateau after its steep fall.

sageikō 下げ意向 [市] selling interest

sageru 下げる lower; reduce; cut down; bring down ¶ The discount rate was *lowered* by ½ percentage point, or was reduced; or *cut down* by ½ percentage point to 5¼ per cent. // to *bring* the level of interest rates *down* and closer to those overseas

sageshiburu 下げ渋る steady; holding up ¶ The market declined fairly steeply on Monday, but it *steadied* on Tuesday. // The market was mixed but then *steadied* and moved higher. // The price for oils was reported to be *holding up*. // Commodity market prices *held up*.

sagesōba 下げ相場 [市] bearish market; short market; [外] adverse exchange ¶ One of the main pegs of the current *bear maket* is prospective countercyclical policy. // Friday's *short market* stemmed from a tumbling of oil shares.

sagurikyaku さぐり客 comparison shopper

sagyō 作業 work ¶ Much conceptual and empirical *work* needs to be done.

sagyōbukai 作業部会 working party

sagyōkeikaku 作業計画 working plan

sagyōnissū 作業日数 working days

saibanetikkusu サイバネティックス cybernetics

saibankankatsu 裁判管轄 jurisdiction ¶ The parties submit to the *jurisdiction* of the English High Court of London.

saibunpai 再分配 redistribution ¶ a systematic *redisribution* of welath amongst nations // *redistribution* of an already inadequate national income, labor, and resources // *redistribution* and transfer of resources within the community // legitimate aspiration for a global *redistribution* of power on a fairer and more equitable basis // the *distributive* function of the State budget

saichōsei 再調整 realignment ¶ international *realignment* of currencies, or international currency *realignment*

saigaifukkyūjūtakukashitsuke 災害復旧住宅貸付 disaster relief housing loan

saigonokashite 最後の貸手 lender of last resort ¶ The central bank is regarded as performing the function of *lender of last resort*. // the central bank as the *lender of last resort* // The bank of issue rediscounts, and acts as *lender of last resort*. // the functions of rediscount and *lender of last resort* // the lack of a clearly defined *lender-of-last-resort* in the Euro-market // to have recourse to the *lender of last resort*

saigonoyoridokoro 最後の拠り所 last resort ¶ →最後の貸手

saihaibun 再配分 reallocation ¶ the *reallocation* of resources within sectors, concentrating then to benefit special groups

saihanbaikakaku 再販売価格 re-sale price ¶ the *re-sale price* maintenance system

saihanbaikakakuijikeiyaku 再販売価格維持契約 resale price maintenance agreement

saihanbukka 再販物価 resale price

saihankakakuijisei 再販価格維持制 [英] retail price maintenance; rpm

saihankakakushiteiseido 再販価格指定制度 resale price designation system

saihensei 再編成 reorganization; reform(ation); restructure; realignment ¶ a sweeping *reorganization* of the banking system, and a drastic *reorganization of* industry // *reorganization* and integration of financial institutions // Japan achieved a substantial *restructuring* of its industry. // international currency *reform*

// a far reaching and lasting international monetary *reform* // the evolutionary *reform* of the banking system // A financial *reform* bill aimed at *restructuring* the banking system. // to stimulate a desirable *restructuring* of the economy towards high-technology // international *realignment* of currencies or currency *realignment*

saihi 歳費 annual expenditure; annual allowance; yearly allowance ¶ total *annual expenditures* of the 1975-76 budget // to give or grant an *annual allowance* of $2,000 for the operations of the project

saihinchi 最頻値 mode

saihinkoku 最貧国 most seriously affected countries; MSAC; "Fouth World"

saihoken 再保険 reinsurance; retrocession (of insurance)

saihokenkin 再保険金 reinsurance claim; reinsurance money

saihokenryō 再保険料 reinsurance premium

saihyōka 再評価 revaluation; reassessment; reappraisal ¶ an upward or downward *revaluation* of assets // to *revalue* upward or downward the national currency // Thailand *revalues* its currency vis-à-vis the U.S. dollar // the regular half-yearly *reassessment* of the value of official foreign exchange items // a *reassessment* of a conventional policy measure // to *reassess* the present method // *revaluation* surplus or loss

saihyōkajōyokin 再評価剰余金 surplus from revaluation

saihyōkason'eki 再評価損益 revaluation profit or loss

saijisshi 再実施 reinstitution; reinstatement ¶ The controls of certain exchange transactions have been *reinstituted*. // The old foreign trade policy has been *reinstated* basically unchanged as from January of this year.

saijunkan 再循環 recycle ¶ Funds laid idle in the oil producing countries were *recycled* into the economic circuit via the international banking system.

saikatonsū 載貨トン数 cargo tonnage

saikei 歳計 budget; annual account; yearly account

saikeikoku 最恵国 the most-favored nation; M.F.N.

saikeikokujōkō 最恵国条項 the most-favored-nation clause; M.F.N.C.

saikeikokutaigū 最恵国待遇 the most-favored-nation treatment; M.F.N. treatment ¶ to accord certain developing countries the *most-favored-nation treatment*

saiken 再建 rebuilding; reconstruction; rehabilitation ¶ financial *reconstruction* and economic *rehabilitation*

saiken 債(券) securities; bond; debenture; bond certificate; debt security; bond; debenture; note; stock

延長債 extended bond
外貨債券 foreign currenay bond
一般財源債 general obligation bond
割賦償還債券 installment bond
継続債 continued bond
期日一括償還債券 bullet bond
記名(式)債券 inscribed bond
工業(=産業)開発債 industrial development bond; industrial revenue bond

交換可能債券 interchangeable bond
更新債 renewed bond
免税債券 tax-exempt bond
無記名(式)債券 bearer bond
無担保債券 unsecured bond
連続償還債券 serial bond
利付債券 interest-bearing bond; coupon bond
利札付債券 coupon bond
政府機関債券 government agency bond
収益債券 income bond
収入引当債券 revenue bond
相互交換式債 interchangeable bond
対外債券 external bond
特別財源債 revenue bond
特別税引当債 special tax bond
登録債券 registered bond
随時償還債券 redeemable bond; callable bond

saiken 債権 credit; claim ¶ Sweden has practically renounced its *claims* to the poorest developing countries.

対外債権 foreign loan; external claim
手形債権 rights on the basis of a bill

saiken'assenkeiyaku 債券斡旋契約 arrangers agreement

saikenbaibai 債券売買 purchase and sale of securities; buying and salling of securities

saikenbaibaisōsa 債券売買操作 buying and selling operations of securities; securities operation; operations in securities

saikenganrikinshiharaijimutoriatsukaikeiyaku 債券元利金支払事務取扱契約 paying agent agreement

saikengenka 債権減価 depreciation of claim.

saikengenkahyō 債券現価表 bond table

saikenhakkō 債券発行 security offering; offer; issuance of securities; securities issue; flotation of bond; bond flotation ¶ Corporate *security offerings* amounted to 10 billion dollars. // The government has approved the *flotation of* Finland's national *bonds* in this country, the first *bond flotation* in Japan. // Japan banned the *issue of* yen-quoted foreign *bonds* in Japan. // A £5 million 6 percent sterling loan priced at 96, is to be *offered* in London by the Japanese Government. // The total volume of corporate *security offerings* amounted to 10.2 billion dollars.

saikenhakkōsetsumeisho 債券発行説明書 placement memorandum

saikenhassei 債権発生 creation of claim ¶ party to *creation,* etc. *of claims*

saikenhō 債権法 law of obligations

saikenhyōkason 債券評価損 depreciation of securities

saikenjōto 債権譲渡 assignment of claim cession an obligation

saikenjun'i 債権順位 order of credit

saikenkaitorikeiyaku 債務買取契約 note purchase agreement

saikenkaitoriken 債券買取権 warrant ¶ Government of Canada 50,000 six-month *warrants* exercisable into 50 million Canadian dollars of the Government's 10.25 percent bonds at a price of 87.50

saikenkaitorikin'yū 債権買取金融 factoring

saikenkakakukakusa 債券価格格差 unamortized discount on interest-bearing debentures

saikenkanjō 債券勘定 debentures account

saikenkoku 債権国 creditor nation; creditor country; (net-)creditor country; creditor nation ¶ 15 *creditor nations* forming the Paris Club

saikenkokukaigi 債権国会議 consortium (of creditor nations)

saikenkurinobekanjō 債券繰延勘定 unamortized discount on debenture accounts

saikennobensai 債権の弁済 liquidation of claim; settlement of claim

saikennokakuzuke 債券の格付 bond (quality) rating ¶ a bond *rated* A-1, a A-1 *rated* bond // →格付

saikennoshōmetu 債権の消滅 extinguishment of claimable asset; extinction of claim

saikenokataisurushorui 債権を化体する書類 document embodying right to claim

saikenrisoku 債券利息 interest on debenture

saikensaimu 債権債務 debts and credits

saikensashiosaenin 債権差押人 garnisher

saikenseibi 再建整備 reconstruction and reorganization

saikensha 債権者 creditor; obligee ¶ national groups of *creditor* banks 善意の債権者 bona fide creditor

saikenshōka 債券消化 subscription; absorption ¶ *subscription* to the loan // The issue was over-*subscribed.* // The banks *absorbed* about one-third of newly issued securities. // large-lot *subrscribers*

saikenshōkan 債券償還 redemption of securities (=bond; debenture) ¶ to *redeem* national *bonds*

saikentanaage 債権棚上げ shelving of a claim

saikentankikaiire 債券短期買入 short-term purchase of securities; purchase of securities for short-term holding

saikentanpo 債権担保 security for obligation

saikentanpokashitsukekin 債権担保貸付金 loan secured by account receivable

saikentorokujimutoriatsukaikeiyaku 債券登録事務取扱契約 recording agent agreement

saikenwaribikiryo 債券割引料 discount on debenture

saikenyuzuriuke 債権譲受け taking over (=take-over) of other's credit claim ¶ to *take over another* bank's credit claims

saikinshi 再禁止 re-prohibition; reimposition of an embargo; reinstitution of ban

金輸出再禁止 re-embargo; re-imposition of a gold embargo

saiko 再興 rehabilitation ¶ Japan's postwar *rehabilitation* // reconstruction and *rehabilitation* of the postwar economy

saikogendo 最高限度 ceiling; (maximum) limit ¶ The *ceiling* on bank note circulation will be raised to Yen 16,300 billion, and the higher *ceiling* is designed to meet growing requirements of funds for the year-end. // The central bank has raised the *ceiling* on debts which domestic banks may contract abroad to 21.5% of each bank's capital and reserves. // a bill raising the Federal debt *ceiling* to $879 billion to the end

of this financial year // The current Federal debt *limit* of $830 billion expired on October 1. // the *maximum limit* for interest rates // the *maximum limit* of overdraft // the *ceiling* on total oil imports fixed at Fr. 58 billion // to set the *ceiling* on the increase in bank lendings // a program containing a *ceiling* on the amount of external debt the country can incur over a specified time (including a *subceiling* on short-term debt) // Overall credit *ceilings* were more likely to hold if *subceilings* on credit to government were observed.

saikohakkogakukusshinseigenseido 最高発行額屈伸制限制度 elastic maximum issue limit system

saikokakaku 最高価格 ceiling (price); maximum price; upper limit (price) ¶ the imposition of a *ceiling price* on new domestic oil // to raise the *ceiling* on domestic crude oil prices by at most 10 percent per year

saikosei 再構成 reconstitution; reform ¶ the requirement of *reconstitution* of SDRs, namely, the obligation to maintain a minimum average balance of SDRs over specified periods

saikoyo 再雇用 rehiring ¶ The company has *rehired* about 2,000 of the 15,000 employees who were laid off last year.

saimu 債務 debt; indebtedness; obligation; liability ¶ to have or owe a large *debt* to someone // to incur or fall into a *debt,* and pay back, pay off, refund, or repay the *debt* // *debt*-plagued Argentina which was on the verge of failing to pay overdue interest on its foreign *debts* // Short-term *debt* is incurred for meeting working capital needs and means *obligations* maturing in five years or less. // satisfaction of the *debt* and all costs to incur and then fulfill financial *obligations* // to accept *liability* for loss or damage // to meet our *liabilities* amounting to 2 million dollars // The *indebtedness* of $10 million became due prior to its stated maturity. // the *obligation* of the company to make any payment of borrowed money when due

長期債務　funded debt

持参人払債務　obligation performable to bearer

公正証書付債務　speciality debt

無証書債務　debt for honor

連帯債務　joint and several obligation

指図人払債務　obligation performable to order

対外債務　external debt; foreign liality

短期債務　floating debt

有証債務　bonded debt; debt of speciality

saimubensai　債務弁済　liquidation of claim; settlement of claim

saimufurikō　債務不履行　default of obligation; delinquency; failure to meet obligation ¶ The bonded indebtedness of many developing countries went into protracted *default*. // a *default* in an agreement // in case of *default* on loans // when a buyer *defaults* on an overseas contract, the exporter's claim is paid based on the sterling rate ruling at the time of *default* // a risk in *delinquency* rates // to prevent the Government from going into *default* // [参考] the danger of the debtor failing to pay interest or principal as due

saimuhensai　債務返済　debt repayment

saimuhensaihiritsu　債務返済比率　debt service ratio ¶ Their *debt service ratio* on long-term foreign borrowing-interest and amortization payments as percentages of exports of goods and services-rose from 18.1 to 22.3 per cent. // the *ratio* of *debt service* payments to exports of the country approximating to 23 per cent

saimuhensaikurinobe　債務返済繰延　∼ rescheduling (of debt) ¶ Mexico signed a big *rescheduling* package covering $11.4 billion of government debt. // Morocco is seeking a *rescheduling* of several hundred million dollars of debt owed to Western governments. // Turkey *rescheduled* foreign debts totaling 3.5 billion dollars. // The amount owed to the companies was *rescheduled* under an agreement which allowed a seven year payback period. // loan *rescheduling* talks with debtors // *Debt* rescheduling amounts to a rearrangement or restructuring, generally involving a stretching out, of the original repayment schedule with respect to a particular debt or a set of debts. // The *rescheduled debt* may include a grace period and a stretched repament schedule.

saimuhikiuke　債務引受　taking of obligation

重畳的債務引受　cumulative taking of obligation

免責的債務引受　non-cumulative taking of obligation

saimuhoshō　債務保証　guarantee of obligation

saimukakuteigaku 債務確定額 assessed amount of debt

saimukiki 債務危機 debt crisis ¶ to alleviate the *debt crisis* // to study solutions to the two-year-old international *debt crisis* // to help countries weather the world *debt crisis* // to ease, not to precipitate, the present international, inter alia, Latin American *debt crisis,* which broke three years ago

saimukoku 債務国 debtor nation, debtor country; indebted country; debt-burdened country; net-debtor country debt-strapped country ¶ the tense situation facing deficit-ridden, *debt-strapped country*

saimumenjo 債務免除 waiver of obligation

saimurikō 債務履行 performance of obligation; fulfillment of obigation; meeting obligation ¶ to *meet* our *obligation;* and to settle the debt

saimusha 債務者 obligor; debtor ¶ various securities of one and the same *obligor*

saimusharijun 債務者利潤 profit for debtor

saimushayokin 債務者預金 deposit of debtor

saimushōkan 債務償還 debt redemption

saimushōkantsumitatekin 債務償還積立金 surplus appropriated for redemption fund

saimushōken 債務証券 debt securities; evidences of debt ¶ to negotiate promissory notes, drafts, bills of exchange, and other *evidences of debt*

saimushōmetsu 債務消滅 expiration of obligation; acquittance

saimutanaage 債務棚上げ consolidation of debt

saimuzandaka 債務残高 outstanding obligations

sainen 再燃 rekindling; re-ignition ¶ The step is likely to *rekindle* inflation. // [参考] another outburst of inflation // →インフレの再燃

sainyū 歳入 annual revenue; annual income; budget receipts ¶ Total *annual revenue* is set at Pts 65.7 billion. // Overall realized *revenue* in the 12-month fiscal year 1975-76 was 2.4 percent below the original budget estimated. // All categories of *budget receipts* were higher than estimated. // attempts to switch *revenue*-raising to new taxes on spending

sainyūbunpaiseido 歳入分配制度 revenue sharing system

sainyūchōshūkan 歳入徴収官 revenue collector

sainyūdairiten 歳入代理店 revenue agency

sainyūjisseki 歳入実績 realized revenue

sainyūkekkan 歳入欠陥 revenue shortfall; budgetary shortfall; budget deficit ¶ New bond issues amounting to ¥2,500 million are planned to compensate for the *shortfall in* fiscal *revenue.* // to repair the city's persistent *budget deficit* // the estimated *shortfall* of D.Kr 31.9 billion for the current year // to make up *revenue shortfalls* caused by tax cuts // to offset *revenue shortfalls* by a raise of indirect taxation

sainyūsaishutsu 歳入歳出 revenue and expenditure

sainyūsaishutsugaigenkinsuitōkanri 歳入歳出外現金出納官吏 accounting official with money in custody

sainyūsaishutsukinsuitō 歳入歳出金出納 (budget) revenues and expenditures; receipts and outlays

sainyūsaishutsuyosan 歳入歳出予算 revenue and expenditure budget; budget revenues and expenditures; estimated expenditures and revenues (=receipts and outlays)

sainyūyosan 歳入予算 estimated revenues (=receipts); budget revenues ¶ *Budget receipts* for 1986 are presently estimated at $65.4 billion. // The fiscal *revenue* for 1979 is *budgeted* at Sw.fr. 14.78 billion.

sainyūyoteigaku 歳入予定額 estimated revenue

sairyō 裁量 discretion ¶ The matter is left to the bank's own *discretion.* // It is within the bank's *discretion* to settle the matter. // expenses subject to a wide range of managerial *discretion*

sairyōkigyōmukekashidashikinri 最良企業向け貸出金利 interest rates charged biggest and most creditworthy borrowers

saisan 採算 cost and profit analysis; cost accounting; commercial profit; margin; profit margin ¶ severe *cost-accounting* of exports
　独立採算 self-support; self-sustenance
　輸入採算 import cost
　輸出採算 export cost

saisanakka 採算悪化 deterioration of profit

saisangai 採算買い buying on a yield basis; sound speculation; investment buying

saisangatorenai 採算がとれない to leave no margin of profit; not to be on a paying basis; not to be paying; unremunerative

saisangatoreru 採算がとれる to be paying; be profitable; to break even ¶ At least 1,000 contracts a day are needed to *break even.*

saisankabu 採算株 income stock

saisansuijun 採算水準 break-even level ¶ to raise volume to the *break even level* of nearly 7,000 contracts a day

saisanten 採算点 break-even point ¶ It has pared costs (notably staff) to lower the *break-even point.*

saisantokka 最算特化 optimum specialization

saisanware 採算割れ below cost; not on a paying basis ¶ to accept orders at *below-cost* price // acceptance of *below-cost* selling prices

saisei 再生 reclamation; reproduction; rejuvenation ¶ to *reclaim* desertified land by reforestation // *rejuvenated,* or *reclaimed,* rubber.

saiseienerugī 再生エネルギー renewable energy ¶ production of *renewable energy,* including biomas, hydroelectric, solar and wind energy

saiseikanō 再生可能 renewable ¶ liquid or gaseous fuels and other *renewable* energy devices // non-conventional and *renewable* sources of energy

saiseisan 再生産 reproduction
　拡大再生産 expanded reproduction; reproduction on an expanded (=a progressive) scale
　縮小再生産 reduced reproduction; reproduction on a diminishing (=regressive) scale
　単純再生産 simple reproduction
　迂回(的)再生産 roundabout reproduction

saiseisanhiyō 再生産費用 reproduction cost

saiseisanhyōshiki 再生産表式 reproduction scheme

saiseisanritsu 再生産率 reproduction rate

saisekigyō 採石業 quarrying industry

saisekijō 採石場 quarry

saisentangijutsu 最先端技術 ultra-advanced technology; ultra-modern technology

sashihiki 差引き balance; remainder; margin; deduction; subtraction

saishiyōfunōginkōken 再使用不能銀行券 non-reusable note

saishiyōkanōginkōken 再使用可能銀行券 re-usable note; fit note

saishōgendonokokuminseikatsusuijun 最小限度の国民生活水準 national minimum

saishōjijōhō 最小二乗法 least squares method; method of least squares

saishōkōritsukibo 最小効率規模 minimum efficient scale

saishokurin 再植林 reforestation

saishūjuekisha 最終受益者 final beneficiary

saishūjuyō 最終需要 final demand; ultimate demand ¶ The *final demand* for goods and services, taken in the aggregate, was well maintained. // *Final demand* (as measured by the aggregate of consumer buying, business investment in plant and equipment, expenditure for housing, net exports, and government purchases) increased all through the year. // The rise in output is adjusted to that in *ultimate demand.*

saishūjuyōsha 最終需要者 final consumer; end user

saishūkariiresha 最終借入者 ultimate borrower; end borrower ¶ the net amount of credit transmitted to *ultimate borrowers*

saishūkōbai 最終購買 final purchase ¶ The upturn in consumer expenditures led the recovery in real *final purchases.* // Total *final purchases,* in constant dollars, turned up and continued to expand.

saishūkyōkyū 最終供給 final supply

saishūrimawari 最終利回り final yield; yield to maturity

saishūseisanbutsu 最終生産物 final product; end product

saishūshōhi 最終消費 end use; final use; final consumption

saishūshōhisha 最終消費者 final consumer; consumer; end user

saishutokukakaku 再取得価格 replacement cost

saishutsu 歳出 annual expenditure; (government annual) expenditure (= oultay); budget expenditure ¶ Total government *annual expenditure* is set at Pts 68.4 billion. // further economies in *government expenditure* // an increase in rearmament *expenditures* // Federal *outlays* on goods and services drifted downward.

saishutsunōtōzenzō 歳出の当然増 increase in appropriation on committed basis

saishutsuyosan 歳出予算 budgeted expenditure ¶ This will bring total *budgeted expenditure* in 1980 to Sw.fr. 16.5 billion.

saishutsuyosan'an 歳出予算案 appropriation bill

saishūyōto 最終用途 end use; final use

saitei 最低　lowest; minimum; bottom; floor ¶ Production hit *bottom*.

saitei 裁定　arbitrage; arbitration; award; decision; ruling; adjudication
地域裁定　space arbitrage
仲裁裁定　decision by arbitration
時間裁定　time arbitrage
金利裁定　interest arbitrage

saiteiatamakinritsu 最低頭金(率)　minimum downpayment

saiteichingin 最低賃金　minimum wage ¶ to allow to pay *wages* lower than the legislated *minimum*

saiteichinginsei 最低賃金制　minimum wage system

saiteihatchūryō 最低発注量　minimum order quantity

saiteiheika 裁定平価　arbitrated par of exchange

saiteihiyō 裁定費用　arbitration expense

saiteijōkō 裁定条項　arbitration clause

saiteikakaku 最低価格　floor (price); minimum price; lower limit (price) ¶ The franc fell through the *floor* to 55. 65 marks to 100 francs. // The *floor level* of the franc is 56. 68 marks. // the administrative guidepost setting forth exportt *floor prices* for some items

saiteikashidashibuai 最低貸出歩合 [英] minimum lending rate

saiteikawase 裁定為替　arbitrated exchange

saiteikawasesōba 裁定為替相場　arbitrated rate of exchange

saiteikazeigendo 最低課税限度　lowest taxable income

saiteikijun 最低基準　minimum standard; minimum requirement

saiteikinri 裁定金利　arbitrated interest rate

saiteikyōbaikakaku 最低競売価格　reserve price

saiteimenzeishotoku 最低免税所得　minimum exempt income

saiteinedan 最低値段　lowest price; minimum price; rock-bottom price; floor price

saiteinogisei 最低の犠牲　minimum sacrifice

saiteirishibuai 最低利子歩合　lowest interest rate

saiteiryōkin 最低料金　minimum charge

saiteiseikatsuchingin 最低生活賃金　subsistence wages

saiteiseikatsuhi 最低生活費　minimum cost of living

saiteiseikatsusuijun 最低生活水準　bare subsistence level of living

saiteiseikatsusuijunshotoku 最低生活水準所得　subsistence income

saiteishōkokinritsu 最低証拠金率　minimum margin requirement

saiteisōsa 裁定操作　arbitrage operation

saiteitorihiki 裁定取引　[外] arbitrage transaction; arbitrage
重複裁定　compound arbitrage
直接裁定　direct arbitrage
単一裁定　single arbitrage

saiteki 最適　optimum; optimal ¶ *optimum* rates of interest // the *optimum* money supply // the *optimum* control of the money supply // *optimal*-sized plants // the *optimum* utilization of capital or *optimum* levels of capital utilization achieved

saitekihaibun 最適配分　optimum allocation; optimum distribution

saitekihensei 最適編成　optimum organization ¶ *optimum organization* of the economic system

saitekijōken 最適条件 optimal condition ¶ *optimal condition* of exchange // *optimal condition* of factor substitution

saitekika 最適化 optimization

saitekikakakuseisaku 最適価格政策 optimal price policy

saitekikakōdō 最適化行動 optimizing behavior

saitekikibo 最適規模 optimum size

saitekimankikōsei 最適満期構成 (国債の) optimal maturity structure (of government debts)

saitekirishiritsu 最適利子率 optimum rate of interest

saitekisei 最適性 optimality パレート最適(性) Pareto optimality

saitekiseichōritsu 最適成長率 optimum rate of growth

saitekiseigyo 最適制御 optimal control

saitekisentakunogenri 最適選択の原理 principle of best alternative

saitekiten 最適点 optimum point ¶ *optimum point* of production

saitenkan 再転換 reconversion ¶ *reconversion* of productive facilities 産業再転換 industrial reconversion

saitori 才取り ［市］ jobber; specialist

saitōshi 再投資 reinvestment

saitōshijunkan 再投資循環 reinvestment cycle

saitōshikatei 再投資過程 plow(ing)-back process

saiwaribiki 再割引 rediscount; rediscounting ¶ bills eligible for *rediscountig* at the central bank window // *rediscount* of bills with the central bank

saiwaribikibuai 再割引歩合 rediscount rate

saiwaribikiritsu 再割引率 rediscount rate ¶ The Central Bank of Ireland *rediscount rate* has been fixed at 5 percent per annum. // The official bank *rediscount rate* was raised in three steps from 3 to 6 percent.

saiwaribikitegata 再割引手形 rediscount bill; bill rediscounted

saiwaribikitekikakushōgyōtegata 再割引適格商業手形 commercial bill eligible for rediscounting (with the Bank of Japan)

saiyō 採用 employment; recruiting

saiyōsen 再用船 sub-charter

saiyōtorikeshi 採用取消し hiring cancellation

saiyūhō 最尤法 maximum likelihood method

saiyunyū 再輸入 re-importation; re-import

saiyunyūmenjō 再輸入免状 re-import permit

saiyunyūshinkokusho 再輸入申告書 re-import entry

saiyushutsu 再輸出 re-exportation; re-export

saiyushutsuwarimodoshi 再輸出割戻し drawback for re-export

saizō 再増 further increase; renewed growth; resurgence ¶ Prices showed a *further increase.* // recent *renewed growth* in bank credit // The renewed *growth* in loan value occurred among banks of all sizes.

sakibosori 先細り tapering-off; trailing-off tailing-off; petering-off ¶ a marked tailing-off of public sector activity // Activity *trailed* off in the afternoon session. // The ex-port boost to GNP is already standing to *trail off.* // The present spurt in sales could *peter out* towards the autumn. // The recession *tailed off* in mid-year and the business climate improved.

sakibosoriyosō 先細り予想 anticipation of decrease; anticipation of tapering off; expectation of petering off

sakidakamikoshi 先高見越し anticipation of a rise (=advance) ¶ to buy in *anticipation of* a (future) *rise* // to buy *anticipating* a further *advance*

sakidori 先取り pre-emption; antedating ¶ to *pre-empt* price increases, or to *antedate* price rises // Institutional funds were cut off from the stock market, because they had been *pre-empted* for investment in property.

sakidorihanbaitesūryō 先取り販売手数料 [市] front-end sales load (= charge)

sakigaiken 先買権 preemption right

sakigiri 先限 [市] future delivery; forward delivery; futures

sakihizukekogitte 先日付小切手 post-dated check

sakiiresakidashihō 先入れ先出し法 [会] first-in first-out method; Fifo

sakimono 先物 futures; forward
物価指数先物 stock index futures
外国通貨先物 foreign currencies futures
金利先物 interest rate futures
金融先物 financial futures

sakimonobaibai 先物売買 forward bargain; arrival sales

sakimonodeisukaunto 先物ディスカウント [外] forward discount

sakimonokaitsukekeiyaku 先物買付契約 purchase contract

sakimonokawase 先物為替 for-

ward exchange; futures ¶ On the London international financial *futures* exchange (LIFFE), gilts *futures* gained 1/16. // Sterling *forward* rates were little changed. // The mark was quoted three months *forward* at the equivalent of 0.3562 dollars.

sakimonokawasesōba 先物為替相場 forward exchange rate; forward quotation

sakimonokawasetorihiki 先物為替取引 forward exchange transaction

sakimonokeiyaku 先物契約 arrival contract; futures contract

sakimonokomittomento 先物コミットメント [市] forward commitment

sakimonomochidaka 先物持高 forward position; contract position

sakimonedan 先物値段 forward price

sakimonopuremiamu 先物プレミアム forward premium

sakimonoshijō 先物市場 futures market

sakimonosōba 先物相場 futures quotation

sakimonotorihiki 先物取引 forward operation; dealing in futures; futures transaction (=trading) ¶ *Futures trading* in gold increased dramatically to dwarf spot trading

sakimonouriwatashikeiyaku 先物売渡契約 sale contract

sakimonoyoyaku 先物予約 forward (exchange) contract

sakin 差金 difference; margin; balance

sakintorihiki 差金取引 [市] speculating for difference; speculation for margin

sakiwatashi 先渡し forward delivery; future delivery

sakiwatashitorihiki 先渡取引 forward trading (＝transaction)

sakiyasukan 先安感 anticipation of low prices

sakiyuki 先行き emerging trend; future course; development; direction; outlook ¶ Much will depend on *emerging trends* in the U.S. payments balance. // The *direction* of U.S. interest rates remains uncertain. // Strikes overshadow the generally positive *outlook* for U.S. industry. // Business executives are less confident about the *future course* of the economy and the prospects for their own industries. // [参考] an ominous shadow hanging over the future

sakiyukifuankan 先行き不安感 uneasiness in the outlook; uncertainty about the outlook ¶ The economy's near-term course is surrounded by a margin of *uncertainty*.

sakiyukikeikaikan 先行き警戒観 cautious outlook

sakiyukimitōshinan 先行き見通し難 uncertain outlook

sakugara 作柄 crop condition; harvest

sakugen 削減 cut(back); cut-off; curtail(ment); reduction; slash; axing; shedding; whittling down; trimming; skim; paring ¶ a plan to help *cut* the country's trade surplus // Still heavier *cuts* in employment are planned. // around 12,500 jobs are being *cut* from the 47,000 workforce. // to achieve the necessary spending *cuts* // to plan a 10 percent *cut* in employment // to *cut* public expenditure by $15 billion // to *cut back* on investment // *cut-offs*

of trade credit to developing countries // to *curtail* production // to *cut back* investment plans // to *reduce* expenditures // to *whittle down* Japan's trade surplus // to *trim* off fiscal expenditures // to *pare* down budgetary expenditures // to achieve a year-by-year net *reduction* in external debt // Its workforce was *slashed* by some 5,000 or 6,000 to leave 2,700 men finishing steel products. // The steel plant is *axing* 8,500 of its 35,800 jobs. // The industry was *shedding* some 1,000 workers a month.

sakuinjunjihenseifairu 索引順次編成ファイル [コン] indexed sequential file

sakushuteki 搾取的 sweatshop ¶ *sweatshop* wages

sakutsuke 作付 planting 米の作付反別 rice acreage

sakutsukemenseki 作付面積 (crop-)planted area; acreage

sakutsuketanbetsu 作付反別 area under cultivation

samagawari 様変り turn-around; making a (sharp) contrast; drartic change ¶ →転換

samuraibondo サムライボンド samurai bond; foreigners' yen borrowing in Japan

sanbantenjō 三番天井 [市] triple top

sanbuhanrikōsai 三分半利公債 3½ % Government Bond

sanbutsu 産物 produce; product ¶ the market for British *produce* // mineral *produce* // agricultural *products* // a native *product* // gross national *product*

sanchakubarai 参着払い payable on demand; payable at sight

銀行参着払い　bank demand try.

sanchakukawase 参着為替 sight
bill; sight draft; demand bill; demand draft

sanchakutegata 参着手形 sight
bill; demand draft; D.D.

sanchō 散超 excess disbursement
(of government funds)

sangaku 産額 production (in money terms); output; yield

sangakukyōdō 産学協同 univer-
sity-business alliance ¶ [参考] Universities should get closer to business and vice versa.

sangokukanbōeki 三国間貿易 triangular trade

sangokukansaitei 三国間裁定 triangular arbitrage; three point arbitrage

sangunfukugōtai 産軍複合体 mil-
itary-industrial complex

sangyō 産業 industry ¶ to establish locally based *industries* geared
to the export market // the establishment of new export-oriented *industries*

防衛産業　defense industry
知識産業　knowledge industry
抽出産業　extractive industry
第一次産業　primary industry
第二次産業　secondary industry
第三次産業　tertiary industry
複合的産業　compound industry
不況産業　depressed industry
原始産業　primitive industry
娯楽産業　amusement industry
兵器産業　weapon industry; am-
munition industry
補助産業　subsidiary industry
庇護産業　sheltered industry
保護産業　protected industry
自動車産業　automobile industry;
automotive industry; auto indus-

情報産業　information industry
助成産業　subsidized industry
住宅産業　housing industry
重要産業　key industry; major industry
過保護産業　over-protected industry
加工産業　processing industry
関連産業　related industry
活況産業　expanding industry
寄生産業　parasitic industry
基礎産業　basic industry
高度技術産業　high technology industry
国営産業　state-run industry
国有化産業　nationalized industry
固有産業　state(-owned) industry
好況産業　thriving industry
構造不況産業　structurally depressed industry
労働集約(的)産業　labor-intensive
industry
流通産業　distribution industry
サービス産業　service industry
再生産業　reproductive industry
成長産業　growth industry
生産財産業　producer goods industry
石油関連産業　petrochemical industry; oil-related industry
斜陽産業　declining industry; dying
industry; 'sunset' industry; depressed industry
資本財産業　capital goods industry
消費財産業　consumer goods industry
省力産業　labor-saving industry
装置産業　process industry
ソフトウエア産業　software indus-
try
素材産業　intermediate products industry
衰退産業　dying industry

宇宙開発産業　space industry
幼稚産業　infant industry
輸出産業　export(ing) industry
輸出集約(的)産業　export-intensive industry

sangyōbetsubunrui 産業別分類 grouping by industry; classification by industry (group)

sangyōbetsurōdōkumiai 産業別労働組合　industrial union

sangyōbetsushūgyōshakōseihi 産業別就業者構成比　composition ratio of employees by industry

sangyōchōsei 産業調整 industrial adjustment ¶ *industrial adjustment* assistance under the Trade Expansion Act of 1962 in the U.S.

sangyōchōseiseisaku 産業調整政策 policy of regulating the industrial structure

sangyōdōin 産業動員 industrial mobilization

sangyōfukkō 産業復興 industial rehabilitation

sangyōgōrika 産業合理化 industrial rationalization

sangyōhaichi 産業配置 industrial location; location of industry

sangyōhaisui 産業排水 industrial waste water

sangyōidō 産業移動 industrial migration

sangyōjunkan 産業循環 industrial cycle

sangyōkabu 産業株 industrial stocks; industrials

sangyōkai 産業界 industrial circles; industrial world ¶ ［参考］ Industrialists are pessimistic about the development of the French economy.

sangyōkakumei 産業革命 industrial revolution

sangyōkankōzō 産業間構造 inter-industry structure

sangyōkatsudō 産業活動 industrial activity ¶ Growth is developing over a broad range of *industrial activity*.

sangyōkeizai 産業経済 industrial economy

sangyōkiban 産業基盤 industrial foundation; industrial base ¶ to build up an *industrial base* of the country

sangyōkikō 産業機構 industrial system

sangyōkin'yū 産業金融 industrial finance

sangyōkōgai 産業公害 industrial pollution; industrial public nuisance

sangyōkōgaku 産業工学 industrial engineering

sangyōkōzō 産業構造 industrial structure; industrial composition ¶ the perpetuation of the least competitive, least needed, parts of Britain's antique *industrial structure* // to look at the totality of *industrial structure* and develop a comprehensive strategy // the export-oriented *industrial structure* of Germany or export-oriented *structure* of German *industry* // a heavily protected *industrial structure*

sangyōkumiai 産業組合 cooperative society

sangyōkyōkō 産業恐慌 industrial crisis

sangyōnaitokka 産業内特化 intra-industry specialization

sangyōnetsu 産業熱 industrialism

sangyōrenkanbunseki 産業連関分析 inter-industry analysis

sangyōrenkanhyō 産業連関表

inter-industry relations table

sangyōrikkoku 産業立国 industrialization of a country

sangyōritchi 産業立地 industrial orientation; location of industry

sangyōrōdōsha 産業労働者 industrial worker

sangyōrōdōshajūtakukashitsuke 産業労働者住宅貸付 loan for industrial worker's housing construction

sangyōsaihensei 産業再編成 reorganization of industry; industrial reorganization; industrial reconstruction; industrial reform(ation) ¶ *Industrial reconstruction*, out of yesterday's growth industries into high knowledge-incentive industries, is coming about.

sangyōsaihenseikōsha 産業再編成公社 ［英］Industrial Reorganisation Corporation

sangyōsaitenkan 産業再転換 industrial reconversion; industrial demobilization

sangyōseisaku 産業政策 industrial policy

sangyōsetsubi 産業設備 industrial facilities; industrial plants and equipment

sangyōshakai 産業社会 industrial society ¶ a diverse and well-organized *industrial society* as in the United States

sangyōshihon 産業資本 industrial capital

sangyōshikin 産業資金 industrial funds

sangyōshūchū 産業集中 industry concentration

sangyōtayōkakeikaku 産業多様化計画 industrial diversification program

sangyōtekiryūtsū 産業的流通 industrial circulation

sangyōtenkan 産業転換 industrial conversion

sangyōtoshi 産業都市 industrial town

sangyōtōshi 産業投資 industrial investment

sangyōyobigun 産業予備軍 industrial reserve laborers; reserve army of industry

sangyōyōkin 産業用金 gold for industrial purposes (＝uses); industrial gold

sanjiseihin 三次製品 tertiary products; highly processed goods

sanjūku 三重苦 triple woes; trilemma

経済運営の三重苦 triple economic woes (of inflation, business recession and aggravation of the international balance of payments situation); trilemma (of economic management)

sanjūnendaifukyō 30年代不況 the Great Depression (of the '30s)

sanjutsuheikin 算術平均 arithmetic average; arithmetic mean

sanka 参加 participation ¶ female labor-force *participation* // to assent in financial *participation* in an international venture // management *participation*, or *participation* in management // Government involvement in a system competitive with private-sector alternatives should be kept to a minimum. // substantial state *participation* in the main steel-producing concerns // to extend worker *participation* in the control of the companies they work for

sankagetsuidōheikin 3カ月移動平均 three-month moving average

sankakigyō 傘下企業 affiliated

business; subordinate companies

sankaritsu 参加率 participation rate ¶ aggregate and female labor force *participation rates*

sankatesūryō 参加手数料 participation fee

sankayūshi 参加融資 participation loan

sankōshagogengyō 三公社五現業 [日] (former) three public corporations and five government enterprises; Japanese National Railways, Nippon Telegraph and Telephone Public Corporation, and Japan Tobacco & Salt Public Corporation; and postal services, printing, minting, and alcohol monopoly enterprises of the government

sannyū 参入 entry ¶ new (=de nove) *entry* into the market ¶ *entry* into each country in the banking area // to obtain *entry* into other markets with reciprocity // [参考] to seek access to foreign markets

sannyūshōheki 参入障壁 barriers to entry; entry barriers

sannyūsoshikakaku 参入阻止価格 entry-preventing price

sanpintorihikisho 三品取引所 [日] Three Staples Exchange

sanpudo 散布度 measure of dispersion

sanpuruchōsa サンプル調査 sample survey

sanraku 惨落 [市] heavy decline; violent fall; drastic slump; drastic loss; drastic setback

sanseihaisui 酸性廃水 acid waste water

sanseihiritsu 酸性比率 acid (test) ratio

sanshutsuryō 産出量 output ¶ labor *output* // industrial *output* // annual *output* of manufacturing industries

完全能力産出量 full capacity output

能力産出量 capacity output

理想産出量 ideal output

sanshutsuryōdanryokusei 産出量弾力性 elasticity of output

sanshutsuryōnokyokudaika 産出量の極大化 output maximization

sanshutsuryōnoragu 産出量のラグ output lag

sanshutsutōnyūhiritsu 産出・投入比率 output-input ratio

santei 算定 computation; calculation; estimate; appraisal

santeikakaku 算定価格 estimated value; appraised price

sanyukoku 産油国 oil producing country (=nation)

sarachi さら地 vacant lot

sararīmannōka サラリーマン農家 salaried farmer

sashidashinin 差出人 sender; addresser; remitter; drawer; fowarder; consignor

sashihikizandaka 差引残高 balance

sashine 指値 [市] limit; limit price; tender; bid price ¶ to increase or raise the limit

売却指値 selling limit

買付指値 buying limit

sashinechūmon 指値注文 [市] limit order; straddle

sashinegai 指値買い [市] limit order; straddle

sashinesanteihō 指値算定法 [市] limit calculation

sashiosae 差押え attachment; attachment of property; taking property into custody

sashizukinshitegata 指図禁止手形

non-order bill

sashizushikikogitte 指図式小切手 check to order ¶ to draw a *check to order* of Mr. John Doe, or a *check to* Mr. John Doe's *order*

sashizushikiuragaki 指図式裏書 endorsement to order

sashō 査証 visa ¶ A *visa* was granted for passage between... // to have the passport *visaed*

sasoimizukōka 誘い水効果 pump-priming effect

sasoimizuseisaku 誘い水政策 pump-priming measure

sasonkin 差損金 loss from difference of price

saya 鞘 spread; margin; difference; brokerage

逆鞘 back spread, backwardation

順鞘 regular spread; contango

本鞘 regular spread; spread

小鞘 narrow spread; narrow margin

大鞘 wide spread; wide margin

sayatori 鞘取り ［市］ arbitration in stock and shares; profit-taking

sayatoribaibai 鞘取り売買 arbitrage operation

sayatorishōnin 鞘取商人 arbitrager; arbitragist

sayatorisuji 鞘取筋 ［市］ arbitragers; arbitragists

sayatoritorihiki 鞘取取引 arbitrage dealing; arbitrage business

sayatoriya 鞘取屋 arbitrage house

sayayose 鞘寄せ narrowing of spread

seginshusshien 世銀出資円 subscribed yen for the IBRD

seibutsukōgaku 生物工学 biotechnology

seibutsushigen 生物資源 living resources

seichō 成長 growth ¶ *Growth* in productivity and real economic *growth* will more or less balance out. // The *growth* of our productivity has been more than 3% annually. // to enhance world economic *growth* // The economy is to continue its lackluster *growth* performance. // The nation's real economic *growth* dipped slightly. // The economy is in moderate or decelerating *growth*, emerging out of high *growth*. // The negative *growth* was followed by a slight positive *growth* in the previous quarter. // to sustain reasonable *growth* in economic activity // to place the economy back on a *growth* path // The *growth* will be seriously disturbed before long. // to *grow* at an unsustainable boom rate // Private consumption provided a notable fillip to economic *growth*. // Real *growth* in the industrial countries is back to something like 3 to 4% a year.

安定成長 stable growth; sustainadle growth

長期の成長 secular growth

不均衡成長 unbalanced growth

逆貿易偏向的の成長 anti-trade-biased growth

実質成長 real growth

持続の成長 sustainable growth; sustained growth

順貿易偏向的の成長 pro-trade-biased growth

循環的成長 cyclical growth

完全成長 full growth

経済成長 economic growth

均衡成長 balanced growth

高(度)成長 high growth; rapid growth

名目成長 nominal growth

趨勢的成長　secular growth
低成長　low growth; slow growth
輸出先行成長　export-led growth

seichōdankaisetsu 成長段階説
stage-of-growth theory

seichōdonka 成長鈍化　slowdown
in economic growth; deceleration of
growth

seichōgensoku 成長減速　slowdown in economic growth; decelerating economic growth; abatement
of economic growth

seichōkabu 成長株　growth stock

seichōritsu 成長率　rate of growth;
growth rate ¶ Greece has achieved
very high *rates* of economic *growth*
現実成長率　actual rate of growth
実質成長率　real rate of growth
名目成長率　nominal rate of growth
最適成長率　optimum rate of
　growth
自然成長率　natural rate of growth
適正成長率　normal growth rate;
　warranted rate of growth

seichōritsujunkan 成長率循環
swing of growth rate

seichōritsuriron 成長率理論　theory of rate of growth; growth-rate
theory

seichōrosen 成長路線　growth
track; growth path ¶ The world
economy was apparently moving
onto a *growth track.* // to place the
economy back on a *growth path* // to
shorten the *path* back to sustainable
growth // the possibility of the world
economy moving along a less than
full capacity *growth path* for a prolonged period of time // The Italian
economy is embarking on a moderate *growth path.* // ［参考］to identify
turning points in growth momentum

seichōsangyō 成長産業　growth industry

seichōtsūka 成長通貨　growth
money; appropriate cash supply for
economic growth; money needed to
finance economic expansion; money
necessary for economic growth;
funds to sustain economic growth ¶
Growth money in an appropriate
amount should be supplied. // ［参考］
The objective was to provide
enough monetary expansion to
accommodate reasonable growth in
economic activity. // growth in the
M_2 money supply to accommodate
economic growth

seichōyokuseizai 成長抑制剤
growth retardant

seichōyosan 成長予算　growth
budget

seido 制度　system; facility ¶ the
well-organized financial *systems* of a
country // reform of the international currency *system* // reorganization and establishment of the banking *system* // to abolish and rein-
stitute the foreign exchange concentration *system* // the evolution of
the international monetary *system* //
the improvement of the world trading *system* // significance of the public borrowing requirement in the
present banking *system* // to improve
communication *facilities* // questions
concerning the adequacy of our
financial *facilities*

seidoka 制度化　institutionalization
¶ a highly *institutionalized* system
of export finance

seidokin'yū 制度金融　institutional
banking

seidoteki 制度的　institutional ¶ an
institutional reform of banking // an
institutional improvement in the

credit market // some *institutional* problems // The Japanese market is now *institutionally* as free as the U.S. or major European markets.

seidozukuri 制度づくり institution building

seifubumon 政府部門 government sector (of the economy)

seifuchōtatsu 政府調達 government procurement

seifuhojokin 政府補助金 government subsidy

seifuhoshōsai 政府保証債 government-guaranteed bond; [米] contingent debt

seifukaihatsuenjo 政府開発援助 official development assistance; ODA

seifukankeikigyō 政府関係企業 government-related enterprises

seifukankōshō 政府間交渉 government-level talks

seifukantorihikigenyu 政府間取引原油 government-to-government crude oil

seifukarakojin'enoiten 政府から個人への移転 current transfers from Government to persons

seifukashitsukekin 政府貸付金 loan to the government

seifukin'yūkikan 政府金融機関 government financial institution; government financial agency

seifukogitte 政府小切手 government check

seifumitōshi 政府見通し government outlook (=forecast) ¶ the *government* economic *outlook* for 1985 // the *government's forecast* for the 1985 economy

seifunoginkō 政府の銀行 bank of the government; bank for the government; banker to the government

seifunojigyōshotoku 政府の事業所得 government income from property and entrepreneurship

seifunozaikasābisukeijōkōnyū 政府の財貨サービス経常購入 Government current expenditure on goods and services

seifusai 政府債 government bond; government note

seifushihei 政府紙幣 government note

seifushishutsu 政府支出 government expenditure (=spending) ¶ *government* current *expenditures* on goods and services

seifushōken 政府証券 government securities

seifusōsashiryō 政府操作飼料 feed handled by the government

seifutankishōken 政府短期証券 government bill; short-term government securities

seifutorihiki 政府取引 government transaction

seifuyokin 政府預金 government deposit

seifuyosan 政府予算 government budget; fiscal budget ¶ [参考] The total accumulated Federal deficit is budgeted to reach Sw.fr. 10.7 billion.

seifuyūkashōken 政府有価証券 government securities ¶ British *Government securities* were mixed with short dates adding about 5 pence, mediums 12 but longs lost about 12.

seigaku 静学 statics

seigen 制限 limit; clamp-down; restraint; restriction; control; curb; check ¶ territorial *limitations* in the performance of the service permitted // A franchise may *limit* a utility company to a single service, such as

operating a telephone system. // a
drastic *limitation* on the total stock
of the country's debt // The country
inclined to *clamp down* on imports
from Japan. // to impose mandatory
restraints // He firmly ruled out any
attemps to slap blanket *control* on
imports but did not rule out *curbs*
on the import of selected goods. //
Japan is discriminated against in the
country-by-country import *restriction* imposed by the U.S. // The
country inclined to *clamp down* on
imports from Japan. // to impose
mandatory *restraints* // He firmly
ruled out any attempt to slap blanket *control* on imports but did not
rule out *curbs* on the import of
selected goods. // Japan was discriminated against in the country-
by-country import *restriction* imposed by the U.S. // the introduction,
substantial intensification, or prolonged maintenance, for balance of
payments purposes, of *restrictions*
on, or incentives for, current transactions or payments // the reduction
or elimination of nontariff *restrictions* (in particular quantitative *restrictions*) to international trade //
the *restrictions* placed on the growth
lending in lire // reliance upon
restrictions on trade and payments
and the discriminatory application
of any existing *restrictions* // statutory Japanese export *curbs* as a
measure of last resort // gradual
elimination of *restrictive* exchange
practices // the *clampdown* on foreign exchange // to exercise tigher
controls on foreign borrowing
譲渡制限 restriction of transfer
持株制限 restriction on stockhold-

ings
利息制限 interest restriction
量的制限 quantitative regulation
質的制限 qualitative regulation
取引制限 trade restriction; restraint of trade
輸入制限 import restriction; import
regulation
輸出制限 export restriction; export
regulation
残存制限 residual restrictions
残存輸入制限 existing quantitative
import restrictions; residual import controls
seigengaihakkō 制限外発行 over-
issue; excess issue; fiduciary issue
seigengyōshu 制限業種 restricted
industry
seigenhikiuke 制限引受け qualified acceptance
seigenhinmoku 制限品目 restricted item ¶ The number of *restricted
items* — *items* whose import remains
on the negative list — has been
reduced to 212.
seigenjōkō 制限条項 reserve
clause
seigenkaijo 制限解除 dismantling
of control ¶ Japan finally got
around to *dismantling* the last con-
trols on capital inflows.
seigenkisoku 制限規則 control regulation ¶ the imposition on more
stringent *control regulations* of capital transactions
seigenmenjo 制限免除 exemption
from restriction
seigentekiseisanyōso 制限的生産要
素 limitational factor
seigentsukikanwa 制限付き緩和
qualified relaxation
seigentsukikōkansei 制限付き交換
性 limited convertibility

seigyo 制御 control; goverance ¶ to place inflation under *control* // inflation running out of *control* // This inflation has been *controllable* in both its severity and duration.

seigyō 生業 occupation

seigyōshikin 生業資金 rehabilitation funds; business funds

seigyotaku 制御卓 ［コン］ console; control desk

seihin 製品 manufactured goods; manufactured products; product; finished goods and merchandise

外注製品 outside product

外国製品 foreign manufactures; foreign products; products of foreign make

自製品 own product

内地製品 home manufactures; domestic products

seihingenzairyō 製品原材料 semi-finished goods

seihinjukyū 製品需給 supply and demand situation of finished goods ¶ The *supply-demand picture* for newsprint depicts a development. // The *demand situation* of durable goods softened. // ［参考］ Markets for copper, rubber and hides strengthened.

seihinjumyō 製品寿命 product life cycle

seihinkakaku 製品価格 quotation for finished goods

seihinkakakuhikiage 製品価格引上げ higher quotation for finished goods (by manufacturers)

seihinkakakuhyōjunka 製品価格標準化 standardization of manufactures

seihinkanjō 製品勘定 finished goods account

seihinnokōkyūka 製品の高級化 im-provement in level of products; level improvement of products

seihinzaikoritsu 製品在庫率 inventory ratio of finished goods to sales; inventory-sales ratio of finished goods; inventory-sales ratio; stock-sales index ¶ The *ratio of stocks to sales* moved from 1.5 months of sales in January to 1.6 months at the year-end. // The *stock-sales* position has remained virtually unchanged holding closely at about 1.3 months of sales.

seihodan 生保団 group of life insurance companies; life insurance syndicate

seiinbunseki 成因分析 component analysis

seijikakaku 政治価格 political price

seijōgaikajunbidaka 正常外貨準備高 normal reserve line

seijukukabu 成熟株 seasoned stock

seijukuki 成熟期 mature phase

seika 正貨 specie

在外正貨 specie holdings abroad; specie holdings overseas

seika 成果 achievement; result; performance ¶ The year was one of extraordinary *achievements* for the F.R. of Germany. // satisfactory *results* of monetary restraints // favorable business *performance* // the satisfactory *performance* of the Belgian economy // The overall *performance* of the economy lacked luster. // The actual *performance* of official development assistance (ODA) has been most disappointing.

seikagagu 生化学 biochemistry

seikagensōten 正貨現送点 specie point; gold point

seikahaibunhōshiki 成果配分方式 payment-by-the-results system

seikahoyūdaka 正貨保有高 gold holdings; specie holdings

seikajunbi 正貨準備 gold reserve; specie reserve

seikaketsubō 正貨欠乏 shortage of specie

seikaryūnyū 正貨流入 inflow of specie; influx of specie

seikaryūshutsu 正貨流出 outflow of specie; efflux of specie

seikashiharai 正貨支払い specie payment

seikatsu 生活 life; existence; livelihood; living; subsistence ¶ to live and have some sort of a decent *life* // the population to be found scratching a bare *living* from the soil // the aspiration of the developing nations to improve the *lives* of their peoples

seikatsuhakusho 生活白書 ［日］ Livelihood White Paper

seikatsuhi 生活費 cost of living; living expenses; living costs

seikatsuhitsujuhin 生活必需品 necessities of life; requirements of life; daily necessaries

seikatsuhitsujukeisū 生活必需係数 coefficient of daily necessities

seikatsuhogo 生活保護 public assistance

seikatsuhogokijun 生活保護基準 standard of livelihood protection

seikatsuhojohi 生活補助費 sustenance money

seikatsujōtai 生活状態 living conditions ¶ the wretched *living conditions* of more than one third of the freeman race // a deterioration of the general *living conditions* of the majority of the rural population

seikatsukaizen 生活改善 improvement of living conditions; better living

seikatsukankyō 生活環境 living environment ¶ standards of *living environment*

seikatsukyū 生活給 minimum wage for living; cost-of-living wage; subsistence wage // the frequency of the *cost-of-living* wage increases

seikatsunan 生活難 hard living; living difficulties

seikatsunoshitsu 生活の質 quality of life ¶ the individual's *quality of life* in a community

seikatsusekkei 生活設計 life design; planning for better family and home living; design of living; life planning

seikatsushikin 生活資金 living funds

seikatsushudan 生活手段 (ways and) means of livelihood; means of living ¶ to flock into cities in search for *means of livelihood*

seikatsusuijun 生活水準 standard of living; living standard; living level ¶ Inflation is measurably reducing the *standard of living*. // improvement of *living standards* // to limit the growth of *living standards* // incomes required to maintain each of the three *living standards*, that is, a hypothetical moderate or "middle-level" *standard of living,* "higher-level" *standard of living,* and "lower-level" *standard of living* // to give small farmers a decent *standard of living* // *Living level* was brought downward among the masses because of the food crisis. // People demand a stop to the continued erosion of their *living standards.*

seikatsutaiyō 生活態様 → 生活様

式

seikatsuyōshiki 生活様式 life-style; way of life; style of life; mode of living ¶ People are accustomed to living a certain *life-style*. // Each country must shape its own *life style*. // profound changes in *life-styles* needed to put western economies back on the track of sustained economic growth // We have significantly improved our *life-style*. // The *way of life* — a moderate climate, plenty of outdoor activity, the residual Southern graces — is attractive. // We have to adapt our *style of life* to current circumstances. // changing *living mode* of Japanese households // westernization of the Japanse *mode of living*

seikei 生計 living; livelihood; sustenance

seikeibunri 政経分離 separation of political and economic affairs; separation of business and politic ¶ U.S. willingness to *separate business and politics* by removing barriers to commerce

seikeifukabunnogensoku 政経不可分の原則 principle of inseparability between political and economic affairs

seikeihi 生計費 cost of living; living cost

seikeihiesukarētājōkō 生計費エスカレーター条項 cost-of-living adjustment; COLA

seikeihishisū 生計費指数 index of living costs; cost of living index; index of living expenses ¶ The *cost-of-living index* (1969=100) rose by 0.9% between mid-January and mid-February to stand at 164.6.

seikeiijisuijun 生計維持水準 sub-sistence level

seikō 性向 propensity ¶ Uncertainties in the monetary field began to inhibit the investment *propensity* of trade and industry. // the marginal *propensity* to consume // the *propensity* to save // the implied *propensity* of governments to finance expenditures from borrowing instead of taxes // The U.S. economy's *propensity* for inflation is vividly demonstrated. // Weak countries have a higher *propensity* to import and a lower *propensity* to export. // Concern provoked by due oil crisis reduced the *propensity* to consume and invest. // The system reduces firms' *propensity* for new investment.

貯蓄性向 propensity to save
保蔵性向 propensity to hoard
控除性向 propensity to withdraw
消費性向 propensity to consume; spending habits
投資性向 propensity to invest
輸入性向 propensity to import
輸出性向 propensity to export

seikō 製鋼 steel making

seikōsho 製鋼所 steel mill; steelwork

seimeihoken 生命保険 life insurance

seimeihokengaisha 生命保険会社 life insurance company

seimeihokenkin 生命保険金 life insurance claim; life insurance money

seimeihokenryō 生命保険料 life insurance premium

seimeihokensaiken 生命保険債券 life insurance policy

seimeisenshōhisuijun 生命線消費水準 lifeline consumption level

seimitsukagakuseihin 精密化学製品 fine chemicals

seimitsukikai 精密機械 precision instrument

seirenkin 精錬金 refined gold

seiri 整理 arrangement; assortment; liquidation; wind(ing-)up ¶ *arrangement* by subjects // to re-*arrange* the grouping of commodity items // *assortment* of bank notes // a company going into *liquidation*

seiridankai 整理段階 [市] liquidating operations

seirikōsei 整理厚生 reorganization (of a company)

seirishōjō 整理商状 [市] liquidating market

seiritōgō 整理統合 reorganization and consolidation; realignment; reorganization and integration

seiryōinryōsui 清涼飲料水 refreshing beverages; nonalcoholic drinks

seisai 制裁 (punitive) sanction

seisaikitei 制裁規定 penal provision

seisaku 政策 policy; policy measure ¶ a stringent monetary *policy* // fiscal and monetary *policies* // to formulate, employ or adopt; carry out, pursue or follow; support or continue; modify; and suspend or discontinue *policy measures* to combat inflation // to dovetail *policies* to attract remittances from migrant workers with a comprehensive and coherent set of *policies* to ensure that these revenues make the optimal contribution

安定化政策 stabilization policy

貿易政策 trade policy

物価安定政策 price stabilization policy

物価政策 price policy

地域開発政策 regional development policy

賃金政策 wage policy; pay policy

超低金利政策 ultra-cheap money policy

中立型金融政策 neutral monetary policy

デフレ政策 deflationary policy

独占禁止政策 anti-monopoly policy; anti-trust policy

販売政策 marketing policy; sales policy

反独占政策 anti-monopoly policy; anti-trust policy

保護政策 protective policy; protectionist policy

保護貿易政策 protectionist policy

補正的支出政策 compensatory spending policy

補正的財政政策 compensatory fiscal policy

人口政策 population policy

自由放任政策 policy of laissez faire

住宅政策 housing policy

需要管理政策 demand management policy

価格支持政策 price-support policy; support price policy; price supporting policy

拡大政策 expansionary policy; expansionist policy; expansive policy

貸出抑制政策 restrictive lending policy

関税政策 tariff policy

景気政策 anti-cyclical policy; contracyclical policy; counter-cyclical policy

景気刺激政策 reflation(ary) policy

金不胎化政策 gold sterilization policy

金利政策 interest rate policy

緊縮政策 restraint policy; retrenchment policy

金融引締め政策　tight money policy; tight credit policy; policy of monetary tightening

金融緩和政策　easy money policy; easy credit policy; policy of monetary relaxation

金融政策　monetary policy; credit policy ¶ →p.268

公開市場政策　open market policy

高金利政策　dear money policy; high interest rate policy

国内政策　domestic policy

国債管理政策　debt management policy

公共政策　public policy

公定歩合政策　bank rate policy

構造政策　structural reform policy

農産物価格支持政策　agricultural price support policy

労働政策　labor policy

再割引政策　rediscount policy

産業立地政策　industrial location policy

積極財政政策　positive fiscal policy

社会政策　social policy

「新経済政策」　New Economic Policy

信用拡張政策　easy credit policy

支出転換政策　expenditure switching policy

支出抑制政策　expenditure damping policy

所得政策　incomes policy

総需要政策　demand management policy

ストップ・ゴー政策　stop and go (= stop-go) policy

対インフレーション政策　anti-inflation policy

低賃金政策　cheap labor policy

低金利政策　cheap money policy; easy money policy

通商政策　trade policy; commercial policy

割引歩合政策　discount rate policy

割引率政策　discount rate policy

割引政策　discount policy

呼び水(＝誘い水)政策　pump-priming policy

予算政策　budgetary policy; budget policy

輸出増強政策　push-exports policy

財政政策　fiscal policy ¶ → p.588

財政金融政策　financial policy; fiscal and monetary policies

善隣外交政策　good neighbor policy

seisakuhandanshiryō 政策判断資料 data to evaluate monetary policy

seisakukadai 政策課題 policy concern; policy task ¶ The foremost and most consistent German *policy concern* over this entire period has been with price stability. // the primary *policy task* for the coming year

seisakukettei 政策決定 policy decision; policy determination ¶ the basic economic *policy decision* facing the Administration // Their dicussions have the purpose of exchanging views rather than arriving at *policy decisions*. // The international ramifications of the present situation severely complicated the *policy determination* of the U.S.

seisakuketteikikan 政策決定機関 policy-making body ¶ The Federal Open Market Committee has been converted into a central *policy-making body* for the Federal Reserve System.

seisakukinyū 政策金融 guidance policy finance; system financing

seisakukyōtei 政策協定 agreement on policy; policy agreement; arrangement on policy

seisakunen 製作年 vintage

seisakunokanri 政策の管理 policy administration ¶ centralized supervision and *policy administration*

seisakunosuikō 政策の遂行 implementation; maneuver; conduct ¶ The Federal System is responsible for the formulation and *implementation* of U.S. monetary policy. // to *implement* national monetary policy // to play a key role in the *implementation* of the monetary policy of the Federal Reserve System // a major instrument for *implementing* monetary policy // The Federal Reserve should devote attention to the behavior of M1 in the *conduct* of monetary policy. // Floating rates give a country more room for maneuver, a greater measure of freedom in the *conduct of* its domestic *policy.*

seisakuragu 政策ラグ policy lag

seisakuritsuan 政策立案 formation of a policy; formulation of policy; shaping of a policy; policy planning; policy-making; policy-setting ¶ to frame, *formulate,* or shape a *policy* // As an operating unit of the U.S. central banking system, each of the two participants in the *formation of* national banking and monetary *policy.* // The central bank is primarily responsible for the *formulation of* U.S. monetary *policy.* // The headquarters of the Federal Reserve System is the seat of the governing and *policymaking* bodies. // They perform a contributory role in *shaping* national monetary *policy.* // The President is primarily responsible for *shaping* and implementing the Federal Government's financial *pol-*

icy. // The watchword of current fiscal and monetary *policy-making* is restraint *policy formulation.* // Both the Federal Reserve and the Congress are exercising restraint in *formulating* monetary and fiscal *policies.* // The Federal Open Market Committee is the Fed's *policy-setting* group. // to be traditionally geared its economic *policy-making* to GNP targets // [参考] a reorientation of the economic policies

seisakurosen 政策路線 policy path; policy course ¶ how best to stay on a sustainable *policy path* // to maintain a steady *course* in economic *policy*

seisakushisei 政策姿勢 policy stance; policy posture ¶ →姿勢

seisakushudan 政策手段 policy instrument (=device; tool; means; weapon) ¶ The various *instruments* of central bank *policy* are to be applied in a flexible, carefully coordinated manner. // a harmonious combination of the three orthodox *policy instruments* // development of the necessary instrumentarium, consisting of financial *instruments*, markets, and data // the value of using interest rates as a credit *policy weapon* to control household saving // The main *weapon* in the government's strategy was a curb on domestic demand, // the 'pieces de resistance' in the Bank's arsenal of *weapons* to counter // Interest rates are not an acceptable permanent *tool* of recourse allocation.

seisakusochi 政策措置 policy measure; policy action; policy move ¶ It could not be seen as a domestic credit *policy move.*

seisakutaido 政策態度 policy stance; policy posture ¶ to ease the restrictive *policy stance* // employment of the more restrictive *posture* of fiscal *policy*

seisakuun'ei 政策運営 policy operation; policy administration; policy maneuver ¶ the continuous *operation* of highly selective *policies* // the extent of Germany's room for *maneuver* on the growth question // Higher prices have reduced the room for *maneuver* in economic *policy* in most countries. // The international slump has severely restricted the room for economic *policy maneuver* in Denmark. // There will be little room for *maneuver* in 1966 as regards of short-term measures.

seisakuun'eimokuhyō 政策運営目標 aim; goal; target; focus; objective; purpose ¶ Market operations would be consistent with overall policy *aims*. // theories on how monetary policy could best meet stabilization *goals* // to emphasize the performance of the monetary aggregates as tactical *targets* for a longer period // to keep immediate money market conditions reasonably aligned with the *targeted* magnitude of the guidance variables back on *target* // the de facto operational *focus* of monetary policy // a short-term horizon with its *focus* on the money market // The Federal Reserve authorities had *focused* on the maintenance of orderly money market conditions as the proximate *objective* of their market operations. // There longer-run effects seem to be a fundamental *focus* for a central bank. // The Federal Open Market Committee determines the broad *objectives* of monetary policy. // to coordinate the Federal Reserve System's monetary *objective* with the broader economic *objectives* of national policy // The *purpose* of its operations is to bring about an expansion in monetary aggregates. // to administer an open market operation for policy *purposes*

seisan 生産 production; manufacture; output

[上昇] ¶ *Production* rose more than proportionately to the rise in shipments. // Industrial *production* is advancing again, slowly but on a broad front. // In a number of lines, *output* has been on an upgrade from lows earlier this year. // Sugar *production* marked a new high record. // Nondurable *manufactures* registered a substantial recovery from August to December. // The upswing in *production* in May was a repeat the April experience. // to regain its *production* peak // *Production* is back to the pre-recession highs of early 1973. // *Production* recovered in June to the April level of 113 percent. // *Output* is to exceed the planned levels. // *Output* is to record advances. // *Output* is to pick up significantly. // *Output* is to rebound from the strike-depressed levels of the previous month.

[不変] ¶ The leveling-off of *output* was widespread, with most sectors showing only marginal changes in either direction // *Production* had an uneven record; some major item rose while others fell back. // *Output* is near to a standstill. // *Output* is at best stagnant.

[下降] ¶ Industrial *production* receded from June onward. // *Output,* after a long increase, declined after July. // *Production* registered a third consecutive monthly decline in August as steel *output* continued falling. // The growth of *output* tended downward. // *Output* is to suffer a sharp setback. // *Output* is to be at diminished levels. // *Output* is to enter its usual summer slowdown. // *Output* is to contract further — by 1.8% over the month. // *Output* is to have still not emerged from a slow downward slide. // A dent in the gross domestic *product* was made by the strike.

大規模生産 mass production; production on a large scale

一貫生産 integated production

重点生産 priority production; production on a priority basis

過剰生産 over-production; excessive production

過少生産 underproduction

傾斜生産 priority production on a priority basis

鉱工業生産 mining and manufacturing production

工業生産 industrial production; manufacturing production ¶ → p.281

国内生産 domestic production

見込み生産 market production

流れ作業生産 flow production

農業生産 agricultural production

市場生産 market production

試験的生産 trial production; production on trial; experimental production; pilot production

商業生産 commercial production; production on a commercial basis

大量生産 mass production; bulk production

迂回生産 indirect production; round-about production; capitalist(ic) production surplus production

seisan 清算 liquidation; settlement; clearing; [市] closing-out (of contract) ¶ to *liquidate* a company, or accounts // to *settle* business accounts // *clearing* of bills and checks

強制清算 forced liquidation; compulsony liquidation

任意清算 voluntary liquidation

差額清算 settlement of difference

seisanbumon 生産部門 producing department

seisanbusoku 生産不足 underproduction

seisanbutsu 生産物 products; produce; output

中間生産物 intermediate product

同質的生産物 homogeneous product

限界価値生産物 marginal value product

限界収入生産物 marginal revenue product

純国民生産物 net national product

工業生産物 industrial product

国民生産物 national product

高所得生産物 high income product

農業生産物 agricultural product

最終生産物 final product

粗国民生産物 gross national product

seisanbutsunosabetsuka 生産物の差別化 product differentiation

seisanchōsei 生産調整 production cutback; production restraints; curtailment of operation; adjustment in output ¶ *Adjustments in output* were made by manufacturers of automobiles.

seisandaiichishugi 生産第一主義 production-first policy

seisandaikin 清算代金 amount of settlement

seisandaka 生産高 amount of production; production; output; yield

seisangaisha 清算会社 liquidation company; liquidated company; company in liquidation

seisangyappu 生産ギャップ output gap ¶ The ratio of actual to potential output is the *output gap*. // Prevailing *output gaps* in manufacturing are large.

seisanhi 生産費 cost of production; production cost

seisanhinohōsoku 生産費の法則 law of cost of production

seisanhyō 清算表 settlement sheet

seisanjisseki 生産実績 actual production

seisanjōyokin 清算剰余金 surplus at liquidation

seisankaishi 生産開始 entry into production ¶ Output of oil rose reflecting the *entry into production* of new oil fields.

seisankajō 生産過剰 over-production; excessive production

seisankakaku 生産価格 price of production

seisankanjō 清算勘定 liquidation account; open account

seisankatsudō 生産活動 productive activity ¶ *Productive activity* revived toward the year-end.

seisankeikaku 生産計画 production plan ¶ the disappearance of the previous contractive tendencies in *production plans* for the next three months

seisankibanshikin 生産基盤資金 funds for basic productive facilities

seisankin 清算金 settlement money; settlement amount

seisankyōtei 生産協定 clearing agreement

seisankyōteikumiai 生産協定組合 producers' cooperative society

seisankyoten 生産拠点 production foothold; manufacturing base; production base ¶ to acquire its first Asian *production base* in the Philippines

seisannin 清算人 liquidator

seisannokakudaikōka 生産の拡大効果 effect on production expansion

seisannōryoku 生産能力 productive capacity ¶ Large additions to *productive capacity* have been made. // *Productive capacity* was still not fully utilized. // Output is well below potential *capacity*. // The utilization of *productive capacity* in manufacturing industry declined from a record 85% in May to 71% in October. // Firms' spare *production capacity* has tended to become smaller. // The *productive capacity* of the economy was only drawn on to the extent of 26.2%. // Industry needs 84.5% of its *capacity for production* in August. // investment with a view to improving, as apposed to expanding *productive capacity* // The greatest slack in *production capacity* exists in the capital goods sector. // Brazil expects nearly to double its steel *capacity* by 1988. // Plants are running at full *capacity* in several sector. // Some branches of industry had not reached their *capacity* limits. // *capacity* limitations on *production*

実際的生産能力 practical capacity

遊休生産能力 idle capacity

seisannōryokuseisanshisū 生 産 能 力生産指数 index of production for production capacity

seisannōryokushisū 生産能力指数 index of production capacity

seisannosaitekijōken 生産の最適条件 optimum point of production

seisanritsu 生産率 rate of production; production rate

seisanrōdōsha 生産労働者 production worker

seisanrōdōshajitsurōdōjikan 生産労働者実労働時間 working hours of production workers

seisanryoku 生 産 力 producing power; productivity; productive force; productive power; productive capacity; productive abilities

限界生産力 marginal productivity

seisanryokukōka 生産力効果 productivity effect

seisansabo 生産サボ production sabotage

seisansaikai 生産再開 resumption of production

seisansei 生 産 性 productivity ¶ One reason for the fall-off in *productivity* is that order-books have shrunk while labor forces have remained unchanged. // *Productivity,* as measured by output per man-hour worked, rose for the first time for some while. // Enterprises raised their output and thus moved into a zone of better *productivity.* // *Productivity* in the economy as a whole went up distinctly. // The increase in *productivity* worked out at 2.5% in 1975. // There seems to have been a sharp fall in *productivity* in industry between these two periods. // Growth in *productivity* per

man-hour worked has been cut from an annual rate of 3.2% to 1.6% recent years. // American's rate-of-*productivity* growth has been below 2%, vs. Japan's 5.5%. // Labor *productivity* in South Korea rose by 11.2% on average in 1977 and 1978. // smaller gains in labor *productivity* // the level of overall labor and capital *productivity* // low and high-*productivity* sectors of the economy // The low rate of *productivity* gains accumulated inflationary measures.

付加価値生産性 productivity of added value

要素生産性 factor productivity

seisanseigen 生産制限 curtailment of production; production cutback; restrained production; production restraint

seisanseikōjōundō 生産性向上運動 productivity drive; productivity efforts ¶ our pragmatic, practical active project-oriented *productivity efforts*

seisanseikyōyaku 生産性協約 productivity deal

seisanseishitsugyō 生産性失業 productivity unemployment

seisanseisokutei 生産性測定 productivity measurement

seisansetsubi 生産設備 plants and equipment; capacity; production (= productive) facilities ¶ Mexico built a hefty *capacity* in petrochemicals and steel.

seisanshabeika 生産者米価 producer's price of rice; producer's rice price

seisanshabukka 生産者物価(指数) (index of) producer price; producer price (index)

seisanshakeikaku 生産者計画 producer's planning

seisanshaseihinzaiko 生産者製品在庫 (index of) producers' inventories of finished goods

seisanshashūkka 生産者出荷 (index of) producers' shipments

seisanshigen 生産資源 productive resources ¶ encouragement of the development of *productive resources*

seisanshihon 生産資本 productive capital

seisanshijō 清算市場 futures market

seisanshisetsu 生産施設 productive facility ¶ reconversion of *productive facility*

seisanshisū 生産指数 production index of industrial products ¶ The general *index of* average daily *industrial output* (1970=100) worked out at 129.0 in March, showing a rise of 1.7 percent on February and a decline of 3.4 percent over the year. // Gains in December raised the *industrial production index* to 115 percent of its 1975 average, continuing the upward trend since the cyclical low in February 1973. // The monthly *index of industrial production* was about 7 percent higher. // *Industrial production* as measured by the Federal Reserve index slipped off a point in June to 111.6 (1957=100). // [参考] The growth of output in industries producing for the home market was about 8 percent greater than a year earlier.

seisanshōgai 生産障害 production impediment ¶ Many industrial firms reported production *impediments* due to insufficient demand.

seisanshotoku 清算所得 income at liquidation

seisanshūchū 生産集中 production centralization

seisanshudan 生産手段 means of production

seisanson'eki 清算損益 profit (or loss) from liquidation

seisanteikei 生産提携 collaboration in production

seisantekijigyō 生産的事業 productive enterprise

seisantekirōdō 生産的労働 productive labor

seisantekirōdōryoku 生産的労働力 productive power of labor

seisantekishishutsu 生産的支出 productive expenditure

seisantekishōhi 生産的消費 productive consumption

seisantekitōshi 生産的投資 productive investment

seisantenkan 生産転換 change-over (of production)

seisantenkankoyō 生産転換雇用 change-over employment

seisantorihiki 清算取引 time bargain; futures transaction; futures trading; clearning contract

seisanwariate 生産割当て production quota

seisan'yoryoku 生産余力 spare (production) capacity; idle (productive) capacity; unutilized (=unused) capacity ¶ a shortage of *spare capacity* // There has been an ample *spare capacity*. // Certain industries had some *idle capacity*. // Ford has spare car-making *capacity* at its big two plants. // the high level of *spare capacity* available // *Unused capacity* margins shrank in the four months to June.

seisan'yōshiki 生産様式 form of production

seisan'yōso 生産要素 agents of production; production factor; factor of production ¶ the classical *factors of production* land, labor, and capital

seiseihin 精選品 choice article

seiseiyakuhin 精製薬品 fine chemicals

seisenshokuryōhin 生鮮食料品 perishable food; perishable foodstuffs

seitaigaku 生態学 ecology ¶ There are numerous impediments to new investment of *ecological* grounds. // the irreversible destruction of *ecological systems*

seitōshojiningensoku 正当所持人原則 holder-in-due-course doctrine ¶ the recent ruling by the Federal Trade Commission on the "*holder-in-due-course*" doctrine

seiyaku 制約 constraint; restriction; bottleneck; condition; limitation; brake ¶ The external *constraint* became compelling. // The major *constraint* under which economic policy has to operate is the risk of renewed acceleration of inflation. // prudential and regulatory *constraints* on bank lending // Some supply *constraints* have been created. // to impose *restrictions* on import trade // to relax and then remove *restrictions* on foreign trade // There were genuine legal and economic *constraints* against a further rise in lending rates. // Serious *bottlenecks* are emerging. // the growth of structural rigidities and *bottlenecks* // arrangements with members involving high *conditionality* in the use of the Fund's resources // to extend stand-by arrangements under highly *conditional*

facilities // Physical *constraints* remained largely unrelieved. // regulatory and other *constraints* are affecting their access to capital markets // Governments accept the necessary *constraints,* primarily on their freedom to alter exchange rates. // Governments face *constraints* on their policies. // to overcome the medium-term *constraint* on growth posed by inflation // The substantial alleviation of supply *constraints* was not feasible over the short run. // Both internal and external *constraints* have been mastered fairly well. // the increasing severity of the liquidity *constraint* // A too rapid upswing might easily run into new *constraints*. // Capacity *limitations* came into play. // Labor shortages are becoming a serious *brake* on growth.

seizai 製材 sawn wood

seizen'undō 西漸運動 [米] westward movement

seizō 製造 manufacture; preparation; fabrication

seizōgenka 製造原価 manufacturing cost; cost of manufacture; cost of production

seizōgyōbumonbetsubukkashisū 製造業部門別物価指数 input-output price index by manufacturing industry sector

seizōgyōsha 製造業者 manufacturer; producer; maker

seizōhin 製造品 products; manufactures; manufactured goods; fabricated goods

seizōhinshukka 製造品出荷 (value of) shipments (of manufacturing industry products) ¶ *Shipments* at the producers' level are stable to slightly higher. // *Shipments* of hopper fabricators slipped marginally.

seizōhō 製造法 manufacturing method; method of production

seizōippankeihi 製造一般経費 manufacturing overhead (expenses)

seizōkōtei 製造工程 manufacturing process

seizonchingin 生存賃金 subsistence wages

seizonhoken 生存保険 endowment insurance

seizonkyōsō 生存競争 struggle for survival; struggle for existence; struggle for life

seizonnōryoku 生存能力 viability

seizōnōryoku 製造能力 production capacity; productive capacity; manufacturing capacity ¶ to shift *manufacturing capacity* to new pictures

seizonsuijun 生存水準 subsistence level ¶ People must be lifted from the *subsistence level.* // whole segments of society exist at bare *subsistence levels*

seizonsuijunshotoku 生存水準所得 subsistence income

sekaijinkōkaigi 世界人口会議 World Population Conference

sekaijuyō 世界需要 world demand ¶ the *world demand* for oil // *World demand* is high.

sekaika 世界化 globalism

sekaikigyō 世界企業 →多国籍企業

sekaishokuryōjōhōshisutemu 世界食料情報システム global information and early-warning on food and agriculture

sekaishokuryōkaigi 世界食料会議 World Food Conference

sekaitsūka 世界通貨 universal currency

sekininjunbikin 責任準備金 liability reserve

sekisaijūryōtonsū 積載重量トン数 deadweight (tonnage); DW

sekiyuakaji 石油赤字 oil-induced deficit; oil deficit ¶ *oil deficit* against non-oil deficit

sekiyuchokusetsutorihiki 石油直接取引 direct-deal trade in oil; bilateral oil deals

sekiyuchōseigurūpu 石油調整グループ Energy Co-ordinate Group

sekiyuigainoakaji 石油以外の赤字 non-oil deficit

sekiyuizondo 石油依存度 dependence on oil

sekiyujikyūkoku 石油自給国 self-sufficient (=self-supporting; self-sustaining) country in oil supply

sekiyukiki 石油危機 oil crisis shortage ¶ the outbreak or emergence of the *oil crisis* // comparison with pre-*oil crisis* levels

sekiyukinkyūyūzūseido 石油緊急融通制度 oil-sharing system in emergencies; emergency allocation scheme

sekiyurōshutsu 石油漏出 oil spill; oil leak

sekiyusaikutsuken 石油採掘権 oil concession

sekiyusaiteikakaku 石油最低価格 floor price of oil

sekiyusanshutsukoku 石油産出国 oil-producing country

sekiyuseihin 石油製品 petroleum products; oil products

sekiyusekitanseihinkōgyō 石油・石炭製品工業 petroleum and coal products industy

sekiyushōhikoku 石油消費国 oil-consumption (=consuming) country (=nation)

sekiyushokku 石油ショック oil shock; oil shock ferment ¶ the situation after the first *oil shock* of 1973-74 // recovery of investment to *pre-oil shock* levels in 1984, in the wake of the *oil shock ferment*

sekiyusutandobai 石油スタンド・バイ stand-by credit for crude oil import

sekiyutanpaku 石油たんぱく petroprotein

sekiyutarenagashi 石油たれ流し →石油漏出

sekiyuyushutsukinshi 石油輸出禁止 oil embargo; ban on oil shipments

sekiyuyushutsukoku 石油輸出国 oil-exporting country (=nation)

sekiyuyushutsukokukikō 石油輸出国機構 Organization of Petroleum Exporting Countries; OPEC

sekkyokutekikoyōseisaku 積極的雇用政策 active employment policy

sekkyokuyosan 積極予算 expansionary budget

sekkyokuzaisei 積極財政 positive financial policy; expansionist fiscal policy

senbai 専売 monopoly ¶ The government holds a *monopoly* on tobacco. // The tobacco business is a government *monopoly*.

senbaihin 専売品 monopoly goods; monopolies

senbaikakaku 専売価格 monopoly price

senbaiken 専売権 monopoly right; monopoly

senbainōfukin 専売納付金 receipts from government monopolies

senbairieki 専売利益 profit of the Monopoly Bureau

senbetsu 選別 sorting ¶ to *sort*

out fit notes from unfit notes

senbetsukijun 選別基準 →選択基準

senbetsukinri 選別金利 selection interest

senbetsuteki 選別的 selective; discretionary ¶ *Selective* policies should include action on industrial bottlenecks and on *selective* import contracts. // Controls became more sophisticated and *selective* with special attention to monopoly industries. // New or intensified restrictions were *selective* in their application. // *selective* and not universal controls of bank lending // *discretionary* items other than daily necessities // Devaluation is a crude, non-*selective* move which would push up prices.

senbetsutekishinyōkisei 選別的信用規制 selective credit control

senbetsutōshi 選別投資 selective investment ¶ The *selective investment* scheme will be extended for another year.

senbetsuyūshi 選別融資 selective lending; selective loan

senbetsuyushutsu 選別輸出 selective exports

senbunhi 千分比 permillage

senchakujunsei 先着順制 first-come-first-served basis; first come system

sendanhōshiki 船団方式 convoy approach

sendenfukyūhanbaiin 宣伝普及販売員 missionary salesman

senden'insatsubutsu 宣伝印刷物 advertising printed matter

sendenkeisaikankōbutsu 宣伝掲載刊行物 ad-carrying publications

sendō 先導 pacemaker; bellwether

¶ the *bellwether* long-term (№ 53) 7.5% issue

sen'igenryō 繊維原料 textile materials

sen'ihin 繊維品 textiles

sen'ikōgyō 繊維工業 textile industry

sen'inhoken 船員保険 seamen's insurance

sen'inuketorisho 船員受取書 mate's receipt

sen'itakokukantorikime 繊維多国間取り決め Arrangement regarding International Trade in Textiles

senjutsu 戦術 tactic ¶ to coordinate *tactically* the use of its several monetary instruments // A change will be necessary in the Committee's operational *tactic.* // to implement a new economic strategy and *tactics* // to be outflanked by the external mercantilist *tactics* of competitors abroad // to switch *tactics* in the attack on inflation // the planned *tactics* President Carter will use to try to gain concessions at the economic summit // The French and Italian authorities have used similar *tactics.* // to use *tactics* which had not been employed // The *tactics* appeared to work very well.

senkei 線型 linear

senkeihōteishiki 線型方程式 linear equation

senken 先見 foresight ¶ from lack of *foresight* // to have little *foresight* as to the future course of prices

senkensei 先験性 apriority

senkō 選好 preference ¶ A marked shift of investor *preferences* toward securities of the highest quality was set in action by market reaction to the financial difficulties of two banks. // changes in consumer *preferences* // Buyer *preferences* shifted from fullsize cars to compacts.

時間選好 time preference

顕示選好 revealed preference

金選好 preference for gold

金融資産選好 preference of financial assets

効用選好 utility preference

流動性選好 liquidity preference

資産選好 assets preference

消費者選好 consumer preference

senkōjōkenki 先行条件期 preconditions period

senkōjunjo 選好順序 order of preference

senkōkikan 先行期間 lead time ¶ Sufficient *lead time* should be provided before this measure becomes effective.

senkōshihyō 先行指標 leading indicator ¶ longer *leading indicators,* which look ahead on average of twelve months

senkukabu 先駆株 forerunner

senmonshōhin 専門商品 specialty goods

senmonshoku 専門職 professionals

senmontekikeieisha 専門的経営者 professional manager

senmutorishimariyaku 専務取締役 senior managing director; managing director

sēnohanrohōsoku セーの販路法則 Say's law of market

senpaku 船舶 ship; vessel

senpakukin'yū 船舶金融 shipping finance

senpatsu 先発 forerunner ¶ The world's latecomers to industrialization can catch up with their *forerun-*

ners in the rich world.

senpōkanjō 先方勘定 their account; vostro a/c

senpuku 船腹 space

senpukuyōsen 船腹用船 lump sum charter; bottom charter

senryaku 戦略 strategy ¶ To formulate and implement a comprehensive *strategy,* geared to the medium term, covering growth, employment, and inflation, which is a coherent and whole, whose parts are interdependent. // The results of this *strategy* of self-defeat litter the economy. // Ministers laid down a broad medium-term *strategy* which will guide their own individual policies. // The central bank resorts to a joint *strategy* of perspectives and targets in policy making. // Such an instructional *strategy* will meet U.S. central banking objectives. // an effective *strategy* for attacking poverty // We work toward mutually consistent economic *strategies* through better cooperation. // France supported the wider concerted growth *strategy* proposed by the OECD. // The Government's current *strategy* against inflation rests on restraints on corporate pricing. // to implement a new economic *strategy* for tackling the country's economic ills // The aim of industrial *strategy* should be investment at home rather than abroad. // The budget's economic *strategy* is to cut inflation at the expense of wages. // The choice of an investment *strategy* by the firm affects the firm's shareholders. // the optimal investment *strategy* for providing social infrastucture // →方略

senryakubichiku 戦略備蓄 strategic stockpile; strategic reserve; strategic storage ¶ to build up our *strategic* oil *reserves* // oil imports for the *strategic storage* program

senryakubusshi 戦略物資 strategic goods

senryakusangyō 戦略産業 strategic industry

senryakutekitōshi 戦略的投資 strategic investment

sensasukyokuhō センサス局法 ［統］ Census method

senshin'ichijisanpinkoku 先進一次産品国 more developed country producing primary product

senshinkoku 先進国 advanced country; industrial(ized) country

sensōhoken 戦争保険 war risk insurance

sensōkiken 戦争危険 war risk

sensokuwatashi 船側渡し free alongside ship; F.A.S.

sensōnarikin 戦争成金 war-made neuveau riche

sentaku 選択 choice; selection ¶ to afford individuals and businesses at least the same breadth of *choice* among alternative suppliers of services as they now have // Competition will generate a broad *choice* of alternative for the public. // to promote wider *choice* for consumers // to offer conusmers a more varied *choice* // *selection* of banks by companies // the joint savings-portfolio *choice* decision // theory of consumer's *choice* // to offer a more varied *choice* for a an occupation

代替選択　substitution choice
最適選択　optimal choice
生産者選択　producer's choice
消費者選択　consumer's choice

sentakugai 選択買い [市] selective buying

sentakujuyō 選択需要 alternative demand

sentakuken 選択権 option ¶ The corporation has exercised its *option* to redeem a part of its outstanding bonds. // *option*-bearing securities with stock purchase warrants, also known as option warrants // to limit the policy *options* that are open to a country // The range of *options* open to the Federal Reserve appears to be narrowing.

sentakunojiyū 選択の自由 freedom of choice ¶ The increased share of bilateral trade has reduced the *freedom of choice* of import.

sentakuseikō 選択性向 selectivity

sentakuteki 選択的 discretionary; selective

sentakutekikashidashikisei 選択的貸出規制 selective restriction on bank loans

sentakutekikoyōzei 選択的雇用税 [英] Selective Employment Tax

sentakutekishin'yōkisei 選択的信用規制 selective credit control (= regulation)

sentakutekishōhishabusshi 選択的消費者物資 discretionary consumer goods

sentakutekitōshi 選択的投資 discretionary investment

sentakutekizaiseiseisaku 選択的財政政策 selective fiscal action (= policy)

sentangijyutsu 先端技術 advanced technology; ultra advanced technology; ultra-modern technology

sen'yōgyogyō 専用漁業 exclusive right fishery

senzaifuwatari 潜在不渡り latent dishonor

senzaiinfurēshon 潜在インフレーション inflationary potential ¶ to limit the *inflationary potential* associated with increases in the money supply

senzaijuyō 潜在需要 latent demand

senzaikyōkyū 潜在供給 latent supply; supply potential

senzairyoku 潜在力 potential ¶ high economic *potentials* of a nation // to improve the employment *potential* of these pursuits // to its full *potential* // the uneven *potential* for energy conservation among countries // to bring the productive capacity of the economy back to its *potential* level, and keep it above *potential* // There is additional productive *potential* both elsewhere in Asia and Africa. // There is considerable *potential* for increasing agricultural output in the developing countries. // The extent of the country's unutilized growth *potential* is substantial. // The growth *potential* in the major economies has been sapped by higher energy costs. // There is a huge, virtually untapped *potential* for the sale of Indian gold to the Arab states. // A prolonged decline in investment will compromise medium-term growth *potential*. // to help the nation's industrial *potentials* materialize // a further strengthening of their scientific and technical *potential* // the rise in national income and the concomitant increase in the population's savings *potential* // the inflationary *potential* of the imbalance in the public finances // the utilization of production *potential*

senzaiseichōryoku 潜 在 成 長 力 growth potential ¶ The government allowed Japan to realize fully its *growth potential*. // *Growth potential* in the electronics industry is enormous. // Stagnating investment will undermine the economy's *growth potential*. // Consumer finance has a vast *potential* for *growth*.

senzaiseisan 潜 在 生 産 potential output ¶ a sharp drop in the rates of growth of *potential output* // to estimate consistent series of *potential output* in manufacturing for industrial countries

senzaiseisanryoku 潜 在 生 産 力 productive potential; latent capacity ¶ the realization of a country's *productive potential*

senzaishitsugyō 潜 在 失 業 latent unemployment; potential unemployment

senzaitekishikin 潜 在 的 資 金 potential holdings of funds

senzaitekishikinjuyō 潜 在 的 資 金 需 要 latent demand of funds

senzaitsūka 潜 在 通 貨 latent currency

senzaiyunyūjuyō 潜 在 輸 入 需 要 absorptive capacity ¶ Their *absorptive capacity* is limited. // countries of low *absorptive capacity* // nations with low-*absorptive capacities* // [参考] a very few "low absorbers" like Saudi Arabia

senzenkijunshisū 戦 前 基 準 指 数 prewar-base index

seronchōsa 世論調査 (public opinion) poll; census ¶ In a *poll* taken last October, 47% said they preferred superstores.

serufusābisuyasuurihyakkaten セ

ルフ・サービス安売り百貨店 ［米］ self-service discount department store; SSDD; self-service department store

sērusuman セ ー ル ス マ ン canvasser; salesman; sales people

sesshūkikinzokutō 接 収 貴 金 属 等 requisitioned precious metals, etc. ¶ to restitute *requisitioned precious metals, etc.*

setaibunpu 世 帯 分 布 distribution of households

setaikibo 世帯規模 family size

setaitan'i 世帯単位 family unit

setogiwaseisaku 瀬戸際政策 brinkmanship

setsubi 設備 facilities; equipment; accommodation ¶ to improve communication *facilities* // to increase manufacturing *facilities* // a complete factory *equipment* // investment in plant and *equipment* // a hotel affording luxurious *accommodation* for 600 guests // sleeping *accommodations* for 20 persons

工場設備 plant and equipment

港湾設備 port facilities; harbor facilities

老朽設備 obsolete equipment

産業設備 industrial facilities

生産設備 productive (=production) facilities

資本設備 capital equipment

省力設備 labor-saving equipment

遊休設備 idle equipment

setsubiidō 設備移動 capacity utilization; operation ¶ The degree of *capacity utilization* has been relatively small. // *Capacity utilization* rates were falling in most major sectors of manufacturing. // As output rose, *capacities* were better *utilized* again.

setsubikadō 設 備 稼 働 capacity utilization; capacity use; factory operation ¶ *Capacity utilization* by manufacturers rose to 85.6% in May. // The recovery from the strike-induced fall in April still left *capacity use* below the March level of 86.2%.

setsubikadōritsu 設 備 稼 働 率 capacity utilization ratio; operation rate ¶ [参考] The economy is pressing against its productive capacity ceiling. // the existing under utilization of industrial capacity // Steel mill operations in July were 42 percent of capacity. // The present overall capacity operating rate in industry is around 86 percent. // →操業率

setsubikindaika 設 備 近 代 化 modernization of equipment

setsubinokaizenjūjitsu 設 備 の 改 善 充実 improvement and expansion of equipment

setsubinōryoku 設 備 能 力 equipment capacity; plant capacity ¶ Only 70% of available *plant capacity* was effectively used. // Manufacturing firms are still working well below *plant capacity*.

setsubishikin 設 備 資 金 funds for equipment investment; equipment funds

setsubishikinkashitsuke 設 備 資 金 貸付 lending of equipment funds

setsubitōshi 設 備 投 資 investment in plant and equipment; plant and equipment investment; equipment investment; fixed investment; spending on plant and equipment; equipment outlay; capital spending ¶ The recent expansion of *equipment investment* has been extremely swift. // Planned *capital spending* by

manufacturers overall is up 16 percent. // Business plans for plant and *equipment outlays* were revised upward. // Enterprises' *fixed capital investment* showed a recovery, after three years of decline. // [参考] to undertake major capacity-expanding outlays for plant and equipment

setsubitōshitaijun'uriagedakahiritsu 設備投資対純売上高比率 ratio of equipment investment to net sales

setsubiyoryoku 設 備 余 力 spare capacity ¶ Many enterprises are first trying to utilize their relatively large *spare capacity* to fill new orders. // Enterprises still had substantial *spare capacity*.

setsubiyunitto 設 備 ユ ニ ッ ト united equipment

setsubiyushutsu 設 備 輸 出 plant export

setsuden'undō 節 電 運 動 [英] SOS; "switch off something now"

setsudo 節 度 discipline ¶ Balance of payments *discipline* re-emerged as a conscious part of economic policy. // fiscal *disciplne* practiced by the government // to be strict in banking *discipline* // a failure to exercise reasonable *discipline* over the international behavior of our economy // The fundamental source of inflation has been the lack of *discipline* in government finances. // a failure to exercise reasonable *discipline* over the international behavior of our economy // Bankers are urged to *discipline* the pace at which they are extending credit. // The borrowing countries were encouraged to accept a greater *discipline* in their economic management. // to maintain a competitive *discipline* in credit pricing // The administration must exercise *discipline* in spending. // concern regarding the adequacy of fiscal *discipline* // The banks have managed to inspire more *discipline* into their customers. // to manage fiscal policy with sufficient *discipline* // the lack of *discipline* in government finances // to *discipline* the pace at which they are extending credit // A *disciplinary* currency system will reinforce Mr. Giscard's economic policy.

金融節度 financial discipline; monetary discipline

国際収支節度 balance-of-payments discipline

通貨節度 montary discipline

財政節度 fiscal discipline

setsugen 節減 retrenchment; reduction; curtailment; cut; economy ¶ to make a *retrenchment* of 500 workers // *retrenchment* in treasury expenditure // a *reduction* in expenses // a drastic *curtailment* of expenses // a 20 percent *cut* in expenses // to practise rigid *economy* in expenditure, time and labor // to *economize* in petroleum // Certain *economies* made in 1975 may affect expenditure in 1976. // [参考] The growth of expenditure will be curbed sharply in view of the tight financial situation. // →節約する

経費節減 retrenchment of expenditures

setsumeihensū 説明変数 explanatory variable

setsuritsuhokki'nin 設立発起人 floater; promoter

setsuyakuchinginbunpaiseido 節約賃金分配制度 gain-sharing plan

setsuyakunogyakusetsu 節約の逆説 paradox of thrift

setsuyakusuru 節約する economize; save; retrench; conserve ¶ means of *economizing* on energy usage // It will *save* the company a lot of time and labor. // labor-*saving* investment // to *retrench* fiscal spendings // to make a *retrenchment* of 1,000 workers // *retrenchment* budget policy // The budget necessitates painful *economies*, probably in the form of staff layoffs. // pressure for *economies* in spending // to extinguish Christmas lights to *conserve* electricity // to make efforts to develop, *conserve* and use rationally the various energy resources // →節減

setsuzoku 接続 link; splice ¶ The national welfare is closely *linked* with industry. // a *link* between the past and present index figures // the *splice* to connect the two series of statistics

setsuzokusen'unchin 接続船運賃 freight of joint carriage ship

setsuzokushisū 接続指数 linked index

settokukōsaku 説得(工作) exhortation; persuasion; suasion; jawboning; appeal; request ¶ continuous *exhortation* by the Bank to restrict lendings // earnest *exhortations* // to *exhort* banks to restrict lendings // much more *jawboning* rather than formal wage-price guidelines // to *appeal* for voluntary reductions in the use of oil // the Board of Governors' statement *requesting* the volutary restriction of lending activity // moral *suasion* // to use Administration's *jawboning* technique to head off high wage settlements // a

jawboning version of incomes policy
道義的説得 moral suasion
穏和な説得 peaceful persuasion
shachō 社長 president
shadanhōjin 社団法人 corporate juridical person
shagai 社外 external; outside
shagaibunpai 社外分配 external distribution
shagaifusai 社外負債 external liability (=debt; obligation)
shagaijūyaku 社外重役 outride director; dummy director
shagairyūshutsu 社外流出 outflow of funds from businesses ¶ These developments combined caused an excessive *outflow of funds from businesses*.
shakai 社会 society; community; world ¶ the upper or lower class of *society* // in modern *society* // in a civilized *community* // an industrialized *community* // rural *communities* // in the industrial, commercial, and financial *world* // the *world* of finance
脱工業社会 post-industrial society
同質社会 homogeneous society
複合社会 plural society
原始社会 primitive society
異質社会 heterogeneous society
結縁社会 blood society
高密度社会 high-density society
共同社会 community
二重社会 dual society
人間尊重への社会 society where human dignity prevails; society where human rights are respected
利益社会 association
産業社会 industrial society
商業社会 commercial society
商業主義的社会 mercantile society
大衆社会 mass society

多民族社会 multi-racial society
豊かな社会 affluent society; opulent society
shakaifujo 社会扶助 social assistance
shakaifukinkō 社会不均衡 social imbalance
shakaifukushi 社会福祉 social welfare; social benefit; community welfare; social service(s) ¶ to replenish *social welfare* // the gap between economic growth and *social welfare* // to build up the *social service*
shakaihiyō 社会費用 social cost
shakaihoken 社会保険 social insurance
shakaihokenfutan 社会保険負担 social security contribution
shakaihōshi 社会奉仕 social job; public service
shakaihoshō 社会保障 social security
shakaihoshōseido 社会保障制度 social security system
shakaijigyō 社会事業 social work; social service; public welfare service
shakaijinkōtōkeitaikei 社会人口統計体系 (system of) social and demographic statistics
shakaikabukikō 社会下部機構 social infrastructure
shakaikaihatsu 社会開発 social development; social planning
shakaikaikei 社会会計 social accounting
shakaikanjō 社会勘定 social accounting
shakaikeiyaku 社会契約 social contract; social compact
shakaikeizaisoshiki 社会経済組織 socio-economic system
shakairentai 社会連帯 social sol-

idarity

shakaiseido 社会制度 social system

shakaiseisaku 社会政策 social policy

shakaishihon 社会資本 social (overhead) capital; infrastructure ¶ *social overhead capital* investment // accumulation of *social overhead capital* // the bank's lending for transport *infrastructure* // finance for *infrastructure* projects // finance for *infrastructure* to improve road and telecommunications links between member countries

shakaishihontōshi 社会資本投資 infrastructural investment; social overhead capital investment

shakaisoshiki 社会組織 social organization; social fabric ¶ *social organization* of the economy // This system is deeply ingrained in the *social fabric*.

shakaitekiben'eki 社会的便益 social benefit; social dividend

shakaitekifubyōdō 社会的不平等 social inequality

shakaitekihitsuyō 社会的必要 social need; social want

shakaitekihizumi 社会的ひずみ social imblance; social distortion

shakaitekikaisōbunka 社会的階層分化 social stratification

shakaitekikankyō 社会的環境 social environment; social climate

shakaitekikansetsushihon 社会的間接資本 social overhead capital ¶ → 社会資本

shakaitekisekinin 社会的責任 social responsibility ¶ *social responsibilities* of banks and of enterprises

shakaitekishin'yōundō 社会的信用運動 social credit movement

shakaitekishishutsu 社会的支出 social expenditure

shakaitekishōhi 社会的消費 social spending

shakaitekishotoku 社会的所得 social income

shakaitekiyokkyū 社会的欲求 social need; social want

shakkan 借款 loan; loan contract; terms and conditions of loan ¶ The *loan*, which will bear interest at 6.5 percent and have a life of 15 years, will be offered for public subscription. // The Export-Import Bank is granting a *loan* of $50 milliard to Algerian State Oil Company, which will be repayable in 25 years after a period of grace of seven years. // to sign 12 *loan contracts* for an amount of $82.5 million // to conclude with Spain a *loan contract* of an equivalent of $3 million dollars // Of this sum, Lit. 10 milliard, granted in two *loans* for eight years at an interest rate of 9%, will go towards a new chemicals plant. // the government's drawing-down of overseas *loans*
　五年据置きの借款 loan unredeemable for 5 years; loan uncallable for 5 years; loan with 5-year gratis

shakkandan 借款団 consortium; syndicate

shakkanhensai 借款返済 repayment of loan

shakkankaishū 借款回収 collection of loan

shakkankyōju 借款享受 loan received

shakkankyōtei 借款協定 loan agreement

shakkankyōyo 借款供与 loan extention

shakki 借記 debit entry; debiting

shakkin 借金 debt; loan; borrowing; borrowed money ¶ to have a *debt,* to be in *debt,* or to owe a *debt* to someone // to incur or fall into *debts,* and to clear off or repay them

shakkinkanjō 借金勘定 debt account

shakkinkoku 借金国 borrower country; debtor nation

shakōkeiyaku 射倖契約 aleatory contract

shakuchi 借地 leasehold (land); leased land; rented land

shakudo 尺度 measuring rod ¶ The ECU is to be a real currency not merely a *measuring* rod.

shakuyō 借用 borrowing; loan; leasing

shakuyōkin 借用金 borrowed money

shakuyōshōsho 借用証書 loan bond; IOU

shanai 社内 internal; intra-company; within company

shanaifusai 社内負債 internal liabilities

shanaihō 社内報 house organ; house magazine

shanairyūho 社内留保 retained profits; reserved profits; internal reserve

shanaishi 社内誌 house magazine; house organ; house journal

shanaiyokin 社内預金 intra-company deposit; employee doposits; deposit within the company

shasai 社債 industrial bond; industrial debenture; debenture; bond; corporate debenture; corporate bond; loan; stock

貯蔵社債 treasury bond
普通社債 straight bond
保証社債 guaranteed bond

一般担保付社債 general mortgage bond
拡張社債 extension bond
株式買取権付社債 warrant bond; bond with warrant
確定利付社債 straight bond
借換社債 refunding bond
仮社債 interim bond
記名社債 registered bond
無期限社債; 永久社債 irredeemable bond; perpetual bond
無担保社債 (unsecured) debenture (bond)
任意償還条項付社債 callable (= retractable) bond
連続発行社債 serial bond
劣後社債 subordinate bond
利益参加社債 participating bond; profit sharing bond
整理社債 adjustment bond
支払引受社債 assumed bond
所持人払い社債 bearer bond; unregistered bond
償還延期社債 deferred bond; extended bond
承継社債 asstumed bond
証券付担保社債 collateral trust bond
収益参加社債 participating bond
収益社債 income bond
出資社債 capital bond
担保付託社債 collateral trust bond
抵当権付社債 mortgage bond; secured bond
転換社債 convertible bond
統合社債 unifying bond; consolidated bond
有期社債 redeemable bond

shasaihakkōdaka 社債発行高 bonds issued; bond issue

shasaihakkōhi 社債発行費 bond issue cost; bond issuing expense

shasaihakkōjōken 社債発行条件

rules for flotation of corporate debentures ¶ to relax the rigid *rules for corporate bond flotation*

shasaihakkōkariirekin 社債発行借入金 bond debt

shasaihakkōsakin 社債発行差金 bond discount; discount on bond

shasaihikiukenin 社債引受人 underwriter

shasaikariirekin 社債借入金 bonded debt

shasaikarikae 社債借換え (bond) refunding

shasaiken 社債券 debenture bond; debenture share

shasaikenjōto 社債券譲渡 debenture transfer (＝assignment)

shasaikensha 社債権者 bond holder

shasaikenshintaku 社債権信託 debenture trust

shasaimihakkōdaka 社債未発行高 bonds unissued

shasainojutakugyōmu 社債の受託業務 business as trustee of bonds and debentures

shasainotōrokugyōmu 社債の登録業務 registration operation of bonds and debentures

shasaiōbo 社債応募 undertaking of corporate bonds

shasairishi 社債利子 debenture interest

shasaisaikōhakkōgendo 社債最高発行限度 (maximum amount of issue of) bonds authorized

shasaishintakushōsho 社債信託証書 trust deed

shasaishōka 社債消化 sales of corporate bonds; absorption of debenture issues

shasaishōkan 社債償還 debenture redemption

shasaishutoku 社債取得 acquisition of debenture

shashi 奢侈 luxury; extravagance

shashihin 奢侈品 luxuries; luxurious articles

shashikanzei 奢侈関税 luxury tariff

shashikinshihō 奢侈禁止法 sumptuary law

shashinkankōzairyō 写真感光材料 photo-sensitized materials

shashinsōba 写真相場 reflex quotation

shashizei 奢侈税 luxury tax

shayōsangyō 斜陽産業 outmoded industry; declining industry

shayōzoku 社用族 entertainment on the expense account; expense-account group; expense-account spenders

shea シェア market share ¶ The downward trend in commercial banks' *market share* of lending business came to a halt, with this banking group accounting for 30 % of all lending. // to build up market *share* rapidly // →市場占有率

shibiruminimamu シビル・ミニマム civil minimum

shibo 私募 private offering; private placement; direct placement ¶ *privately offered* bond issues

shibōhoken 死亡保険 mortality insurance

shibōritsu 死亡率 death rate ¶ The *death rate* in middle-income countries, at 12 per thousand of population, was down within sight of the 10 per thousand rate in the industrial countries.

shiburi 仕振り practice; behavior; attitude; manner ¶ overreaction to the bad *practices* of a few bankers //

the *behavior* of construction activity // a positive *attitude* of banks toward lending // in an earnest *manner*

shichiireuragaki 質入裏書 endorsement for pledge

shichiken 質権 right of pledge

shichikensettei 質権設定 establishment of the right of pledge

shichikensha 質権者 pledgee; pawnee; mortgage creditor

shichikentōroku 質権登録 registration of the right of pledge

shichizunminimamu シチズン・ミニマム citizen minimum

shichū 市中 (open) market

shichūginkō 市中銀行 (commercial) bank ¶ The *commercial banks* in Sweden expanded their lending operations.

shichūginkōkashidashizōkagaku-kisei 市中銀行貸出増加額規制 regulatory controls on bank lending increase; measures to check the increase in city bank lendings; measures to restrain commercial bank lendings; ceiling on bank credit expansion; quantitative limits on the increase in bank lending

shichūkashidashi 市中貸出 commercial bank discounts and loans; (commercial) bank credit ¶ The expansion of *commercial bank credit* has been accelerated. // *Bank credit* has been constricted rapidly. // the large *credit* expansion by the commercial banks // *Commercial bank loans* expanded.

shichūkinri 市中金利 market interest rates; open market rates; money market rates; interst rates ¶ *Interest rates* tend generally to move downward in times of arrested

growth. // *Interest rates* turned upward again after last week's leap to 3.6 percent. // *Interest rates* charged by large city banks on prime loans to business have lagged behind changes in *open market rates*.

shichūtemoto 市中手許 fund position of banks; reserve position of banks ¶ maldistribution of *bank reserves* between regions

shichūwaribikibuai 市中割引歩合 (open) market discount rates

shidō 指導 guidance; guideline ¶ to issue *guidance* to the banks on the direction of their lending // The Fund shall adopt specific principles for the *guidance* of all members with respect to their exchange rate policies. // The *guidance* takes time to work through. // The *guide-lines* reflect a general agreement that behavior of governments with respect to exchange rates is a matter for consultation in the Fund. // "*Guidelines* for the Management of Floating Exchange Rates" adopted by the Executive Directors of the Fund. // →ガイドライン

shidōgenri 指導原理 guiding principle

shidōkakaku 指導価格 guided price; price guideline

shidōkijun 指導基準 guideline; guiding post; guidepost; guiding principle ¶ *guiding principles* for the lending activities of the credit institutions // the Accounting Manager's "money market condtions" *guideline*

shienzairyō 支援材料 [市] encouraging stimulant

shifuto シフト passing-through; passing-over; passing-on; transfer ¶

Increases in wage cost are *passed on* in prices. // a dollar-for-dollar *passing-through* to prices // →転稼

shigaichikakakushisū 市街地価格指数 land price index of urban districts

shigaika 市街化 →都市化

shigaikachōseikuiki 市街化調整区域 urbanization control area

shigaikakuiki 市街化区域 urbanization promotion area

shigeki 刺激 stimulus; incentive; fillip; impetus; prodding ¶ A substastial *stimulus* to import renewed dynamism to the economy. // regional fiscal *incentives* to attract economic activity to specific regions applied in some countries // The good response to the Treasury auction of three-year notes gave the U.S. bond market a *fillip*. // the major *impetus* behind the dollar's strength // Under *prodding* from the Government, corporations began to set up sogoshosha. // The main *impetus* for the growth in demand comes from private consumption. // The main *stimulus* to growth came from the industrial sector. // The economy is receiving considerable *stimulus* from domestic expansionary forces. // New *stimuli* are forthcoming. // to give the economy a dose of *stimulus* just when it was least needed // to prefer every possible *stimulation* to business investment // to seek high economic growth by risklessly *stimulating* its economy with fiscal expenditures // The monetary policy was over-*stimulating* the economy. // public spending provided a strong *stimulus* to economic activity // to import a *stimulus* to the economy through investment in the public sector // to avoid giving any extraneous *stimulus* to prices // to draw up an economic *stimulus* package // to offset the fall in the *stimulus* to growth coming from foreign demand // A general contractionary *impulse* is felt throughout the economy. // Favorable economic developments abroad provide the main *impetus* to Germany's upswing in exports which in turn is *stimulating* domestic firms' inclination to import. // Output has responded to the *impetus* given by fiscal and monetary policy. // It would give an added *impulse* to inflation. // The market acquired an *impetus* taking some rates beyond appropriate levels. // It will generate very limited *incentives* for encouraging exports. // [参考] a shot in the arm to stimulate business

shigekisaku 刺激策 stimulatory measure; measure to stimulate business ¶ a package of *stimulatory measures*

shigekizairyō 刺激材料 [市] incentives

shigen 資源 resources ¶ The Fund's *resources* were increasingly called upon by its member countries. // members' access to Fund *resources* to finance their temporary balance of payments needs // to redirect *resources* to the more productive sectors // to deplete the world of precious *resources* // the exploration and anticipated exploitation of the ocean beds' vast mineral *resources* // to devote more *resources* to these projects // Oil may be a finite *resource*, which we are squandering. // to allocate inherently limited *resources* to a variety of uses // The *resource* picture for the world as a whole is not discouraging. // the availability and longevity of natural *resources* // the physical depletion of natural *resources* // Needs are fully met from local *resources*. // to be beset by national differences in *resource* endowment // alternative energy *resources* to oil // *resource* exporting developing, *resource* importing, *resource* self-sufficient, and *resource* poor developing countries

物的資源 material resources; visible resources; physical resources

永久的資源 permanent resources

エネルギー資源 energy resources

非永久的資源 non-permanent resources

非再生資源 non-renewable resources

人的資源 human resources; man-power; invisible resources

かけがえのない資源 irreplaceable resources

金融資源 financial resources

国家資源 national resources

未開発資源 undeveloped resources; untapped resources

未利用資源 unused (=untapped) resources

生産資源 productive resources

天然資源 natural resources (= wealth)

shigen'eikyūshuken 資源永久主権 permanent sovereignity over natural wealth and resources

shigengaikō 資源外交 diplomacy on resources

shigenhaibun 資源配分 resources allocation ¶ the efficiency and planning of *resources allocation* // *allocation* of existing capital *resources*

shigenhoyūkoku 資源保有国 resource-rich country

shigenkaihatsu 資源開発 development of resources; tapping of resources

shigenkaisei 資源回生 resources recovery; recycling of resources

shigenkikin 資源飢饉 famine of resources

shigenkōkyūshuken 資源恒久主権 permanent sovereignty over natural wealth and resources

shigennokokatsu 資源の枯渇 exhaustion of resources

shigenriyō 資源利用 resource utilization

shigensetsuyaku 資源節約 resource conservation; resource saving

shigentekiseihaibun 資源適正配分 optimum allocation of resources; reasonable distribution of resources

shigoto 仕事 work; job ¶ These shutdowns will throw 2,000 men out of *work*. // to manage to duck *work* and live on the public dole // These industrial investments created some 300 new *jobs*. // These projects offer new opportunities for skilled *work*. // Many wives *work* in low-paying *jobs*. // the creation of 100,000 *jobs* in four years at Fl.100,000 per *job*

shigotobetsuchingin 仕事別賃金 wages by jobs

shigotochūdoku 仕事中毒 →働き中毒

shigotonoshikumisōtenkenkaizen 仕事の仕組み総点検・改善 system inspection and improvement program; SIP

shihai 支配 domination ¶ to join the ranks of advanced nations and escape foreign politico-economic *domination*

shihan 市販 marketing ¶ to *market* VTRs in the U.S.

shihankeiro 市販経路 marketing channel

shihanki 四半期 quarter (of the year) ¶ the first, second, third, or fourth *quarter* of a calendar or fiscal year

shiharai 支払い payment; defrayment; disbursement ¶ wage and salary *payments* // the balance of external *payments* // to make and receive the *payment* of $50 in cash for it // the amount *defrayed* for the expense // "prompt", "delayed", or "slow" *payments,* or "no complaints" made about *payments*

shiharaibashohenkō 支払場所変更 change of the place for payment

shiharaibi 支払日 date of payment

shiharaichi 支払地 place of payment; domicile

shiharaichōka 支払超過 net payment; excess payment (over receipt) ¶ Treasury accounts with the public showed a *net payment* of ¥123 million.

shiharaidairinin 支払代理人(国債 の) paying agent (for government bonds)

shiharaidaka 支払高 amount paid; disbursement

shiharaidenpyō 支払伝票 debit slip; payment slip (=ticket)

shiharaienki 支払延期 deferment of payment

shiharaifunō 支払不能 insolvency ¶ the number of cases of business *insolvency* // *insolvents* or *insolvent*

companies // to become *insolvent*

経済的支払不能 economic insolvency

金融的支払不能 financial insolvency

強制的支払不能 involuntary insolvency

任意(的)支払不能 voluntary insolvency

shiharaihoshō 支払保証 certification of payment

shiharaihoshōginkō 支払保証銀行 certifying bank

shiharaihoshōkogitte 支払保証小切手 certified check

shiharaijōken 支払条件 terms and conditions of payment; terms of payment; payment terms

shiharaijunbikin 支払準備金 reserve fund for payment; payment reserve; cash reserve

shiharaijunbiritsu 支払準備率 required reserve percentage; mandatory reserve requirement; ratio of cash reserves to deposits; required reserve requirement; reserve ratio ¶ The *required reserve percentages* against demand deposits may be changed separately by deposit category alone or by depsit category and class of bank. // the differential in the level and range of demand deposit *reserve ratios* for reserve city banks as compared with country banks // to fix and change the *ratios* // the *ratios required* of net *demand deposits* // The effective minimum *reserves* for *demand deposits* are set at 15 percent. // The *ratios required* of country member banks range from 7 to 14 percent against net *demand deposits.* // the authority to vary the *required* *reserve ratios* of the member banks // to establish member bank *ratios of reserve cash to deposit* liabilities, within a range fixed by statute // to determine for each of these bank classes a graduation in *reserve ratios* up to a maximum falling within the statutory limits // These supervisors vary the *ratios of required reserves.* // The mandatory *reserve requirements* both on the stock and on the float of bank deposits would be inceased by ½.

shiharaijunbiseido 支払準備制度 system of (legal minimum) reserve (deposit) requirement ¶ The *reserve requirements* of member banks against the net demand deposits shall be graduated. // the liabilities of member banks to be classed as deposits subject to a *reserve requirement* // an increase in the *minimum reserves* for demand *deposits* from 10 percent to 15 percent

shiharaijunbishisan 支払準備資産 reserve requirement asset

shiharaikawase 支払為替 bill payable

振出地支払為替 foreign bill payable

自国支払為替 home bill payable

通貨支払為替 currency bill payable

shiharaikanjō 支払勘定 account payable

shiharaikanjōdate 支払勘定建 giving quotation

shiharaikeiyaku 支払契約 contract del credere; del credere contract

shiharaikigen 支払期限 due date for payment; maturity

shiharaikigenkeika 支払期限経過 overdue ¶ an *overdue* loan

shiharaikijitsu 支払期日 date of payment

shiharaikijitsuheikinhō 支払期日平均法 equalization of payment

shiharaikogitte 支払小切手 certified check

shiharaikurinobe 支払繰延べ deferment of payment; postponement of payment; deferred payment; payment deferral

shiharaikyōtei 支払協定 payments agreement

shiharaikyozetsu 支払拒絶 repudiation; protest; nonpayment ¶ to *repudiate* some or all of its foreign indebtedness // loans which are clearly uncollectable, such as those that have been *repudiated* by a country

shiharaikyozetsukogitte 支払拒絶小切手 protested check

shiharaimeirei 支払命令 order for payment; draft

shiharainin 支払人 payer; drawee

shiharainōryoku 支払能力 solvency; financial ability; ability to pay ¶ institutions of recognized *solvency* // to seriously jeopardize the *solvency* of the corporation

shiharairishi 支払利子 interest expense

shiharairisokuhiritsu 支払利息比率 ratio of interest expenses to interest-bearing liabilities

shiharaisaiken 支払債券 guaranteed bond

shiharaiseikyū 支払請求 demand for payment

shiharaishōdaku 支払承諾 acceptance and guarantee

shiharaishōdakumikaeri 支払承諾見返 customer's liability for acceptance and guarantee

shiharaishudan 支払手段 means of payment; payment means; payment media

内国支払手段 domestic means of payment

対外支払手段 foreign means of payment

shiharaitegata 支払手形 bill payable; note payable

shiharaiteishi 支払停止 suspension of payment; moratorium; bank suspension

shiharaiteishitsūchi 支払停止通知 stop-payment order

shiharaitesūryō 支払手数料 del credere commission

shiharaiwaribikiryō 支払割引料 discount paid

shiharaiwatashi 支払渡し documents against payment; D.P.

shiharaiwatashikawase 支払渡為替 documents against payment; D/A bill

shiharaiyakkan 支払約款 promise-to-pay clause

shiharaiyūyo 支払猶予 delay of payment (of money due); postponement of payment; grace; indulgence; moratorium ¶ →モラトリアム

shiharaiyūyokikan 支払猶予期間 period of grace; days of grace; grace period ¶ to give a *day's grace* // with the *grace of* three *years* // The previously typical *grace periods* of two to three years before amortization payments were supplanted by those of four to five years.

shiharaiyūyorei 支払猶予令 moratorium ¶ Creditor banks agreed to a request for a 90-day *moratorium* on principal payments. // a 180 day extension of principal payments *moratorium* on public sector foreign debt // →モラトリアム

shiharaizatsurisoku 支払雑利息 miscellaneous interest paid

shiharaizumi 支払済み paid ¶ a *paid* check

shiharaizumikogitte 支払済小切手 canceled check; paid check

shihei 紙幣 paper money; paper currency; bank note; note; bill ¶ to issue and withdraw *bank notes* // the face, obverse, or front; and back or reverse of a *bank note* // new or crisp *notes,* and old but fit *notes* // damaged, mutilated, worn-out *notes* defiled or soiled *notes* // unfit and retired *notes*

不換紙幣 inconvertible note

贋造紙幣 counterfeit note

無準備紙幣 fiduciary note

shiheihakkō 紙幣発行 note-issue

shiheihakkōginkō 紙幣発行銀行 bank of issue; issuing bank; issue bank

shiheihakkōken 紙幣発行権 right of issue

shiheihon'i 紙幣本位 paper standard

shiheiranpatsu 紙幣乱発 excessive note-issue

shiheiryūtsūdaka 紙幣流通高 note circulation ¶ bank *notes in circulation*

shihon 資本 capital stock; capital; stockholders' equity; owner's equity; funds ¶ The authorized *capital* consists of 100,000 shares of the par value of $ 100,000 or a total $ 10,000,000. // a company with a *capital* of $5 million // to increase or decrease the *capital* // to redeem (＝repatriate) a *capital* invested

安全資本 security capital

募入資本 subscribed capital

募集資本　issued capital
物的資本　physical capital
長期資本　long-term capital
独占資金　monopoly capital
営業資本　operating capital; working capital
不変資本　constant capital
不利用資本　unused capital
不生産(的)資本　unproductive capital; dead capital
外部資本　external capital; borrowed capital; outside capital
銀行営業資本　banking capital
擬制資本　fictitious capital; watered capital
発行(済)資本　issued capital; subscribed capital; outstanding capital
払込(済)資本　paid-up capital; paid-in capital
避難資本　→逃避資本
自己資本　owned capital; own capital; net worth
人的資本　human capital
実物資本　real capital
自由資本　free capital
受権資本　authorized capital
株主資本　owner's capital
株式資本　equity capital
可変資本　variable capital
借入資本　borrowed capital
貸付資本　loan capital
過少資本　excessively small capital
活動資本　active capital
金銭資本　money capital
金融資本　financial capital
危険(負担)資本　risk capital; venture capital
国際資本　international capital
期首資本　initial capital
国家資本　state capital
固定資本　fixed capital
高利貸資本　usury capital

公称資本　authorized capital; nominal capital
共同資本　joint capital
未発行資本　unissued capital
未払込資本　unpaid capital; uncalled capital
民間資本　private capital
民族資本　national capital
水増し資本　watered capital
無形資本　immaterial capital
利子を生む資本　interest-bearing capital
流動資本　floating capital; liquid capital; circulating capital
産業資本　industrial capital
生産的資本　productive capital
生存資本　subsistence capital
社会資本　social capital
社会的間接資本　social overhead capital; (social) infrastructure
使用資本　employed capital
商業資本　commercial capital
自然資本　natural capital
他人資本　borrowed capital; outside capital
短期資本　short-term capital
他人資本　borrowed capital; outside capital
逃避資本　flight capital; refugee capital ¶ the recent influx of Italian *flight capital* on the national currency
投下資本　invested capital
凍結資本　locked-in capital
運転資本　working capital; operating capital
遊休資本　unemployed capital

shihonchikuseki 資本蓄積　accumulation of capital; capital accumulation

shihonchōsei 資本調整　capital control and adjustment

shihondōin 資本動員　capital mobilization

shihonfusaihiritsu 資本負債比率
net worth to debts ratio; capital and
liabilities ratio

shihongenkaikōritsu 資本限界効率
marginal efficiency of capital

shihongenmōhikiate 資本減耗引当
capital consumption allowance

shihongenmōhikiatekin 資本減耗
引当金 provision for the consumption of fixed capital

shihonhōfukoku 資本豊富国 capital rich country

shihon'idō 資本移動 capital flow;
capital movement; migration of capital ¶ the countries of origin and
the host countries of international
migration of capital // *Capital flows*
were reversed. // to encourage *capital* to *flow* from Germany to Belgium // to suffer from volatility of
capital movements between the dollar and the Deutsche Mark, which
are determined by market confidence // *Capital movements* by enterprises and individuals closed with
a deficit of BF. 1.7 milliard.

shihonjiyūka 資本自由化 liberalization of capital transactions

shihonjōyokin 資本剰余金 capital
surplus

shihonjōyokinkeisansho 資本剰余
金計算書 capital surplus statement

shihonjunbikin 資本準備金 capital reserve

shihonjunkan 資本循環 circulation of capital

shihonka 資本化 capitalization ¶
capitalization of income

shihonka 資本家 capitalist; financier

shihonkadai 資本過大 overcapitalization

shihonkaishūkikan 資本回収期間
pay-out period

shihonkaitenritsu 資本回転率
turnover ratio of capital
使用総資本回転率 turnover ratio of
total liabilities and net worth

shihonkanjōhōkokusho 資本勘定
報告書 capital statement

shihonkazei 資本課税 capital levy

shihonkeisei 資本形成 capital formation ¶ Inflation has depressed
business *capital formation*.

shihonkeiseikanjyō 資本形成勘定
gross saving and capital formation
account

shihonkangenkachi 資本還元価値
capitalized value

shihonkin 資本金 capital; capital
stock; capitalization ¶ a company
with *capital* of ¥100 million, or
capitalized at ¥100 million // →資本

shihonkingaku 資本金額 capitalization value ¶ companies with
capitalization value of more than 1
billion yen

shihonkinkanjō 資本金勘定 capital account

shihonkinriekiritsu 資本金利益率
ratio of net income to common
stock

shihonkōsei 資本構成 capital composition; capital structure

shihonkoteihiritsu 資本固定比率
net worth to fixed capital ratio

shihonkumiire 資本組入れ recap-
italization; capital incorporation;
capitalization; conversion into capital stock

shihonnonagare 資本の流れ capital inflow (=influx) ¶ The *inflow of*
private *capital* increased.

shihonnogenkaikōritsu 資本の限
界効率 marginal efficiency of capi-

tal

shihonnogōdō 資本の合同 pooling of capital

shihonnohiidōsei 資本の非移動性 immobility of capital

shihonnoidō 資本の移動 migration of capital

shihonnokaininkikan 資本の懐妊期間 gestation period of capital

shihonnokokusairyūtsū 資本の国際流通 international flow of capital

shihonriekiritsu 資本利益率 ratio of profit to capital

shihonritokusonshitsu 資本利得・損失 capital gain (or loss)

shihonrōdōhiritsu 資本労働比率 capital labor ratio

shihonrōdōryokuidō 資本労働力移動 capital and labor movement ¶ liberalization of *capital and labor movement*

shihonsanka 資本参加 capital participation; equity participation ¶ The way is opened for *equity participation* by foreign banks in domestic financial institutions. // banks created with foreign *participation* // [参考] to take equity in Filipino financial institutions

shihonsanshutsuryōhiritsu 資本産出量比率 capital-output ratio

shihonshijō 資本市場 capital market ¶ to access the *capital markets* at the finest rates possible // a country whose *capital markets* are rudimentary // The government drew on the long-term *capital markets* for $2 billion of funds. // The *capital market* was subjected to steadily increasing pressures. // proceeds of *capital market* financings

長期資本市場 long-term capital market

国際資本市場 international capital market

短期資本市場 short-term capital market

shihonshijōrimawari 資本市場利回り capital-market yields

shihonshishutsu 資本支出 capital outlay; capital expenditure

shihonshōhi 資本消費 capital consumption

shihonshotokuhiritsu 資本・所得比率 capital income ratio

shihonshugi 資本主義 capitalism

経営者資本主義 managerial capitalism

国家独占資本主義 state monopoly capitalism

国家資本主義 state capitalism

労働者資本主義 labor capitalism

shihonshūyakudo 資本集約度 capital intensity; capital labor ratio ¶ industry of high *capital intensity*

shihonshūyakuteki 資本集約的 capital intensive ¶ the establishment of *capital-intensive* industries and use of *capital-intensive* techniques

shihonshūyakutekikōgyōhin 資本集約的工業品 capital intensive industrial products

shihonsōbiritsu 資本装備率 capital equipment ratio; tangible fixed assets per regular employee; capital-labor ratio; capital intensity

shihonsutokkuchōseigenri 資本ストック調整原理 capital stock adjustment principle

shihonteikei 資本提携 capital tie-up

shihontōhi 資本逃避 capital exodus; capital refuge; capital flight ¶ Short-term *capital flight* was virtually arrested.

shihontokeieinobunri 資本と経営 の分離 separation between capital and administration

shihontorihiki 資本取引 capital transaction

shihontorihikinojiyūka 資本取引 の自由化 liberalization of capital transactions

shihon'yojōkoku 資本余剰国 capital surplus country (=nation) ¶ the *capital surplus* oil exporting *nations*

shihon'yushutsu 資本輸出 export of capital; capital export

shihon'yushutsukoku 資本輸出国 countries having deficit in capital transactions

shihonzai 資本財 auxiliary capital; capital goods

shihonzei 資本税 capital levy; capital stock tax

shihonzōka 資本増加 capital increment; capital appreciation

shihyō 指標 indicator; index; measure ¶ A cyclical recovery has been signalled by various economic *indicators*. // Most other *indicators* show a bleak picture. // Economic *indicators* are pointing downwards in almost all sectors. // The index of short-leading *indicators* looking ahead an average of five months fell. // The index of coincident *indicators* — pointing to current activity — dropped. // The index of lagging *indicators* — an average of eleven months behind the turning point — fell. // broad fluctuations in comprehensive *measures* of economic activity // a forward-looking *indicator* to point to the likely rate of growth of private credit demand // the longer leading *indicator* generally foreshadows eco-

nomic activity of about a year // Two sets of economic *indicators* are showing amber-to-green. // a key *indicator* for the operation of monetary policy // There are merely rough *indicators* of the absolute state of poverty. // the simple most valued *indicator* of business to come

物的指標 physical indicator

遅行指標 lagging indicator

福祉指標 welfare indicator

一致指標 coinciding indicator; coincidence indicator; coinciding indicator

景気指標 business indicator; business barometer

政策指標 indicator of policy; policy indicator ¶ The central-bank money supply, the Bundesbank's main monetary *policy indicator,* has been growing less strongly.

先行(=先駆)指標 leading indicator

社会指標 social indicator

早期警戒指標 early warning indicator

統計指標 statistical indicator

shihyōmeigara 指標銘柄 bellwether (issue); benchmark (issue) ¶ Coupon issue prices rose 1/32 to 1/8, with the *bellwether* 12 percent bonds of 2013 advancing 1/8 to 95-15/16. // The yield of *benchmark* 7.5 percent 10-year government bonds due 1993 rose to a high of 7.530 percent.

shihyōten 指標点 indicator point

shiire 仕入 purchase; buying-in; laying in stock

shiirechō 仕入帳 purchase book

shiiredaka 仕入高 amount of goods laid in stock; amount of goods purchased

shiiregenka 仕入原価 buying (= purchase) cost; prime cost; original cost; first cost; purchase cost

shiirehin 仕入品　stock in trade

shiiremodoshidaka 仕入戻し高　purchases returns

shiirenebikidaka 仕入値引高　purchases allowances

shiirenedan 仕入値段　cost price; purchasing price

shiiresaki 仕入先　supplyer vendor; seller; source of supply

shiiresakimaebaraidaikin 仕入先前払代金　deposits paid to trade creditors; advances on accounts of sellers

shiiresakimotochō 仕入先元帳　purchase ledger

shiireshiwakechō 仕入仕訳帳　purchase journal

shiirewaribikidaka 仕入割引高　purchases discounts

shiji 支持　support ¶ The main *support* to activity came from brisk domestic demand. // major elements of continuing *support* to general business activity // international flanking *support* to adequate action // to *support* the peseta exchange rate by artificial means

shijikakaku 支持価格　supported price

shijisuijun 支持水準　Support level ¶ Sellers withdrew at the important 680-point *support level*.

shijō 市場　market; market-place; mart; exchange ¶ to place on the *market* // to bring to the *market* // to come into the *market* // to find a *market* for... // to extend the *market* // *Markets* for copper strengthened. // The tending for prices to increase on the domestic *market* intesified. // The *market* remains bearish. // *Markets* for these products will retain the buoyancy characteristic of recent years. // *Markets* have become more strongly competitive. // The developing world constitutes an important and growing *market* for the exports of industrial nations. // The Arabian Gulf states are setting up their own localized capital *market*. // The company is looking to new *markets* in Asia for its rising production of lead. // The aggressive return of the USSR to world grain *markets* is boosting the price of wheat. // Individuals and firms have equal access to the capital *market*. // Access to the *market* was open to a large variety of borrowers. // Some producers are denied competitive access to expanding *markets*. // The housing *market* was still dominated by a large overhang of unsold units. // Twenty millions dollars in bonds were raised in the *market-place*. // The Europeans and the Japanese are urged to open more of their *markets* to U.S. exports. // There are clearly defined and separate business and leisure *markets*. // The phrenetic nature of the gold *market* has tended to infect other *markets* to the detriment of normal *market* trading conditions. // The foreign exchange *market* is a world-wide, round-the-clock telephonic *market*. // building-up of broadly-based domestic *markets* products // The strain between supply and demand on the commodity *market* remained unchanged. // The housing *market* is still dominated by a large overhang of unsold units. // The stock *market* advanced to another peak. // The *market* recouped some of the losses to close a little above the day's low. // The *market* was higher at the start, turned mixed, then steadied and moved higher.

青空市場 bazaar
物産市場 produce exchange
第一市場 first market
第二市場 second market
独占市場 monopolistic market; market of monopoly
独占的競争市場 market of monopolistic competition
不完全競争市場 market of imperfect competition
外国市場 foreign market; overseas market; market abroad
(外国)為替市場 (foreign) exchange market
現物市場 spot market
発行市場 issue market; primary market
はめ込み市場 placement market
直物市場 spot market
自由市場 free market
海外市場 overseas market
完全競争市場 perfect competitive market; market of perfect competition
寡占市場 oligopolistic market
起債市場 bond flotation market
公開市場 open market; market overt
国内市場 domestic market; home market; markets at home
国際金融市場 international financial market; international banking market; international money market
顧客市場 negotiated market
コール市場 call (money) market
公社債市場 bond market
小売市場 retail market

共同市場 common market
競争市場 competitive market
求人市場 job market
卸売市場 wholesale market
連続市場 continuous market
労働市場 labor market
流通市場 trading market; secondary market; distribution sector; wholesalers' and retailers' level
債券市場 bond market
先物市場 futures market
世界市場 world market
資本市場 capital market
商品市場 commodity market
証券市場 securities market
大衆消費市場 mass (consumption) market
短期金融市場 (short-term) money market; short-term credit market
短資市場 call market; short-term credit market
手形市場 commercial paper market; bills market
定期商品市場 futures market for commodities
投資市場 investment market; capital market
売手市場 seller's market
割引市場 discount market
若者市場 youth market
闇市場 black market
ユーロ金融市場 Euro-currency banking market

shijōchiiki 市場地域 market area
shijōchokkanryoku 市場直感力 market instinct
shijōchōsa 市場調査 market survey; market research
shijōchōsahi 市場調査費 expenses for market research
shijōdaiichibu 市場第一部 [日・市] First Section of the (Tokyo) Stock Exchange

shijōdainibu 市場第二部 ［日・市］ Second Section of the (Tokyo) Stock Exchange

shijōdankai 市場段階 marketing level; stage of marketing

shijōgaizaika 市場外在荷 invisible supply

shijōgenri 市場原理 market mechanism; market forces; free market process; market discipline ¶ a free functioning of the *market mechanism* // the effective utilization of *market forces* // the equalization of rate of return, wages and prices by the *market mechanism* // to leave the *forces of market* largely unobstructed // to allow *market forces* to determine where the rate should be // to allow the rate to move in response to *market forces* // The exchange rate of the dollar was devalued by *market forces*.

shijōheisa 市場閉鎖 market closure

shijōkachi 市場価値 market value ¶ The surtax will distort the true *market value* of the dollar. // redemption of bonds at *market value*

shijōkakaku 市場価格 →市価

shijōkeiyugaikokutōshi 市場経由外国投資 foreign investment via the stock market

shijōkeiyukabushiki 市場経由株式 stock purchased on the market; stock acquisition through the market

shijōkeizai 市場経済 market economy ¶ The *market economies* suffer most from opaqueness about the future. // This constitutes a departure from the self-regulatory principles of the *market economy*.

shijōkinō 市場機能 →市場原理

shijōkinri 市場金利 market rate of interest ¶ availability of credit at below-*market rates* of interest // →市中金利

shijōkinrirendōgatayokinshōsho 市場金利連動型預金証書 money market certificate; MMC

shijōkōdō 市場行動 market behavior

shijōkōdōsetsu 市場行動説 theory of market behavior

shijōkonran 市場混乱 market disruption

shijōkyōtei 市場協定 market-sharing arrangement

shijōmukenokeizai 市場向けの経済 market-directed economy

shijōnaibuyōin 市場内部要因 technical factor; internal market forces ¶ *Technical factors* may have aided the market's firming. // The upswing stemmed largely from *internal market forces* after the decline of the past several weeks.

shijōninki 市場人気 market psychology; market sentiment ¶ *Market psychology* responsible for the rise of the yen subsided. // *Market sentiment* became more positive following a series of anti-inflation measures. // *Market sentiment* toward the dollar remained very bearish. // These developments gave a boost to *market sentiment*.

shijōnoanteisei 市場の安定性 market stability

shijōokaitakusuru 市場を開拓する cultivate (=exploit; develop) the market

shijōriritsu 市場利率 market rate

shijōsaibunka 市場細分化 market segmentation

shijōsaikō 市場最高 all-time high;

historical high ¶ to record an *all-time high* of 92 percent

shijōsannyu 市場参入 market entry ¶ advertising facilitates *market entry* for new brands // →参入

shijōsei 市場性 marketability; salability ¶ to be *salable* under ordinary circumstances with reasonable promptness at fair value

shijōseinakiyūkashōken 市場性なき有価証券 non-negotiable securities; non-marketable securities

shijōseisan 市場生産 market production

shijōseishōken 市場性証券 marketable issue

shijosenkyoritsu 市場占拠率 →市場占有率

shijōsen'yūritsu 市場占有率 share; maket share; share in the market ¶ This forecast implies gains in *market shares*. // The downward trend in commercial banks' *market share* of lending business came to a halt. // Their *share* of aggregate loans is 12 percent. // a drive to expand its *market share* // to recapture their odd *market shares* and gain a large *share* of the American *market* // The *share of* the international *market* captured by Italian products went up from 5.9 to 6%. // Italy regained a good part of the *share* in world *markets* that it had lost. // a continued steady erosion in foreign banks' *share of* the loan *market*

shijōshihai 市場支配 (dominant) market control; control over the market

shijōshihairyoku 市場支配力 market power ¶ The company increased its *market power* through industry concentration.

shijōshinri 市場心理 → 市場人気

shijōshisatsudan 市場視察団 market survey mission

shijōsōba 市場相場 market rate; going market price; market quotation; price in the market ¶ *quotations on* commodity *markets* // commodity *market quotations* // commodity *prices in the market* // evaluation at the *going market price*

shijōsōsa 市場操作 market operation; market manipulation ¶ *market operations* in bills // securities *market operations* // buying *operations in the market* // The floating yen is being kept undervalued by *market manipulation* from the Bank of Japan. // The exchange rate is kept high by *market manipulation* from the central bank.

shijōsuji 市場筋 market participants; market sources

shijōwaribikibuai 市場割引歩合 market discount rate

shijōyōin 市場要因 market factor; market force ¶ the seven organic *market factors* requiring due consideration in orderly market operations // to achieve policy objectives through the ordinary *market forces*, i.e., influencing supply or demand // to allow the yen rate to move in response to *market forces*

shijōzaika 市場在荷 visible supply

shijōzaiko 市場在庫 visible stock

shijūtekikōsai 死重的公債 deadweight debt

shika 市価 market price; marketable price; current price; prevailing price ¶ to force up, raise, or lower the *market price* for the article

shikachūmon 市価注文 market order; open order

shikahendō 市価変動 market fluctuation

shikahendōjōkō 市価変動条項 fluctuation clause

shikakarihin 仕掛品 work in process; goods in process; partly-finished goods

shikakarihinkurikoshidaka 仕掛品繰越高 inventory of work in process at the beginning of period

shikakarihinmotochō 仕掛品元帳 work in process ledger

shikakōtō 市価高騰 soaring of market prices ¶ →物価

shikakugizuke 市価釘付 pegging of prices

shikakukyū 資格給 wages for job qualification

shikarieki 市価利益 market return

shikashōkan 市価償還 redemption at market value

shikateiraku 市価低落 sagging of market prices ¶ →物価

shikenchōsa 試験調査 pilot test; pilot survey

shikenhatsubai 試験発売 test marketing

shikenkōjō 試験工場 pilot factory (=plant)

shikennōjō 試験農場 pilot farm

shikentekiseisan 試験的生産 pilot production; experimental production

shiki 士気 morale ¶ *Morale* among many of the employees is scraping bottom.

shikichi 敷地 site; lot
建築敷地 building site; building lot
工場敷地 factory site; plant site ¶ →用地

shikichōsa 士気調査 morale survey

shikihō 四季報 quarterly (report)

shikikin 敷金 deposit; caution-money; [参考] foregift; premium for lease

shikikingire 敷金切れ no deposit

shikin 資金 funds; capital; financial resource ¶ International capital markets are well supplied with *funds*. // The *funds* for capital purposes are sometimes obtained through liquidation of excess inventories. // to raise *funds* and appropriate them for a project // to channel *funds* from abroad towards financing productive activity // to reconstruct the energy sector through the injection of public *funds* // The considerable volume of liquid *funds* placed internationally with the commercial banking system. // a government-*funded* independent research body. // business-*funded* projects // The *funding* required for the commission's work would be modest. // The facilities were funded with *resources* borrowed by the Fund.

安定資金 stabilization funds
蓄積資金 accumulated funds
長期資金 long-term funds
営農資金 farming funds; farm management funds
外貨資金 foreign currency funds
外国資金 foreign capital
減産資金 funds for production curtailment; fund demand relating to production cutbacks
罷業資金 strike funds
非流動資金 illiquid funds
維持資金 maintenance funds; upkeep funds
事業資金 enterprise funds
自己資金 owned funds; own funds; funds on (=in) hand

準備資金　reserve funds
貸出資金　lendable funds; loanable funds
緊急資金　urgent funds
季節的資金　seasonal funds
救済資金　relief funds
農業資金　cultivation funds
見返り資金　counterpart funds
民間資金　private funds
流動資金　liquid funds
政府資金　government funds
設備資金　plant and equipment funds
新規コール資金　fresh (call) money
即時資金　immediate funds
手許資金　funds on (=in) hand
投資資金　investment funds
運転資金　working funds; operating funds
財政資金　government funds; Treasury funds

shikinchōsei 資金調整　fund adjustment; fund control

shikinchōtatsu 資金調達　raising of funds; fund raising; raising of money; obtainment of funds; funding; financing; finance; funding ¶ to arrange for *raising* needed *funds* on the most desirable // how *funds* have been *procured* for a business // Foreign depositors provided the bulk of the bank's *funding* in recent month. // banks *funding* capabilities // the Treasury's *funding* requirements for the first quarter // the Treasury *financing* in the February refunding // to *finance* a new investment through sale of fresh debt // the lower cost of debt *finance* as compared with equity *finance* // Borrowers have a wider choice of methods of *fund-raising*. // Argentina's ability to *raise money* in the Euromarket on favorable terms could be impaired. // The government is allowed to *raise* over Esc.91 billion in internal and external loans to meet the budget deficit. // The margin between the return on lending and the cost of *obtaining funds* has narrowed. // The supplementary budget is designed to help *fund* the yen 2,500 billion package of stimulatory measures. // stable and sufficient access to long-term yen *funding*

shikinchōtatsukosuto 資金調達コスト　cost of procuring money; cost of raising funds; fund cost

shikinchōtatsuryoku 資金調達力　fund raising capacity

shikinfusoku 資金不足　shortage of funds; fund shortage; financial deficit; funding gap ¶ to play the *funding gap* now filled by the 7.5 billion dollar goverment and commercial deal package

shikinfusokuzuki 資金不足月　month of seasonal tight money; month of seasonal monetary stringency; month of seasonal monetary tightening

shikingen 資金源　source of funds (=funding; finance); financial resources ¶ the best possible mix chosen from the available *sources of* external *finance* – whether loans, grants, or direct investment // to have sufficient access to *funds* from private *sources* // It has provided another major *source of funds* for local borrowers. // to tap a new *source of funds* for loans // Nonbank *sources* and uses *of funds* channeled through the market. // the single largest *source of* external *finance* to developing countries // The World Bank is now by far the largest single *source* of external *funding* for agriculture in the developing world.

shikinguri 資金繰り fund management; management of funds; fund position; liquidity position; reserve position; solvency ¶ the tight corporate *fund position* // easy *liquidity positions* of businesses // stringent *reserve positions* of banks // *Fund positions* of businesses were tight. // business feelings of tight *fund position*, or the sense of tightness of business *fund positions*

shikingurihanbō 資金繰繁忙 tight liquidity position of fund management

shikinhōshutsu 資金放出 release of funds

shikin'idō 資金移動 movement of funds; transfer of funds

shikin'idōten 資金移動点 transfer point

shikinjukyū 資金需給 supply and demand of funds

shikinjukyūkeikaku 資金需給計画 funds supply and demand program

shikinjukyūsetsu 資金需給説 loanable funds theory

shikinjunkankanjō 資金循環勘定 flow of funds (accounts); money flow ¶ to drastically alter the volume, direction, and terms of the *flow of funds* within and among national economies

shikinjuyō 資金需要 credit (= fund) requirement; funding need credit demand; fund demand ¶ Corporate *credit requirements* toward the year-end mounted. // inventory *credit requirement* // active *credit requirements* of smaller business for

expansive business purposes // to meet growing *requirements of funds* for the year-end // Private *credit demand* continued to clash with public *funding needs*. // The *demand for funds* is essentially calm. // The active *demand for funds* continued. // Business *demand for funds* in credit and equity markets was heavy. // active *demand for* loanable and investable *funds* // →借入需要

shikinkabi 資金化日 value date

shikinkafusoku 資金過不足 shortage and overage of funds; financial surplus and deficit

shikinkōritsu 資金効率 efficiency of fund operations

shikinkosuto 資金コスト cost of money; cost of funds ¶ higher *cost of funds* in the capital markets

shikinkyōkyū 資金供給 fund supply; funding ¶ the *supply* and demand of *funds* // a reduced *supply of funds* emanating from exchange-market intervention by the surplus countries // a program practically *funded* by the government to finance the search for new oil funds

shikinkyūshū 資金吸収 absorption of funds; fund collection

shikinmaewatashikanri 資金前渡官吏 accounting official with cash funds advanced

shikinnan 資金難 financial difficulty; short of funds; fund shortage

shikinnohongokusōkan 資金の本国送還 repatriation of funds; funds repatriation

shikinnokaiten 資金の回転 turnover of capital

shikinnokanryū 資金の還流 reflow of funds

shikinnougoki 資金の動き movement of funds ¶ *movements of funds* induced by frequent changes in expectations concerning the dollar

shikinpojishon 資金ポジション fund position; liquidity position ¶ the Bank's guidance for banks in the *liquidity position* // *fund position* guidance // →資金繰り

shikinryoku 資金力 financial ability; pecuniary ability

shikinshito 資金使途 purpose for funds; use of funds; fund employment ¶ the breakdown of assets by final *use of funds* // the analysis of how *funds* have been *employed*

shikintoriireatsuryoku 資金取入れ圧力 hastened intake of funds

shikintōsei 資金統制 fund control

shikin'ukewatashi 資金受渡し [市] delivery

shikin'unyōhyō 資金運用表 fund statement

shikin'unyōsōsa 資金運用操作 banking operation; fund operation

shikin'yūin 資金誘引 attracting funds; inducing capital

shikiri 仕切り partition; division; separation; invoice; settlement of accounts; [市] transaction on dealer's basis

shikiribaibai 仕切売買 [市] transaction on dealer's basis

shikirichō 仕切帳 invoice book

shikirichūmon 仕切注文 stop-order

shikirijō 仕切状 invoice

shikirirēto 仕切レート [外] provisional rate

shikisannyū 新規参入 new (=de nove) entry ¶ Advertising may deter new *entry* into the market.

shikkaichōsa 悉皆調査 complete

enumeration

shikkari しっかり firm; steady; strong ¶ The tone of the market was quite *firm*. // The market became *steady*. // Prices have been relatively *strong*. // The market *steadied* down. // Prices were *firming* down.

shikkarishōjō しっかり商状 steady market; steadiness; strong market

shikkenkabu 失権株 forfeited share

shikkō 失効 lapse; losing effect; invalidation; becoming null and void

shikkōbi 失効日 expiry date

shikkōhokenshōken 失効保険証券 lapsed policy

shikkōkabu 失効株 lapsed share

shikkōkeiyaku 失効契約 void contract

shikkōkikan 執行機関 executive organ

shikkōshōken 失効証券 nullified bond

shikkōsoshiki 執行組織 operating organization; executing organization

shikkōtsūka 失効通貨 invalid currency

shikō 指向 orientation ¶ Private consumption is heavily import-*oriented*. // The bank resolved to *orientate* monetary policy towards a gradual decline in the liquidity ratio. // *orientation* towards price raises // export-*oriented* economy // policy having a distinct medium-term *orientation* // the child-*oriented* market for goods and services, including some hospital facilities // to *orientate* economic policy towards balancing the external accounts // a shift to welfare-*orientated* national expenditure // defense-*oriented* industries // a welfare-*oriented* economy // an international financial service organization with strong retail *orientation* // [参考] The U.S. is directing its fiscal policy toward a reduction of the government deficit. // Government policy is geared to promote the direction of financial savings.

shikōgata 指向型 -oriented ¶ the thift to a welfare-*oriented* economy from the conditional growth-*oriented* one // The stock market advanced with export-*oriented* issues leading the way. // an independent and free-enterprise-*oriented* populace // export-*oriented* nations // →指向

shikōsakugo 試行錯誤 trial and error; learning ¶ to modify the fee by *trials and errors*

shikumi 仕組み setup ¶ The new product line fit logically into the marketing and management *setups*.

shikutsu 試掘 exploratory drilling; trial digging; prospect

shikyō 市況 tone of market; conditions of market; market conditions; market ¶ The *tone of* the *market* was generally quite firm. // the easier *conditions of* the *market* // *Market conditions* eased. // A firm *tone* reappeared in the *market*. // The commodity *market* operated smoothly. // There were from time to time stringencies in the *market*.
沈滞市況 depressed market; inactive market; stagnant market
鈍重市況 sluggish market
逼迫市況 stringent market; taut market; stiff market; tight market

¶ The *market* is *stringent*. // [参考] The market hardened.

shikyōchōsa 市況調査 market research

shikyōhinhanbai 試供品販売 approval sale

shikyōhōkoku 市況報告 market report

shikyōkaifuku 市況回復 market recovery; rally

shikyōkansan 市況閑散 quiet market; slack market ¶ The *market* is *quiet (= slack)*.

shikyōkappatsu 市況活発 brisk market; active market; animated market ¶ The *market* is *active (= brisk; animated)*.

shikyōsangyōkabu 市況産業株 cyclical stocks

shikyōshōhin 市況商品 market-leading commodities; sensitive commodities

shikyōtaisaku 市況対策 measures to support the market; price supporting measure; market counter-measure; action in coping with the market conditions

shimaigaisha 姉妹会社 sister company

shimaikikan 姉妹機関 sister institution

shimedashi 締め出し crowding-out ¶ Business requirements are *crowding out*. // personal demands being *crowded out* as corporate requirements mounted // Private borrowers are not being "*crowded out*" by high interest rates resulting from heavy government competition for credit. // The those government securities may *crowd out* private money demand. // → クラウディング・アウト

shimekiri 締切 [会] ruling-off

shiminkeiyaku 市民契約 civil contract

shiminseikatsu 市民生活 civil life

shimintekihankō 市民的反抗 civil disobedience

shimoki 下期 the second half of the year; latter half of the year; second half-year; latter half-year; second half; latter half ¶ in *the second half* of fiscal 1976

shimonkikan 諮問機関 consultative organization; advisory organization ¶ an *advisory organization* to the Finance Minister

shimuke 仕向け destination

shimukechiten 仕向地点 point of destination

shimukekō 仕向港 port of destination

shimukesōkinkawase 仕向送金為替 remittance abroad ¶ to draw a *remittance abroad*

shimuketen 仕向店 sending office

shinagire 品切れ out of stock; sold out ¶ to be *out of stock, sold out,* or exhausted

shinagiresōba 品切相場 famine price

shinario シナリオ scenario ¶ "the Growth *Scenario* to 1980" presented on 28/7 the Secretariat of the OECD.

shinausukabu 品薄株 scarce stock; narrow market securities

shinausunedan 品薄値段 scarcity price

shinchō 慎重 prudence ¶ The attitude to these borrowers has hardened as a matter of normal banking *prudence*.

shinchōnahikishime 慎重な引締め prudent restraint

shinchōnakanrishajunsoku 慎重

な管理者準則 prudent-man rule

shinchōnakanwa 慎重な緩和 prudent relaxation

shinchōnarakkan 慎重な楽観 cautious optimism; guarded optimism

shinchōnatōshinogensoku 慎重な投資の原則 prudent-man rule

shindanrūtin 診断ルーティン [コン] diagnostic routine

shindōriron 振動理論 oscillation theory

shindotōsei 進度統制 progress control

shingai 侵害 infringement; disturbance; violation

商標権侵害 trademark infringement

特許侵害 infringement of patent right

shingi 審議(予算の) deliberation ¶ budget new under *deliberation*

shingijutsukenkyūkaihatsu 新技術研究開発 research and development of new technology

shingō 信号 signal ¶ to give a clear *signal* for a general reduction in interest rates for domestic credits // The *signals* are set for expansion. // to hoist a *signal* of danger // to flash a danger *signal* // The Board *signaled* its intention by reducing the Federal funds rate.

shinise 老舗 shop of old standing; long established house; goodwill ¶ to sell the *goodwill*

shinjikētorōn シンジケート・ローン syndicat(ed) loan

shinjun 浸潤 saturation ¶ Amex Co. has largely *saturated* the market for high-income holders of credit cards.

shinkabu 新株 new share; new stock

shinkabuhakkōhi 新株発行費 new

share issuing expense

shinkabuhikiukeken 新株引受権 subscription right; stock purchase right; pre-emptive right

shinkabuochi 新株落ち ex new (allotment); new share off

shinkabutsuki 新株付き cum new; new share on

shinkaiteishigenkaihatsu 深海底 資源開発 deep sea-bed mining

shinkigakusotsurōdōryoku 新規学 卒労働力 new school graduates (= school-leavers) on the labor market

shinkihakkōshasai 新規発行社債 newly-issued (corporate) bond

shinkijikuriron 新機軸理論 theory of innovation

shinkikyūjin 新規求人 new employment offer; new job offer; new offer; new employment wanted

shinkin'yūchōsetsuhōshiki 新金融 調節方式 [英] new scheme for monetary controls; Competition and Credit Control ¶ The new *"Competition and Credit Control"* system of monetary regulation introduced from 1971. // the new freer *Competition and Credit Control* policy introduced in 1971

shinkiroku 新記録 new record; new high; record high; all-time high ¶ Output was at *record* rates. // mark a *new all-time high record* // to rise to a *record high* of 191 percent // to *renew the* (past) *record* // [参考] to exceed (top) the past peak // the shapest fall on record

shinkisaiyō 新規採用 (labor) recruiting; new hiring; recruitment ¶ Companies are extremely cautious in *recruiting* new employees. // a clamp-down on *recruiting* // *New hiring* remained unchanged at 24

workers per 1,000. // a halt to public service *recruitment* // [参考] Manufacturers added workers to their payrolls at the highest rate since June.

shinkisotsugyōsha 新規卒業者 school-leaver ¶ Including *school-leavers*, total unemployment fell by 6.8% of the labor force. // → 新卒者

shinkiyushutsuseiyaku 新規輸出成 約 new export contracts

shinkōchūnoseisankatsudō 進行中 の生産活動 carry-on-activity

shinkōkoku 新興国 young country

shinkoku 申告 declaration; notice; return
青色申告 [日] blue-form return
原産地申告 declaration of origin
確定申告 final return
庫入申告 declaration for warehousing
所得申告 income return
所得税申告 income tax return
積出し申告 declaration for shipping
積戻し申告 declaration for reshipment
輸入申告 import declaration; notice of import
輸出申告 export declaration; notice of export
予定申告 provisional return

shinkokudosōgōkaihatsukeikaku 新国土総合開発計画 new overall national land development program

shinkokunōzei 申告納税 tax payment by self-assessment

shinkokusaikeizaichitsujo 新国際 経済秩序 New International Economic Order; NEO

shinkokusairaundo 新国際ラウンド New International Round; NIR

shinkokusha 申告者 reporter

shinkokushimekirikijitsu 申告締切期日 final date for filing; deadline for filing report

shinkokusho 申告書 declaration; notice; report; statement

貨物申告書 merchandise declaration

shinkokuyōshi 申告用紙 declaration form; return blank

shinkokuzei 申告税 taxes assessed by taxpayers' report

shinkutanku シンク・タンク think tank

shinne 新値 record price; new high ¶ to record or mark a *new high* // to hit a *new high*

shinnin 信認 confidence ¶ The *confidence* in the dollar had at times wavered. // to undermine consumers' *confidence* // loss of confidence // renewed *confidence* in the dollar // → コンフィデンス

shinnyūka 新入荷 new arrival

shinpatsusaishōka 新発債消化 sale of newly-issued bonds

shinpo 進歩 progress; advance ¶ Inventory adjustment is fully in *progress*. // The revival of business made marked *progress*. // disembodied technological *progress*

技術進歩 technological progress; advancement in technics

経済進歩 economic progress

shipuku 振幅 amplitude; magnitude of fluctuation

shinrai 信頼 faith; confidence ¶ Inflation undermined public *confidence* in financial assets. // Public *confidence* in the economic outlook was blighted by the virulent rise of prices. // *Confidence* in the dollar deteriorated both at home and abroad. // investors who have lost *faith* in the dollar // Oil industry *confidence* in government policy has been seriously eroded by recent decisions. // Foreign *confidence* in the Danish economy was waning markedly, and was to be restored. // significant erosion of public *confidence* in the banking system // Drastic cuts in public spending helped preserve foreign *confidence* in pound sterling. // the recovery of *confidence* in the pound sterling // an incipient loss of *confidence* in a currency // a return of *confidence* in the U.S. dollar // *Faith* in the Japanese economy limited the dollar's advance against the yen. // →コンフィデンス

shinraisei 信頼性 credibility ¶ Discrepancies between target and result lead to a loss of *credibility* of the published money-supply targets.

shinraiseikōgaku 信頼性工学 reliability engineering

shinrenpōshugi 新連邦主義 ［米］ New Federalism (of 1969)

shinrinkumiairengōkai 森林組合連合会 federation of forestry cooperatives

shinritekieikyō 心理的影響 psychological influence

shinritekikeikiriron 心理的景気論 psychological theory of business cycle

shinritekikōbōsen 心理的攻防線 psychological barrier ¶ The pound sterling has broken the *psychological barrier* of 2 dollars.

shinritekishotoku 心理的所得 psychic income

shinritekiyōin 心理的要因 psychological factor; psychological force

shinryoku 伸力 strength ¶ The

market lacks in *strength*. // The market increases *strength*.

shinsa 審査 screening; scrutiny ¶ to *screen* new lending applications // to be subject to a close, careful, and rigid *scrutiny* // to *scrutinize* keenly // Trading companies strengthened their *screening* of credit requests.

shinsakijun 審査選別基準 screening standard criteria for screening

shinsangyōtoshi 新産業都市 new industrial cities

shinsankin 新産金 newly mined gold

shinsashiryō 審査資料 data for credit examining

shinseijunbi 真正準備 true reserve

shinseishōhin 真正商品 genuine goods

shinseishōhinnoheikōyunyū 真正商品の並行輸入 parallel import of genuine goods

shinsetsujūtakuchakkōsū 新設住宅着工数 new housing starts; new residential construction starts

shinsetsukigyō 新設企業 newly established corporation

shinshanendo 新車年度 model year

shinshatōrokudaisū 新車登録台数 new car registration ¶ *New car registrations* numbered 96, 948, a rise of 34.08 %.

shinshikyōtei 紳士協定 gentlemen's (= gentleman's) agreement ¶ Six major industrial nations finalized a "*gentlemen's agreement*" on the terms for granting export credits to Third countries. // only under a non-legally binding *gentleman's agreement* reached last year // The bank has renewed unchanged for one year two *gentleman's agreements* on exchange-market operations.

shinshōkenhakkōsetsumeikai 新証券発行説明会 due diligence meeting

shinshukujōkō 伸縮条項 escalator (clause)

shinshukusei 伸縮性 flexibilty; resiliency; elasticity
　価格伸縮性 price flexibility
　構造的価格伸縮性 structural price flexibility

shinshutsu 進出 advance; penetration; inroad; intrusion ¶ Japanese industry *penetrated* deeply into foreign markets. // economic *penetration* of Indonesia // to make *inroads* into the American economic scene // Japanese economic *advance* in the form of investment in Europe // Compared with European companies, Japanese *advancement* in the United States is still relatively new and small. // The foreign banks made their *inroads* through competitive pricing. // The U.S. auto manufacturing industry realized capital *inroads* into Japan. // foreign banks' *penetration* of commercial lending markets in the U.S. // a closed market for foreign companies to *penetrate* // Motor-vehicle import *penetration* rose to a peak 25%. // [参考] The time was ripe for an American export push into Japan. // to protect trust banks and other segments of the financial industry from encroachments by other-types of financial institutions

shinsotsusha 新卒者 school-leaver; new school graduate ¶ the absorption of 41,470 previously unemployed *school-leavers* into the labor force

shintakane 新高値 new high; record high; all-time high; new high level; new high mark; high record price ¶ to hit (=record; mark; register) a *new high*

shintaku 信託 trust

便益信託 benefit trust

永続信託 perpetual trust

不動産信託 real estate trust

不法信託 illegal trust

議決権信託 voting trust

貸付信託 loan trust

金銭貸付信託 cash loan trust

金銭信託 money trust; money in trust

オープン型投資信託 open(-end) investment trust

証券投資信託 securities investment trust

担保付社債信託 mortgage debenture

特定金銭信託 specified money trust

取消不能信託 irrevocable trust

取消可能信託 revocable trust

投資信託 investment trust

遺言信託 testamentary trust

有価証券信託 securities trust; securities in trust

有価証券運用信託 securities operation trust

有期信託 limited trust

ユニット型投資信託 unit-(type) investment trust

shintakubutsu 信託物 trust; things in trust

shintakugaisha 信託会社 corporate fiduciary; trust company

shintakuginkō 信託銀行 trust bank; trust and banking company

shintakugyō 信託業 trust business

shintakukanjō 信託勘定 trust account

shintakukeiyaku 信託契約 trust ageement; indenture

shintakukeiyakusho 信託契約書 trust deed

shintakusha 信託者 fiduciant; truster

被信託者 trustee; fiduciary

shintakushōsho 信託証書 trust indenture; deed of trust; trust certificate

shintakuyokin 信託預金 trust deposit

shintakuzaisan 信託財産 trust assets; trust estate; trust property

shinten 進展 progress ¶ to avoid disruptions of international economic *progress*

shintō 浸透 permeation; pervasion; passing-through infiltration; trickling down; working through; spread; filtering (=passing) through ¶ a fuller *permeation* of effects // The effect *passed through* the economy. // The economy is *pervaded* with inflationary mood. // gradual *permeation* of the policy effect through the economy // quick *infiltration* of stringency in major sectors // The measures worked their way through into the economy. // to let wealth *trickle down* through layers of middlemen // to encourage the *penetration* of manufactured consumer goods into the region // slow *penetration* of American goods into the Japanese market // The policy may take a long time to *work through* properly to the balance of payments. // The measures *worked* their way *through* into the economy. // The recovery in activity has *spread* to most sectors. // Recent rises in commodity prices are beginning to *work* their way *through* to the retail level. // Higher costs for materials have *worked through* to output prices. // The anti-inflation measures are *working through* into economic performance. // Italy increased its *penetration* of foreign markets, especially in oil-exporting countries. // to restrict import *penetration*, that is, imports as a proportion of domestic consumption // Goods for which any significant market *penetration* is still quite limited. // Monetary policy had time to *work through* the economy. // Policy to keep recent oil price increases from *filtering through* to the rest of the economy. // Recent rises in commodity prices are beginning to *work* their way through to the retail level.

shin'yasune 新安値 new low; record low ¶ to register, mark, or reach a *new* or *record low*

shin'yō 信用 credit; confidence; reliance; reputation ¶ Outstanding *credit* of the banking system increased by 21%. // Total consumer *credit* outstanding amounted to $41 billion. // Business and consumer demands for *credit* slackened. // The expansion of bank *credit* has been accelerated. // to buy goods on *credit*, or to purchase for *credit* // high or good *credit* of a person // people's *confidence* in money // *reliance* on the correctness of figures // a high *reputation* of a great businessmen // →信認; コンフィデンス

長期信用 long-term credit
中期信用 medium-term credit; intermediate credit
不動産信用 real estate credit

銀行信用 bank credit
企業間信用 trade credit; intra-business credit; inter-enterprise credit intermediate credit
国内信用 local credit
紙券信用 paper credit
商業信用 commercial credit
消費者信用 consumer credit
証券市場信用 stock market credit
対物信用 real credit
対人信用 personal credit
短期信用 short-term credit
低金利信用 low-interest credit
追加信用 additional credit

shinyōben'eki 信用便益 credit facilities

shin'yōbōchō 信用膨張 credit expansion

shin'yōbunseki 信用分析 credit analysis

shin'yōchōsa 信用調査 credit investigation; credit analysis ¶ report on *credit investigation*

海外信用調査 overseas credit inquiry
国内信用調査 credit inquiry in Japan

shin'yōchōsetsushudan 信用調節手段 credit control techniques; credit control instrument (=device; tool; means; weapon)

shin'yōdo 信用度 credibility; credit standing; creditworthiness; credit status; confidence ¶ business of high *creditworthiness* // Their *creditworthiness* is badly strained. // The bank's excellent *credit standing* in the capital markets will not suffer. // different lending rates depending on market perceptions of borrowers' *creditworthiness* // The *confidence* of the international capital markets in the Bank is absolute. // to evaluate the *creditworthiness* of a potential borrower // the market perception of their *creditworthiness* // to support the *creditworthiness* of developing market // *Creditworthiness* considerations carry even more weight in the Eurobond market. // to wish to remain *creditworthy* for lending by private financial institutions // Some borrowers' *creditworthiness* has been upgraded. // the efforts of countries to safeguard their external *creditworthiness* // to restore Italy's international *creditworthiness* which had slumped at the height of the crisis // the system of country *creditworthiness* ratings // Loan demand from more *creditworthy* borrowers expanded. // rating of the *credit* standing of the company // to supplement the *credit* standing // The money-supply explosion undermined the *credibility* of the stability policy.

shin'yōfuan 信用不安 financial uncertainty; concern over the financial situation ¶ *financial uncertainty* in the U.S. banking sector triggered by Continental Illinois Corp.

shin'yōgai 信用買い margin buying; buying on margin; buying futures stocks; bull account ¶ Traders do about 60 percent of their *buying* on *margin*.

shin'yōgari 信用借り confidential debt; debt of honor; unsecured loan

shin'yōgashi 信用貸し credit loan; fiduciary loan; unsecured loan
短期信用貸し short credit

shin'yōgin'kō 信用銀行 credit bank

shin'yōhanbai 信用販売 conditional sale; time sale; installment sale

shin'yōhantei 信用判定 rating of credit standing; credit rating; (composite) credit appraisal

shin'yōhoken 信用保険 credit insurance; fidelity insurance; insurance of credit guarantee

shin'yōhoshō 信用保証 credit guarantee

shin'yōhoshojo 信用保証状 letter of guarantee; L/C

shin'yōhoshōkin 信用保証金 margin requirement

shin'yōhosokuseido 信用補足制度 system for supplement of credit standing

shin'yōjō 信用状 letter of credit ¶ to open or receive *letters of credit* for (=in favor of) companies, and advise the beneficiaries of the banker's confirmation thereof
確認信用状 confirmed credit
無確認信用状 unconfirmed credit
旅行(者)信用状 traveler's letter of credit
償還請求不許可信用状 without recourse credit
手形売買銀行不指定信用状 open credit; general credit
手形売買銀行指定信用状 restricted credit; special credit
取消不能信用状 irrevocable credit
取消可能信用状 revocable credit

shin'yōjōkaisetsuhoshōkin 信用状開設保証金 L/C margin money

shin'yōjōkaisetsutesūryō 信用状開設手数料 L/C opening charge (=fee)

shin'yōjōkakunintesūryō 信用状確認手数料 L/C confirmation charge (=fee)

shin'yōjōnosetsujukaisetsu 信用状の接受・開設 to receive or open a letter of credit

shin'yōjōtai 信用状態 credit standing; credit status ¶ The *credit-standing* of sound borrowers would probably gain if more complete data could be made available. // →信用度

shin'yōjōtōitsukisoku 信用状統一規則 Uniform Custom and Practice for Documentary Credits

shin'yōjunbi 信用準備 fiduciary reserve

shin'yōkakuzuke 信用格付け credit rating; grading of credit standing

shin'yōkinko 信用金庫 credit association

shin'yōkisei 信用規制 credit control; credit regulation ¶ The *credit control* on security purchases curbed a contemplated purchase of securities.

不動産信用規制 real estate credit control

一般信用規制 general credit control

量的信用規制 quantitative credit control

選別的信用規制 selective credit control

質的信用規制 qualitative credit control

証券市場信用規制 stock market credit control

shin'yōkumiai 信用組合 credit association; [英] credit union

shin'yōkyōdōkumiai 信用協同組合 credit cooperative

shin'yōkyōyo 信用供与 credit accommodation; credit extension; credit granting; provision of credit ¶ Their Bank's *credit accommodation* of any member is safely and reasonably extended. // to regulate the *extension of credit* for the purpose of carrying securities // Altogether the bank's *credit-granting* amounted to 826.4 transferable roubles. // The bank stepped up its *credit-granting* substantially, expanding it by 22%. // to be more liberal or more restrictive in *granting* new *credit* // The volume of *credits granted* rose by about one-third to $2.0 billion. // The bank *granted* its first-ever *credit* for a non-member country. // to regulate any and all *extensions* of *credit* // rapid growth in the *provision of credit* by the international capital markets // to *provide* both short- and long-term *credit accommodations* // to *provide credit* to countries for long periods

shin'yōkyōyogendo 信用供与限度 line of credit; credit line ¶ The bank often waives fees on unused *credit lines*. // This bank adopted a much tougher attitude towards commitment fees on the overdraft *lines* it extends to costomers.

shin'yōmeigara 信用銘柄 [市] stocks open to futures transactions; speculative stocks

shin'yōnoabeirabiriti 信用のアベイラビリティ credit availability ¶ → アベイラビリティ

shin'yōnōgyōkyōdōkumiairengō-kai 信用農業協同組合連合会 credit federation of agricultural cooperatives

shin'yōnosōzō 信用の創造 creation of credit; credit creation

shin'yōnoyokinsōshutsu 信用の預金創出 multiple creation of deposit; multiple deposit creation

shin'yōrisuku 信用リスク credit risk

shin'yōseido 信用制度 credit system ¶ to maintain and foster the *credit system*

shin'yōshōkaisaki 信用照会先 trade reference

shin'yōshōken 信用証券 credit instrument

shin'yōshūshuku 信用収縮 credit contraction

shin'yōshusshi 信用出資 fiduciary contribution

shin'yōsōzō 信用創造 credit creation ¶ The banks' facilities for recourse to the central bank represent a *credit creation* potential more than sufficient to satisfy private and public credit demand.

shin'yōsōzōkinō 信用創造機能 credit creating (function) ¶ The relatively low-cost funds generated through the *credit-creating function* of banks.

shin'yōtegata 信用手形 credit bill; unsecured bill

shin'yōtorihiki 信用取引 sale on credit; [市] margin transaction; stock margin trading; futures transaction ¶ Traders do about 60 percent of their buying on *margin*.

shin'yōtorihikikisei 信用取引規制 regulation of margin trading activities; restrictive measures on stock margin trading

shin'yōtsūka 信用通貨 credit currency

shin'yōuri 信用売り short sale; short selling; bear account ¶ to sell short // to *sell* a *bear*

shin'yōwariate 信用割当 credit rationing

shin'yōyokuseisaku 信用抑制策 credit control measures; credit squeeze measures

shippāzuyūzansu シッパーズ・ユーザンス shippers' usance

shiraji 白地 blank

shirajihikiuke 白地引受け blank acceptance

shirajishikikogitte 白地式小切手 blank check

shirajishikitegata 白地式手形 blank bill

shirajishoshiki 白地書式 blank form

shirajiuragaki 白地裏書 blank endorsement

shiren 試練 ordeal; trial ¶ a year of *ordeal* for the British economy // undergoing a situation of stresses and *trials* // The nation is now facing "a year of *ordeal*".

shirinuke しり抜け loophole ¶ *loopholes* in the current domestic tight money supply // a *loophole* for the present monetary stringency // [参考] Many large conglomerate mergers are able to slip through the net of existing antitrust laws.

shiryō 資料 data; material ¶ a work relying on the *data* drawn from 64 developing countries // the collection of in-depth socio-economic *data* // the reliability and timely availability of monetary *data* // a range of the most recent internationally comparable statistical *data* designed for cross-country analysis preliminary *data* and estimates confirm that sales have increased. // Incomplete *data* for July show an acceleration of inflation. // revised balance-of-payments *data* for the United Kingdom // Market participants are concentrating on upcoming *data* including retail sales, industrial production, and personal income. // Economic *data* point to rising U.S. interest rates.

shiryō 飼料 feed grains; feedstuffs; fodder (crops)

shiryoku 資力 solvency; financial capacity; pecuriary resources; means ¶ companies of recognized *solvency* // to seriously jeopardize the *solvency* of the corporation // Individuals of large *means* save almost automatically.

shiryōseizōgyō 飼料製造業 feedstuff manufacturing industry

shisai 市債 municipal loan; municipal bond; municipals

shisaishōsho 市債証書 municipal warrant

shisakuhi 試作費 experimental manufacturing cost

shisan 試算 trial computation; tentative calculation; trial calculation; pro forma calculation; provisional calculation; provisional estimation

shisan 資産 asset; property; estate
簿外資産 unlisted asset
陳腐化資産 obsolete asset
現金資産 cash asset
減耗資産 depleting asset
擬制資産 fictitious asset
隠匿資産 hidden asset
純資産 net assets
準備資産 reserve asset
換価不可能資産 unrealizable asset
換価可能資産 realizable asset; available asset
危険資産 risky asset
焦付資産 frozen asset
固定資産 fixed asset
名目資産 nominal asset
水割(=水増)資産 watered assets
無形固定資産 intangible fixed asset
無形資産 intangible asset; invisible asset

流動資産 liquid asset; floating asset; circulating asset; quick asset
資本資産 capital asset
消耗資産 wasting asset
当座資産 quick asset
運用資産 operating asset; working asset
有形固定資産 tangible fixed asset
有形資産 tangible asset; visible asset
在外資産 overseas asset

shisanchōka 資産超過 net assets

shisanchōsa 資産調査 means test; status inquiry

shisanfusaihyō 資産負債表 financial statement; statement of assets and liabilities

shisanfusaikanri 資産負債管理 asset-liability management; ALM

shisanhikiatekin 資産引当金 assets reserves

shisanhyō 試算表 trial balance sheet
合併試算表 compound trial balance
合計試算表 trial balance of totals
残高試算表 trial balance of balances

shisanhyōkaron 資産評価論 theory of asset valuation

shisanjōtai 資産状態 financial standing

shisankabu 資産株 income stock; asset issue

shisankanri 資産管理 portfolio management

shisankeijō 資産計上 capitalization

shisanmokuroku 資産目録 statement of assets

shisannaiyō 資産内容 quality of assets; asset components

shisan'okurijō 試算送り状 pro

forma invoice

shisansaihyōka 資産再評価 revaluation of assets; assets revaluation

shisansenkōriron 資産選好理論 theory of asset preference; theory of portfolio selection

shisansentaku 資産選択 portfolio selection

shisanshōkyaku 資産償却 depreciation of assets

shisantofusai 資産と負債 assets and liabilities

shisantōketsu 資産凍結 freezing of assets

shisan'un'yō 資産運用 asset management

shisanun'yōtōshi 資産運用投資 portfolio investment ¶ *portfolio investment* in Japanese stocks by non-residents

shisatsu 私札 private note; paper money issued by individuals or civil groups

shisei 姿勢 posture; stance; attitude ¶ an easy policy *stance* // a restrictive *stance* of policy administration // restrictive *attitudes* of banks toward lending // to keep holding the continuously restrictive *posture* in policy actions // The central bank was not wavering from its anti-inflation *stance*. // The Federal Reserve shifted to a less accommodative *stance* in the domestic money market. // The *stance* of monetary policy has been tightened over this period and may be operating more restrictively than fiscal policy. // The Bank continues to observe a restrictive *stance* in the field of credit policy. // In this context, what is the proper *stance* for economic policy? // the deliberately easy *stance* on

monetary policy adopted by the National Bank for exchange rate reasons // Government policy must still maintain a restrictive *posture* modified to protect against an excessive reduction in real income. // →態度

shisetsu 施設 facility ¶ to finance the power, port, and other infrastructure and production *facilities* // companies operating the mining *facilities*

shishagonyū 四捨五入 fractions less than half unit being omitted and those of half unit or more counted as unit; counting 5 and higher fractions as units and disregarding the rest; half-adjust ¶ *Fractions* of a cent equalling or exceeding five mills shall be *regarded* as one cent and *fractions* of a cent less than five mills shall be *disregarded*. // [参考] Rates are rounded up to the nearest $1/8$ percentage point. // to round the resultant figure to the nearest cent (half a cent being rounded upwards)

shishutsu 支出 outlay; disbursement; expenditure; spending ¶ "*Expenditures* rise to match all available revenues", Perkinson's second law // taxpayers' outcries against injudicious *spending* // large and recurrent defense *expenditures* // to hold down public *expenditure* // to reduce the relative size of Federal *expenditures* // *Expenditures* for medicare and medicaid rose even faster. // Total government *spending* exerted a restrictive impact on aggregate demand. // Industrial consumer *spending* increased. // a rise in capital *spending* on a construction basis // cuts in Federal *spending* as per cent of GNP // a stringent *spending* crackdown designed to cut the U.S. budget deficit // Carter proposed a 10% boost in defense *spending* to $122.8 billion. // to check Federal *spending* // Mr. Carter's *spending* plan for the fiscal year would increase *outlays* by 3.1%. // Defense *spending* accounts for a high proportion of total budget *outlays*. // a fiscal program leading to lower *outlays*, which have been unacceptably high // to cut fiscal *disbursement* // Business plans for plant and equipment *outlays* were revised upward. // Government *expenditures* on public work projects

防衛支出 defense expenditure

非生産的支出 nonproductive expenditure

移転支出 transfer expenditure

実質支出 real expenditure

国防支出 defense expenditure

個人消費支出 personal consumption expenditure

国民総支出 gross national expenditure; GNE

国内総支出 gross domestic expenditure

公共支出 public expenditure

経常支出 current expenditure

民間支出 private expenditure

臨時支出 extraordinary expenditure

政府支出 government expenditure

生産的支出 productive expenditure

資本支出 capital expenditure

消費支出 consumption expenditure

対外支出 external expenditure

対内支出 internal expenditure

財政支出 fiscal expenditure; government spending

shishutsuchōka 支出超過 deficit spending

shishutsufutankōi 支出負担行為 act resulting in Treasury expenses

shishutsufutankōijisshikeikaku 支出負担行為実施計画 execution plan of obligation

shishutsufutankōitantōkan 支出負担行為担当官 official for Treasury obligation

shishutsukakuchōkeiro 支出拡張経路 expenditure expansion path

shishutsukan 支出官 disbursing official

shishutsukankogitte 支出官小切手 government check issued by disbursing official

shishutsuyaku 支出役 disbursing official

shisonhin 仕損品 spoiled goods; defective goods

shisonnotamenochochiku 子孫のための貯蓄 saving for posterity

shisū 指数 index (figure; number) ¶ The *index* of leading economic indicators fell by 0.1% in March, following a revised gain of 0.5% in February and a 1.3% decline in January. // The monthly drop left the *index* at 134.1 (1967=100), up 3.2% from a year earlier. // The consumer price *index* rose by 0.8%, reasonably adjusted, in March; it was 6.5% higher than twelve months earlier. // The *index* of wholesale prices (1935-39=100) worked out at 588 in February, representing a rise of 1.2% over the month and one of 8.7% over the year. // The official *index* of industrial production (1979=100) fell by 4.1% over the month in August to the provisional figure. // In the three months to the end of August the all-industries *index* showed a rise of

1% compared with the previous three months, while the *index* measuring output in the manufacturing industry was 0.3% over the same period. // The *index* of industrial output on an unadjusted basis (1970=100) showed a downward movement of 0.1% and stood at 78.5 in August. // The production *index* receded after moving up 0.3 percent in the previous month. // The unit price *index* of trade has been on the decline. // price expressed as *index* numbers with 1975=100 // the *index number* of producer's finished goods inventories // *Indexes* (=*indices*) of wholesale and consumer prices fluctuated narrowly.

貿易額指数　trade value index
貿易単価指数　unit price index of trade
物価指数　price index
賃金指数　wage (rate) index
ダウ平均株価指数　Dow-Jones average index
不快指数　discomfort index; D.I.; temperature humidity index: T.H.I.
複合要素交易条件指数　double factoral terms of trade index
販売業者製品在庫指数　index of dealer's inventory
平均指数　average index
秤量指数　weighted index
一般物価指数　general price index
常用労働者賃金指数　wage index of regular workers
株価指数　stock price index
稼働率指数　index of capacity utilization
加重指数　weighted index
拡散指数　diffusion index; D.I.
季節調整済指数　seasonally adjusted index

季節指数　seasonal index
個別価格指数　individual price index
交易条件指数　terms of trade index
鉱工業生産　mining and manufacturing production index; industrial production index
小売物価指数　retail price index
小売売上高指数　retail sales index
農業パリティ指数　agricultural parity index
農村物価指数　price index of commodities in agricultural community
卸売物価指数　wholesale price index; W.P.I.
パリティ指数　parity index
パーシェ指数　paasche index
ポアソン分散指数　poisson index of dispersion
連鎖指数　chain index
労働生産性指数　labor productivity index
生計費指数　cost-of-living index; living cost index
生産者物価指数　producer's price index
生産者製品在庫指数　index of producers' inventories of finished goods
生産者出荷指数　index of producers' shipments
生産指数　production index
戦前基準指数　prewar base index
商業販売額指数　index of wholesale and retail sales
消費者物価指数　consumer price index; C.P.I.
消費者コンフィデンス指数　consumer confidence index
消費数量指数　consumption quantity index
所得指数　income index

出荷指数　shipment index

操業率指数　index of operating ratio

総合指数　aggregate index

数量指数　quantum index

スタンダード・プア物価指数　Standard & Poor's Stock Price Index

帯状指数　zonal index

単位指数　unit value index

単純相対指数　simple relative index

単純総和指数　simple aggregate index

輸入物価指数　import price index

輸出物価指数　export price index

輸出マインド指数　index of export incentives

輸出入単価指数　index of unit price of trade value

輸出数量指数　export volume index

在庫率指数　index of inventory-sales ratio; index of stock-price ratio

shisūkyūsū　指数級数　exponential series

shisūsanshiki　指数算式　index formula

shisutemugijutsu　システム技術　system technology

shisutemukaihatsu　システム開発　system(atic) development

shisutemukaihatsufutan　システム開発負担　load of system development

shisutemukōgaku　システム工学　System(s) engineering

shisutemusangyō　システム産業　System(s) industry

shisutemusekkei　システム設計　system design

shitabanare　下放れ　[市] falling off

shitadori　下取り　part exchange ¶ Four out of five new model cars are sold in *part exchange* for used cars.

shitadorikakaku　下取り価格　turn-in value; trade in value

shitadorishōhin　下取り商品　trade-in items; turn-in items

shitahikiukegaisha　下引受会社　sub-underwriter

shitahikiukegyō　下引受業　[市] selling group

shitamawaru　下回る　lower ¶ The value of retail sales was 1.5 percent *lower* than the year-ago figure. // [参考] Sales at department stores showed a less than seasonal decline in July.

shitanaga　下長　[市] buyers over

shitane　下値　lower price; lower quotation

shitaoshi　下押し　easing; weakening; falling; declining; sagging; downturn; downgrade ¶ →下降

shitauke　下請け　subcontract

shitaukekigyō　下請企業　sub-contractor

shitaukekōjō　下請工場　sub-contracting factory

shitaukekōjōmaebaraikin　下請工場前払金　advance to sub-contractor

shitazasae　下支え　underpinning; basic support; underlying support; propping up ¶ Increased consumer confidence *underpinned* spendings // to provide the market with a *basic support* // Forecasts of a fall in the money supply gave *underlying support* to the credit markets. // Expectations of an increase in U.S. M_1 money supply also provided the dollar with *underlying support*.

shitazuminimotsu　下積荷物　goods in lower layer

shite　仕手　operator; trader; rigger; speculator

shitei 指定 designation ¶ India *de*-signated trade with eastern Europe in rupees.

shiteigōdōun'yōkinsenshintaku 指定合同運用金銭信託 designated joint operating money trust

shitekabu 仕手株 speculative stock; speculative leader

shitekankei 仕手関係 operators' maneuver; technical position

shitekibuntankin 私的分担金 membership fee

shitenginkōseido 支店銀行制度 branch banking system

shitenmō 支店網 network of branches; branch network

shitenshūeki 支店収益 earnings of branches

shitentōshi 支店投資 investment to branches

shitesen 仕手戦 technical struggle; deal between speculators

shitofumeikin 使途不明金 expenditure for unexplained purposes

shitsu 質 quality ¶ The stress must be on the quality of opportunity, not the *quality* of income. // superlative *quality* which was seen as incompatible with quantity

shitsubō 失望 [市] disappointed; disappointing

shitsugyō 失業 unemployment; joblessness ¶ *Unemployment* remains at a high rate. // Today's high *unemployment* hit most savagely at women. // *Unemployment* remained stubbornly unresponsive; indeed, the *unemployment* rate increased by 0.2 percent. // The number of wholly *unemployed* rose by 0.1 percent over the month.

現実の失業 actual unemployment
技術失業 productivity unemploy-ment

偽装失業 disguised unemployment; hidden unemployment

半失業 under-employment; partial unemployment

非自発的失業 involuntary unemployment

自発的失業 voluntary unemployment

循環的失業 cyclical unemployment

過渡的失業 transitional unemployment

構造的失業 structural unemployment

慢性的失業 chronic unemployment

摩擦的失業 frictional unemployment

生産失業 productivity unemployment

潜在(=隠れた)失業 hidden unemployment

周期的失業 cyclical unemployment
大量失業 mass unemployment

shitsugyōchōsa 失業調査 unemployment census

shitsugyōhoken 失業保険 unemployment insurance

shitsugyōhoshō 失業補償 unemployment compensation ¶ The present programs for *unemployment compensation* may be providing benefits on a generous scale.

shitsugyōkyūfu 失業給付 unemployment benefit

shitsugyōkyūsai 失業救済 unemployment relief; unemployment benefit

shitsugyōritsu 失業率 unemployment rate; jobless rate ¶ the official *unemployment rate* with the fixed-weight measure which weights the unemployment rates of the major age-sex groups by their relative importance in the labor force // high *unemployment rates* for women and teen-agers // The U.S. *unemployment rate* dropped to 7.6 %. // The *jobless rate* for men aged twenty-five and older was about equal to the peak rate in 1962.

shitsugyōsha 失業者 person out of work; jobless person; those who lost their job; the unemployed; unemployed person; out-of-work empoyee ¶ The number of *persons out of work* rose no further in the final months of 1975, after adjustment for seasonal influences. // The official count of *jobless persons* has hovered around the 5 million mark. // Some of *those who lost their jobs* did not seek new employment. // Italy absorbed its *unemployed* into working force. // The total number of *unemployed* registered at the labor exchanges was smaller than originally expected. // The number of *unemployed persons,* and particularly that of short-time workers, decreased. // Some *out-of-work* female *employees* have not looked for new jobs. // [参考] These shutdowns will throw 2,000 men out of work with little hope of finding other jobs.

完全失業者 wholly unemployed

shitsugyōshameibo 失業者名簿 unemployment roll ¶ It added 120,000 people on the *unemployment rolls.*

shitsugyōtaisaku 失業対策 measures for the unemployment; counter-unemployment measures ¶ expenses for *measures for the unemployment*

shitsugyōteate 失業手当 unemployment benefit; [英] dole ¶

legislation-determined *unemployment benefit* periods of relatively fixed length // Recession boosts Federal spending mainiy through higher outlays for *unemployment benefits.* // to manage to duck work and live on the public *dole*

shitsugyōtōkei 失業統計 unemployment statistics

shitsutekikōjō 質的向上 qualitative repletion; qualitative improvement ¶ realization of a *qualitative repletion* rather than quantitative expansion

shitsutekikyōsō 質的競争 quality competition

shitsutekishin'yokisei 質的信用規制 qualitative credit control (=regulation)

shitsutekitenkan 質的転換 qualitative turn (=change)

shitsutekitōsei 質的統制 qualitative control

shiwakechō 仕訳帳 journal; journal-book

shiyō 仕様 specifications; description ¶ to produce nightwear to Host's *specifications* for export // sale on *description* // *description* leaflet // *specifications* of the machine

shiyōhanbai 試用販売 approval sale

shiyōkikan 試用期間 probation (period)

shiyōshahiyō 使用者費用 user cost

shizenchitsujo 自然秩序 natural order

shizengenshū 自然減収 natural decrease ¶ the *natural decrease* in tax revenue

shizenkankyōhozenchōsa 自然環境保全調査 green Japan survey;

vegetation survey; survey of the state of vegetation

shizenrishiritsu 自然利子率 natural rate of interest

shizenseichōritsu 自然成長率 natural rate of growth

shizenshokuhin 自然食品 organic food

shizensonmō 自然損耗 natural wastage

shizentōta 自然淘汰 natural selection

shizenzō 自然増 natural increase; unearned increase ¶ on *natural increase* in tax revenue // *unearned increase* in estates

shizenzōkaritsu 自然増加率 natural rate of increase

shizenzōshū 自然増収 natural increase (in tax revenue)

shizōhin 死蔵品 dead stock

shō~ 省~ saving; economy; conservation ¶ energy-*saving* investment // labor-*saving* equipment // oil-*economy* measures

shōbatsu 賞罰 rewards and punishments

shobun'uri 処分売り [市] flattening out

shōchō 消長 vicissitude; rise and fall; up and down; prosperity and decay ¶ to pass through various *vicissitudes* // to experience many *vicissitudes* // stable growth after many *vicissitudes*

shōdan 商談 negotiation; deal; bargain; transaction; business confab ¶ Given time, the intricate *negotiations* could have worked out for the proposed buyout of a business.

shōdōgai 衝動買い purchase on the spur of the moment; impulse buying; impulse shopping ¶ to become a

nation of *impulse shoppers* // Clothing is clustered by size instead of type to encourage *impulse buying*.

shōenerugī 省エネルギー energy-saving ¶ investements in *energy-saving* equipment

shōfudō 小浮動 moderate fluctuation; slight ups and downs

shōfudōsuru 小浮動する to fluctuate in a narrow range; to waver narrowly

shōgai 障害 hurdle; impediment ¶ European countries cleared bigger *hurdles* in their efforts to expand trade with China. // The numerous *impediments* to new investment on ecological grounds // to raise all kinds of monetary *hurdles*

shōgaihoken 傷害保険 (personal) accident insurance

shōgaiun'yugaisha 渉外運輸会社 overseas transportation company

shogakari 諸掛り charges; expenses

特別諸掛り special charges

追加諸掛り additional charges

shogakarikaitemochi 諸掛買手持ち all charges for buyer's account

shogakarikanjōsho 諸掛勘定書 bill of charges

shogakarisakibarai 諸掛先払い charges forward

shogakarishiharaizumi 諸掛支払済み charges prepaid; charges paid

shōgaku 少額 small amount; small sum; petty sum

shōgakuchochikuhikazeiseido 少額貯蓄非課税制度 non-taxable system on small savings

shōgakuginkōken 小額銀行券 fractional (bank) notes; bank notes of small denominations

shōgakuhoken 少額保険 petty-sum insurance

shōgakukamotsu 少額貨物 goods of small amount

shōgakukōsaibetsuwakuhikazeiseido 少額公債別枠非課税制度 special nontaxable system on small government bonds

shōgakusaiken 少額債券 small bond

shōgakushihei 小額紙幣 notes of small denominations; small notes

shōgi 商議 consultation; negotiation

shōgijyōkō 商議条項 consultation clause

shōgitaoshiriron 将棋倒し理論 domino theory

shōgō 商号 trade name; firm name

shōgōhenkō 商号変更 change of trade name

shōgōki 照合機 [コン] collator

shōgōsuru 照合する collate; match; check

shōgyō 商業 commerce; trade; business

shōgyōbēsunokariire 商業ベースの借入 borrowing on a commercial basis ¶ [参考] The low-income countries can borrow little commercially. // to be well placed to borrow much from private commercial sources // to borrow on commercial terms

shōgyōbēsunoseisan 商業ベースの生産 production on a commercial basis

shōgyōchi 商業地 commercial district; business district

shōgyōchūshinchi 商業中心地 business center; commercial center

shōgyōdōtoku 商業道徳 commercial morality

shōgyōginkō 商業銀行 commer-

cial bank

shōgyōhanbaigakushisū 商業販売額指数 index of wholesale and retail sales

shōgyōinsatsubutsu 商業印刷物 commercial printing

shōgyōka 商業化 commercialization

shōgyōkaigisho 商業会議所 chamber of commerce

shōgyōkakumei 商業革命 commercial revolution

shōgyōkin'yū 商業金融 commercial finance

shōgyōkōshinjo 商業興信所 mercantile agency; credit bureau

shōgyōkuiki 商業区域 business section; business quarter; trade area

shōgyōkumiai 商業組合 trade association; merchant association; guild

shōgyōmeikan 商業名鑑 business directory

shōgyōseisaku 商業政策 commercial policy

shōgyōshihon 商業資本 commercial capital

shōgyōshin'yō 商業信用 commercial credit

shōgyōshin'yōjō 商業信用状 commerial credit; commercial letter of credit

shōgyōtegata 商業手形 commercial bill; commercial paper

shōgyōtegatanijunzurutegata 商業手形に準ずる手形 bills almost equivalent to commercial bills; bills corresponding in credibility to commercial bills

shōgyōtegatawaribikibuai 商業手形割引歩合 discount rate of a commercial bill

shōgyōtōki 商業登記 commercial

registration

shōgyōwaribiki 商業割引 commercial discount

shōgyōzaikogakushisū 商業在庫額指数 index of wholesale and retail inventories

shōhanraku 小反落 slight reactionary drop (=fall)

shōharan 小波乱 flurry

shohatsukabu 初発株 original issue stock

shōhcki 障壁 barrier; wall ¶ The Japanese language constitues a trade *barrier*. // Market people felt 200 was unfairly substantial *barrier* of the rise in the year against the U.S. dollar. // The recent proliferation of protectionist *barriers*. // to remove or reform entrenched structural and institutional *barriers* // to remove technical *barriers* to trade in industrial products // to bear down artificial geographic *barriers* into the banking industry // to reduce the *barriers* to exports from developed countries // to raise protective *barriers* against imports // to drop trade-tariff and non-tariff *barriers* // the rush to erect protectionist trade *barriers* // to reduce the *barriers* to exports from developing countries // to raise protective *barriers* against imports // to avoid the imposition of new trade *burriers* // to promote the dismantling of non-tariff *barriers* // the lowering of many of Canada's trade *barriers* // to raise the £44.50 low pay *barrier* // international trade is menaced by national *barriers* openly erected at the frontier // *barriers* to entry, or trade *barriers* // to insulate its monopoly position by raising entry *barriers* through ac-

quisition of its customers // subtle Japanese non-tariff *barriers* to import

貿易障壁　trade barrier

非関税障壁　nontariff barrier

関税障壁　tariff barrier

参入障壁　entry barrier

輸入障壁　import barrier

shōhi 消費 consumption; spending ¶ daily, monthly, or annual domestic or home *consumption* // personal and industrial consumer *spending* // The upsurge in *consumption* declined. // Personal *consumption* in real terms, adjusted for seasonal factors, has changed little since the beginning of the year. // *Consumption* showed a strong upward trend in the first seven months of the year. // the over*consumption* of the rich and the under*consumption* of the poor

不生産的消費　unproductive consumption

月間消費(量)　monthly consumption

現実消費　actual consumption

一時的消費　transitory consumption

家計消費　household consumption

高度大衆消費　high mass consumption

個人消費　personal consumption ¶ *Personal consumption* has been running at very little above last year's level.

誇示的消費　conspicuous consumption; ostentatious consumption

恒常的消費　permanent consumption

国内消費　domestic consumption ¶ *Domestic consumption* dipped slightly below the rate in the previous year.

民間消費 private consumption ¶ *Private consumption* at current prices rose by 9.7 percent.

最終消費 final consumption ¶ *Final consumption* of goods and services is well maintained.

政府消費 government consumption; public consumption ¶ *Public consumption* rose by 3.0 percent at current prices and private consumption by 9.7 percent.

shōhibūmu 消費ブーム consumer spending spree ¶ In line with the recent *consumer spending spree* department store sales are rising.

shōhibusshinokyōdōkōnyū 消費物資の共同購入 joint purchases of consumption goods

shōhidaka 消費高 amount of consumption; consumption

shōhigentai 消費減退 decrease of consumption; under-consumption

shōhiiyoku 消費意欲 motivation to spend; spending intentions ¶ Building up strength of the *motivation to spend* means a decrease in savings.

shōhijōtai 消費状態 condition of consumption

shōhikanren'yūnyū 消費関連輸入 consumption-related imports

shōhikeiki 消費景気 consumption boom; spending boom

shōhikeizai 消費経済 economy of consumption

shōhikisei 消費規制 control of consumption

shōhikōbairyoku 消費購買力 consumers' purchasing power

shōhikōzō 消費構造 (nation's) consumption structure

shōhikumiai 消費組合 consumers' cooperative society

shōhikumiaibaiten 消費組合売店 cooperative store

shōhin 商品 merchandise; commodity; goods; product ¶ introduction of a new financial *product* for retail banking

買回(商)品 shopping goods

最寄(商)品 convenience goods

専門(商)品 specialty goods

shōhin'aridaka 商品有り高 inventory; amount of stock; mechandise inventories

shōhindemawaridaka 商品出回り高 visible supply (=stock)

shōhin'enjo 商品援助 commodity aid

shōhingun 商品群 commodity group

shōhinhoken 商品保険 commodity insurance

shōhinka 商品化 commercialization

shōhinkachi 商品価値 commercial value; commodity value ¶ low-grade timber of little *commercial value*

shōhinkahei 商品貨幣 commodity money; merchandise money

shōhinkaitenritsu 商品回転率 merchandise turnover

shōhinkakeikaku 商品化計画 merchandising

shōhinkanri 商品管理 merchandise control

shōhinken 商品券 merchandise certificate; merchandise coupon; exchange ticket; present ticket; gift voucher

shōhinmihon 商品見本 sample

shōhinmikaerikashitsuke 商品見返貸付 loan secured by commodities collateral

shōhinnakagainin 商品仲買人 commodity broker

shōhinseisannōka 商品生産農家 commercial farms

shōhinshijō 商品市場 commodity market

shōhinsōko 商品倉庫 merchandise warehouse

shōhintorihiki 商品取引 commodity transaction

shōhintorihikisho 商品取引所 commodity exchange

shōhipatān 消費パターン consumer expenditure income pattern

shōhiseigen 消費制限 restriction on consumption

shōhiseikō 消費性向 propensity to consume; spending

shōhisetsuyaku 消費節約 economy in (=on) consumption; retrenchment in consumption; saving ¶ *economy in* oil *consumption* // oil *saving* drives

shōhisetsuyakuundō 消費節約運動 movement to economize on consumption

shōhisha 消費者 consumer; user ¶ As a *consumer,* Japanese requirements will be no larger per person than in West Germany.
　最終消費者 final consumer; ultimate consumer; end user
　限界消費者 marginal consumer

shōhishabukka 消費者物価 consumer prices ¶ The effect of higher wholesale prices is bound to show up at the *consumer price* level.

shōhishabukkashisū 消費者物価指数 consumer price index; CPI

shōhishadantai 消費者団体 consumer group

shōhishadōkō 消費者動向 consumer attitudes; consumers' behavior

shōhishajuyō 消費者需要 consumer demand ¶ Once erratic *consumer demand* is now much steadier.

shōhishakakaku 消費者価格 consumer prices; price to consumers; consumer's prices

shōhishakiken 消費者危険 consumer's risk

shōhishakin'yū 消費者金融 loan to consumers; consumer lending; consumer credit; consumer banking ¶ the Bank's assault on *consumer banking* markets worldwide

shōhishakin'yūgaisha 消費者金融会社 consumer finance company

shōhishakōbai 消費者購買 consumer buying ¶ The slide-off in *consumer buying* occured in durable goods.

shōhishakōdō 消費者行動 consumer('s) behavior

shōhishakōdōnoriron 消費者行動の理論 theory of consumer's behavior ¶ to be generally consistent with the tenets of the *theory of consumer behavior*

shōhishakyōiku 消費者教育 consumer education

shōhishamaindo 消費者マインド consumer confidence; consumer expectation; consumer sentiment ¶ *Consumer sentiment* picked up. // *Consumer confidence* continued to falter. // *Confidence* among *consumers* in all income groups improved sharply between January and March. // The Index of *Consumers Sentiment* (1966=100) rose to 84.1. // *Consumer cofidence* now stands at its highest spring level since the survey was started in 1976. // The recovery in *consumer confidence,* which emerged in early

February, was sustained in March. // Fear of inflation undermines fragile *consumer confidence*. // The University of Michigan general index of *consumer sentiment* continued its long decline from its May 1977 peak of 89.1. // *Consumer confidence* remains at too low a level.

shōhishamaindochōsa 消費者マインド調査 survey of consumers' confidence; consumer survey ¶ Of late, *consumer surveys* have indicated some improvement in confidence.

shōhishamaindoshisū 消費者マインド指数 consumer-confidence index

shōhishaseikatsu 消費者生活 consumer life

shōhishasenkō 消費者選好 consumer('s) preference

shōhishasentakunoriron 消費者選択の理論 theory of consumer's choice

shōhishashin'yō 消費者信用 consumer credit

shōhishashin'yōhogohō 消費者信用保護法 [米] Consumer Credit Protection Act of 1968

shōhishashin'yōkisei 消費者信用規制 consumer credit control

shōhishashishutsu 消費者支出 consumer spending; consumption expenditure; consumers' outlay ¶ *Consumer expenditures* on services seldom show much departure from their up ward trend. // The future course of *consumer spending* is shrouded in uncertainty. // Industrial *consumer spending* was restrained by the tax surcharge. // New housing starts and car sales are the classes of *consumer outlays* that are mostly closely related to cyclical developments in the economy.

// Private *consumer spending* is expected to stagnate, and to recover later on. // household *consumption expenditure* on an all household basis

shōhishashūkan 消費者習慣 consumer habits ¶ to familiarize Yugoslavian exporters with *consumer habits* in EFTA countries

shōhishashuken 消費者主権 consumer('s) sovereignty

shōhishaundō 消費者運動 consumer movement ¶ the standard-bearer of the *consumer movement*

shōhishayojō 消費者余剰 consumer's rent; consumer's surplus

shōhishihon 消費資本 consumption capital

shōhishishutsu 消費支出 →消費者支出

shōhisuijun 消費水準 level of consumption

shōhitaishaku 消費貸借 mutual; loan for consumption

shōhitōshihōhō 消費・投資方法 consumption-investment method

shōhizai 消費財 consumer goods; consumption goods

shōhizei 消費税 consumption tax; excise

shōhizeishinkoku 消費税申告 consumption entry

shōhyō 商標 trade-mark; brand; trade name
　　自家商標 private brand
　　商業者商標 private brand

shōhyō 証票 voucher; evidence
　　払出証票 voucher for disbursement
　　受入証票 voucher for receipt

shōhyōimēji 商標イメージ brand image

shōhyōken 商標権 right of trade-mark

shōhyōkenshingai 商標権侵害

trade-mark infringement

shōhyōshikikogitte 証票式小切手 voucher check

shōjigaisha 商事会社 trading concern; commercial company

shojinin 所持人 holder; bearer
正当所持人 holder in due course; bona fide holder

shojininbaraikogitte 所持人払小切手 check payable to bearer

shojininbaraitegata 所持人払手形 bill (or draft) payable to bearer

shōjō 商状 market conditions; conditions of the market; market ¶ The commodity *market conditions* somewhat relaxed. // *Conditions of the commodity market* were slightly easier than before. // The *market* stiffened. // The tone of the *market* was a shade firmer. // The *market* tone was quite taut. // →市況; 商況

shōka 消化 absorption; digestion ¶ *absorption* of government bond issues // to *absorb* newly-issued corporate bonds // smooth *absorption* of public and industrial bonds

shōkaikyakukakutoku 紹介客獲得 radiation

shōkaisaki 照会先 reference
同業者信用照合先 trade reference
銀行信用照合先 bank reference

shōkan 償還 redemption; repayment; refunding; amortization; reimbursement ¶ A bond issue may be made *redeemable* before maturity in whole or in part. // bonds repaid by installment *repayments* // issues *redeemable* on demand at definite schedules of prices // *redeemable* for cash plus accrued interest at the option of the holder // the probable amount of *repayment* of public loans by a lump sum at maturity // to

present notes for *redemption* in specie // *reimbursement* on drawings
抽籤償還 redemption by drawing
買入償還 redemption by purchase
繰上償還 advanced redemption
満期償還 redemption at maturity
満期前償還 prior redemption; redemption prior to maturity
無費用償還 redemption without cost
年賦償還 amortization

shōkan'enkikōsai 償還延期公債 extended bond

shōkanginkō 償還銀行 reimbursing bank (=agent)

shōkanhoshōjō 償還保証状 letter of commitment

shōkankabushiki 償還株式 redeemable stock

shōkankakaku 償還価格 call price

shōkankeisan 償還計算 recourse account

shōkankigen 償還期限 term of redemption; maturity ¶ bonds of various *maturities* // to pay at *maturity*

shōkankijitsu 償還期日 maturity date

shōkankikin 償還基金 sinking fund for redemption

shōkankinkajitsu 償還金果実 redeemed principal and interest

shōkanseikyū 償還請求 recourse

shōkanseikyūfukyokashin'yōjō 償還請求不許可信用状 without-recourse credit

shōkanseikyūken 償還請求権 right of recourse ¶ with or withourt *right of recourse*

shōkanseikyūkyoyōshin'yōjō 償還請求許容信用状 with-recourse credit

shōkansentakuken 償還選択権

optional call

shōkanshikin 償還資金 redmption fund

shōkanshū 商慣習 business practice; commercial practice; business customs; customary practices in business ¶ according to the international *business practice* // a universally established *business practice*

shōkanshūhō 商慣習法 lex mercatorum; law merchant

shōkantsumitatekin 償還積立金 sinking fund for redemption; redemption fund

shōken 商圏 market area; trading area

shōken 証券 security; instrument; deed; bill; bond certificate; bond; certificate

預り証券 securities in trust

売却制限証券 restricted securities

長期証券 long-term securities

中期証券 medium-term securities

代用納付証券 securities received for cash

不確定利付証券 unfixed interest bearing securities

不活発証券 inactive securities

船荷証券 bill of lading

船積証券 shipping documents

外貨証券 foreign curreney securities; bonds and securities in non-yen currencies

外国証券 foreign securities

払込付証券 assessible securites

非公開証券 restricted securities

保険証券 insurance policy

本邦証券 domestic securities

一時払い証券 non-amortizable securities

受益証券 beneficiary certificate

確定利付証券 fixed interest bearing securities

金(貨)証券 gold certificate

個人保証証券 personal securities

国際市場証券 intercourse securities

持分証券 equity securities

無取引証券 uncurrent securities

納税引当証券 tax anticipation bill or note

大蔵省証券 [日] Treasury bill; [英] Exchequer bill

利潤証券 profit sharing securities

流通証券 negotiable securities

債権証券 debt securities

指図人証券 bill to order

政府証券 government securities

仕入証券 instrument of pledge

社外証券 oustanding securities

市証券 municipal securities

出資証券 investment securities

倉庫証券 warehouse warrant; warehouse receipt

短期証券 short-term securities

投資有価証券 investment securities

有価証券 negotiable securities

優良証券 gilt-edged securities; blue chip securities

優先証券 senior securities

財務(省)証券 Treasury bill; TB

shōken'anarisuto 証券アナリスト security analyst

shōkenbaibaisho 証券売買所 security house

shōkendaikōnin 証券代行人 (securities) transfer agent

shōkendairigyōmu 証券代理業務 agent business on securities

shokendīrā 証券ディーラー investment dealer

shōken'en 証券円 special non-residence free yen account with securities company

shōken'enkatokubetsukanjō 証券円貨特別勘定 yen-denominated special securities account; special yen accounts of securities companies

shōkengaisha 証券会社 securities company (=house); security corporation; [英] security dealer

shōkengyōmu 証券業務 securities business

shōkengyōsha 証券業者 (securities) broker-dealer

shōkenhikikaebarai 証券引替払い payment against document

shōkenhoyū 証券保有 securities holding; security portfolio; portfolio ¶ The banks increased their *portfolios* by nearly DM3.8 billion. // a marked increase in the commercial banks' *security portfolio*

shōkenka 証券化 conversion into securities

shōkenkibangō 証券記番号 serial letter and number of the bond

shōkenkin'yū 証券金融 securities financing; security loan; collateral loan

shōkenkin'yūgaisha 証券金融会社 securities finance corporation

shōkenkin'yūkisei 証券金融規制 control on security financing

shōkenniokerushinjitsu 証券における真実 [米] Truth-in-Securities

shokenri 諸権利 [市] all rights ¶ ex *all rights,* or *all rights* off // cum all rights, or all rights on

shokenriochi 諸権利落ち [証市] ex all; all rights off

shokenritsuki 諸権利付き [証市] cum all; all rights on

shōkenshijō 証券市場 security market; securities market

shōkenshojinin 証券所持人 bondholder

shōkenshoyūsha 証券所有者 holders of securities; security holder

shōkentanpokawasetegata 証券担

保為替手形 security bills

shōkentanposhasai 証券担保社債 collateral trust bond

shōkentorihikihō 証券取引法 [日] Securities and Exchange Law; [米] Securities Exchange Act (of 1934)

shōkentorihikiiinkai 証券取引委員会 [米] Securities and Exchange Commission; SEC

shōkentorihikisho 証券取引所 stock market; stock exchange; security market

shōkentōshi 証券投資 securities investment; portfolio investment; investment in securities ¶ foreigners' *investment in* Japanese *securities*

shōkentōshishintaku 証券投資信託 securities investment trust ¶ sales, repurchases and redemption of open-end *securities investment trusts*

shōkentōshishintakuhanbaigaisha 証券投資信託販売会社 securities investment trust sales company

shōkentōshishintakuitakugaisha 証券投資信託委託会社 securities investment trust management company

shōkentanpokashitsuke 証券担保貸付 advance against securities

shōki 商機 business opportunity; business chance; chance of business

shokijōken 初期条件 initial condition

shōkin 正金 specie; cash; gold

shōkinbarai 正金払い payment in gold; payment in cash

shōkin'yushutsu 正金輸出 specie shipment

shōkin'yusōten 正金輸送点 specie (export) point; gold (export) point

shokirishi 初期利子 vocation; trade; profession; occupation

shokku ショック shock (wave;

effect; ferment); impact; impulse ¶ recovery to pre-oil-*shock* levels // to tide over the *shock-wave* // The record balance-of-payments deficit really *shocked* the market // The economic recovery looks vulnerable to external *shocks* // The Canadian economy received a relatively small initial reflationary *shock* from the increase in oil prices. // The *shock wave* of President Nixon's declaration of his new economic policy has been almost dissipated. // The *shocks* to which the non-oil developing countries were subjected in 1973-75. // The *shock waves* of two years ago have left their mark in international lending trends. // The oil crises have had *shock effects* on the world economy. // to minimize the *impact* of adjustment on their growth economies // insulation of the domestic economy from external *impulses* // to offset the disequilibrating *impulse* from abroad

shōko 証拠 evidence; proof ¶ There is still no clear *evidence* of a wide spread increase in capacity utilization rates. // All the *evidence* indicates that the rate of economic growth will be the fastest in more than half a decade. // *Evidence* has accumulated of a significant strengthening in the pace of economic expansion. // *Evidence* accumulated that economic expansion was quickening. // It constitutes eloquent *proof* of the confidence placed in the solidity of the economy.

shōkō 小康 ease; lull; pause; respite ¶ The money market is easy. // Prices have been *easing*. // The market has been in a *lull*. // The market was in a *lull*. // Demand picked up after a *lull*. // The long *lull* in the U.S. recovery finally ended. // →中だるみ

shōkokin 証拠金 margin money; warrant money; down payment

shōkokinritsu 証拠金率 ［市］ margin requirement; down payment; investor's rate of guarantee for margin trading deals ¶ The exchanges raised *margin requirements* on 18 stocks and debentures of 13 companies. // Member firms are ordered to require a 75% *down payment* on these stocks instead of the general *requirement* of 50% set by the Federal Reserve Board.

shōkokintorihiki 証拠金取引 margin transaction

shōkōkumiai 商工組合 commercial and industrial association

shōkoshorui 証拠書類 documentary evidence; voucher

shoku 職 job ¶ to guarantee *jobs* to those who will work at them // *Jobs* for about 1.2 million persons are to be created. // to create some 90,000 new *jobs* in the next three years // to create more lasting *jobs* over time // Chrysler UK's underproductive workforce of 25,000 was slimmed by 8,000 *jobs*. // The preservation of redundant *jobs* // to provide *jobs* in sectors where productivity keeps growing // This large number of new *jobs* will be filled. // Around 12,500 *jobs* have been cut from the 47,000 workforce of the group. // 40,000 *jobs* have vanished, bringing the workforce in the industry to 720,000. // The number of people without *jobs* increased to 6.19 million.

shokubadaihyōsei 職場代表制

shop stewardship

shokubahaichitenkan 職場配置転換 job rotation

shokubahōki 職場放棄 absenteeism

shokubai 触媒 catalizer; catalytic agent ¶ the World Bank's *catalytic* role in the sphere of cofinancing

shokubaiinkai 職場委員会 shop committee

shokubakankyō 職場環境 workplace environment

shokubakiritsu 職場規律 disciplinary rules

shokubasōon 職場騒音 on-the-job noise

shokubatōsō 職場闘争 workshop struggle

shokugyō 職業 vocation; trade; profession; occupation; pursuit ¶ the rural labor force primarily engaged in off-farm *pursuits* // technical and economic *pursuits*

shokugyōanteisho 職業安定所 public labor exchange; public employment agency; employment security office

shokugyōbetsurōdōkumiai 職業別労働組合 occupationally-classified trade (or labor) unions

shokugyōishiki 職業意識 job consciousness

shokugyōkōzō 職業構造 occupational structure

shokugyōsaikunren 職業再訓練 job retraining

shokugyōshōkai 職業紹介 job introduction; employment placements (through labor exchanges)

shokugyōshōkaijo 職業紹介所 employment agency; employment exchange; labor exchange

shokugyōtekiseikensa 職業適性検査 vocational test

shokugyōyōgu 職業用具 professional instruments

shokuminchiginkō 植民地銀行 colonial bank

shokumubunseki 職務分析 job analysis; occupational analysis

shokumuhyōka 職務評価 job rating; job evalution; job valuation

shokumukengen 職務権限 official authority

shokumukyū 職務給 job wage; wage attached to the post; wage on job evaluation

単一職務給 single wage rate for job

shokumushokunōkyūsei 職務・職能給制 formula for determining wages by evaluation or job performing ability

shokunō 職能 job performing ability

shokunōbunka 職能分化 functional specialization

shokunōbunri 職能分離 segregation of the functions

shokunōkōka 職能考課 performance rating; assessment of performance

shokunōkyū 職能給 wage on job-evaluation

shokunōkyūsei 職能給制 formula for determining wages by job performing ability

shokurin 植林 afforestation; reforestation

shokuryō 食糧 foodstuff; provisions; food

配給食糧 food ration; allocated food

shokuryōbichikukōsō 食糧備蓄構想 world grain's reserve system

shokuryōbusoku 食糧不足 food shortage

shokuryōhi 食料費 food expenses

shokuryōhinkōgyō 食料品工業 foods (and beverages) industry

shokuryōjōhōshisutemu 食糧情報システム global information and early warning on food and agriculture

shokuryōkanrihi 食糧管理費 expenses for foodstuff control

shokuryōkiki 食糧危機 food crisis

shokuryōyōnōchikusuisanbutsu 食料用農蓄水産物 edible agricultural, livestock, and aquatic products

shokusei 職制 staff organization

shokuseikatsu 食生活 dietary life; dietary habits; food habits (of the nation)

shokushubetsuchingin 職種別賃金 prevailing wages by occupation

shokushunaishōshin 職種内昇進 job promotion

shōkyaku 消却 cancellation

shōkyaku 償却 repayment; refundment; redemption; amortization; depreciation; write-off (=-down)

抽籤償却 redemption by drawing

減価償却 depreciation; writing off; writing down

買入償却 depreciation by purchase

加速償却 accelerated depreciation

shōkyakufusoku 償却不足 underdepreciation; inadequate depreciation; insufficient depreciation; shortfall in depreciation

shōkyakujunbikin 償却準備金 contingency reserve; depreciation reserve

shōkyakushikin 償却資金 sinking fund; depreciation fund

shōkyakushisan 償却資産 depreciable asset

shōkyō 商況 market; market conditions; market situation; market tone; market trend ¶ The extremely tight *market* points to further rises in quotations. // The strain between supply and demand on commodity *markets* remained unchanged. // All signs indicate the tautness of the *market*. // The *market* experienced the usual year-end strains. // dull, inactive, slack, or subdued, or depressed, *market* // active, buoyant, brisk, or animated *market* // booming or rising *market* // [市] bearish or bear *market* // bullish or bull *market* // →市況; 商状

shōkyōkō 小恐慌 flurry

shōkyōshisatsu 商況視察 market survey

shokyūyo 諸給与 fringe benefits ¶ to supplement contractual wage by *fringe benefits*, such as paid holidays, sick leaves, lunch vouchers and medical care

shomeikan 署名鑑 specimen signature

shōmetsujikō 消滅時効 negative prescription; extinctive prescription

shomiharaikin 諸未払い金 miscellaneous accounts payable

shomin 庶民 common people; people

shominjūtaku 庶民住宅 popular dwellings

shominkinko 庶民金庫 people's bank; popular bank

shominkin'yū 庶民金融 petty loans for the public; people's loan; consumer financing

shominkin'yūkikan 庶民金融機関 financial institution of petty loans for the public

shomishūkin 諸未収金 miscellaneous accounts receivable

shōmōhin 消耗品 consumables

shōmōshisan 消耗資産 current assets; liquid assets

shomōtekikeihi 消耗的経費 exhaustive expenditure

shōmu 商務 commercial affairs; business affairs

shōnin 承認 authorization; approval; surety

shōnin 商人 merchant; dealer; trader; tradesman; peddler; hawker
小売商人 retail trader; retailer
卸売商人 wholesale trader; wholesaler
闇商人 black-marketeer

shoninkyū 初任給 starting wage; starting salary; initial salary; entrance salary ¶ The *starting wages* for newly recruited school graduates rose steeply.

shōnō 小農 small farmer; peasant

shōnōkaikyū 小農階級 peasantry

shōnōsei 小農制 intensive farming system

shōōrai 小往来 [市] fluctuation within a narrow range; slight rise and fall; moderate fluctuation

shōraku 小落 slight decline; slight fall; slight setback; slight recess

shōrei 奨励 encouragement ¶ curbing of imports, or artificial *encouragement* of exports

shōreichinginsei 奨励賃金制 incentive wage system

shōreikin 奨励金 subsidy; bounty; incentive payment ¶ neither ask nor receive any *subsidies* from the government // a government *bounty* granted on exports

shōreisaku 奨励策 incentive ¶ The most widely used export *incentives* are fiscal *incentives*. // to use credit *incentives* intensively

shorijikan 処理時間 [コン] turn-around time

shoriryō 処理量 [コン] throughput

shōruibetsu 小類別 [統] sub-group

shoruihikikaebarai 書類引換払い payment against document; p.a.d.

shōryokugijutsu 省力技術 labor-saving technology

shōryokuka 省力化 economizing on manpower; labor saving ¶ *labor-saving* efforts // to *economize manpower* // increasing need for *labor-saving* devices

shōryokukikai 省力機械 labor-saving machinery

shōryokunōgyō 省力農業 labor-saving technique of agriculture

shōryokusangyō 省力産業 labor-saving machinery industry

shōryokusetsubi 省力設備 labor-saving equipment

shōryokutōshi 省力投資 labor-saving invensment

shōsa 照査 reconciliation ¶ a *reconciliation*, or *reconciling* the monthly statement with the balance by the cash book

shōsajimu 照査事務 reconciliation (process)

shōsen 商船 merchant vessel; mercantile marine; merchant ship; merchant fleet

shōsentai 商船隊 merchant fleet ¶ a *merchant fleet* of five hundred vessels

shōsha 商社 firm; concern; trading house; (general) trading firm; trading company; trading concern
総合商社 general merchants

shōshagaikahoyūseido 商社外貨保有制度 system authorizing limited open position of foreign exchange holdings of trading firms

shōshakōgokeisanseido 商社交互

計算制度 inter-office offsetting accounting system

shōshatōgaikayokin 商社等外貨預金 limited foreign exchange holdings by non-banks

shōshatōhonshitenkōgokeisanseido 商社等本支店交互計算制度 inter-office offsetting accounting system between the principal office and its overseas branch

shōshatōhoyūgaika 商社等保有外貨 foreign currency holdings by trading and manufacturing companies

shōshigengatakeizai 省資源型経済 resource-saving economy

shoshinkawase 書信為替 credit note

shōsho 証書 bond; deed; instrument; paper; note; bill; certificate; diploma
借用証書 IOU
信託証書 deed of trust
預金証書 certificate of deposit

shōshokashitsuke 証書貸付 loans on deed

shōsūkabunushigaisha 少数株主会社 closely held company

shōsūkabunushiken 少数株主権 minority stockholder right

shōsūshihai 少数支配 minority control

shoteigaichingin 所定外賃金 wage drift

shoteigairōdōjikan 所定外労働時間 nonscheduled hours worked

shōtō 小騰 slight advance; small gain

shotoku 所得 income; earning ¶ The average family *income* had risen to $14,000 by 1975. // The well-off family is defined as having twice that *income* in a year, and the wealthy family as having four times as much. // The surge in prices has sharply depressed real *earnings*.

分配国民所得 national income by distributive share; national income distributed

分配所得 distributive income

賃貸(料)所得 rental income

超過所得 excess income

営業外所得 non-operating income

営業所得 operating income

不労所得 unearned income

現物所得 non-money income

現実の所得 measured income

限界所得 marginal income

配当所得 dividend income

変動所得 transitory income

非課税所得 non-taxable income

一人当り所得 per capita income; income per capita

法人所得 corporate income

一時(的)所得 occasional income

移転所得 transfer income

事業所得 income from entrepreneurship

実質国民所得 national income in real terms; real national income

実質所得 real income

純所得 net income

稼働所得 earned income

貨幣所得 money income

可処分所得 disposable income

課税最低限所得 minimum taxable income

課税所得 taxable income

勤労所得 earned income

個人賃貸料所得 personal rental income; rental income of persons

個人業所得 income from unincorporated enterprise

個人配当所得 personal dividend income

個人可処分所得 personal disposable income; disposable personal income

個人所得　personal income; individual income

恒常的所得　permanent income

国民所得　national income

高所得　high income

名目所得　nominal income; income in nominal terms

年間所得　annual income

農業外所得　income from non-farming business

農家所得　farm income

市場価格表示国民所得　national income at market price

支出国民所得　national income expenditure

総所得　gross income

利子所得　interest income

留保所得　retained income

生産国民所得　national income produced

生存(水準)所得　subsistence income

社会的所得　social income

心理所得　psychic income

資産所得　assets income

相対所得　relative income

低所得　low income

要素費用表示の国民所得　national income at factor cost

財産所得　income from property

税引き所得　after-tax income

税込み所得　before-tax income

shotokubaizō 所得倍増　income-doubling; doubling of income

shotokubaizōkeikaku 所得倍増計画　doubling national income plan; income-doubling program

shotokubunpu 所得分布　income distribution ¶ equitable (=even) distribution of national income // to reduce the disparity in *income distribution*

shotokubunseki 所得分析　income analysis

shotokudanryokusei 所得弾力性　income elasticity

shotokugaku 所得額　amount of income

shotokuhoshōseido 所得保証制度　income maintenance policy

shotokukaisō 所得階層　income group; income bracket; income class ¶ people in the lower, middle, and higher-*income brackets*

shotokukakusa 所得格差　income differential

shotokukeisansho 所得計算書　income statement

shotokuketteinochochikutōshiri-ron 所得決定の貯蓄投資理論　saving-investment theory of income determination

shotokukōjo 所得控除　deduction (from taxable income)

shotokukōka 所得効果　income effect

shotokunofubyōdō 所得の不平等　inequality of incomes

shotokuryūtsūsokudo 所得流通速度　income velocity (of money)

shotokusaibunpai 所得再分配　income redistribution

shotokuseisaku 所得政策　incomes policy ¶ The government is planning a tough "stage two" *incomes policy* when the current wage arrangements expire. // It is desirable to bring *incomes policy* into play to assist demand policy in slowing inflation.

shotokusha 所得者　income earner ¶ large, or small, *income earners* // wage and salary *earners* // Women are a family's second *income earner*.
中所得者　middle-income earners

高所得者　high(=upper)-income earners

低所得者　low-income earners

shotokushinkoku　所得申告　income return

shotokusokudo　所得速度(貨幣の)　income velocity (of money)

shotokusuijun　所得水準　income level; level of income

shōtsunagi　正繋ぎ　hedging

shōwasanjūhachinenhakkōeikakōsai　昭和38年発行英貨公債　Japanese Government 6% Sterling Loan 1983/88.

shōyo　賞与　bonus

年末賞与　year-end bonus

特別賞与　special bonus

shōyosei　賞与制　premium system

shōyowarimashisei　賞与割増制　bonus premium system

shoyūdōsanfudōsan　所有動産不動産　real estate and properties

shoyūjunbi　所有準備　owned reserve

shoyūken　所有権　ownership; proprietorial right; proprietorship ¶ Australian-based companies with 25% or more Australian *ownership*.

shoyūsha　所有者　owner; proprietor; holder ¶ the *owners* on record as at the close of business // two individuals as co-*owners*, and one individual as *owner*

shoyūshashihai　所有者支配　owner control

shoyūtokeieinobunri　所有と経営の分離　separation of ownership and control; separation of ownership and management

shozappi　諸雑費　miscellaneous expenses; sundry expenses

shozokudantaikashitsuke　所属団体貸付　lending to member bodies

shuchikunōgyō　主畜農業　farming with priority to livestock raising

shuchikunōgyōnōka　主畜農業農家　farm household based on livestock raising

shūchū　集中　concentration; convergence ¶ In many industries *concentration* is negligible or being reduced. // There are excessively large *concentrations* of bond-holdings in some areas. // to reduce the undesirable country *concentration* of borrowing slightly // a system of *concentration* of foreign exchange holdings // The funds are *concentrated* on the financing of infrastructure projects. // British manufacturing is getting more *concentrated*. // to enhance the *convergence* of economic policies towards greater stability // greater *convergence* in economic performance of the member countries

shūchūdo　集中度　concentration ratio

shūchūgimu　集中義務　surrender requirement

shūchūgimunomenjo　集中義務の免除　exemption from responsibility of concentration (of foreign exchange)

shūchūgōutekiyushutsu　集中豪雨的輸出　flooding exports (into specific markets); downpour export(ing)

shūchūhaijo　集中排除　deconcentration; decentralization

shūchūnorieki　集中の利益　economics of concentration (=agglomeration)

shūchūsōba　集中相場　[外] exchange rate under concentration system

shudan 手段 instrumentality; tool; device; instrument; weapon; means ¶ money as an *instrumentality* for saving one's purchasing power, and a *device* for transporting value from one place to another // Checks are widely accepted as a *means* of payment. // The main *instrument* being used to bring the rate of inflation down further is incomes policy. // The European currency unit can serve as a new *instrument* for settling claims and liabilities between central banks. // an *instrument* for influencing the level of advances of commercial banks // the use of direct *instruments* of monetary management // active and co-ordinated use of the *instruments* at its disposal // the usefulness of published money-supply targets as an *instrument* of monetary policy // the principal effective protective policy *instrument* // The most powerful *weapon* for reducing unemployment // to diminish the tariffs as protective *tools* // a less attractive commercial policy *tool* // to employ fiscal *tools* actively in order to promote economic growth // many forms of disguised trade restricting *devices* // This policy measure was a necessary addition to our arsenal of economic stabilization *weapons*, to be used occasionally — but nevertheless vigorously — when needed. // the development and use of active counter-cyclical policy *weapons* to reduce fluctuations in demand

伝達手段 means of communication; vehicle
交換手段 means of exchange
生活手段 means of living
生産手政 means of production
支払手段 means of payment
輸送手段 means of transport

shūdanchūseishin 集団忠誠心 group loyalty

shūdanka 集団化 collectivization

shūdankōkaihanbaiseido 集団公開販売制度 collective open sales system

shūdankyōyaku 集団協約 collective agreement

shūdannōjō 集団農場 collective farm

shūdanrikigaku 集団力学 group dynamics

shudōgata ～主導型 ～-led ¶ The prospects were good for an export-*led* boom.

shūeki 収益 profit; earnings; return ¶ investment to earn a *profit* // to secure a *return* in the form of interest, dividends, rents, or capital appreciation // A further boost to foreign exchange *earnings* comes from tourism. // Korea receives many foreign visitors, generating *earnings* in the region of $450 millions. // Bank *earnings*, hurt by large loan losses, leveled off or declined after their sharp rise. // *Earnings* remain depressed as a result of unsatisfactory prices. // a pre-tax *return* of 3% over costs, or 12% on capital // investment media offering a better *return* // The projected *return* on capital diminished. // Companies are still producing *profits*, albeit slim. // →収入; 利益

平均収益 average earnings
純収益 net earnings
総収益 gross earnings
予定収益 estimate(d) earnings

shūekihotenritsu 収益補填率

earnings coverage

shūekijōkyō 収益状況 profits position; earning position; profit performance ¶ The corporate *profits position* is improving moderately. // The *earnings position* of enterprises is still unsatisfactory. // The Bank's strong *profit performance* in 1984 in part reflected better domestic business.

shūekijōyo 収益剰余 earned surplus

shūekikakujitsusei 収益確実性 income certainty

shūekikanzainin 収益管財人 receiver

shūekikōritsu 収益効率 profit earning efficiency

shūekikōzō 収益構造 structure of corporate profits ¶ Inflation caused serious distortions in the *structure of corporate profits* by boosting nominal profiits.

shūekiritsu 収益率 rate of return ¶ The projects must produce an acceptable *rate of return*. // an economic *rate of return* at least equal to the opportunity cost of capital
時間加重収益率 time weighted rate of return
内部収益率 internal rate of returns
市場収益率 market rate of returns
総収益率 ratio of total expenses to total revenues

shūekiryoku 収益力 profitability; earning power; profitableness; profit performance; capacity to earn profit ¶ The *profitability* of companies has shown a long-term leading to decline. // Competitive practices destroyed the *earning power* of weaker banks. // an enterprise showing a strong *profit performance*

shūekisai 収益債 revenue bond

shūekisei 収益性 profitability ¶ The outlook for corporate *profitability* is less depressing than a year ago. // →収益力

shūekishasai 収益社債 income bond

shūekishisan 収益資産 live assets

shūekitaika 終駅滞貨 terminal congestion

shūekiteigennohōsoku 収益逓減の法則 law of diminishing returns

shūekiyoryoku 収益余力 margin of safety

shūgyōjinkō 就業人口 employed workforce; occupied population ¶ Another 883,000 people found work pushing the *employed workforce* up to 107 million.

shūgyōkikai 就業機会 job opportunity; opportunity of work ¶ When *jobs* have been scarce, tourism has provided some much needed *opportunities*. // a project designed to create many *job opportunities* // The economy became incapable of creating sufficient *opportunities of work* for young people. // to provide the *opportunity* of permanent *work* for the army of unemployed // →雇用機会

shūgyōkisoku 就業規則 work rules

shūgyōkōzō 就業構造 structure of employment; employment structure

shūgyōnenrei 就業年齢 working age ¶ the male *working-age* population actively seeking work // active job-seekers among *working-age* women

shūgyōsha 就業者 employed person; persons holding jobs ¶ The number of those *holding jobs* rose by 613,000 to 97.51 million.

shūhen 周辺 periphery ¶ foreign

trade financing on the *periphery* of our banking system

shūhengyōmu 周辺業務 areas incidental to ordinary operations; fields beyond traditional operations; other services incidental to ordinary operations; fields beyond conventional services; peripheral business; peripheral fields; subsidiary business; fringe business activities ¶ *peripheral business* operations of banking institutions

shūhensōchi 周辺装置 peripheral equipment

shūhōginkō 州法銀行 state bank

shūitsukarōdōsei 週5日労働制 five-day week

shūka 集荷 cargo booking; collection (=assembly) of goods

shūkakikan 集荷機関 collecting agency; purchasing agency

shūkaku 収穫 harvest; crop; return; fruit

shūkakudaikin 収穫代金 harvest proceeds

shūkakuteigennohōsoku 収穫逓減の法則 law of diminishing returns

shūkakuyosō 収穫予想 crop estimate

shūkanan 集荷難 difficulty of booking cargoes

shūkanin 集荷人 assembler

shukankachisetsu 主観価値説 subjective (=utility) value theory

shukantekikakuritsu 主観的確率 subjective probability

shūkashikin 集荷資金 fund for collecting goods

shūkeichigainen 集計値概念 aggregate concept

shūkeinomondai 集計の問題 aggregation problem

shuken 主権 sovereignty ¶ to

impinge on a country's *sovereignty* and limit its policy options // to preserve the exercise of *sovereignty* over national resources

shukenmenjo 主権免除 sovereign immunity (from taxation, etc.)

shukka 出荷 shipment; delivery ¶ *Shipments* of finished products at the producer's level slightly dropped. // *Shipments* have been stable to slightly higher. // In volume terms, *deliveries* in May showed a decline of 4% on last year. // →売上

shukketsu 出血 hemorrhage ¶ The huge and unchecked *hemorrhage* of U.S. dollars caused by massive oil imports.

shukketsujuchū 出血受注 acceptance of an order at below-cost price; acceptance of below cost orders

shukketsukakaku 出血価格 below-cost price ¶ This resulted in the acceptance of *below-cost* selling *prices*.

shukōgyō 手工業 handicraft

shukushō 縮小 curtailment; cutback; diminution ¶ voluntary, or self-active *curtailment* of production // drastic *cutbacks* of production, or production *cutbacks* // Manufacturers started *cutting back* production. // a substantial *diminution* of the present large deficit

shukushōhendōhaba 縮小変動幅 [外] narrow margin of exchange rate; narrow margins

shukushōkinkō 縮小均衡 balance at a reduced level; diminishing equilibrium; balanced contraction ¶ the situation of a *balanced contraction* of both exports and imports

shukushōsaiseisan 縮小再生産 reproduction on a regressive scale;

reproduction on a diminishing scale

shukushōteki 縮小的 contractionary; restrictive ¶ the *contractionary* effect // *contractionary* measures // *restrictive* credit policies // to pursue a *restrictive* course

shūkyūfutsukasei 週休2日制 five-day-workweek (system)

shūmanpuran シューマン・プラン Schuman plan (of 1950)

shūmatsuteatejakkan 週末手当若干 [市] some end-week covering

shuninkaikeikan 主任会計官 chief accountant

shūnō 収納 receipt

shūnōbuai 収納歩合 ratio of collection to budgetary revenue

shūnōdenpyō 収納伝票 receipt slip (=ticket); credit slip

shunōkaigi 首脳会議 summit (meeting) ¶ topics on the agenda of the Western economic *summit* opening in London on June 7

shūnōzumigaku 収納済額 collected amount

shuntō 春闘 (annual) spring labor offensive; spring wage offensive; spring wage negotiations; "shunto" ¶ The first act of Japan's *spring wage offensive* was staged this week.

shuntōdaiippa 春闘第一波 first wave of spring labor offensive

shuntōsōba 春闘相場 spring wage settlements ¶ *Spring wage settlements* average substantially less than last year's 32 percent.

shūnyū 収入 income; earning; revenue; receipt; return; fruit ¶ to derive, earn, draw, obtain, yield, receive, make, or bring a good, large, or small *income* from business operations // Medium family *income* rose by 37.0% during the 1960s. //

Brokers' *income* on transactions in the secondary market is rocketing. // fiscal *revenue;* tax *revenue* // business *returns* // Japanese banks' *returns* on equity and investment are unattractive to think of purchasing Japanese banks. // Economic *returns* on investment in education exceed returns on alternative kinds of investment. // to tap the full potential *revenues* of the mining industry // the high dependence of the economy on fiscal and foreign exchange *revenues* emanating from the mining sector // principal and *fruit* of investment

営業収入 operating income

限界収入 marginal revenue

純収入 net income; net revenue

内国(税)収入 inland revenue

臨時収入 casual revenue

粗(=総)収入 gross income; gross earnings

租税外収入 non-tax revenue

租税収入 tax revenue

対外収入 external receipt

財産的収入 receipt for property

財政収入 fiscal revenue

shūnyūgen 収入源 revenue source ¶ The community's existing *revenue sources* are being wholly sucked up by farm spending.

shūnyūinshi 収入印紙 revenue stamp

shūnyūkanri 収入官吏 revenue official

shūnyūkyokudaika 収入極大化 revenue maximization

shūnyūshishutsu 収入支出 receipts and payments; income and outgo; income and expense; revenue and expenditure

shūnyūyaku 収入役 treasurer; revenue officer

shuppanken 出版権 publication right; copyright

shūrōdōjikan 週労働時間 work-week; working week ¶ a decline in the average *workweek* // The increase in output is attributed to a larger *workweek*. // to cut the maximum *working week* to 36 hours // [参考] to demand the shorter week // Workers earned an average 85 for 46 hours' work.

shuryoku 主力 leading; major; principal; star performer ¶ *leading* shares // *major* companies in this line of industry // The *principal* forces at work in the revival of business activity so far have been increases in consumer and government spending. // The *star performers* have been cars, with exports up 56% over a year earlier.

shuryokuginkō 主力銀行 main bank; principal banker

shuryokukabu 主力株 leading shares; pivotal shares; (market) leaders

shuryokushōhin 主力商品 most influential commodity; mainstay item

shūsanchi 集散地 distributing center; trading center

shūsei 修正 revision; amendment; modification ¶ the upward-*revised* figure // Planned investment was *revised* downward. // an *amendment* to the law // a *modification* of the measures in force // the law requires some substantial *modifications* // a downward-*revised* estimate of F1. 50.0 billion // The upgrading of growth forecasts follows the normal summer *revision* of the national in-

come forecast.

shūseihendōkawasesōbasei 修正変動為替相場制 modified system of flexible exchange rate

shūseison'eki 修正損益 revised profit and loss

shūseizai 集成材 laminate lumber

shūsekikairo 集積回路 integrated circuit: IC

shūsekinorieki 集積の利益 economies of concentration; economies of agglomeration; advantage of economic integration

shūshi 収支 income and expenditure; receipts and spending; revenue and expenditure; income and outlay ¶ to keep *expenditures and revenues* realistically in line

対民間収支 Treasury accounts with the public; government-to-public balance

shūshikessan 収支決算 settlement of accounts

shūshimikomi 収支見込 prospective income and expenditure

shūshin 終身 life; whole life; lifetime; life-long

shūshinnenkin 終身年金 life annuity

shūshinhoken 終身保険 straight life insurance; whole life insurance

shūshinkoyō 終身雇用(制) career-long-employment (system); life-time job-security; employment for life; "lifetime" (system of) employment; life-long employment ¶ the traditional Japanese practice of guaranteeing *lifetime employment*

shūshoku 就職 job placement ¶ the training and *job placement* of young Canadians

shūshokuguchi 就職口 opening; vacancy; job offer ¶ It was planned to provide *openings* for 50,000 young people a year in productive activity. // unemployment-benefit applicants who have turned down previous *job offers*

shūshuku 収縮 contraction; shrinkage; constriction ¶ the expected *shrinkage* of imports in response to higher prices // →減少

通貨収縮 deflation; contraction of money in circulation

shūshukuteki 収縮的 contractionary ¶ The mounting disorders in the money and capital markets have *contractionary* effects on the nonfinancial sectors.

shussankyūka 出産休暇 maternity leave

shussanritsu 出産率 birth rate; fertility rate

shusseikakaku 出井価格 wellhead price

shusseishibōtōkei 出生死亡統計 vital statistics

shusshi 出資 capital subscription; subscription to the capital ¶ to regulate the receiving of *capital subscriptions*

shusshiharaikomi 出資払込 payment of subscription

shusshikintanpokashitsuke 出資金担保貸付 share account loan

shusshimochibun 出資持分 subscriber's share on the capital

shusshisha 出資者 subscriber ¶ *subscribers* to the bank's capital

shusshishōken 出資証券 equity issue; subscription certificate

shusshitokeieinobunri 出資と経営の分離 separation of investment and management

shusshiyoyakuchokin 出資予約貯金 savings for capital subscription

shutchō 出超 excess of exports (over imports); favorable balance of trade; trade surplus

shutchōhanbai 出張販売 traveling sale

shutchōsho 出張所 sub-branch

shutoken 首都圏 metropolitan areas; metropolitan region; national capital region

shutokenjūtakuchiiki 首都圏住宅地域 residential quarters in the metropolitan area

shutoku 取得 acquisition; obtainment

shutokukakaku 取得価格 acquisition cost; initial cost; purchase price

shutsuryoku 出力 output ¶ a generating plant with a maximum *output* of 625,000 kilowatts

shūyakudo 集約度 intensity
労働集約度 labor intensity
資本集約度 capital intensity

shūyakunōgyō 集約農業 intensive agriculture; intensive farming

shūyakuteki 集約的 intensive ¶ energy-*intensive* industries such as iron-steel and chemicals industries

shūyakutōshi 集約投資 intensive investment

shūyō 収用 expropriation
土地収用権 land expropriation right

shuyōkigyōkeieibunseki 主要企業経営分析 financial statements of principal enterprises

shuyōkigyōtankikeizaikansoku 主要企業短期経済観測 short-term economic survey of principal enterprises

shuyōsangyō 主要産業 key industry; staple industry ¶ South Wales' two and *staple industries* of coal and steel

shuyōshōhinsakumotsu 主要商品作物 stable crop

shuyōtsūka 主要通貨 major currency; leading currency; key currency

shuyōtsūkakoku 主要通貨国 key currency nation

sinjikētoginkō シンジケート銀行 syndicate bank

sinjikētokeiyaku シンジケート契約 syndicate agreement

sinjikētorōn シンジケートローン syndicate(d) loan

soakuka 粗悪化 adulteration

sōba 相場 quotation; market price; rate; speculation ¶ *Quotations* of shares rose. // Oils were *quoted* high. // higher, or lower, *quotations* for the yen

  売買相場 buying and selling rates
  電信相場 T.T. rate
  ドル相場 dollar rate
  現物相場 spot rate
  銀行間相場 inter-bank rate
  直物相場 spot rate
  人為相場 forced quotation; artificial market
  上限相場 upper support rate
  実際相場 actual rate
  裸相場 flat rate
  期限付手形相場 usance bill rate
  基準相場 basic rate
  気迷い相場 ［市］ mixed market
  小刻み相場 split quotations
  公定 official rate
  屈伸 flexible rate
  恐怖相場 ［市］ near-panic market
  名目 nominal rate
  熱狂相場 ［市］ feverish market
  ポンド相場 sterling rate
  先物相場 forward rate; futures quotation
  市場相場 market rate

  品切相場 famine price
  写真相場 reflex quotation
  大衆相場 ［市］ public market
  天井相場 ceiling rate
  受取勘定建相場 receiver (=receiving) quotation
  輸入手形決済相場 acceptance rate
  要求払相場 demand rate

sōbahonnō 相場本能 market instinct

sōbahyō 相場表 list of quotations; course of exchange; current prices

sōbahyōjiki 相場表示器 ticker

sōbakan 相場観 forecast for market tendency

sōbakankakusa 相場間格差 discrepancies between exchange rates

sōbanateki 総花的 all-embracing ¶ an *all-embracing* budget under *all-embracing* fiscal policy

sōbanatekiyosan 総花的予算 all-embracing budget

sōbanatekizaisei 総花的財政 all-embracing fiscal policy

sōbashijisōsa 相場支持操作 official supporting operation ¶ ［参考］ The central bank intervened in the exchange market to support the dollar. // The Bank bought some $300 million in support of the dollar.

sōbasōjū 相場操縦 manipulation (of quotation)

sōbatatene 相場建値 exchange quotation; fixing of exchange rate

sochi 措置 measure; action; step; practice; expedient ¶ *Measures* that will save energy became operational. // One of the *measures* which lifts the 10% value added tax on gold transactions is already operative. // to choose moderate *measures* over drastic ones suitable to the occasion // the usefulness and feasibility of other *measures* designed to increase investment flows // Far-reaching monetary policy *measures* were instrumental in bringing about a business upturn. // to take tough *measures* to redress the situation // energy-saving *measures* are a necessary adjunct to appropriate demand management. // to identify the major *actions* that are being taken to counter inflation // to take a temporary and extraordinary *step* of calling for moderation in exports // They should be part of a package of interlocking expansionary *actions*. // a concerted *action* to comfort inflation // *action* on tax cuts // to take a timely preventive *action* to defend the dollar // a temporary *action*, not directed against any other country // the stimulative fiscal *actions* proposed by the president // harsh *action* to hold down the growth in expenditure // to introduce a series of harsh economic *measures* aimed at reducing France's high inflation rate // a patchwork of piecemeal protection *measures* that vary in scope and toughness from country to country // the need for taking more pragmatic policy-oriented *action* toward the promotion of imports // the scale and timing of expansionary *action* // to shift away from defensive *action* to prop up weak sectors // internationally concerted *action* featuring tax cuts // Australia should take determined *action* towards reducing import tariffs. // abatement of the numerous cost and price raising *actions* of the government // the EEC's growth rate, needed to be

boosted by energetic joint *action* // to adopt and implement a series of anti-inflationary *measures* // to enforce at once a package of policy *measures* for cutting the trade surplus // restrictive *steps* taken by the monetary authorities to arrest inflation in its early stages // to take many *steps*, both legislative and administrative, to encourage economic expansion // to eliminate discriminatory currency *practice* // the type and scope of *measures* needed to ensure that... // to incorporate adequate environmental protective *measures* in the projects // to discuss concrete and practical *steps* // to help re-establish vulgar and short-term *expedient*

直接措置　direct action
経済措置　economic measure
金融措置　monetary measure
政策措置　policy measures; policy action
財政措置　fiscal action

sochōsei 粗調整 rough tuning

sōdaikai 総代会 general meeting of share subscribers

sōdairiten 総代理店 sole agency; sole agent ¶ to accept the *sole agency* of a U.S. company in Japan

sōdan 相談 consultation ¶ to provide *consultancy* services for emigrant entrepreneurs

sōdatsusen 争奪戦 scramble ¶ The oil embargo sparked a *scramble* for crude oil among refiners. // The *scramble* for long-term supply contracts is spreading.

sōekikin 総益金 gross profits; gross receipts; gross earnings

sōekiritsu 総益率 gross profit rate

sofutorōn ソフト・ローン soft loan

sofutoueasangyō ソフトウエア産業 software industry

sogaiyōin 阻害要因 drag; impediment; check; constraint; hindrance; stunting; *disincentive* ¶ This was a major *drag* on trade expansion. // *constraints* placed on supply by the oil embargo // a serious *hindrance* to trade // to be *stunted* in growth // to remove existing *disincentives* in order to stimulate exports

sōgakarihi 総掛費 general (administrative) expenses

sōgakuhikiukehōshiki 総額引受方式 firm commitment

sogenzairyō 素原材料 raw materials ¶ *raw materials* for textile-making, or textile raw materials

sōgi 争議 dispute; strike ¶ →ストライキ

　小作争議 tenancy dispute
　労働争議 labor dispute

sōgidan 争議団 strikers

sōgikōi 争議行為 acts of dispute

sōgo 相互 mutual; reciprocal

sōgō 総合 synthesis; generalization; coordination; integration; totaling; consolidation

sōgobōeki 相互貿易 reciprocal trade; two-way trade

sōgochochiku 相互貯蓄 mutual savings

sōgoenjo 相互援助 mutual aid

sōgoginkō 相互銀行 mutual loan and savings bank

sōgōginkō 総合銀行 universal bank; do-all bank

sōgohoken 相互保険 mutual insurance

sōgohokengaisha 相互保険会社 mutual insurance company

sōgohokenkikin 相互保険基金 mutual insurance fund

sōgoizonkankei 相互依存関係 mutual-dependence relation

sōgojōyaku 相互条約 bilateral treaty; reciprocal treaty

sōgojuyōkintōnohōsoku 相互需要均等の法則 law of reciprocal demand

sōgōkazei 総合課税 taxation upon total income; consolidated taxation

sōgōkeikaku 総合計画 comprehensive plan

sōgōkeizaishihyō 総合経済指標 composite economic indicator ¶ The *composite economic indicator* published by the National Bank of Belgium rose by 1.5% in October to 87.5%.

sōgōkikaika 総合機械化 general mechanization; over-all mechanization; general computerization

sōgōmochidaka 総合持高 overall position

sōgōnōsei 総合農政 overall agricultural policy

sōgorieki 相互利益 mutual benefit; reciprocity

sōgōseisaku 総合政策 integrated policy; comprehensive policy; general policy; over-all policy ¶ to envisage and implement an *integrated policy* package

sōgōshisaku 総合施策 package deal; package of measures ¶ →総合対策

sōgōshisū 総合指数 composite index; overall index ¶ The *composite index* of leading economic indicators was unchanged in August at 137.1, which represents a fall of 2% over the year. // The *overall* wholesale price *index* (1980 equals 100) stood at 100.9 for September. // The New York Stock Exchange's *composite index* rose 0.75 to 54.55.

sōgōshōkengyōsha 総合証券業者
integrated (securities) firm

sōgōshokuryōseisaku 総合食糧政策
general food policy

sōgōshōsha 総合商社 general trading firm; general merchant; trading conglomerate

sōgōshotokuzei 総合所得税 consolidated income tax

sōgoshugi 相互主義 reciprocity

sōgōshūshi 総合収支 overall balance; overall accounts

sōgōtaisaku 総合対策 package (of measures) ¶ The Federal Government approved a *package of* economic *measures*. // A *package of* stimulatory *measures* designed to sustain real GNP growth. // to see the energy *package* through Congress // a N.Kr. 412 million *package of measures* to aid industry // The November *package* of dollar supports announced came in two distinct parts.

sōgōtekiippankinkō 総合的一般均衡 comprehensive general equilibrium

sōgōtekisekkin 総合的接近 global approach

sōgōtekitaisaku 総合的対策 integrated counter-measures ¶ →総合対策

sōgotekitsūkahoyū 相互的通貨保有 mutual currency holding

sōgotekizōyo 相互的贈与 mutual gift

sōgotsūkakanjō 相互通貨勘定 mutual currency account

sōgōun'ei 総合運営 integrated management; (well-)coordinated management

sōgōyokinkōza 総合預金口座 deposit combined account; special deposit account

sōgōyosan 総合予算 master budget

sōgōyosanhōshiki 総合予算方式 unified budget system; integrated budget formula

sōgōyosanseisaku 総合予算政策 "single annual budget" policy; fiscal policy calling for no supplement budgets; unified budget system

sōgyō 創業 inauguration; initiation; establishment

sōgyō 操業 operation; work ¶ *Work* on the new steel plant was stopped.

周年操業 year-round operation

sōgyōdo 操業度 →操業率

sōgyōhi 創業費 initial expenses; organization expenses; preliminary expenses; promotion expenses

未償却創業費 unamortized initial expenses

sōgyōhi 操業費 operating expenses

sōgyōhishōkyahu 創業費償却 amortization of initial expenses

sōgyōjikan 操業時間 hours of operation; office hours

sōgyōnissu 操業日数 operated days

sōgyōritsu 操業率 rate of operation; operation rate; rate of capacity utilization ¶ The economy is *operating* below full capacity *rates*. // to be temporarily *operating* below capacity // to *operate* close to *capacity* // to *operate at* a high *rate* // ［参考］the level of under-utilized capacity // idle capacity // →設備稼働率

sōgyōsha 創業者 founder; promoter

sōgyōsharitoku 創業者利得 founder's profit

sōgyōtanshuku 操業短縮 reduction of operation; curtailment of operation; cutback of operation; production cutbacks; production curtailment; output reduction; short-time working ¶ A further increase in lay-offs' *short-time working* and shiftdowns is expected. // There were 2,667 firms *working short-time* in Febuary. // The number of persons on *short-time* fell to 102,864.

sōhigyō 総罷業 general strike

sōhōdokusen 双方独占 bilateral monopoly

sohōnōgyō 粗放農業 extensive farming

sōjōkōka 相乗効果 multiplier effect ¶ the *multiplier effect* of increase in fiscal spending

sōjōtekijōshōkōka 相乗的上昇効果 spiral influence

sōjunbi 総準備 gross reserves; aggregate reserves

sōjunbipojishon 総準備ポジション gross reserve position

sōjuyō 総需要 total demand; schedule demand; aggregate demand ¶ levels of *aggregate demand* commensurate with supply availabilities // the recession and the subsequent low *aggregate demand* // a temporary shortfall of *aggregate demand*

sōjuyōseisaku 総需要政策 demand management ¶ In 1979 *demand management* is again expansionary. // the role of *demand management* in the fight against inflation

sōjuyōyokusei 総需要抑制 restrictive demand management; restriction of aggregate demand

sōkachūshutsuhō 層化抽出法 stratified sampling

sōkaheikin 相加平均 arithmetic mean

sōkaiya 総会屋 professional hecklers and blackmailers (threating to disrupt shareholders' meetings); professional hirelings employed by corporations (to obstruct anti-management moves at shareholders' meetings); professional stockholder; corporate gadfly

sōkamusakuichūshutsuhō 層化無作為抽出法 stratified random sampling method

sōkanjōmotochō 総勘定元帳 general ledger

sōkankankei 相関(関係) relationship; (cor)relation ¶ A broad *relationship* was drawn between a particular share and the market as a whole. // There is no consistent empirical verification of this *relationship* — the interest elasticity of investment. // to verify the hypothesized behavioral *relationship* between the interest rate and investment decisions // The *relationship* between unemployment and inflation implicit in an econometric model is usually not rigid. // The *relation* of money and growth can be viewed in purely statistical terms. // the regression expressing the *relation* of economic growth to money creation // Without the investment variable the *relationship* was not significant. // a high *correlation* existing between increases in money supply and economic growth // the whole *relationship* between money supply and income // the positive *relation* between money supply and growth // Foreign assets show up as not positively and significantly *related* to growth. // Rates of growth in real income seem to be positively *related* with rates of increases in money supply. // The concurrent *relation* between growth and inflation over longer periods was examined. // A positive year by year *relation* seemed plausible.

逆相関 negative (cor)relation ¶ A *negative correlation* was found between growth and government borrowing. // The openness of an economy is *negatively related* to growth.

時差相関 timing relation(ship); lead lag relation(ship)

系列相関 serial correlation

sōkatsuhoken 総括保険 blanket insurance

sōkatsukeiei 総括経営 general administration

sōkatsukeieisha 総括経営者 general management executive

sōkatsukeieisō 総括経営層 administrative function; general management

sōkatsuteitō 総括抵当 general mortgage; blanket mortgage

sōkatsuteitōkentsukisaiken 総括抵当権付債券 blanket bond

sōkei 総計 aggregate; total; sum ¶ to take in the *aggregate* // to *total* $5,000 in the *aggregate* // This makes a *total* of $200. // Sales *total* over $100. // Expenditures *total* the huge sum of nearly $2 billion. // Outlays *sum up to* $4 million

sōkeiyosan 総計予算 overall budget

sōkin 送金 remittance

移住者送金 immigrant remittance; expatriate remittance

海外送金 overseas remittance; remittance abroad

為替送金 remittance by draft

sōkingaku 送金額 amount of remittance

sōkinirainin 送金依頼人 remitter; debtor

sōkinkawase 送金為替 remittance bill; remittance draft

被仕向送金為替 remittance from abroad; inward remittance; incoming remittance

仕向送金為替 remittance abroad; outword remittance; out-going remittance

sōkinkogitte 送金小切手 remittance check

sōkinnin 送金人 remitter

被送金人 remittee

sōkintesuryō 送金手数料 remittance charge

sōkin'uketorinin 送金受取人 recipient; creditor

sokkin 即金 spot cash; prompt cash; immediate payment

sokkinbarai 即金払い cash payment; immediate payment

sokkinnedan 即金値段 spot price; price for cash

sokkintorihiki 即金取引 cash transaction

soko 底 trough; bottom; nadir; low; valley ¶ to decline gradually to the *trough* month of February // The decline appears to have reached *bottom*. // 1964 was probably the *nadir* of an inventory cycle. // The trade situation is approaching its *nadir* and should begin to improve around the mid-year. // to be on an upgrade from *lows* earlier this year // The downward cycle has passed its *nadir*. // the peak and *trough* of the business cycle // The recession has passed its *trough*. //

The cyclical *trough* has not yet been left behind. // The recession *trough* is deeper than estimated. // The price decline reached *bottom*. // The *bottom* fell out of the market. // The market hit a two-year *bottom*. // April will prove to be the *bottom* month of the recession. // to hurt bargains at *bottom*

二番底　double bottom (=valley) ¶ The decline touched the *double bottom*. // a *"double-bottomed"* recession // The market goes lower than the last *valley*.

sokō 粗鋼 crude steel

sōko 倉庫 warehouse; godown; store house

普通倉庫　private warehouse; free warehouse

保税倉庫　bonded warehouse

港湾倉庫　port warehouse; pier warehouse

sokobanare 底離れ bottoming out ¶ Exports increased in the wake of the *bottoming out* of overseas business. // The recession seems to have *bottomed out* in the course of the autumn.

sōkogaisha 倉庫会社 warehouse company

sokogatai 底堅い steady undertone; firm undertone ¶ The *undertone* of the market was steady. // The market has been *firm* in its *undertone*. // The *tone underlying* the market was firm. // [参考] The market tone was basically firm.

sokogatame 底堅め firming (down); touching (rock) bottom; tamping ¶ Prices *firmed down*. // Prices presumably *touched* (= *hit*) *bottom*. // The U.S. was *tamping* down its economy to fight infla-

tion. // the likelihood of a *firming* of interest rates

sokogatasa 底堅さ firmness ¶ the *firmness* of the Belgian franc // [参考] The dollar has returned to terra firma.

sōkogyō 倉庫業 warehousing business

sōkogyōsha 倉庫業者 warehouse man

sokoi 底意 undertone; underlying tone; underlying tendency; basic tone ¶ The *undertone* is firm. // The tone *underlying* the market has been a shade firmer. // A weak *tone underlied* the market.

sokoire 底入れ touching bottom; hitting bottom ¶ The decline in prices *hit bottom*. // Prices already *hit bottom*.

sokoirekan 底入れ感 sentiment of bottoming-out

sokojikara 底力 underlying strength; underlying vitality ¶ the *underlying strength* and resilience of the U.S. economy // The Italian economy has displayed an *underlying vitality*, without which any progress would be impossible.

sokōken 租鉱権 mining lease

sokone 底値 bottom price; floor price

sokonejigen 底値示現 hitting bottom; bottoming out; touching bottom ¶ The market *hit* a two-year *bottom*. // The price touched *bottom*.

sokoneken 底値圏 vicinity of the lower limit

sokoni 底荷 ballast

sokonukesōba 底抜け相場 bottom falling out of the market ¶ The bottom has *fallen out of the market*.

sōkoshōken 倉庫証券 warehouse

receipt; warrant

sōkowatashi 倉庫渡し ex warehouse; in bond; ex store

sokozumi 底積み bottom stowage

sokuhō 速報 advance report; advance announcement; interim report; urgent message; preliminary report (=figures)

sokuhōkeisū 速報計数 preliminary figure; quick estimate; flash estimate ¶ a 7.2 percent *flash estimate* made by the Commerce Department earlier of GNP

sokuhōsei 速報性 necessity to report speedily

sokujikankinsei 即時換金性 ready convertibility into cash

sokujiōtōshisutemu 即時応答システム [コン] on-demand system

sokujishori 即時処理 [コン] real time processing

sokujitekikōbaiyoryoku 即時的購買余力 ready purchasing power

sokujitsuriyōkanōshikin 即日利用可能資金 immediately available funds

sokunō 即納 spot payment; immediate payment

sokutei 測定 measurement ¶ the productivity *measurement*, or *measurement* of productivity // An M2 *measurement* of money available in the system on a weekly basis may be a steadier *measurement*.

sokuteishakudo 測定尺度 measurement rod ¶ to much dependence on one simple *measurement rod*, ie., the Ml money supply figure

sōkuzure 総崩れ [市] collapse; debacle; sweeping crash

sokyū 遡及 retroaction; retrospection; recourse ¶ with-*recourse* credit // The law is *retroactive* to

1971. // to review 1975 in *retrospect*

sokyūhō 遡及法 retroactive law

sokyūhoken 遡及保険 retroactive insurance

sokyūhyōka 遡及評価 retroactive appraisal

sokyūkeisan 遡及計算 retrogressive accounting

sokyūkōryoku 遡及効力 retroaction

sokyūteki 遡及的 retroactive; retrospective; backdated

sokyūwarimashihaitō 遡及割増配当 reteroactive bonus

somōbō 梳毛紡 worsted (yarn) spinning

somōshi 梳毛糸 worsted yarn

sōmubōeki 双務貿易 bilateral trade

sōmujōyaku 双務条約 bilateral treaty; bilateral contract; reciprocal agreement

sōmutorihiki 双務取引 bilateral transaction

son'ekibunkibunseki 損益分岐分析 break-even analysis

son'ekibunkiten 損益分岐点 break-even point

son'ekibunkitensōgyōdo 損益分岐点操業度 break-even rate of operation ¶ enterprises that have a low *break-even rate of operation*

son'ekikin 損益金 profit and loss

songai 損害 damage; loss ¶ The local *damage* is estimated at $5 million. // to suffer serious *damage* from a flood // The damage was covered by *damage* insurance.

songaibaishō 損害賠償 compensation; indemnity; reparation

songaibaishōkin 損害賠償金 indemnity; compensation money for damages; damages ¶ to sue for *damages* // to make a claim for *damages* against a company

songaigaku 損害額 amount of damage

songaihoken 損害保険 property and casualty insurance; insurance against loss; insurance against damage; non-life insurance; casualty insurance

songaihokengaisha 損害保険会社 non-life insurance company

songaihokenkin 損害保険金 casualty insurance claim; casualty insurance money

songaihokenryō 損害保険料 casualty insurance premium

songaihyōkagaku 損害評価額 appraisal of damage

songaikamotsu 損害貨物 damaged cargo; damaged goods

songaimikomi 損害見込 estimated loss; estimated damage

sonmō 損耗 wear and tear

sonryō 損料 rent; hire

sonshitsu 損失 loss ¶ the danger of *loss* from (=due to) bank failures // a sudden business slump inflicted heavy *losses* to (=on) creditors // *losses* recorded when realized // to incur, and make up for, a substantial *loss* on investments // The *loss* on disposal meant that the group incurred a net *loss* of $325m.

sonshitsubuntan 損失分担 share of loss

sonshitsuhoten 損失補塡 loss compensation; making up (=covering; filling up; making good) a deficit

sonshitsukeijō 損失計上 registering a deficit; going into the red

sonshitsukin 損失金 expenses; loss

sonshitsunissū 損失日数 total working days lost

sonshōkahei 損傷貨幣 worn(-out) coin; damaged coin

sonshōken 損傷券 worn(-out) coin; damaged note; mutilated note

sontokunashinotorihiki 損得なしの取引 even bargain

sōonbōshikatsudō 騒音防止活動 Anti-noise activity

sōonhannin 騒音犯人 noise-maker

sōonkanwa 騒音緩和 noise abatement

sōonkijun 騒音基準 noise level

sōonkōgai 騒音公害 noise pollution; environmental pollution from intolerable noise

sōonseigen 騒音制限 noise limit

sōon'yokushiki 騒音抑止器 noise suppressor

sōrahausu ソーラ・ハウス solar house

sorishi 粗利子 gross interest

sōrōdōjikan 総労働時間 total hours worked

sōryūdōseipojishon 総流動性ポジション whole liquidity position

sōsa 操作 operation; practice; manipulation ¶ The company plans to shut assembly *operations* at five plants. // The industry sought to resume normal *operations* in the aftermath of the strike. // to *operate* the national economy // policy *operations* // market *operations* // machines in full *operation* // deliberate *manipulation* of the books to deceive supervisory authorities

公開市場操作 open market operation

表口操作 front-door operation

裏口操作 back-door operation

sōsai 相殺 offset; compensate; countervail; counterbalance; cancel out ¶ Outlays drifted lower in each of the third and fourth quarters, but these were *offset* by rising expenses elsewhere. // These largely *offsetting* movements gave a slight upward tilt to the index. // These large divergent movements were largely *offsetting,* and the overall index changed little. // The rise in exports was more than *offset* by the increase in imports. // to *compensate* the lender for the erosion in the future value of the debt // The large gain in exports *compensated* for most of the gain in imports. // The adverse effect of it has been more than *counterbalanced* by expansion in other directions. // The lira was 12% lower against the D. mark, which over-*compensates* for the 10% inflation gap with West Germany. // The fall of 3.7% *canceled out* the expansion of 3.4% that had been recorded in the previous year.

sōsaikanzei 相殺関税 countervailing duties

sōsamokuhyō 操作目標 operating target ¶ →政策運営目標

sōshihainin 総支配人 general manager

sōshihon 総資本 total liabilities and net worth

sōshihonkaitenritsu 総資本回転率 turnover ratio of total liabilities and net worth

sōshihonshūekiritsu 総資本収益率 ratio of net profit to total liabilities and net worth

soshiki 組織 fabric ¶ Aggressive policies would erode the economic *fabric* on which the international banking system depends. // to undermine the social *fabric* of the country

soshikikaihatsu 組織開発 organization development

soshikikitei 組織規程 organization regulations

sōshikinkeijōgenka 総資金経常原価 current cost of funds; ratio of interests and expenses on funds to total funds

sōshikinkeijōrimawari 総資金経常利回り current yield on funds; ratio of total income on funds to total funds

soshikirōdōsha 組織労働者 organized labor; organized worker

soshikitekihanbaikanri 組織的販売管理 systematized sales management

soshikitekihanbaikatsudō 組織的販売活動 system marketing

soshikitekishijō 組織的市場 organized market

soshikizu 組織図 organization chart

sōshūeki 総収益 gross earnings; gross income; total profit

sōtai 相対 contra; relative

sōtaihōshisū 相対法指数 index number by relative method

sōtaikachi 相対価値 relative value

sōtaikakaku 相対価格 relative price ¶ Changes in *relative prices* —particularly those stemming from the sharp rise in the price of energy —had the effect of reducing the effective capital stock. // *Relative prices* in machinery sectors are moving, toward a lower level.

輸出相対価格 relative export price ¶ Japan's *relative export prices* (= Japanese export price divided by world export price) continue to drop.

sōtaikanjō 相対勘定 contra account

sōtainomondai 総体の問題 aggregation problem

sōtaishotokukasetsu 相対所得仮説 relative income hypothesis

sōtaitekikyūbōka 相対的窮乏化 relative impoverishment

sōtaitekiwakemae 相対的分け前 relative share

sōtan 操短 →操業短縮

sōtōgaku 相当額 equivalent ¶ to pay a sum as an *equivalent* for the supply of ores // to receive the yen *equivalent* of 100 U.S. dollars // →等価

sōtokei 総解け合い enforced liquidation; all-out liquidation

sotomuki 外向き outward-looking ¶ the whole *outward-looking* strategy

sōtonsū 総トン数 grossweight (tonnage); G/T

sōtōshi 総投資 gross investment

sotosotogaisai 「外-外」外債 out-to-out external bond

sotouchigaisai 「外-内」外債 out-to-in external bond

sōuriagedaka 総売上高 gross sales

sōwahōshisū 総和法指数 index number by aggregative method

sōyosan 総予算 general budget

sozai 素材 material ¶ (the metal) *materials* for minting 10-yen coins

sozei 租税 taxes; local taxes; rates

sozeichōshū 租税徴収 collection of taxes; tax collection

sozeifutan 租税負担 tax burden; incidence of tax(ation)

sozeifutanritsu 租税負担率 tax burden ratio; tax bearing rate; percentage of the total annual taxation to the total annual national income

sozeifutansha 租税負担者 taxpayer; ratepayer

sozeigensoku 租税原則 canon of taxation

sozeihinanchi 租税避難地 tax haven ¶ Global transfers of a colossal amount of funds to dodge taxes or in quest of lucrative investments are facilitated in various ways by *tax havens* like the Caymans. // to move plants to *tax havens* // Many of the *tax haven* corporations are nothing but dummies.

sozeihōteishugi 租税法定主義 no taxation without representation

sozeijōyaku 租税条約 taxation convention

sozeikanpukin 租税還付金 tax refund; tax rebate

sozeikeigen 租税軽減 tax reduction

sozeikōka 租税公課 taxes and public charges

sozeimenjo 租税免除 exemption of taxes; exemption from taxation; tax exemption

sozeinojuekishafutangensoku 租税の受益者負担原則 benefit theory of taxation; benefits-received principle of taxation; compensatory principle of taxation

sozeinonukeana 租税の抜け穴 tax loophole

sozeinoshizenzō 租税の自然増 excess in tax revenues; natural increase of tax revenues

sozeiōnōgensoku 租税応能原則 ability-to-pay principle

sozeishōken 租税証券 tax anticipation bill

sozeishūnyū 租税収入 tax revenue

sozeitaikei 租税体系 system of taxation

sozeitenka 租税転嫁 shift of taxes

sōzoku 相続 succession; inheritance

sōzokuken 相続権 right of inheritance

sōzokunin 相続人 heir; heiress; successor

sōzokuzaisan 相続財産 inheritance; inherited property; heirloom

sōzōtekihakai 創造的破壊 creative destruction

sūchi 数値 value; figure ¶ 2.9 on average in 1980, a *figure* in excess of the long-term value

sūchiseigyoki 数値制御機 ［コン］ numerical control machine tools

sueoki 据置き deferred; unredeemed; unredeemable; uncallable; stationary; noncallable ¶ The bonds will be *noncallable* for the first five years after issuance. // to allow it to *defer* principal payments on loans coming due in the next three years // to present its *deferment* proposal to its creditor banks

sueokibarai 据置払い deferred payment

sueokichokin 据置貯金 deferred savings; fixed savings

sueokihaitōkin 据置配当金 deferred dividend

sueokikikan 据置期間 grace period; term of deferment; waiting period ¶ bonds redeemable after a *grace period* of three years, or after a five years' *grace* // The loan is repayable over 40 years after a ten-year *grace period*. // the expiration of *grace periods* on some loans // the *waiting period* for the repatriation of foreign capital invested in Japanese stocks // ［参考］ bonds not redeemable for three years

sueokinenkin 据置年金 deferred annuity

sueokitanpo 据置担保 fixed collateral

sūgakutekikeikaku 数学的計画 mathematical programing

sugushō 直ぐ正 ［証市］ immediate delivery

suichokubōeki 垂直貿易 vertical trade

suichokutekidankaisoshiki 垂直的段階組織 vertical hierarchy

suichokutekikigyōrengō 垂直的企業連合 vertical combination

suichokutekikokusaibungyō 垂直的国際分業 vertical international specialization

suichokutōgō 垂直統合 vertical integration

suiden 水田 paddy-field; rice field

suidōryōkin 水道料金 water rates (=charges)

suigai 水害 flood damage; flood disaster

suigaichi 水害地 flooded district

suigaihoken 水害保険 flood insurance

suigaikaoku 水害家屋 submerged houses

suigairisaisha 水害罹災者 flood sufferers

suigaitaisaku 水害対策 flood control measure; relief measure for flood sufferers

suigaiyobō 水害予防 flood control

suigin'osen 水銀汚染 mercury pollution

suiheibōeki 水平貿易 horizontal trade

suiheibungyō 水平分業 horizontal division of labor

suiheitekigappei 水平(的)合併 horizontal amalgamation

suiheitekikokusaibungyō 水平的国際分業 horizontal international specialization

suiheitekirenkei 水平的連携 horizontal association

suiheitekitōgō 水平(的)統合 horizontal integration

suii 推移 movement; change; trend ¶ *movements* in selected monetary aggregates // major price *trends* // → 動き

suijun 水準 level; standard; norm ¶ to attain a high *level* // to keep, or maintain a *level* of prices // to raise, increase, elevate, heighten, reduce, decrease, or bring down the general *level* of prices // to reach or touch higher *levels* // to keep at low *levels* or on high *levels* // rises and falls in the *level* of prices // high and low *levels* of activity // the gain over the year-ago *level* // the disappointing or encouraging *level* of sales // prices at peak *levels* // people on a low *level* of civilization // to *level* up or down prices // the fall in living *standards* // to elevate the *standard* of living // below or above the prewar *standard* // to fall short off or be up to the newly set *standard* // as measured from past *standards* // The index was 3.5% above the year-ago *level*. // to bring the growth of the monetary aggregates down to *levels* commensurate with the real growth rate of the economy // to push the value of the dollar below *levels* justified by the underlying economic situation // sales exceeding the record *levels* achieved in 1974 // *levels* higher than normal for the time of the year // the prevalence of historically high *levels* of unemployment // to return to a more tolerable *level* // to upgrade the *level* of technology, which is well below the best international *standards* // Imports recovered to a more normal *level*. // to be pushed upward to unaccustomed *levels* in recent years // to recede toward historical *levels* // to even out benefit *levels* // an income equal to 65% of the local poverty *level* // to keep imports to a reasonable *level* // not to carry demand to unsustainably high, or unacceptably low *levels* // an exorbitant *level* of government expenditures // to strive to raise employment to acceptable *levels* // Unemployment, although coming down from the record *level* seen in the recession, is expected to remain at a *level* well above post-war *norms*. // The low *level* of the reserves was rendered more serious by the limitations on the use of gold. // The indicator rose to 87.58, its highest *level* for two years. // International capital movements have risen to enormous—some might even say excessive—*levels*

物価水準　price level
文化水準　cultural level
賃金水準　wage level; level of wages
価格水準　price level; level of prices
許容水準　permissible level
給与水準　wage level; level of wages
最低生活水準　minimum standard of living
産業水準　level of industry
生活維持水準　subsistence level
生活水準　level of living; plane of living; living standards; standard of living
生産水準　level of production
支持水準　support level
消費水準　consumption level; level

of consumption

所得水準 income level; level of income

抵抗水準 resistance level; holding level

suikei 推計 estimate; estimation ¶ the volume on the most conservative *estimate* // *Estimates* for this year are favorable, with exports projected to expand. // The final outturn corresponds to the *estimates*. // The decline is provisionally *estimated* by the Federation at 10%.

suikeichi 推計値 estimated value

suiminkōza 睡眠口座 dormant account; sleeping account

suingugendo スイング限度 swing ceiling; swing limit

suiryokuhatsuden 水力発電 hydraulic (=hydroelectric; water) power generation

suisan 水産 fishery

suisanbutsu 水産物 aquatic products; marine products; sea-food

加工水産物 processed aquatic products; processed marine products; processed sea-food

suisangyō 水産業 fishery; fisheries industry; fishing industry; marine products industry

suisankumiai 水産組合 fishery cooperative; marine products guild

suisanshikenjō 水産試験場 fisheries experiment station

suishin 推進 drive; promotion ¶ The United States continues its *drive* for self-sufficiency in energy. // to conduct an all-out savings *drive*

suishinryoku 推進力 thrust; driving power; driving force; forward momentum; motive power; stimulus; boost; propellant ¶ The main *thrust* in previous recoveries came from business investment. // to take positive initiatives to impart a *forward momentum* // The major *driving force* of business activity was active demand. // Government expenditure will be the main *driving force* behind the econmy's upturn. // Exports were the principal *driving force* of the economy. // The major *driving force* of business activity is active demand. // The *driving force* of economic expansion was blunted. // The main *stimulus* to economic activity is being provided by the consumer goods sector. // The main *boost* to the Norwegian economy this year is coming from North Sea oil and gas. // Expenditure on machinery and equipment was the main *propellant* of domestic business activity.

suishitsuosen 水質汚染 water pollution

suisokutōkeigaku 推測統計学 inductive statistics

suisukasai スイス貨債 Swiss franc bond

suiteikessan 推定決算 tentative closing of accounts

suitō 出納 receipt and payment; receipts and disbursements

suitōbo 出納簿 cash-book

suitōdenpyō 出納伝票 cash slip

suitōkanri 出納官吏 accounting official

suitōkanrikogitte 出納官吏小切手 government check issued by accounting official; red check

suitōkikan 出納機関 accounting organ

suitōmadoguchi 出納窓口 tellers' station

suitōmadoguchikakariin 出納窓口係員 teller ¶ *tellers* at tellers' station

suitōseiriki 出納整理期 settlement period

suitōyaku 出納役 accounting official

suitōyokin 出納預金 cash deposits

suiun 水運 water transport; water carriage; transportation by water

sūji 数字 number; figure; digit; numeric character; numeral ¶ to reach its fourth *number;* to run into four *figures,* or a four-*digit figure* // an untold *number,* or astronomical *figure*

sūjishikikeisanki 数字式計算機 digital computer

sukueapojishon スクエア・ポジション square position ¶ exchange holdings in a *square position* // to keep the *position square* // to *square* the exchange *position*

sumikomisei 住込制 live-in system

sumisoniangōi スミソニアン合意 Smithsonian agreement

sumisoniantaisei スミソニアン体制 Smithsonian monetary system; Smithsonian regime

sunēku スネーク "snake"; "snake in the tunnel" ¶ the *"snake,"* i.e., the European common margins agreement // The spot mark moved up from the bottom of the European *"snake."* // Switzerland is not a member but actually follows the *"snake."* // Central-bank interventions keep exchange rates on a level with the *"snake."* // The consequences of the franc's latest desertion from the *snake* are being weighed. // The French currency's withdrawal from the *snake* is being questioned.

sūpāgōrudotoranshe スーパー・ゴールド・トランシェ ［外］ super gold tranche

supairaru スパイラル spiral ¶ Raises in product prices set in motion a price-wage and a wage-price *spiral* feeding on each other. // to break the pernicious *spiral* of nominal incomes and prices // to put an end to the vicious wage-price *spiral* // an uncontrollable living cost *spiral*

suraidochingin スライド賃金 wage in slide scale

suraidosei スライド制 sliding scale ¶ the *sliding* pay *scales* // the *sliding scale* of wages

suranpufurēshon スランプフレーション slumpflation ¶ When slump and inflation are combined in *slumpflation,* negative real interest rates are necessary.

sūryō 数量 quantity; physical volume; volume

sūryōbunseki 数量分析 quantitative analysis

sūryōkeiki 数量景気 quantitative boom; prosperity without inflation; non-inflationary growth

sūryōshisū 数量指数 quantum index

sūryōtekihaaku 数量的把握 quantification ¶ →計量化

sūryōwaribiki 数量割引 quantity discount

sūsei 趨勢 secular movement; trend ¶ a *secular uptrend* in shipments // Output has *trended* downward since late 1971. // the recent *trend* in price movements // The *trend* of prices is disquieting. // to be consistent with continuing real growth of the economy at its long-term *trend* rate of increase of close to 5% a year //

Lagging indicators tend to trail economic *trends*. // The slack demand for credit followed a weaker than expected *trend* in economic output. // The economic and demographic *trends* of recent years will hold. // These *trends* are inherently inflationary. // The year 1978 witnessed a major reversal of these *trends*. // Though hesitantly, the *trend* in employment turned up again. // the worldwide upward *trend* of the price level // The expansionary *trend* appears to be firmly established for the year. // temporary deviations of M2 from its underlying *trend* // The annual figure is way off *trend*. // The year witnessed a major reversal of those *trends*. // to reverse a 36-year *trend* upward // →基調

sūseibunseki 趨勢分析 trend analysis

sūseichōsei 趨勢調整 adjustment for trend

sūseichōseizumi 趨勢調整済 adjusted for trend

sūseihendō 趨勢変動 secular trend

sūseihiritsu 趨勢比率 trend ratio

sūseiseichōritsu 趨勢成長率 trend rate of growth

sūseisen 趨勢線 trend line ¶ The year's ratio of capital stock to labor fell shorter of its earlier growth-*trend line*.

sūseitekifukinkō 趨勢的不均衡 secular disequilibrium

sūseitekihendō 趨勢的変動 secular change

sūseitekikinkō 趨勢的均衡 secular equilibrium

sūseitekiseichō 趨勢的成長 secular growth

sūseizōkaritsu 趨勢増加率 rate of increase on trend; trend rate of growth ¶ to gradually moderate the *trend rate of growth* of the money supply // to allow to *grow* but at a below-*trend rate*

sūshikishorigengo 数式処理言語 [コン] formula symbolic manipulation language

sutagufurēshon スタグフレーション stagflation; a mixture of economic stagnation and inflation

sutandādopuakabukashisū スタンダード・プア株価指数 Standard & Poor's Stock Price Index

sutandobaikurejitto スタンド・バイ・クレジット stand by credit

sutanpu スタンプ trade stamp; stamp

sutāringuchiiki スターリング地域 sterling area

sutebe ステベ stevedore

sutene 捨値 sacrifice price; sacrificial price

sutērubīeru ステール・ビー・エル [外] stale B/L

suteuri 捨売り sacrifice sale

sutokku ストック stock; balance; outstanding amount ¶ the money supply as measured on a *stock* basis // The nation's *stock* of plant and equipment has become obsolete. // to replenish the nation's capital *stock*

sutoppugōseisaku ストップ・ゴー政策 stop-go policy ¶ to stop the *stop-go policy*

sutoraiki ストライキ strike; labor dispute ¶ The unions have threatened to launch a one-day *strike* tomorrow to back pay demands. // to decide when and where to call *strikes* over demands for a five-hour cut in the working week // Altogether 3,783 workers and employees took part in *strikes*, i.e. 0.14% of all workers. // They went on *strike* for a total of 57,948 hours. // The average duration of a *strike* was 12 hours and 39 minutes in 1975. // Railway workers performed a 24-hour *strike*.

同情スト sympathy strike

示威スト(ライキ) demonstration strike

抗議スト(ライキ) protest strike

縄張り争いのスト(ライキ) jurisdictional strike

政治スト(ライキ) political strike

座り込みスト sit-in strike; sitdown strike

山猫スト wildcat strike

sutoraikiken ストライキ権 right to strike; right of general strike

sutoraikishirei ストライキ指令 strike order

sutoyaburi スト破り strike breaker; fink; scab

suwapputorihiki スワップ取引 swap transaction; swap operation changing over; spot-forward transaction; sale of spot against purchase of forward exchange ¶ the spot exchange being *swapped* against forward exchange

suwapputorikime スワップ取決め swap arrangement; reciprocal currency agreement

suwarikomi 座り込み stay-down; stay-in (strike)

T

TB rēto TBレート Treasury bill rate

tachiai 立会 attendance; presence; [市] call; session ¶ in the morning and afternoon *sessions* of the market

後場(の立会) afternoon session

前場(の立会) morning session

tachiaiba 立会場 [市] board-room; floor; walk

tachiaijikan 立会時間 [市] market hours

tachiainin 立会人 witness; watcher

tachiaiteishi 立会停止 [市] suspension of transactions

tachiba 立場 footing ¶ to incorporate the foreign banking community into the U.S. banking system

on an equal *footing* with domestic banks

tachinaori 立直り rally; firming up; revival; recovery

tachinokiryō 立退料 compensation for removal

tadanchūshutsuhō 多段抽出法 multi-stage sampling

tafutohātorēhō タフト・ハートレー法 [米] Taft-Hartley Act

tagenshakai 多元社会 heterogeneous society

tahentekikyōtei 多辺的協定 multilateral agreement

tahentekimusabetsutekibōeki 多辺的無差別的貿易 multilateral and non-discrimination trade

taibō 耐乏 austerity ¶ A greater

austerity in the living is required.

taibōseikatsu 耐乏生活 austerity life; belt tightening

taibutsukashitsuke 対物貸付 loan on real estate

taibutsukeiyaku 対物契約 real contract

taibutsushin'yō 対物信用 real credit

taibutsushin'yōkashitsuke 対物信用貸付 loan on real credit

taido 態度 attitude; stance; posture; disposition; stand ¶ a more cautious *attitude* taken by banks toward lending // a case illustrative of the "public demand" *attitude* of corporate officials towards stockholders // a strictly restrictive *stance* in policy actions // a positive *posture* of banks to lend money // consumers' *disposition* to buy // "Buy-now-before-prices-rise" *attitudes* are at a record level. // More of a restrictive *attitude* toward lending was assured by banks. // The wait-and-see *attitude* prevailed among investors. // Lending *attitudes* of financial *institutions* are accommodative. // a smooth transition to a moderate stimulative monetary *posture* of the Bank // Banks maintained an accommodative lending *posture*. // the appropriate modifications of the policy *stance* // Governments appear to be taking a tougher *stand* against inflation. // [参考] The lending behavior of banks has become more prudent. // →姿勢

taidorōn タイド・ローン tied loan; conditional loan; project loan

taigai 対外 foreign; external; overseas; off-shore

taigaibōeki 対外貿易 overseas trade

taigaienjo 対外援助 aid to a foreign country; foreign aid

taigaienjokeikaku 対外援助計画 foreign aid program

taigaihukinkō 対外不均衡 external imbalance; external disequilibrium

taigaijunbiryūdōsei 対外準備流動性 variability (=liquidity) of payments reserves

taigaijunshisan 対外純資産 net foreign claims

taigaikachi 対外価値 external value ¶ The *external value* of the Deutsche Mark then rose slightly against all currencies. // Adjustment of the currency's *external value* could provide a stimulus to economic activity.

taigaikankei 対外関係 foreign relations; external relations

taigaikariire 対外借入 overseas borrowing

taigaikariirenōryoku 対外借入能力 potentiality of overseas borrowing; ability for overseas borrowing

taigaikeizai 対外経済 external economy ¶ to rectify the imbalance in the *external economy* // to bring about an improvement in the *external economy*

taigaikinkō 対外均衡 external equilibrium

taigairiken 対外利権 overseas interests

taigaisaiken 対外債権 foreign credit (=claimable asset); external credit

taigaisaimu 対外債務 external debt; external indebtedness; foreign debt; external liabilities ¶ The long-term *external debt* of non-oil developing countries increased. // Their *external indebtedness* has been mounting. // to experience *external debt* difficulties // The German banks' outstanding short-term *external liabilities* reached the amount of DM50 billion, DM46 billion of which was invested with foreign banks. // A degree of centralized control over the incurrence of *foreign debt* is required. // to service and reimburse their high *foreign debts*, which were mainly incurred vis-à-vis the industrial nations // *Foreign indebtedness* was built up rapidly.

taigaisaimushiharaiteishisochi 対外債務支払停止措置 transfer moratorium

taigaishakkan 対外借款 external loan

taigaishakkankyōyo 対外借款供与 loans to overseas countries

taigaishiharaishudan 対外支払手段 foreign means of payment

taigaishin'yōkyōyo 対外信用供与 credit extensions to overseas non-residents

taigaitankishisanfusai 対外短期資産負債 short-term assets and liabilities vis-à-vis non-residents

taigaitōshi 対外投資 overseas investment; investment in foreign countries

taigaitōyūshi 対外投融資 overseas loan and investment

taigyō 怠業 sabotage; slowdown; idling strike; go-slow sabotage ¶ a railroad sabotage // They *sabotaged* railroads. // to go on a *slowdown* // Some 350,000 workers have been *idled* in the 20-day series of strikes, lockouts, strike-related layoffs and forced vacations.

taiheiyōberutochitai 太平洋ベルト地帯 Pacific belt zone

taiheiyōbōekikaihatsukaigi 太平洋貿易開発会議 Conference for Pacific Trade and Development

taiheiyōkeizaiiinkai 太平洋経済委員会 Pacific Basin Economic Cooperation Committee

taiheiyōkeizaiken 太平洋経済圏 Pacific economic community

taiinfureshori 対インフレ処理 inflation-proofing ¶ to introduce *inflation-proofing* in pensions

taijin 対人 personal

taijinkankei 対人関係 personal relations

taijinkeiyaku 対人契約 personal contract

taijinsin'yō 対人信用 personal credit

taijinsoshō 対人訴訟 personal action

taijintanpo 対人担保 personal security

taijinzei 対人税 personal tax

taika 対価 equivalent; compensation; price remuneration; counter value; quid pro quo ¶ It was purchased for $100, paying the *equivalent* of $100 in U.S. dollars.// to pay a sum as *compensation* for the loss // Interest rates represent the *price* charged borrowers by lenders for the use of money.// to work at high *remuneration* // an assignment with or without *quid pro quo*

taika 滞貨 accumulated stock; accumulation of (unsold) stock; congestion of cargo

海港滞貨 port congestion

船舶滞貨 shipping congestion

終駅滞貨 terminal congestion

鉄道滞貨 railroad congestion

taikakin'yū 滞貨金融 stockpile financing; financing for carrying unsold inventories

taikasanseki 滞貨山積 heavy congestion of freight; huge unintended accumulation of stocks; sizable involuntary inventory accumulation

taikasaretagijutsushinpo 体化された技術進歩 embodied technical progress

taikashikinshōkyaku 滞貨金償却 writing off bad loan

taiki 貸記 credit entry; crediting

taikikijun 大気基準 air standard

taikikikan 待機期間 waiting period

taikōkigyō 対抗企業 countervailing company (power)

taikokyakukaiyoyaku 対顧客買予約(残高) (balance of) buying contracts

taikokyakusōba 対顧客相場 customer rates; [外] bank's rates for customers; merchant rates; rates quoted to customers

taikyojūshagaikagashiseido 対居住者外貨貸制度 system concerning foreign currency loans to residents

taikyū 耐久 durability; endurance; permanence

taikyūhiritsu 対級比率 inter-class ratio

taikyūryoku 耐久力 durability; lasting quality; endurance; lasting power; persistence

taikyūsei 耐久性 durablility; durableness; endurance; persistence; lastingness; permanence

taikyūshiken 耐久試験 endurance test

taikyūshōhizai 耐久消費財 durable consumer goods; consumer durables

taimeikikan 待命期間 waiting period

taimeikyūshokusei 待命休職制 system of awaiting orders

taimuragu タイム・ラグ time lag ¶ the *time lags* between changes in policy and changes in economic activity // the *lag* before a policy begins to take effect // The *time-lags* before new policies take effect often defeat their original purpose. // →ラグ

taimurekōdā タイムレコーダー time clock

tainō 滞納 (tax) delinquency; default; failure (to pay); arrears

taiōgenri 対応原理 correspondence principle

taiōsaku 対応策 →対処案

tairyō 大量 large quantity; enormous volume; vast; huge; immense; sizable; substantial; great amount; bulk; heap

tairyōchūmon 大量注文 bulk order, large order

tairyōgenshō 大量現象 mass phenomenon

tairyōgyokutorihiki 大量玉取引 block transaction

tairyōhanbai 大量販売 mass sale

tairyōhanbaiten 大量販売店 mass sale store; big store

tairyōkaiire 大量買入れ bulk purchase(=bying)

tairyōkaitsuke 大量買付け [市] bulk-buying(=purchase)

tairyōkansatsu 大量観察 mass observation

tairyōkōnyūharaimodoshi 大量購入払戻し quantity rebate

tairyōkōnyūkyōtei 大量購入協定 bulk-purchase agreement

tairyōkouriten 大量小売店 mass retail outlet ¶ distributing products through *mass retail outlets* such as supermarkets and drugstores

tairyōseisan 大量生産 mass production; large-scale production; quantity production; bulk production

tairyōseisanshi 大量生産紙 mass-producible paper

tairyōshitsugyō 大量失業 mass unemployment

tairyōshōhishakai 大量消費社会 mass consumption society

tairyōshōhizai 大量消費財 goods for mass consumption

tairyōyusō 大量輸送 mass transport(ation)

tairyūkikan 滞留期間 retaining period ¶ the *retaining period* of deposits at banks

taisaku 対策 countermeasure ¶ to take *countermeasures* against depopulation of rural areas // to take *measures* to *counter* foreign competition
景気対策 counter-cyclical policy (measure); anti-cyclical policy (measure)

taisei 大勢 general situation; general trend; current tide; overall state of things

taisei 体制 regime ¶ to settle the future price *regime* for natural gas

taiseikan 大勢観 long-term market outlook

taiseizukuri 体制づくり formulation of the structure; initiating a structure; institutionalization

taisenryō 滞船料 demurrage

taishaku 貸借 borrowing and lending; debt and credit; loan ¶ Banks are *borrowing* short and *lending* long in their international business.
使用貸借 loan for use

消費貸借 loan for consumption

taishakukanjō 貸借勘定 debtor and creditor accounts; current accounts

taishakukankei 貸借関係 loan accounts

taishakukigen 貸借期限 term of the loan

taishakutaishōhyō 貸借対照表 balance sheet; B/S; account of finance
連結貸借対照表 consolidated balance sheet

taishakutaishōhyōkansa 貸借対照表監査 balance sheet audit

taishakutanpokin 貸借担保金 margin transaction guarantee money

taishakutorihikikashitsuke 貸借取引貸付 loan on margin transaction

taishitsukaizen 体質改善（企業の） qualitative improvement of business; enterprise's constitutional improvement; improvement of corporate structure

taishoan 対処案 contingency plan; countermeasure; planned counteraction

taishōkanjō 対照勘定 contra account

taishoku 退職 retirement (from office; from service); resignation

taishokuichijikin 退職一時金 retirement allowance (payment in lump sum)

taishokukin 退職金 retirement allowance; severance payment; termination allowance; superannuation

taishokukyūyo 退職給与 retirement allowance; severance payment; retiring allowance

taishokunenkin 退職年金 (com-

pany) retirement pension ¶ *Retirement pensions* are financed entirely by employers and employees.

taishokunenrei 退職年齢 age of retirement

taishokuteateihikiatekin 退職手当引当金 reserve for employees' retirement allowance

taishokuteateshikin 退職手当資金 reserve for retirement allowances

taishū 大衆 masses; populace; (general) public ¶ The Democrats are the party of the lower-income *populace*. // The announcement met with widespread approval among the *general public*. // the lower-income *populace*
勤労大衆 working masses

taishūbaitai 大衆媒体 mass media

taishūdankō 大衆団交 public negotiations; mass bargain; collective bargain

taishūdentatsu 大衆伝達 mass communication

taishūkazei 大衆課説 taxation upon the general public

taishūkōbairyoku 大衆購買力 mass purchasing power

taishūkokusai 大衆国債 people's bond

taishūshakai 大衆社会 mass society

taishūshōhisha 大衆消費者 consuming public ¶ The *consuming public* is leading the way.

taishūshōhishijō 大衆消費市場 mass market

taishūtekihinkon 大衆的貧困 mass poverty

taishūtōshika 大衆投資家 public investors; investing public

taisō 大宗 mainstay; leader; chief support; staple article; pace setter ¶

Agriculture is the *mainstay* of the country. // Textiles are a *staple article* of exports.
輸出の大宗 mainstay for export ¶ Silk was the *mainstay* of Japanese *exports*.

taitekitorihikihō 対敵取引法 ［米］ Trading With the Enemy Act

taitōgappei 対等合併 merger on equal terms; amalgamation on an equal basis

taiwa 対話 dialogue; colloquy ¶ the tone and content of the North (developed countries)-South (developing countries) *dialogue* // to inject a discordant note into the so-called North-South *dialogue* // the World Bank's policy *dialogue* maintained with member countries // The *dialogue* between the developed and developing nations will achieve concrete results. // The North-South *dialogue* between advanced countries and developing nations has been held through various international conferences. // increased consumer producer *dialogue* // ［参考］ a proposal for a summit-level "trialogue" among European, Arab and African leaders

taiyo 貸与 lending; loan; leasing

taiyōkokutensetsu 太陽黒点説 sun-spot theory

taiyōnensū 耐用年数 durable years; useful life; life cycle
銀行券耐用年数 life cycle of bank notes

taizaihi 滞在費 sojourn expenses; non-transportation charges

taizō 退蔵 hoarding; concealment; caching ¶ speculative *hoarding* associated with a boom in demand for basic commodities

taizōbusshi 退蔵物資 hoarded goods; cached goods; goods in caches

taizōgenkin 退蔵現金 hoarded cash

taizōkahei 退蔵貨幣 hoarded money

taizokin 退蔵金 hoarded gold; gold held by hoarders

takadonae 高唱え [市] quoting high

takainukitorikensahō 多回抜取り 検査法 multiple sampling inspection

takakubōeki 多角貿易 multilateral trade

takakuka 多角化 multipolarization ¶ *multipolarization* of the world economy

takakukashūchū 多角化集中 conglomerate

takakukeiei 多角経営 diversified management; multiple operation

takakukeieikigyō 多角経営企業 multi-divisional enterprise

takakukessai 多角決済 multilateral settlements

takakutekigappei 多角的合併 multi-merger

takakutekikanshi 多角的監視 multilateral surveillance

takakutekikyōdōshingi 多角的共 同審議 multilateral surveillance

takakutekinōgyō 多角的農業 multiple agriculture

takakutekisēfugādo 多角的セーフ ガード multi-national safeguard

takakutekishiharaikyōtei 多角的 支払協定 multilateral payment agreements

takakutekitsūkachōsei 多角的通貨 調整 multilateral currency realignment

takamochiai 高保合 holding high ¶ Prices have *held high*.

takane 高値 [市] high; highest price; high price; record price; best level

新高値 new high; record high

takanebike 高値引け closing high ¶ International oils *closed high*.

takanekeikaikan 高値警戒観 cautious attitude toward high prices; cautious mood for fear of another dip; cautiousness on higher prices ¶ The market became *cautious on higher prices*.

takanemachi 高値待ち [市] anticipation of a rising market

takaneotonaeru 高値を唱える [市] quoted higher ¶ Motors were *quoted higher*.

takaneoyobu 高値を呼ぶ [市] to excite high bidding ¶ Oils *excited high bidding*.

takaneteisei 高値訂正 corrective (price) decline ¶ Coppers marked a *corrective decline* after a two-week straight rise.

takarakuji 宝くじ [日] takara lottery; lottery ¶ to buy tickets of a *lottery* // to win a prize in a *lottery* // to take a draw in a *lottery*

takayori 高寄り opening high ¶ The market *opened higher*. // [参考] The market was higher at the start.

takazairyō 高材料 [市] bullish factor

takika 多岐化 diversification; ramification ¶ growing *diversification* of demand and taste // for *diversification* of monetary control instruments // further reserve *diversification* away from the dollar into other currencies // The growth of investment shows greater *diver-*

sification within the various sectors. // money demand for *diversification* of lines of business // *Diversification* into currencies other than the U.S. dollar was noticeable. // A certain *diversification* of a so-called portfolio out of the dollar into other currencies is under way. // to *diversify* their economies into lines of production with more favorable market prospects // the *diversification* of revenues and the *ramification* of expenditure in all directions // Needs for financial services became more *diverse*.

takikanseisan 多期間生産 polyperiodic production

takohaitō 蛸配当 bogus dividend

takokukankeizaikyōryoku 多国間経済協力 multi-economic cooperation

takokukankigyōnokōdōkijun 多国間企業の行動基準 the code of conduct on multinational corporations

takokusekiginkō 多国籍銀行 multinational bank

takokusekikigyō 多国籍企業 multinational enterprise (=corporation; company); transnational corporation; world enterprise

takokutsūkadatesōba 他国通貨建相場 rate in foreign money; direct rate

takuchi 宅地 dwelling land; residential land; site for dwellings; dwelling site

takuchichintaikakaku 宅地賃貸価格 dwelling land rent

takuchizōsei 宅地造成 land reclamation for housing purposes; residential land formation; development of home building land (lot);

curtilage development ¶ *curtilage development* loan

takyokuka 多極化 multipolarization

takyokukasekai 多極化世界 multipolar world

takyokuteki 多極的 multipolar ¶ to live in a *multipolar* world, not a bipolar one

tamatsukidainoriron 玉突台の理論 billiard table theory

tameginshōnin 為銀承認 approval by an authorized foreign exchange bank

tamensōka 多面層化 multiple stratification

tamenteki 多面的 multifarious; multifacet(ed) ¶ *multifarious* endeavors // to play a central and *multifaceted* role in the monetary sphere

tamokutekidētabēsu 多目的データベース [コン] general purpose data base

tamokutekikeikaku 多目的計画 multiple purpose project; multipurpose project

tamōsaku 多毛作 multiple cropping

tanaage 棚上げ pigeonholing; shelving; suspension ¶ They *shelved* the project for another year. // Many building projects are being *shelved*.

tanaagekabu 棚上げ株 frozen stock

tanabota たなぼた (unexpected) windfall gain; windfall profit ¶ *windfall gains* of revaluation

tanaoroshi 棚卸し stock-taking; clearance ¶ to *take stock* of merchandise, or to make an inventory

tanaoroshigenmōhi 棚卸し減耗費 stock losses and shrinkage

tanaoroshihin 棚卸し品 stock in the inventory; inventory; clearance goods

tanaoroshihyō 棚卸し表 inventory; list of property

tanaoroshishisan 棚卸資産 inventories; working asset; stock on hand
運転棚卸資産 working inventory

tanaoroshishisangenzaidaka 棚卸資産現在高 opening inventory

tanaoroshishisanhyōkahikiatekin 棚卸資産評価引当金 inventory valuation reserve

tanaoroshishisankaitennissū 棚卸資産回転日数 inventory turnover period

tanaoroshishisankaitenritsu 棚卸資産回転率 inventory turnover; turnover ratio of inventories

tanaoroshishisankurikoshidaka 棚卸資産繰越高 closing inventory

tanaoroshishōhin 棚卸商品 goods in trade; stock in trade

tanaoroshiuridashi 棚卸売出し clearance sale

tan'atarishūryō 反当り収量 production per 'tan'

tanazarashi 店晒し dead stock; shop-worn stock; old stock.

tanbetsu 反別 area of land; acreage
作付反別 area under cultivation; acreage; planted area

tanchōrōdō 単調労働 monotonous work

tandokukaisontanpo 単独海損担保 with average; w.a. ¶ to cover shipments on *W.A.* for the sum equal to US $5 bil.

tanhon'ironsha 単本位論者 monometallist

tan'i 単位 unit; denomination; numeraire; term; module ¶ The

family is an economic *unit*. // a *unit* for regulating the proportions of parts // international statistical *unit* // SDRs, the *numeraire.* or *unit* of account of the new system // ECU is used as the *denominator* for the exchange rate mechanism.

売買取引単位 [市] round lot; full lot; bound lot; even lot
物量単位 physical unit
原単位 basic unit
実質単位 real term
実用単位 practical unit
費用単位 cost unit
重量単位 unit of weight
価値単位 unit in terms of value
貨幣単位 money term
勘定単位 unit of account
計算単位 unit of account
経済単位 economic unit
労働単位 labor unit
生産力単位 unit of productive power
速度単位 unit of velocity
測定単位 measuring unit
通貨単位 monetary unit; unit in terms of money
容積単位 unit of volume
誘導単位 derived unit
絶対単位 absolute unit

tan'ihitsuyōrōdōryō 単位必要労働量 unit labor requirement

tan'ikabu 単位株 round-lot shares

tan'ikumiai 単位組合 unit (individual) association; unit labor union

tan'imiman 単位未満 fraction less than a unit ¶ to omit *fractions less than a unit,* or to count as a unit

taninshihon 他人資本 borrowed capital; outside capital

tan'irōdōkosuto 単位労働コスト unit labor costs

tan'iryō 単位量 unitage

tan'itsu 単一 single; sole; simple; solo

tan'itsuginkōmochikabugaisha 単一銀行持株会社 [米] one-bank holding company

tan'itsuginkōseido 単一銀行制度 unit banking system

tan'itsuhōka 単一法貨 simple legal tender

tan'itsuhokenryō 単一保険料 simple premium

tan'itsuhōteishikisuiteihō 単一方程式推定法 single-equation estimation

tan'itsukawaserēto 単一為替レート single exchange rate

tan'itsusaiteikawase 単一裁定為替 simple arbitration of exchange

tan'itsuseigyo 単一制御 unicontrol

tan'itsusekaitaisei 単一世界体制 one-world system

tan'itsushōhinsenmongaisha 単一商品専門会社 one-item company

tan'itsushokumukyū 単一職務給 single wage rate for job

tan'itsutegata 単一手形 sole bill, single bill

tan'itsuzeiritsusei 単一税率制 simple tariff system

tanjunheikinkabuka 単純平均株価 simple arithmetical stock price average

tanjunhikiuke 単純引受け general acceptance; clean acceptance

tanjunkakuchōtōshi 単純拡張投資 simple expansion investment

tanjunkeiyaku 単純契約 simple contract

tanjunrōdō 単純労働 unskilled labor

tanjunsagyō 単純作業 monotonous work

tanjunsaitei 単純裁定 simple arbitrage

tanjunsanjutsuheikinshisū 単純算術平均指数 simple arithmetic average index

tanjunshisū 単純指数 simple index

tanjunsōwa 単純総和 simple aggregate

tanjuntokkentsukibaibai 単純特権付売買 single option

tanka 単価 unit price; piece rate ¶ export and import *unit prices*

tankashisū 単価指数 unit value index

tankaukeoi 単価請負 unit cost contract

tankibarai 短期払い payment at short date

tankifusai 短期負債 current liabilities; quick liabilities; floating liabilities; short-term liabilities; short-term debt

tankigari 短期借り borrowing short

tankihoken 短期保険 short-period insurance

tankijitsuwatashijōkensakimonokawase 短期日渡条件先物為替 (forward exchange) for short date

tankikariirekin 短期借入金 short-term borrowing; short-term loans payable

tankikashitsuke 短期貸付 short-term loan; short loan; short-term loans receivable

tankikawasesōba 短期為替相場 short exchange rate; short rate

tankikeizaiyosokumoderu 短期経済予測モデル short-term economic forecast model

tankikinri 短期金利 short-term rate of interest; short-term interest rate; near-term rates

tankikin'yūshijō 短期金融市場 short-term credit market; (short-term) money market

tankikin'yūshijōshisan 短期金融市場資産 money market instruments

tankikin'yūshijōshōken 短期金融市場証券 money market paper; money market instrument

tankikokusai 短期国債 short-term government securities

tankimikoshibaikyaku 短期見越売却 short sale (=selling)

tankimokuhyō 短期目標 short-run target ¶ a *short-run target* of monetary policy actions

tānkīsei ターン・キー制 turn-key system; turn-key basis

tankishasai 短期社債 short-term debenture; short-term bond

tankishihon 短期資本 short-term capital ¶ to control internal flows of *short-term capital*

tankishihonshūshi 短期資本収支 short-term capital (transactions) balance

tankishijō 短期市場 call loan market; call market; money market (narrowly defined)

tankishikiboki 単記式簿記 bookkeeping by single entry

tankishikin 短期資金 short-term funds

tankishin'yō 短期信用 short credit; short-term credit

tankitegata 短期手形 short-dated bill; short exchange bill; short exchange; short bill

tankitejimai 短期手仕舞い ［市］ in and out

tankiteki 短期的 short-term; near-term; short-range; short-run; short period; short time; short date(d);

short-lived ¶ Recessions have been *short-lived* and shallow. // →一時的

tankitorihiki 短期取引 short-term transaction; short delivery

tankiyūshi 短期融資 call loan; demand loan; money at call

tankyoriyusōki 短距離輸送機 short-haul plane

tanmatsuki 端末機 ［コン］ terminal (unit); remote terminal equipment

tanmeitegata 単名手形 single-name paper; one-name paper

tannendoyosanseisaku 単年度予算政策 single-annual-budget policy

tannōjukuren 単能熟練 one-job skill

tanpo 担保 security; mortgage; collateral; collateral security ¶ to lend money on good *security* // to borrow without *security* // to deposit *security* for 100,000 yen with a bank // to tender goods as *collateral security* for... // to put up *security* as *collateral* for a loan // to post *collateral,* and dispose of it // to pledge securities as *collateral* for a loan // direct loans usually *collateraled* by securities

遊担保 counter-security

換価担保 convertible security

共通担保 common collateral

増し担保 additional collateral

見返り担保 collateral security

債権担保 security for an obligation

据置担保 fixed collateral

適格担保 security eligible for collateral

tanpogashi 担保貸し loan on security; loan against security; secured loan; collateral loan

tanpogire 担保切れ running off of the (collateral) margin

tanpokahiteijōkō 担保化否定条項 negative pledge clause

tanpokaijo 担保解除 release of security

tanpokakaku 担保価格 collateral value

tanpokakeme 担保掛目 assessment rate of collateral; collateral value; loan value

tanpokeiyakusho 担保契約書 (letter of) hypothecation

tanpokentōroku 担保権登録 registration of pledge

tanpokōkan 担保交換 change of (collateral) security

tanpomokuroku 担保目録 inventory of security

tanposashiireshō 担保差入証 letter of confirmation of collateral

tanposashiireyūkashōken 担保差入有価証券 securities deposited as collateral

tanposei 担保性 collateral qualities

tanpoteikyōshisan 担保提供資産 asset subject to lien

tanpotsuki 担保付 secured; collateral; mortgage(d)

tanpotsukirōn 担保付ローン secured loan; collateral loan

tanpotsukishasai 担保付社債 mortgage bond; mortgage debenture; secured debenture; secured bond

部分担保付社債 divisional mortgage bond

第一順位担保付社債 first mortgage bond

閉鎖担保付社債 closed-end mortgage

一般担保付社債 general mortgage bond

開放担保付社債 open-end mortgage bond

借換担保付社債 refunding mortgage bond

後順位担保付社債 junior mortgage bond

先順位担保付社債 senior mortgage bond

証券担保付信託社債 collateral trust bond

統合担保付社債 consolidated mortgage bond

特別直接抵当付社債 special direct lien bond

tanpotsukishasaishintaku 担保付社債信託 mortgage debentures in trust

tanpotsukishōken 担保付証券 secured bond

tanpotsukishūekishasai 担保付収益社債 collateral income bond

tanpotsukitegata 担保付手形 bill with collateral security; secured bill; bill as collateral

tanpoyokin 担保預金 deposit as collateral

tanpoyoryoku 担保余力 (collateral) margin

tanrihō 単利法 method of simple interest

tanririmawari 単利利回り yield by simple interest

tansakuchitai 単作地帯 single crop area

tanshi 短資 short-term loan; short-term credit; call loan; call money

越月短資 overmonth short-term loans; overmonth call loan

tanshigaisha 短資会社 money market dealer; short-term credit dealer

tanshigyōsha 短資業者 short-term credit broker; call loan broker; money market broker; money market dealer; short-term money house

tanshikisei 短資規制 control of short-term capital

tanshinoryūshutsunyū 短資の流出入 international flow of short-term capital

tanshishijō 短資市場 call money market; call market; call money and discount markets

tanshitegata 短資手形 call loan dealer's bill

tanshitorihikitanposaiken 短資取引担保債券 securities in pledge of call loan transaction

tanshuku 短縮 curtailment; reduction; shortening; contraction; cutback

労働時間の短縮 reduction of working hours; reduction of office hours; shorter hours

操業短縮 curtailment of operation; operation cutback

tanshukujikan 短縮時間 reduced hours

tanshukunengen 短縮年限 shortened years

tansōgyō 単操業 single-shift operation

tanzeiryoku 担税力 taxable capacity; ability to pay (taxes)

tarenagashi たれ流し spillage ¶ Most of the *spillages* of crude of roughly 4,000 tonnes was successfully dispersed at sea.

tārusando タール・サンド tar sand

taryōbaibaitorihiki 多量売買取引 block sale

tasen 多占 polypoly; multiple monopoly

tashobaraikogitte 他所払小切手 out-(of-)town check

tashobaraitegata 他所払手形 out-(of-)town bill

tashutsūkasentakujōkōtsukikashitsuke 多種通貨選択条項付貸付 loan subject to multi-currency selection; multi-currency loan

tasūshōhinseizōgaisha 多数商品製造会社 multi-product firm

tatekabu 建株 listed stock

tatekae 立替え advance; loan; payment for another

一時立替え temporary advance

tatekaebarai 立替払い ［会］ charges forward

tatekaekin 立替金 advance; advance money

受託販売立替金 advance consignment-in

買付委託立替金 advance on indent

tatekaekinkanjō 立替金勘定 disbursement; advance account

tatemono 建物 building; structure; edifice; premises

tatemonogaisha 建物会社 building company

tatemonogenkashōkyaku 建物減価償却 depreciation of building

tatemonokanjō 建物勘定 premises account; building account

tatemonooyobifuzokusetsubi 建物および付属設備 buildings and building fixtures

tatenaoshi 建て直し reconstruction ¶ *reconstruction* of the deficit-ridden state finances // →再建

tatene 建値 quotation ¶ *Quotations,* particularly of shares, rose gradually. // The *quoted* value of all stocks listed on the Now York stock exchange fell an estimated $1,286,000.

tatenmawashichūmon 他店回し注文 give-out order

tatenpokeiei 多店舗経営 multi-store operation

tateurijūtaku 建売住宅 house for installment sale

tayōka 多様化 diversification

tayōkanotamenokaheijuyō 多様化 のための貨幣需要 money demand for diversification

tayōsei 多様性 multiplicity ¶ the *multiplicity* of clients in easy reach // the *multiplicity* of production inputs, or a wide variety of inputs // [参考] to attract a diverse set of manufacturing activities from urban areas

teate 手当 allowance; perquisite (= perk); dole; compensation; cover; procurement; purchase ¶ family *allowance* // to give a regular monthly *allowance* for personal expenses // a whole varieties of "*perks*" to retain and reward staff-free housing, directorship fees and the like // lavish pay and *perks* for the civil service // to *cover* the loss // to *procure* necessary materials // to *purchase* raw materials

別居手当 separation allowance

物価手当 allowance for price increase; cost of living allowance

扶養手当 family (support) allowance; sustenance allowance

育児手当 child care allowance (for nursing mothers)

インフレ手当 anti-inflation allowance

児童手当 children's allowance

時間外勤務手当 overtime (work) allowance

住宅手当 housing allowance

家族手当 dependent allowance; family allowance

危険手当 danger allowance

勤続手当 long service allowance

臨時手当 temporary allowance

子女教育手当 educational allowance for children; education grant

失業手当 unemployment benefit; unemployment compensation; dole

傷病手当 accident and sickness allowances

宿直手当 night duty allowance

出産手当 childbirth allowance

退職手当 retirement allowance; retiring allowance; severance pay

特別勤務手当 specific duty allowance

特別手当 special allowance

残業手当 allowance for overtime work

teategai 手当買い short covering; covering short; covering purchase for immediate needs; purchase made to cover requirements; hand-to-mouth buying

teawase 手合せ transaction; dealing; bargain; business

teawasedaka 手合せ高 volume of business; amount of dealings ¶ →取引高

teawasenedan 手合せ値段 price agreed upon

teawaseōki 手合せ多き [市] free

teawasesukunaki 手合せ少なき [市] narrow

tebari 手張り [市] trade on (one's) own account

tebikaeru 手控える to hold off; refrain from acting

tēburushōsha テーブル商社 small trading company

tedori 手取り proceeds; net pay; take-home pay ¶ *proceeds* from the sale

正味手取り net proceeds

総手取り gross proceeds

tedorikyūryō 手取り給料 take-home pay ¶ the real value of the *take-home pay*

tegata 手形 bill; note; draft; paper

複名手形　double-name paper; two-name paper

不渡り手形　dishonored bill

外貨為替手形　bill in foreign exchange

外貨手形　foreign currency bill

外国為替手形　foreign exchange bill

銀行引受手形　banker's acceptance; bank acceptance

銀行為替手形　bank draft

銀行手形　bank bill; bank draft

早受け手形　bill for premature delivery

引受手形　bill accepted; acceptance

引受渡荷為替手形　document against acceptance bill

日付後定期払手形　bill payable at a fixed period after sight

邦貨為替手形　bill in domestic currency

邦貨手形　home currency bill

一覧払手形　sight bill; demand bill

一流手形　gilt-edged bill; prime bill

自己宛手形　house bill; self-addressed bill

自己指図手形　self-order bill

持参人払手形　bill to bearer

確定日払手形　bill payable at a fixed date

空手形　fictitious bill

為替手形　bill of exchange; draft

期限付手形　usance bill; time bill

期限付輸出手形　export usance bill

期限付輸入手形　import usance bill

金融手形　finance bill

工業手形　industrial bill; industrial paper

個人手形　personal bill; private bill

組手形　set bill

満期手形　matured bill

綿花手形　cotton bill

並（＝一般）手形　ordinary bill

荷為替手形　documentary bill

流通手形　running bill

再割引手形　rediscounted bill

参差払手形　bill on demand

指図禁止手形　non-order bill

指図人払い手形　bill to order

支払手形　bill payable

支払渡荷為替手形　document against payment bill

信用手形　unsecured bill

白地手形　blank bill

商業手形　commercial bill; trade bill

商業手形に準ずる手形　bills corresponding in creditability to commercial bills

倉庫証券付手形　bill accompanied by warehouse receipt

単一手形　sole bill; sola

単名手形　single-name paper; one-name paper

担保手形　bill as collateral

担保付手形　secured bill

短資手形　call loan dealer's bill

他所払手形　out-of-town bill

適格手形　eligible bill

取立手形　bill for collection; collection bill

受取手形　bill receivable

裏書禁止手形　mon-negotiable bill

裏書手形　endorced bill

約束手形　promissory note

優遇手形　preferential bill

輸入貿易手形　import trade bill

輸入決済手形　import settlement bill

輸入運賃手形　import freight bill

優良手形　prime bill; hot bill

輸出貿易手形　export trade bill

輸出前貸手形　export advance bill

ユーザンス手形　usance bill

融通手形　accommodation bill; finance bill

割引手形　bill discounted ¶ commercial *bills* that commercial

banks *discount* with the National Bank

tegatahikiukenin 手形引受人 acceptor

tegatai 手堅い steady; firm

tegataishikyō 手堅い市況 steady market ¶ The *market* then *steadied* and moved higher.

tegatakaitoriginkōfushiteishin'yōjō 手形買取銀行不指定信用状 general credit; open credit

tegatakaitoriginkōshiteishin'yōjō 手形買取銀行指定信用状 special credit; restricted credit

tegatakaitorijukensho 手形買取授権書 authorization to purchase

tegatakaitoritesūryō 手形買取手数料 negotiation charge

tegatakankeinin 手形関係人 parties to a bill

tegatakashitsuke 手形貸付 loans on bills; advance on a promissory note

tegatakashitsukeentairisoku 手形貸付延滞利息 overdue interest on loans on bills

tegatakashitsukerisoku 手形貸付利息 interest on loans on bills

tegatakashitsuketanpo 手形貸付担保 collateral on loans on bills

tegatakashitsuketsuichōrisoku 手形貸付追徴利息 additionally collected interest on loans on bills

tegatakōkan 手形交換 bank clearing; bill clearing

tegatakōkandaka 手形交換高 (bill) clearing; clearance

tegatakōkanjiri 手形交換尻 balance of clearing; clearing house balance

tegatakōkanjo 手形交換所 clearing house

tegatakōkanjokumiaiginkō 手形

交換所組合銀行 member banks of clearing house ¶ *member banks of* the London *clearing house*

tegatakōkankashikatadenpyō 手形交換貸方伝票 clearing house credit ticket

tegatakōkankessanhyō 手形交換決算表 clearing house proof; clerk's sheet

tegataoperēshon 手形オペレーション operation of bills; operation in bills

tegatashiharaijukensho 手形支払授権書 authorization to pay

tegatatoritate 手形取立 collection of bills; bill collection

tegatauridashi 手形売出 sale of bills ¶ the system for *sale of bills* drawn by the Bank of Japan

tegatawaribiki 手形割引 discount of bills; bill discount

tegatawaribikikawarikin 手形割引代り金 proceeds of a discount on bill

tegatawaribikiryō 手形割引料 discount on bills

tegatawaribikishijō 手形割引市場 bills market; discount market

teianseido 提案制度 improvement proposing system

teibukkaseisaku 低物価政策 low price policy

teichaku 定着 entrenchment; embedding; establishment; rooting; taking hold ¶ Restrictions became *entrenched* (=rooted) in the economy. // deeply *embedded* wage rigidities // Expectations of business recovery have become *entrenched*. // The process of recovery in the industrial world is firmly *established*. // This became a deep-*rooted* practice the world over. // The tightening of controls began to *take hold*.

teichingin 低賃金 low wages; cheap labor

teichinginrōdō 低賃金労働 cheap labor

teichō 低調 inactive; sluggish; [市] bearish ¶ Trading was *sluggish* for a while. // The market rose to another new peak after some initial *sluggishness*. // The main peg of the *bear* market was the reflationary package.

teigakuhō 定額法 [会] straight-line method; fixed installment method

teigakukogawase 定額小為替 postal money order with fixed amount

teihaikabu 低配株 low-dividend stock

teiikabu 低位株 low-price stock; low grade stocks; lesser grade stocks

teiji 呈示 presentation
引受呈示 presentation for acceptance
支払要求呈示 presentation for payment

teijibarai 呈示払い payment at sight; on demand

teijibaraitegata 呈示払手形 sight bill; demand bill

teijikikan 呈示期間 time of presentation; presentation period

teijishidai 呈示次第 on presentation; when presented

teikahō 低価法 [会] "cost or market" method; cost or market, whichever is lower; the lower of either cost or market price ¶ inventories stated at the *lower of cost or market*

teikaihatsuchiiki 低開発地域 underdeveloped area (=region)

teikaihatsukoku 低開発国 less developed countries; LDCs; underdeveloped country ¶ financial assistance to the *LDCs* // →発展途上国; 後進国

teikan 定款 by-laws of corporation; articles of association; statute; articles of incorporation; articles of partnership; memorandum of association
仮定款 provisional by-laws; provisional articles of association

teikei 提携 affiliation; tie-up ¶ to form a business *affiliation* with another corporation // countries with particularly strong economic and financial *ties* with the community. // a technological *tie-up* between the two companies // to enter into an extensive business *tie-up* with Armco Inc. // *tie-up* in terms of personnel and capital
業務提携 business tie-up
技術提携 technological tie-up
販売提携 sales tie-up
資本提携 capital tie-up

teikeiginkai 定型銀塊 silver ingot

teikeikinkai 定型金塊 gold ingot

teikeitorihikijōkennokaishakuni-kansurukokusaikisoku 定型取引条件の解釈に関する国際規則 International Rules for the Interpretation of Trade Terms; Incoterms

teikibaraitegata 定期払手形 time bill; usance bill

tekijisei 適時性 timeliness

teikihokenshōken 定期保険証券 time policy

teikikariire 定期借入れ time money; term money

teikikashitsuke 定期貸付 time loan; term loan

teikikōro 定期航路 regular service;

regular line; line

teikinenkin 定期年金 term annuity

teikinri 低金利 low interest rate; low cost of money; cheap money ¶ to provide *low-cost* credit to farmers

teikinriseisaku 低金利制策 low interest policy; cheap money policy; low interest rate policy; easy money policy

teikinrishikin 低金利資金 low-interest credit; cheap money

teikiseiyokin 定期性預金 deposits with prescribed terms; time and savings deposits; deposits with certain contracted periods

teikisen 定期船 regular liner; liner

teikitorihiki 定期取引 dealing in futures; time bargain; settlement dealing

teikitsumikin 定期積金 installment savings

teikiyokin 定期預金 time deposit; term deposit; fixed deposit; fixture

teikiyokinshōsho 定期預金証書 time deposit certificate; certificate of time deposit; CD

teikiyokintanpokashidashikinri 定期預金担保貸出金利 interest rate on loans secured by time deposit

teikiyōsenryōshisū 定期用船料指数 time charterage index

teikōgaisha 低公害車 low-pollution car

teikōkaiyōsen 定航海用船 voyage charter; trip charter

teikōkaiyōsen'unchin 定航海用船運賃 trip charter money; trip charter rate

teikōsen 抵抗線 resistance area; resistance level; resistant level; support level; barrier ¶ The dollar failed to break through the 233.80

yen chart *resistance level* in New york.

teikuofu テイクオフ take-off ¶ the *take-off* into self-sustained growth

teimei 低迷 slackening in (the rate of) growth; sluggish rise; slower growth; sluggishness; stagnancy; leveling-off at a low level; wavering low; ［市］dull tone; featureless; slack; wavering low; hovering low

teinen 定年 (mandatory) retirement age ¶ He will retire as president on June 30, when he will have reached the traditional *retirement age* of 65. // to specify age 65 as the normal *retirement age* for male employees // Employees resign on reaching the *mandatory retirement age*. // the proposed extension of the worker *retirement age* // to lower the *retirement age* // Unions are asking for later *retirement*. // ［参考］Workers are supposed to retire at 68.

teinentaishokusha 定年退職者 employee resigned ·on reaching (mandatory) retirement age; retired worker ¶ *"Retired"* 55-year-olds get new jobs with the same firms' subcontractors.

teinōritsu 低能率 ¶ →非能率

teiraku 低落 ［市］decline; fall; slump; collapse; easing off; slipping off; setback

teireika 定例化 routinization

teireikyūyo 定例給与 regular salary and allowances

teiri 低利 low interest

teirikarikae 低利借換え conversion at low interest rate

teirikashitsuke 低利貸付 low interest loan

teirikin'yū 低利金融 cheap credit;

cheap money

teirishikin 低利資金 low interest funds

teiritsuhō 定率法 ［会］composite-line method; fixed percentage method

teiritsutesūryō 定率手数料 flat fee

teiryū 底流 undertone; undercurrent; underlying tone; basic tone; key note

teisei 訂正 correction; rectification; revision

teiseichō 低成長 reduced growth; slow-growth; modest-growth; moderate-growth; less-rapid-growth; decelerating growth; lower level of growth; low-rate growth ¶ institutions' intent of working toward *lower levels of* monetary *growth* over time

teiseidaka 訂正高 ［市］corrective rise

teiseigai 訂正買い ［市］corrective buying

teiseikiun 訂正気運 ［市］corrective mood ¶ The market was lower in a *corrective mood.*

teiseiokurijō 訂正送状 corrected invoice

teiseisōba 訂正相場 corrective market

teiseisūji 訂正数字 revised figure

teiseiuri 訂正売り ［市］corrective selling

teishikika 定式化 formulation

teishikyori 停止距離 braking distance ¶ Some *braking distance* is necessary when a restrictive policy has to be applied.

teishutsu 提出 presentation; submittance ¶ to *present* the budget to the Diet for deliberation // to *submit*

the question to the commission for its consideration

teisōgenkin 逓送現金 cash in transit

teitai 停滞 stagnancy; stagnation; doldrum; torpor; torpidness ¶ the present *stagnancy* in the economy // *stagnancy* of business activity, or *stagnant* business // Much of the rest of the economy is still wavering in the *doldrums*. // business in *torpor* // to revive from *torpor* // *torpid* economic activity // Private investment is out of the *doldrums* if not recovering. // With the summer *doldrums* ahead, production is unlikely to gather much momentum. // to extricate the economy from prolonged virtual *stagnation* // to end the *stagnation* of world economic trends // to revive from the prolonged *stagnation* of business activity // ［参考］→不冴え

teitō 抵当 mortgage; hypothec; hypothecation ¶ to *mortgage* a house to the lender // to hold the land in *mortgage* // to have a *mortgage* of 2 million dollars on the property

分割式抵当 development mortgage; open mortgage

動産抵当 chattel mortgage

副抵当 collateral mortgage

一番抵当 first mortgage

上層抵当 overlying mortgage

満額抵当 closed mortgage

根抵当 fixed mortgage

二番抵当 second mortgage

二重抵当 double mortgage

総括抵当 blanket mortgage

総括式抵当 general mortgage

低次抵当 junior mortgage

優先抵当 senior mortgage

teitōbutsu 抵当物 security; collateral; pledge; pawn; thing mortgaged ¶ to give, put, or lay, and to take, or accept a thing for *security* // an eligible *collateral* for the loan // construction loans not *collateralized* by real estate

teitōgashi 抵当貸し loan on security; secured loan

teitōhikiateshōken 抵当引当証券 mortgage-backed securities

teitōhoken 抵当保険 mortgage insurance

teitōken 抵当権 mortgage; hypothec

teitōkensettei 抵当権設定 settlement of mortgage

teitōkensetteisha 抵当権設定者 mortgagor; mortgager; mortgage debtor

teitōkensetteitōki 抵当権設定登記 register of settlement of mortgage

teitōkensha 抵当権者 mortgagee; mortgage creditor

teitōkin'yūgaisha 抵当金融会社 mortgage company

teitōnagare 抵当流れ mortgage forfeit; foreclosure ¶ The mortgagee may *foreclose* on and take title to pledged realty.

teitōnagarekōbai 抵当流れ公売 foreclosure sale

teitōnagaretetsuzuki 抵当流れ手続 foreclosure proceeding

teitōsaiken 抵当債券 mortgage-backed bond

teitōshōken 抵当証券 mortgage (securities); mortgage pass-through certificate; mortgage certificate

teitōshōkengaisha 抵当証券会社 mortgage (acceptance) company

teitōshōsho 抵当証書 mortgage bond; mortgage debenture

teitōshōshorui 抵当証書類 mort-gage documents

teitōshūtoku 抵当収得 foreclosure

teitōtsukisaiken 抵当付債券 →抵当証券

teizōhi 逓増費 progressive cost

tejimai 手仕舞い clearance; ［市］liquidation; closing (account); clearing; awaying; cover; evening up; closing trade

　硬派の手仕舞い liquidation of bulls; liquidation of longs

　軟派の手仕舞い liquidation of bears; liquidation of shorts

　商品の手仕舞い clearance sale of goods

　短期手仕舞い in and out

tejunkettei 手順決定 routing

tekikakusei 適格性 eligibility ¶ current legislation concerning the *eligibility* for benefits // the criteria of *eligibility* of trade bills for rediscounting at the central bank window // to be allowed in the Euroyen bond market under specific *eligibility* criteria // government securities are *eligible* for bank investment. // ［参考］Readily possible sales at fair value make it appropriate for bank purchase.

tekikakushasai 適格社債 eligible corporate bond (for collateral for a loan) ¶ ［参考］bank-eligible government securities, which have come within 10 years of their maturity or call dates

tekikakutanpo 適格担保 security eligible for collateral (for a loan)

tekikakutegata 適格手形 eligible paper; eligible bill (for rediscount; as collateral security for a loan) ¶ the types of *paper eligible* for Federal Reserve banks' discount // advance on *eligible paper*

tekiō 適応 adaptation ¶ *adaptation* to lower rates of growth and productivity // to *adapt* their products to Japanese

tekiseichingin 適正賃金 fair wage

tekiseigaikajunbidaka 適正外貨準備高 adequate gold and foreign exchange reserve; optimum reserve of gold and foreign exchange

tekiseikakaku 適正価格 fair price

tekiseikensa 適性検査 aptitude test

tekiseikyōsō 適正競争 fair competition

tekiseirijun 適正利潤 reasonable profit

tekiseiryūdōsei 適正流動性 adequate liquidity

tekiseishorikonnanbutsu 適正処理困難物 inappropriate disposable waste

tekiseitsūkaryō 適正通貨量 optimum quantity of money; optimum money supply; money supply within an adequate amount; adequate amount of the money supply

tekisetsuseijōnajunbizandaka 適切・正常な準備残高 appropriate normal stock of reserves; optimum stock of reserves

tekishōhinshitsu 適商品質 good merchantable quality; GMQ

tekiyōteishijōkō 適用停止条項 escape clause

tekkō 鉄鋼 iron and steel; iron and steel products; ferrous metals; ferrous metal products

tekkōgenzairyō 鉄鋼原材料 materials related to steel making; materials for steel making; steel-making materials; steel-making (raw) materials

tekkōgyō 鉄鋼業 iron and steel industry

tekkōkōhansei 鉄鋼公販制 collective open sales system for steel products

tekkōkuzu 鉄鋼くず iron and steel scrap; ferrous scrap; scrap iron and steel

tekkōseki 鉄鉱石 iron ore

tekoire てこ入れ support; jacking up; propping ¶ The market must have *support*. // to give *support* to the market // The main *support* came from... // Major elements of *support* to general business activity are...

tekoritsu 挺率 leverage ratio; debt ratio ¶ the tremendous *leverage* conferred by the low margin requirements

temashigoto 手間仕事 piece work

temochi 手持ち holdings; stock on (＝in) hand; stockpile; ⌊市⌋ position ¶ banks' foreign exchange *holdings*; banks' *holdings* of foreign exchange
買手持 long position
売手持 short position

temochichūmon 手持注文 unfilled orders; backlog of orders; order stock

temochisaiken 手持債券 portfolio bonds; securities in portfolio

temochishizai 手持資材 materials on hand

temochizaiko 手持在庫 stock on hand

temotogenkin 手許現金 ready money; cash on hand; vault cash; till cash

temotoryūdōseihiritsu 手許流動性比率 liquidity ratio

temotousu 手許薄 light holdings; small stock

temotozandaka 手許残高 balance in hand

ten 点 point
限界点 critical point
飽和点 saturation point
最適点 optimum point
正貨現送点 specie point
転換点 turn-around point; turning-point ¶ This year will mark a *turning-point* in the job situation.

tenaoshisochi 手直し措置 corrective action (=measure)

tenaoshisuru 手直しする mend; amend; better; improve; rectify; correct; modify; [コン] debugging ¶ to *mend,* or *amend* the law, or to make an *amendment* to the law // to need *betterment* // a *correction* to the present policy // to *modify* regulations

tenbai 転売 resale; liquidation sale

tenbaikinshi 転売禁止 prohibition of resale

tenbiki 天引き reduction; deduction; withholding ¶ the employer's *withholding* of part of employees' wages or salaries

tenbikichokin 天引貯金 deposit through deduction from monthly pay; savings deducted at source

tenbō 展望 perspective; outlook; looking forward; prospect; forecast; preview; vista ¶ a medium-term *perspective* // The *outlook* for production remains promising. // The *prospects* are favorable for further rises. // *Prospects* for the long-run future are clouded with uncertainties. // pessimistic *forecasts* about likely behavior of the economy // Two important factors are progressively enhancing the *outlook* for the British economy. // The exact timing of a change in the economic climate is difficult to *forecast.* // The economy now can *look forward* to a period of sound growth. // The *prospects* for the current year point to no marked change in the trends of the domestic economy. // The entrepreneurs are generally optimistic as far as short-term *prospects* are concerned. // Their assessment of the medium-term *outlook* is cautious. // the government's economic *preview* for the next year // [参考] →予測; 見通し

tengashi 転貸し sublease; subtenancy underletting; subletting

tengashinin 転貸人 sublessor

tengyō 転業 occupational change; change of occupation; change of employment; change of trade

tengyōshikin 転業資金 funds for the change of trade

tengyōtaisaku 転業対策 measures for occupational changes

tenhaigyō 転廃業 shift or quitting of trade

tenimotsuunchin 手荷物運賃 baggage fee

tenjō 天井 ceiling; peak; top; highest level; constraint ¶ with the yen at its *ceiling* // output hitting a *ceiling* // the balance of payments' *ceiling* // The market goes higher than the last *peak,* to mark a double or triple *peak.* // The March high ran higher than the horizontal *tops.* // Production reached a *ceiling.* // A *ceiling* existed on the level of attainable production. // Output is bumping against *ceilings* of productive capacity and skilled manpower. // The balance of payments will continue for some time to be a major *constraint* on growth policies.
二番天井 double peak ¶ to eventually form a *double* or triple *peak*

tenjōken 天井圏 vicinity of the upper limit

tenjōoutsu 天井を打つ reaching the top price; hitting peak; hitting the ceiling

tenjōshirazunosōba 天井知らずの相場 skyrocketing price; sky's-the-limit price

tenjōsōba 天井相場 ［市］ ceiling rate; ceiling price

tenjōtsukami 天井摑み buying at top price

tenka 転嫁 shift; pass-through; passing-on; transfer ¶ Distributors are allowed a dollar-for-dollar *pass-through* of rising farm prices. // Distributors may have abstained from *passing on* to final buyers all the increase in their import prices. // A change in the payroll tax cannot be *shifted* directly into changes in prices. // to *shift* more of the cost of doctors' fees to patients // The margin for *passing* on higher costs has diminished. // Firms can *pass* along all cost increases to the buyer. // The higher costs of imported fuel and materials are being *passed on* as price boosts on domestic manufactured products. // the scope for *passing on* price and cost increases directly and effectively // The lower prices for imported goods are *passed on* to the retail level. // to abstain from *transfer* to final buyers all the increase in import prices // ［参考］ OPEC price rises feed rapidly through to the consumer. // →シフト

tenkai 展開 development; evolution ¶ *development* of economic policy // *development* of the monetary policy

tenkaimachi 展開待ち ［市］ wait-

ing for further developments

tenkaiten 転回点 turning point ¶ the upper turning point of the business cycle

tenkan 転換 shift; conversion; transition; veer; changeover; switchover; turn (=turnabout; turnaround; swing; reorientation ¶ a *shift* in the policy posture from expansionary to restrictive one // to *convert* foreign funds into yen funds // net *conversion* of funds out of domestic currency, for Euro-currency lending by banks // to make the *transition* from rapid expansion to growth at sustainable rates // a *shift* in the lending posture to a more positive one // restriction on the *conversion* of foreign currencies into yen // a *shift* in the monetary policy to a more restrictive direction // The partial choking-off of the fund supply compelled businesses to *veer* away from excessive dependence on bank loans. // a noticeable *changeover* in business opinions from all-out optimism to cautious optimism // a drastic *switchover* in economic policy forced by the oil crisis // a rapid *turn* for the better of the payments balance // a *turnaround* of the economy incited by the oil embargo // a vigorous effort to *swing* resources from current consumption into industrial investment // The less developed countries managed the structural *shift* from agriculture to industry. // geographical *shifts* in population and job opportunities—broadly from north to south // a *shift* away from the consumer oriented growth to a model with the emphasis on improving economic plant and equipment // Japan was *shifting* its trade away from the developed towards the developing world. // a *turnaround* in the monetary policy // The *turnaround* comes when the economy is at a very deep level. // The economy is now in the process of *turning around*. // The *turnaround* point moved deep into the autumn. // *Reorientation* of the nation's economic policy to emphasize supply management will take time. // a premature *switch* in economic policy from fighting inflation to stimulating a sluggish economy // Britain's labor scene is witnessing a gradual *transition* from an unsustainable situation to a much more sustainable situation.

tenkankakaku 転換価格 conversion price

tenkanki 転換期 turning-point; turnaround point ¶ A major *turning point* for the dollar may be reached in about three months.

tenkankyūfukin 転換給付金 benefit for the change of job

tenkanseikyūkanōkikan 転換請求可能期間 life of conversion privilege

tenkanseikyūkikan 転換請求期間 conversion period

tenkanshasai 転換社債 convertible bond; convertible debenture ¶ *bond convertible* at market price

tenkanshasaitōshin 転換社債投信 convert fund

tenkanshōken 転換証券 convertible securities

tenki 転記 ［会］posting; transfer

tenkibaikaibo 転記媒介簿 posting medium

tennengasu 天然ガス natural gas

tenpo テンポ pace; tempo; rate ¶ Economic expansion is proceeding at a fairly rapid *pace*. // Its *pace* has slackened. // the torrid first-quarter *pace* of the growth rate // evidence of an increased *tempo* of industrial production // The *tempo* of investment picked up its speed.

tenpo 店舗 establishment; office; shop ¶ the number of banking establishments

tenpohaichi 店舗配置 location of offices

tenpushorui 添付書類 accompanying document; supporting document

tenro 転炉 converter

tensaiyūshiseido 天災融資制度 natural disaster loan (system)

tentōkabu 店頭株 counter share; over-the-counter issue (=share; stock)

tentōkehaihappyōseido 店頭気配発表制度 ［市］system of publishing quotations of over-the-counter issues

tentōshijō 店頭市場 over-the-counter market

tentōtorihiki 店頭取引 ［市］over-the-counter transaction; trading on the over-the-counter market; OTC (=over-the-counter) market trading ¶ securities actively traded on the unorganized and decentralized market, known as the *over-the-counter* (=*OTC*) market // securities selected for the Board's list of *OTC* margin stocks // to meet the criteria for *OTC* listing

tenzuhyō 点図表 dot diagram

terebifukyūritsu テレビ普及率 diffusion ratio of television sets (=TVs)

terebihōeiken テレビ放映権 television broadcasting rights

terebijuzōki テレビ受像機 television set; TV

teretaiputsūshinmō テレタイプ通信網 teletype communication network

teritorīsei テリトリー制 sales territory system

tesagyō 手作業 manual work; manual operation; manual labor

tesūryō 手数料 fee; charge; commission; brokerage; load
銀行手数料 banker's commission
販売手数料 selling commission
幹事手数料 management fee
買付手数料 buying commission
先取手数料 [市] front-end (sales) load
参加手数料 participation fee
支払保証手数料 debt-credere commission
受入手数料 commission received

tesūryōbaibai 手数料売買 commission sale

tesūryōkanjō 手数料勘定 commission account

tetsudōtaika 鉄道滞貨 railroad congestion

tetsukekin 手付金 earnest(-money); deposit (money); bargain deposit; bargain-money; deposits paid on contracts; security money; hand money

tetsuzuki 手続き procedures ¶ to comply with international trade bureaucratic *procedures*

tetteitekikeikenshugi 徹底的経験主義 radical empiricism

tezume 手詰め [市] forced liquidation; stop-loss selling

tezumeuri 手詰売り liquidation sale

tobikaesu 跳返す [市] rally; rebound

tochi 土地 land; landed property; real estate; land tract; tract; plot ¶ a desirable lot of *land* // a big *tract* of *land* // a *tract* of country // a *plot* or a *tract* of *land* // to acquire twelve drilling *tracts*

tochibaibaigyōsha 土地売買業者 estate agent; land jobber; realtor

tochibaibaishūsennin 土地売買周旋人 land broker; realtor; real estate broker

tochichintaiken 土地賃貸権 lease of land

tochidaichō 土地台帳 land ledger; land register

tochifudōsan 土地不動産 landed estate; landed property

tochiginkō 土地銀行 land bank; soil bank

tochikabu 土地株 realty shares

tochikaihatsu 土地開発 land development

tochikaihatsugyōsha 土地開発業者 land developer

tochikairyōshikinkashitsuke 土地改良資金貸付 land improvement loan

tochikangenfunōno 土地還元不能の bioundegradable

tochikangenkanōno 土地還元可能の biodegradable ¶ *biodegradable* plastics

tōchikenrisuku 統治権リスク sovereign risk; country risk

tochikokuyūka 土地国有化 nationalization of land; state ownership of land

tochinosanshutsuryoku 土地の産出力 fertility of land

tochisaiken 土地債券 land bond

tochisenkōshutoku 土地先行取得

land acquisition for future developments

tochisen'yūsha 土地占有者 tenant; occupant

tochishoyūken 土地所有権 land ownership

tochishūyō 土地収用 expropriation of land

tochishūyōken 土地収用権 right of eminent domain

tochitatemono 土地建物 land and building; real estate; premises

tochitatemonochinshakuryō 土地建物賃借料 rent on real estate

tochitatemonogaisha 土地建物会社 real estate and building company

tochitōkisho 土地登記所 land registry

tochizōseigyō 土地造成業 land developing business; land formation business; land developer

tōdori 頭取 president

tōeikanjō 投影勘定 shadow account

tōgeokosu 峠を越す passing a peak; passing the worst ¶ The rush to borrow *passed* its *peak*. // Business already *passed the worst* of the recession.

tōgiri 当限 current month delivery

tōgō 統合 integration; unification; combination ¶ economic integration // implicit and closer *integration* of the Scandinavian currencies // to inhibit the *integration* of developing countries into the world economy // the inevitable international *integration* of financial markets // the rapid progress of international financial *integration* // the strategy of vertical *integration* which may be employed in circumstances where ownership

integration is inferrible

所有権統合 ownership integration

垂直統合 vertical integration

水平統合 horizontal integration

tōgōkabu 統合株 consolidated stock

tōhi 逃避 flight; refuge; escape ¶ *flight* of capital from the market // signs of *flight* from money to goods // Land is being bought as a

tōhijōkō 逃避条項 escape clause ¶ resort to *"escape clause"* actions to protect domestic industries against injury from imports // to invoke the GATT *escape clause* provision

tōhishihon 逃避資本 refugee capital; refugee funds

tōhishikin 逃避資金 refugee funds; capital refugee ¶ [参考] to liquidate domestic investment assets and purchase gold as a more politically safe investment

tōhōkanjō 当方勘定 [外] our account; nostro account

tōhyōken 投票権 voting right; voting power ¶ the restructuring of *voting rights* in the World Bank // While *voting rights* have been revised over time, they still represent the balance of economic, financial, and political power. // The United Kingdom continues to have twice the *voting power* of West Germany. // Iran has a lower *voting power* than India.

tōitsu 統一 uniformity; unity ¶ Little *uniformity* prevails in the form and content of financial statements.

tōitsukaikeiseido 統一会計制度 uniform accounting

tōitsukanshūkisoku 統一慣習規則 uniform practice code

tōitsukeirikijun 統一経理基準 uniform criteria of accounting; accounting code

toitsukōdō 統一行動 concerted action ¶ a *concerted action* to combat inflation

toitsukōshō 統一交渉 multiemployer bargaining

tōitsutegatayōshi 統一手形用紙 uniform note

toiya 問屋 wholesaler; wholesale trader; factor; wholesale merchant; commission merchant; commission house

toiyagyō 問屋業 wholesale trading; commission business

toiyakōsen 問屋口銭 commission; factorage

tōjikogitte 透字小切手 perforated check

tōkakōkan 等価交換 exchange of the equivalents; equivalent exchange

tōkatsuten 統轄店 controlling office

tokeai 解け合い ［市］ liquidation of compromise

tōkei 統計 statistics; figures ¶ The range and depth of these national *statistics* proved extremely varied. // The clear message from the study's *statistics* is that...

貿易業態統計 statistics of foreign trade activity

貿易統計 foreign trade statistics

賃金統計 wage statistics

動態統計 dynamic statistics

外国為替統計 foreign exchange statistics

漁業統計 fishery statistics

平均残高統計 statistics on the average balance

人口統計 population statistics;

vital statistics; census; official count of inhabitants

経済統計 economic statistics

企業統計 business statistics

記述統計 descriptive statistics

金融統計 financial statistics

工業統計 industrial statistics

農業統計 agricultural statistics

静態統計 static statistics

社会統計 social statistics

市場統計 market statistics

商業統計 commercial statistics

推測統計 inductive statistics

通関統計 customs clearance statistics

通貨統計 monetary statistics

tōkeichōsa 統計調査 statistical research

tōkeigaku 統計学 statistics

記述統計学 descriptive statistics

tōkeihōkoku 統計報告 statistical report; statistical return

tōkeihyō 統計表 statistical table; statistical tabulation; statistics

tōkeihyōsakusei 統計表作成 statistical table (tabulation)

tōkeijōnofutotsugō 統計上の不突合 statistical discrepancy

tōkeijōtaizu 統計状態図 pictogram

tōkeikaiseki 統計解析 statistical analysis

tōkeishihyō 統計指標 statistical indicator

tōkeishiki 統計式 statistical equation

tōkeishiryō 統計資料 statistical data; statistical material

tōkeisuiriron 統計推理論 theory of statistical inference

tōkeitekihinshitsukanrihō 統計的品質管理法 statistical quality control

tōkeitekikasetsu 統計的仮説 statistical hypothesis

tōkeitekikeiretsu 統計的系列 statistical series

tōkeitekikenshō 統計的検証 statistical prediction

tōkeitekisokutei 統計的測定 statistical measurement

tōkeitekisūji 統計的数字 statistical figure

tōkeizuhyō 統計図表 statistical chart (＝diagram; graph)

tōketsu 凍結 freeze; sterilization; pause; immobilization ¶ price *freeze; freeze* on prices; *freezing* of prices // wage *pause*; pay *pause* // The countervalue of the issue of the loan was *sterilized* at the central bank. // to ease the 90-day price-*freeze* rules // the wage price-rent *freeze* in all business dealings // The raise of the minimum reserve ratios will *immobilize* DM4 milliard of bank liquidity. // Such *immobilization* is necessary to prevent the already high bank liquidity from increasing further. // to lift the temporary price *freeze* // to introduce a *freeze* on all prices with retroactive effect from Sept. 1 // to continue the monetary *freeze* that has been enforced over the past two months // to order a *freeze* on all prices and wages // to extend the 90-day wage-price *freeze* to all dividends // A nine-month price *freeze* was pledged until June 30.
　賃金凍結　wage freeze
　価格凍結　price freeze
　資産凍結　freezing of assets
　所得凍結　income freeze

tōketsushisan 凍結資産 frozen asset

tōki 当期 current period; current term; present term; present period; term under review

tōki 投機 speculation; venture ¶ a wild *speculation* in stocks on the stock market // to buy dollars on *speculation* // to make a project as a *venture* // to *venture* money in *speculation* // to *venture* risk at a work // pursuit of *speculative* gains // The increase in the down payment cooled rather than cured feverish *speculation* that has caused gambling shares to trifle in price. // The lira came under *speculative* attack. // to buy the yen on *speculation*, or to *speculate* in the yen // to *venture* money in *speculation* // A craze for *speculation* dominated the market. // *speculation* over declining interest rates

tōki 登記 registration; register; registry; official record ¶ to make or effect *registration* // to have *registered* // to be entered in the *register*
　変更登記　registration of alteration
　抵当権設定登記　register of settlement of mortgage

tōki 騰貴 rise; advance; jump; appreciation; surge ¶ Some countries experienced significant currency *appreciation*. // Most of the renewed *appreciation* of the Deutsche mark took place towards the year-end. // The speculative *surge* in the yen exchange rate continued. // →上昇; 物価

tōkiatsuryoku 投機圧力 speculative pressure; speculative attack

tōkibo 登記簿 register book; registry; official record

tōkiboshōhon 登記簿抄本 extract from the register book

tōkibotōhon 登記簿謄本 exemplified copy of the register book

tōkigai 投機買い bull speculation; speculator buying ¶ Petroleum soared as *speculator* buying surged.

tokihogushi 解きほぐし unwinding ¶ *unwinding* of leads of lags of current payments

tōkikabu 投機株 speculative stock

tōkimasshō 登記抹消 cancellation of register

tōkimisai 登記未済 non-registered

tōkinetsu 投機熱 craze for speculation; speculative enthusiasm ¶ when *speculative enthusiasm* is rampant

tōkiriekikin 当期利益金 profit for the current term

tōkirijun 投機利潤 speculative gain ¶ pursuit of *speculative gains*

tōkiryō 登記料 registration fee

tōkishi 投機師 professional speculator; operator

tōkishijō 投機市場 speculative market

tōkishijō 騰貴市場 buoyant market

tōkisho 登記所 registry office; registry

tōkisonshitsukin 当期損失金 loss for the current term

tōkisuji 投機筋 speculators; professionals

tōkitekikaimochi 投機の買持 ［市］ bull position

tōkitekinaengainitaisurukanri 投機的な円買いに対する管理 controls on speculative yen buying

tōkitekiurimochi 投機的売持 ［市］ bear position

tōkitetsuzuki 登記手続 registration formalities

tōkitorihiki 投機取引 speculative

transaction; speculative operation

tōkiuri 投機売り speculative selling; bear speculation ¶ *Speculator selling* pushed copper below £1,000 a tonne.

tōkizumi 登記済み registered

tokka 特化 specialization ¶ The business is now highly *specialized*. // →分業

　国際特化 international specialization

　最適特化 optimal specialization

　産業内特化 intra-industry specialization

tokka 特価 special price; specially reduced price; bargain price ¶ *bargain priced* articles

tokkahin'uriba 特価品売場 bargain counter

tokkateikyō 特価提供 offering of lower priced articles

tokkauridashi 特価売出し bargain sale; bargain; sale; sale at special prices

tokkeikanzei 特恵関税 preferential tariff benefits; trade preferences; preferential duties; tariff preferences; preferential tariffs ¶ to approve *preferential tariffs* for developing countries // to grant *favorable tariff* treatment to developing nations // special *tariff preferences* for developing countries

tokkeitaigū 特恵待遇 preferential treatment

tokkōyaku 特効薬 nostrum ¶ There is no *nostrum* or panacea for inflation. // economic *nostrums*

tokkyoginkō 特許銀行 chartered bank

tokkyoken 特許権 patent right

tokkyokenshiyōryō 特許権使用料 royalty

tokkyokenshoyūsha 特許権所有者 patentee

tokubaihin 特売品 articles for special sale

tokubetsuchōikinkokkosaiken 特別弔慰金国庫債券 Non-Interest Treasury Bond for Special Condolence

tokubetsugenkashōkyaku 特別減価償却 specially recognized depreciation; accelerated depreciation

tokubetsugenzeikokusai 特別減税国債 special tax reduction bond

tokubetsuhaitō 特別配当 plum

tokubetsuhikidashiken 特別引出権 (IMF) special drawing rights; SDR; "paper gold" ¶ The Fund has agreed to a purchase by the Govt. of Cameroon of the equivalent of 17.5 million *special drawing rights* in currencies — *SDR* 10 million in Austrian schillings and SDR 7.5 million in Norwegian kroner. // The total use of *SDRs* by participants was SDR 826 million. // world export unit values in terms of *SDRs*

tokubetsuhikidashikenrisoku 特別引出権利息 interest on Special Drawing Rights

tokubetsuhikidashikenhoyūgaku 特別引出権保有額 holdings of Special Drawing Rights

tokubetsukōritsu 特別高率 higher rate; penalty rate; penal high rate

tokubetsukyūfu 特別給付 fringe benefits ¶ →諸給与

tokubetsukyūfukinkokkosaiken 特別給付金国庫債券 Non-Interest Special Benefit Treasury Bond

tokubetsumaruyūseido 特別マル優制度 →少額公債非課税制度

tokubetsutsumitatekin 特別積立金 special reserve

tokubetsuyūshi 特別融資 special loan; special finance

tokuchō 特徴 characteristic; feature; trait ¶ the important *characteristic* of the last year // to show signs *characteristic* of a year of recovery // Growth *characteristics* are still evident. // a regular *feature* of periods of economic adjustment // salient *features* in the business sector // an event *featured* in the report // to reflect the *traits* of its people and its economic life // higher living costs *characteristic* of larger cities

tokuisaki 得意先 customers; clientele; regular customer

tokuisakikanjō 得意先勘定 customer's account

tokuju 特需 special procurement (by the U.S. forces)

tokumeishain 匿名社員 sleeping partner; anonymous partner; silent partner

tokusei 特性 peculiarity; characteristic ¶ regulatory and economic *peculiarities* of public utilities // the uneven male-female distribution of productive *characteristics* endowments // differences in observable *characteristics* // →特徴

tokushoku 特色 peculiarity ¶ a *peculiarity* of the present situation in that... // →特性

tokushuazukarikin 特殊預り金 specific deposits

tokushuginkō 特殊銀行 special bank

tokushukashitsuke 特殊貸付 special loan

tokushukō 特殊鋼 special steel

tokuteikinsenshintaku 特定金銭信託 designated money in trust

tokuteimeigara 特定銘柄 ［市］ designated speculative stock; specified stock

tokuteisangyōikusei 特定産業育成 industrial targeting

tokuteisenbikikogitte 特定線引小切手 special crossed check

tokuyakujōkō 特約条項 rider

tokuyakunimotozukukaimodoshi 特約に基づく買戻し contractual repurchase

tōkyōkouribukkashisū 東京小売物価指数 Tokyo retail price index

tōkyōshōhishabukkashisū 東京消費者物価指数 Tokyo consumer price index

tōkyūjoretsu 等級序列 rank ordering ¶ This *rank ordering* of countries by dollar GNP per head is rough and ready.

tōmeisei 透明性 transparency

tōmen 当面 for some time to come; in the foreseeable future; for months ahead; for the immediate future; in the near term; for the time being

tomenechūmon 留値注文 ［市］ stop (loss) order

tomodaoreno 共倒れの internecine ¶ The consortium was formed to lay aside the usual *internecine* competition.

tomokasegikatei 共稼ぎ家庭 two-income family; family in which both spouses work

tonae 唱え ［市］ quoting ¶ Motors were *quoted* high.

tonaene 唱え値 asked price; asked quotation

tōnanhoken 盗難保険 burglary insurance

ton'ya 問屋 → toiya

tōnyūryō 投入量 input ¶ Changes in labor *inputs,* quantitative and qualitative, are important determinants of economic growth.

tōnyūsanshutsubunseki 投入産出分析 input-output analysis

tōnyūsanshutsuhyō 投入産出表 input-output table

tōnyūsanshutsuritsu 投入産出比率 input-output ratio

tōraku 騰落 rise and fall; up and down; fluctuation

tōrakukabusen 騰落株線 advance-decline line

tōrakuritsu 騰落率 percent(age) change; rate of increase or decrease ¶ *percentage changes* in production by industry over the month // the annual *rate of increase or decrease* in prices

torēdoofu トレード・オフ trade-off (relation) ¶ the *trade-off relation* between inflation and unemployment // The selection of countries, variables, and years represents a *trade-off*; more better data are available for fewer countries for shorter periods. // One theory is that people have a "liquidity-savings *trade-off.*" // ［参考］ the increasing degree of unemployment and wage-price inflation

toriatsukai 取扱い ［証市］ best-efforts underwriting; underwriting on a best-efforts basis

torigākakaku トリガー価格 trigger price

torihiki 取引 trading; transaction; dealing; bargain; trade; traffic; sales; business; operation ¶ to open business *dealings* with a bank // The yen was little changed against the dollar in quiet *trading.* // The dollar opened flat in subdued *business.* // The combination of a spot and forward *transaction* is called a swap *operation*. // Commodity *transactions* on the black-market are brisk. // The Act permits banks of high calibre to *deal* in the interbank market. // August gold futures were *trading* to 375.80 dollars an ounce. // [参考] The dollar has changed hands around 2.80 marks.

相対取引 negotiated transaction

アウトライト取引 outright transaction

売買一任勘定取引 discretionary account transaction

貿易外取引 invisible trade

貿易取引 visible trade; merchandise transaction

外国為替取引 foreign exchange transaction

現物取引 spot sale; spot transaction

現金取引 cash transaction; bargain for cash

直取引 direct transaction; spot sale

実物(為替)取引 spot (exchange) transaction

実務取引 actual transaction

場外取引 off-mart dealing; outside dealing; curb dealing; trading on the curb

株式取引 stock dealing; stock exchange

掛繋取引 hedge transaction

空取引 fictitious transaction; short sale

経常取引 current transaction

期近物取引 transaction of near delivery

金融的取引 financial transaction

民間取引 private transaction

無条件取引 outright transaction

内部取引 internal transaction

仲間取引 trader's transaction

思惑取引 speculative transaction

先物(為替)取引 forward (exchange) transaction; futures transaction

差金取引 speculation for margin

政府取引 govenmental transaction

清算取引 time transaction

資本取引 capital transaction

信用取引 sale on credit

商業取引 commercial transaction; business transaction; bargaining transaction

商品取引 commodity transaction

証券取引 securities transaction

証拠金取引 margin transaction

スワップ取引 swap transaction

定期取引 time bargain; settlement dealing

torihikiaitekoku 取引相手国 →貿易相手国

torihikibetsusaisan 取引別採算 profit analysis by transactions

torihikibi 取引日 business day

torihikidaka 取引高 trade volume; trading; volume of business dealings; turnover; volume; transactions; sales ¶ Retail trade *turnover* showed a year-to-year decline of 4.8% in June. // *Turnovers* have risen steeply both in exports and in imports. // Volvo is at the top of the list for the sixth year running with *sales* at S. Kr. 14.9 milliard. // The "milliard club" comprises firms with a *turnover* in excess of S.Kr. 1 millard. // *Trading* continues thin. // →出来高; 売上高

torihikidōki 取引動機 transaction motive

torihikiginkō 取引銀行 correspondent bank; one's bank; banker

torihikiin 取引員 broker agent; regular member; regular trader;

authorized broker

torihikiinshikkakusha 取引員失格
者 [市] defaulter

torihikijikan 取引時間 business
hours

torihikijōkensho 取引条件書
schedule of terms and conditions

torihikikankei 取引関係 business
relations (=relationship)

torihikikeiyaku 取引契約 correspondent agreement (=arrange-
ments)

torihikimabara 取引まばら [市]
spotty trading

torihikiryūtsūsokudo 取引流通速度
transactions velocity of money

torihikisaki 取引先 correspondent;
customer; client; clientele ¶ →顧客

torihikisakigakari 取引先係 can
vasser

torihikiseigen 取引制限 restraint
of trade ¶ Manufacturers acted
unlawfully in *restraint of trade* in
the distribution and sale of color TV
sets.

torihikishin'yō 取引信用 trade
credit

torihikijo 取引所 exchange; bourse
米穀取引所 grain exchange
株式取引所 stock exchange
穀物取引所 grain exchange
砂糖取引所 sugar exchange

torihikijokaiin 取引所会員 exchange members

torihikijonakagainin 取引所仲買人
exchange broker

torihikiteishishobun 取引停止処分
disposition by suspension of trade

torihikiteishishobunkensū 取引停
止処分件数 number of cases of
suspension of business transactions
with banks

torihikiten 取引店 office in trans-

action

toriire 取入れ intake ¶ The country's *intake* of foreign capital increased. // supplies equivalent to the
necessary basic *intake* of food grains
of some 180 million persons // an
active foreign currency short-term
loan *intake* by Japanese firms

toriirekibōkinri 取入れ希望金利
bid rate

torikae 取替え replacement ¶ to
replace inventories and plant // Capital assets which outlived their
usefulness must be *replaced* in whole
or in part. // to encourage companies
to *replace* existing assets
同種設備の取替え like-for-like replacement

torikaegenka 取替原価 replacement cost

torikaejuyō 取替需要 replacement
demand

torikaekachi 取替価値 replacement value

torikaetōshi 取替投資 replacement investment

torikaetsumitatekin 取替積立金
replacement reserve fund

torikeshi 取消し(予約の) cancellation (of exchange contract)

torikeshifunōshin'yōjō 取消不能信
用状 irrevocable (letter of) credit

torikeshikanōshin'yōjō 取消可能
信用状 revocable credit

torikowashihi 取壊し費 demoli-
tion expense

torikumi 取組み drawing of bill;
[市] technical position
為替取組 money-order exchange

torikumidaka 取組高 turnover;
volume ¶ →出来高

torikumikankei 取組み関係 [証
市] ratio of money loans to stock

loans

torikumisaki 取組先 drawee (of a bill)

torikumiten 取組店 sending office

torikuzushi 取崩し disposition; drawing (down); running down; drawdown; liquidation ¶ *disposition* of reserves // The increase in orders was met by *drawing* on the previously accumulated buffer stock. // The smaller sales were met partly through *running down* stocks. // *drawdown* on available stock // *liquidation* of stocks of imported raw materials // to keep up their lending by *drawing* on their reserves

torirenma トリレンマ trilemma; "magic triangle" ¶ the *trilemma* of inflation, recession, and payments imbalances // to achieve the goals of the *"magic triangle"*, i.e., high employment, external equilibrium and price stability

torishimariyaku 取締役 director
代表権限を有する取締役 director who has authority to represent the company
代表取締役 representing director
常務取締役 managing director
専務取締役 senior managing director

torishimariyakukai 取締役会 board of directors

torishimariyakukaikaichō 取締役会会長 chairman of the board of directors

tōrisōba 通り相場 ruling price

toritate 取立て collection ¶ inward and outgoing *collections* // the *collection* of foreign credit instruments forwarded for *collection* abroad

toritatehiyō 取立費用 collection expenses

toritateinin'uragaki 取立委任裏書 endorsement for collection

toritatekawase 取立為替 exchange for collection

toritatekittetegata 取立切手手形 checks and bills for collection; collections outstanding

toritatemisaikittetegata 取立未済切手手形 checks and bills in process of collection; bank float

toritateryō 取立料 collection charge

toritatetegata 取立手形 bill for collection; collection bill

torite 取り手 [市] borrower; bidder; taker

toritsugi 取次ぎ agency; commission; intermediation

toritsugigyō 取次業 agency business

toritsugihanbai 取次販売 sale on commission

toritsuginin 取次人 agent; middleman; commission broker

toritsugiten 取次店 agent
一手取次店 sole agent

toritsuke 取付け run on a bank; drawing; cashing ¶ A *run* is made *on a bank*. // The *bank* had a *run*.

tōroku 登録 registration; register; entry; record ¶ The notes are in *registered* form and are nontransferable. // *registration* of nationality of a ship // cancellation of *register* of bonds
証券登録 registration of securities ¶ a security *registered* with the Commission by filing a registration statement.

tōrokubo 登録簿 register

tōrokuhenkō 登録変更 registration of transfer

tōrokuishō 登録意匠 registered design

tōrokujimu 登録事務 registration business

tōrokujokyaku 登録除却 discharge from registration

tōrokukikan 登録機関 registrar

tōrokukokusaigankinrishi 登録国債元金利子 principal and interest of registered government bonds

tōrokukōsai 登録公債 registered bond

tōrokumeiginin 登録名義人 registered owner; owner on record

tōrokunin 登録人 registrant; one on record; registered owner (=holder) ¶ owners *on record* as at the close of business

tōrokuryō 登録料 registration fee

tōrokusei 登録制 registration system ¶ [参考] All government backed securities should be in registered and not bearer form.

tōrokuseikyū 登録請求 application for registration

tōrokushōhyō 登録商標 registered trade mark

tōrokutodokedesho 登録届出書 registration statement

tororugyogyō トロール漁業 trawl fishery

tōsan 倒産 insolvency; bankruptcy; business failure ¶ the number of *business failures,* or of cases of *bankruptcy* // to go *bankrupt* // The country's corporate *bankruptcies* rose by 28% over the month in March. // The number of *bankruptcies* stood at 1,409. // The number of *bankruptcy* proceedings instituted rose to 424, while the number of proceedings closed came to 317. // a company on the verge of *bankruptcy* // a biggest

ever instance of *business failure*, involving ¥200,000 million in liabilities // *Business failures* may visit upon well-established firms.

tōsei 統制 control; regimentation ¶ foreign exchange *controls* // tools of monetary *controls* // monetary *control* devices // monetary *regimentation* // *controlled* economy // to *regiment* banking activity // The threat of inflation led to imposition of wage and price *controls* which proved to be unworkable, inequitable and ineffective. // strict exercise of war-time mandatory *controls* over production and prices // to cast off the centralized state *controls* // Maintenance of direct statutory *controls* is undesirable. // Excessive state *regimentation* of industry and commerce for war purposes came to be removed.

tōsei 騰勢 upward trend; up-trend

tōseiippuku 騰勢一服 slowdown of rise; deceleration; ceasing of rise ¶ The *rise* in prices *slowed down.* // The increase in output *decelerated.* // Prices *ceased to rise.*

tōseikaijo 統制解除 decontrol; deregulation; dismantling (=abolition; removal lifting, freeing; ruling out) of controls ¶ Spain was moving towards *decontrol* of prices. // Carter's plan of phased fuel price *decontrol* // a plan for *decontrolling* foreign trade // to completely *rule out* a beef price freeze // Insurance premiums will be *freed of controls.* // to *dismantle* the foreign exchange restrictions to *deregulate* foreign trade // the gradual oil price *decontrol* proposal // Most of export *controls* will be *removed.* // to *lift* *regulations* on capital transactions

tōseikeizai 統制経済 controlled economy

tōshi 投資 investment ¶ The *investment* initially scheduled for iron and steel for 1979 was somewhat delayed and the planned program could not be carried out in full. // the systematic permanent *investment* of surplus production in reproductive works // Two kinds — portfolio and direct — *investment* nosedived befor picking up. // increased liquidations by foreign investors of portfolio *investments* in Japanese bonds // The rise in terms of value, in *investment* in manufacturing industry probably represents replacement and rationalization *investments*. // The dollar is a desirable *investment* outlet. // outward and inward capital *investment* transactions // *Investment* in machinery and equipment and in building expanded fairly equally. // The scale of equipment *investment* appears extensive. // Privately financed *investment* and publicly financed *investment* both are running below the 1980 average. // Plant and equipment *investment* declined and the pace of inventory *investment* slackened from the earlier boom levels. // Business *investment*, which had grown steadily and very fast since 1974, weakend progressively in the course of the following year. // Fixed *investment* by industry rose strongly. // Business fixed *investment* leveled off. // *Investment* probably contracted. // [参考] Businessmen plan to increase sharply their spending on equipment. // Capital spending will climb to an estimated $73 billion. // Business plans for equipment outlays in 1976 were revised upward.

冒険投資　risky investment

分散投資　diversification investment

長期投資　long-term investment

直接投資　direct investment; equity investment

独立投資　autonomous investment

負の投資　negative investment

外人対日証券投資　foreigners' investment in Japanese securities

技術革新投資　investment in technological innovation

意図しない(=せざる)投資　unintended investment; unplanned investment

意図した投資　intended investment; planned

事後的投資　ex-post investment

人的投資　human investment

自生的投資　autonomous investment

実物投資　real investment

事前的投資　ex-ante investment

受動的投資　passive investment

純投資　net investment

住宅投資　housing investment

株式投資　stock investment

海外投資　overseas investment; investment abroad

過剰投資　over-investment ¶ Some concern has arisen about the possibility of *over-investment*.

拡張投資　expansion investment

間接投資　indirect investment; portfolio investment

計画投資　planned investment; projected investment; designed investment

継続投資　investment project already undertaken

研究開発投資　research and development investment

健全投資　sound investment

子会社株式投資　stock investment in a subsidiary

国内投資　domestic investment; investment at home

国際投資　international investment

公共投資　public investment; investment in public utilities

更新投資　replacement investment

コスト削減投資　cost-reducing investment

固定資本投資　fixed capital investment; fixed investment; capital spending; capital outlay ¶ Business *fixed investment* levelled off. // *Fixed investment* by industry presumably contracted. // *Capital spending* grew steadily and very fast and then weakened progressively.

民間設備投資　private plant and equipment investment

民間住宅投資　private housing investment

民間投資　private investment

能動的投資　active investment; positive investment

置換投資　replacement investment

労働代替投資　investment in substitution for labor

累積投資　accumulated investment; [市] installment trade

生産的投資　productive investment

戦略投資　strategic investment

設備拡大投資　capacity-widening investment

設備投資　plant and equipment investment; equipment investment; fixed assets investment; fixed investment; investment in plants and equipment

資産運用投資　portfolio investment

証券投資　portfolio investment; securities investment

省力投資　labor-saving investment

粗投資　gross investment

総投資　aggregate investment

対外投資　overseas investment; external investment; investment abroad; outward investment

余裕資金投資　"leeway" investment

誘発(的)投資　induced investment

在庫投資　inventory investment; investment in inventories

tōshibukken 投資物件　investment instrument

tōshichūkainin 投資仲介人　investment broker

tōshifunanishōken 通し船荷証券　through bill of lading

tōshigai 投資買　investment buying

tōshigaisha 投資会社　investment company; management company; unit investment trust company

toshiginkō 都市銀行　city bank; large city-based commercial banks
上位都銀　largest city banks

tōshiginkō 投資銀行　investment bank; investment banking firm

tōshihiyō 投資費用　investment cost

tōshiiyoku 投資意欲　investment intention; investor interest; willingness to invest ¶ *Investment intentions* are still rising. // A recent survey of *investment intentions* in industry indicates a slowdown in capital outlays. // waning *investor interest* // *Investment intentions* for 1979 improved relative to 1978 *intentions*. // The strength of *investment intentions* is notable. // The continuing rise in *investment intentions* indicates the need to improve efficiency. // to stimulate firms' *inclination to invest*

tōshijikkō 投資実行 execution of investment

tōshijikkōryoku 投資実行力 ability to invest

tōshijunkan 投資循環 investment cycle ¶ The year saw the ending of a medium-run *investment cycle.* // The near complètion of a massive *investment cycle* was an autonomous force. // It is difficult for a new *investment cycle* of the traditional type to get under way. // A downward phase of the medium-term *investment cycle* has commenced.

tōshijuyō 投資需要 investment demand; investment need ¶ to sell bonds to supply *investment demands* // a back-log of unfilled *investment needs*

tōshijuyōhyō 投資需要表 investment-demand schedule

toshika 都市化 urbanization

tōshika 投資家 investor ¶ *Investors* prove to be less capable than ever of withstanding a certain investment euphoria.
　機関投資家 institutional investor
　大衆投資家 investing public

tōshikabu 投資株 investment stock

toshikachōsa 都市化調査 urbanization control

toshikaihatsu 都市開発 urban development

tōshikamotsu 通し貨物 through cargo

tōshikankyō 投資環境 investment climate (=environment) ¶ The *investment climate* presented a mixed picture.

toshikanosokushin 都市化の促進 urbanization promotion

tōshikatsudō 投資活動 investment activity ¶ Resumption of *investment activities,* which was once mere conjecture, has become a reality. // The sustained *investment* boom of the past three years has run its course and is now entering a period of lower *activity.*

toshikeikaku 都市計画 urban planning; city planning

tōshikeikaku 投資計画 investment plan (=program; project); planned investment ¶ Supply constraints motivated large increases in *planned investment.* // *Investment plans* were expanded more than compatible with sales prospects. // a downward or upward revision of business *investment plans* for the coming year. // Business *plans* for plant and equipment *investment* were revised upward appreciably. // Second quarter *investment programs* were scaled down. // An *investment project* can be postponed at any stage of the planning and construction process. // Each country must review critically the content and direction of its public *investment program.* // Business firms are laying *plans* for increases in *investment* outlays. // *Planned investment* reached $37 billion, compared with total realized investment of $34 billion in the previous year.

tōshikeiki 投資景気 investment boom

tōshikikai 投資機会 opportunities of making investment; investment opportunities ¶ *Opportunities* to *make* cost-reducing *investment* will decrease in the future. // to provide safe and profitable *investment opportunities* for Euro-dollars // *Opportunities* to make cost-reducing *investment* will decrease in the future.

tōshikikan 投資期間 investment period

toshikōhai 都市荒廃 urban decay

tōshikomongyō 投資顧問業 investment adviser

toshikoshimono 年越物 ［市］ over-year-end (＝overyear) loan

tōshikurabu 投資クラブ investment club

tōshikurinobe 投資繰延べ deferment of investment; postponement of investment

toshinomukeikakukakudai 都市の無計画拡大 sprawling urban areas; urban sprawl ¶ Populations are growing, as are *sprawling urban areas.*

tōshinonijūkōka 投資の二重効果 dual effect of investment

toshiosen 都市汚染 urban pollution

toshisaikaihatsu 都市再開発 urban redevelopment; urban renewal

tōshisaiken 投資債券 investment bond

tōshisaki 投資先 investee; investment outlet ¶ Funds were attracted to more profitable *investment outlets.*

toshisangyōmō 都市産業網 urban-industrial network

tōshiseikō 投資性向 propensity to invest; investment propensity ¶ Uncertainties in the monetary field began to inhibit the *investment propensity* of trade and industry. // Financial changes contributed to the weakening of the *propensity to invest.* // industrialists' *propensity* to embark on new capital spending projects

toshisekkei 都市設計 urban design

tōshishijō 投資市場 investment market

tōshishikin 投資資金 investment capital; investible funds ¶ to determine the direction of *investible funds* into the various market compartments // the continued abundance of both official and private *investible funds*

tōshishintaku 投資信託 investment trust; mutual fund ¶ securities for *investment trust* // securities held for *investment trust*

　オープン型投資信託 open investment trust

　債券投資信託 bond open investment trust

　ユニット型投資信託 unit investment trust

tōshishintakuitakugyōmu 投資信託委託業務 management business of investment trust

tōshishintakukumiireshōken 投資信託組入れ証券 securities for investment trust

tōshishintakusōba 投資信託相場 investment trust prices

tōshishintakuyūkashōken 投資信託有価証券 securities held for investment trust

tōshishintakuzanzonganpon 投資信託残存元本 outstanding principal of investment trust

tōshishishutsu 投資支出 investment outlay (＝expenditure) ¶ The value of *investment outlays* in the national economy, in current prices, amounted to about \$1,670 billion.

tōshishōken 投資証券 investment security ¶ to buy bonds, notes, or debentures commonly known as *investment securities*

toshishūchūka 都市集中化 urban concentration; concentration in cities

tōshishudōgatakeiki 投資主導型景気 business boom spearheaded by investment; business boom led by investment

tōshisōdan 投資相談 investment counsel

tōshisuji 投資筋 investors; investment interest ¶ The large volume reflects widespread *investment* and speculative *interest*.

tōshisujikaimono 投資筋買物 [市] investment demand

tōshitaishō 投資対象 investment outlet ¶ The surest *outlets* for *investment* then were land and scarce commodities.

tōshitegata 投資手形 investment bill

tōshitsūka 投資通貨 investment currency ¶ U.S. bonds are attractive, supporting the dollar as an *investment currency*.

tōshiunchin 通し運賃 through rate

tōshiun'yō 投資運用 portfolio management

tōshiyūin 投資誘因 inducement of investment

tōshizai 投資材 investment goods

tōshizeigakukōjo 投資税額控除 investment (tax) credit

tōshizeikōjo 投資税控除 investment tax credit

tōshokabu 当所株 stock exchange share

tōshōshūseikabukaheikin 東証修正株価平均 Tokyo Stock Exchange (＝T.S.E.) stock price average

tōshoyosan 当初予算 original budget; initial budget

tōshoyusoku 当初予測 original prediction; original estimate; intial estimate; earlier estimate

tōyōgai 当用買い hand-to-mouth buying; purchase only for the present use; conservative purchase; restrained buying

tōyūshi 投融資 investmest and loan ¶ treasury *investment and loan* program

tōzafurikomi 当座振込 credit to current account

tōzagashi 当座貸し loan on short notice; cash credit

tōzahiritsu 当座比率 quick ratio; acid (test) ratio

tōzaibōeki 東西貿易 East-West trade

tōzakanjō 当座勘定 account current; current account; running account; open account; checking account

tōzakanjōnyūkinhyō 当座勘定入金票 paying-in slip for current deposit; current deposit credit slip

tōzakanjōtsukekae 当座勘定付替 transfer on current account

tōzakanjōzandakashōmei 当座勘定残高証明 certificate of current deposit

tōzakarikoshi 当座借越 overdrafts with banks; debt on short notice; overdrawing account; bank overdraft; overdraft; bank credit

tōzakashikoshi 当座貸越 overdraft; overdrawn account

tōzakashikoshibuai 当座貸越歩合 rate on overdraft

tōzakashikoshigendogaku 当座貸越限度額 maximum limit of overdraft

tōzakashikoshitsukiteikiyokin 当

座貸越付定期預金　time deposit with overdraft facilities

tōzashisan　当座資産　liquid asset

tōzayokin　当座預金　current deposit; current account; checking account ¶ Consumers will soon be able to open interest-bearing *checking accounts* even at credit unions.

小口当座預金　petty current deposit

特別当座預金　special current deposit

tōzenzō　当然増　mandatory increase ¶ a sharp *mandatory increase* in government expenditures

tsūshōchitsujoijihō　通商秩序維持法 [米] Orderly Trade Act

tsūbaifōhōshiki　ツーバイフォー方式　2×4-inch lumber method; platform frame construction

tsubushine　潰し値　residual value; scrap value

tsūchi　通知　notice; notification; advice ¶ Any *notice* required to be given must be in writing and sufficiently given if delivered in person or sent by mail. // The *notice* of change of address must be deemed to have been given when received. // to *notify* the bank that the check was raised

tsūchiginkō　通知銀行　advising bank; notifying bank

tsūchitesūryō　通知手数料　advising charge; advising fee

tsūchiyokin　通知預金　deposit at notice; notice deposit

tsūchō　通帳　passbook

tsuichō　追徴　penalty collection; additional collection

tsuichōkin　追徴金　additional assessment; forfeit; surcharge ¶ →追加料金

tsuichōshobun　追徴処分　punishment on penalty tax

tsuichōzei　追徴税　penalty tax

tsuigekiuri　追撃売り　[市] follow-up bearing

tsuika　追加　addition; supplement; addendum; appendix

tsuikachūmon　追加注文　additional order

tsuikahiyō　追加費用　additional expense

tsuikajuyō　追加需要　additional demand

tsuikanyūsatsu　追加入札　supplementary bid

tsuikaryūdōsei　追加流動性　additional liquidity

tsuikashin'yō　追加信用　additional credit

tsuikashogakari　追加諸掛り　additional charges

tsuikashōkokin　追加証拠金　additional margin; re-margin

tsuikashusshi　追加出資　additional investment; amount added to capital

tsuikauntenshikin　追加運転資金　additional operating funds

tsuikayosan　追加予算　supplementary budget

tsuisekichōsa　追跡調査　follow-up check; follow-up

tsuisekirūtin　追跡ルーティン [コン] tracer; tracing routine

tsūka　通貨　currency; money ¶ expansion and contraction of *money* in circulation // to put a new *currency* into circulation // a considerable withdrawal of *money* from the market // *Currencies* of countries in strong surplus strengthened. // The inflation differential weakened the national *currency*.

安定通貨　stabilized currency

貿易通貨　trade currency

第三の通貨　third reserve component; SDR

越年通貨　year-end note (=currency) issue balance

補助通貨　subsidiary currency; fractional currency

不換通貨　inconvertible currency

不足通貨　scarce currency

減価通貨　depreciated currency

現金通貨　cash currency

合法通貨　lawful currency (=money)

非常通貨　emergency currency

準備通貨　reserve currency

受領容認通貨　acceptable currency

10進法通貨　decimal currency ¶ the adoption of *decimal* coinage in New Zealand with the present 10 schillings as the basic monetary unit // Pakistan has been in the process of introducing *decimal coinage*, without change in either the value or nomenclature of the rupee.

介入通貨　intervention currency

管理通貨　managed currency; controlled currency

計量通貨　currency by weight

計算通貨　currency by tale

健全通貨　sound currency

決済通貨　currency of settlement

基軸通貨　key currency; basic currency

基準通貨　basic currency; key currency

金属通貨　metallic currency

交換可能通貨　convertible currency

国内通貨　domestic currency; local currency

国際準備通貨　international reserve currency

混合通貨　mixed currency

強制通貨　forced currency

共通通貨　common currency

無制限通貨　free currency

流通不便通貨　currency unfit for circulation

世界通貨　universal currency

潜在通貨　latent currency

伸縮通貨　elastic currency; flexible currency

信用通貨　credit currency

資産通貨　asset currency

指定通貨　designated currency

小額通貨　fractional currency

主要通貨　principal currency

大陸通貨　continentals

強い通貨　strong currency

預金通貨　depositary money

弱い通貨　weak currency

tsūkaantei　通貨安定　stabilization of currency; monetary stabilization

tsūkaanteiken　通貨安定圏　zone of monetary stability; monetary stability zone ¶ the creation of a *zone of monetary stability* in Europe, encompassing greater stability at home and abroad

tsūkaanteisei　通貨安定性　currency stability, monetary stability ¶ to achieve greater *currency stability* // The country's *monetary stability* was foreefeited because of our excessively lenient monetary policy.

tsūkaanteishakkan　通貨安定借款　currency stabilization loan

tsūkabasukettohōshiki　通貨バスケット方式　currency basket system

tsūkabōeki　通過貿易　transit trade

tsūkachitsujo　通貨秩序　monetary order ¶ a more equitable and stable *monetary order*

tsūkadaiyōkokusai　通貨代用国債　note in substitution for currency

tsūkafuan　通貨不安　monetary unrest; monetary uncertainties; international monetary unrest; international currency disturbances; currency upheavals; monetary turbulences; currency nervousness; unrest over currency; currency unrest; currency turmoil ¶ emergence of *international currency disturbances* // inflation-induced *unrest over* the major *currencies* // The international market was hardly affected by last week's *currency unrest.* // The yen exchange rate is to be directly affected by *currency turmoil* in Europe. // *Monetary turbulence* of a quite different kind has affected sterling and Italian lira. // The "snake" itself can become a source of *currency unrest.* // The *uncertainties* surrounding both sterling and lira will disappear soon. // We have experienced some considerable *turbulence* in the European currency field.

tsūkafukuhon'isei 通貨複本位制 bimetal(l)ism

tsukaisute 使い捨て disposable; throwaway; use-and-dispose; use-and-discard ¶ a *disposable* watch // a *throwaway* car // a *use-and-discard* cigaret lighter // Japan's *throwaway* consumers are becoming interested in secondhand cars.

tsūkajunbi 通貨準備 monetary reserve ¶ the constitution or liquidation of *monetary reserves* denominated in Deutsche Mark

tsūkakachi 通貨価値 currency value; value of money; monetary value ¶ an erosion of the *value of money* by inflation // a change in either *value* or the nomenclature of the rupee // to maintain the *value* of their *currencies* in relation to the

value of the *currency* or currencies of other members, or to allow it to vary // to link the *value* of its *currency* to one key currency // a persistent decline in the external *value* of the *currency* // to keep the *value of money* stable // *Monetary values* continue to be eroded by irresponsible governments.

tsūkakachinogeraku 通貨価値の下落 currency depreciation ¶ Many countries experienced significant *currency depreciation.* // Some countries suffered from a *depreciation of* their *currencies.* // the *depreciation* of the U.S. dollar on the exchange markets

tsūkakachinoiji 通貨価値の維持 maintenance of a value for its currency (in terms of the special drawing right or another denominator); maintenance of monetary stability; stability in the value of money

tsūkakachinotōki 通貨価値の騰貴 currency appreciation ¶ Some countries experienced significant *currency appreciation* // to enjoy the advantage of an *appreciation of* their *currency* // the *appreciation* of the yen in exchange markets

tsūkakaikaku 通貨改革 currency reform; monetary reform ¶ the difficult process of world *monetary reform*

tsukakanri 通貨管理 management of currency; currency management; currency (=monetary) control; monetary administration; money management ¶ gritty and sophisticated *money management*

tsūkakiki 通貨危機 monetary crisis ¶ There has been an average of one international *monetary crisis* every year.

tsūkakōbairyoku 通貨購買力 purchasing power of money ¶ The replacement of the present ruble by a new one does not affect the *purchasing power of monetary* claims.

tsūkakōkansei 通貨交換性 convertibility ¶ to suspend and restore the free *convertibility* of the national currency

tsūkakonran 通貨混乱 currency turmoil; currency disturbance; monetary upheaval; monetary convulsion; monetary turbulence ¶ a series of international *monetary convulsion* // →通貨不安

tsūkakyōkyūryō 通貨供給量 money supply ¶ →マネー・サプライ

tsūkamihon 通貨見本 specimen currency

tsūkan 通関 entry; customs clearance; passage through the customs house

tsūkanbēsu 通関ベース ［統］ customs basis; customs clearance basis

tsūkanhikomi 通関費込み cleared

tsūkanjisseki 通関実績 trade (balance) on a customs (clearance) basis; statistics of customs clearance

tsūkankō 通関港 port of entry

tsūkanmenjō 通関免状 entry; clearance; permit

tsūkanmisainedan 通関未済値段 duty unpaid

tsūkanokōkansei 通貨の交換性 currency convertibility

tsūkan'okurijō 通関送り状 customs invoice

tsūkanoryūtsūsokudo 通貨の流通速度 velocity of circulation of money

tsukanshōmeisho 通関証明書 delivery verification

tsūkanshorui 通関書類 document for clearance

tsūkanshūshi 通関収支 trade balance on customs clearance basis

tsūkantesūryō 通関手数料 customs fee

tsūkantetsuzuki 通関手続 customs procedure; customs formalities; customs clearance; customs entry

tsūkantōkei 通関統計 customs clearance statistics

tsūkan'yōokurijō 通関用送状 customs invoice

tsūkanzumi 通関済み customs-cleared; cleared; entered ¶ *customs-cleared* exports and imports in June on a dollar base

tsūkaryōchōsetsu 通貨量調節 control of the money supply (＝stock)

tsūkaryūtsūdaka 通貨流通高 currency in circulation; money in circulation; monetary circulation ¶ *Money in circulation* dropped some lempira 7 million below the figure reached one year earlier. // expansion in the *monetary circulation* // a substantial return of *currency* from public *circulation* // The *note circulation* declined slightly but then expanded. // ［参考］ →マネー・サプライ

tsūkaryūtsūryō 通貨流通量 stock of money ¶ to manage the *stock of money* perfectly // →マネー・サプライ

tsūkasei 通貨性 moneyness

tsūkaseido 通貨制度 monetary system; ¶ to dislocate the international *monetary system* // the difficult process of reforming the international *monetary system*

tsūkaseiyokin 通貨性預金 monetary deposit

tsūkasensō 通貨戦争 monetary

war; currency war ¶ to take the world back to the *monetary wars* of the 1930s

tsūkashijō 通貨市場 monetary market ¶ African gold sales to the *monetary market*

tsūkashugi 通貨主義 currency principle; metal(l)ism

tsūkashūshuku 通貨収縮 (monetary) deflation; currency deflation, monetary contraction; currency contraction

tsūkasochi 通貨措置 currency practice ¶ to avoid discriminatory *currency practices*

tsūkasōzō 通貨創造 money creation ¶ The Bundesbank has seen no reason to stimulate the *money creation* of the domestic banking system any further. // This component of *money creation* lost some of its importance. // the size of the *money creation* of the banking system // funds provided by the central bank for the banks' *money creation* // to effect unlimited *money creation* which is inconsistent with stabilization policy // to finance the budget deficit without excess *money creation*

tsūkatan'i 通貨単位 currency unit; monetary unit ¶ The new *currency unit,* the "new franc," equal to 100 old francs, became the only legal tender in Metropolitan France and the Departments of Algeria and Sahara. // the basic *monetary unit*

tsūkatōgō 通貨統合 currency unification

tsūkatōkyoku 通貨当局 monetary authorities

tsukene 付値 bid price; offered price

tsukigake 月掛け monthly installment (payment)

tsukigakechokin 月掛貯金 monthly savings

tsukiheikin 月平均 monthly average; average daily figures of the month ¶ The *daily* output *averaged* 20 percent over the previous month. // the *monthly average* output in June // the *average daily balance* of bank note issues in December

tsukiikkaidoyōkyūjitsu 月1回土曜休日 one Saturday off in a month

tsukikoshi 月越し standing over the month-end

tsukikoshikanjō 月越し勘定 last month's bill

tsukikoshimono 月越物 over-month-end loan; loan standing over the month-end

tsūkinsei 通勤制 live-out system

tsukiwarichōshū 月割徴収 collection by monthly installment

tsukiwarigaku 月割額 amount allocated per month; monthly installment

tsukiwarikeisan 月割計算 accounting by month

tsukkominedan 突込値段 all-round price; gross price; blanket price

tsukkomiuri 突込売り aggressive selling

tsumikae 積換え reshipment; transshipment

tsumimodoshi 積戻し reshipment; re-exportation

tsumimodoshihin 積戻品 reshipments; returned goods

tsuminihoken 積荷保険 cargo insurance

tsuminimokuroku 積荷目録 manifest

tsuminokoshi 積残し short shipment; shutout; crowding out ¶ Many were *crowded out* of the train. // →クラウディング・アウト

tsumitateen 積立円 reserved yen

tsumitatekin 積立金 reserve; provision reserve fund; appropriation of surplus for reserves

別途積立金 special reserve; general reserve; unconditional reserve

減債基金積立金 sinking fund reserve

配当平均準備積立金 reserve for equalization of dividend

配当準備積立金 reserve for dividend

秘密積立金 secret reserve; hidden reserve

法定積立金 legal reserve

事業拡張積立金 reserve for business expansion

貸倒準備積立金 reserve for bad debts; reserve for dead loans

欠損補塡積立金 reserve for losses

任意積立金 voluntary reserve

余剰予備積立金 surplus contingency reserve

増改築積立金 additions and betterments reserve

tsumitatekinkanjō 積立金勘定 reserve account

tsumitatekinkuriire 積立金繰入れ additions to reserve

tsumitatekinmodoshiire 積立金戻入れ surplus reserves transferred to income

tsumitateteiki 積立定期 installment time deposit

tsumitorihiritsu 積取比率 loading rate

tsunagi 繋ぎ bridging; hedge ¶ for *bridging* over brief cash deficits

買繋ぎ hedge-buying

売繋ぎ hedge-selling

tsunagibaibai 繋ぎ売買 [市] hedging

tsunagihazushi 繋ぎ外し hedge-lifting

tsunagimono 繋ぎ物 [市] hedge

tsunagishikin 繋ぎ資金 stop-gap funds; emegency fund

tsunagiyūshi 繋ぎ融資 bridging finance; relief loan; emergency loan ¶ to provide *bridge finance* to the IMF to help it meet its commitments until year-end // continuous emergency *bridging loans* to the most troubled debtor nations from other governments // to advance new *bridging* finance to debtor nations

tsunagu 繋ぐ to hedge; buy (or sell) forward against a spot sale (or purchase)

tsuriagekabu 吊上げ株 ballooned stock

tsūsenryō 通船料 launch hire

tsūshinhanbai 通信販売 mail order trading; sale by post

tsūshinhi 通信費 communication expenses

tsūshinmō 通信網 telecommunication network

tsūshō 通商 commerce; trade

tsūshōdaihyōbu 通商代表部 trade representation

tsūshōjōyaku 通商条約 treaty of commerce; commercial treaty

tsūshōkōheitaigū 通商衡平待遇 equitable treatment of commerce

tsūshōkōkaijōyaku 通商航海条約 Treaty of Commerce and Navigation

tsūshōro 通商路 trade route

tsūungaisha 通運会社 transport company; express company; forwarder; forwarding agent

tsuyofukumi 強含み ［市］ strengthening; stiffening; hardening; rising firmly; firmer tone; higher tone ¶ The market started a shade *firmer*.

tsuyoki 強気 strong feeling; strong sentiment; ［市］ bullish tone ¶ The market was construed to be *bullish*. // More *bullish* influences were the rise in exports and boost in living costs. // The market *bulled* ahead to new highs.

tsuyokigai 強気買い ［市］ bull buying

tsuyokishikyō 強気市況 ［市］ bull market; strong market

tsuyokisuji 強気筋 ［市］ long account; long interest; longs; bulls clique; bull ¶ It was a *bull* market in steels and other stocks related to defense needs.

tsuyokiuri 強気売り ［市］ long pull

tsuyokizairyō 強気材料 ［市］ bullish factor

tsuyomochiai 強保合い ［市］ firmer; gaining; consolidating upward; firm with an upward tendency; steady and tending upward

U

uchibarai 内払い payment on account (=in part); part (=partial) payment

uchiirekin 内入金 money paid on account (=in part); partial payment; bargain deposit; bargain money

uchikehai 内気配 undertone; underlying sentiment

uchikinbarai 内金払い →内払い

uchikinryōshūsho 内金領収書 part receipt

uchimuki 内向き inward-looking ¶ *inward-looking* bilateral and regional approaches to trade policy

uchiwake 内訳 items; breakdown; itemization; disaggregated data ¶ a *breakdown* of production by industry group // a full country *breakdown* of the reporting banks' liabilities and assets

uchiwakekanjōsho 内訳勘定書 itemized bill

uchiwakesho 内訳書 statement of items ¶ An invoice is an *itemized statement* of money owed.

uchiwatashi 内渡し part payment; part delivery

uchūkaihatsusangyō 宇宙開発産業 space exploitation (industry)

ueito ウエイト weight ¶ to revise the percentage *weights* assigned to each currency in the basket

ugoki 動き tendency; trend; tide; movement; development; accomplishment; performance; behavior; exercise; pursuit; move; fluctuation ¶ Certain seasonal *tendencies* have come to the fore. // There is a pronounced *tendency* towards a further price rise. // The upward *movement* of prices showed as yet little *tendency* to abate. // to apply or brake on expansionary *tendencies* // Currency fluctuations distort the *trend* in commodity prices. // There is a clear and rising *trend* toward hurried buying. // No homogeneous *trend* can be detected within each group of industries. // The *trend* in stock prices reversed. // The year witnessed a major reversal of these *trends*. // The *tide* of foreign trade during the year was running against the United States. // The market turned in as indecisive *performance*. // The economic *performance* for the year is as good as expected previously. // to review the *performance* of the real economy // For the behavior of exchange rates, and the associated *behavior* of current-account deficits and surpluses, variety of factors may be held responsible. // to smooth or neutralize erratic and exaggerated *movements* in the dollar/DM rates // disruptive short-term *movements* in the exchange value of the currency // The market is waiting for the next *move*. // speculative *moves* against the yen // Price *movements* were small. // Oil prices joined the general downward *movement*. // The *movement* of stock prices tended upward. // There are some signs of *movement* in fixed investment. // leading and lagging of the actual physical *movement* of goods // *movement*, or *moves*, to economize on consumption // →動向

uikuserunoruishinkatei ウイクセルの累進過程 Wicksell's cumulative process

ukaibōeki 迂回貿易 roundabout trade

ukaikawase 迂回為替 circuitous arbitration of exchange

ukaiseisanhōshiki 迂回生産方式 roundabout method of production

ukechō 受超 net receipts (over pay-

ments) surplus (balance)

ukeharaitankikashitsuke 受払短期貸付 ［市］ short-term loan of settlement funds

ukeharairitsu 受払率 receipt-payment ratio; ratio of receipts to payments

ukeirekanjōkaitenritsu 受入勘定回転率 receivable turnover

ukemodoshiken 受戻権 right of redemption

ukemodoshikensōshitsu 受戻権喪失 foreclosure

ukeoi 請負 contract

ukeoichingin 請負賃金 piece wage

ukeoigyō 請負業 contracting business

ukeoijikan 請負時間 time work

ukeoikōsaku 請負耕作 contract farming

ukeoinin 請負人 contractor

ukeoinyūsatsu 請負入札 contract tender

ukeoiseido 請負制度 contract work system

ukeoishigoto 請負仕事 contract work; job-work; piece-work

uketori 受取 receipt ¶ the large net *receipts* in the Foreign Exchange account

uketoricho 受取帳 receipt book; chit book

uketorihaitōkin 受取配当金 dividend received

uketorihunanishōken 受取船荷証券 received B/L; received for shipment B/L

uketorikanjō 受取勘定 account to receive; account receivable; receiving

uketorinin 受取人 recipient; payee; remittee; beneficiary; consignee

uketorisaikenhiritsu 受取債権比率

receivable ratio

uketorisaikenkaitenritsu 受取債権回転率 receivable turnover

uketorisōba 受取相場 receiving quotation (=rate)

uketoritegata 受取手形 bill (=note) receivable

uketoriwaribikiryō 受取割引料 discount earned

ukewatashi 受渡し delivery; transfer ¶ trading in bonds made for deferred *delivery* up to 7 days
即日受渡 cash delivery
翌日受渡 regular delivery

ukewatashibi 受渡日 date of delivery; [市] settlement day; [外] value date

ukewatashifurikō 受渡不履行 non- delivery

ukewatashifurikō 受渡不履行 non-delivery

ukewatashikurinobe 受渡繰延べ [市] carry-over

ukewatashinedan 受渡値段 delivery price

ukigashi 浮貸し off-record lending; kiting

ukigoshino 浮腰の [市] unsteady

umetate 埋立て land reclamation

umetatechi 埋立地 reclaimed land

unchin 運賃 freight; rate; carriage; portage; cartage; (transport) fare ¶ Standard *fares* on short and medium-haul in Europe average 75% higher for equivalent distances in the United States. // Cheap air *fares* are here to stay.
不積運賃 dead freight
販売運賃 freight-out; freight outward
引取運賃 freight-in; freight inward
帰り荷運賃 homeward freight
航路相当額運賃 pro rata freight

戻し荷運賃 return freight
旅客運賃 passenger fare
低率運賃 cheap freight
特別運賃 extra freight
通し運賃 through freight
往き荷運賃 outward freight

unchin'atobarai 運賃後払い freight to collect

unchindōmei 運賃同盟 freight conference; tariff agreement; shipping conference

unchinhokenryōkomi 運賃保険料込み cost, insurance and freight; c.i.f. price

unchinhyō 運賃表 tariff; freight list

unchinkominedan 運賃込値段 c.&f. price

unchinkyōsō 運賃競争 tariff war

unchinkyōtei 運賃協定 tariff agreement; freight agreement

unchinmaebarai 運賃前払い freight paid in advance; freight prepaid

unchinmuryō 運賃無料 freight free

unchinnobemodoshisei 運賃延戻制 deferred rebate system

unchinpūru 運賃プール freight pool

unchinritsu 運賃率 freight (=carriage) rate

unchinsakibarai 運賃先払い freight forward; freight payable at destination; freight to collect

unchinseikyūsho 運賃請求書 freight note

unchintōhōmochi 運賃当方持ち carriage paid; carriage prepaid

unchinwarimashi 運賃割増 hat money

unchinwarimodoshi 運賃割戻し freight (=carriage) rebate

undō 運動 campaign; movement

un'eihōshin 運営方針 policy of operation; operation policy; principle of operation; operation principle; principle underlying operations; manner of working; modus operandi; modality of operation ¶ the objectives and *modus operandi* of the compensatory financing facility // to develop a *modus operandi* for financial decision making // to define the *modalities of operation* of an organization

un'eikanri 運営管理 administration (of operations)

unsō 運送 transportation; transport

unsōchū 運送中 on passage; in transit

unsōgyō 運送業 carrying trade

unsōgyōsha 運送業者 carrier; transportation company

unsōhi 運送費 freight; carriage; shipping charge; transportation expense

unsōhoken 運送保険 transit insurance; transport insurance

unsōjō 運送状 way-bill; consignment note

unsōryō 運送料 forwarding charge; carriage; cartage

unsōten 運送店 forwarding agent; carrier; forwarder

untenshikin 運転資金 operating funds; working capital

untenzaiko 運転在庫 running stock

un'yō 運用 operation; mobilization; implementation ¶ fund *operations* // cofinancing to *mobilize* additional funds // to simplify, streamline, and update the *operations* of the fund // The *implementation* of this system will henceforth be much more flexible.

un'yōrimawari 運用利回り yield on investment

un'yōshisan 運用資産 working assets; operating assets

uragaki 裏書 endorsement (＝indorsement)

不規則裏書 irregular endorsement
限定裏書 restrictive endorsement
銀行裏書 bank endorsement
偽造裏書 forged endorsement
一部裏書 partial endorsement
条件付裏書 conditional endorsement
譲渡裏書 endorsement for transfer
完全裏書 full endorsement; complete endorsement
記名式裏書 special endorsement
無記名式裏書 general endorsement
無償還裏書 endorsement without recourse
指図式裏書 endorsement to order
制限裏書 qualified endorsement
正当裏書 authorized endorsement
質入裏書 endorsement for pledge
白地式裏書 blank endorsement
承認裏書 endorsement confirmed
連名裏書 joint endorsement
取立委任裏書 endorsement for collection
融通手形裏書 accommodation endorsement
有償裏書 endorsement for value
絶対裏書 absolute endorsement

uragakihoshō 裏書保証 guarantee(d) by endorsement

uragakikinshitegata 裏書禁止手形 non-negotiable bill

uragakikinshiuragaki 裏書禁止裏書 non-negotiable endorsement

uragakinin 裏書人 endorser (＝indorser)

被裏書人 endorsee
融通裏書人 accommodation en-

dorser

uragakirenzokunokenketsu 裏書
連続の欠缺 defect in successive en-
dorsements; discontinuity of endorsement

urahoshō 裏保証 guarantee in
favor of the primary guarantor (for
the account of the debtor); back-up
¶ a commercial paper *back-up*
credit agreement

urame 裏目 ［市］ outwitted market

uran'yushutsukokukikō ウラン輸
出国機構 Association of Uranium
Exporting Countries

urasaku 裏作 after crop

urenokori 売れ残り unsold stock;
frozen stock; dead stock; goods left
unsold; remainders; dead stock; (involuntary; unintended) inventory
accumulation; ［市］ undigested securities ¶ to reduce *inventory accumulation*

urenokorizaiko 売れ残り在庫
over- hang ¶ The housing market
is still dominated by a large *overhang* of unsold units. // → 売れ残り

uri 売り sale; selling ¶ exchange
rate smoothing dollar *sales* by the
Bundesbank on the spot exchange
market // forward *sales* of Swiss
francs to foreigners

uriagari 売り上がり ［市］ selling on
a rising scale

uriagechō 売上帳 sales book

uriagedaka 売上高 sales; (sales)
proceeds; takings; turnover; sales
amount (=value) ¶ Nondurable
goods *sales* were well maintained. //
Sales at durable *goods* outlets
remained at advanced levels. //
Retail *sales* were sluggish. // dismal
sales performance // In terms of
value retail *sales* rose by 15% in the

year to June. // The volume of *sales*
was 3.5% above the average for
1978. // Unit *sales* of new automobiles remained at a high level. //
Their *sales* volume just kept ahead
of inflation. // *Turnover* in April
showed a year-to-year increase. //
Retail trade *turnover* was above
year-earlier levels. // In terms of
value, the year-to-year increase in
turnover came to 4.5%.

純売上高 net sales
総売上高 gross sales
当期売上高 sales for the (current)
term
予想売上高 estimate of sales; estimated sales

uriagedakachōsa 売上高調査
sales research

uriagedakaeigyōhihiritsu 売上高
営業費比率 ratio of operating
expenses to sales

uriagedakajunriekiritsu 売上高純
利益率 ratio of net profit to sales

uriagedakariekiritsu 売上高利益率
profit ratio of sales

uriagedakarishifutanritsu 売上高
利子負担率 ratio of interest expenses to sales

uriagedakasōriekiritsu 売上高総利
益率 gross income on sales

uriagefushin 売上不振 stagnant
(=sluggish; inactive) sales

uriagegenkaritsu 売上原価率
sales-cost ratio

uriagehingenka 売上(品)原価 cost
of goods sold

uriagejun'eki 売上純益 net profit
on sales

uriagejunriekiritsu 売上純利益率
net profit rate to sales

uriagekanjō 売上勘定 sales account

uriagekin 売上金 (sales) proceeds; proceeds from sales

uriagekinkaishū 売上金回収 collection of (sales) proceeds

uriagemotochō 売上元帳 customer's (sold) ledger

uriageriekiritsu 売上利益率 sales profit ratio

uriageryō 売上量 volume of sales; sales volume [参考] →売上高

uriagesaiken 売上債権 [会] trade receivables; customers' receivables

uriagesaikenhiritsu 売上債権比率 ratio of trade receivables; receivables to sales ratio; receivables turnover

uriagesaikenkaitennissū 売上債権回転日数 receivables turnover period

uriagesaikenkaitenritsu 売上債権回転率 receivables turnover

uriagesōeki 売上総益 gross profit on sales

uriagesōriekiritsu 売上総利益率 ratio of gross profit to sales

uriagetesūryō 売上手数量 selling commission

uriagewarimodoshi 売上割戻し sales rebate

uriagezei 売上税 sales tax

uriba 売場 salesroom

urichūmon 売注文 [市] sell order; offer; selling order

uridashi 売出し sales drive; bargain sale; special sale; clearance sale; [証市] secondary offering (of bonds)

uridashikabu 売出株 publicly offered share

uridashikakaku 売出価格 offering price; sale price; [証市] issue price

uridashitegata 売出手形 bill drawn for sale

uridashitegataseido 売出手形制度 [日] system for sale of bills drawn by the Bank of Japan

urigyoku 売り玉 [市] short account; bear account

urihanatsu 売放つ [市] unload

uriichijun 売一巡 [市] sold-out condition ¶ the market in *sold-out condition*

uriisogi 売急ぎ rushed sale; active inclination to sell

urikake 売掛け credit sales

urikakedaikin 売掛代金 sales credit; credit account; [会] account receivable

urikakekinkin'yū 売掛金金融 accounts-receivable financing

urikakesaiken 売掛債権 account receivable; sales credit; book credit

urikata 売方 seller; [市] bear; short; bear interests

urikatakata 売方過多 bears over

urikatanosakudō 売方の策動 bear raid

urikatazeme 売方攻め squeezing bears

urikawase 売為替 selling exchange; exchange sold; bill sold

urikawasesōba 売為替相場 giving quotation

urikomi 売込み canvassing for sales; [市] heavy selling

urikominohandō 売込みの反動 reaction of heavy selling

urikoshi 売越し selling on balance

urikuzushi 売崩し [市] gunning; banging the market; depressing the market; bear raid; selling off

urimochi 売持ち [外] oversold position; short position; [市] bear position

urimodoshi 売戻し resale; reselling; [市] long-liquidation

urimodoshijōkentsukikaioperē-shon 売戻条件付買いオペレーション open-market transactions involving repurchase agreement; buying operation under repurchase agreement

urimodoshijōkentsukikaiire 売戻条件付買入 purchase (of government and other securities) with repurchase agreements (=under repurchase agreement); [米] repurchase agreement; RP ¶ The Manager of the System Account engages in short-term *repurchase agreements* (= *RP's*)with dealers. // The Account Manager offers *RP's* to dealers.

urimodoshiyakujōbi 売戻約定日 contractual value date

urimodoshiyakujōkigen 売戻約定期限 contractual reselling (= resale) date

urimōshikomi 売申込み [外] selling order

urimukai 売向い [市] bear drive ¶ to make a *bear drive*

urine 売値 selling price; [市] asked price

urininki 売人気 [市] bearish sentiment; selling support

urinoki 売退き [市] realization; liquidation

urinose 売乗せ [市] putting on more

urinushi 売主 seller; vendor

urioperēshon 売オペレーション market selling operation

urioshimi 売惜しみ restrained sales; reluctant selling; holding back of selling

urisōba 売相場 [外] selling rate ¶ The Bank set the dollar's *selling rate* at ¥310.00 for cash transactions.

urisugi 売過ぎ [市] overselling

urisuginohandō 売過ぎの反動 reaction of overselling

urisuginosōba 売過ぎの相場 short market; oversold market

uritataki 売叩き bear raid; gunning for a stock; drive; hammering; underselling ¶ to *bear* the market

uritate 売建 [市] short commitment; short interest

urite 売手 seller; vendor

uriteginkō 売手銀行 selling bank

uritekata 売手過多 sellers over

uriteopushon 売手オプション seller's option

uritesentaku 売手選択 seller's option

uriteshijō 売手市場 seller's market

uritonae 売唱え [市] asked price

uritsunagi 売繋ぎ [市] hedge-selling

uriwatashigaikokukawase 売渡外国為替 foreign exchange sold

uriyasui 売り易い marketable ¶ Fabrics are precut to more *marketable* sizes.

uriyobine 売り呼び値 asked price

urizairyō 売材料 [市] bearish factor

usagigoya 兎小屋 rabbit hutch 兎小屋の中の働き中毒 'workaholics living in rabbit hutches'

ushiromukishikin 後ろ向き資金 fund for non-expansionary purposes

ushiromukizaiko 後ろ向き在庫 involuntary (=unintended) inventory

usuakinai 薄商い [市] meager market; thin trading; light trading; light turnover; narrow market; poor dealings; inactive market ¶ The market moved lower in *thin trading*. // *Trading* remained *thin* Friday morning amid the wait-and-see attitude. // Spot *dealing* remained *thin* amid a lull in the Christmas holidays. // *Turnover* was *light*. // The market was lower in *light trading*. // Prices of leading shares dropped in *light trading* on the London stock exchange Monday.

usuyamishijō 薄やみ市場 grey (= gray) market

uwabanare 上放れ [市] jump; sudden rise; conspicuous rise; upside penetration; break away; break out

uwamawaru 上回る exceed; surpass; top; overtop; override; out-match; outbalance ¶ Total output in May *surpassed* the 1975 peak. // Exports *exceeded* imports by $4 million. // to *top* the past high

uwamuki 上向き upturn; upward turn; upswing; rebound; revival; upward trend; [市] improvement; hardening ¶ to expect an *upturn* in business activity // Prices *rebounded*.

uwane 上値 [市] higher quotation

uwaya 上屋 shed
保税上屋 bonded shed
税関上屋 customs shed

W

waidābando ワイダー・バンド [外] wider band ¶ a *wider band* of fluctuations around fixed international currency rates

wakamonoshijō 若者市場 youth market

wakeuri 分け売り split sale; split

waku 枠 framework ¶ greater reliance on market forces within the general *framework* of economic planning

wakugaiyūshi 枠外融資 special loan (outside prescribed limitations beyond the ceiling)

wanganshokoku 湾岸諸国 Gulf countries

wanryokusōba 腕力相場 forced quotation; forced market

wariai 割合 rate; proportion; ratio; percentage; share ¶ The *proportion* of firms planning to expand output has risen further. // a decline in the *proportion* of bank deposits subject to Federal Reserve reserve require-ments // Comecon's debt and debt service have been kept in manageable *proportions*. // Official development assistance slipped back as a *share* of GNP to 0.3%. // to receive their fair *share* of procurement under World Bank-financed projects // a long downtrend in the military *share* of the budget // The *share* of employment earnings in total income fell below 10%. // Company profits increased their *share* of total domestic income.

wariate 割当 allotment; allocation; quota; rationing; appropriation; assignment ¶ the net cumulative *allocation* of SDRs to a participant (allocations minus cancellations by the Fund) // The Ministry is receiving a DM5.6 billion budgetary *allocation* next year. // *allotment* of new shares to relatives // *Quotas* were imposed on imports of clothing and textiles. // a mandatory *rationing* of

gasoline

按分割当　pro rata allotment

縁故者割当　allotment to relatives

事前割当　pre-allocation

株主割当　allotment to stockholders

供出割当　delivery quota

wariatechōseihōshiki　割当調整方
式　allocation adjustment formula

wariatekin　割当金　allotment; appropriation

wariatekyōshutsu　割当供出　quota
delivery

wariatemōshikomisha　割当申込者
allottee

wariatesei　割当制　quota system;
allocation system; rationing

自動割当制　automatic funds allocation system

wariateshigoto　割当仕事　taskwork

waribiki　割引　discount; reduction
¶ The services of female employees
can be purchased at a substantial
discount below those of comparable
male employees.

団体割引　group-rate discount; par-
ty-trip reduction

同業割引　trade discount

複利割引　compound discount

現金割引　cash discount

銀行割引　bank discount

時間割引　time discount

卸売割引　trade discount

数量割引　quantity discount

手形割引　bill discount

特別割引　extra discount; special
discount

waribikibuai　割引歩合　discount rate
¶ The *discount rate* of commercial
bills was reduced by a full percentage point to 10 percent. // Italy is to
cut its base *discount rate* from 9%
to 8%. // The official central bank
discount rate was increased to

7.5%. // the *discount rate* applied
the central bank in the fixing of it
buying and selling of foreign exchange bills

基準割引歩合　basic discount rate;
base discount rate

公定割引歩合　official discount rate

市中割引歩合　(open) market dis-
count rate

waribikiginkō　割引銀行　discount-
(ing) bank

waribikigyōsha　割引業者　discount
house

waribikihakkō　割引発行　issue of
bond at discount

waribikikokusai　割引国債　discount government bond

waribikinedan　割引値段　reduced
price; discount(ed) price

waribikioyobikashitsukebuai　割引
および貸付歩合　interest rate of discounts and loans; lending and discount rates

日本銀行再割適格商業手形等信用度の
高い手形の割引および貸付歩合　in-
terest rate of discounts and loans
on prime bills in the credit standing such as bills eligible for the
Bank of Japan rediscount

輸出前貸手形のうち日本銀行再割引適
格手形以外の手形の割引および貸付
歩合　interest rate of discounts
and loans on export advance bills
other than bills eligible for the
Bank of Japan rediscount

waribikiritsu　割引率　discount rate
¶ → 割引歩合

waribikiryōkin　割引料金　cut-rate
fare; reduced rate; discount rate
Fully 80% of Pan American's tra
atlantic passengers take advant
of *cut-rate fares.* // *Cut-rate fares*
of less consideration to bu

travellers. // There is a total of nine rates, ranging from the standard first-class and economy tariffs to age-related *reduced rates*.

waribikishijō 割引市場 discount market

waribikishōsha 割引商社 ［英］ discount house

waribikitegata 割引手形 bill discounted; bills receivable discounted

waribikitegatakanjō 割引手形勘定 bills discounted account

waribikitegatakijitsuchō 割引手形期日帳 bills discounted daily list; bills discounted diary

waribikitegatakinyūchō 割引手形記入帳 discount cash book; discount register

waribikitegatamikaeri 割引手形見返り bills receivable discounted on accounts of customers

waribikitegatamotochō 割引手形元帳 discount ledger

warimashi 割増し extra; premium; bonus

warimashichingin 割増賃金 extra wage; extra pay; premium wage

warimashihaitōkin 割増配当金 extra dividend; bonus

warimashihokenryō 割増保険料 extra premium

warimashikin 割増金 premium

warimashikintsukichochiku 割増金付貯蓄 premium-bearing savings

warimashikintsukisaiken 割増金付債券 premium-bearing debenture

warimashikyūseido 割増給制度 pre- mium plan

warimashiritsu 割増率 additional rate

warimashiryōkin 割増料金 extra charge

warimashisei 割増制 premium system

warimashishōkan 割増償還 redemption with premium

warimashiteikiyokin 割増定期預金 time deposit with premium

warimashiunchin 割増運賃 extra freight

warimodoshi 割戻し rebate; drawback; bonus
延期払割戻し deferred rebate
仕入割戻し purchase rebate
売上割戻し sales rebate
運賃割戻し carriage rebate

warimodoshiryōkin 割戻料金 rebate

warimodoshitesūryō 割戻手数料 return commission

wariyasuno 割安の comparatively cheap; moderate; reasonable in price

watashi 渡し delivery
着荷渡し delivery on arrival
埠頭渡し ex-wharf
艀渡し ex-lighter
本船渡し ex-ship
直渡し prompt delivery
甲板渡し delivery on board; free on board; f.o.b.
貨車渡し delivery on rail
近日渡し near delivery
先渡し forward delivery
桟橋渡し ex-pier
倉庫渡し ex-warehouse
定期渡し delivery on term
鉄道渡し free on rail; free on truck; free on wagon
税関構内渡し ex-customs compounds
税関上屋渡し ex-customs shed

watashikabu 渡し株 delivery share

Y

yachin 家賃 house-rent; rent; rental
前受家賃 prepaid rents on buildings
yachinfubaraidōmei 家賃不払同盟
rent strike
yachinhikiage 家賃引上げ rent increase
yachinnotodokoori 家賃の滞り back rent; rent in arrears
yachinseigen 家賃制限 rent ceiling
yagyō 夜業 night-work; night-shift
半夜業 half-night operation
深夜業 midnight-work
yagyōteppai 夜業撤廃 abolition of night-shifts
yajirushizushiki 矢印図式 arrow system
yakin 夜勤 night duty; night-work; night shift
yakinjikan 夜勤時間 night-shift hours
yakinsha 夜勤者 night-shift; night worker
yakinteate 夜勤手当 night-work allowance
yakujō 約定 promise; engagement; contract; bargain; agreement; commitment; arrangement; convention; stipulation
仮約定 provisional contract
yakujōhin'i 約定品位 contract grade
yakujōkamotsu 約定貨物 contract goods
yakujōkigen 約定期限 stipulated time
yakujōkinri 約定金利 contractual interest rate; contracted rate (of interest); agreed interest rate ¶ The

average *contracted interest rates* for lending by all Japanese banks fell by 0.07 percentage points in July to a record low of 6.173% per annum.
yakujōnedan 約定値段 contract price
yakujōriritsu 約定利率 contractual interest rate; contracted interest rate; agreed interest rate
yakujōryō 約定料 commitment fee
yakujōsho 約定書 written contract; written agreement; letter of agreement
yakujōzumi 約定済み engaged; promised (for)
yakushokuteate 役職手当 assignment allowance
yakusoku 約束 promise; undertaking ¶ to perform this obligation by observing certain specified *undertakings* with respect to domestic and external financial policies
yakusokufurikō 約束不履行 breach of a promise
yakusokutegata 約束手形 promissory note; advance note; note of hand
外国約束手形 overseas promissory note
一覧払約束手形 demand note; sight note
持参人払約束手形 note to bearer
記名式約束手形 special note
国内約束手形 inland promissory note
連帯約束手形 joint promissory note
指図式約束手形 note to order

支払約束手形　note payable
定期約束手形　time note
受取約束手形　note receivable

yakutō 躍騰 soaring; buoyancy; steady advance; to jump by leaps and bounds

yama 山 peak ¶ The rate of growth of the world's population passed its explosive *peak*. // Output in May surpassed the 1978 *peak*. // to slip below its *peak* 1978 level // to recede somewhat from the *peaks* reached at the turn of the year // to regain its previous *peak*

yamanekosuto 山猫スト "wildcat" strike

yamaoyobitani 山および谷(景気の) peak and trough (of the business cycle)

yamerukeizai 病める経済 sick (= ailing) economy ¶ Tax cuts may serve as a quick fix for a *sick economy*.

yamerusangyō 病める産業 ailing industry ¶ to give the then *ailing* U.S. *industry* time to re-tool and re-structure in the face of Japanese competition

yamigai 闇買い black market purchase

yamikehai 闇気配 [市] undertone

yamikin'yū 闇金融 black market financing

yamikyūyo 闇給与 distribution of clandestine salaries; underhand allowance

yamine 闇値 black market quotation; black market price; black mart price

yamirūto 闇ルート clandestine channel; black-marketeering channel; illegal channel; black market outlet

yamishijō 闇市場 black market; black mart; underground market; black bourse

yamitaiji 闇退治 uprooting of black marketeers

yamitorihiki 闇取引 black marketeering; underground (=undercover; illegal; shady; off-the-books) dealing (=transaction)

yamiuri 闇売り black market sale; black marketeering

yamiya 闇屋 blackmarketeer; bootlegger

yarikurikessan 遣繰決算 makeshift settlement; manipulated account

yasuagarinoseifu 安上がりの政府 cheap government; inexpensive government

yasufukumi 安含み bearish indications

yasukehai 安気配 [市] bearish tone; weak tone

yasune 安値 [市] low(price) ¶ The market closed a little above the day's *low*.

yasunehiroi 安値拾い [市] bargain hunting ¶ Institutional *bargain hunting* sent prices higher on the London stock exchange.

yasunejuchū 安値受注 order of less value

yasunemachi 安値待ち [市] anticipation of falling market

yasuuri 安売り bargain sale; sacrifice sale ¶ to *sell* at a *bargain*

yasuzairyō 安材料 [市] bearish factor; damping factor

yatoiire 雇い入れ hiring ¶ direct *hiring* at the gate of unsolicited applicants

yatoinin 雇人 employee

yatoininhoken 雇人保険 fidelity

insurance

yatoininhoshō 雇人保証 fidelity guarantee

yatoinushi 雇主 employer; management

yatōkeihōsōchi 夜盗警報装置 burglar alarm system

yobichōsa 予備調査 preliminary survey

yobidēta 予備データ preliminary data

yobihi 予備費 reserve fund; emergency fund; miscellaneous expenses; incidental expenses

yobihin 予備品 spare parts

yobikiki 予備機器 stand-by machine

yobikin 予備金 contingencies; reserve fund; emergency fund

yobimizu 呼び水 pump-priming; prime-the-pump ¶ all-out *pump-priming* effort to stimulate business activity

yobimizuseisaku 呼び水政策 pump-priming policy

yobinaatenin 予備名宛人 reference in case of need

yobine 呼び値 nominal price (= quotation); asked price; bidding

yobishiharainin 予備支払人 referee in case of need

yobishōken 予備証券 reserve bond certificate; preliminary bond certificate

yobitekijuyō 予備的需要 precautionary demand

yobiurinin 呼売人 hawker; huckster

yobō 予防 prevention; precaution ¶ A *preventive* measure was taken against a possible excessive credit expansion. // A *precautionary* policy of restricting credit expansion was adopted. // to adopt tactical policies as *preventive* measures for avoiding... // to organize *precautionary* measures to fend off another revaluation // Saving is undertaken as a *precaution* against uncertain asset returns.

yobōhoshu 予防保守 preventive maintenance

yochi 余地 scope; room; leeway ¶ efforts to reduce the *scope* for undesirable speculative transactions // It gave the National Bank welcome *scope* to resume foreign exchange interventions on a large scale. // Occasional large-scale interventions confirmed the limited *scope* available for influencing a general movement in the rate effectively. // The *room* for financial deficits has to be measured in terms of the rate of interest. // There is less *room* for autonomous maneuvering here than in the U.S. // Budget *room* became available for tax reduction. // Governments are likely to have less *room* for maneuver in their economic policy than in the past. // Every central bank has some *room* for discretion, and the range is considerable in the more independent central banks. // There is *room* for sales of comparable goods by others. // to prevent additional *scope* for price increases from emerging on the monetary side // to provide *scope* for inflation in the longer run // Severe external constraints greatly narrow the *scope* for policy maneuver. // Increased export competitiveness broadened the *scope* for more expansive policies. // The government gave the Central Bank greater *leeway* to adjust currency rates without government intervention.

yochokin 預貯金 deposits and savings

yōchūikashidashi 要注意貸出 doubtful loan; inferior loan

yōchūikashidashihiritsu 要注意貸出比率 ratio of doubtful loans to total loans; ratio of inferior

yōekiken 用益権 servitude

yōgyo 養魚 fish-farming; fish-breeding; fishculture

yōgyō 窯業 ceramic industry

yōgyochi 養魚池 fish-pond

yōgyōdosekiseihinkōgyō 窯業・土石製品工業 ceramics, stone and clay products industry

yōgyojō 養魚場 fish-hatchery; fish-farm

yōgyoka 養魚家 fish-farmer; fish-breeder

yōgyōseihin 窯業製品 ceramics

yōhō 養蜂 bee-keeping; apiculture

yōhōjō 養蜂場 bee-farm; bee-yard

yōin 要因 factor; ingredient; element ¶ deficits stemming from adverse transitory external, or internal, *factors* // Environmental considerations need to be *factored* into the planning process. // The short-covering of dollar positions was the main *factor* accounting for the dollar's recovery. // Exports will be the most dynamic *factor* supporting activity. // stimulating *factors* in the domestic business picture // The nation's trade surplus remains a key *factor* in its recovery plans. // the *factors* affecting the growth in domestic liquidity, and inhibiting production // Many *factors,* both structural and cyclical, seem to un-

derlie the resurgence of protectionist sentiments. // A multiplicity of *factors* — economic and social — are at work. // The major *factor* working to reduce deficit was a gain in exports. // the *factors* which have adversely affected the reserve position // the underlying *factor* in the country's difficulties // to take into consideration all income, plus *factors*, and deduct all costs and expenses, minus *factors* // A major positive *factor* in the increase in profit was the decrease in cost of sales. // a further contributory *factor* and disturbing *factors* in the working of the market // The combination of these special *factors* has played a decisive role in driving up prices. // The return of currency reflected cyclical as well as seasonal *factors*. // The rise was caused by seasonal and accidental *factors*. // the dominant *factor* underpinning strong import performance // to advance supported by various favorable *factors* // the decisive *factor* behind a change of course in policy // an *ingredient* in the preparation of the policy guidelines // All the *factors* that are pro-dollar are very firmly in place.

悪化要因 adverse factor; unfavorable factor; discouraging factor

補完的要因 complementary factor

好転要因 favorable factor; encouraging factor

マイナス要因 minus factor

プラス要因 plus factor

制限的要因 limitational factor

生産要因 factor of production; productive factor

心理的要因 psychological factor

主要因 prime factor; key factor

yōinbunseki 要因分析 factor analysis

yojō 余剰 surplus; excess; overhang ¶ The *surplus* on the market was absorbed through calling-in of loans. // to reduce the world's dollar *overhang* of excess dollar holding // The *overhang* of excessive wages is still there. // ［参考］→ 剰余

　減資余剰 surplus from capital reduction

　評価余剰 appraisal surplus

　株式余剰 surplus from forfeited stock

　海外余剰 external surplus

　買手余剰 buyer's surplus

　生産者余剰 producer's surplus

　再評価余剰 surplus at liquidation

　資本余剰 capital surplus

　消費者余剰 consumer's surplus

　償還余剰 surplus from stock redemption

yojōjin'in 余剰人員 unneeded workers ¶ Manufacturers are carrying about 3 million *unneeded workers* on their payrolls.

yojōkinshobunkeisansho 余剰金処分計算書 surplus appropriation statement

yojōnohakeguchi 余剰のはけ口 vent for surplus

yojōnōsanbutsushorihō 余剰農産物処理法 ［米］ Agricultural Trade Development and Assistance Act of 1954

yojōrōdōryoku 余剰労働力 redundant labor force; surplus labor

　企業内余剰労働力 surplus labor retained within enterprises

yojōseisan 余剰生産 surplus production

yojōshikin 余剰資金 idle funds; surplus funds; glut of funds ¶ a means of utilizing *idle funds* // *surplus (funds)* in the market // Foreign tourists have given the *glut of funds* in the international markets.

yojōshikinnokyūshū 余剰資金の吸収 absorption of surplus funds; mopping up of excess liquidity from the market

yojōshokuryō 余剰食糧 surplus food

yojōzaiko 余剰在庫 overhang of stocks; surplus inventories; surplus stock ¶ The *overhang of stocks* accumulated during the year will be a drag on output levels. // *Surplus stocks* contributed to a reduction in imports.

yōkei 養鶏 poultry-farming; poultry-raising

yoken 与件 data

yokimeisū 予期命数 expectation of life; life expectancy

yokin 預金 deposit; money on deposit; bank account ¶ to place *money on deposit* with a bank // to have a large *deposit* in a bank // Total *deposits,* including current *accounts* at *banks* and other credit institutions, rose by Fmk 50 billion. // There has been considerable withdrawal of *deposits* from commercial banks. // Because of the shift from demand *deposits* to time *deposits,* the growth of over-all bank *deposits* did not affect the money supply. // The Bank of Spain has provisionally reimposed mandatory special *deposits*, amounting to 100% of any rise in foreign accounts. // The banks are allowed to take *deposits.* // ［参考］ More of the Arab surplus is banked in the region rather than dispersed to Europe.

別段預金　special deposit
歩積預金　bill discount deposit
貯蓄(性)預金　savings deposit
同業者預金　inter-bank deposit
不活動預金　idle deposit
粉飾預金　window-dressing deposit
普通預金　ordinary deposit
外貨預金　foreign currency deposit; non-yen denominated deposit
現金預金　cash deposit
派生(的)預金　derivative deposit
非居住者(円)預金　non-resident (yen) deposit
法人預金　corporate deposit
本源的預金　primary deposit
表面預金　nominal deposit
一般預金　private deposit
実質預金　real deposit
活動預金　active deposit
系統外預金　deposit with outside organization
期日指定預金　maturity-designated deposit
基礎的預金　core deposit
個人預金　personal deposit
公金預金　public deposit
拘束性預金　limited withdrawal deposit; derivative deposit
くじ付定期預金　lottery-attached time deposit
無記名(定期)預金　uninscribed (time) deposit; anonymous (time) deposit
両建預金　compensatory deposit
流動性預金　liquid deposit; floating deposit
債務者預金　deposit of debtor
政府預金　government deposit
社内預金　deposit within the company
所得預金　income deposit
担保預金　deposit as collateral
定期性預金　time and savings deposits; deposits with prescribed terms; deposits with some contracted periods
定期預金　time deposit; fixed deposit
特別保護預金　special safe deposit
特別預金　special deposit
当座預金　current deposit
通知預金　deposit at notice
通貨性預金　monetary deposit
積立定期預金　installment time deposit
要求払預金　demand deposit; checking deposit; bank money
割増金付定期預金　time deposit with premium
預金自動継続定期預金　automatic renewable time deposit

yokindairiten 預金代理店　deposit agency
yokinfusokukogitte 預金不足小切手　short check
yokinginkō 預金銀行　deposit bank
yokinharaimodoshiteishi 預金払戻停止　suspension of repaying monetary deposits
yokinhokenkikō 預金保険機構　deposit insurance system; [日] Deposit Insurance Corporation
yokinjimu 預金事務　deposit business
yokinjisseki 預金実績　deposit achievement results
yokinjunbiritsu 預金準備率　(required) reserve ratio against deposits
yokinkakutokukyōsō 預金獲得競争　competition for securing deposits; competition in the collection of deposits; competition to attract deposits
yokinkanjō 預金勘定　deposit account ¶ to open and maintain a

deposit account at (=with; in) a bank

yokinkan'yū 預金勧誘 solicitation of deposits (for banks)

yokinkihinofūchō 預金忌避の風潮 tendency to avoid making deposits

yokinkinri 預金金利 deposit rate; interest (rate) on deposits

yokinkosuto 預金コスト cost of deposits; ratio of interest and expenses on deposits to deposits

yokinkyūshū 預金吸収 collection of deposits; deposit inducement; attraction of deposits; absorption of deposits

yokinmeberitaisaku 預金目減り対策 steps to prevent an inflation-caused decrease in the real value of deposits and savings; steps to make up for the reduced (=eroded) value of postal savings and deposits caused by inflation; steps to make up for the depreciation of postal savings and bank deposits caused by inflation; measures to provide relief from the inflationary bite on deposits

yokinnohimitsusei 預金の秘密性 privacy of deposit

yokinriritsu 預金利率 deposit rate ¶ The Bank of Japan formally decided to raise the officially-controlled bank *deposit rate* by between 0.75 and 1% from October 3. // The *rate* for one-year *deposits* will be increased by 1% to 7%.

yokinrishi 預金利子 deposit interest; interest on deposits

yokinrishikazei 預金利子課税 tax on deposit interest

yokinsaimokukinri 預金細目金利 itemized deposit interest rates; itemized rates on deposits

yokinsaimu 預金債務 deposit liability

yokinseido 預金制度 deposit system

yokinsha 預金者 depositor ¶ corporate *depositors* with a bank // private *depositors* in a savings bank

yokinshahogo 預金者保護 protection of depositors ¶ to *protect* bank *depositors* from future losses due to bank failures // the *protection of depositors* against the risk of bank failures

yokinshanokimitsusei 預金者の機密性 confidentiality of depositors ¶ to violate the policy of *confidentiality of* individual *depositors*

yokinshanoseikyūken 預金者の請求権 validity of claim for (insured) deposit

yokinshiharaijunbiseido 預金支払準備制度 reserve deposit requirement system

yokinsōshutsu 預金創出 deposit creation

yokintsūchō 預金通帳 bankbook; passbook; deposit book (=passbook)

yokintsūchōkōza 預金通帳口座 passbook account

yokintsūka 預金通貨 deposit money; demand deposit; quasi-money; deposit currency; bank money

yokin'ukeirekikan 預金受入機関 deposit-taking institution

yokinzandakabusoku 預金残高不足 short (deposit) balance

yokinzōkaritsukisei 預金増加率規制 ［英］ corset ¶ →コルセット

yokinzōkyō 預金増強 campaign for deposit augmentation

yokkyū 欲求 want; appetite; desire; need; demand; yen ¶ to meet the public and social *wants* // to whet the public *appetite* for speculative securities // the natural *desire* of the investment banker to realize a profit // to gratify certain more temporary *desires*, such as a car, clothes, or a vacation // to serve adequately the customer's diversifying *needs* // to stand ready to satisfy current *demands* // to satisfy their *yen* for the good life // [参考] →要求; 需要

yokobai 横這い leveling-out; leveling-off; flattening-out; flattening-off; marginal change; marking time; (remaining) unchanged; moving sideways; leveling; horizontal movement; sideways movement; sidewise movement; crab-like movement ¶ The index *leveled off* in the following week. // The *leveling-off* in production was widespread. // April and May saw a *leveling-out* of output. // Production showed definite signs of *leveling-out* on a high plateau. // Prices fluctuated narrowly around *horizontal* trends. // Prices remained virtually *unchanged* during the year. // the continued movement, *sidewise movement* of prices, still at the same level as a year before // → 保合い

yokonagare 横流れ flow into illegal trade; leakage into illicit trade

yokonagashi 横流し diversion to the black market; resale through illegal (=unlawful) channels; diversion to illicit trade; illegal disposal

yokozahyōjiku 横座標軸 axis of abscissa

yokugetsumono 翌月物 over-month loan

yokugetsuukewatashi 翌月受渡し [市] over-the-month delivery

yokujitsubaraikashitsuke 翌日払い貸付 overnight money

yokujitsumono 翌日物 overnight call loan; day-to-day accommodation; overnight delivery ¶ The U.S. dollar for *overnight delivery* closed at yen 193.50.

yokujitsuwatashi 翌日渡し [市] overnight delivery

yokusei 抑制 restraint; restriction; clamp; squeeze; rein; brake; suppression; containment; constraint; constriction; arrest; check; hold-down; curb; choking off; squeeze; pruning; subdual ¶ The trend was *arrested.* // *arrested* growth // to place a *check* on price rises // The advance was *checked* by a counter-measure. // to place a *curb* on price increase // to *curb* inflation // to amount to unlawful *suppression* of competition // A wage *hold-down* may hurt recovery. // to *suppress* demand // a partial *choking-off* of credit supply // to *arrest* inflation and population growth rates // to succeed in *containing* wage rises // Business and labor will use *restraint* in future price and wage rises. // A large-scale *restraint* program was successful. // to exercise strict *restraint* on lending or provision of facilities for other purposes // The government is committed to continued wage *restraint* in the public sector. // to *clamp* down on excessive activities // demand-*squeezing*, investment-*pruning* and export-promoting policies // A few big companies agreed to *rein* in salary increases. // to *check* price rises and, if possible, reverse them // to strive to *hold down* the growth of money and credit

yokuseikōka 抑制効果 inhibiting

effect; restrictive effect; contractive effect

yokuseisochi 抑制措置 restrictive measure; control; dampening measure; braking measure; restraint; curb; check ¶ to apply *braking measures* in suppressing rising production // to take more exhaustive expenditure-*dampening measures* // additional *measures* needed to *dampen* domestic expenditures // to put on the credit *brakes* to fight inflation

yokushigensoku 抑止原則 abstention principle

yokushirain 抑止ライン abstention line

yōkyū 要求 demand; requirement; need; claim ¶ to be paid on *demand* // to meet the *requirement* of the times // to be more responsive to its clients' *needs* // to make a *claim* for the damage // the satisfaction of basic human *needs* // to meet the *needs* of community // to make an unreasonable *claim* against a company for compensation // to accept the *claim* for pay raise // [参考] → 欲求; 需要

yōkyūbarai 要求払い payable on demand; payable at call

yōkyūbaraitegata 要求払手形 demand bill (=note; draft)

yōkyūbaraiyokinshōsho 要求払預金証書 certificate of demand deposit

yōkyūbeika 要求米価 rice price demand

yonasannokōhīten ヨナサンのコーヒー店 [英] Jonathan's Coffee House

yōnashisōba 用なし相場 [市] sluggish market

yonyū 預入 inpayment ¶ net *inpayments* to savings accounts, i.e. interest credited

yoritsuki 寄付き [市] opening session ¶ The market *opened* higher, turned mixed, then steadied. // The dollar *opened* higher on firm interest rates. // to buy or sell at the *opening session* // The market was slightly lower at the *opening,* then firmed.

yoritsukikehai 寄付気配 [市] opening tone

yoritsukinedan 寄付値段 [市] opening quotation (=price)

yosan 予算 budget; appropriation; estimate; estimated cost ¶ The Ministry's *budget* over the four-year financial plan covering 1980-83 is planned at DM26.5 billion. // The Federal *budget* for the fiscal year 1980 would be limited to $500.8 billion, with a $57.7 billion deficit. // The *budget* has been sent to the House of Representatives for consideration. // The *budget* provides for defence spending of $116.6 billion, which is $1.2 billion above Mr. Carter's original proposal. // The Diet approved the General Account *budget* for the fiscal year 1971/72. // In this *budget*, expenditure is estimated at ¥9,414 billion, an increase of 18.4 percent over the budget estimate. // The year's capital *budget*, originally set for $2.5 billion, is being cut drastically. // Someone has to hold the line on the *budget*.

赤字予算 deficit budget; adverse budget

膨張予算 inflated budget

超均衡予算 balanced budget with surplus

中立(型)予算 neutral budget

不均衡予算　unbalanced budget
複数予算　multiple budget
外貨予算　foreign exchange budget
軍事予算　military budget
行政予算　administrative budget
平時予算　peace(-time) budget
変動予算　variable budget
本予算　main budget
補正予算　supplementary budget
実行予算　working budget
純計予算　net budget
会計予算　fiscal budget
間接費変動予算　flexible overhead budget
経費予算　estimated appropriation
経常予算　current budget
企業予算　business budget
均衡予算　balanced budget
緊縮予算　austerity budget; restrictive budget; restrained budget
骨格予算　skeleton budget
国防予算　national defense budget
国民経済予算　nation's economic budget
臨時予算　extraordinary budget
作業別予算　performance budget
歳入予算　revenue budget; estimated revenues (=receipts); budget revenue
歳出予算　expenditure budget; estimated expenditures; budget expenditure
政府予算　government budget
戦時予算　war(-time) budget
資本予算　capital budget
支出予算　payment estimate
修正予算　revised budget
総合予算　unified budget
総予算　general budget
単年度予算　one-year budget
当初予算　original budget
追加予算　additional appropriations; additional budget; supplementary budget
財政予算　fiscal budget
暫定予算　provisional budget
ゼロ・ベース予算　zero-based budget
yōsan 養蚕　sericulture; silk-raising
yosan'an 予算案　budget bill; budget proposals; estimates ¶ The House of Representatives has passed a *budget bill* which *proposes* spending of \$529.9 billion, against anticipated revenues of \$509 billion. // the *budget proposals* to be tabled in Parliament // The full *budget proposals* will be presented to Parliament by the Minister of Finance. // ［参考］→予算原案
yosan'annonaiji 予算案の内示　informal showing of the budget to respective ministries and agencies
yosan'arainaoshiseido 予算洗い直し制度　zero-base budget(ing)
yosanbeika 予算米価　budgeted rice price
yōsanchi 養蚕地　silk-raising district
yosanchōka 予算超過　excess over the estimates; budget overrun ¶ to accommodate the *budget overrun* caused by high farm support expenditure
yosanfuseiritsu 予算不成立　rejection of a budget bill
yosangaikokkofutan 予算外国庫負担　national treasury charge out of the budget
yosangaishishutsu 予算外支出　expenditure unprovided for in the budget
yosangaishūnyū 予算外収入　receipts outside of the budget
yosangen'an 予算原案　estimate budget; estimates of revenues and expenditures; draft budget; pro-

posals ¶ The 1976 *draft budget* presented by the Federal government last autumn had a volume of DM168 billion (+4% over the 1975 *estimates*) and envisaged a deficit of DM39 billion. // The Finance Minister has presented *budget proposals* for 1980 which show a record deficit of D. Kr. 41.5 billion // a program to cut public spending *estimates* by Fl. 10 billion // ［参考］ →予算案

yosanhensei 予算編成 preparation of budget; compilation of budget; budget drafting ¶ to *prepare the budget* and submit it to the Diet // Quality matters more than quantity in the process of *budget compilation.* // Mr. Fraser's annual *budget preparations* this winter are a severe test of his economic policies.

yosanhenseihōshin 予算編成方針 budget drafting policy; principles for compiling budget; budget drafting principles

yosan'iinkai 予算委員会 budget committee; Standing Committee on Budget; ［米］ Appropriations Committee

yōsanjo 養蚕所 cocoonery

yosanjōyo 予算剰余 budget surplus

yōsanka 養蚕家 sericulturist; silkworm-raiser

yosankaikaku 予算改革 budgetary reform

yosankinkōkashikin 予算均衡化資金 budget equalization fund

yosanmitsumorisho 予算見積書 estimation of budget

yosannaijikai 予算内示会 preliminary budget committee

yosannofukkatsusesshō 予算の復活折衝 negotiations for additional appropriations; negotiations for the

restoration of reduced (=curtailed) funds

yosannoshikkō 予算の執行 execution of the budget

yosansakusei 予算作成 budgeting; budget drafting

yosansatei 予算査定 budget making

yosanseikyū 予算請求 budgetary request; budget demand ¶ Governmental departments present their *budgetary requests.* // the ceiling on fiscal 1781 *budget demands*

yosanseiyaku 予算制約 budget constraint

yosansengiken 予算先議権 priority in budgetary discussion

yosanshikkōritsu 予算執行率 ratio of budget execution

yosanshinchokuritsu 予算進捗率 ratio of payments to the budget

yōsanshitsu 養蚕室 silkworm nursery

yosansōsoku 予算総則 general provisions of the budget

yosantōsei 予算統制 budgetary control

yosanwariategaku 予算割当額 appropriations ¶ Extravagant *appropriations* by Congress prevented accumulation of revenues.

yōsen 用船 charter
　裸用船 bare charter; bare-boat charter
　日決め用船 per diem charter
　航海用船 voyage charter; trip charter
　再用船 sub-charter
　定額用船 lump sum charter
　定期用船 time charter

yōsenkeiyaku 用船契約 charter; charter party; charter hire
　予定用船契約 open charter

yōsenryō 用船料 charter money; charterage; hire

yōsensha 用船者 charterer

yōsenshijō 用船市場 chartering market

yoshingyōmu 与信業務 credit (extending) business

yoshinshinsa 与信審査 credit administration

yōshōkyakumikomikashidashihiritsu 要償却見込貸出比率 ratio of estimated depreciation (loss) of loans to total loans; ratio of estimated loss of loans to total loans

yosō 予想 expectation; anticipation; estimate; prediction; projection ¶ Economic growth in 1975 fell considerably short of *expectations*. // *Expectations* for the U.S. dollar's exchange rate will improve. // Today's figure was still outside market *expectations*. // Computer *predictions* said that... // The Bureau *predicts* that... // The government has *projected* a deficit for the full year of around 7.25 billion pounds. // →予測; 見通し

yōso 要素 element ¶ loans containing (=incorporating) a grant *element* of at least 25 per cent // an important stabilizing *element* in international banking

yōsō 様相 showing; appearance ¶ The U.S. steel industry is rebounding from last year's poor *showing*. // the present doubtful *appearances* of business conditions // to present a threatening *appearance*

yosōdaka 予想高 estimate; estimated amount

yosōhaitōritsu 予想配当率 prospective dividend rate

yōsohiyōhyōjinokokunaisōseisan

要素費用表示の国内総生産 gross domestic product at factor cost

yōsokōekijōken 要素交易条件 factoral terms of trade

yosoku 予測 expectation; expectancy; anticipation; forecast; estimate; projection; prospect; assessment; perspective; prognosis ¶ There was little *expectation* of a boisterous recovery. // The strength of business *expectations* is evident in the capital spending plans. // But inflationary *expectations* dominated the thinking of many businessmen. // to give businessmen the *expectancy* of expansionary impulses from abroad // to look forward with dull *expectancy* to the future // to look forward with the keenest *anticipation* to... // The exact timing of a change in the economic climate is difficult to *forecast*. // a series of pessimistic *forecasts* about the likely behavior of the economy // conflicting *forecasts* of U.K. economic trends // business *estimates* of output // In a 1976 *projection* for the U.S. economy, a number of *forecasters* are in general agreement on the following *projections*. // Investors mostly appear to be taking a sanguine view of future economic *prospects*. // This *forecast* is more pessimistic than the official government *forecast* of 3.7% growth next year. // These *forecasts* are clouded by numerous uncertainties. // Under the plan public investment is *projected* to grow at a lower rate than GNP. // → 見通し; 予想

yosokumoderu 予測モデル forecasting model

yosōrieki 予想利益 expected (=

anticipated; prospective; projected) profit; imaginary profit

yosōrimawari 予想利回り prospective yield

yosōshūekiritsu 予想収益率 prospective return (=income; earning) ¶ the *prospective return* on plant and equipment

yosōshūkakudaka 予想収穫高 crop estimate

yosōzaimushohyō 予想財務諸表 financial statement forecast

yotaiheishin 預貸併進 increases of both deposits and loans; *increase* in tandem of deposits and loans; parallel increases in loans and deposits

yotaikinritsu 預貸金率 bank loan-deposit ratio; ratio of (bank's) loans to deposits ¶ Eurodollar balances are counted as deposits in the computation of the *loan-deposit ratio*.

yotakushōsho 預託証書 depository receipt

yoteishinkoku 予定申告 provisional (tax) return

yowai 弱い [市] weak; soft; easy ¶ Sterling was *softer* against most currencies and stood marginally *weaker* against the dollar.

yowaitsūka 弱い通貨 weak currency

yowaki 弱気 [市] bear; short; bearish sentiment; bearish tone

yowakika 弱気化 clouded prospects ¶ *Prospects* for sales became *clouded*.

yowakikanjō 弱気勘定 [市] short account

yowakishikyō 弱気市況 [市] bear market; short market

yowakisuji 弱気筋 [市] bear interests; bears; shorts

yowakiuri 弱気売り selling a bear

yowamochiai 弱保合 unchanged with easy undertone

yowazairyō 弱材料 [市] bearish factor; dampening factor ¶ The *bearish factor* dragged wheat futures lower.

yoyakukeiyakusho 予約契約書 [外] contract slip

yoyakunokōshin 予約の更新 [外] renewal of exchange contract

yoyū 余裕 leeway ¶ still to have fund *leeway*

yōyūscido 遙有制度 absentee ownership; absenteeism

yuatsukikiseizōgyō 油圧機器製造業 hydraulic equipment manufacturing industry

yūbinchokin 郵便貯金 postal savings

yūbinchokinrishihikazeiseido 郵便貯金利子非課税制度 tax exemption system for interest on postal savings

yūbinfurikaechokin 郵便振替貯金 postal book-transfer savings

yūbinfurikaekikan 郵便振替機関 [英] national giro

yūbinkansho 郵便官署 government agency for postal administration; postal service office

yūbinkyoku 郵便局 post office

yūbinnenkin 郵便年金 postal annuity

yūbinryōkin 郵便料金 postal rate (=charge); mail rate (=charge); postage

yūchi 誘致 attraction; enticement; introduction ¶ the *attraction* of foreign investment, and of factories and enterprises // to *attract* and retain foreign capital in the U.S. // A factor that could *entice* manufacturing into the rural areas would be low labor costs.

yudaku 油濁 oil pollution; oil leak

yūdohikentei 尤度比検定 likelihood ratio test

yūfuku 裕福 affluence ¶ to live in *affluence* // a land *affluent* in minerals

yūgengaisha 有限会社 limited private company

yūgūkinri 優遇金利 advantageous interest rates; preferential (low) interest rate; prime rate

yūgūkin'yū 優遇金融 priority financing

yūgūsochi 優遇措置 incentive; privilege; favor; preferential treatment ¶ Fiscal *incentives* reduced the cost of capital goods. // Tax *incentives* on inputs commonly pertain to the purchase or modernization of fixed assets. // to accord *privileges* among countries according to their industrial maturity // The Act provides *preferential treatment* as regards commissions. // *preferential treatment* accorded development investment // curtailment of tax *incentives* for exporters // tax *privileges* granted in respect of owner-occupied flats // The present interest rate differential in *favor* of imports will be abolished. // to extend the agreement on *preferential* credit *treatment* for the export industry for further six months

yūgūtegata 優遇手形 preferential bill

yūgyōjinkō 有業人口 gainfully-occupied population

yūhatsusaretaidō 誘発された移動 induced movement

yūhatsusuru 誘発する spark; induce; generate; provoke; prompt; inspire; whet; engender; incite; stimulate; touch off; trigger; ignite ¶ Pressures on the sterling *sparked* an interest rate hike. // to *ignite* another round of inflation // The pressure, *triggered* by overseas nervousness about trade union rejection of the proposal sent the pound down to a new low. // to *provoke* unfavorable psychological reactions // price inflation *ignited* by the oil embargo // oil-*induced* inflation

yūhatsutekishihon'idō 誘発的資本移動 induced capital movement

yūhatsutekiyunyū 誘発的輸入 induced import; consequential import

yūhatsutōshi 誘発投資 induced investment

yūi 有意 significant ¶ The coefficient for the sales change variable is positive and statistically *significant*.

yūi 優位 advantage; superiority; ascendancy; preponderant position; edge ¶ to gain an unfair competitive *advantage* over other members // to come into the *ascendancy*. // It once played the *preponderant position* in this line. // Primary producing countries have an actual or potential comparative *advantage*. // to give the producers of the import-competing product a relative price *edge* to protect their share of the market

比較優位 comparative advantage
絶対優位 absolute advantage

yūin 誘引 inducement; attraction; enticement; temptation; introduction ¶ Falling interest rates played a major role in *inducing* borrowers to come to market and in *attracting*

investment funds out of the money markets and into the bond market. // It was *enticing* for market arbitrageurs to take this route out of francs. // Rising yields are *tempting* investors.

yūin 誘因 inducement; incentive; stimulus ¶ The investment grant gave industry a greater *inducement* than had generally been expected to start postponed building projects. // to offer *incentives* to *induce* bondholders to agree to an extension of maturity, such as a higher maturity value // *Incentives* to save were eroded as interest rates lagged behind inflation. // The more favorable financing terms presumably acted as *inducements*. // Prospective price rises provided *incentives* for increased investment in this line. // The principal *stimulus* in 1975 came from the domestic side. // large interest-*induced* money and capital exports // The program includes financial *incentives* to encourage labor mobility. // a rebound in car sales brought on by various *incentives* offered by the car manufacturers // This resulted in reduced *incentive* to export. // The government spells out their official *incentives* and deterrents to international direct investment. // benefits on such a generous scale as to blunt *incentives* to work // The price increases are intended as *incentives* to U.S. oil companies to increase domestic production in marginal wells. // a series of *incentives* to induce shipowners to scrap old vessels // For the developing countries there has been more *incentive* to

take bank credits than to issue bonds. // to provide the strongest short-term *incentive* in our history to invest // effective *incentives* for business to increase investment // There is not much *incentive* for buying.

yūino 有意の significant; meaningful ¶ This relationship remains *significant* when investment is brought into the relationship. // The relation becomes *insignificant* when investment enters into the regression. // Foreign assets show up as not *significantly* related to growth. // The monetary variable remains *meaning,* or *meaningful.*

yūisei 有意性 significance; meaning ¶ The following regressions have only limited *significance.* // at a lower level of *significance* // The *significance* of the coefficients is overstated. // It will retain *significance.* // The *significance* level of the monetary variable will deteriorate. // The following regressions have only limited *significance.*

yūkashōken 有価証券 (negotiable) securities; stocks and bonds
　一時払有価証券 non-amortizable securities
　借入有価証券 securities borrowed
　貸付有価証券 securities loaned
　投資有価証券 investment securities
yūkashōkenbaikyakueki 有価証券売却益 profits on securities sold
yūkashōkenbaikyakukinyūchō 有価証券売却記入帳 securities sold register
yūkashōkenbaikyakuson 有価証券売却損 losses on securities sold
yūkashōkenhikiukegyōmu 有価証券引受業務 investment banking
yūkashōkenhō 有価証券法

Securities Act of 1933

yūkashōken'itenzei 有価証券移転税 securities transfer tax

yūkashōkenjunbi 有価証券準備 securities reserve

yūkashōkenkaiire 有価証券買入 securities purchase; purchase of securities ¶ Net U.S. *purchases* of foreign *securities* decline by \$2 billion.

yūkashōkenkaiirekinyūchō 有価証券買入記入帳 investment purchased register

yūkashōkenkanjō 有価証券勘定 securities account

yūkashōkenkanrishintaku 有価証券管理信託 securities administration trust

yūkashōkenkinyūchō 有価証券記入帳 bonds and securities register; securities register

yūkashōkenmotochō 有価証券元帳 securities ledger

yūkashōkenshintaku 有価証券信託 securities (in) trust

yūkashōkentaisōyokinhiritsu 有価証券対総預金比率 ratio of securities to total deposits

yūkashōkentanpokashitsukekin 有価証券担保貸付金 loan secured by stocks and bonds

yūkashōkentodokedesho 有価証券届出書 registration statement

yūkashōkentōshi 有価証券投資 securities investment; investment in securities; portfolio investment

yūkashōken'un'yōshintaku 有価証券運用信託 securities operation trust

yūkeibōeki 有形貿易 visible trade

yūkeikoteishisan 有形固定資産 tangible fixed assets

yūkeishisan 有形資産 tangible assets; material property; visible

means

yukidoke "雪どけ" thaw; detente ¶ to suggest a *thaw* of monetary stringency // a *detente* between the two nations // the economy waiting for a vibrant bloom growth after the *thaw*

yūkikagakuseihin 有機化学製品 organic chemical products

yukiniunchin 往き荷運賃 outward freight

yūkiseihaikibutsu 有機性廃棄物 organic waste

yūkitekisoshikitai 有機的組織体 organism

yūkitekitōitsutai 有機的統一体 organic whole

yūkōjumyō 有効寿命 service life

yūkōjuyō 有効需要 effective demand; effectual demand

yūkōjuyōnogenri 有効需要の原理 principle of effective demand

yūkōkikan 有効期間 term of validity; term of availability; life

yūkōkyūjinbairitsu 有効求人倍率 ratio of effective labor demand to effective supply; (cumulative) demand-supply ratio of labor force; ratio of effective job offers to effective job openings; ratio of cumulative job vacancies to offers

yūkōkyūjinsū 有効求人数 effective job openings; effective job offers

yūkōkyūshokusha 有効求職者 effective labor supply; job-seekers in the present period and those carried over from the previous period

yūkōna 有効な effective; vali available

yūkōrakusa 有効落差 effect head

yūkōryūdōseisuijun 有効流動性 effective liquidity level

yūkōsei 有効性 effective

effectiveness ¶ the *effective range* of the financial policy // the *effectiveness* of the financial adjustment policy

yūkyū 有給 paid; salaried

yūkyū 遊休 idle; unused; out of operation; unutilized

yūkyūkyōikukyūka 有給教育休暇 paid educational leave

yūkyūkyūka 有給休暇 holidays with pay; paid holiday; paid days-off; paid vacation

年次有給休暇 annual paid vacation

yūkyūsetsubi 遊休設備 idle equipment; unutilized capacity; idle capacity

yūkyūsetsubihi 遊休設備費 idle capacity cost

yūkyūsetsubinōryoku 遊休設備能力 idle capacity; under-utilized capacity ¶ The margin of *idle capacity* was still large. // Widespread *under-utilization* of *capacity* was down by more than half.

yūkyūshihon 遊休資本 unemployed capital; idle capital

yūkyūshikin 遊休資金 idle money; idle funds; unused funds

yūkyūshisan 遊休資産 idle properties; dormant assets

yūkyūshisetsu 遊休施設 idle facilities; unutilized facilities

yūkyūtochihoyūzei 遊休土地保有税 land hoarding tax

yūkyūzandaka 遊休残高 idle balance ¶ investors' *idle balance*

yūmeiseihin 有名製品 well-known products with name recognition

yūmeiten 有名店 prestige store

yunittochinretsu ユニット陳列 unit display

yunittogatatōshishintaku ユニット型投資信託 unit-type investment

trust; unit trust

yunyū 輸入 import; importation; overseas buying ¶ *Imports* from the West made up 31.1% of total Comecon *imports* last year.

貿易外輸入 invisible import

直接輸入 direct import

外貨輸入 import of foreign capital

技術輸入 import of technologies

並行輸入 parallel import; non-exclusive import-distribution system

見込み輸入 anticipated import

無為替輸入 import without foreign exchange; non-draft import

無税輸入 (duty) free import

先行輸入 export-incentive import

資本輸入 capital import

商品輸入 visible import; merchandise import

yunyūbōeki 輸入貿易 import trade

yunyūbōekitegata 輸入貿易手形 import trade bill

yunyūchōka 輸入超過 excess of imports over exports; unfavorable balance of trade

yunyūchūijikō 輸入注意事項 notes on import; matters to be attended on import

yunyūdaitai 輸入代替 import substitution; import replacement ¶ incentives to *import-replacement* activities given by import restrictions // to protect infant *import-replacement* (=replacing) industries // reduction of *import-replacement* protection // the existing incentive system favoring *import substitution*

yunyūdaitaiseisan 輸入代替生産 production of substitutes of imported goods

yunyūgendo 輸入限度 import limit; ceiling on imports

yunyūgenka 輸入原価 cost of import; import cost

yunyūgenzairyōzaikoritsu 輸入原材料在庫率 inventory ratio of imported raw material to production

yunyūhaneshikin 輸入ハネ資金 yen finance after foreign currency credit for imports

yunyūhappyō 輸入発表 import announcement

yunyūhin 輸入品 imports; imported articles; imported goods

yunyūhiritsu 輸入比率 import content ¶ the generally low *import content* of housing

yunyūhoshōgaku 輸入保証額 guaranteed value of import

yunyūhoshōkin 輸入保証金 import guarantee money

yunyūizondo 輸入依存度 degree (=rate) of dependence on imports of goods

yunyūkabāritsu 輸入カバー率 import cover ratio

yunyūkachōkin 輸入課徴金 import surcharge; tax surcharge on imports

yunyūkawase 輸入為替 import bill

yunyūkessai 輸入決済 payment for import

yunyūkessaitegata 輸入決済手形 import settlement bill

yunyūkinshi 輸入禁止 import prohibition; import ban; ban on import

yunyūkō 輸入港 port of entry

yunyūkōhyō 輸入公表 import announcement; import notice

yunyūkōsei 輸入構成 construction of imports; import structure

yunyūkyoka 輸入許可 import license (=permit)

yunyūkyokasei 輸入許可制 import licensing system

包括輸入許可制 open general license

yunyūkyōsōsangyō 輸入競争産業 import-competing industry

yunyūmaebaraikin 輸入前払金 import prepayment; prepayment for import

yunyūmenjō 輸入免状 import permit (=license)

yunyūnitomonaugaikasaiken 輸入に伴う外貨債権 foreign claimable assets incidental to import

yunyūookonauseizōgyōsha 輸入を行う製造業者 importing manufacturer

yunyūsaki 輸入先 origin country of imports

yunyūseigen 輸入制限 import restriction

緊急輸入制限条項 safeguard clause

yunyūseikō 輸入性向 propensity to import

平均輸入性向 average propensity to import

yunyūsenko 輸入先行 export-incentive import; import first; import priority

yunyūshikinkashitsuke 輸入資金貸付 import financing credit; loans for import financing (to the authorized foreign exchange banks)

yunyūshinkoku 輸入申告 declaration of import; import declaration

yunyūshin'yōjō 輸入信用状 import letter of credit

yunyūshogakari 輸入諸掛り import charges

yunyūshōmeisho 輸入証明書 import certificate

yunyūshōninshō 輸入承認証 import license

yunyūshōnintōkei 輸入承認統計 import statistics on a licensed basis

yunyūshōreikin 輸入奨励金 subsidy for import; import bounty

yunyūsōdairiten 輸入総代理店 sole distributorship; sole agent; import general agent

yunyūsūryōshisū 輸入数量指数 import volume index

yunyūtanponimotsuhikitorihoshō 輸入担保荷物引取保証 guarantee for delivery (of goods) without bill of lading

yunyūtanposeido 輸入担保制度 advanced deposit requirement system on import

yunyūtegatakessaishikingashi 輸入手形決済資金貸 import bills settlement account, Dr.

yunyūtegatanohikiukekessai 輸入手形の引受・決済 acceptance and settlement of import bills

yunyūtetsuzuki 輸入手続 import procedure; import formalities

yunyūtodokede 輸入届出 import declaration

yunyūtokaigaienoshotoku 輸入と海外への所得 imports of goods and services and factor income paid abroad

yunyūtozetsu 輸入途絶 suspension of imports

yunyūtsūkantetsuzuki 輸入通関手続 customs clearance procedure for import

yunyūunchintegata 輸入運賃手形 import freight bill

yunyūwariate 輸入割当 import quota

yunyūwariateseido 輸入割当制度 import quota system; IQ system

yunyūwariateshōmeisho 輸入割当証明書 import quota certificate

yunyūyōchūihinmokujōkō 輸入要注意品目条項 sensitive item clause (under the GATT)

yunyūyotakukin 輸入預託金 import deposit ¶ 20% ad valorem *import deposits*

yunyūyūzansu 輸入ユーザンス import usance facilities (extended by banks in Japan)

yunyūzei 輸入税 import duty

yunyūzeiritsu 輸入税率 import tariff

yūreigaisha 幽霊会社 bogus company

yūreijinkō 幽霊人口 bogus population; fraudulently-registered population

yūreikabu 幽霊株 bogus stock

yūrina 有利な profitable; lucrative; remunerative; paying; advantageous; favorable; expedient

yūrinajigyō 有利な事業 profitable enterprise; lucrative business; paying business; remunerative business

yūrinajōken 有利な条件 advantageous terms; favorable conditions

yūrishiyokin 有利子預金 interest-bearing deposit

yurō 油漏 oil leak

yūrodarā ユーロ・ダラー Euro-dollars

yūrodarāshijō ユーロ・ダラー市場 Euro-dollar market ¶ to tap the *Euro-dollar market* for large amounts

yūroginkō ユーロ銀行 Euro-(currency) banks ¶ The attitudes of *Euro-banks* toward expanding commitments in the Euro-currency markets were cautious. // long-term *Euro-currency bank* financing // the formation of the hundreds of *Euro-banks* which are based in financial centers such as London, Singapore, Hongkong and Luxemburg // London based *Euro-bank* executives

yūrokarenshīshinjikētorōnshijō ユーロカレンシー・シンジケート・ローン市場 Euro-currency syndicated loan market

yūrokinri ユーロ金利 interest rate on the Euro-currency market

yūrokin'yūshijō ユーロ金融市場 Euro-currency banking markets; Euro-currency banking system ¶ sources and uses of funds in the *Euro-currency banking markets* // The Western European countries in which the Euro-banks reside provided the largest flow of funds into the *Euro-currency banking markets*. // The OPEC countries have been the dominant suppliers of funds flowing through the *Euro-currency system*.

yūromanē ユーロ・マネー Euro-currency ¶ givers and takers of *Euro-currency*

yūronodashitetotorite ユーロの出し手と取り手 giver and taker of Euro-currency

yūrosai ユーロ債 Euro-bond; Euro-market loan ¶ The majority of *Euro-bond* issues have been denominated in U.S. dollars; in 1974 nearly 60 percent of *Euro-bonds* sold were dollar-denominated. // Offerings of German mark denominated *Euro-bonds* increased. // During this period mark-denominated *Euro-bond* yields have generally been below the yields on dollar-denominated *Euro-bond* issues. // a $380 million *Euro-market loan* for the Mexican State company // a seven-year *Euro-currency loan* of $300 million to Austria

yūrosaishijō ユーロ債市場 Euro-bond markets ¶ Long-term borrowing costs in the *Euro-bond markets* were exceptionally high.

yūroshijō ユーロ市場 Euro-currency markets; Euro markets ¶ Credit uncertainties developed in the *Euro markets*. // The investable surpluses of OPEC member countries have been held in the *Euro-currency markets*. // Lending through the *Euro-currency* banking *markets* slowed down.

yūroshinjikattosōgōhyakushukabukashisū ユーロシンジカット総合100種株価指数 Eurosyndicat General Share Index

yūroshin'yō ユーロ信用 Euro-currency credit ¶ An increase in 1974 in the proportion of total Euro-bank lending in maturities greater than 1 year is reflected in the data on publicized medium- and long-term (generally 5 to 7 years) *Euro-currency credits*. // Medium- and long-term *Euro-currency credits* were denominated almost exclusively in U.S. dollars.

yūrotoriirezandaka ユーロ取入残高 Euro-currency liabilities

yurui 緩い ［市］ easy; easier

yurumu 緩む ease off; relax

yūryōchūkenkigyō 優良中堅企業 superior, medium-ranking business

yūryōkigyō 優良企業 enterprise of good standing; prime business

yūryokusuji 有力筋 ［市］influential interests; leading operators

yūryōshisan 優良資産 prime asset

yūryōtegata 優良手形 prime bill

yūryōtegatawaribikibuai 優良手形割引歩合 fine rate; prime rate

yūryōtorihikisaki 優良取引先 prime customer

yūsen 優先 priority; preference ¶ to give special *priority* for materials to export industries // to give housing the highest *priority* // with special *priority* given to exports // *Preference* is given for welfare over growth.

公益優先 preference of public interest ¶ policy giving an unequivocal *priority* to... // [参考] Safety of principal must be banks' predominant consideration.

yūsenhaitō 優先配当 preference dividend; preferred dividend

yūsenjun'i 優先順位 priority; preference ¶ *Priority* will go to export-promoting and energy-saving projects. // Such investment will have to be a *priority* over any increase in other spending. // objectives that must command the *priorities* of us all // They gave a high *priority* to keeping inflation under control. // The first *priority* for policy is to effect a further reduction of inflation. // to reduce growth with investment being given more *priority* to consumption // The control of inflation should receive a top *priority* in national economic policy. // to reorder the budget *priorities* // to make a careful reassessment of the country's development *priorities* // reordering of national *priorities* so as to emphasize the "quality of life" // Inflation has tended to have lower *priority* in Iceland's economic policy than full employment. // Control of inflation will need to assume higher *priority*. // to conflict with national planning *priorities* // Bank credit will continue to be extended on a *preferential* basis to *priority* sectors.

yūsenjun'hyō 優先順位表 priority ranking schedule

yūsenkabu 優先株 preference share (=stock)

累積優先株 cumulative preference share (=stock)

参加優先株 participating preference share (=stock)

yūsenken 優先権 priority; preferential right; precedence

yūsensaikensha 優先債権者 preferential creditor

yūsensei 優先制 priorities system; preferential basis; priority basis ¶ bank credit accommodation on a *preferential basis*

yūsenshasai 優先社債 preference debenture

yūshi 融資 accommodation of funds; financing; lending (of money); loan (of money); (financial) accommodation; credit facility ¶ The banks have been *accommodating* a growing volume of loans. // Banks' *lending* operations expanded. // Bank *loans* and discounts fell. // A member bank can obtain *accommodation* from a Federal Reserve Bank. // the granting of credit *accommodation* in the form of discounts or collateral advance // to obtain *accommodation* from a bank // to apply for *accommodation* to a bank // to maintain second credit *accommodations* // to provide more ample *credit facilities*

別枠融資 special loan

公害防止用融資 anti-pollution loan

協調融資 participation loan

共同融資 syndicate financing; joint financing

選別融資 selective lending

yūshi 遊資 idle capital; idle money

yūshiassen 融資斡旋 loan facilitation

yūshigaisha 融資会社 financing corporation

yūshigendo 融資限度 loan value ¶ The maximum *loan value* of stocks works out at 35%. // →掛け目

yūshihōshin 融資方針 credit extending policy; lending policy ¶ → 貸出方針

yūshijunsoku 融資準則 financing regulation; regulation on funds to be supplied by financial institutions

yūshikatsudō 融資活動 lending operation (=activity)

yūshikisei 融資規制 loan restrictions; regulation of lending

yūshimōshikomi 融資申込み loan application ¶ Withdrawals of *loan applications* by potential borrowers are becoming more frequent.

yūshisankashōsho 融資参加証書 participation certificate

yūshitaido 融資態度 lending attitude; attitude toward lending; lending posture; stance in lending ¶ Banks hold restrictive, not accommodative *lending attitudes*. // a less restrictive *attitude* held by banks *toward lending*

yūshitekikakumeigara 融資適格銘柄 [証市] stocks (=issues) qualified for loans

yūshiyokuseitaido 融資抑制態度 restrictive attitude toward lending; restrictive lending posture; restrictive stance in lending

yūshiyoyaku 融資予約 loan commitment

yūshizaidan 融資財団 consortium ¶ A U.S. concern was part of a Japanese-led *consortium* bidding on a $220 million contract.

yūshōkeiyaku 有償契約 contract made for a consideration

yūshōkōi 有償行為 juristic act done for a consideration

yūshōno 有償の for consideration; with payment; with quid pro quo; paid

yūshōshutoku 有償取得 acquisition for value

yūshōwariate 有償割当 paid-in capital allotment

yūshōzōshi 有償増資 paid-in capital increase

yushutsu 輸出 export; exportation; overseas sale ¶ Trade frictions could soon stunt *export sales*. // *Overseas sales* doubled between 1975 and 1976.

現地組立て輸出 knock-down export

技術輸出 export of technologies

飢餓輸出 hunger export

無為替輸出 export on consignments; export without foreign exchange; non-draft export

無形輸出 invisible export

延払輸出 export by deferred payment

プラント輸出 plant export

正貨輸出 specie export

資本輸出 capital export

郵便による輸出 export by mail

有形輸出 visible export; merchandise export

yushutsuatsuryoku 輸出圧力 export pressure

yushutsubōeki 輸出貿易 export trade

yushutsubōekitegata 輸出貿易手形 export trade bill

yushutsuchitsujo 輸出秩序 order in exports; orderly exports

yushutsuchōka 輸出超過 excess of exports over imports; favorable balance of trade

yushutsudaikin 輸出代金 export proceeds; proceeds from export

yushutsudaikinhoken 輸出代金保険 export cost insurance

yushutsudaikinkaishū 輸出代金回収 collection of export proceeds

yushutsudairishō 輸出代理商 export agent

yushutsudama 輸出玉 export goods; goods available for export; exportable goods; products for export ¶ the shortage of French *products for export*

yushutsudanseichi 輸出弾性値 elasticity coefficient of exports

yushutsugyō 輸出業 export business

yushutsuhendōhoshōyūshiseido 輸出変動補償融資制度 compensatory financing facility (of the IMF)

yushutsuhenkōtekigijutsushinpo 輸出偏向的技術進歩 export-biased progress

yushutsuhin 輸出品 export goods; exports

yushutsuhinmeisaihyō 輸出品明細表 shipping list

yushutsuhinseisangyōsha 輸出品生産業者 producer for export

yushutsuhintenrankai 輸出品展覧会 exports exposition; exports exhibition

yushutsuhojokin 輸出補助金 export subsidy

yushutsuhoken 輸出保険 export insurance ¶ to suspend *export insurance* cover on transactions with 25 countries

yushutsuhoshō 輸出補償 export indemnification

yushutsujishukisei 輸出自主規制 voluntary restriction on export; voluntary export restriction

yushutsujoseikin 輸出助成金 export bounty

yushutsukamotsudaikinmaeuke 輸出貨物代金前受 receipt of export prepayment

yushutsukankeikashidashi 輸出関係貸出 export-related loan

yushutsukaruteru 輸出カルテル export cartel

yushutsukawase 輸出為替 →輸出手形

yushutsukensakikan 輸出検査機関 export inspection organ

yushutsukensashōmeisho 輸出検査証明書 export inspection certificate

yushutsukenteiseido 輸出検定制度 export inspection system

yushutsukinshi 輸出禁止 export ban; embargo

金輸出禁止 embargo on gold; gold embargo

対日輸出禁止 embargo on shipments to Japan

yushutsukin'yū 輸出金融 export financing; financing for export

yushutsukin'yūhoken 輸出金融保険 export financing insurance

yushutsukōzō 輸出構造 export structure

yushutsukumiai 輸出組合 export association

yushutsukyokasei 輸出許可制 export licensing system

yushutsukyokasho 輸出許可書 export license (=permit)

yushutsukyōsōryoku 輸出競争力 competitiveness in exports

yushutsumaegashi 輸出前貸し export advance

yushutsumaegashishin'yōjō 輸出前貸信用状 packing credit; red clause credit

yushutsumaegashitegataseido 輸

出前貸手形制度 export advance bill system

yushutsumaeukekin 輸出前受金 export prepayment

yushutsumaeukenojizenkyoka 輸出前受の事前許可 prior permission for prepayment of (Japanese) exports

yushutsumenjō 輸出免状 export permit

yushutsumokuhyō 輸出目標 export target

yushutsuninshōtetsuzuki 輸出認証手続 export certification procedure

yushutsuninshōtōkei 輸出認証統計 export statistics on certified basis

yushutsunobebarai 輸出延払 deferred payment on export

yushutsunobebaraishin'yō 輸出延払信用 export credit on deferred payment

yushutsunyūbukkashisū 輸出入物価指数 export and import price index

yushutsunyūkaitenkikin 輸出入回転基金 export and import revolving fund

yushutsunyūkin'yūtaisei 輸出入金融体制 export-import financing structure

yushutsunyūninshōgaku 輸出入認証額 import and export permit validations

yushutsunyūnobebarairishi 輸出入延払利子 deferred interest on trade credit

yushutsunyūrinkusei 輸出入リンク制 export-import link system

yushutsunyūritsu 輸出入率 export-import cover ratio

yushutsunyūtōkeihinmokuhyō 輸出入統計品目表 commodity classification for foreign trade statistics

yushutsusaiteikakaku 輸出最低価格 check price for export

yushutsusangyō 輸出産業 export industry

yushutsuseigen 輸出制限 export restriction

yushutsuseisandaiichishugi 輸出生産第一主義 export-production-first policy

yushutsusenkōtekiseichō 輸出先行的成長 export-led growth

yushutsushikōsangyō 輸出指向産業 export-oriented industry

yushutsushinkokusho 輸出申告書 export declaration (form)

yushutsushinkōsaku 輸出振興策 export drive; export-incentive program (=scheme); export promotion program

yushutsushinsa 輸出審査 examination on export

yushutsushin'yōhoken 輸出信用保険 export credit insurance

yushutsushin'yōjōsetsujudaka 輸出信用状接受高 export letters of credit received

yushutsushōninshinseisho 輸出承認申請書 application for license to export

yushutsushōrei 輸出奨励 export encouragement; export drive; export promotion ¶ an economically desirable level of *export promotion*

yushutsushōreikin 輸出奨励金 export subsidy; export bounty

yushutsushudōgatakeizaikakudai 輸出主導型経済拡大 export-led growth

yushutsushudōgatanoseichō 輸出主導型の成長 export-led expansion; growth led by exports

yushutsushudōkigyō 輸出主導企業 export-centered enterprise

yushutsushūeki 輸出収益 export earnings (=income; receipts) ¶ to keep its *export earnings* at an acceptable multiple of its debt servicing payments

yushutsusūryōshisū 輸出数量指数 export volume index

yushutsutegata 輸出手形 export bill

yushutsutegatakaitori 輸出手形買取り purchase of export bills

yushutsutesūryōdairiten 輸出手数料代理店 export commission house

yushutsutetsuzuki 輸出手続 export formalities

yushutsutokaigaikaranoshotoku 輸出と海外からの所得 exports of goods and services and factor income received from abroad

yushutsutokubetsushōkyaku 輸出特別償却 accelerated depreciation for exporters

yushutsutsūkantetsuzuki 輸出通関手続 customs clearing procedure for exports

yushutsuwariate 輸出割当 export quota

yushutsuyoryoku 輸出余力 export capacity

yushutsuzei 輸出税 export duty

yushutsuzeimoku 輸出税目 table of export duties

yusō 輸送 transport; transportation; carriage; transit; traffic

　海上輸送 transport by sea; sea transport; carriage by sea; marine transport

　陸上輸送 land transport; surface transport

　鉄道輸送 transport by rail; railway transport; carriage by rail

yūsō 郵送 forwarding by post; forwarding by mail; sending by mail

yusōhi 輸送費 transportation cost

yusōkikai 輸送機械 transport equipment; transport machinery

yūsōmuryō 郵送無料 postage free

yusōnan 輸送難 transportaion difficulty

yusōryoku 輸送力 transport capacity; carrying power

yusōsen 輸送船 transport boat; transport ship

yusōsen 輸送線 line of transportation

yūtaishisan 有体資産 tangible asset

yutakanashakai "豊かな社会" "affluent society"; opulent society

yūtesōsa 融手操作 financing of accommodation

yūyo 猶予 grace; extension of time 支払猶予 indulgence

yūyokikan 猶予期間 grace period; period of grace; days of grace; probationary period; elimination period; waiting period; [保険] renewal period ¶ to give another four *months of grace* to comply with the regulations // The *grace periods* for amortization operative in many of the earlier loan agreements are beginning to expire.

yūyonissū 猶予日数 days of grace; days of indulgence

yūzansu ユーザンス usance (facility)

　自行ユーザンス usance extended by the bank's own funds

　輸入ユーザンス import usance

　輸出ユーザンス export usance

yūzansukinri ユーザンス金利 interest on usance bills

yūzei 郵税 postage

　外国郵税 foreign postage

　国内郵税 domestic postage

yūzeibusoku 郵税不足 short postage

yūzeihin 有税品 taxable goods; dutiable goods; assessable goods

yūzeimuryō 郵税無料 postage free

yūzeisenpōbarai 郵税先方払い postage paid on delivery

yūzeishiharaizumi 郵税支払済み postage paid

yūzeishōzappi 郵税小雑費 postage and petties

yūzū 融通 accommodation ¶ to provide *accommodation* of $1,000

yūzūshōken 融通証券 treasury accommodation bill

yūzūtegata 融通手形 accommodation bill; kite; windbill

yūzūtegatafuridashi 融通手形振出し kite-flying; cross drawing

yūzūtegatahikiukenin 融通手形引受人 accommodation acceptor

yūzūtegatauragaki 融通手形裏書 accommodation endorsement

yūzūtōjisha 融通当事者 accommodation parties

Z

zahyō 座標 coordinate
角座標 angular coordinate
球面座標 spherical coordinate
斜角座標 oblique coordinate
縦座標 ordinate
躍線座標 curvilinear coordinate
横座標 abscissa

zahyōjiku 座標軸 axis of coordinate

zahyōkei 座標系 coordinate system

zaibatsu 財閥 industrial conglomerate; financial clique; plutocracy; plutocrats; "zaibatsu"

zaibatsukaitai 財閥解体 dissolution of financial cliques; liquidation of financial plutocrats

zaidan 財団 foundation; financial group; syndicate; estate
破産財団 bankrupt's estate
融資財団 consortium

zaidanhōjin 財団法人 foundation; incorporated foundation

zaidanteitōkashitsukekin 財団抵当貸付金 loan secured by factory foundation mortgage

zaigaifusai 在外負債 overseas liabilities

zaigaihōjin 在外邦人 Japanese resident abroad

zaigaihoyūdaka 在外保有高 amount held abroad; overeas holdings

zaigaiseika 在外正貨 specie holdings abroad

zaigaishisan 在外資産 overseas assets; assets abroad ¶ U.S. *assets abroad* rose by $58 billion, while foreign assets in the U.S. increased by $63 billion.

zaigen 財源 source of revenue; financial resources; fiscal · resources; treasury resources; ways and means ¶ Companies' internal *resources* amounted to DM73 billion. // to cover 97% of their gross investments from their own *resources* // search for fiscal *resources* // shortage of fiscal *resources* // to find *ways and means,* and spend within *ways and means*

隠し財源　hidden treasury reserves

zaigennan 財源難　shortage of financial resources; resourcelessness

zaigennenshutsu 財源捻出　search for financial resources; finding ways and means

zaika 在荷　stock; goods in stock; visible supplies

市場外在荷　invisible supplies

市場在荷　visible stock (=supplies)

zaika 財(貨)　goods ¶ The upturn of output has been confined to intermediate *goods,* rather than consumer or investment *goods.*

中間財　intermediate goods; intermediary goods

独立財　independent goods

半耐久財　semi-durable goods

非耐久消費財　nondurable consumer goods; consumer nondurables

非耐久財　nondurable goods; nondurables

補完財　complementary goods

一般資本財　capital goods excluding transport equipment

実物財　real goods

上級財　superior goods

下級財　inferior goods

関連財　related goods

完全代替財　perfect substitute goods

経済財　economic goods

希少財　scarcity goods

国内財　domestic goods

国際財　international goods

公共財　public goods

共同消費財　collective consumption goods

競争財　competitive goods

劣等財　inferior goods

再生産可能財　reproducible goods

最終財　final goods

生産者耐久財　producers' durable goods

生産財　producer goods; production goods

資本財　capital goods

私的財　private goods

消費財　consumer goods; consumption goods

消耗財　perishable goods

粗代替財　gross substitute goods

即時財　instantaneous goods

耐久消費財　durable consumer goods; consumer durables

耐久財　durable goods; hard goods; durables

耐用財　durable use goods

低級財　inferior goods

投資財　investment goods

輸入競争財　import-competing goods

zaikafuttei 在荷払底　inventory shortage; dearth of goods in stock

zaikai 財界　financial world; financial circles; financial quarters; financial world; financial community ¶ various segments of the *financial community*

zaikainoantei 財界の安定　financial stability

zaikainofuan 財界の不安　financial unrest

zaikainokiki 財界の危機　financial crisis

zaikainoōdatemono 財界の大立物　financial magnate

zaikainotatenaoshi 財界の建直し　financial reconstruction; financial rehabilitation

zaikakata 在荷過多　glut; overstock

zaikasābisu 財貨・サービス　goods

and services ¶ purchases of *goods and services*

zaikei 財形 building-up of personal financial assets

zaikeichochikukeiyaku 財形貯蓄契約 property accumulation savings (contract)

zaiko 在庫 inventory; stock ¶ There were large increases of purchased-materials *inventories* by durable goods producers, and of work-in-process inventories by manufacturers. // *Stocks* of finished goods combined with those in process expanded moderately. // Retailers' *stocks* dipped slightly, then picked up moderately through June and have since leveled off. // Manufacturing *inventories* grew to $190 billion, while retail *inventories* went up to $92 billion. // By contrast, *inventories* of the wholesale trade decreased to $75 billion. // The rundown in manufacturing industry's *stocks* came to a virtual halt after a record fall last year. // *Stocks* generally have remained lean relative to sales. // *Stocks* of oil are building up nicely. // The high cost of carrying commodity *stocks* requires disposal of surplus *stocks*.

原材料在庫 raw material(s) inventory

販売在庫 dealers' inventories; trade inventory

過剰在庫 excess inventory; surplus inventory; inventory glut

企業在庫 business inventory

基準在庫 basic inventory

小売在庫 retail inventory

卸売在庫 wholesale inventory

流通在庫 dealers' inventories; trade inventory

製品在庫 finished goods inventory

生産者在庫 manufacturing inventory; inventory with manufacturers;

後ろ向き在庫 involuntary inventory

zaikoberashi 在庫減らし disinvestment; inventory run-off; inventory curtailment; inventory liquidation; inventory cutback; inventory reduction; inventory decumulation; destocking; inventory squeeze; inventory pruning ¶ The rate of *inventory liquidation* has sharply abated. // There were no *decumulation* of *inventories*. // The year-to-year *reduction in stocks* paralleled the decline in sales. // [参考] Excess inventories were to be worked off and eliminated. // Wholesalers' inventories, after a slight reduction, were held even. Retailers were making sizable cuts in inventories. // Stocks have been run down. // The stockpiles were worn down. // Business was working down excessive stocks.

zaikochikuseki 在庫蓄積 stockpiling ¶ The Company will spend £50 million this year on a countercyclical *stockpiling* scheme.

zaikōchosei 在庫調整 inventory adjustment; inventory curtailment; inventory cutback; stock reduction ¶ The *inventory adjustment* had about run its course. // →在庫減らし

zaikochōseikatei 在庫調整過程 inventory adjustment process ¶ The *inventory adjustment process* appears to be now largely completed.

zaikochōseiniyorukeikikōtai 在庫調整による景気後退 inventory recession

zaikogenshō 在庫減少 decline in inventories; run-down of stocks; in-

zaiseienjo 財政援助 financial support; financial aid

zaiseifutan 財政負担 fiscal burden on the nation; financial burden ¶ increased *financial burdens* on citizens

zaiseihikishime 財政引締め fiscal austerity; fiscal restraint

zaiseijōtai 財政状態 financial situation (=position); financial standing; fiscal condition ¶ The company's *financial condition* is "strong", "good", "fair", or "limited". // to be in a strong *financial position* to be able to ... // to maintain the superb *financial condition* that currently exists // The Government's *financial situation* will deteriorate further. // Many consumers feel that their *financial situation* has become more favorable. // sustained progress in the *fiscal position* of the government // countries whose *financial standing* is the weakest // countries whose *financial position* seemed no longer to justify further expense // [参考] The national finances were in a bad way.

zaiseikansa 財政監査 investigation on fiscal operations

zaiseikekkan 財政欠陥 shortfall of revenue ¶ The total *shortfall of revenue* to the Federal Government was partially offset by a rise in value added tax.

zaiseikiki 財政危機 financial crisis ¶ Italy, in a serious *financial crisis,* plans severe cuts in government spending. // to pass through many acute *financial crises*

zaiseikin'yūseisaku 財政金融政策 fiscal and monetary policies

zaiseikōchokuka 財政硬直化 in-flexibility of public finance; in flexibility in budget preparations becoming rigid and inflexible of public finance; budget rigidity; fiscal inflexibility

zaiseimenkaranokeikishigekisaku 財政面からの景気刺激策 fiscal stimulus ¶ the massive *fiscal stimulus* to combat recession

zaiseinan 財政難 financial difficulty; financial embarrassment; pecuniary difficulty ¶ to alleviate, not aggravate, the *financial difficulties* // to tide over *financial embarrassments* // to overcome repeated *financial difficulties* // financially *embarassed* public entities // to salvage industrial firms from *financial difficulties* // [参考] Most financially pressed universities welcome the aid. // They were facing financial problems.

zaiseiseisaku 財政政策 fiscal policy ¶ Mr.Healey threatened tougher *fiscal policies* to counteract a pay explosion. // the continuation of sound and growth-oriented *fiscal policy* by the Government

補正的財政政策 compensatory fiscal policy

zaiseishikin 財政資金 financial funds; treasury funds; (特に国家の) fiscal funds; government funds; Treasury funds

zaiseishikinshūshi 財政資金収支 receipts and payments of Treasury (=Government) funds

zaiseishikintaiminkanshūshi 財政資金対民間収支 (receipts and payment of) Treasury (=Government) accounts with the public

zaiseishishutsu 財政支出 fiscal expenditure; government expenditure;

ventory run-off ¶ the much-needed continued *run-down* of high *stocks* as a result of growing export demand // There was a huge *run-off* of auto *inventories*. // Business began to slow *run-off* of stocks. // →在庫減らし

zaikohakidashi 在庫吐出し destocking; inventory liquidation ¶ →在庫減らし

zaikohin 在庫品 goods in stock; stocks in (=on) hand

zaikohinhikaechō 在庫品控帳 stock book

zaikohinhoken 在庫品保険 stock insurance

zaikohinmotochō 在庫品元帳 stock ledger

zaikohojū 在庫補充 restocking; replenishment of inventories ¶ *restocking* at a rate faster than the increase in sales

zaikohyōka 在庫評価 inventory valuation; inventory pricing ¶ a reserve for fluctuation in *inventory valuation* // changes in *inventory pricing* methods, or methods used to *value inventories*

zaikohyōkachōsei 在庫評価調整 inventory valuation adjustment

zaikojunkan 在庫循環 stock cycle; inventory cycle ¶ The evidence on hand is rather scanty for an accurate assessment of *stock cycle* trends. // The depressive effects of the *stock cycle* are likely to cease soon. // The appearance of a *stock cycle* reinforced the depressive effects on the growth of output of the weakening propensity to invest.

zaikojushi 在庫需資 inventory financial requirements; credit needs to carry inventories; credit require-ments for carrying inventories

zaikokachitōki 在庫価値騰貴 stock appreciation

zaikokajō 在庫過剰 excess inventories; surplus stocks; inventory glut; overstock; overhang of stock ¶ *Excess inventories* were to be worked off and eliminated. // programs for disposal of *surplus stocks* // There is the threat of an *inventory glut.*

zaikokin'yū 在庫金融 inventory financing; inventory finance

zaikoritsu 在庫率 stock-sales ratio; inventory-sales ratio; stock-output ratio; ratio of inventory holdings to production; inventory-sales relationship ¶ *Inventory-sales ratios* have remained high by past standards. // The steady rise in sales lowered the *stock-sales ratio.* // an *inventory-sales ratio* of 1.2 months of sales // *Inventory-sales relationships* are being brought into better alignment. // [参考] Stocks were equivalent to a 45 selling-day supply. // Inventories at that were adequate for the going rate of sales.

製品在庫率 inventory ratio of finished goods to sales; inventory (=stock)-sales ratio of finished goods

輸入原材料在庫率 inventory ratio of imported raw materials to production

zaikoruiseki 在庫累積 accumulation of inventories; inventory accumulation; stock accumulation ¶ Involuntary, or unintended, *accumulation of stocks* became important. // Business sought to limit *accumulation* in some lines. // *Accumulated stocks* of unsold cloth with the mills mounted to 31 million yards. // the strong *inventory accumulation* that preceded the recession

zaikoteate 在庫手当 stockbuilding; stockpiling; stock buildup ¶ → 在庫積み増し；在庫補充

zaikoteatenotebikae 在庫手当の手控え conservative stock purchase

zaikotōshi 在庫投資 inventory investment; investment in inventories ¶ At home there was a sharp fall in *inventory investment.* // The amount of *investment* and disinvestment in *inventories* is the result of differing movements in various categories of stocks.

意図せざる在庫投資 unintended (= unplanned) inventory investment

意図した在庫投資 intended (= planned) inventory investment

zaikotsumimashi 在庫積み増し rebuilding of inventories; inventory buildup; stock reconstitution; stockbuilding ¶ Signs of a *buildup* of finished goods inventories appeared. // We experienced some *rebuilding of inventories.* // The low level of *stockbuilding* was bound to give way to a *rebuilding of stocks.*

zaikousu 在庫薄 short stock

zaimu 財務 financial affairs

zaimubunseki 財務分析 financial analysis

zaimudairinin 財務代理人 fiscal agent

zaimudairikeiyaku 財務代理契約 fiscal agency agreement

zaimuhi 財務費 financial expenses

zaimuhiritsu 財務比率 financial ratios

zaimuhōkoku 財務報告 financial report(ing)

zaimukaikei 財務会計 financial accounting

zaimukanri 財務管理 financial management

zaimukansa 財務監査 financial audit

zaimukansakan 財務監査官 comptroller (of the treasury)

zaimukeikaku 財務計画 financial planning

zaimukomon 財務顧問 financial adviser

zaimukōsei 財務構成 financial structure ¶ the soundness of borrowing businesses' *financial structure*

zaimunaiyō 財務内容 composition of finances ¶ It is important to reform the *composition of finances* and improve the efficiency of capital.

zaimuseigenjōkō 財務制限条項 additional debt restriction

zaimushohyōbunseki 財務諸表分析 analysis of financial statements

zaimushohyōkisoku 財務諸表規則 regulation concerning financial statements

zaimushōshōken 財務省証券 ［米］ (1年以下) certificate of indebtedness; (1年超5年迄) Treasury note; (5年超) Treasury bond; (90-93日) Treasury bill; TB

zaimuyosan 財務予算 financial budget

zainichigaigin 在日外銀 foreign banks with branches in Japan; foreign bank in Japan

zairyō 材料 material; factor; data ［市］factor; impetus; incentive; news ¶ Trading was quiet in the absence of fresh market *factors.* // The dollar drifted lower with no fresh *impetus.* // Trading remained sub-

---

dued on lack of fresh *incentive.* // no fresh trading *incentive* evident // There was little *news* to stimulate the market. // The market is waiting for new *incentives.*

悪材料 ［市］damper; adverse factor

弱材料 ［市］bearish factor

建築材料 building material

好材料 ［市］favorable factor; encouraging factor

強材料 ［市］bullish factor

zairyōgenzaidaka 材料現在高 closing inventory

zairyōhi 材料費 material costs

zairyoku 財力 financial ability; pecuniary ability financial power; means ¶ →資力

zairyōkurikoshidaka 材料繰越高 opening inventory

zairyōmachi 材料待ち ［市］waiting for new factors; waiting for new incentives; waiting for the next move; absence of fresh news ¶ Dollar trade was inactive in the *absence of fresh news.* // The market held generally quiet *awaiting new incentives.*

zaisan 財産 property; asset; estate

団体財産 corporate property

個人財産 personal property

国有財産 state-owned property

公共財産 public property

共有財産 joint estate; common property

無形財産 immaterial property; intangible property; non-visible property

世襲財産 hereditary property; hereditary estate; heritage; freehold

私有財産 private property

残余財産 residual property

zaisanbaikyakueki 財産売却益 profits on assets sold

zaisanhenkan 財産返還 escheat; reverting of property

zaisanhaitō 財産配当 property dividend

zaisanhyōka 財産評価 property valuation; income from appreciation of assets

zaisanjōto 財産譲渡 conveyance of estate

zaisankanrinin 財産管理人 custodian of property; administrator of property; receiver

zaisankeisei 財産形成 building-up of personal financial assets

zaisankeiseikyūfushintaku 財産形成給付信託 employees' property formation benefit trust

zaisanken 財産権 property rights

zaisankensa 財産検査 inspection of property

zaisanmokuroku 財産目録 inventory; list of property

zaisansashiosae 財産差押え attachment of property

zaisanshotoku 財産所得 property income

zaisantekishūnyū 財産的収入 receipt for property

zaisei 財政 finance ¶ The government *finances* remain in a weak state. // restoration of health to public *finance* by reducing government bond issues // ［参考］to restore fiscal health

赤字財政 deficit finance

地方財政 local finance

健全財政 sound finance

均衡財政 balanced finance

国家財政 national finance

zaiseiakaji 財政赤字 budget deficit ¶ The Carter *budget deficit* for 1979 originally pegged at $60.6 billion came in significantly lower.

fiscal (=government) spending ¶ *Federal* Government *expenditure* in 1980 is estimated to decline to 9.9% of the expected gross national product.

zaiseishishutsunokurinobe 財政支出の繰延べ deferment (=postponement) of fiscal expenditure; carrying over budget(ary) expenditures (=outlays; spendings)

zaiseishūshi 財政収支 fiscal (=government; budgetary) revenue and expenditure ¶ *expenditure*-cutting and *revenue*-raising

zaiseitatenaoshi 財政建て直し financial reconstruction ¶ the *financial reconstruction* of local governments // how to *reconstruct* local *finances*

zaiseitokureihō 財政特例法 ［日］ bill authorizing the government to issue special deficit-financing bonds

zaiseitōyūshi 財政投融資 fiscal investment and loans ¶ ［参考］ Investments under the budget projections are to advance to DM 35 billion.

zaiseiyosan 財政予算 fiscal budget; government budget

zakka 雑貨 sundry goods; miscellaneous goods; general merchandise; general cargo

zakkoku 雑穀 minor cereals; minor grain

zandaka 残高 balance; remainder; outstanding amount ¶ the month-end *balance,* or the *amount outstanding* at month-end // a country bank with most deposit *balances* under $5,000 // The *balance outstanding* on loans from European Investment Bank's own resources, plus guarantees provided, rose by 22.8%. // to redress the adverse *bal-*

ance // an increase in the red (=deficit) *balance* // to add to the surplus (=favorable) *balance* // an unusually large increase in undisbursed *balances*

期首残高 initial balance
繰越残高 balance brought forward; balance carried forward
日々残高 daily balance
遊休残高 idle balance

zandakachō 残高帳 balance book

zandakahyō 残高表 balance sheet

zandakakanjō 残高勘定 balance account

zandakashōgō 残高照合 collation of balance ¶ to *collate* the *balance* with the ledger

zandakashōninsho 残高承認書 confirmation of balance

zangakuhikiuke 残額引受 ［証市］ stand-by commitment

zangyō 残業 overtime work

zangyōteate 残業手当 allowance for overtime work; overtime pay; overtime premium

zankaritsu 残価率 ratio of remaining value

zanpin 残品 unsold goods; remaining stock; dead stock

zanpinseiri 残品整理 clearing-off of remaining stock

zansonganpon 残存元本 outstanding principal (of investment trust funds)

zansonkachi 残存価値 residual value; salvage value

zansonkikan 残存期間 remaining life ¶ a bond with a *remaining life* of five years, or a bond with five years to run // securities with a *remaining life* of up to four years (=with four years to run)

zansonseigen 残存制限 remaining

restrictions; existing restrictions ¶ The *remaining restrictions* on current invisibles will be removed step by step.

zansonyunyūseigenhōshiki 残存輸入制限方式 residual import restriction formula

zansonzaisan 残存財産 residual asset; residue

zantei 暫定 provisional; preliminary

zanteieki 暫定益 provisional profit

zanteihyōka 暫定評価 provisional appraisal

zanteikeisū 暫定計数 preliminary figure; provisional figure ¶ *Provisional* seasonally adjusted *figures* issued by the Ministry show that the number of unemployed rose sharply to 204,100.

zanteikeiyaku 暫定契約 open contract

zanteimitsumori 暫定見積り provisional estimate

zanteishisan 暫定試算 tentative estimation

zanteitekitorikime 暫定的取決め stopgap arrangement

zanteiyosan 暫定予算 provisional budget

zan'yokachi 残余価値 residual value; scrap value

zan'yozaisan 残余財産 residual property; surplus assets ¶ evalution of *residual property*

zappi 雑費 sundry expenses; miscellaneous expenses; out-of-pocket expenses

zappin 雑品 miscellaneous articles; sundry goods

zaraba ザラ場 ［市］ continuous session

zasshuzei 雑種税 miscellaneous local taxes

zatsueki 雑益 miscellaneous incomes

zatsukabu 雑株 miscellaneous shares; minor stocks

zatsukanjō 雑勘定 sundry accounts; miscellaneous accounts; miscellaneous credits; miscellaneous credits and debits

zatsushūnyū 雑収入 miscellaneous receipts; sundry receipts; miscellaneous incomes

zatsuson'eki 雑損益 petty losses and profits

zatsutesūryō 雑手数料 miscellaneous charges and commissions

zeibiki 税引き after tax; net of tax ¶ *after-tax* prices, or prices *after tax*; net of tax // the profit *net of* income *taxes*

zeibikikyūyo 税引給与 take-home pay

zeibikinedan 税引値段 prices minus tax; prices less tax; after tax prices; prices after taxes

zeibikirieki 税引利益 after-tax profits; taxed profits; profit after tax payments

zeibikiriekikiritsu 税引利益率 after-tax profit rate

zeibikirimawari 税引利回り net yield

zeibikizenrieki 税引前利益 pretax profit

zeifutan 税負担 tax liability; tax burden; tax load ¶ to alleviate, or lighten, presently heavy Federal *tax burdens* // to reduce wealthy individuals' *tax load*

zeigaifutan 税外負担 non-tax burden

zeigaishūnyū 税外収入 non-tax receipt (=revenue)

zeigakukōjo 税額控除 tax credit; tax deduction ¶ to increase the *tax credit* that companies get on spending for new plant and equipment // a 10 percent job development (*tax*) *credit* for one year
外国税額控除 foreign tax credit
投資税額控除 investment tax credit
zeikan'okurijō 税関送状 customs invoice
zeikin 税(金) tax; duty (on goods); imposition; impost; charge; dues; rates ¶ to pay or collect *taxes* on earnings // to assess and impose, levy, or lay a heavy *tax (up)on goods* // to raise or reduce *taxes* // to impose *surcharges* upon certain imports // articles liable to (customs) *duty,* i.e., customable articles // to impose a 10 percent *surtax* on dutiable-goods imports // to broaden the base and bring *rates* down for *tax* simplification
分類所得税 classified income tax
物納税 tax in kind
物品税 commodity tax
物税 impersonal tax; real tax; tax on goods and properties
地方交付税 local allocation tax
地方贈与税 national tax revenue transferred to local treasuries
超過利得税 extra tax on corporate profit
付加価値税 value added tax; VAT
付加税 surtax; surcharge
富裕税 net worth tax
外国人入国税 alien tax
源泉課税 withholding tax
源泉所得税 income tax collected at the source; withholding income tax
逆進的所得税 regressive income tax

逆進税 regressive tax
逆所得税 negative income tax
ハイウェイ利用者税 highway-user tax
比例税 proportional tax
法人所得税 corporate income tax
法人税 corporation tax
移転税 transfer tax
人頭税 poll; poll tax; head tax; caption tax
住民税 local inhabitants tax
従価税 ad valorem tax; tax ad valorem
従量税 specific tax; per-unit tax
家屋税 tax on house
間接税 indirect tax
加算税 tax for default
経費税 outlay tax
個人所得税 individual income tax
(個)人税 personal tax
興業税 entertainment tax
国境税 border tax
国内消費税 excise (tax)
雇用税 employment tax
鉱山税 tax on mine
空閑地税 vacant land tax
給与税 payroll tax
目的税 special purpose tax; objective tax
入場税 amusement tax
利子平衡税 interest equalization tax
利子税 interest tax
利潤税 profit tax
累進税 progressive tax
流通税 tax on transaction
再評価税 tax on revaluation
選択雇用税 selective employment tax
戦時利得税 war (time) profit tax
奢侈抑止税 sumptuary tax
奢侈税 tax on luxury
社会保障税 social security tax

消費税　consumption tax
収入税　revenue tax
総合所得税　consolidated income tax
相続税　accession tax
単一税　single tax
定率税　rated tax
取引高税　sales tax
取引税　turnover tax; tax on transaction
登録税　registration tax
都市計画税　city planning tax
通行税　passenger tax
売上税　sales tax
有価証券取引税　securities transaction tax
遊興税　amusement tax; entertainment tax
財産税　property tax

zeikinchōshū 税金徴収 collection of tax

zeikinhinanchi 税金避難地 tax-haven ¶ →租税避難地

zeikinjōkō 税金条項 tax clause

zeikinnoansokuchi 税金の安息地 →租税避難地

zeikinnōfu 税金納付 payment of tax; tax payment

zeikomi 税込み including tax; pretax; before tax ¶ to chalk up $100 million in *pre-tax* recurring deficits

zeikomikakaku 税込価格 price including tax

zeinokangen 税の還元 amortization of taxes; tax rebate

zeinokeigen 税の軽減 tax relief ¶ to rule out elimination of *tax relief* on interest on home mortgage loans

zeinokokuminshotokudanseichi 税の国民所得弾性値 elasticity of tax to national income

zeinoshizengenshū 税の自然減収 natural decrease in tax revenue

zeinoshizenzōshū 税の自然増収 natural increase in tax revenue; unearned increase (in tax revenues)

zeinoshōten 税の消転 transformation of tax

zeinotenka 税の転嫁 shifting and incidence of tax

zeinoyūgūsochi 税の優遇措置 preferential tax measure

zeiritsu 税率 tax rate ¶ [参考] Japan's tax bite is low by industrialized-world standards.

zeiritsuhyō 税率表 tax table

zeisei 税制 taxation system; tax structure; tax system ¶ to raise additional taxes by reforming the *tax structure*

zeiseijōnoyūgūsochi 税制上の優遇措置 tax incentive; tax preference; tax benefit; tariff preference ¶ *tax incentives* on inputs and on profits // *tax preferences* to foreign partners in joint ventures // to use *tax incentives* for capital spending // to reduce special *tax benefits* // to negotiate a pioneering exchange of *tariff preferences*

zeiseikaikaku 税制改革 tax reform

zeiseiseiri 税制整理 readjustment of the taxation system

zeishū 税収 tax revenue

zeitakuhin 贅沢品 luxuries; luxurious articles; luxurious goods

zenba 前場 [市] morning session; morning market; first call

zenesuto ゼネスト general strike

zengaku 全額 total amount; total sum; total; grand total

zengakuharaikomi 全額払込み fully paid-up

zengakuhoken 全額保険 full insurance

zengakujunbiseido 全額準備制度 simple reserve system; total reserve system

zengakuryōshūsho 全額領収書 receipt in full

zengakushiharai 全額支払 full payment

zengakushusshi 全額出資 wholly owned ¶ its *wholly-owned* foreign subsidiaries

zengakushusshigaishikogaisha 全額出資外資子会社 100 percent self-financed foreign company

zengetsunami 前月並み on the same level with the previous month; no change over the month

zen'inodaisansha 善意の第三者 third parties in good faith; bona fide third parties

zen'inomushi 善意の無視 benign neglect; kindly negligence ¶ policy of *benign neglect*

zen'inoshojinin 善意の所持人 bona fide holder

zenjunkan 善循環 virtuous circle ¶ Japan is the outstanding example of the *virtuous circle* of rapid growth, high investment, considerable productivity gains and stable or falling industrial costs.

zenki 前期 previous term; preceding period; first half (of the year); first half-year

zenkikurikoshikessonkin 前期繰越欠損金 deficit at the beginning of the period

zenkikurikoshikin 前期繰越金 balance brought over from the last account

zenkikurikoshiriekikin 前期繰越利益金 surplus at the beginning of the period

zenkison'ekikin 前期損益金 profit

or loss brought forward from previous business term

zenkokuginkōdētatsūshinshisutemu 全国銀行データ通信システム all-bank data telecommunication system

zenkokuginkōjisshitsuyokinzandaka 全国銀行実質預金残高 deposits outstanding deducted by checks and bills in process of collection

zenkokuginkōkashidashiyakujō-heikinkinri 全国銀行貸出約定平均金利 average interest rates on loans and discounts of all banks

zenkokuginkōkashidashizandaka 全国銀行貸出残高 outstanding lendings of all banks

zenkokuginkōtaikai 全国銀行大会 national convention of bankers

zenkokuginkōyokinzandaka 全国銀行預金残高 deposits outstanding of all banks

zenmenfukyō 全面不況 full-blown depression; full-fledged depression

zenmenkanwa 全面緩和 overall relaxation

zenmenshūchūsei 全面集中制 ［外］ foreign exchange concentration system

zenmenyasu 全面安 fall across the board

zennendo 前年度 preceding fiscal year; previous financial year

zennendojōyokin'ukeire 前年度剰余金受入 surplus in preceding fiscal year

zennendōkihi 前年同期比 as compared with the corresponding period of the previous year; over the same period of the preceding year; compared with the same month a year ago; over the year-ago month; over the year ¶ Production in June rose 20 percent *over the year*. // Output increased by 20 percent *on the year-ago figure*. // Shipments declined by 5 percent from that *in the same month a year before*.

zennenhi 前年比 against the previous year; in a year-to-year (=year-on-year) comparison; over a year ago; over the year; yearly change; change from a year ago ¶ Prices increased by 2.0 percent *over a year earlier*. // The *yearly change* in output was up 15 percent.

zennijūtsūshin 全二重通信 ［コン］ full duplex

zenraku 漸落 easing off; edging downward; gradual sagging; gradual decline; slight setback; receding

zenshinshugi 漸進主義 gradualism ¶ *Gradualism* is the only feasible course.

zenson 全損 total loss

zensūchōsa 全数調査 complete enumeration

zenteijōken 前提条件 precondition; prerequisite; premise; assumption ¶ the essential *precondition* for effective monetary policy // an essential *prerequisite* to a successful working of the system // conclusion on false *premises* // on the *assumption* that... // *Assuming* that..., ...

zentō 漸騰 gradual rise

zentokin 前渡金 advanced funds

zentoshishōhishabukkashisū 全都市消費者物価指数 consumer price index for all cities

zenzō 漸増 gradual increase; gradual expansion ¶ The *gradual increase* in output will continue into the next month. // The note circulation *expanded gradually*.

zeroseichō ゼロ成長 zero economic growth; ZEG; no growth; zero growth; nil growth ¶ The economy is experiencing *no growth*. // Britain's wide monetary base aggregate showed little or *no growth* in the banking month to April 18. // The government applied "*zero growth*" or "lower-than-earlier" limitations on budgetary requests.

zetchō 絶頂 culmination ¶ The ten-year stretch of inflation *culminated* in the deep recession. // *culminating* period of the cyclical rise dating from mid-1955

zettaichi 絶対値 absolute value

zettaichidai 絶対地代 absolute ground-rent

zettaijōshōgendo 絶対上昇限度 absolute ceiling

zettaikakaku 絶対価格 absolute price

zettaishotokukasetsu 絶対所得仮説 absolute income hypothesis

zettaitekihinkon 絶対的貧困 absolute poverty ¶ to reduce the prevalence of *absolute poverty* // all aspects of *absolute poverty*, malnutrition, ill health, and illiteracy, as well as low incomes

zettaitekikoteihi 絶対的固定費 absolute fixed cost

zettaitekikoteishihon 絶対的固定資本 absolute fixed capital

zettaitekiseisanhisa 絶対的生産費差 difference of absolute costs

zōchi 造地 land reclamation

zōdai 増大 expansion; increase; growth; gain; bulge; increment; augmentation; magnification; prolification ¶ The pace of sales *expansion* slowed down. // *Expansion* in output stopped. // Production tended to *expand*. // The *increase* in sales came to a halt. // a sharp *increase* in prices by 4 pecent over the previous month // Production made widespread and good *gains.* // The *incremental* capital output ratio averaged 3.0 for 1980-83. // Exports *gained* or held firm. // Above average *growth* may occur in shipments. // The *growth* of investment accelerated. // The evergoing surplus *augmented* by seasonal factors. // These indications *magnified.* // the price *bulge* after the oil crisis // intensification of restrictions through a *proliferation* of bilateral arrangements

zōgenritsu 増減率 percentage change ¶ monthly *percentage change* in production // *percentage change* in output over the year

zōhai 増配 increased ration; increased dividend

zōhatsu 増発 increased issue; additional issue ¶ The bank note *issue* showed an *increase* of ¥10 billion, or bank notes in circulation increased by ¥10 billion.

zōhei 造幣 coinage; mintage

zōheihika 造幣比価 mint par of exchange

zōheikōken 造幣高権 coinage prerogative

zōheikyoku 造幣局 mint

zōheirisa 造幣利差 seigniorage

zōheiryō 造幣料 mintage; brassage

zōka 増加 increase; increment; gain; expansion; addition ¶ This brought a substantial *addition* to the budgetary expenditure. // →増大

自然増加 natural increment; natural increase

zōka 増価 appreciation; increase in value

機械増価 machinery appreciation
建物増価 building appreciation
土地増価 land appreciation

zokaritsu 増加率 increasing rate; rate of increase; rate of growth; growth rate; percentage increase ¶ The *growth* of exports reversed from a negative 0.8 percent to a positive 17 *percent* annually.

zōkashihon 増加資本 additional capital

zōkauntenjushi 増加運転需資 additional operating funds

zōkazaigen 増加財源 revenue expected to be added; increase in revenue

zokuraku 続落 further decline; continued fall; continuous drop; another setback

zokurakuhochō 続落歩調 edging down(ward)

zokushin 続伸 continuous rise; continued advance; incessant rise; continued rise; persistent advance; uninterrupted rise; spiraling escalator hiking; further rise; another increase

zokutō 続騰 →続伸

zōsaku 造作 fittings

zōsei 増勢 increasing trend; growing trend; upward trend; uptrend

zōseidonkakiyoritsu 増勢鈍化寄与率 percentage contribution to the slowdown of the uptrend

zōsendaikin 造船代金 ［外］ sales proceeds of exported ships

zōsetsu 増設 extension; enlargement; addition

zōsetsukanjō 増設勘定 construction in process

zōsetsutsumitatekin 増設積立金 reserve for additions

zōshi 増資 capital increase

額面払込方式の増資 capital increase in the form of paid-in capital increase through par value allocation

過大増資 stock watering; capital watering; capital padding

zōshian 増資案 capital increase plan

zōshiharaikomikin 増資払込金 subscription to the increased capital

zōshikabu 増資株 newly issued share; new issue

zōshikawarikin 増資代り金 proceeds of the capital increase

zōshikenritsukikabushiki 増資権利付株式 stocks cum rights

zōshikijun 増資基準 standards for capital increase

zōshū 増収 increased income; increased revenue; increased earnings; increased yield; increased receipts

zōshūzōeki 増収増益 increase both in sales and profits

zōsuisangyō 造水産業 water re-use industry

zōyo 贈与 donation; presentation

zōyobutsu 贈与物 gift; present

zōyojōyokin 贈与剰余金 surplus from donation

zōyokabushiki 贈与株式 donated stock

zōyosha 贈与者 donator; donor; giver

zōyozaisan 贈与財産 donated property

zōyozei 贈与税 donation tax

zōzei 増税 increased tax; tax increase

zuijishōkan 随時償還 optional redemption

zurekomijuyō ずれ込み需要 demand carried forward; demand carry-over; postponed demand

zutsukae 頭閊え ［市］ top-heavy; toppy

付　　　　　録

1. 財政・金融関係法律名

Laws concerning Financial Affairs

(1) 財政関係

財　　政　　法	Finance Law
会　　計　　法	Accounts Law
国　税　通　則　法	National Tax Collection Law
所　　得　　税　　法	Income Tax Law
法　　人　　税　　法	Corporation Tax Law
租　税　特　別　措　置　法	Special Taxation Measures Law
食　糧　管　理　法	Foodstuff Control Law
地　方　財　政　法	Local Finance Law
地　方　交　付　税　法	Local Allocation Tax Law
国　債　に　関　す　る　法　律	Law Concerning Government Bonds
国債整理基金特別会計法	Law Concerning Special Account of Government Bonds Consolidation Fund
外貨公債の発行に関する法律	Law Concerning Issuance of Foreign Currency Bonds
外　貨　債　処　理　法	Law Relating to the Treatment of the Foreign Currency Bonds
旧外貨債処理法による借換済外貨債の証券の一部の有効化等に関する法律	Law Concerning Revalidation of Certain Categories of Certificates of Foreign Currency Bonds Converted under the Old Law Relating to the Treatment of the Foreign Currency Bonds and Other Incidental Matters

(2) 通貨・金融関係

貨　　幣　　法	Coins Law
臨　時　通　貨　法	Temporary Currency Law
通貨及び証券模造取締法	Law Concerning the Regulation of Counterfeit Currency and Securities
紙幣類似証券取締法	Law Concerning the Regulation of Securities Resembling Paper Currency

すき入紙製造取締法	Law Concerning the Regulation of Manufacturing Watermarked Paper
補助貨幣損傷等取締法	Law Concerning the Regulation of Damaging, etc. of Subsidiary Coins
日 本 銀 行 法	Bank of Japan Law
準備預金制度に関する法律	Law Concerning Reserve Deposit Requirement System
銀 行 法	Banking Law
銀 行 法 等 特 例 法	Law Concerning Exceptions to Banking Law, etc.
日 本 開 発 銀 行 法	Japan Development Bank Law
日 本 輸 出 入 銀 行 法	Export-Import Bank of Japan Law
信 託 業 法	Trust Business Law
長 期 信 用 銀 行 法	Long-Term Credit Bank Law
外 国 為 替 銀 行 法	Foreign Exchange Bank Law
相 互 銀 行 法	Mutual Loan and Savings Bank Law
貯 蓄 銀 行 法	Savings Bank Law
信 用 金 庫 法	Credit Association Law
労 働 金 庫 法	Labor Credit Association Law
保 険 業 法	Insurance Business Law
国 民 金 融 公 庫 法	People's Finance Corporation Law
農 業 協 同 組 合 法	Agricultural Cooperatives Law
水 産 業 協 同 組 合 法	Fisheries Cooperatives Law
中小企業等協同組合法	Law for Cooperatives of Small Business, etc.
証 券 投 資 信 託 法	Securities Investment Trust Law
貸 付 信 託 法	Loan Trust Law
担 保 付 社 債 信 託 法	Mortgage Debentures Trust Law
中 小 企 業 信 用 保 険 法	Small Business Credit Insurance Law
住 宅 融 資 保 険 法	Housing Finance Insurance Law
信 用 保 証 協 会 法	Credit Guarantee Association Law
公 益 質 屋 法	Public Pawn-Shop Law
無 尽 業 法	Mutual Loan Business Law
割 賦 販 売 法	Installment Sale Law
証 券 取 引 法	Securities and Exchange Law
社 債 等 登 録 法	Law for Registration of Corporate Debentures, etc.
抵 当 証 券 法	Mortgage Certificate Law

利 息 制 限 法	Law Concerning the Restriction of Interest
臨 時 金 利 調 整 法	Temporary Money Rates Adjustment Law
出資の受入，預り金及び金利等の取締等に関する法律	Law Concerning the Regulation of Receiving of Capital Subscription, Deposits and Interest on Deposits
預金等に係る不当契約の取締に関する法律	Law Concerning Control of Unjust Contracts Relative to Deposits, etc.
普通銀行等の貯蓄銀行業務又は信託業務の兼営等に関する法律	Law Concerning Concurrent Operation, etc. of Savings Bank Business or Trust Business by Ordinary Bank, etc.
金融機関の合併及び転換に関する法律	Law Concerning Amalgamation and Conversion of Financial Institution

(3) その他

手 形 法	Law on Bills
小 切 手 法	Law on Checks
労 働 基 準 法	Labor Standard Law
労 働 組 合 法	Trade Union Law
労 働 関 係 調 整 法	Labor Relations Adjustment Law
農 業 基 本 法	Law for Orientation of Agriculture
農 産 物 価 格 安 定 法	Farm Products Price Stabilization Law
農 地 法	Agricultural Land Law
農 業 災 害 補 償 法	Agricultural Disaster Indemnity Law
特 許 法	Patent Law
実 用 新 案 法	Utility Model Law
意 匠 法	Design Law
商 標 法	Trade Mark Law
私的独占の禁止及び公正取引の確保に関する法律（独禁法）	Law Concerning Prohibition of Private Monopoly and Security of Fair Trading (Anti-Trust Law)
会 社 更 生 法	Corporation Reorganization Law
企 業 合 理 化 促 進 法	Law for Acceleration of Rationalization of Enterprises
中小企業団体の組織に関する法律	Smaller Industries Organization Law
中 小 企 業 基 本 法	Medium and Small Enterprise Modernization Promotion Law
国 民 年 金 法	National Pension Law

国 民 健 康 保 険 法	National Health Insurance Law
消 費 者 保 護 基 本 法	Consumers Protection Basic Law
生 活 保 護 法	Daily Life Security Law
倉 庫 業 法	Warehousing Business Law
商 品 取 引 所 法	Commodity Exchange Law
勤 労 者 財 産 形 成 促 進 法	Law Concerning the Promotion of Workers' Property Ownership
外国為替並に外国貿易管理法	Foreign Exchange and Foreign Trade Control Law
外 資 に 関 す る 法 律	Law Concerning Foreign Investment
輸 出 入 取 引 法	Export and Import Trading Law
輸 出 保 険 法	Export Insurance Law
地 方 自 治 法	Local Autonomy Law
統 計 法	Statistics Law

2. 現行金融組織

Present Financial Organization

(1) 日 本 銀 行
政 策 委 員 会 室	Secretariat of the Policy Board
秘 書 室	Secretary's Office
総 務 局	Coordination and Planning Department
業 務 管 理 局	Management and Budget Control Department
人 事 局	Personnel Department
検 査 局	Inspection Department
発 券 局	Cash Department
営 業 局	Banking Department
外 国 局	Foreign Department
国 庫 局	Government Depositary Department
総 務 課	Coordination Division
代 理 店 課	Agency Supervision Division
業 務 課	Business Division
計 理 課	Accounting Division
国 債 局	Government Bond Department
証 券 局	Securities Department
考 査 局	Bank Relations and Supervision Department
調 査 統 計 局	Research and Statistics Department
文 書 局	Administration Department
管 財 局	Real Property Department
電 算 情 報 局	Computer and Data Processing Department

(2) 民 間 金 融 機 関
商 業 銀 行	commercial banks
都 市 銀 行	city banks
地 方 銀 行	regional banks
外 国 銀 行	foreign banks
外 国 為 替 金 融 機 関	financial institutions for foreign exchange
外 国 為 替 専 門 銀 行	specialized foreign exchange bank

外 国 為 替 公 認 銀 行	authorized foreign exchange banks
長 期 金 融 機 関	financial institutions for long-term credit
長 期 信 用 銀 行	long-term credit banks
信 託 銀 行	trust banks
中 小 企 業 金 融 機 関	financial institutions for small business
相 互 銀 行	mutual loan and savings banks
全 国 信 用 金 庫 連 合 会	National Federation of Credit Associations
信 用 金 庫	credit associations
全国信用協同組合連合会	National Federation of Credit Cooperatives
信 用 協 同 組 合	credit cooperatives
労 働 金 庫 連 合 会	National Federation of Labor Credit Associations
労 働 金 庫	labor credit associations
商 工 組 合 中 央 金 庫	Central Bank for Commercial and Industrial Cooperatives
農 林 水 産 金 融 機 関	financial institutions for agriculture, forestry and fisheries
農 林 中 央 金 庫	Norin Chukin Bank
信用農業協同組合連合会	credit federations of agricultural cooperatives
農 業 協 同 組 合	agricultural cooperatives
信用漁業協同組合連合会	credit federations of fishery cooperatives
漁 業 協 同 組 合	fishery cooperatives
森 林 組 合 連 合 会	federations of forestry cooperatives
森 林 組 合	forestry cooperatives
全国共済農業協同組合連合会	National Mutual Insurance Federation of Agricultural Cooperatives
共済農業協同組合連合会	mutual insurance federations of agricultural cooperatives
保 険 会 社	insurance companies
生 命 保 険 会 社	life insurance companies
損 害 保 険 会 社	non-life insurance companies
短 資 会 社	short-term credit dealers (=call money brokers)
証 券 金 融 機 関	securities finance institutions
証 券 金 融 会 社	securities finance corporations

抵 当 証 券 会 社	mortgage companies
証 券 会 社	securities companies

(3) 政府金融機関

日 本 輸 出 入 銀 行	Export-Import Bank of Japan
日 本 開 発 銀 行	Japan Development Bank
国 民 金 融 公 庫	People's Finance Corporation
庶 民 金 庫	Peoples' Bank
恩 給 金 庫	Pension Bank
復 興 金 融 金 庫	Reconversion Bank
中 小 企 業 金 融 公 庫	Small Business Finance Corporation
中 小 企 業 信 用 保 険 公 庫	Small Business Credit Insurance Corporation
医 療 金 融 公 庫	Medical Care Facilities Finance Corporation
環 境 衛 生 金 融 公 庫	Environmental Sanitation Business Finance Corporation
農 林 漁 業 金 融 公 庫	Agriculture, Forestry and Fisheries Finance Corporation
住 宅 金 融 公 庫	Housing Loan Corporation
北 海 道 東 北 開 発 公 庫	Hokkaido and Tohoku Development Corporation
沖 縄 振 興 開 発 金 融 公 庫	Okinawa Development Finance Corporation
公 営 企 業 金 融 公 庫	Finance Corporation of Local Public Enterprise
預 金 保 険 機 構	Deposit Insurance Corporation
農水産業協同組合貯金保険機構	Savings Insurance Corporation for Agricultural and Fishery Cooperatives
海 外 経 済 協 力 基 金	Overseas Economic Cooperation Fund
郵 便 局	Post office
資 金 運 用 部	Trust Fund Bureau
簡易保険・郵便年金資金	Assets of Postal Life Insurance

3. 資金循環勘定項目

Flow of Funds Accounts

通貨	Currency & Demand Deposits
現金通貨	Currency
当座性預金	Current Deposits
短期性預金	Short-term Deposits
政府当座預金	Government Current Deposits
定期性預金	Time Deposits
外貨預金	Foreign Currency Deposits
信託	Trust
保険	Insurance
有価証券	Securities
政府短期証券	Short-Term Govenment Securities
長期国債	Government Bonds
その他債券	Other Bonds
株式	Stocks
投資信託受益証券	Securities Investment Trust
外貨債	Bonds in Foreign Currency
中央銀行貸出金・借入金	Central Bank Loans
コール	Call Money
買入手形・売渡手形	Bills Bought & Sold
貸出金・借入金	Loans
市中貸出金・借入金	Loans by Private Financial Institutions
政府貸出金・借入金	Loans by Government
証券会社貸付金	Loans by Securities Companies
企業間信用	Trade Credit
出資金	Equities other than Stocks
外貨準備高	Gold & Foreign Exchange Reserves
短期貿易信用	Short-Term Foreign Trade Credits
長期貿易信用	Long-Term Foreign Trade Credits
直接投資	Foreign Direct Investment
その他対外債権債務	Other Foreign Claims & Debts
その他	Others
金過不足(一)	Financial Surplus or Deficit (一)

4. 政府会計名・国庫計算科目・租税名

Titles and Items of Budget, Treasury Accounts, and Taxes

(1) 一般会計予算主要科目

一 般 会 計	General Account
歳 入	Revenue
租税および印紙収入	Tax and Stamp Receipts
専 売 納 付 金	Monopoly Profits
官業益金および官業収入	Receipts from Government Enterprises and Properties
政 府 資 産 整 理 収 入	Receipts from the Disposal of Government Properties
雑 収 入	Miscellaneous Receipts
公 債 金	Public Bonds
前年度剰余金受入	Carried-over Surplus
歳 出	Expenditure
社 会 保 障 関 係 費	Social Security Expenses
生 活 保 護 費	Public Assistance Expenses
社 会 福 祉 費	Social Welfare Expenses
社 会 保 険 費	Social Insurance Expenses
保 健 衛 生 対 策 費	Expenses for Public Health Service
失 業 対 策 費	Expenses for Measures for the Unemployed
文教および科学振興費	Expenses for Education and Science
義務教育国庫負担金	National Government's Share of Compulsory Education Expenses
国立学校特別会計へ繰入	Transfer to the National Schools Special Account
科 学 技 術 振 興 費	Expenses for Promotion of Science and Technology
文 教 施 設 費	Expenses for Public School Facilities
教 育 振 興 助 成 費	Expenses for School Education Assist*
育 英 事 業 費	Expenses for Scholarships on Loan ⌐ Students
国 債 費	National Debt Expenses

恩 給 関 係 費	Pensions and Other Expenses
文 官 等 恩 給 費	Pensions for Civil Servants
旧 軍 人 遺 族 等 恩 給 費	Pensions for Veterans and War-bereaved Families of Soldiers
恩 給 支 給 事 務 費	Administrative Expenses for Pension Payments
遺族および留守家族等援護費	Expenses for Aid to War-bereaved Families and Families of the Unrepatriated
地 方 交 付 税 交 付 金	Distribution of Local Allocation Tax
臨 時 地 方 交 付 税 交 付 金	Temporary Local Special Grants
防 衛 関 係 費	National Defense Expenses
防 衛 庁 費	Expenses for Defense Agency
防 衛 施 設 庁 費	Expenses for Defense Facilities Administration Agency
国 防 会 議 費	Expenses for National Defense Agency
公 共 事 業 関 係 費	Public Works Expenses
治 山 治 水 対 策 事 業 費	Expenses for Erosion and Flood Control
道 路 整 備 事 業 費	Expenses for Road Improvement
港湾漁港空港整備事業費	Expenses for Improvement of Harbors, Fishing Ports and Airports
住 宅 対 策 費	Housing Expenses
生 活 環 境 施 設 整 備 費	Expenses for Public Service Facilities
農 業 基 盤 整 備 費	Expenses for Improvement of Conditions for Agricultural Production
林 道 工 業 用 水 等 事 業 費	Expenses for Forest, Roads and Water for Industrial Use
調 整 費	Adjustment Works Expenses
災 害 復 旧 等 事 業 費	Disaster Reconstruction Expenses
貿 易 振 興 および 経 済 協 力 費	Expenses for Promotion of Foreign Trade and Economic Cooperation
海 運 対 策 費	Measures for Shipping Expenses
中 小 企 業 対 策 費	Measures for Small Business Expenses
業 保 険 費	Agricultural Insurance Expenses
糧 管 理 費	Expenses for Foodstuff Control
管理特別会計へ繰入	Transfer to the Foodstuff Control Special Account
特別会計へ繰入	Transfer to the Industrial Investment Special Account

609

予　　備　　費	Miscellaneous Expenses

(2) **特別会計名**

事 業 特 別 会 計	Special Accounts for Government Enterprises
造 幣 局 特 別 会 計	Mint Bureau Special Account
印 刷 局 特 別 会 計	Printing Bureau Special Account
国 有 林 野 事 業 特 別 会 計	National Forest Service Special Account
特定土地改良工事特別会計	Specific Land Improvement Special Account
アルコール専売事業特別会計	Alcohol Monopoly Special Account
港 湾 整 備 特 別 会 計	Harbor Improvement Special Account
空 港 整 備 特 別 会 計	Airport Improvement Special Account
郵 政 事 業 特 別 会 計	Postal Services Special Account
郵 便 貯 金 特 別 会 計	Postal Savings Special Account
道 路 整 備 特 別 会 計	Road Improvement Special Account
治 水 特 別 会 計	Flood Control Special Account
保 険 特 別 会 計	Special Account for Insurance
地 震 再 保 険 特 別 会 計	Earthquake Reinsurance Special Account
厚 生 保 険 特 別 会 計	Welfare Insurance Special Account
船 員 保 険 特 別 会 計	Seamen's Insurance Special Account
国 民 年 金 特 別 会 計	National Pensions Special Account
農業共済再保険特別会計	Special Account for Agricultural Mutual Aid Reinsurance
森 林 保 険 特 別 会 計	Forest Insurance Special Account
漁船再保険および漁業共済保険特別会計	Special Account for Fishing Boat Reinsurance and Fishery Mutual Aid Reinsurance
中小漁業融資保証保険特別会計	Special Account for Reinsurance of Loans to Fisheries
輸 出 保 険 特 別 会 計	Export Insurance Special Account
機械類信用保険特別会計	Special Account for Machinery Installment Credit Insurance
木 船 再 保 険 特 別 会 計	Wooden Boat Reinsurance Special Accou
自動車損害賠償責任再保険特別会計	Special Account for Reinsurance of C pensation for Motor-car Accidents
簡易生命保険および郵便年金特別会計	Special Account for Post-Office Lif ance and Postal Annuity

労働者災害補償保険特別会計	Special Account for Laborer's Accident Insurance
失 業 保 険 特 別 会 計	Unemployment Insurance Special Account
管 理 特 別 会 計	Special Account of Management
貴 金 属 特 別 会 計	Precious Metals Special Account
外 国 為 替 資 金 特 別 会 計	Foreign Exchange Fund Special Account
国 立 学 校 特 別 会 計	National Schools Special Account
国 立 病 院 特 別 会 計	National Hospitals Special Account
あ へ ん 特 別 会 計	Opium Special Account
食 糧 管 理 特 別 会 計	Foodstuff Control Special Account
自作農創設特別措置特別会計	Special Account for Special Measures for Establishment of Landed Farms
自動車検査登録特別会計	Special Account for Motor-car Inspection and Registration
融 資 特 別 会 計	Special Account for Public Investment and Loans
資 金 運 用 部 特 別 会 計	Trust Fund Bureau Special Account
産 業 投 資 特 別 会 計	Industrial Investment Special Account
開 拓 者 資 金 融 通 特 別 会 計	Finance for Settlers Special Account
都市開発資金融通特別会計	Finance for Urban Development Special Account
整 理 特 別 会 計	Special Account to Consolidate Funds
国 債 整 理 基 金 特 別 会 計	National Debt Consolidation Fund Special Account
賠償等特殊債務処理特別会計	Special Account for Reparations and Special Obligations
特定国有財産整備特別会計	Special Account for National Property Special Consolidation Fund
交付税および譲与税配付金特別会計	Special Account for Allotment of Local Allocation Tax and Transferred Tax
石 炭 対 策 特 別 会 計	Coal Mining Industry Special Account

その他の国庫計算科目

税 収 納 金 整 理 資 金	National Tax Receipts Adjustment Fund
支 払 未 済 繰 越 金	Deferred Government Expenditure Brought Forward

国税資金支払未済繰越金	Deferred National Tax Refundments Brought Forward
預　　　託　　　金	Deposits of Accounting Officers
保　　　管　　　金	Money in Custody of Treasury
供　　　託　　　金	Deposited Money
特　別　調　達　資　金	Special Procurement Fund
在外公館等借入金返済資金	Fund for Repayment of Borrowings of Government Overseas Offices
経 済 基 盤 強 化 資 金	Fund for Strengthening the Foundation of the Economy
外 国 為 替 運 営 資 金	Fund for Operation of Foreign Exchange
補 助 貨 幣 回 収 準 備 資 金	Reserve Fund for Subsidiary Coins
資 金 運 用 部 資 金	Trust Fund Bureau Fund
産 業 投 資 資 金	Fund for Industrial Investment
公 債 利 子 支 払 資 金	Fund for Payment of Interest on Government Securities
借入金および一時借入金利子支払資金	Fund for Payment of Interest on Borrowings and Temporary Borrowings
外 債 元 利 払 資 金	Fund for Payment of Principal and Interest of External Bonded Debts
国 債 運 用 資 金	Fund for Operation of Government Securities
貴 金 属 買 入 資 金	Fund for Purchase of Precious Metals
主要食糧買入代金支払資金	Fund for Purchase of Staple Foodstuffs
国有林野事業特別積立金引当資金	Fund for National Forestry Service Special Reserves
農 業 近 代 化 助 成 資 金	Fund for Promotion of Farming Modernization
国 庫 内 為 替	Intra-Treasury Remittance
郵 便 局 受 払 金	Post-Office Account
国 庫 余 裕 金 繰 替	Treasury Surplus Temporarily Transferred
特 別 会 計 補 足 繰 入	Transfer to Special Accounts
国 庫 金 未 整 理	Treasury Suspense Account
小 額 紙 幣 発 行 高	Government Fractional Notes Issued
戦 時 未 整 理	War-Time Accounts Unsettled
各 店 間 未 整 理	Inter-Office Accounts Unsettled
公 債 発 行 収 入 金	Proceeds of Government Securities Issued

借　　　　　入　　　　　金	Borrowings
大 蔵 省 証 券 発 行 高	Treasury Bills Issued
食 糧 証 券 発 行 高	Food Bills Issued
融 通 証 券 発 行 高	Accommodation Bills Issued
一 時 借 入 金	Temporary Borrowings
公 債 償 還 資 金	Fund for Redemption of Government Securities
借 入 金 償 還 資 金	Fund for Repayment of Borrowings
大 蔵 省 証 券 償 還 資 金	Fund for Redemption of Treasury Bills
食 糧 証 券 償 還 資 金	Fund for Redemption of Food Bills
融 通 証 券 償 還 資 金	Fund for Redemption of Accommodation Bills
一 時 借 入 金 償 還 資 金	Fund for Repayment of Temporary Borrowings
基金通貨代用証券発行収入金	Proceeds of International Monetary Fund Securities
基金通貨代用証券償還資金	Fund for Redemption of International Monetary Fund Securities

(4) 租　税　名

国　　　　　　　　　税	National Tax
所　　　得　　　税	Income Tax
源 泉 所 得 税	Income Tax Withheld at Source
申 告 所 得 税	Income Tax Paid by Self-Assessment
法　　　人　　　税	Corporation Tax
相　　　続　　　税	Inheritance Tax
贈　　　与　　　税	Gift Tax
酒　　　　　　　　税	Liquor Tax
砂 糖 消 費 税	Sugar Excise Tax
揮　発　油　税	Gasoline Tax
石 油 ガ ス 税	Liquefied Petroleum Gas Tax
物　　　品　　　税	Commodity Tax
ト ラ ン プ 類 税	Playing Cards Tax
取　引　所　税	Bourse Tax
有 価 証 券 取 引 税	Securities Transaction Tax
通　　　行　　　税	Travel Tax
関　　　　　　　　税	Customs Duty
と　　　ん　　　税	Tonnage Duty

自 動 車 重 量 税	Automobile Weight Tax
印 紙 収 入	Stamp Revenue
日 本 銀 行 券 発 行 税	Bank of Japan Note Issue Tax
入 場 税	Admission Tax
地 方 道 路 税	Local Road Tax
特 別 と ん 税	Special Tonnage Duty
原 重 油 関 税	Crude Petroleum Customs Duty
地 方 税	Local Tax
道 府 県 税	Prefectural Tax
道 府 県 民 税	Prefectural Inhabitants Tax
事 業 税	Enterprise Tax
不 動 産 取 得 税	Real Property Acquisition Tax
道府県たばこ消費税	Prefectural Tobacco Consumption Tax
娯 楽 施 設 利 用 税	Local Entertainment Tax
料 理 飲 食 等 消 費 税	Eating, Drinking and Lodging Tax
自 動 車 税	Automobile Tax
鉱 区 税	Mine-Lot Tax
狩 猟 免 許 税	Hunters License Tax
固 定 資 産 税	Prefectural Fixed Assets Tax
軽 油 引 取 税	Light-Oil Delivery Tax
入 猟 税	Hunting Tax
自 動 車 取 得 税	Automobile Acquisition Tax
市 町 村 税	Municipal Tax
市 町 村 民 税	Municipal Inhabitants Tax
固 定 資 産 税	Municipal Fixed Assets Tax
軽 自 動 車 税	Light Vehicle Tax
市町村たばこ消費税	Municipal Tobacco Consumption Tax
電 気 ガ ス 税	Electricity and Gas Tax
鉱 産 税	Mineral Product Tax
木 材 引 取 税	Timber Delivery Tax
入 湯 税	Bathing Tax
都 市 計 画 税	City Planning Tax
水 利 地 益 税	Water and Land Utilization Tax
共 同 施 設 税	Common Facilities Tax
宅 地 開 発 税	Residential Land Formation Tax
国 民 健 康 保 険 税	National Health Insurance Tax

5. 資産負債表・損益計算書項目例

Items of Typical Financial Statement and Statement of Profit and Loss

(1) 資産負債表 — (1) FINANCIAL STATEMENT

資 産 — ASSETS

現金	Cash
手元現金，当座性預金	On hand, and unrestricted in banks
受取手形	Notes Receivable, Not Discounted
子会社等以外の取引先からの受取手形で未割引のもの	From customers, except subsidiaries, etc.
割引手形	Notes Receivable, Discounted
銀行，金融会社等で割引いた受取手形	With banks, finance companies, etc.
売掛金	Accounts Receivable (Current & Collectable)
子会社等以外の取引先からの売掛金	From customers, except subsidiaries, etc.
子会社および関連会社との一般商品取引勘定	Due From Subsidiaries & Affiliates
通常の商品取引期間の短期債権勘定	Current accts. only for goods, within regular terms
商品―素原材料	Merchandise—Raw Materials
―原材料	—Supplies
―仕掛品	—Goods in Process
―完成品	—Finished
保険解約払戻金	Life Insurance, Cash Surrender Value
（借入控除前）	(Do not deduct loans)
流通有価証券	Securities, Readily Marketable
証券取引所上場株式債券等	Stocks, bonds, etc. listed on Stock Exchange, etc.
流動資産合計	Total Current Assets
土地建物	Land and Buildings, Used in Business

減価償却引当前	Before depreciation reserves
非営業用土地建物	Land and Buildings, Not Used in Business
減価償却引当前	Before depreciation reserves
機械設備	Machinery and Equipment
減価償却引当前	Before depreciation reserves
什器備品	Furniture and Fixtures
減価償却引当前	Before depreciation reserves
トラック，車両等	Trucks, Autos, etc.
減価償却引当前	Before depreciation reserves
子会社および関連会社への出資貸出勘定等を除く	Investments in Subsidiaries & Affiliates Not including loans, advances, accounts, etc.
子会社および関連会社への債権延滞貸出	Due from Subsidiaries & Affiliates Loans, advances, slow receivables
役員，株主，従業員への債権	Due from Officers, Stockholders, Employees
受取勘定および受取手形	Accounts & Notes Receivable
延滞ないし回収困難	Slow or doubtful of collection
前払い費用	Prepaid Expenses
税金，保険，利子，家賃地代等	Taxes, insurance, interest, rent, etc.
型見本，著作権等	Patterns, Dies, Lasts, Copyrights, etc.
特許権	Patents
営業権	Good Will
資産合計	Total Assets
負　債	LIABILITIES
無担保銀行支払手形	Notes Payable to Banks, Unsecured
担保付銀行支払手形	Notes Payable to Banks, Secured
割引手形	Customers' Notes Discounted
銀行金融会社等で割引いた受取手形	With banks, finance companies, etc.
保険契約者借入金	Loans on Life Insurance

機械設備代金支払手形	Notes Payable for Mach'y, Equip't, etc.
期限1年以内	Payable within one year
商品代金支払手形	Notes Payable for Merchandise
支払勘定	Accounts Payable
子会社および関連会社への買	Due to Subsidiaries & Affiliates
掛金等	
商品購入代金支払勘定支払	Current accounts & notes, for purchase
手形等	of goods, etc.
子会社および関連会社からの	Due to Subsidiaries & Affiliates
債務借入金	Loans and advances
役員，株主，従業員からの債	Due to Officers, Stockholders, Employees
務	
未払い負債	Accrued Liabilities
賃金，利子，保険等に対す	For wages, interest, insurance, etc.
る未払い負債	
抵当借入金および社債	Mortgage and Bonded Debt
期限1年以内	Due and payable within one year
租税公課	Taxes and Assessments
流動負債合計	Total Current Liabilities
不動産抵当借入	Real Estate Mortgages Payable
期限1年超	Due after one year
社債	Bonded Debt
期限1年超	Due after a year
の据置債務	Other Deferred Liabilities
債合計	Total Liabilities

減価償却引当金―建物	Depreciation Reserve—Buildings
―機械設備	—Mach'y & Equip't.
―什器備品	—Furn. & Fixt's.
―トラック等	—Trucks, etc.
優先株	Preferred Stock
配当率	Dividend Rate
普通株	Common Stock
営業外または資本剰余金	Unearned or Capital Surplus
利益剰余金	Earned Surplus
負債合計および正味資産	Total Liabilities & Net Worth

(2) 損益計算書 / (2) STATEMENT OF PROFIT & LOSS

総売上高―子会社及び関連会社への	Gross Sales—To Subsidiaries and Affiliates
―その他への	—To Others
控除：返戻，および値引	Less : Returns and Allowances
（現金割引を除く）	(Except cash discounts)

純売上高	**NET SALES**
期首在庫高	Inventory, Beginning Period
期中仕入高（現金割引前）	Purchases During Period (Before cash discounts)
直接労務費	Direct Labor
その他費用	Other Costs
合計	Total
控除：期末在庫高	Less : Inventory, End of Period
商品販売コスト	Cost of Goods Sold

総利益	**GROSS PROFIT**
経営管理費および一般経費	**Administrative & General Expenses**
役員給与	Officers' Salaries
その他給与	Other Salaries
利息	Interest
不良債権	Bad Debts
減価償却（他に計上されていないもの）	Depreciation (Not applicable elsewhere)

合計	Total
経営管理費，一般経費および 　販売費	Total Administrative, General, and Selling Expenses

純営業利益　　　　　　　　**NET OPERATING PROFIT**
　その他収入　　　　　　　　　**Other Income**
現金割引収入　　　　　　　　Cash Discounts Received
その他収入合計　　　　　　　Total Other Income
その他収入支出への追加控除　Net Addition or Deduction for Other In-
　純計　　　　　　　　　　　come and Expense

期中純収入　　　　　　　　**NET INCOME FOR PERIOD**
期首営業収益　　　　　　　　Earned Surplus, Beginning of Period
　収益からの控除分　　　　　**Deductions from Surplus**
控除合計　　　　　　　　　　Total Deductions
収益純増減　　　　　　　　　Net Surplus Change
期末営業収益　　　　　　　　Earned Surplus, End of Period

　販売費用　　　　　　　　**Selling Expenses**
給与　　　　　　　　　　　　Salaries
手数料　　　　　　　　　　　Commissions
出張費等　　　　　　　　　　Traveling, etc.
宣伝費　　　　　　　　　　　Advertising
合計　　　　　　　　　　　　Total

　その他費用　　　　　　　**Other Expenses**
現金割引　　　　　　　　　　Cash Discounts Given
その他費用合計　　　　　　　Total Other Expenses

　収益への追加分　　　　　**Additions to Surplus**
追加分合計　　　　　　　　　Total Additions

6. 主要経済指標

Key Economic Indicators

マネー・サプライ	Money stock
銀行券発行高	Bank note issues
中央銀行信用増減	Central bank credit increase or decrease
銀行勘定	Bank accounts
預金	Deposits
貸出	Loans & discounts
銀行貸出約定平均金利	Average contractural interest rates on bank loans and discounts
コール・レート	Call money rates
財政資金対民間収支尻	Net receipts or payments on treasury transactions with the public
一般財政資金	General funds
国債	Government bonds
国際収支	Balance of payments
経常収支	Current balance
貿易収支	Trade balance
輸出	Exports
輸入	Imports
長期資本収支	Long-term capital
基礎的収支	Basic balance
総合収支	Overall balance
外貨準備高	Gold & foreign exchange reserves
貿易（通関統計）	Foreign trade (customs clearance)
輸出	Exports
輸入	Imports
生産・出荷・在庫指数	Production, shipment & inventory indexes
鉱工業	Mining & manufacturing
生産	Industrial production
生産者出荷	Producers' shipments
生産者製品在庫	Producers' inventory of finished goods
製造工業原材料在庫	Manufacturing industries' raw materials inventories

主要物資生産高	Output of principal products
電力	Electric power
粗鋼	Crude steel
乗用車	Passenger cars
テレビ受像器	TVs
鋼船（しゅん工量）	Steel ships (completion)
機械受注額（民需，除船舶）	Orders received for machinery (private, excluding ships)
住宅着工（新設住宅）	Residential construction (new starts)
百貨店売上高（全国）	Sales at all department stores
賃金指数・雇用指数	Wage & employment indexes
名目賃金（製造業）	Nominal wage (manufacturing)
実質賃金（製造業）	Real wage (manufacturing)
常用雇用（製造業）	Regular workers (manufacturing)
労働生産性指数	Labor productivity index
求人倍率	Ratio of labor demand to supply
完全失業者	Unemployed (wholly)
物価指数	Price indexes
卸売物価	Wholesale price
輸出物価	Export price
輸入物価	Import price
消費者物価	Consumer price
消費水準	Consumption expenditure levels
非農家	Non-farm households'
農村	Rural
国民総生産	Gross national product
名目	Nominal
実質	Real

7. 国民所得項目

National Income Items

(1) 国民総生産と総支出勘定

(1) **Gross National Product and Expenditure**

国民所得（要素費用表示の国民純生産）	National Income (Net National Product at Factor Cost)
資本減耗引当	Provisions for the Consumption of Fixed Capital
間接税	Indirect Taxes
（控除）経常補助金	Less : Current Subsidies
統計上の不突合	Statistical Discrepancy
市場価格表示の国民総生産	Gross National Product at Market Prices
個人消費支出	Private Consumption Expenditure
政府の財貨サービス経営購入	General Government Consumption Expenditure
国内総固定資本形成	Gross Domestic Fixed Capital Formation
在庫品増加	Increase in Stocks
輸出と海外からの所得	Exports of Goods and Services and Factor Income Received from Abroad
（控除）輸入と海外への所得	Less : Imports of Goods and Service and Factor Income Paid Abroad
市場価格表示の国民総支出	Expenditure on Gross National Product at Market Prices

(2) 国民所得分配勘定

(2) **Distribution of National Income**

雇用者所得	Compensation of Employees
個人業主所得	Income from Unincorporated Enterprises
個人の財産所得	Income from Property
法人企業から個人への移転	Corporate Transfers to Households and Private Non-profit Institutions
法人税および税外負担	Direct Taxes and Charges on Private Corporate
法人留保	Saving of Private Corporations

政府の事業所得および財産所得	General Government Income from Property and Entrepreneurship
（控除）一般政府負債利子	Less : Interest on the Public Debt
（控除）消費者負債利子	Less : Interest on Consumers' Debt
要素費用表示の国民所得	National Income of Factor Cost
国民所得（要素費用表示の国民純生産）	National Income (Net National Product at Factor Cost)
法人所得	Income from Private Corporations

(3) 個人勘定   (3) **Households and Private Non-profit Institutions**

個人消費支出	Private Consumption Expenditure
個人税および税外負担	Direct Taxes and Charges
社会保険に対する負担	Social Insurance Contributions
個人から政府へのその他の移転	Other Current Transfers to General Government
個人から海外への移転	Transfers to the Rest of the World
個人貯蓄	Saving
個人所得の処分	Disbursements
雇用者所得	Compensation of Employees
個人業主所得	Income from Unincorporated Enterprises
個人の財産所得	Income from Property
法人企業から個人への移転	Current Transfers from Private Corporations
（控除）消費者負担負債利子	Less : Interest on Consumers' Debt
政府から個人への移転	Current Transfers from General Government
海外から個人への移転	Transfers from the Rest of the World
個人所得	Receipts (Personal Income)
個人可処分所得	Disposable Income of Persons
個人貯蓄率	Saving Ratio of Persons

(4) 政府一般勘定   (4) **General Government**

政府の財貨サービス経常購入	Consumption Expenditure
経常補助金	Current Subsidies
政府から個人への移転	Current Transfers to Households and Non-profit Institutions

政府から海外への移転	Transfers to the Rest of the World
政府経常余剰	Saving
経常支出	Disposal of Current Revenue
個人税および税外負担	Direct Taxes and Charges on Households and Non-profit Institutions
法人税および税外負担	Direct Taxes and Charges on Private Corporations
間接税	Indirect Taxes
社会保険に対する負担	Social Insurance Contributions
個人から政府へのその他の移転	Other Current Transfers from Households and Non-profit Institutions
海外から政府への移転	Transfers from the Rest of the World
政府の事業所得および財産所得	Income from Property and Entrepreneurship
（控除）一般政府負債利子	Less : Interest on Public Debt
経常収入	Current Revenue

(5)　資本形成勘定 / (5) Gross Saving and Capital Formation

国内総固定資本形成	Gross Domestic Fixed Capital Formation
在庫品増加	Increase in Stocks
海外に対する債権の純増	Net Lending to the Rest of the World
総資本形成	Disposal of Gross Saving
資本減耗引当	Provisions for the Consumption of Fixed Capital
法人留保	Saving of Private Corporations
個人貯蓄	Saving of Households and Private Non-profit Institutions
政府経常余剰	Saving of General Government
統計上の不突合	Statistical Discrepancy
総貯蓄	Gross Saving

(6)　海外勘定 / (6) External Transactions

| 輸出と海外からの所得 | Exports of Goods and Services and Factor Income Received from Abroad |
| 海外から個人への移転 | Transfers to Households and Private Non-profit Institutions |

海外から政府への移転	Transfer to General Government
受取り	Receipts
輸入と海外への所得	Imports of Goods and Services and Factor Income Paid Abroad
個人から海外への移転	Transfers from Households and Private Non-profit Institutions
政府から海外への移転	Transfers from General Government
海外に対する債権の純増	Net Lending to the Rest of the World
支払い	Disbursements
海外からの純所得	Net Factor Income from Abroad
海外からの要素所得受取り	Factor Income Received from Abroad
（控除）海外への要素所得支払い	Less : Factor Income Paid Abroad

(7) **要素費用表示の産業別国民純生産**	(7) **Industrial Origin of Net National Product at Factor Cost**
農林水産業	Agriculture, Forestry and Fishing
鉱業	Mining
製造業	Manufacturing
建設業	Construction
電気・ガス・水道業・運輸業・通信業	Electricity, Gas, Water Supply, Transportation and Communication
卸・小売業	Wholesale and Retail Trade
金融・保険・不動産業	Banking, Insurance and Real Estate
サービス業	Services
公務	Public Administration
要素費用表示の国内純生産	Net Domestic Product at Factor Cost
海外からの純所得	Net Factor Income from Abroad
要素費用表示の国民純生産	Net National Product at Factor Cost

(8) **国民所得の分配**	(8) **Distribution of National Income**
雇用者所得	Compensation of Employees
賃金・俸給	Wages and Salaries
その他の給与および手当	Other Pays and Allowances
社会保険雇用主負担	Social Insurance Contributions of Employers
個人業主所得	Income from Unincorporated Enterprises

農林水産業	Agriculture, Forestry and Fishing
その他	Others
個人の財産所得	Income of Property
賃貸料	Rent
利子	Interest
配当	Dividends
法人企業から個人への移転	Corporate Transfers Enterprises to Households and Private Non-profit Institutions
法人税および税外負担	Direct Taxes and Charges on Private Corporations
法人留保	Saving of Private Corporations
政府の事業所得および財産所得	General Government Income from Property and Entrepreneurship
政府企業の利潤	Profits of Government Enterprises
賃貸料，利子および配当	Rent, Interest and Dividends
（控除）一般政府負債利子	Less : Interest on Public Debt
（控除）消費者負債利子	Less : Interest on Consumers' Debt
国民所得	National Income
（在庫品評価調整額）	(Stock Valuation Adjustment)
法人所得	Income from Private Corporations

(9) 国民総支出　(9) **Gross National Expenditure**

個人消費支出	Private Consumption Expenditure
家計消費支出	Expenditure of Households
飲食費	Foods, Beverages and Tobacco
被服費	Clothing
光熱費	Fuel and light
住居費	Housing
地代・家賃	Rent
その他	Others
雑費	Miscellaneous
民間非営利団体の消費支出	Expenditure of Private Non-Profit Institutions
海外における居住者の消費支出など	Expenditure of Residents Abroad, etc.
政府の財貨サービス経営購入	General Government Consumption Expenditure
国内総資本形成	Gross Domestic Capital Formation

総固定資本形成	Gross Domestic Fixed Capital Formation
民間	By private
住宅	Dwellings
企業設備	Others
政府	By Government
住宅	Dwellings
企業設備	Machinery and Equipment
一般政府	General Government
在庫品増加	Increase in Stocks
民間企業	Private Enterprises
政府企業	Government Enterprises
経常海外余剰	Surplus of the Nation on Current Account
輸出と海外からの所得	Exports of Goods and Services and Factor Income Received from Abroad
（控除）輸入と海外への所得	Less : Imports of Goods and Services and Factor Income Paid Abroad
市場価格表示の国民総支出	Gross National Expenditure at Market Prices
（在庫品評価調整額）	(Stock Valuation Adjustment)

8. 主要統計調査資料名

Selected Statistical Reports

地方財政統計年報,自治省	Local Public Finance Statistics Annual, MOHA
賃金構造基本統計,労働省	Wage Structure Statistics, MOL
賃金労働時間制度総合調査報告,労働省	General Survey on Wage and Working Hour Systems, MOL
貯蓄動向調査,総務庁	Family Savings Survey, MCA
中小企業動向調査,中小企業金融公庫	Survey on Small Business Trend, Small Business Finance Corporation
中小企業業況調査,中小企業金融公庫	Survey on Smaller Firms' Business Sentiments, Small Business Finance Corporation
エネルギー統計月報,通産省	Energy Statistics Monthly, MITI
エネルギーバランス表,日本エネルギー経済研究所	Energy Balance Table, Institute of Energy Economics
不動産経済調査月報,不動産経済研究所	Real Estate Business Survey Monthly Report, Japan Real Estate Economic Research Institute
外国貿易概況,通産省	Summary Report on Trade of Japan, MITI
外国技術導入年次報告,科学技術庁	Annual Report on Foreign Technology Introduction, Science and Technology Agency
外資導入実績,大蔵省	Foreign Capital Inflow, MOF
原材料統計速報,通産省	Raw Materials Statistics, MITI
銀行局金融年報,大蔵省	Monetary Annual of Banking Department, MOF
銀行取引停止処分者負債状況,全国銀行協会連合会	Report on Indebtedness of Insolvent Persons, Federation of Bankers' Associations of Japan
漁業養殖業生産統計年報,農林水産省	Fishery, Fish Farm Production Annual Reports, MAFF
業種別貸出統計,日本銀行	Statistics of Lendings by Industry Group, Bank of Japan

販売業者在庫統計，通産省	Distribution Inventory Statistics, MITI
発注者別保証実績表，保証事業会社協会	Guaranteed Public Works, Society of Public Works Underwriting Companies
法人企業統計季報，大蔵省	Quarterly Report of Statistical Survey of Incorporated Enterprises, MOF
法人企業統計年報，大蔵省	Statistical Annual Report of Incorporated Enterprises, MOF
法人企業投資動向調査，経企庁	Survey on Corporate Businesses' Investment, EPA
百貨店統計月報，通産省	Department Store Statistics, MITI
医療施設調査，厚生省	Survey on Medical Facilities, MHW
自動車統計月報，日本自動車業会	Automobile Statistics Monthly, Japan Automobile Manufacturers' Association
事業所統計調査，総務庁	Census of Japan Establishments, MCA
人口動態統計，厚生省	Population Statistics, WHM
住宅需要実態調査，建設省	Housing Demand Survey, MOC
住宅金融月報，住宅金融公庫	Monthly Report on Housing Finance, Housing Loan Corporation
住宅敷地価格調査報告，住宅金融公庫	Survey Report on Residential Land Prices, Housing Loan Corporation
住宅統計調査報告，総務庁	Report on Housing Statistics Survey, MCA
乗用車燃費一覧，運輸省	Handbook on Passenger Car Fuel Efficiency, MOT
家畜基本調査，農林水産省	Basic Survey on Livestock, MAFF
科学技術白書，科学技術庁	White Paper on Science and Technology, Science and Technology Agency
科学技術研究調査報告，総務庁	Survey Report on Research and Development Activities, MCA
化学工業統計月報，通産省	Chemical Industry Statistics, MITI
家計調査報告，総務庁	Familiy Income and Expenditure Survey, MCA
紙パルプ統計月報，通産省	Paper-Pulp Statistics Monthly, MITI
カントリー・データ・シート，国際金融情報センター	Country Data Sheet, Japan Center for International Finance
経営指標ハンドブック，日本開発銀行	Handbook on Business Performance Indicators, Japan Development Bank
経済統計月(年)報，日本銀行	Economics Statistics Monthly (Annual), Bank of Japan

建設部門分析用産業関連表, 建設省	Input-Output Table for Analysis of Construction Sector, MOC
建設動態統計調査, 建設省	Dynamic Construction Statistics Survey, MOC
建設業務統計年報, 建設省	Annual Report on Construction Business Statistics, MOC
建設工事費デフレーター, 建設省	Deflator for Construction Expenditure, MOC
建設労働・資材原単位調査, 建設省	Survey on Unit Labor and Materials Input for Construction, MOC
建設総合統計, 建設省	Comprehensive Construction Statistics, MOC
企業経営者見通し調査, 経企庁	Business Outlook Survey, EPA
機械受注統計, 経企庁	Machinery Orders Statistics, EPA
機械統計月報, 通産省	Machinery Orders Statistics Monthly, MITI
耕地面積調査, 農林水産省	Survey on Cultivated Land Area, MAFF
耕地及び作付面積統計, 農林水産省	Statistics on Arable Land and Crop-Planted Area, MAFF
工業統計表, 通産省	Industrial Census, MITI
鉱工業生産指数, 通産省	Industrial Production Index, MITI
国民経済計算(新 SNA), 経企庁	Report on National Accounts (New SNA), EPA
国民所得統計年報, 経企庁	Annual Report on National Income Statistics, EPA
国際比較統計, 日本銀行	Comparative International Statistics, Bank of Japan
国際金融局年報, 大蔵省	Annual Report of International Finance Bureau, MOF
国際収支統計月報, 日本銀行	Balance of Payments Monthly, Bank of Japan
国勢調査, 総務庁	Census, MCA
公共事業に関する世論調査. 総務庁	Opinion Survey on Public Works, MCA
公共工事着工統計, 建設省	Statistics on Public Works Construction Starts, MOC

公社債月報，公社債引受協会	Bond Review, Bond Underwriters' Association
公社債月報，東京証券取引所	Bond Market Monthly Report, Tokyo Stock Exchange
小売物価統計，総務庁	Retail Price Survey, MCA
求人等実態調査，労働省	Field Survey on Job Openings, etc., MOL
毎月勤労統計調査，労働省	Monthly Labor Statistics Survey, MOL
民間土木工事着工統計，建設省	Statistics on Private Civil Engineering Construction Starts, MOC
民間住宅建設資金実態調査，建設省	Survey on Financing of Private Residential Construction, MOC
民間企業粗資本ストック統計，経企庁	Capital Stock Statistics of Corporate Businesses, EPA
民間設備投資デフレーター，経企庁	Deflator for Private Investment, EPA
生コンクリート統計4半期報，通産省	Ready-Mixed Concrete Statistics Quarterly, MITI
日本貿易月報，通産省	Japan Exports and Imports Monthly, MITI
日本貿易精覧，東洋経済新報社	Japan Trade Statistics Manual, Toyo Keizai Shimposha
日本外国貿易年報，通産省	Japan Exports and Imports Annual, MITI
日本食糧標準成分表，科学技術庁	Analysis of Japan Food Product Ingredients, Science and Technology Agency
日本統計年鑑，総務庁	Japan Statistical Handbook, MCA
農業調査，農林水産省	Agricultural Survey, MAFF
農家経済調査，農林水産省	Survey of Farmers' Household Economy, MAFF
農家就業動向調査，農林水産省	Survey of Agricultural Employment Trend, MAFF
農林水産試験研究年報，農林水産省	Annual Report on Agricultural, Forestry and Fishery Experiments and Research, MAFF
農産物生産費調査，農林水産省	Survey on Agricultural Production Costs, MAFF
農村物価賃金調査，農林水産省	Survey on Prices, Wages in Agricultural Areas, MAFF

卸売物価統計月報，日本銀行	Wholesale Price Statistics Monthly, Bank of Japan
陸運統計要覧，運輸省	Summary Land Transport Trends, MOT
労働経済動向調査，労働省	Survey on Labor Economic Trends, MOL
労働力調査統計，総務庁	Labor Force Statistics, MCA
産業連関表，通産省	Input-Output Tables, MITI
生産農業所得統計，農林水産省	Statistics on Production Income from Agriculture, MAFF
生産性統計，日本生産性本部	Productivity Statistics, Japan Productivity Center
製造業部門別投入産出物価指数，日本銀行	Price Indexes of Input and Output of Manufacturing Industries, Bank of Japan
繊維統計月報，通産省	Textile Statistics Monthly, MITI
セルフサービス店に関する統計表，通産省	Statistics on Self-Service Stores, MITI
設備投資動向調査，日本長期信用銀行	Survey on Plant and Equipment Investment Trend, Long-Term Credit Bank of Japan
設備投資計画調査，日本開発銀行	Survey of Investment Plans, Japan Development Bank
社会福祉施設調査報告，厚生省	Survey Report on Social Welfare Institutions, MHW
資源統計月報，通産省	Resources Statistics Monthly, MITI
四半期別民間企業資本ストック，経企庁	Quarterly Statistics on Private Business Capital Stock, EPA
資金循環勘定，日本銀行	Flow of Funds Account, Bank of Japan
資金循環勘定応用表，日本銀行	Flow of Funds Applied Table, Bank of Japan
信託財産調，信託協会	Trust Property, Trust Association
商業動態統計，通産省	Current Survey of Commerce, MITI
商業統計調査，通産省	Census of Commerce, MITI
消費動向調査，経企庁	Consumption Trend Survey, EPA
消費者物価指数，総務庁	Consumer Price Index, MCA
消費と貯蓄の動向，経企庁	Consumption and Savings Trend, EPA
就業構造基本調査，総務庁	Employment Structure Survey, MCA
出入国管理統計年報，法務省	Immigration Control Statistics Annual Report, MOJ
主要企業経営分析，日本銀行	Financial Statements of Principal Enterprises, Bank of Japan

主要国自動車統計，日本自動車工業会	Automobile Statistics for Major Countries, Japan Automobile Manufacturers' Association
主要企業短期経済観測，日本銀行	Short-Term Economic Survey of Principal Enterprises, Bank of Japan
主要産業の設備投資計画，通産省	Investment Plans of Major Industries, MITI
職業安定業務月報，労働省	Monthly Report on Employment Security Agency, MOL
食料需給表，農林水産省	Food Supply-Demand Statistics, MAFF
食糧管理主要指標，農林水産省	Major Indexes of Food Control Operations, MAFF
総合エネルギー統計，通産省	Comprehensive Energy Statistics, MITI
対外直接投資許可統計，大蔵省	License Statistics of Direct Investment in Foreign Countries, MOF
鉄鋼統計月報，通産省	Steel Statistics Monthly, MITI
特許庁公報，通産省	Patent Agency Gazette, MITI
東京消費者物価指数，総務庁	Tokyo Consumer Price Index, MCA
通産統計，通産省	Industrial Statistics, MITI
わが国企業の経営分析，通産省	Financial Analysis of Japanese Enterprises, MITI
輸出入物価動向調査，経企庁	Survey on Price Trend of Exported and Imported Products, EPA
輸出入物価指数月報，日本銀行	Export and Import Price Index Monthly, Bank of Japan
窯業・建材統計月報，通産省	Ceramics, Construction Supplies Statistics Monthly Report, MITI
財政統計，大蔵省	Budgetary Statistics, MOF
全国物価統計調査報告，総務庁	Report on National Prices Survey, MCA
全国道路交通情勢調査，建設省	National Survey on Road Traffic Situation, MOC
全国銀行財務諸表分析，全国銀行協会連合会	Analysis of Banks' Financial Statements, Federation of Bankers' Associations of Japan
全国人口・世帯数表，自治省	National Population, Household Statistics, MOHA

全国企業短期経済観測調査, 日本銀行	Short-term Business Survey of All Enterprises, Bank of Japan
全国マンション市場動向, 不動産経済研究所	Trend in National Market for Condominiums, Japan Real Estate Economic Research Institute
全国市街地価格指数, 不動産経済研究所	National Urban Land Price Index, Japan Real Estate Research Institute

(注)EPA : Economic Planning Agency
MAFF : Ministry of Agriculture, Forestry and Fisheries
MCA : Management and Coordination Agency
MHW : Ministry of Health and Welfare
MITI : Ministry of International Trade and Industry
MOC : Ministry of Construction
MOF : Ministry of Finance
MOHA: Ministry of Home Affairs
MOJ : Ministry of Justice
MOL : Ministry of Labor
MOT : Ministry of Transport

編者略歴

花田　實（はなだ　みのる）

1921年生まれ。1941年大阪外国語学校（現大阪外国語大学）英語部卒業。1942年日本銀行入行。為替管理局，外国局，調査局などに勤務。1980年退職。現在，協和銀行国際部顧問。著書に『和英・経済英語辞典』，『経済英語基本文例事典』（ジャパンタイムズ刊）などがある。

和英・金融用語辞典

1985年 7 月25日　初 版 発 行
1990年 8 月20日　第 4 刷発行

編　者　花田　實
　　　　© Minoru Hanada, 1985
発行者　太田　良久
発行所　株式会社　ジャパン タイムズ
　　　　〒108 東京都港区芝浦 4 丁目 5 番 4 号
　　　　電話 東京（03）453-5311
　　　　振替口座　東京9-64848
印刷所　新興印刷製本株式会社

装幀　㈱CADEC
定価は箱に表示してあります。

ISBN4-7890-0279-9